Henry Austin Wilson

The Gelasian Sacramentary

liber sacramentorum romanae ecclesiae

Henry Austin Wilson

The Gelasian Sacramentary
liber sacramentorum romanae ecclesiae

ISBN/EAN: 9783741140129

Manufactured in Europe, USA, Canada, Australia, Japa

Cover: Foto ©Lupo / pixelio.de

Manufactured and distributed by brebook publishing software (www.brebook.com)

Henry Austin Wilson

The Gelasian Sacramentary

The Gelasian Sacramentary

LIBER SACRAMENTORUM
ROMANAE ECCLESIAE

EDITED

WITH INTRODUCTION, CRITICAL NOTES
AND APPENDIX

BY

H. A. WILSON, M.A.

FELLOW OF S. MARY MAGDALEN COLLEGE

WITH TWO FACSIMILES

Oxford
AT THE CLARENDON PRESS
1894

PREFACE

THIS edition of the Gelasian Sacramentary was originally taken in hand in order to provide, for the use of persons studying the Western service-books, a text more convenient and more easily accessible than those of the earlier editions, and more accurate than that which is included in Migne's *Patrologia Latina*. For this purpose it was at first proposed to reproduce Tommasi's text, with an introduction, and possibly with notes critical and explanatory. Before adopting this course, however, it seemed desirable to examine not only the Vatican manuscript *Reginae* 316, from which Tommasi's text was taken, but also other manuscript authorities. The result of this examination was an enlargement of the original design. The Sacramentaries of Rheinau and S. Gallen proved not only to be likely to furnish better means of emending the text of the Vatican MS. than those which were at the disposal of Tommasi or Vezzosi, but to be themselves of such importance as to warrant an endeavour to make their contents, their arrangement, and their text more fully known. The task of comparing these later 'Gelasian' Sacramentaries with the earlier text of the Vatican MS. has been a slow and laborious one, since the differences of arrangement made it somewhat hard to trace, in the different recensions, the matter common to the three MSS.; even now, though the greater part of the contents of the text has been traced in one or both of the later

'Gelasian' books, it is probable that the portions marked as found in the MSS. denoted by the symbols R. and S. do not form absolutely the whole of the common matter. The marginal references, however, will show what parts of the text have actually been identified and compared with R. and S., while it is hoped that the references to various printed texts, though less numerous, may also be found useful. The references to Gerbert's *Monumenta Veteris Liturgiae Alemannicae* in particular may, in conjunction with the Appendix, enable readers to see in what surroundings the particular prayers and benedictions appear in the later 'Gelasian' books. The Appendix is intended to assist in this matter readers to whom Gerbert's work is not easily accessible, and to enable those who have his book at hand to find their way more safely in the labyrinth of his 'triple' Sacramentary, by showing what parts of that text are actually contained in the two 'Gelasian' books which he discarded in favour of a later manuscript.

An account of the method which has been followed in the reproduction and correction of the text of the Vatican MS. will be found in the Introduction. It may be well to say here that corrections have been more sparingly made in the rubrics of the manuscript than in the text of the prayers, since it often appears that the errors of the latter are due to the mistakes of the scribe, and are absent from the text of other books of a date either earlier, or practically contemporary as belonging to the period before the literary reforms of Charles the Great. In the case of the rubrics, on the other hand, the evidence of other manuscripts is scantier, and it is often on the whole more probable that the ungrammatical form is the earliest in which the rubric appeared.

With regard to the notes appended to the text, it should be observed that except where the spelling of a manuscript seems to be of any importance for the determination of the true reading, no notice has been taken of variations in cases where manuscripts are in substantial agreement with each other or with the printed texts marked as agreeing with them in a certain reading. To have taken account of all the divergences of spelling between the Rheinau and S. Gallen MSS., or between the first and second hands of the latter, would probably have been both wearisome and useless, and would certainly have added a great deal to the notes, which may even now seem unduly long. Except in cases where it seemed for any reason worth while to record the exact form, the grammatical errors of R. are similarly passed over: but the editor has endeavoured, as far as possible, to take note of all those which seem to be of any moment. In the Appendix, the same plan has been followed: the opening words of the prayers and prefaces are given (spelling excepted) as they appear in the original hand of the S. Gallen MS.

The numbers marked on the inner margin of the text refer to the columns of the first volume of Muratori's *Liturgia Romana Vetus* (Venice, 1748). They are added not only for the benefit of those who may wish to compare the present text with that of the earlier edition, but also for the assistance of students who may wish to compare the readings of the 'Gelasian' books with those of Muratori's Gregorian text, and to employ for that purpose an Index to the Roman Sacramentaries of Muratori, which was compiled by the editor to serve as an instrument in the preparation of the present work, and has since been published by the Cambridge University Press.

In conclusion, the editor desires to express his gratitude to all those who have, in one way or in another, assisted him in his work. His thanks are especially due to Dr. Bright, Regius Professor of Ecclesiastical History, at whose instigation that work was undertaken; to Dr. Ince, Regius Professor of Divinity, to whose kindness he owes the collation of the Vatican MS. *Reginae* 316; to the authorities of the Chapter Library of S. Gallen, and of the Library of the Canton of Zürich, who most considerately sent to the Bodleian Library for his use the S. Gallen and the Rheinau Sacramentaries; to the Rev. F. E. Brightman, the Rev. F. A. Overton, and Mr. C. H. Turner, for preliminary enquiries made on his behalf as to certain manuscripts; to Herr Jakob Werner, for a specimen collation of a portion of the Rheinau MS.; to Dr. Wickham Legg, for the loan of collations of the *Canon Actionis*; to the Rev. W. A. B. Coolidge, for information on the history of the Bishops of Chur; and to Mr. Falconer Madan, for guidance and help in determining the dates of handwritings and the arrangement of gatherings in the Rheinau and S. Gallen MSS. He desires also gratefully to acknowledge the kindness of the Delegates of the University Press in undertaking the publication of his work, and to record his sense of the attention and care which have been bestowed upon the book by the officials and the workmen concerned in its production.

S. MARY MAGDALEN COLLEGE, OXFORD:
January 10, 1894.

CONTENTS

		PAGE
INTRODUCTION		xvii–lxxvi
LISTS OF ABBREVIATIONS		lxxvii–lxxviii
LIBER I		1–160

I.	Orationes et Preces in Vigiliis Natalis Domini	1
II.	Item de Vigilia Domini. In Nocte	2
III.	Item in Vigilia Domini. Mane prima	3
IV.	Item in Natale Domini. In Die	4
V.	Item Orationes de Natali Domini	5
VI.	In Natali S. Stephani Martyris	6
VII.	In Natali S. Ioannis Evangelistae	7
VIII.	In Natali Innocentium	8
IX.	In Octavas Domini	9
X.	Prohibendum ab Idolis	10
XI.	In Vigiliis de Theophania	10
XII.	In Theophania. In Die	11
XIII.	In Septuagesima	12
XIV.	In Sexagesima	13
XV.	Orationes et Preces super Poenitentes	14
XVI.	Ordo agentibus publicam poenitentiam	15
XVII.	Orat. et Preces a Quinquagesima usque ad Quadragesimam	15
XVIII.	Orat. et Preces. Dominica in Quadragesima	17
XIX.	Orat. et Preces in xii Lect. mense primo	21
XX.	Ordo qualiter in Romana sedis apostolicae ecclesia Presbyteri, Diaconi vel Subdiaconi eligendi sunt	22
	Ad Ordinandos Presbyteros	22
XXI.	Capitulum S. Gregorii Papae	26
XXII.	Ad Ordinandos Diaconos	26
[XXIII.]	Ad Consummandum Diaconatus officium	28
XXIV.	Orationes et Preces ad Missam	29
XXV.	Secunda Dominica in Quadragesima	30
XXVI.	Tertia Dominica	34
XXVII.	Quarta Dominica	38
XXVIII.	Quinta Dominica	42
XXIX.	Denuntiatio pro Scrutinio	45
XXX.	Orationes super Electos	46
XXXI.	Benedictio salis dandi Catechumenis	47

CONTENTS.

		PAGE
XXXII.	Benedictio post datum salem	47
XXXIII.	Exorcismi super Electos	48
XXXIV.	Expositio Evangeliorum in aurium apertione	50
XXXV.	Praefatio Symboli ad Electos	53
XXXVI.	Praefatio Orationis Dominicae	57
XXXVII.	Dominica in Palmis	60
XXXVIII.	Orationes in Quinta Feria	63
	Ordo agentibus publicam poenitentiam	63
	Reconciliatio Poenitentis ad mortem	66
XL.	In Quinta Feria. Missa Chrismatis	69
	Missa ad Vesperum	72
XLI.	Ordo de Feria vi, Passione Domini	74
XLII.	Sabbatorum die	78
XLIII.	Orat. per singulas lectiones in Sabbato Sancto	82
XLIV.	Benedictio Fontis	84
XLV.	Orat. et Preces ad Missam in Nocte	88
XLVI.	Dominicum Paschae	90
XLVII.	Totius albae Orationes et Preces. Feria ii	91
XLVIII.	Feria iii	92
XLIX.	Feria iv	93
L.	Feria v	94
LI.	Feria vi	94
LII.	Feria vii	95
LIII.	Octavas Paschae	96
LIV.	Orat. et Preces de Pascha annotina	97
LV.	Orat. et Preces in Parochia	98
LVI.	Orationes Paschales vespertinales	99
LVII.	Orat. et Preces Dom. post Octavas Paschae	102
LVIII.	Secunda Dom. post Clausum Paschae	102
LIX.	Tertia Dom. post Clausum Paschae	103
LX.	Quarta Dom. post Clausum Paschae	104
LXI.	Quinta Dom. post Clausum Paschae	105
LXII.	Sexta Dom. post Clausum Paschae	106
LXIII.	Orat. et Preces in Ascensa Domini	107
LXIV.	Item alia Missa	108
LXV.	Orat. et Preces Dom. post Ascensa Domini	109
LXVI.	Aegrotanti catechumeno imposita manuum	110
LXVII.	Impositio manus, energumenum catechumenum	111
LXVIII.	Item alia pro parvulo energumeno	112
LXIX.	Oratio super catechumenum infirmum	112
LXX.	Super catechumenum infirmum si fuerit baptizandus	113
LXXI.	Ad catechumenum ex pagano faciendum	113
LXXII.	Ad succurrendum catechumenum infirmum	114
LXXIII.	Benedictio Fontis	115
LXXIV.	Alia ad succurrendum	116
LXXV.	Item alia Benedictio	116
LXXVI.	Ad succurrendum. Benedictio olei exorcizati	118
LXXVII.	Orat. per singulas lectiones in Sabb. Pentecosten	118
LXXVIII.	In Vigilia de Pentecosten	120
LXXIX.	Item aliter in Vigilia Pentecosten	121
LXXX.	Orationes et Preces Dom. Pentecosten	122

CONTENTS.

		PAGE
LXXXI.	Orat. ad Vesperos infra Octavas Pentecosten	124
LXXXII.	Denuntiatio Ieiuniorum iv, vii et x mensis	124
LXXXIII.	Orat. et Preces mensis quarti	125
LXXXIV.	Orat. et Preces in Dominica Octav. Pentecosten	129
LXXXV.	Benedictio super eos qui de Ariana ad Catholicam redeunt unitatem	130
LXXXVI.	Pro eos qui de diversis haeresibus redeunt	131
LXXXVII.	Reconciliatio rebaptizati ab Haereticis	131
LXXXVIII.	In Dedicatione Basilicae novae	133
LXXXIX.	Orat. et Preces ad Missas in Ded. Basilicae novae	137
XC.	Item alia Missa	139
XCI.	Orat. et Preces in Ded. Basilicae quam conditor non dedicatam reliquit	140
XCII.	In eiusdem conditoris agendis	141
XCIII.	Orat. et Preces in Dedicatione loci ubi prius fuit Synagoga	141
XCIV.	Orat. et Preces in Dedicatione Fontis	142
XCV.	Ordo de sacris ordinibus benedicendis	144
XCVI.	Benedictiones super eos qui sacris ordinibus benedicendi sunt	147
XCVII.	In Natale consecrationis Diaconi	149
XCVIII.	In Natale consecrationis Presbyteri qualiter sibi Missam debeat celebrare	150
XCIX.	Orationes de Episcopis ordinandis	151
C.	Missa quam pro se Episcopus die ordinationis suae cantat	153
CI.	In Natalitio Episcopi, si infirmus aut absens fuerit, qualiter Presbyter debeat celebrare missam	154
CII.	Missa pro alio Sacerdote	155
CIII.	Consecratio sacrae Virginis	156
CIV.	Oratio super ancillas Dei, quibus conversis vestimenta mutantur	158
CV.	Orationes ad Missas eiusdem	159
CVI.	Item alia eiusdem	160

LIBER II		161-223
I.	Denuntiatio Natalitii unius Martyris	161
	Denuntiatio quum reliquiae ponendae sunt martyrum	161
II.	In Nat. S. Felicis Confessoris	162
III.	In Nat. S. Marcelli Confessoris	162
IV.	In Nat. Sanctorum Martyrum Sebastiani, Mariae, Martae, Audifax et Abacuc	163
V.	In Nat. S. Fabiani	164
VI.	In Nat. S. Agnetis Virg. de Passione sua	164
VII.	In Nat. eiusdem de Nativitate	165
VIII.	In Purificatione S. Mariae	165
IX.	In Nat. S. Agathae	166
X.	In Nat. S. Soteris	166
XI.	In Nat. Valentini, Vitalis, et Feliculae	167
XII.	In Nat. S. Iulianae	168
XIII.	In Nat. S. Perpetuae et Felicitatis	168
XIV.	In Annuntiatione S. Mariae	169
XV.	In Nat. S. Euphemiae	170
XVI.	In Nat. Philippi et Iacobi Apostolorum	171

CONTENTS

		PAGE
XVII.	In Nat. S. Iuvenalis	172
XVIII.	De Inventione Sanctae Crucis	172
XIX.	In Nat. Sanctorum Nerei et Achillei fratrum et S. Pancrati	173
XX.	In Nat. Sanctorum Petri et Marcellini	174
XXI.	In Nat. Sanctorum Cyrini, Naboris, et Nazari	174
XXII.	In Nat. S. Viti	175
XXIII.	In Nat. Sanctorum Marci et Marcelliani	175
XXIV.	In Vigil. Sanctorum Martyrum Gerbasi et Protasi	176
	In Natali ut supra	176
XXV.	In Vigil. S. Ioannis Baptistae	177
XXVI.	In Nat. unde supra	178
XXVII.	In Vigil. martyrum Ioannis et Pauli	179
XXVIII.	In Nat. eorumdem	180
XXIX.	In Vigil. Apostolorum Petri et Pauli	180
XXX.	In Nat. S. Petri proprie	181
XXXI.	In Nat. Apostolorum Petri et Pauli	181
XXXII.	In Nat. S. Pauli proprie	182
XXXIII.	Orationes ad Vesperum	183
XXXIV.	De Vigil. omnium Apostolorum	184
XXXV.	In Nat. omnium Apostolorum	185
XXXVI.	In Octav. Apostolorum	186
XXXVII.	In Nat. Sanctorum Simplici, Faustini, et Viatricis	186
XXXVIII.	In Nat. Abdo et Senis	187
XXXIX.	In Nat. Machabaeorum	188
XL.	In Nat. S. Sixti	188
XLI.	In Nat. S. Donati	189
XLII.	In Vigil. S. Laurenti	189
XLIII.	In Nat. eiusdem	190
XLIV.	In Nat. S. Tiburti	192
XLV.	In Nat. S. Ypoliti	192
XLVI.	In Oct. S. Laurenti	192
XLVII.	In Assumptione S. Mariae	193
XLVIII.	In Nat. S. Agapiti	194
XLIX.	In Nat. S. Magni	194
L.	In Nat. S. Ruffi	195
LI.	In Nat. S. Hermis	195
LII.	In die Passionis S. Ioannis Baptistae	196
LIII.	In Nat. S. Prisci	196
LIV.	In Nativitate S. Mariae	197
LV.	In Nat. S. Gurgoni	198
LVI.	In Exaltatione sanctae Crucis	198
LVII.	In Nat. Sanctorum Corneli et Cypriani	199
LVIII.	In Nat. Sanctorum Cosmae et Damiani	199
LIX.	In [Dedic. Basil.] S. Archangeli Michaelis	200
LX.	Orat. in Ieiunio mensis septimi	200
LXI.	In Nat. Sanctorum Marcelli et Apulei	202
LXII.	In Nat. Sanctorum Quatuor Coronatorum	203
LXIII.	In [Vigilia] S. Caeciliae	203
LXIV.	In Nat. eiusdem	204
LXV.	In Nat. S. Clementis	205
LXVI.	In Nat. S. Felicitatis	205

CONTENTS. xiii

		PAGE
LXVII.	In Nat. Sanctorum Martyrum Saturnini, Crisanti, Mauri, Dariae et aliorum	206
LXVIII.	In Vigil. S. Andreae	206
LXIX.	In Nat. eiusdem	207
LXX.	In Oct. S. Andreae Apostoli	208
LXXI.	In Nat. S. Thomae Apostoli	208
LXXII.	Orat. in Nat. plurimorum sanctorum	209
LXXIII.	Item alia Missa	209
LXXIV.	Item alia Missa	210
LXXV.	Item alia Missa	211
LXXVI.	Item alia Missa	211
LXXVII.	Item alia Missa	212
LXXVIII.	Item alia Missa	213
LXXIX.	Item alia Missa	213
LXXX.	Orat. de Adventum Domini	214
LXXXI.	Item alia Missa	215
LXXXII.	Item alia Missa	216
LXXXIII.	Item alia Missa	217
LXXXIV.	Item alia Missa	218
LXXXV.	Orat. et Preces mensis decimi	220
	LIBER III	**224–315**
I.	Missa pro Dominicis diebus	224
II.	Item alia Missa	225
III.	Item alia Missa	225
IV.	Item alia Missa	226
V.	Item alia Missa	226
VI.	Item alia Missa	227
VII.	Item alia Missa	228
VIII.	Item alia Missa	228
IX.	Item alia Missa	229
X.	Item alia Missa	229
XI.	Item alia Missa	230
XII.	Item alia Missa	231
XIII.	Item alia Missa	231
XIV.	Item alia Missa	232
XV.	Item alia Missa	232
XVI.	Item alia Missa	233
	Canon Actionis	234
	Postcommuniones	236
[XVII.]	Benedictiones super Populum	240
XVIII.	Orat. quotidianis diebus ad Missas	242
XIX.	Item alia Missa	242
XX.	Item alia Missa	243
XXI.	Item alia Missa	243
XXII.	Item alia Missa	244
XXIII.	Item alia Missa	244
XXIV.	Orat. ad proficiscendum in itinere	245
XXV.	Orat. ad iter agentibus	247
XXVI.	Orat. pro caritate	247

xiv CONTENTS.

		PAGE
XXVII.	Item alia Missa	248
XXVIII.	Orat. in tribulatione	248
XXIX.	Item alia Missa	249
XXX.	Item alia Missa	249
XXXI.	Item alia Missa	250
XXXII.	Item alia Missa	250
XXXIII.	Item alia Missa	251
XXXIV.	Item alia Missa	252
XXXV.	Item alia Missa	252
XXXVI.	Item alia Missa	253
XXXVII.	Item alia Missa	253
	Orat. in Natali Presbyteri qualiter sibi Missam debeat celebrare	254
XXXVIII.	Orat. tempore, quod absit, mortalitatis	255
XXXIX.	Item alia Missa	255
XL.	Item alia Missa	256
XLI.	Item alia Missa	256
XLII.	Orat. pro mortalitate animalium	257
XLIII.	Orat. de sterilitate	258
XLIV.	Orat. ad pluviam postulandam	258
XLV.	Item alia Missa	259
XLVI.	Orat. ad poscendam serenitatem	260
XLVII.	Orat. post tempestatem et fulgura	261
XLVIII.	Orat. pro his qui Agape faciunt	261
XLIX.	Item orat. ad Missas	262
L.	Missa in monasterio	263
LI.	Item orationes monachorum	264
LII.	Actio nuptialis	265
LIII.	Orat. in Natale genuinum	268
LIV.	Orat. ad Missam pro sterilitate mulierum	269
LV.	Benedictio viduae quae fuerit castitatem professa	271
LVI.	Orat. pro pace	271
LVII.	Orat. tempore belli	272
LVIII.	Item alia Missa	273
LIX.	Item alia Missa	274
LX.	Item alia Missa	275
LXI.	Item alia Missa	275
LXII.	Missa pro regibus	276
LXIII.	Missa contra iudices male agentes	277
LXIV.	Item alia Missa	278
LXV.	Orat. in contentione ad Missas	278
LXVI.	Item alia Missa	279
LXVII.	Orat. ad Missam contra obloquentes	279
LXVIII.	Orat. ad Missas pro irreligiosis	280
LXIX.	Orat. super infirmum in domo	281
LXX.	Orat. ad Missam pro infirmum	282
LXXI.	Oratio pro reddita sanitate	282
LXXII.	Orationes intrantibus in domo	283
LXXIII.	Item orat. ad Missas	283
LXXIV.	Orationes super venientes in domo	284
LXXV.	Benedictio aquae spargendae in domo	285
LXXVI.	Item alia	285

CONTENTS.

		PAGE
	Orationes pro aspersione aquae	287
LXXVII.	Orationes pro fulguribus	288
LXXVIII.	Benedictio aquae exorcizatae ad fulgura	289
LXXIX.	Orationes in area nova	289
LXXX.	Orationes in monasterio	290
LXXXI.	Oratio in domo ancillarum Dei	290
LXXXII.	Oratio pro renuntiantibus saeculo	290
LXXXIII.	Oratio pro eo qui prius barbam tondet	291
LXXXIV.	Orationes ad matutinas	291
LXXXV.	Orationes ad vesperum	292
LXXXVI.	Orationes ante cibum	293
LXXXVII.	Orationes post cibos	294
LXXXVIII.	Oratio ad fruges novas benedicendas	294
LXXXIX.	Benedictio pomorum	294
XC.	Benedictio arboris	295
XCI.	Orationes post obitum hominis	295
XCII.	Missa pro defuncto Sacerdote	301
XCIII.	Item alia pro Sacerdote	302
XCIV.	Item alia pro Sacerdote sive Abbate	302
XCV.	Orat. ad Missa in Natale sanctorum sive agenda mortuorum	303
XCVI.	Missa pro defuncti nuper baptizati	304
XCVII.	Item alia Missa	305
XCVIII.	Orat. ad Missas pro defunctis desiderantibus poenitentiam et minimum consecutis	306
XCIX.	Orat. pro defunctis laicis. Item unius defuncti	307
C.	In agenda plurimorum	308
CI.	Item alia Missa	308
CII.	Item alia Missa	309
CIII.	Item alia Missa in Coemeteriis	310
CIV.	Item alia Missa	311
CV.	Item Missa in Depositione defuncti, tertii, septimi, tricesimi dierum sive annualem	312
CVI.	Item Orat. ad Missam pro salute vivorum	313
	Ad Poenitentiam dandam	314

APPENDIX 317-371

INDEX OF LITURGICAL FORMS 373-395

INDEX OF SUBJECTS 396-400

INTRODUCTION

AMONG the few service-books of the Western Church which have come down to us from a time before the days of Charles the Great, one of the most important is the manuscript commonly called the Gelasian Sacramentary. It was written most probably in the seventh, or in the early years of the eighth century, evidently for use in some church in the Frankish dominions, possibly for the abbey of S. Denis[1]. It is now in the Library of the Vatican, where it is known as MS. *Reginae* 316, being part of the collection formed by Queen Christina of Sweden. Before it came into her possession, it was for some time in the collection of the Senator Paul Petau, at Paris, where it was examined by Morinus and by Cardinal Bona. Both of these writers regarded it as a representative of the Sacramentary attributed to S. Gelasius[2].

This view was adopted by the first editor of the Sacramentary, Joseph Maria Tommasi[3], who argued in his preface in support of the Gelasian origin of the book: but he did not give to it in his edition any other title than that which the manuscript itself supplied; and it therefore appeared under

---

[1] This is the view of Abbé Duchesne (*Origines du Culte Chrétien*, p. 124), and is supported by the fact that the names of the three patron saints of S. Denis are mentioned in the *Canon Actionis* of the manuscript, before the names of S. Hilary and S. Martin. The three names have, however, been erased; and this may suggest that the codex, even if written for S. Denis, was afterwards used elsewhere. Mabillon, in the preface to his treatise, *De Liturgia Gallicana*, remarks that the greater part of the liturgical MSS. of Petau's collection came from the abbey of Fleury.

[2] Morinus, *Commentarius Historicus de disciplina in administratione sacramenti Poenitentiae*, App., pp. 51, 52; Bona, *De Rebus Liturgicis*, Lib. II, c. v, § 4 (vol. iii, p. 99, ed. Sala).

[3] Afterwards Cardinal of S. Martin *in montibus*. He was beatified by Pius VII. The Sacramentary was first published in his collection entitled *Codices Sacramentorum nongentis annis vetustiores* (4to, Romae, 1680).

the title *Liber Sacramentorum Romanae Ecclesiae*. The name of *Sacramentarium Gelasianum* was assigned to it, when it next appeared in print, by Muratori, who included in his *Liturgia Romana Vetus*[1] a reprint of Tommasi's text, preface, and notes. Muratori added but little of his own: but in the preface to his whole book he declared his adhesion to Tommasi's view of the origin of the Sacramentary, and supported that opinion by some further arguments.

The Sacramentary was published once more, a few years later, under its former title, in the sixth volume of Vezzosi's edition of the collected works of Cardinal Tommasi, which appeared at Rome in 1751. This edition was more than a mere reprint. . It reproduced Tommasi's text, with corrections of typographical errors, and with additional notes. These gave the results of a new collation of the manuscript, and of a comparison not only with the Gregorian texts edited by Pamelius and by Ménard, which Tommasi had himself frequently cited, but also with the Gregorian text published by Rocca, and with the *Codex Ottobonianus*. This last authority, a Gregorian Sacramentary, had been partly made known by Muratori, and had been examined by Tommasi, after the publication of his *Codices Sacramentorum*. Another source of additional notes was found in a copy of Tommasi's work in which the editor had himself made manuscript additions and corrections (including observations as to the readings of the *Codex Ottobonianus*), possibly with a view to a new edition. The more important of these memoranda were incorporated by Vezzosi with the notes of Tommasi's own edition, being distinguished by asterisks from the earlier notes. Thus Vezzosi's edition is the most complete of those which have hitherto appeared[2]; but since its publication some further means have become available for the critical study of the text.

When Tommasi published his *editio princeps*, the Vatican manuscript stood by itself. It was, professedly, a Roman Sacramentary: but while it contained a good many things in common with the Roman Sacramentaries of the 'Gregorian' type, it differed very widely from these later books not only in date,

---

[1] 2 vols. fol. (Venice, 1748).
[2] The edition contained in the seventy-fourth volume of Migne's *Patrologia Latina* is merely an incorrect reproduction of Muratori's reprint of the first edition. It is the only edition which can easily be obtained; but it has no other recommendation.

but also in arrangement and in contents. Its division into three books, and some other indications, seemed to show that it was really a specimen of that older Roman Sacramentary which writers of the ninth century alleged to have been recast by S. Gregory, and which they connected with the name of S. Gelasius. But there were no other 'Gelasian' Sacramentaries known to its editors: and although here and there the Gregorian books which they were able to employ might throw light on the text of the Vatican manuscript, where this was faulty or obscure, they were of less value for such a purpose than books more nearly approaching to the date of the Vatican manuscript, and more nearly allied to it in structure.

Before Muratori issued his reprint, or Vezzosi issued his new edition, Pierre Le Brun, the learned French Oratorian, had published, under the title of *Explication de la Messe*[1], his valuable dissertations on the Liturgy. He also recognizes, in the manuscript published by Tommasi, a representative of the Sacramentary of S. Gelasius; but he regards it as only one specimen of a class of manuscripts of which he knew other examples. Some of these, he tells us, he proposed to publish in his projected *Bibliotheca Liturgica*; and while he specifies several points of distinction between the 'Gelasian' and the 'Gregorian' Sacramentaries, his language suggests that his statements as to the former class were based upon a considerable number of instances[2]. Unhappily the *Bibliotheca Liturgica* never appeared, and Le Brun's mention of 'Gelasian' books had not the effect of producing an enquiry as to their place or their contents.

In 1777 Dom Martin Gerbert, Abbot of S. Blaise in the Black Forest, published, in the first volume of his *Monumenta Veteris Liturgiae Alemannicae*[3], a text which was in part professedly 'Gelasian,' and concerning which there could be little, if any, doubt that it was in part actually drawn from a Sacramentary of the class which was in the ninth century known as 'Gelasian.' At first sight, therefore, it would seem that Gerbert's text must have a high value for the purpose of comparison with the text of the Vatican manuscript. His work has certainly

---

[1] This work appeared at Paris, in 4 vols. 8vo, between 1715 and 1726. It has been reprinted in 4 vols. 8vo (Paris, 1860).

[2] Le Brun, *Expl. de la Messe*, Diss. II, Art. ii. (vol. ii, pp. 131-3, 147-9, in 1860 ed.).

[3] 4to, Typis San-Blasianis, 1777.

been of much service in the preparation of the present edition, and it seems almost ungrateful to criticise the method and execution of a scholar of the last century, to whom students of Liturgy owe so much as we owe to Gerbert. But it must be said that his text is one which requires to be used with caution, that the plan which he followed in this part of his work was chosen with an unfortunate want of judgement, and that his mode of handling his materials, and of explaining what those materials were, is at times exceedingly confused and misleading.

Of the three principal manuscripts used by Gerbert in editing, or compiling, the text of his Sacramentary, two, the *Codex Rhenaugiensis* and *Codex Sangallensis antiquior*, belonged to the class of books known as 'Gelasian.' The third, a manuscript of a peculiar character, of which he sometimes speaks by the title *Sangallensis recentior*, sometimes simply by the title *Sangallensis*, was, when he used it, not at S. Gallen, but at Zürich. He calls it in one passage 'Sangallensis olim nunc Turicensis, ex triplici ritu Gelasiano, Gregoriano, et Ambrosiano compositus[1].' To this third manuscript, of much later date

---

[1] The two 'Gelasian' manuscripts, the Rheinau and the S. Gallen, have been collated for this edition, and are frequently referred to by the symbols R. (for the *Codex Rhenaugiensis*) and S. (for the *Codex Sangallensis*). The third of Gerbert's principal MSS. is sometimes indicated in the following pages by the symbol T. (for *Turicensis*): but, for reasons which will be apparent, it is not often mentioned. Even if it had been of more value for the purposes of this edition than there is any reason to suppose, it cannot now be traced. Its presence at Zürich is most probably to be explained by supposing that it was one of the manuscripts which fell to the share of the town of Zürich, and were removed to its Town Library, when the Library of S. Gallen was plundered in the religious war of 1712 by the forces of Zürich and Bern, and that it was not among those which were returned to S. Gallen a few years later. Both in a Zürich list of manuscripts brought from S. Gallen, drawn up in 1713, and in a S. Gallen list of losses suffered by the Library of the monastery in 1712, there appears a volume described as *Collectae Missales*: the S. Gallen list adds the further description 'seu Missae Gregorianae et Ambrosianae,' a phrase which seems to point to a compound Sacramentary, and may not impossibly be a description of the Sacramentary which Gerbert, later in the eighteenth century, found at Zürich. (Weidmann, *Gesch. der Bibliothek von S. Gallen*, pp. 435, 440.) In the Catalogue of the S. Gallen MSS. edited by G. Scherrer (Halle, 1875), in the notice of the S. Gallen MS. 348, reference is made to Gerbert's work, and the triple Sacramentary used by him is described as 'jetzt Zürcher codex C. 389.' It does not appear whence Scherrer derived this information. But the manuscript now bearing the mark C. 389 in the Town Library of Zürich is not a Sacramentary, but a collection of miscellaneous fragments. Curiously enough, however, it contains the following extract from a letter, written in 1764 by Gerbert to the

than either of the others, Gerbert gave the first place in his estimation; and it was this manuscript which he chose, rather than either of the other two, as the basis of the greater part of his text. The reason for this preference, and some of its consequences, must be very briefly stated.

Gerbert considered the *Codex Sangallensis* (S.) to be a manuscript of the latter part of the eighth century ('vix assurgit ad mille annos'); the *Codex Rhenaugiensis* (R.) he supposed to be earlier than S. 'aliquot annorum decadibus.' The third manuscript was of the tenth century, and he believed it to have been written at S. Gallen. It was, as has been said, a Sacramentary of an unusual type. The compiler had had for his object the combination in a single volume of the services for the various days of the Church year according to the rites which were known to him as 'Gelasian,' 'Gregorian,' and 'Ambrosian.' In carrying out this task he appears to have used the *Codex Sangallensis* (S.) as one of his authorities, transcribing its contents, or great part of its contents, and distinguishing as 'Gelasian' the portions of his triple text which were derived from this source[1].

The special interest attaching to the combination of rites presented by T. gave to that manuscript, no doubt, part of its special importance in Gerbert's eyes: a Sacramentary which included not only Gelasian forms but also Gregorian and Ambrosian *missae* for the same days appeared to him to possess a character of completeness which the older manuscripts could not claim: but he was influenced also by other reasons. He conceived that the resemblance between R. and S. was so close

Librarian of Zürich:—'Remitto codicem Turicensem incomparabilem, cui forte parem in re liturgica non fert orbis litterarius. Si otium fuerit, edam cum singulari commentario.'

[1] This makes it clear that S. (and therefore also R., which is certainly a book of the same type as S.) would in the tenth century have been described as 'Gelasian.' It was, presumably, on the connexion between S. and T. that Gerbert, in part at least, relied in supposing that T. was written at S. Gallen. He seems to have had no doubt as to the relation of the two manuscripts; indeed the comparison of S. with his printed text leaves very little room for hesitation in accepting his view. The 'Gelasian' portions of his text are in very close agreement with S., as the latter now stands; and the case is still further strengthened by the fact that the compiler of T. seems, in almost all cases, to have given effect to certain marginal notes which appear in S., intended for the guidance of a copyist, as to the order of *missae* and prayers. In one case a marginal gloss in S., explanatory of a word in one of the prayers, has been incorporated with the text of the prayer as it appears in Gerbert's Sacramentary (see note 18 on p. 12 of this volume).

as to leave no doubt that both had been copied from the same source, though S. contained some *missae* for festivals and some other matter which had been added in the interval between the dates at which the two had been written. It was true, he thought, that the latter part of R. contained a good deal which was not to be found in S.: but so far as the first part, containing the services for the yearly round of Sundays and festivals, was concerned, S. seemed to him to contain practically everything that was to be found in R., with valuable additions. As between these two, therefore, he would have given the preference to S. as an authority, even if it had not possessed what he regarded as an advantage of special importance. Originally, he says, R. and S. had agreed 'ad apicem usque... in corrupto etiam dicendi scribendique genere, erroribus grammaticalibus ac sphalmatis aevo Merovingico propriis[1].' But the original text of S. had been revised and corrected by a later hand, which had 'restored the true sense' by emending the errors of the original scribe: and these improvements in the text were to be found also in T., since the compiler of this manuscript had followed the corrected text of S. Thus, in Gerbert's view, while S. contained, in its round of services, all, or nearly all, that was to be found in the parallel portion of R., T. also contained the whole, or nearly the whole, of what was to be found in S., in a corrected and improved form, and with further additions.

He accordingly determined to reproduce the text of T., distinguishing by special type those parts of the 'triple text' which were to be found in S., and marking by brackets those portions which, though contained in S., were not to be found in R. Where T. was defective, he used one or other of the two older manuscripts as the basis of his text, and he also reproduced from R. a good deal of matter not contained in S. or T., while he occasionally added, in his footnotes to the text, some particulars as to the readings or arrangement of the two older manuscripts. Unfortunately, in carrying out his plan, he

---

[1] An examination of the two MSS. does not bear out Gerbert's statement on this point. The text of the two agrees, in the common matter, very closely, but they do not by any means exactly accord with one another in the matters of grammar and spelling. The grammar of R. is more faulty than that of S., and its spelling much more variable and incorrect. As to the nature and extent of the agreement which Gerbert alleges to exist between them in respect of the matter contained in the two Sacramentaries, more will be said at a later stage.

was not always careful in the employment of his marks of differentiation. Some entire *missae* and many portions of *missae* which are contained in S. are not distinguished by the type which ought to mark the matter found in the older books, while a large number of *missae* which are absent from R. appear in his text without the brackets which ought to have indicated their absence from that manuscript[1].

But besides this defect of accuracy in following out the plan he had laid down for himself (a defect which seriously diminishes the value of the information conveyed by his method) Gerbert's way of regarding his materials had another unfortunate result. As he was inclined to minimise the differences of text between R. and S., he was also inclined to underrate, or to misunderstand, the importance of the changes introduced into the latter manuscript by the hand of the corrector. These changes were, in many cases, much more than mere corrections of mistakes in grammar or variations in spelling. The effect, if not the purpose, of the corrector's work has generally been the alteration of the original text into closer agreement with the text of the later Sacramentaries of the type known as 'Gregorian.' Hence it comes to pass that the 'Gelasian' portions of the 'triple text' of T. (and therefore of Gerbert's printed text) do not represent the original text of the 'Gelasian' books, but a revision of that text, apparently based upon the text of the Sacramentaries of the 'Gregorian' type[2].' The evidence for this statement will be found in the notes of the present volume, where it will again and again appear that the text of R. and the original text of S. are in agreement with the readings of the Vatican manuscript, while the readings of the later hand of S., followed by Gerbert's printed text, are in agreement with the

---

[1] Gerbert himself apologizes, in his preface, for the omission, in two specified cases, of these distinguishing brackets: but the instances of such omission are far more numerous. As a matter of fact he has failed to mark in this way more than sixty entire *missae*, and a large number of Collects and Prefaces. It is quite impossible to gather from his text the real state of the case as to the amount of matter common to R. and S.

[2] This does not of course apply to the portions of Gerbert's text where R. has been employed as his authority. In these portions he reproduces the readings of the original text, not literally, but with substantial accuracy for the most part. He has, however, occasionally failed to read the manuscript correctly, or to notice the existence of a gap occasioned by the loss of a leaf, and has thus perpetrated one or two amazing blunders. In anything which he extracts directly from S., he appears as a rule to follow the readings of the second hand.

'Gregorian' Sacramentaries edited by Pamelius and by Ménard, or with the Sacramentary known as the 'Leofric Missal.'

Thus, while Gerbert's text contains a larger proportion of prayers derived from 'Gelasian' sources than the text of Pamelius, or even of Ménard, its value as a means of elucidating the text of the Vatican manuscript is practically not much greater than that of the 'Gregorian' books, except where it is directly taken from the older Sacramentary which Gerbert, for a large part of his work, deliberately set aside, or where the tenth century manuscript which he preferred to follow has retained unaltered the original reading of one or both of the older books. The actual text, as well as the actual arrangement of those older manuscripts is, as M. Duchesne remarks [1], 'very imperfectly known' to us from his work, in spite of the labour and pains which that work must have cost him.

On the other hand, however, the evidence of these two manuscripts, to which Gerbert was the first to direct attention, appears upon examination to be of considerable importance in its bearing upon the text of the Vatican manuscript. The later manuscripts furnish us, in some cases, with the means of correcting that text: they sometimes show us, by their agreement with the Vatican manuscript in readings apparently faulty, that the errors of that manuscript, to whatever cause they are to be assigned, are not always due to the aberrations of a single scribe. Further, it may perhaps be found that a comparison of the contents and arrangement of the three 'Gelasian' sacramentaries may throw some light on the history of the class of Sacramentaries to which they belong, and on the origin of the particular Sacramentary to which the name 'Gelasian' has now been for a long time attached.

Before proceeding to touch upon these questions it will be best to give some account of the manuscripts themselves, of other manuscripts used in the revision of the text, and of the use which has been made of the manuscript and printed material employed.

I. The manuscript which has furnished the text of this edition is that commonly known as the 'Gelasian' Sacramentary, the Vatican MS. *Reginae* 316. This manuscript is distinguished in the notes appended to the text as V. It has been twice

---

[1] *Origines du Culte Chrétien*, p. 120.

described by M. Léopold Delisle[1], and from his descriptions the following brief account of its external features is drawn. The manuscript contains 245 leaves, measuring 263 by 164 millimetres (or about 10¼ by 6½ inches), and is written throughout in uncial characters with the exception of the Latin versions of the bilingual texts of the Lord's Prayer[2] and the Creed[3].

The Greek versions are written in Roman uncials, while the Latin versions, between the lines of the Greek, are in a minuscule hand of a Lombardic type. The contents of the manuscript are divided into numbered sections, the headings of which are written in red and green. The last page of each gathering of the manuscript bears a signature in Roman numerals: and in these signatures, as in the numeration of the sections of the text, the number six is occasionally denoted by the *Episemon*. Each of the three books into which the Sacramentary is divided is preceded by an ornamental design covering the *verso* of a leaf the *recto* of which is left blank. The design in each case is that of an arch enclosing a cross having the letters Alpha and Omega dependent from its arms[4]. The titles prefixed to the three books are as follows:—

(i) 'In nomine Domini Ihesu Salvatoris. Incipit liber Sacramentorum Romanae aecclesiae ordinis anni circuli.'

(ii) 'Incipit liber secundus. Oraciones et praeces de nataliciis sanctorum.'

(iii) 'Incipit liber tercius. Oraciones et praeces cum canone per dominicis diebus.'

The third book is closed with the words 'Explicit liber Sacramentorum. Deo gracias.'

On palaeographical grounds, M. Delisle assigns the manuscript to the seventh, or the early part of the eighth, century. The fact that it was written for some church in the Frankish kingdom is shown not only by the names of saints mentioned in the Canon, but also by the mention of the 'Imperium Francorum' in the Good Friday prayers. The Sacramentary itself

---

[1] In the *Bibliothèque de l'Ecole des Chartes*, vol. xxxvii. (1876), pp. 475-7. and again in his most valuable *Mémoire sur d'Anciens Sacramentaires* (*Mémoires de l'Académie des Inscriptions*, vol. xxxii.).

[2] This stands on the *verso* of fol. 2, at the end of the remains of the table of contents, which was prefixed to the Sacramentary proper.

[3] This begins on fol. 45 *v*. of the MS. See pp. 53-4 of this edition. A facsimile of part of the bilingual Creed is to be found in the plates accompanying M. Delisle's *Mémoire* (Plate iv).

[4] See *Mémoire sur d'Anciens Sacramentaires*, Plate ii.

is complete, but the first part of a list of its contents, prefixed to the whole, has been lost. The remains of this list, with the bilingual text of the Lord's Prayer, occupy the first and second leaves.

When we pass from considering the outward appearance of the book to the examination of its contents, we find that the matter contained in its three divisions does not in any one case exactly correspond with the title. The first book contains several sections, relating to Episcopal functions, which would in later times have formed part of the 'Pontifical,' and which do not, strictly speaking, fall under the description of the contents of the book as 'ordinis anni circuli.' These portions do not stand together, but while some of them are to be found at the end of the book, others are fitted into the series of *missae* and prayers for the course of the Church year from Christmas to Pentecost, which occupies the first half of the book. This method is also followed with regard to certain offices and forms which would in later times have been included in the Missal, but would also have found their place in the 'Manual' or 'Rituale.' Thus the forms for the Ordination of Deacons and Priests are placed after the *Orationes et preces in xii lectiones mense primo* which follow the *missae* for the first week in Lent, while the other forms of Ordination stand near the end of the book. The prayers *super Poenitentes* are, not unnaturally, placed at the beginning of Lent, and the forms for the public reconciliation of the Penitents, and for the hallowing of the Oils and Chrism, find their place in the section relating to the Thursday *in Coena Domini*. It may be regarded as a natural arrangement that the forms relating to the preparation of the Catechumens should be intercalated with the series of Lent *missae*, and that those relating to the *Consecratio Fontis* and to Baptism and Confirmation should stand in the section relating to Easter Even. But it is not at first sight clear why other forms relating to Penitents should be joined with those belonging to the order of Maundy Thursday, and perhaps still less clear why the forms relating to the Baptism of the Sick should be placed between the prayers of Ascensiontide and those of Pentecost. To this point reference will be made again, in treating of the arrangement of the Rheinau Sacramentary, which seems to throw some light on the structure of the first book of the Vatican manuscript. Another instance of inserted matter is evidently to be found in the form for the *Benedictio cerei*, which finds its natural place in the section relating to Easter Even, but is shown, by the rubric which follows it [1], to have been drawn, not from a *Liber Sacramentorum*, but from some document corresponding to an '*Exultet* Roll.' It is right also to notice here the fact, which is pointed out by M. Duchesne [2], that, among what may be called the Pontifical sections of this book, the series of forms relating to the minor Orders contained in sections xcv and xcvi are not of Roman origin, and that certain forms relating to the ordination of Deacons and Priests are also probably drawn from a Gallican source. But it seems certain that the basis of the first part of the book, containing the services for the Church year from Christmas to Pentecost, has been a Roman Sacramentary of early date. Here and there we may find indications that the Roman book has been adapted to Gallican usages, in the use of the phrase 'post clausum Paschae,' in the absence of any reference to the Roman 'Stations,' and perhaps in the presence, in the *missae* of Christmas and Eastertide, of prayers which seem to have the characteristics of Gallican rather than of Roman collects, and of other prayers which are found in the Gallican Sacramentaries. The Roman book employed by the compiler was probably of a date earlier than 731, since there are no *missae* for the Thursdays of Lent, while we know that the 'Stations' on these days were established by Gregory II (715-731) [3]. On the other hand, the presence of *missae* for the Wednesday, Friday and Saturday before the first Sunday of Lent seems to point to a date later than S. Gregory the Great for the Roman book, while the presence of a *Capitulum S. Gregorii Papae* in section xxi makes it quite clear that the present arrangement of the text belongs to a date not earlier than the year 600.

The second book contains not only *missae* for the Saints' Days, but also certain sections which would seem properly to belong to the series contained in the first book, namely, the *missae* for the September and December Ember days, and those for the Sundays of Advent (Book II. lx, lxxx–lxxxv). The presence of these portions of the text in a division of the Sacramentary which is professedly devoted to the *Sanctorale* may perhaps

---

[1] See p. 81 of this edition.
[2] *Origines du Culte Chrétien*, pp. 125, 338, 349 sqq.
[3] *Liber Pontif.* i. p. 402.

suggest a doubt whether the method of division which we find in the Vatican manuscript was adopted in the Roman Sacramentary used by its compiler. It seems possible that the severance of the Advent *missae* from the series contained in the first book may have been due to a division, awkwardly carried out, of the contents of a Sacramentary which, like the Rheinau and S. Gallen manuscripts, had the *Proprium de Tempore* and the *Proprium Sanctorum* placed together in a single series, and which, like the S. Gallen manuscript[1], described that series as 'ordinis anni circuli,' or '[per] anni circulum.'

With regard to the contents of the *Proprium Sanctorum* we may here notice that almost every festival included in this portion of the Vatican manuscript finds a place also in the S. Gallen Sacramentary, and that in a very large proportion of cases the *missa* assigned to a festival in the S. Gallen book agrees, in whole or in part, with that which belongs to the same festival in the Vatican manuscript. The *Proprium Sanctorum* of the Rheinau manuscript is much more limited in extent, but this also contains a good deal in common with this portion of the Vatican manuscript. The presence of *missae* for the four festivals of the Blessed Virgin seems to point to a date later than the beginning of the seventh century for the source from which they were taken, if this was a Roman Sacramentary[2]: and the *missa* for the festival of the Exaltation of the Cross probably dates from some time after 628.

The third book begins with a series of *missae* for Sundays, the contents of which (except for the fact that none of the *missae* contains a proper Preface) correspond almost exactly with a portion of the series of *missae* assigned in the Rheinau and S. Gallen books to the Sundays between Pentecost and Advent. Then follows the *Canon Actionis*, with two series, one of Postcommunions, the other of benedictions *super Populum*. Next come several *missae* for ordinary days; and the remainder of the book is occupied by a collection of *missae* and prayers for special purposes, including forms relating to Marriage, and to the Burial of the Dead. The first part of this book (the series of Sunday *missae*) is found, as has been said, in the Rheinau and

---

[1] It is very possible that the case was the same with the Rheinau manuscript, but this has now no title; the leaf which probably contained the title is lost.

[2] Perhaps some part of the contents of the *missa* for the Annunciation may be thought to show traces of a Gallican rather than a Roman origin.

S. Gallen books: these also contain a similar set of *missae* for ordinary days, with the *Canon Actionis* and appended series of Postcommunions and Benedictions. But with the last of these the S. Gallen book now ends, so that that Sacramentary has nothing corresponding to the latter part of the third book. The Rheinau Sacramentary, on the other hand, contains a similar series of special *missae* and occasional prayers, having much in common with the parallel portion of the Vatican manuscript.

In the third book, once more, we find some indications that the Roman Sacramentary used by the compiler was probably later than the beginning of the seventh century. In the *Canon Actionis* the clause *Diesque nostros*, said to have been added by S. Gregory, is present, and the name of S. Gregory is mentioned among those of the saints [1]. But we may notice on the other hand, that many of the special *missae* in the latter portion of the book, which have clauses for insertion in the Canon, take no notice of the clause *Diesque nostros*, but pass directly from the end of the *Hanc igitur* to the *Quam oblationem*. This may indicate for these sections an origin earlier than the time of S. Gregory's pontificate: but the inference is not a certain one.

The spelling and grammar of the manuscript are, as might be expected in a manuscript of the Merovingian period, exceedingly capricious and irregular. The method which has been adopted in reproducing its text is one which is certainly open to some objections, but it appeared, after careful consideration, to be on the whole the most satisfactory for practical uses.

From one point of view it would no doubt have been desirable to aim at an exact literal reproduction of the text of the manuscript, with all its errors. But the conditions under which the preparation of this edition has been carried on rendered this course practically impossible, since it would have required, not only the making of an exact transcript, but also, if the work were to be done with the minute care which such a method would demand, the careful correction of the proof-sheets by comparison with the manuscript itself. It would have required also, for the completeness of the work, careful notice of the

---

[1] We also find, in the latter part of the book, a prayer which includes a petition that benefit may be obtained by the intercession of S. Gregory (see p. 270). It is perhaps not quite certain, but it seems most likely, that the saint referred to is S. Gregory the Great.

variations of spelling in the kindred manuscripts ; and the result of this would have been a very large addition to the bulk of the notes appended to the text, and therefore to the size of the volume. Another possible method would have been to adopt an arbitrary standard of spelling based on what might be called the normal spelling of the manuscript: but this method would not have had the advantage of an exact reproduction of the text, while it would have been found impossible, in some cases, to say what the normal spelling of the scribe really is. The best course therefore seemed to be that of following the example of the former editors, in adopting a modern standard of spelling, and of carefully noting the readings of the manuscript, where there seemed to be any doubt as to a particular word or phrase, arising from the possibility of rendering a misspelt word in more ways than one. For this purpose, a careful collation of the manuscript seemed to be all that was necessary, and upon such a collation the present text is based [1].

But a further question presented itself, the question of rejecting or retaining obviously ungrammatical readings : and this was a point on which it was more difficult to arrive at a decision. It has seemed best, on the whole, to set aside those readings which are probably due to the errors of the scribe. Sometimes, as when an ablative and an accusative are both made to depend upon the same verb, or when a reading may be treated either as an ungrammatical construction, or as a simple error of spelling, these corrections have been made *sub silentio*. But in cases where an ungrammatical reading is set aside, either on the evidence of the manuscript itself, which elsewhere gives the phrase in a form grammatically correct, or on the evidence of other texts, the rejected reading, and the evidence in favour of the more grammatical form, are given in the notes. It has seemed reasonable to use, as the means of such corrections, not only the earlier text of the Leonine Sacramentary, and the practically contemporary texts of the Gallican books, but also the later texts of the Rheinau and S. Gallen manuscripts, and of

---

[1] The collation, with which the editor was furnished by the kindness of Dr. Ince, the Regius Professor of Divinity, was made by Signor Rappagliosi, who was recommended by the authorities of the Vatican Library for the performance of the work. This collation has been tested by a comparison with other collations of particular portions of the text, and appears to have been very carefully and accurately carried out.

documents reproduced by Martène, since these later texts, though later, still serve to show that the grammatically correct form was current before the literary reforms of Charles the Great, or in manuscripts which contain a sufficient amount of error to make it clear that their texts owed little or nothing of their correctness to these reforms. Where no such evidence for the early existence of a grammatical reading of a passage is to be found, or where the kindred manuscripts of Rheinau and S. Gallen clearly support the ungrammatical reading, that reading has been retained in the text, and its character, in most cases, indicated by the appended notes.

The most notable grammatical errors of the manuscript are the following:—

(*a*) The abuse of cases. The ablative and accusative cases are frequently interchanged: in some instances the apparent misuse of the ablative may be due to the accidental omission of a superscribed *m*: but this theory would not account for the whole of the instances. In one or two places the accusative seems to be used for the nominative[1]: but these cases may be due to the loss of some word in the text.

(*b*) The use of the imperative mood for the subjunctive, following *ut*. This may perhaps, at least in the majority of instances, be explained by supposing that *ut* is a clerical error for *et*: but the fact that the verb, rather than the conjunction, has been altered in the later recension of the text, must be taken into account in estimating the character of the error.

(*c*) The present participle is occasionally used (probably with a suppression of the verb substantive) in an imperative sense[2].

The interchange of certain letters, which is a marked feature of the spelling of the manuscript, is no doubt due in many cases to similarity of sounds. The following are the chief cases of substitution or variation[3]:—

a is used for ae, e, in some instances for i (e.g. *turabulis* = *thuribulis*).

ae (or its equivalent ę) is used for a, e, oe, i.

---

[1] e.g. Adesto Domine ... et populum tuum ... salvetur (p. 5); Ascendant ad te, Domine, preces nostras (pp. 304, 305).

[2] See the rubric on p. 80.

[3] These irregularities have most commonly been corrected without remark: in cases where there is a doubt as to the word intended, the reading of the manuscript, if rejected, has been given in the note. In the case of certain proper names, where the spelling of the manuscript is constant, it has been retained (e.g. Gerbasius, Ypolitus).

b is used for p, v.

c is used for ch, g, qu, s, t; it is also sometimes inserted (e. g. *uncxisti*), and sometimes omitted.

d is used for t.

e is used for a, for i (very frequently), and perhaps for u; it is sometimes inserted (e.g. *offeret = offert*).

ę is used not only for ae, but also for e and oe.

f is used for ff, and for ph.

ff is used for f.

g is occasionally used for i (e. g. *genuam = ianuam*).

h is sometimes prefixed, inserted, and omitted.

i is used for ae, for e (very frequently), and u, rarely for g, and often for y: it is sometimes doubled, sometimes omitted.

l is used for ll, and ll for l.

m is used for mm.

n is used for nn, sometimes inserted before s.

o is used for u (very frequently).

oe is used for ae, and for e.

p is used for b, and for pp: sometimes inserted and sometimes omitted in words like *sollempnis*.

qu is used for c, and for ch.

s is used for c; sometimes for ss; sometimes inserted, sometimes not inserted, in such words as *exequi*.

t is used for c, d, th, tt, and sometimes doubled.

u is sometimes used for i, and frequently for o.

v is used for b, and for f.

y is used frequently for i.

The assimilation of consonants in composition sometimes takes place, but they are perhaps more commonly left unassimilated.

II. The Rheinau MS. 30, now in the Kantonsbibliothek at Zürich [R.], has been briefly described by M. Delisle, who has been misled by Gerbert's somewhat confused expressions into supposing it to be the same Zürich manuscript which furnished Gerbert with his triple text[1]. It was actually used by Gerbert, who made considerable extracts from the latter part of its con-

---

[1] *Mémoire sur d'Anciens Sacramentaires*, p. 83. M. Delisle has also made a slip, in which he is followed, not unnaturally, by Abbé Duchesne (*Origines du Culte Chrétien*, p. 119, note 2), in speaking of the MS. as forming part of the *Reichenau* collection at Zürich. It actually belonged to the monastery of Rheinau, near Schaffhausen, the MSS. of which were transferred to the Zürich Library on the suppression of the monastery in 1862.

tents: but except as regards the latter part, it may be said that Gerbert fails to give any accurate information as to its text or arrangement.

The volume now contains 189 leaves of parchment, the size of the leaves being about $11\frac{1}{2}$ by $6\frac{3}{4}$ inches. The leaves have been numbered by *pages*, beginning with the verso of the first leaf. The numeration has been made rather carelessly; only one side of each leaf has been numbered; the numbering is not consecutive in some cases where nothing is wanting in the manuscript[1]; one leaf bears the same number as that which precedes it[2]; and there are three unnumbered leaves[3]. The binding is not ancient.

An examination of the gatherings shows that, besides being defective at the end, the volume has, at some time anterior to the numbering of the pages, lost several leaves. It now contains twenty-three gatherings, each of which appears to have consisted of eight leaves. Only one of these is now signed, the old numbering having probably been cut off in the case of the others. The collation may be given summarily as follows, the gatherings being indicated by letters:—

A^8 B^8 (5, 7, 8 lost) C^8 D^8 (1, 5, 8 lost) E^8 (1 lost) F^8 G^8 H^8 (4, 5 lost) I^8 K^8 L^8 (5 lost) M^8 N^8 O^8 P^8 Q^8 R^8 S^8 T^8 (4, 5 lost) V^8 X^8 Y^8 Z^8 (1, 7, 8 lost).

The only one with a signature is the gathering V, which is marked xvi. This is the sixteenth gathering of the Sacramentary proper, which begins with the fifth gathering of the volume, at the page marked 54. Hence it may be inferred that the first four gatherings of the present book did not originally form part of the same volume with the Sacramentary. They are apparently of about the same date with the Sacramentary itself, with the exception of the last two leaves, which are in a rather later hand. The contents of these preliminary leaves are as follows:—

(1) Portions of a Gradual[4], beginning on p. 1, and occupying thirteen leaves.

(2) Portions of a Penitential, beginning on p. 28, and occupying eleven leaves.

---

[1] The numerals ignored are 20, 21, 66, 67, 78, 105, 226, 227.
[2] The number repeated is 146, which implies, of course, the repetition of 147.
[3] The leaves which follow those bearing the numbers 138, 318, 326.
[4] See Gerbert, *Mon. Vet. Lit. Aleman.* vol. i. pp. 353 sqq.

c

(3) 'Missa pro salute vivorum.'
(4) 'Benedictio super Ramos Palmarum.'

The portions (3) and (4) occupy the leaves marked 50 and 52.

The Sacramentary itself is written in a hand which cannot be very precisely dated, but may confidently be assigned to the eighth century. It shows some of the characteristics of the Lombard type of writing, but these are not very strongly marked. The spelling and grammar of the manuscript are very frequently faulty; the most notable errors of spelling are the use of *ae* not only for *e* and *a*, but also occasionally for *i*, and the interchange of *u* and *o*. The ablative and accusative cases are frequently interchanged; the present participle appears at times to take the place of an imperative, while the imperative is occasionally used with *ut*, as in the Vatican MS. In a few cases errors of grammar and spelling have been corrected by a later hand.

The Sacramentary has, as Gerbert remarks, no title: but the absence of a title is probably due to the loss of a leaf, as the first leaf of the gathering with which the Sacramentary begins is wanting. In the S. Gallen MS. the title occupies the verso of the first leaf of the Sacramentary, facing the first page of the text, and it is quite likely that the same arrangement was formerly to be found in the Rheinau manuscript, the contents of which so far correspond with those of the S. Gallen book as to favour the conjecture that both codices bore the same title. The differences between the two Sacramentaries in respect of contents and arrangement will, it is hoped, be clearly seen from the Appendix to the present volume. In the matter common to the two, if allowance be made for the more irregular orthography of the Rheinau MS., the correspondence of readings is well marked: and there can be little doubt that both are derived from a text of the 'Liber Sacramentorum' which, though perhaps differing in arrangement from that which was employed by the compiler of the Vatican manuscript, was yet closely related to that earlier text.

The Rheinau Sacramentary, according to a tradition recorded in the written catalogue of the Rheinau MSS., now at Zürich, was believed by the community of Rheinau to have been brought to the monastery by S. Fintan, who, though not the founder, was afterwards regarded as the patron saint of the community. The note in the catalogue states that S. Fintan entered the

THE RHEINAU MS. (R.)

monastery of Rheinau about the middle of the ninth century: but it is most probable that this event took place earlier, about the year 800. Before making his monastic profession, S. Fintan, according to the tradition concerning him, had travelled through several countries: he is said in particular to have visited both Tours and Rome. Hence the tradition which connects the Sacramentary with him (a tradition with which the apparent date of the manuscript is quite compatible) does not furnish any clear indication as to the probable place from which the book was brought, or in which it was written. The internal evidence of the book itself, however, makes it pretty clear that it was written at some place within the Frankish kingdom.

The Good Friday prayers mention the 'King' as well as the 'Christiani imperatores,' and the 'imperium Francorum' as well as the 'imperium Romanorum.' The appearance of prayers for the Rogation Days points to a district where Gallican usage was influential [1]. Again, while the *missae* which make up the *Proprium Sanctorum* of the Sacramentary are few in number, and most of the saints commemorated (other than the Blessed Virgin, the Apostles, and S. John Baptist) are saints connected with Rome, there is here to be found what looks like a mark of Gallican influence, in the presence of a *missa* for the festival of S. Leodegarius (Oct. 2). Further, the *Martyrologium*, a fragment of which remains at the end of the Sacramentary, contains names which seem to M. Delisle to point to some district of northern Gaul as the place where the manuscript was written and used [2]. The peculiar feature presented by the *Canon Actionis*, the insertion before the clause *Communicantes* of a commemoration of the departed, may be due to a local usage: but the lack of other instances prevents any certain inference on this point [3]. A more clear trace of Gallican usage is to be found in the latter part of the manuscript, in a *missa* printed by

---

[1] The observance of these days, ordered by the Council of Orleans in 511, was general in those regions where Gallican influence prevailed. It was not introduced at Rome till the time of Leo III, about the year 800, or later. (*Liber Pontificalis*, vol. ii. p. 12, and p. 40, note 58.)

[2] The *Martyrologium* is printed, with additions, by Gerbert (*Mon. Vet. Lit. Alem.* vol. i. pp. 455 sqq.), and more exactly reproduced by M. Delisle in the appendix to his *Mémoire sur d'Anciens Sacramentaires*.

[3] See p. 238, note 13, in the present volume. A somewhat similar insertion is to be found in the Canon contained in the Bodleian MS., B. N. Rawlinson 99 (fol. 163). There is some reason for supposing that this document belongs to the north of France; but it is of a date (c. 1200) far later than that of the Rheinau Sacramentary.

Gerbert (*Mon. Vet. Lit. Alem.* vol. i. p. 282), where the Secret takes the form of a 'bidding-prayer' and begins with the words 'Auditis nominibus offerentium,' which clearly point to a previous recitation of the names.

The contents of the first portion of the manuscript show, as has been already said, a close resemblance to those of the S. Gallen Sacramentary. The *missae* for saints'-days, however, are far less numerous in the Rheinau than in the S. Gallen, and the orders for the consecration of the Chrism and for the public reconciliation of the Penitents on Maundy Thursday are absent from the Rheinau manuscript. The inference to be drawn from the non-appearance of these sections seems to be that the manuscript was written for the use of a priest, and not for that of a bishop; and this view concerning it will be found to explain some points with regard to the second part of its contents. The headings of the *missae* of the first portion contain mention of the Roman 'stations' for the days of Lent, the Ember days, and for certain festivals, a fact which testifies to the Roman origin of the Sacramentary[1]. The presence of *missae* for the Thursdays in Lent shows that this part of its text is of a date as late as the time of Gregory II (715-31).

The second part of the Sacramentary is almost all included by Gerbert in his Sacramentary, but he does not follow the order in which the parts stand in the manuscript. This will be seen, it is hoped, more clearly in the Appendix to the present volume. The second part begins after the series of Post-communions and Benedictions which follow the *Canon Actionis*, and is preceded by the words 'Expliciunt benedictiones anni circuli est numerus lxxii. Incipit Liber secundus de extrema parte.' The 'benedictiones anni circuli' here referred to cannot be the Benedictions which stand immediately before the words: for these are not by any means so numerous. It seems most likely that the words were copied by the scribe from a manuscript in which they stood at the close of a series of Episcopal Benedictions such as were used in Gaul, and might be included in a Sacramentary intended for use by a bishop, but would naturally be omitted in a book intended for a priest, by whom

---

[1] M. Duchesne (*Origines du Culte Chrétien*, p. 124) seems to include both the Rheinau and S. Gallen MSS. in his statement that the 'Gelasian' books have no mention of the Roman churches: but these headings occur, not always in exactly the same form, in both manuscripts.

these Benedictions would not be given. The peculiar phrase 'Incipit Liber secundus de extrema parte' may be similarly accounted for. If the 'Liber secundus' of the Sacramentary before the scribe contained, as it very likely would contain, such forms as would, at a later time, have been included in a 'Pontifical,' and these forms stood at the beginning of the 'Liber secundus'[1], the portion which remained, after their omission, would naturally enough be described as 'de extrema parte.' In this case, the first portion of the 'Liber secundus' probably included the forms of Ordination, the 'Consecratio Virginum,' the forms for Dedication of Churches, and perhaps also the order for the Reconciliation of the Penitents, and such forms for the Reconciliation of Heretics as we find in sections lxxxv–lxxxvii of the first book of the Vatican manuscript.

The 'Liber secundus,' as we have it here, contains none of these. It begins with a selection of Collects for Mattins, Vespers, and other Hours. Next comes the *Ordo Baptisterii*, including not only the actual Baptismal rites, with the form for hallowing the font, but also the *missae* for the 'Scrutinies,' the exorcisms to be said over the catechumens, and the forms relating to the Baptism of the Sick, and to the admission of a heathen to the *status* of a catechumen. These correspond very closely with the various sections of the Vatican manuscript which provide for the same purposes; but they do not include the forms for the *Expositio Evangeliorum*, the *Praefatio Symboli*, or the *Praefatio Orationis Dominicae*. Nor do they include the form of Confirmation which in the Vatican manuscript stands at the end of the Baptismal order : the reason for this omission is probably the same which has dictated the omission of the *missa Chrismalis*. But it is to be observed that in the Rheinau Sacramentary the *Ordo Baptisterii* forms one whole. In the Vatican manuscript, the different parts of it are separated ; the *missae* for the 'Scrutinies' are placed among the Lent *missae*, and assigned to

---

[1] It may be remarked that if a series of Episcopal Benedictions for use at Mass, such as is here supposed to be referred to in the phrase 'benedictiones anni circuli' were placed (as it conveniently might be placed) just after the *Canon Actionis* and the accompanying series of Postcommunions and *Orationes super Populum*, it would be all the more natural that the offices for the bishop's use should stand at the beginning of the 'Liber secundus': while, if the 'Pontifical' formed the first part of the Liber secundus of a *Roman* Sacramentary, into which these Gallican benedictions were inserted, the latter would be most conveniently placed just before the Pontifical.

the third, fourth, and fifth Sundays of Lent[1]: the hallowing of the font and the actual order of Baptism are placed among the sections relating to Easter, while the rubric, which in the Rheinau manuscript follows the order of Baptism, and directs that the order at Pentecost is to be the same as at Easter, is in the Vatican manuscript placed after the *missa* for the Sunday before Pentecost, and has carried along with it into this place the forms for the Baptism of the Sick, which in the Rheinau Sacramentary also follow the rubric, but there form a natural appendix to the first part of the *Ordo Baptisterii*. The result of this arrangement in the Vatican manuscript is the placing of these forms in a position where there is no obvious reason for their presence, and where they interrupt the regular order of the Sacramentary.

The inference to be drawn from these facts seems perfectly clear. The compiler of the Vatican manuscript had before him an *Ordo Baptisterii* agreeing closely with that contained in the 'Liber secundus' of the Rheinau manuscript, though perhaps including certain things which are not to be found in the Rheinau book[2]. But instead of transcribing it as a continuous whole, he divided it, intending to graft the several portions of it into the Sacramentary at convenient points: and the process of grafting has been carried out, in one instance, so awkwardly as to leave a plain indication of what has taken place. A similar process seems to have been attempted with the forms of Ordination. The sections of the Vatican manuscript which contain the forms for ordaining Deacons and Priests have been placed at what seemed to be a convenient point, after the *missae* for the first of the Ember seasons, near the beginning of the first book, while the forms of admission to the Minor Orders, and that for the Consecration of Bishops stand near the end of the same book, in conjunction with other parts of what, for convenience sake, may be called the Pontifical. And in this case again we have an indication that what is now divided formed,

---

[1] The *Denuntiatio pro Scrutinio*, however, in the Vatican manuscript as well as in the Rheinau manuscript, speaks of the 'Scrutiny' as beginning 'secunda feria.' Both follow a common form, while in each there is an indication that the Scrutiny actually took place on another day of the week than that mentioned in the form.

[2] The form of Confirmation may have been included in the *Ordo Baptisterii*, or may have been placed apart from it with other forms for the use of the bishop. The forms for the exposition of the Gospels, the Creed, and the Lord's Prayer may have formed part of the *Ordo Baptisterii*: but it is also possible that they were taken from a Gallican source.

in the manuscript used by the compiler, a consecutive whole. The forms relating to the Consecration of Churches are followed by the sections relating to the Minor Orders: these are followed by *missae* for the anniversaries of the ordination of the celebrant as Deacon and as Priest. Next come the prayers for the Consecration of Bishops, which are followed by anniversary *missae*; and these are succeeded by the *Consecratio sacrae virginis*, which again is followed by a series of *missae* for the anniversary of the profession. It seems that there can be little doubt that the Ordination forms which now stand at the beginning of the book have been transferred to a new place by the compiler, who has failed to transfer along with them the anniversary *missae* which were annexed to them in their original position. Thus we may see that the forms of Ordination, and the form for the benediction of nuns were probably, in the manuscript which he used, all placed together[1]. Such a collection would include the greater part of the matter which, as has been suggested above, the scribe of the Rheinau MS. discarded from the 'Liber secundus,' as not required for the purpose which his book was intended to serve.

Returning to the actual contents of the Rheinau MS. we find that it contains, after the *Ordo Baptisterii*, a collection of *missae*, benedictions, and prayers for special purposes, corresponding in general character, and sometimes closely agreeing in arrangement and in text, with the similar collection in the third book of the Vatican MS. We find also the form for the reconciliation of a penitent at the point of death, the *Commendatio Animae*, and the order for the Burial of the Dead (in somewhat more minute detail than the parallel portion of the Vatican MS.); and these are followed, as in the Vatican MS., by a collection of *Missae pro defunctis*. There are also some forms for the exorcism of 'possessed' persons, which in part agree with the parallel portion of the Vatican MS. With these the Sacramentary ends; for the *Breviarium Apostolorum*[2]

---

[1] The forms of admission to the Minor Orders, and the section (or the greater part of the section) containing canonical regulations on the subject of Ordination, are probably of Gallican origin, and derived from another source. (See Duchesne, *Origines du Culte Chrétien*, pp. 338, 350.) From the same Gallican source, probably, were drawn the forms which appear in the Vatican manuscript annexed to the Roman forms for the Ordination of Deacons and Priests (pp. 24, 28 of the present volume), and perhaps that for the Dedication of a Church (pp. 133-6). See Duchesne, *Or. du Culte Chrétien*, pp. 350 sqq., 389 sqq.

[2] This, as well as the *Martyrologium*,

and the fragment of the *Martyrologium* already mentioned are not, strictly speaking, parts of the Sacramentary itself, but are rather of the nature of an Appendix.

It may be noted that in the Rheinau MS. as in the Vatican MS. the name 'Secreta' is used as the heading of the prayer which in the S. Gallen MS. has the title of 'Super oblata': while some of the Prefaces are marked by the heading 'Contestatio' or 'Contestata.'

III. The S. Gallen MS. 348 [S.] is also described by M. Delisle (*Mémoire sur d'anciens Sacramentaires*, pp. 84–6). It is a small volume, bound in stamped white sheepskin or pigskin on oak boards, with leather clasps, and now contains 388 numbered *pages*, including eight pages of paper at the beginning[1] and six at the end of the volume. The paper and the binding are both of the same period (c. 1400), and are perhaps only a little earlier than the inscription 'Collectarium vetustum' upon the binding.

The parchment leaves, now numbering 184 (pp. 9–376), are arranged in eighteen gatherings, of which the first two appear to be a later addition to the original volume. These two gatherings are signed at the end with the marks I and II, those which next follow being marked at the beginning as III and IIII, but bearing also at the end their original signatures I and II. The fifth gathering, and those which follow it, with the exception of the last[2], are signed at the end with letters, beginning with C. The collation, summarily stated, is as follows:—

I^6 II^4 I II^8 CD^{10} E^{12} F^{10} GH^{12} (H^7 now lost) I^{10} K^{12} L^{10} M^{14} NOPQ^{12} (Q^{12} now lost).

The original Sacramentary begins on p. 32 (i. e. on the verso of the second leaf of gathering I), with an illuminated title, filling the whole page: 'In nomine sancte Trinitatis. Incipit liber sacramentorum anni circulum Romane ecclesie.' The recto of the leaf is blank, and the first leaf of the gathering was probably also left blank by the original scribe. The pages

---

is printed by Gerbert (*Mon. Vet. Lit. Alem.* vol. i. p. 453).

[1] The first of these pages bears the S. Gallen press-mark, the second is blank. The third contains a note with the signature of 'Martin Gerbert Abbas S. Blasii,' which shows that the MS. is identical with his 'Sangallensis antiquior.' The fourth, fifth, and sixth pages are blank, while the seventh and eighth contain some notes on the contents of the MS.

[2] The last leaf of this gathering, which probably bore the signature Q, is now lost.

from 9 to 30 inclusive contain additional matter, written by different hands, at different times. The earliest portions are apparently but little later than the body of the MS. while the latest may belong to the early years of the tenth century[1]. The Sacramentary itself is written in a hand which may be best described as of a 'modified Lombardic' type, and which seems to belong to the beginning of the ninth or the end of the eighth century[2]. Traces of Lombardic writing appear also throughout the later additions on pp. 9–30, though they are less strongly marked than those which are to be found in the Sacramentary itself. In the ornamentation of the initial letters, and in the decorative use of red dots, there may perhaps be found some indication of Irish influence.

The spelling of the MS. presents few peculiarities: the use of *e* for *i* is rather frequent, and there are occasional instances of the use of *o* for *u*. But both in spelling and in grammar the manuscript shows a much smaller proportion of errors than the Rheinau codex. The errors which it does contain have been generally corrected, and further emendations of the work of the original scribe have been made, by a second hand, probably

---

[1] The contents of these added leaves may be briefly noted:—

P. 9 (mutilated) contains prayers for use at the time of the Oblation of the Eucharistic elements.

Pp. 10–12, 17–18 contain *missae* and prayers for the Festival of S. Gall, and its Vigil and Octave. These are interrupted by the insertion of other matter on pp. 13–16 (see below).

Pp. 18–21 contain *missae* for All Saints Day and for its Vigil. [These portions are written in a hand probably of the latter part of the ninth century.]

Pp. 13–16, which now form the middle sheet of the gathering, contain a *Missa quam sacerdos pro semetipso debet canere*: the prayers of this *missa* are in a hand of about the year 900, the Epistle and Gospel being added at the end, in a hand probably of the early part of the tenth century.

Pp. 22–3 contain a 'Horologium' or table showing the length of a shadow at certain hours of the day in each month of the year.

Pp. 24–8 contain *missae* with the following headings:—(a) *Missa S. Mariae*. (b) *Alia Missa in Sanctorum* [sic]. (c) *Item alia Missa*. (d) *Missa de Trinitate*. (e) *Item Missa pro quemcunque* [sic] *cupis*. (f) *Missa pro peccatis* (incomplete).

Pp. 29–30 are in a hand different from that of the preceding pages. They contain the end of a *missa* for the Vigil of the Assumption, and a *missa* for the Festival. [There is clearly a break between the contents of p. 28 and those of p. 29 (i.e. between the whole of the gatherings 11 and I): but the whole of the contents of pp. 22–30 are probably of about the same date, most likely before 830.]

[2] This phrase is borrowed from Dr. Maunde Thompson (*Handbook of Greek and Latin Palaeography*, p. 218), who points out that the most distinctly Lombardic character attaches only to certain letters in the MS. A page of the MS. has been reproduced in facsimile in the collection of the Palaeographical Society. [Plate 185 (or vol. iii. no. 9).] Another appears in the present volume.

of the ninth century. Sometimes the original writing has been altogether erased, and in some other cases it is not quite clear what the reading of the first hand has been: but in the great majority of instances the original reading can be quite clearly made out. In citing the readings of the MS. in the notes to the present volume, the original text is indicated by the symbol S^1 (a query being added where the reading seems probable, but not absolutely certain) and the emended text by the symbol S^2. Speaking generally, it may be said that in the matter common to this MS., the Vatican MS., and Gerbert's text, the readings of S^1 are in agreement with the Vatican MS. and those of S^2 with Gerbert's text. But the portions of the MS. where the corrector has used the greatest freedom are the Prefaces, the greater number of which are not contained in the Vatican MS. In these portions also, the readings of S^2 generally agree with those of Gerbert's text.

A further point to be noted with regard to the MS. is the appearance in many places of notes, most of which may be assigned to the tenth century, which have apparently been intended, as M. Delisle remarks, for the guidance of a scribe who was engaged in writing a Sacramentary, using the MS. as his model, but making some variations from its order, and incorporating matter from other sources. It may be observed that in its divergences from the text of the S. Gallen MS., as corrected, the 'Gelasian' text of Gerbert's triple Sacramentary almost always follows these marginal directions: and this fact strongly supports Gerbert's view that the S. Gallen MS. was that employed by the scribe of his triple Sacramentary ('Sangallensis olim, nunc Turicensis') for the 'Gelasian' part of his compilation.

It seems most likely that the manuscript, though it had very possibly passed into the possession of the monastery of S. Gallen before the time when Gerbert's triple Sacramentary was written, was not written in that house. It is most improbable that it would in that case have contained no *missa* for the Festival of S. Gall: and there is no such *missa* in the Sacramentary itself, though the deficiency is, as we have seen, supplied by some of the leaves added at a later time. Among the notes already mentioned is one at the point (p. 307) where the Festival would fall, 'Hic scribe de Sco. Gallo': and in Gerbert's text we find the services for the Vigil and Festival inserted.

Another piece of internal evidence, of a more positive kind, bearing upon the question of the date of the manuscript, as well as upon that of the place where it was written, is to be found at p. 368, where at the bottom of the page there appear in red uncial letters the words 'Memento Domine famuli tui Remedii Episcopi.' The purpose of the insertion has evidently been that Remedius should be mentioned by name in the 'Memento vivorum': and it is at least a most probable conjecture that the Remedius thus referred to is the great Bishop Remedius of Chur. The inference that the Sacramentary belonged to Remedius himself[1] is perhaps hardly warranted: but it seems clear that it must have been written during the life of Remedius, and in some place where his name would receive such a special mention.

This mention is given to him, apparently, not as the Bishop of the diocese, since the *Canon Actionis* also contains the words 'et antistite nostro *Ill*.,' and it seems most likely that its presence is due to the peculiar position of Remedius as a temporal prince. The see of Chur, in the seventh and eighth centuries, was hereditary in the family known as the Victoridae. The Bishops exercised temporal as well as spiritual authority in the district known as 'Rhaetia Curiensis' (an entirely un-Teutonized district, the boundaries of which nearly corresponded with those of the diocese), and bore the title of 'Praeses.' The last of the Victoridae, Bishop Tello, died about 773, and his successor in the see, Constantius, received probably in that year, from Charles the Great, the title and powers of 'Rector[2].' The purpose of Charles in this grant was no doubt to secure his power in a district which had as yet remained, by reason of its isolated situation, practically untouched by Teutonic colonists. It was not until 806 that he took the further step of withdrawing this temporal office from the hands of the Bishop and of organizing the province according to the German fashion, under two 'Grafen[3].' Thus from 773 to 806 the occupants of the see of Chur practically retained, under Charles' sanction, the temporal power which had belonged to their predecessors. The

---

[1] This seems to be the view of M. Delisle (*Mémoires sur d'Anciens Sacramentaires*, p. 85), and of Dr. Maunde Thompson (*Handbook of Greek and Latin Palaeography*, p. 218).

[2] See P. C. Planta, *Geschichte von Graubünden*, p. 20, and Abel-Simson, *Karl der Grosse*, vol. i. p. 141 (note 4).

[3] See P. C. Planta, *Geschichte von Graubünden*, p. 28, and the same author's *Das alte Raetien*, p. 357.

exact date of Remedius' episcopate is not known. The dates commonly assigned for his accession (800) and for his death (820) do not seem to rest on any very good authority. It is certain that he was Bishop in the year 800, since Alcuin mentions him as such in a letter of that year, addressed to Anno of Salzburg: and it is not impossible that he may have become Bishop before that year. On the other hand, in view of the fact that he seems to have been in high favour at the court of Charles, it has been supposed that his death had already taken place before the change in the administration of the province in 806, a change for which the death of an active and capable 'Rector' would possibly give occasion [1].

If this view as to the date of Remedius' death is correct, the date of our manuscript cannot be later than 806: and the same consequence will follow if we adopt the view that the mention of his name in the manuscript is due to his possession of a temporal dignity which came to an end in that year. On the other hand, it does not seem that the evidence as to the date of his accession to the see of Chur, and to the temporal dignity annexed to that see, necessarily points to the year 800 as the earliest possible date. It is perhaps hardly safe to lay much stress on such phrases as 'pro Christianissimis imperatoribus nostris[2]' as an indication of date. But the presence of this phrase in the manuscript is perhaps most easily accounted for if we suppose that it was written before the coronation of Charles the Great, and that the phrase is a survival, having reference to the Eastern imperial house. If the words are to be taken strictly[3], and interpreted of the new Western dynasty, they would point to a date as late as 813[4]. But on the whole it may be said that whether the true date of the manuscript is to be found in the eighth or in the ninth century, it is probably within a short distance of the year 800, while the evidence seems to point to the district of Rhaetia as the place where it was written.

That district was, as we have said, but little affected by

---

[1] See P. C. Planta, *Das alte Raetien*, pp. 309, 357.

[2] This appears in one of the Good Friday 'bidding prayers' of the MS.

[3] It is perhaps more likely that they should be taken strictly, if the date is later than 800, than if it is earlier. A vague plural might continue to be used before the coronation of Charles; we should hardly expect to find it during his reign.

[4] In this year Louis was crowned and associated in the empire; and he in turn associated his son Lothair with himself a few years later, in 817.

Teutonic influence; and we find in the contents of the Sacramentary but few traces of 'Gallican' usage, and none (except for the mention of Remedius, already referred to) of the recognition of any other temporal power than the Roman. There is no mention of the 'regnum Francorum' such as we find in the Vatican and Rheinau MSS. Apart from the evidence of the *Proprium Sanctorum* the most notable point in which Gallican influence may be discerned is the mention of S. Hilary and S. Martin in the 'Communicantes' clause of the Canon. If M. Duchesne's suggestion as to the origin of the two forms which appear at the end of the *Missa Chrismalis* in the Vatican MS.[1] is correct, we must reckon their appearance in the S. Gallen MS. as a sign of possible Gallican influence. The form of blessing the Paschal candle is the same as that which appears in the Gallican books, but it is probable that this form, as well as the usage of the benediction, had already found its way into Italy before the end of the eighth century. The form for blessing the lamb at the close of the Canon in the *Missa in Nocte Sancta* (see Gerb. p. 90) illustrates a custom which, though probably not general, was apparently sufficiently common in the middle of the ninth century to furnish Photius with one of his accusations against the Western Church[2]; and its presence in the manuscript, though showing that the latter was adapted, in this respect, to local custom, gives no sure indication as to any particular locality.

On the other hand, the absence of any notice of the Rogation Days may be taken as evidence that the Gallican influence was not strong in the district to which the manuscript belongs[3]: while the presence of the prayers for the Great Litany of April 25, with mention of the Roman 'stations,' points to the following, in this respect, of the Roman custom. A similar inference may be drawn from the list of saints mentioned in the *Proprium Sanctorum*. Here also it would appear that Roman, rather than Gallican, usage has determined the local practice, and influenced the local kalendar.

The points in the *Proprium Sanctorum* which suggest Galli-

---

[1] See p. 72 of the present edition, and Duchesne, *Or. du Culte Chrét.* p. 296, *note*.
[2] See Bona, *De Rebus Liturg.* II. viii. 5, and Sala's notes. (Vol. iii. pp. 185 sqq. of Sala's edition.)
[3] As we have seen, there are prayers for these days in the Rheinau MS., which omits the Roman usage of the Great Litany.

can influence are few in number. First, perhaps, may be mentioned the commemoration of S. Praejectus on Jan. 25, since he may be probably identified with the Bishop and martyr commemorated in Auvergne. Another trace of Gallican influence may be found in the double commemoration of S. Euphemia, whose name appears not only on Sept. 16, as in the Leonine and Gregorian Sacramentaries, but also on April 13, as in the Vatican MS. and in the Eastern Kalendars[1]. Possibly the appearance of the names of SS. *Mary* and Martha on Jan. 19, as in the Rheinau MS., may be due to Gallican influence[2]. On the other hand, the correspondence with what may be said to be known, with tolerable certainty, as to the Roman Kalendar of the latter part of the eighth century is well marked, while the great majority of the saints especially commemorated belong, if not to Rome itself, at any rate to Italy.

M. Battifol, in his luminous book upon the origin and history of the Roman Breviary, furnishes us with a Kalendar including the names of those saints who may be said to have been certainly, or almost certainly, especially commemorated at Rome in the time of Adrian I[3]. If we compare this Kalendar with the *Proprium Sanctorum* of the S. Gallen MS., we find that the two are in close agreement. The S. Gallen MS. omits the mention of S. Anastasius (Jan. 22), of S. Matthias (Feb. 24), of S. Mark (April 25), and of S. Epimachus (May 10)[4]. It omits the feasts of S. Potentiana or Pudentiana (May 11), S. Cyrus (July 15), S. Praxedes (July 21), and S. Apollinaris (July 23)[5]. It assigns the festival of S. Leo not to June 28 (the date of the translation of his relics by Sergius I in 688), but to

---

[1] See Duchesne, *Origines du Culte Chrétien*, p. 127.

[2] The Vatican MS. also substitutes the name *S. Mariae*, for the name *S. Marii*, but shows the connexion of the festival with the Roman usage by adding the names of Audifax and Habacuc, the sons of S. Marius and S. Martha, according to the tradition which makes the latter martyrs at Rome. Gerbert, it may be remarked, is mistaken in his statement that the Rheinau MS. gives the name of Marius.

[3] Battifol, *Histoire du Bréviaire Romain*, pp. 125 sqq. The Kalendar is constructed by a comparison of the later Antiphonary according to the use of S. Peter's church at Rome with the *Proprium Sanctorum* of the early Gregorian Sacramentaries, and with the Carolingian Lectionaries.

[4] It mentions S. Vincent, who in Battifol's Kalendar is joined with S. Anastasius, on Jan. 22, and S. Gordianus, who is coupled with S. Epimachus, on May 10; the prayers of the Great Litany are assigned to April 25.

[5] The mention of SS. Cyrus, Praxedes, and Apollinaris in Battifol's Kalendar is due to the Lectionaries; S. Potentiana is the only one of these four whose festival appears in the Sacramentaries.

April 11, which is the date indicated as that of his 'deposition' in the *Liber Pontificalis* (vol. i. p. 239), and probably the date intended in the inscription cited by M. Duchesne, in the notes to his edition of the same work (*Liber Pontificalis*, vol. i. p. 379, note 35), where the name of the month is omitted. The festival of All Saints is not noticed, that of S. Caesarius being alone mentioned on Nov. 1. The mention of SS. Chrysanthus and Daria is not on Oct. 25, but on Nov. 29, where they (with S. Maurus) are joined, as in the Vatican MS., in the same commemoration with S. Saturninus. In connexion with this juxtaposition it may perhaps be worth while to note the restoration by Adrian I of the basilica of S. Saturninus 'una cum cymeterio sanctorum Crisanti et Dariae' (*Lib. Pontif.*, vol. i. p. 509).

Other saints' days mentioned in S., but not in M. Battifol's list, are SS. Emerentiana and Macarius (Jan. 23); S. Sotheris, and SS. Zoticus, Irenaeus, and Hyacinthus (Feb. 10); SS. Vitalis, Felicula, and Zeno (with S. Valentinus on Feb. 14); S. Juliana (Feb. 16); SS. Perpetua and Felicitas (March 7); S. Juvenalis (May 3); the *Dedicatio Ecclesiae beatae Mariae ad Martyres* (May 13); S. Vitus (June 15); S. Benedict (July 11); the 'Maccabees' (Aug. 1, where mention is also made of the veneration of S. Peter's chains); S. Donatus (Aug. 7); S. Magnus (Aug. 19); S. Rufus (Aug. 27); S. Priscus (Sept. 1); S. Gurgonius (Sept. 9); S. Augustinus[1] (Nov. 17); and S. Damasus (Dec. 11). Of these festivals, those of SS. Perpetua and Felicitas and of S. Gurgonius appear in the Philocalian list of 'Depositiones Martyrum'; that of the Maccabees was apparently of general observance; that of S. Augustinus appears to be the festival of a Capuan martyr, who has been confused, at least by the later scribe, with the Bishop of Hippo. All the remaining names of Saints, with the exception of S. Macarius, may be connected with places in Italy, while some of them are certainly Roman[2]. It may be noted also that the festival of S. Nicomedes (June 1) and that of S. Michael (Sept. 29) are shown by the titles of the S. Gallen MS. to be connected, like that of

---

[1] This is marked as *Natl. S. Agustini Epi.* by the original hand. The corrector has altered *Natl.* to *Translatio.*

[2] S. Sotheris, and the other three saints commemorated on the same day, belong to Rome; SS. Vitalis, Felicula, and Zeno either to Rome or to Spoleto; S. Juliana is assigned by the old Roman Martyrology to Cumae; S. Juvenalis was Bishop of Narni; the 'Diaconia S. Viti' and a 'monasterium S. Donati' were already in existence at Rome in the time of Leo III (*Liber Pontif.* ii. pp. 21, 24): S. Donatus is perhaps the Bishop of Arezzo. The

S. Mary *ad Martyres*, with the anniversaries of the dedications of churches at Rome: while the festival of the Purification has, as in the Rheinau MS., the title 'S. Simeonis.'

As in the Rheinau MS., the Roman 'stations' are marked throughout Lent, for the Ember Days, and also for certain festivals. The Secret has always the title 'Super oblata,' or 'Super oblatam'; the Preface is marked only by the initials of 'Vere Dignum,' having no separate title. The Lent *missae*, as in the Rheinau Sacramentary, include *missae* for the Thursdays in each week.

Whether the S. Gallen Sacramentary originally agreed with that of Rheinau in containing a 'Liber secundus,' including the *Ordo Baptisterii*, and other special offices and *missae* such as those which occupy the latter part of the first and third books of the Vatican MS., we cannot now say: but it seems not unlikely that this was the case. If so, the loss of the *Liber secundus* is the more to be regretted, since it seems that the S. Gallen MS. was so constructed as to include forms for the use of a bishop[1]. It might therefore have been expected (on the theory already stated as to the significance of the words 'Liber secundus de extrema parte' in the Rheinau MS.), that the *Liber secundus* of the S. Gallen book, if it existed, would have contained the forms of Ordination and other Episcopal offices, and so have furnished material for comparison with the text of the Vatican Sacramentary which is not supplied by the contents of the *Liber secundus* of the Rheinau book.

But in what it now contains, the S. Gallen MS. does supply the defects of that of Rheinau to a very considerable extent. As we have seen, the *Proprium Sanctorum* of the Rheinau Sacramentary is much less full than that of the S. Gallen: and the additional *missae* contained in the latter cover a very large part of the second book of the Vatican MS. In fact, there are only a very few sections of the *Proprium Sanctorum* of the Vatican Sacramentary which do not appear, either in whole or in part, in the S. Gallen text. The precise extent of the agreement between the two will, it is hoped, be sufficiently shown by the marginal references appended to the text

---

name of S. Magnus may be connected with Anagni, and those of SS. Rufus and Priscus with Capua.

[1] It contains the forms for hallowing the Oils and Chrism, and for the Reconciliation of the Penitents, which, as we have seen, the Rheinau Sacramentary omits.

of the present volume, and by the scheme of the contents of the S. Gallen manuscript, which will be found in the Appendix.

From what has already been said of the Rheinau and S. Gallen Sacramentaries, it will appear that there are strong grounds for regarding them as independent witnesses. The Rheinau manuscript shows traces of Gallican influence which are absent from the S. Gallen manuscript: there is reason to think that the two manuscripts were written in different localities: they are not, indeed, very widely separated in date; but the limited character which marks the *Proprium Sanctorum* of the Rheinau manuscript may be taken as an indication that it was copied from a text a good deal earlier than that employed by the scribe of the S. Gallen manuscript. The amount of irregularity of spelling and of grammar exhibited by the two, while it is sufficient in each case to show that the text has not been much affected by the movement for reform in these matters, is so much greater in the one than in the other as to supply a further reason for regarding them as mutually independent: while this view is also supported by the absence from one of prayers and Prefaces contained in the parallel sections of the other. When we compare them with the Vatican Sacramentary, hitherto known as the 'Gelasian,' we find that, taken together, they include by far the greater part of its contents. They differ from it in the arrangement of the common matter: and the differences of arrangement are by no means few or unimportant. But of these differences, and of the inferences to be drawn from them, it will be more convenient to treat at a later stage. It is sufficient here to note two facts: first, that the proportion of matter common to these three Sacramentaries of the 'Gelasian' type is very large; and second, that in cases where such common matter is also found in the Sacramentaries of the later or 'Gregorian' type, the three 'Gelasian' Sacramentaries[1] are very often in agreement with one another, as against what appears to be the later recension of the text, presented by the 'Gregorian' Sacramentaries.

For these reasons it would seem to be clear that in the task of verifying or correcting the readings of the Vatican manuscript, the two Sacramentaries of Rheinau and S. Gallen must, as a general rule, be our principal authorities; though in some

[1] This statement, so far as the S. Gallen manuscript is concerned, has reference to the original readings, not to the later corrections or alterations.

cases their evidence may be set aside in favour of that supplied by earlier authorities, such as the 'Leonine' Sacramentary, it must outweigh that of the later Sacramentaries of the 'Gregorian' type, such as those edited by Pamelius or Ménard, to which, as the best authorities accessible in their time, Tommasi and Vezzosi were naturally led to refer.

IV. The Bodleian MS. Bodl. Add. A. 173 has been occasionally cited in the notes to the present volume, where it is denoted by the symbol A. This manuscript also is described by M. Delisle[1], from notes furnished by Mr. Falconer Madan. It is a small volume containing fifty-two parchment leaves, not uniform in size. It is written in a Carolingian minuscule hand which may be assigned to a date near the end of the ninth century. The phrase 'Christianum Francorum Romanorumque imperium' in the Good Friday prayers, may be taken as evidence that it was written in the Frankish kingdom, but there is nothing else in the manuscript itself to show clearly the place where it was written or used. It may be said to consist of four fragments, each incomplete at the beginning and at the end, while there are also several gaps in the first and fourth fragments. The *missae* contained in this manuscript are of the Gregorian, not of the Gelasian type: but in some portions of its contents it presents certain points of interest for the purpose of the present edition. The peculiar form in which the Creed which it contains was written by the original scribe shows several curious instances of agreement with the text of the Vatican manuscript: and certain portions of the forms relating to Ordination, which make up one of the fragments[2], show a text closely agreeing with that of the Codex Gellonensis, as cited by Martène.

V. Another Bodleian manuscript, formerly included in the Canonici collection, now MS. Liturg. Miscell. 319, has also furnished some material for the notes of this edition, where it is cited by the symbol B. It is professedly a Gregorian Sacramentary, and appears to have been once used at Aquileia, since the later insertions in its Kalendar include the names of certain Aquileian saints[3], and notices of the obits of six Patri-

---

[1] *Mémoire sur d'Anciens Sacramentaires*, pp. 152–3.

[2] This fragment consists of two leaves only (fol. 41, 42), which are misplaced, interrupting, as they now stand, the consecutive text of the leaves now numbered 40 and 43.

[3] S. Hermagoras (July 12) and SS. Thecla, Erasma, and Dorothea (Sept. 25).

archs of Aquileia. Its date may be after the year 1000, but is probably before 1019[1]. The manuscript is beautifully written throughout, and contains some fine miniatures and illuminated letters. The portions of its contents which have been used for this edition are the *missae* for special purposes, which include several collects parallel to those in the Vatican manuscript, and its order for the Burial of the Dead, which in several portions agrees with the parallel orders in the Vatican and in the Rheinau Sacramentaries.

VI. For one portion of the order for the Burial of the Dead, reference has been made to a manuscript Pontifical of English use, of the twelfth century, which seems to have at one time belonged to Hereford Cathedral. It is now in the Library of Magdalen College, Oxford (MS. Magd. 226).

The use made of printed texts has been chiefly for the purpose of comparison; but some of these texts have appeared to be of sufficient value to be employed also for purposes of correction. Foremost among these is the text of the Leonine Sacramentary. The references to this Sacramentary are to the columns of Muratori's *Liturgia Romana Vetus*, but the readings of his edition have been compared with the more trustworthy text contained in the second volume of the edition of S. Leo's works prepared by the Ballerini, in which every divergence from the readings of the manuscript is professedly indicated in the notes. Next in importance, as regards the use made of them, are the Gallican Sacramentaries edited by Tommasi and Mabillon, and the *Ordines* reproduced by Martène from certain early manuscripts. To the Gallican books, reference is made by the columns of Muratori's *Liturgia Romana Vetus*, but for greater security his readings have been compared, where that was possible, with the edition of Neale and Forbes[2]. For the *Canon Actionis* recent collations of the parallel portion of the *Missale Francorum* and the *Sacramentarium Gallicanum* have been employed as well as the printed texts. Where the Rheinau and S. Gallen manuscripts furnish no material for comparison, recourse has been had to early texts included in the second volume of Gerbert's *Monumenta Vet. Lit. Alemannicae*, and to *Ordines*

---

[1] This is the latest date assigned to the decease of John, Patriarch of Aquileia, the first of the six whose obits are noted in the Kalendar. He occupied the see of Aquileia for more than thirty years.

[2] *Ancient Liturgies of the Gallican Church*, 8vo, Burntisland, 1855-1867.

printed by Martène in his *De Antiquis Ecclesiae Ritibus*[1]. Some use has also been made of the 'Ambrosian' text contained in the first volume of Pamelius' *Liturgicon Latinum*[2], of the Gregorian text in Muratori's *Liturgia Romana Vetus*, and of Mr. Warren's edition of the Leofric Missal[3].

Three other printed texts have been employed much more largely, and their readings cited much more frequently. But the purpose of the citations is rather that of comparison than of emendation. They serve as the means of showing the relation between the text of the Vatican manuscript and the kindred texts of Rheinau and S. Gallen on the one hand, and the later recension of the text on the other. These are the text contained in Gerbert's Sacramentary, already mentioned, and the Gregorian Sacramentaries edited by Pamelius[4] and Ménard[5]. The Sacramentary of Ménard is of some special importance, as it contains a good deal of matter closely parallel to parts of the contents of the third book of the Vatican manuscript, which find no place in the Rheinau Sacramentary.

To attempt anything like a full discussion of the questions relating to the history and development of the Roman Sacramentaries is not the purpose of this Introduction, and would be beyond its scope. But it may be well, for the sake of clearness, before discussing the variations of the Rheinau and S. Gallen Sacramentaries from the Vatican manuscript, or the points of resemblance and of difference which they exhibit, as compared with the Gregorian Sacramentaries, to state certain facts which form the most important data of the general problem.

The Vatican manuscript itself furnishes us with evidence that before the time of Charles the Great books bearing the title of 'Liber Sacramentorum Romanae Ecclesiae' were known and used within the Frankish kingdom. It is itself one of these books: and the fact that it contains a certain admixture of Gallican elements, and is clearly not a simple transcript of a Roman book, may be taken as evidence, to a certain extent, of

---

[1] Those most frequently used are taken from the *Codex Gellonensis*, from a MS. Pontifical at Jumièges, and from Egbert's Pontifical.

[2] The edition used is that of 1609.

[3] 4to, Oxford, 1883.

[4] In the second volume of the *Liturgicon Latinum*.

[5] The references are given to the reprint contained in the third volume of the Benedictine edition of S. Gregory's works (1705).

the introduction of the Roman book from which it is in the main derived, at some time earlier than the date of the manuscript itself. The Sacramentaries commonly known as Gallican, the 'Missale Francorum,' the 'Missale Gothicum,' the 'Missale Gallicanum Vetus,' and possibly the 'Sacramentarium Gallicanum [1],' show signs of the influence of Roman books in the modification of the Gallican rite within the Frankish dominions: but they give us no evidence as to the name by which the Roman books in question were known. The Rheinau manuscript, though rather later, and though now possessing no title, may be taken as another instance of a Frankish Sacramentary, in the main Roman, and based to some extent on a Sacramentary closely akin to that from which the Vatican manuscript is derived.

In the latter part of the eighth century, probably between 784 and 791, Pope Adrian I sent to Charles the Great, at his request, a copy of the Roman Sacramentary in the shape which, as it was believed, had been given to it by the revision of S. Gregory. This forms the basis of the class of Sacramentaries known as Gregorian, of which all the earliest specimens known to us appear to have been written north of the Alps. The earliest Gregorian Sacramentaries are all divided into two parts, which are in some manuscripts separated by a list of the contents of the second part, in others also by a short preface to the second part, drawn up by the person to whose arrangement that portion of the Sacramentary is to be assigned. In this preface it is stated that the first part of the Sacramentary, which stands before the preface, is (with certain specified exceptions) the Sacramentary set forth by S. Gregory, while the second part, which follows the preface, is a compilation from other sources, containing 'alia quaedam quibus necessario utitur sancta ecclesia,' which S. Gregory had omitted in his Sacramentary, in view of the fact that they had been already set forth by others. The second part is of the nature, in fact, of a supplement to the first part, compiled from service books other than that ascribed to S. Gregory. This preface, and therefore also the second part of the Gregorian Sacramentaries, are sometimes ascribed to Grimoldus, who was Abbot of S. Gallen from about 850 to 872: but a more probable view is that expressed by the writer of the

---

[1] Mabillon supposed this manuscript to have had its origin in the province of Besançon, but it seems not unlikely that it belongs rather to the north of Italy. (See Duchesne, *Origines du Culte Chrétien*, pp. 150, 151).

treatise *De Ecclesiasticis Observationibus*, who ascribes the authorship of the preface and the compilation of the supplement to Alcuin [1].

The desire of Charles the Great was to make the adoption of the Gregorian Sacramentary universal and exclusive throughout his dominions, and it was no doubt partly with the view of assisting such a general adoption that the second part, or supplement, was added to the text furnished by Adrian, which, as we may infer, did not contain all that was required. If, as seems most likely, we may judge from the contents of the supplement what Adrian's copy of the Sacramentary left to be provided from other sources, it would appear that what was sent to Charles as the Roman Sacramentary of S. Gregory contained no *missae* for ordinary Sundays, such as those after Epiphany and after Pentecost, and no *missae* for special purposes such as those which are contained in the third book of the Vatican manuscript. M. Duchesne argues that Adrian's book was a copy of the Sacramentary prepared for the use of the Pope, and included only the prayers for festivals and 'stational' days, which would be said by the Pope himself [2]. With the addition of the supplement, however, the Gregorian Sacramentary was suitable for general use, and was accordingly generally adopted, according to Charles' direction.

It was not, however, at once adopted so completely as to exclude the use of the older Roman Sacramentaries, which we find, in the ninth century, distinguished by the name of 'Gelasian.' Thus in the Chronicle of the Abbey of S. Riquier, we find in an inventory drawn up in 831, the following entry:—

'De libris sacrarii qui ministerio altaris deserviunt Missales Gregoriani tres: Missalis Gregorianus et Gelasianus modernis temporibus ab Albino ordinatus i: Lectionarii Epistolarum et Evangeliorum mixtim et ordinate compositi v: Missales Gelasiani xix [3].'

Here the 'Missales Gregoriani' are no doubt some of the copies of Adrian's book which were multiplied and distributed, under Charles' direction, soon after its reception: the 'Missalis

---

[1] Micrologus, *De Eccl. Observ.* cap. 60. See for a recent argument on this subject a paper 'Ueber das sogenannte Sacramentarium Gelasianum,' by Dom Suitbert Bäumer, O. S. B., in the *Historische Jahrbuch*, vol. xiv. pp. 252 sqq.

[2] *Origines du Culte Chrétien*, pp. 115 sqq.

[3] *Chronicon Centulense*, in the *Spicilegium* of d'Achery, vol. iv. p. 485.

CONTINUANCE OF 'GELASIAN' BOOKS.

Gregorianus et Gelasianus . . . ab Albino ordinatus' is most probably a copy of the Gregorian Sacramentary including the supplement: if so, we have here a confirmation of the view which ascribes that supplement to Alcuin. The 'Missales Gelasiani,' far more numerous, are Sacramentaries of the older type, of which it is expressly said that they are among the 'libri sacrarii' and employed in the service of the altar.

Le Brun, in commenting on this passage, notes it as an argument in favour of the view that the Benedictines retained the older or 'Gelasian' Sacramentary after the introduction of the Gregorian[1]. But its retention was not confined to the monastic communities. In a record of a diocesan visitation by Hincmar of Rheims, held probably about the year 850, we find, in the inventories of books belonging to parish churches, the mention of 'Gelasian' as well as of 'Gregorian' missals: in one case the only missal of the church seems to have been 'Gelasian[2].'

How long the use of the 'Gelasian' Sacramentary continued, side by side with that of the Gregorian, can hardly be determined. But the evidence of the triple Sacramentary used by Gerbert would seem to show that in the tenth century the 'Gelasian' rite was still not a mere survival, but was so far in practical use as to rank, for the purposes of the compiler of that collection, which can hardly be supposed to have been merely antiquarian, with the Gregorian and Ambrosian rites. Traces of its partial use may also be found. Thus in a Poitiers Pontifical, cited by Martène, who supposed it to have been written about the year 900, we find provision for the possibility of the lessons on Easter Even being either 'secundum Gelasium' or 'secundum Gregorium[3],' while in another manuscript mentioned by Vezzosi, certain *Missae Dominicales* (presumably a series such as that in

---

[1] Le Brun, *Explication de la Messe*, vol. ii. p. 143 (ed. 1860).

[2] See the paper by Dom Suitbert Bäumer, to which reference has been made above. (*Hist. Jahrb.* vol. xiv. p. 248.) The author argues that the term 'Gelasian' must have been, in popular as well as in learned use, applied to the Missals (or Sacramentaries) of the older type.

[3] Martène, *De Antiq. Eccl. Ritibus*, lib. iii. cap. 24 (vol. iii. p. 155 in 1764 ed.). The passage is erroneously cited from Martène by Vezzosi (*Thomasii Opera*, vol. vi. p. 70 *note*) as being contained in the Pontifical of Troyes, the *Ordo* from which immediately precedes that from the Poitiers Pontifical in Martène's series of extracts. Gerbert (*Mon. Vet. Lit. Alem.* vol. i. p. 83 *note*) reproduces Vezzosi's statement.

the supplement to the Gregorian Sacramentary) are called 'Orationes Dominicales S. Gelasii Papae[1].' Another instance of the same kind of reference is to be found in the Irish book known as the Stowe Missal, where the Canon is entitled 'Canon Dominicus Papae Gilasi[2].'

We have already seen that Le Brun speaks of several 'Gelasian' Sacramentaries as known to him: and the points which he notes as distinguishing them from the Gregorian Sacramentaries may be sufficiently traced in R. and S. to warrant us in supposing that these two manuscripts, if not among those with which Le Brun was acquainted, belong to the same type which he distinguished as 'Gelasian.' He does not notice any Sacramentary divided, like the Vatican manuscript, into three books, and we may perhaps fairly infer that he knew of none, except the Vatican manuscript, in which this division was to be found. The manuscripts of the 'Gelasian' type now known to us are few in number. Besides R. and S., it would seem that we may assign to this class the Sacramentary of Gellone, from which Martène extracted several of the *Ordines* included in his work *De Antiquis Ecclesiae Ritibus*, and to which, as reproduced by Martène, reference is occasionally made in the following pages[3]; and also a manuscript now known as *Codex* O. 83 in the Chapter Library of Prague[4]. To the same class, perhaps, belongs the Sacramentary of Angoulême, described by M. Delisle[5]; but this

---

[1] *Thomasii Opera*, vol. vi. Preface, p. xxxv.

[2] F. E. Warren, *Liturgy and Ritual of the Celtic Church*, p. 234. The date of the part of the MS. including the Canon and its title is rather uncertain: but it seems most likely that here, as in other cases, the name is employed to distinguish something taken from a Sacramentary not professedly Gregorian. The Canon actually contains the words said to have been added by S. Gregory, agreeing in this point, as well as in some others, with the Canon of the 'Gelasian' Sacramentaries.

[3] This manuscript, now in the National Library at Paris (MS. Lat. 12048), bears the title 'Liber Sacramentorum.' It has been described by M. Delisle (*Mém. sur d'Anc. Sacram.* pp. 80, 81), who considers it to date from the latter half of the eighth century.

[4] This MS. has recently been made known by Dom S. Bäumer, who mentions it more than once in his paper, already referred to, in vol. xiv. of the *Historische Jahrbuch*. He is of opinion that both the Sacramentary of Gellone and the Prague manuscript, though showing (especially the latter) traces of Gregorian influence, should be classed as 'Gelasian.'

[5] *Mém. sur d'Anc. Sacram.*, pp. 91–96. The contents of the codex, as noted by M. Delisle, show some apparent correspondences with the Vatican manuscript; but the general arrangement seems to agree more with the later Gelasian Sacramentaries, the whole *Proprium de Tempore* and *Proprium de Sanctis* forming one series. The Canon, as in the Gelasian

apparently is so far 'Gregorianized' as to have led to its being classified, as M. Delisle tells us, as 'Missale vetus ex Gelasiano et Gregoriano mixtum.'

In addition to these manuscripts mention may be made of a fragment, hitherto unnoticed, in the Bodleian Library at Oxford[1]. This is of very small extent, consisting only of portions of four leaves, which seem to have been used in the old binding of one of the printed books of the Douce collection, and to have been rescued from that position by Mr. Douce when the volume was rebound, and attached to one of the fly-leaves. They have now been removed from this situation, and bound up in a separate cover. The fragment contains part of the *Missa Chrismalis* (including a portion of the Exorcism and Preface which are to be found on p. 72 of the present work), the end of the *missa* for the night of Easter Even, and part of that for Easter Day, parts of the *missa* and other prayers for the Nativity of S. John Baptist, and of the *missae* for the vigil and the festival of SS. John and Paul, the latter part of the *missa* for the sixth Sunday after Pentecost, and the heading of that for the vigil of SS. Peter and Paul. The sections, as in the Vatican manuscript and the Angoulême Sacramentary, appear to have been numbered, and the Roman 'station' for Easter Day is noted in the heading of the *missa*. The order of the prayers agrees exactly with that of the S. Gallen manuscript, while the readings of the text, save for some minor variations of spelling, agree very closely with those of the first hand in the same manuscript[2].

books, is not at the beginning, but at the end of the *Proprium* and *Commune*. It may be noted that the second part of the book contains a series of Episcopal Benedictions such as that which, as already suggested, may be referred to in the heading of the 'second book' of R. M. Delisle assigns the Angoulême Sacramentary to the latter part of the eighth, or the beginning of the ninth, century, apparently inclining to the later date, which he gives in the list of manuscripts appended to his text. Another manuscript, now lost, which is mentioned by M. Delisle, was probably of the Gelasian class—a 'Liber Sacramentorum Romanae Ecclesiae' written in silver letters on purple parchment, which perished when the Library of Strasburg was destroyed in

1870 (*Mém. sur d'Anc. Sacram.*, pp. 89–91).

[1] MS. Douce, f. 1. A 'collotype' facsimile of one page of the fragment (fol. 3 verso) is included in the present volume.

[2] One exception may be noticed. In the Preface which stands at the end of the *Missa Chrismalis* (see p. 72 *infra*) the fragment reads, 'Qui mysterium (*sic*) tuorum secreta revelans pacificum nemus ore columbe gestatum,' &c. This differs from the reading of S[1]. by the insertion of the word 'pacificum,' but supports the reading of 'nemus' found in V. and S[1]., and adopted in the text in preference to 'munus,' which is substituted by S[2]. The change is no doubt due to the corrector's failure to understand the original word, which is used in a rather rare sense.

The treatment which the leaves have at different times received prevents the formation of any trustworthy estimate of their date from their present general appearance, and the character of the handwriting furnishes the only test by which the date of the fragment can be determined. The writing is of a rather unusual type, presenting affinities with both the Merovingian and the Lombardic, and may point to a date nearly as early as that of the Vatican manuscript. It probably does point to a date earlier than that of either S. or R. The fragment is thus perhaps the oldest among the known specimens of the later type of 'Gelasian' Sacramentaries, and its agreement with S. seems to give additional weight to the evidence of that manuscript.

None of the manuscripts classed as 'Gelasian' contains any mention of S. Gelasius corresponding to the mention of S. Gregory, which we find in the titles of the Gregorian Sacramentaries. Those which have a title at all are called either 'Liber Sacramentorum Romanae Ecclesiae,' or simply 'Liber Sacramentorum.' Their claim to the name 'Gelasian' rests chiefly on what seems to have been the general usage of the eighth and ninth centuries, when they were distinguished by this epithet from the Sacramentaries which claimed to be, and were believed to be, the work of S. Gregory. But the further question as to the foundation of this usage is one which we can hardly now decide. It may have been the consequence of a tradition which ascribed to S. Gelasius the origin of the 'Liber Sacramentorum' from which they were derived. But we do not find any clear evidence of such a tradition before the time when the name appears in use. Gennadius, in the account of S. Gelasius contained in the treatise *De Viris Illustribus*, speaks of 'tractatus diversarum scripturarum et sacramentorum' composed by him. The 'Liber Pontificalis,' while it does not say expressly that S. Gelasius compiled a Sacramentary, does attribute to him the composition of 'sacramentorum praefationes et orationes'—of forms, that is to say, such as those of which a Sacramentary is an organized collection [1]. Walafrid Strabo, writing in the first half of the ninth century, goes a step further, and tells us that S. Gelasius is said to have arranged prayers composed by himself and others. He may be understood to

---

[1] *Liber Pontificalis*, vol. i. p. 255.

say also that the prayers arranged by S. Gelasius were in use in the churches of Gaul[1].

By the time when Walafrid wrote, however, the term 'Gelasian' was already in use, as we see by the inventory of S. Riquier, and his statement may rest simply on that usage. John the Deacon, writing in the latter half of the ninth century, is more explicit and detailed in his statement. He tells us[2] that S. Gregory compressed 'in unius libri volumine' the 'Gelasianum codicem de missarum solemniis,' and that he effected this object 'multa subtrahens, pauca convertens, nonnulla vero superadiciens pro exponendis evangelicis lectionibus.' It is upon this statement that Tommasi and others who have followed him have principally relied in their argument in favour of the Gelasian origin of the Vatican manuscript. This Sacramentary seemed to correspond with the indications contained in John's statement as to the character of the 'Gelasianus codex.' It is certainly the case that it is divided into three books, while the Gregorian Sacramentary contains, or forms, a single book. But here the correspondence seems to end. The differences of arrangement between the Vatican manuscript and the Gregorian Sacramentary are such that the work of the person who compiled the latter from the former could hardly be adequately described by the phrases which John employs, if those phrases are to be taken strictly. The quantity of matter which, on this theory, would have been discarded, is certainly considerable: but the amount of matter which has changed its place is also very large: the 'multa subtrahens' may fit the case well enough: but the 'pauca convertens' does not seem to apply. It would be more applicable, as we shall see, if we suppose that the 'Gelasianus codex' of which John speaks was a Sacramentary of which the *missae* were arranged like those in R. or S.: and R., though not divided into three books, contains more books than one. But if we are to suppose the 'Gelasianus codex' which John had in view to have been a Sacramentary resem-

---

[1] *De Rebus Ecclesiasticis*, cap. 22. The phrase is also capable of another interpretation—that the churches of Gaul used 'prayers of their own,' and as referring to the Gallican Sacramentaries. Walafrid goes on to speak of S. Gregory as the compiler of the 'Liber Sacramentorum' which bears his name: but his words suggest the view that S. Gregory drew his material from various sources, rather than the view expressed by John the Deacon, that S. Gregory's Sacramentary was based on a similar work of S. Gelasius.

[2] *De Vita Gregorii*, ii. 17.

bling R. or S., it becomes more probable that his statement was based simply on a comparison of what in his own day was known as the 'Gelasian' Sacramentary with what was known as the Gregorian, and therefore less likely that his statement expresses an early tradition, uncoloured by the opinion of the writer or his contemporaries. The question seems, however, to be rendered more difficult, whatever view we take as to the character of the 'Gelasian codex,' by his mention of another point with regard to S. Gregory's work. If the words 'nonnulla vero superadiciens' stood by themselves, they might apply to either of the supposed cases, at least as exactly as the phrases 'multa subtrahens' and 'pauca convertens.' But it is difficult to see how the phrase 'nonnulla vero superadiciens pro exponendis evangelicis lectionibus' is to be explained as a reference to anything contained in the Gregorian Sacramentary as we have it now, or as we know it to have been received before the time at which John the Deacon wrote. Possibly an explanation might be found by a comparison of the degrees in which the Gelasian and Gregorian books serve by their arrangement to illustrate the Liturgical Gospels. But it seems also possible that we have here an indication that John's statement does not rest simply on the impression which he had formed of the comparative contents of the 'Gelasian' and 'Gregorian' codices of his own day, but in part depends upon some source of information now unknown to us, as to the actual work of S. Gregory[1].

The only authority, therefore, which can be alleged with certainty for the use of the term 'Gelasian,' as applied to the class of Sacramentaries which includes V., R., and S., is to be

[1] It may be worth while to notice the fact that Bede, writing at a date much nearer to S. Gregory's own time than either John the Deacon or Walafrid Strabo, and dwelling at some length upon the literary labours of S. Gregory, does not attribute to him either the formation or the revision of a Sacramentary, though he does mention the addition which S. Gregory is said to have made to the clause 'Hanc igitur oblationem' in the Canon of the Mass. Nor does the *Liber Pontificalis*, which briefly passes over S. Gregory's literary work, make any mention of his compilation of a 'Liber Sacramentorum,' though here also we find mention of the addition to the Canon. But the resemblance between Bede's account of S. Gregory and the account in the *Liber Pontificalis* is sufficiently strong to suggest that there may be a close relationship between the two, which would account for the non-appearance in the one of what is omitted in the other. John the Deacon seems to have used other sources of information, independent of either account.

found in the fact that such Sacramentaries were actually distinguished by this name while they were still in use, and that, in accordance with this usage, certain forms, such as the lessons on Easter Even, agreeing with the order prescribed in these Sacramentaries, were also described as 'secundum Gelasium.' The usage may have been the result of an early tradition as to their origin; but we cannot be certain that this was so. It may, as M. Duchesne supposes, have sprung up in the eighth or ninth century, when it was desired to distinguish the older form of Sacramentary from that which bore the name of S. Gregory, and have owed its origin to the tradition preserved in the 'Liber Pontificalis,' that S. Gelasius was the author of 'prefaces and prayers [1].' In any case, it would have been admitted by those who used the term that the whole 'Gelasian' Sacramentary, as they knew and used it, had not proceeded from S. Gelasius: and it is hard to think that, if there had been a general belief, in the early part of the eighth century, that the main body of the 'Gelasian' Sacramentary, apart from certain things obviously of much more recent origin, was really due to S. Gelasius, the compiler of the supplement to the Gregorian Sacramentary would have refrained from citing the authority of S. Gelasius for the forms which he transferred from the older Sacramentaries to his own compilation, and would have been content, as he was content, to state in his introductory preface that his material was drawn from the work of authorities other than S. Gregory.

For the use of the term in our own day, and especially for its use as applied to the Vatican manuscript, we may plead not only the usage of the time when these Sacramentaries were still employed, but the current use of liturgical scholars. The name is a convenient one, so long as we do not use it as a 'question-begging epithet': it has, ever since Tommasi's time, been generally applied to the one Sacramentary of this class which has been really known to students of the Western Liturgies, and it would be unreasonable, unless some clear advantage could be expected from a change, to attempt to alter the title by which the book has so long been known.

In comparing the arrangement of the Vatican manuscript with that of the later 'Gelasian' codices, as represented by R. and S.,

---

[1] See Duchesne, *Origines du Culte Chrétien*, pp. 121-123.

perhaps the first point which strikes our attention is the absence in the latter of the division into three books, which marks the earlier manuscript, and which was, in the eyes of its first editor, a weighty argument in favour of the identity of that manuscript with the Sacramentary of S. Gelasius. If we assume that the early Roman Sacramentary which furnished the basis of V. was divided, like V. itself, into three books, of which the first contained the partially developed *Proprium de Tempore*, the second the *Proprium Sanctorum* and *Commune Sanctorum*[1], and the third a series of unappropriated Sunday *missae* with the *Canon Actionis* and certain *missae in quotidianis diebus*, we find on turning to R. and S. that these three divisions have been combined, augmented, and in part revised. The *Proprium de Tempore* has been developed by the appropriation of the *missae Dominicales* to particular Sundays, and by the addition of other Sunday *missae* assigned to Sundays not provided for by this appropriation; the *Proprium Sanctorum* has also received additions, and no longer forms a separate division, but is broken up, and its parts interspersed with the Sunday *missae*. The group of Sunday *missae* being thus removed from their position immediately before the *Canon Actionis*, the *missae quotidianae* are moved into that place, so that the Canon, with its attendant series of Postcommunions and Benedictions *super Populum*, stands at the end of the whole collection. Thus the whole of the Sacramentary has received a certain amount of rearrangement, and almost all its parts show a certain amount of change in their position.

But the process of rearrangement has not been confined to this general shifting of material. There has been also, it would seem, in many cases, a rearrangement of the contents of particular portions. Thus, while the greater part of the prayers which in V. make up the *missae* from Christmas to the Epiphany are found also in the corresponding portion of R.

---

[1] The second book of V. contains, as we have seen, some portions which belong to the *Proprium de Tempore*; whether this was the original arrangement may perhaps be doubtful, but the point is not of much importance for the present purpose. In the following discussion of the contents of V., R., and S., we may leave out of our consideration the portions of the first book of V. which are not strictly 'ordinis anni circuli,' and the contents of the latter part of the third book (sections xxiv–cvi): we may also leave out of our reckoning the portion of R. which is parallel to these portions of V., and forms in R. the second book of the whole collection.

and S., they there appear in a different order: so also with the prayers which in V. make up the *missae* from Easter to Pentecost, and so again with the Advent *missae* and with the prayers of the *missae* for the Ember seasons. The case is the same, in several instances, with the prayers for particular festivals in the *Sanctorale*, while here we also find that in R. and S. some of the *missae* which form the *Commune Sanctorum* of V. have been assigned to particular festivals, and the *Commune Sanctorum* has been reconstructed. The *missae* for the whole of Lent and Advent have been revised and rearranged, those for Septuagesima, Sexagesima, and Quinquagesima have been slightly altered. As a general rule, the form of the *missa* in R. and S. corresponds with that which we find in V.: each *missa*, that is to say, contains two Collects before the Secret: many are also provided with a Preface[1], and with a *Benedictio super Populum*. But while R. and S. thus preserve, in the structure of their *missae*, the characteristic features of the 'Gelasian' Sacramentary, the general result of the revision is such that the individual *missae* are brought into closer agreement with the Gregorian *missae* for the same days than those of V. Looking merely at the prayers contained in a particular *missa* of R. or S., as they stand in Gerbert's text, and comparing them with those of the corresponding *missa* in the Gregorian Sacramentary of Muratori, we might often be disposed to think that the *missa* of R. or S. had been constructed by simply adding to the Gregorian *missa* such forms as were needed to make up a *missa* of the 'Gelasian' type: or, if we chose to look at the matter from another point of view, we might say that the Gregorian *missa* seems to have been formed from the 'Gelasian' *missa* of R. or S. by simply discarding the forms which were not required in a *missa* of the Gregorian type. If, however, we take the differences of readings presented

---

[1] The large number of proper Prefaces in R., and still more in S., is a feature in which the two later Sacramentaries show a marked difference from the earlier one. The number in R. is less than in S.; for (as will be seen from the Appendix) R. not only omits a good many Saint's day *missae*, which appear in S., and which there include a proper Preface, but also omits in many cases a Preface contained in S., where the rest of the *missa* is common to both manuscripts. Even so, the number of Prefaces in R. exceeds that in V.: but the Prefaces of S. outnumber those of V. in the proportion of nearly three to one. The greater part of the Prefaces of S. find a place, though frequently with some alteration of their text, in the supplementary portion of the Gregorian Sacramentaries.

by the different Sacramentaries into account, the question of the relation of R. and S. to V. on the one hand, and to the Gregorian Sacramentary on the other, will sometimes appear, even in such cases, to be rather more intricate. If, in addition to this, we further consider the fact that R. and S. contain many *missae* which, while they owe, or seem to owe, some part of their contents to the Gregorian Sacramentary, are for the most part composed of prayers which find no place in the first portion of that Sacramentary, but can be traced in V., and contain also other *missae* which are not represented in the Gregorian Sacramentary at all, it seems impossible to avoid the conclusion that the type of Sacramentary represented by R. and S. rests, at least to a very large extent, and probably as its principal foundation, upon a Roman Sacramentary very closely allied to that which forms the basis of the text of V. On the other hand, it can hardly be doubted that this later type of 'Gelasian' Sacramentary is closely related to that other recension of the Roman Sacramentary which is represented by the first portion of Muratori's Gregorian text[1].

The use which is made in R. and S. of the material furnished by the Advent *missae* of V. may be seen, to some extent, from the notes appended to those *missae* (Book II, sections lxxx–lxxxv, pp. 214–223). But it may be worth while, as an illustration of what has been said, to examine the result, as it appears in R. and S., in comparison with the parallel portion of Muratori's Gregorian text.

The two 'Gelasian' books contain five *missae* for the Sundays before Christmas: Muratori's Gregorian text has only four. In S. each of the five *missae* has a Preface: the Gregorian *missae* have none, and those of S. are not all contained in V. The Collects, Secret, and Postcommunion of the first *missa* in R. and S. are all found in V.: the two Collects are also found in the *Aliae orationes de Adventu* of the Gregorian text: as regards readings, S[1] and R. preserve in one of these two Collects the reading of V., in the other they agree with the

---

[1] The Gregorian Sacramentary edited by Pamelius contains, in its first portion, a large amount of material common to R. and S. But much of this material, as it would seem, has been inserted by the same hand which compiled the supplement, and did not form part of the recension which the compiler attributed to S. Gregory. The relation of this added matter to the 'Gelasian' Sacramentaries is the same as that of the supplement.

Gregorian text, and differ from V. The Secret and Postcommunion are not in the Gregorian text. In the *missae* for the other four Sundays R. and S. agree with the Gregorian text as to the first Collect, Secret, and Postcommunion; some of these prayers are not contained in V. On the other hand, the second Collect in each of the four *missae* is to be found in V., while none of them is contained in the Gregorian text. The two 'Gelasian' books contain a series of *missae* 'quotidianis diebus,' which is not to be found either in V. or in the Gregorian text: the greater part of the prayers of which the *missae* are made up are contained in V., and most of them are absent from the Gregorian text. The same is the case with the series of additional Advent collects. The *missae* for the Ember days, while differing from the parallel series both in V. and in the Gregorian text, have more in common with the former than with the latter. There are some cases, in this portion of R. and S., of prayers in which the text of the later 'Gelasian' manuscripts shows agreement with that of the earlier, where they differ from the Gregorian text: but the instances are few, and the points of agreement or difference somewhat slight.

The *missae* of V. for Septuagesima and the two following Sundays are found in R. and S. with but little change. Each of them has, in the later manuscripts, a proper Preface: the Preface for Sexagesima appears elsewhere in V., while all three find a place in the supplement to the Gregorian Sacramentary, in a form corresponding, on the whole, rather to that which is given to them by the second hand of S. than to that in which they are to be found in R. Apart from these Prefaces, there is not much to connect the *missae* of R. and S. with the Gregorian text. One prayer is common to R., S., and the Gregorian in each of the three *missae*. In that for Septuagesima, the *Super Populum* of R. and S. is identical with the Collect of the Gregorian *missa*: it is found elsewhere in V., which here has no *Super Populum*[1]. In the *missae* for Sexagesima and Quinquagesima, R. and S. adopt, as the first Collect, the Collect of the Gregorian *missa*, and transfer to the second place the Collect which stands first in the *missa* of V. This is perhaps more to be noted in the case of the Sexagesima

---

[1] The title *Super Populum* is in V. prefixed to what is obviously the Postcommunion: the absence of a *Super Populum* is probably due to this clerical error of the scribe, which has been corrected in the text of this edition.

missa, where the peculiar significance of the Gregorian Collect depends upon the Roman usage, which made the 'station' that day at the church of S. Paul, and where the remaining prayers of the *missa* are not found in the Gregorian text [1].

The *missae* of the Sundays of Lent in R. and S. present fewer points of comparison with V., since in that manuscript the *missae* for the 'Scrutinies' are assigned to the third, fourth, and fifth Sundays: these *missae* are to be found also in R., but not assigned to the same, or indeed to any particular days [2]. In the *missa* which R. and S. assign to the first Sunday of Lent, the first Collect is the same, with a slight variation, as in Muratori's Gregorian text, the second the same as the first Collect of V., the Secret is common to V. and to the Gregorian, the Postcommunion is in the Gregorian *missa* but not in V., while the *Super Populum* is the same as in V., not appearing in Muratori's Gregorian text, but being found in the *Codex Ottobonianus*. For the second Sunday, the first Collect is Gregorian, while the remaining prayers agree with V.; the Postcommunion appears elsewhere in the Gregorian books, and the *Super Populum* is in the *missa* for the same day in the *Codex Ottobonianus*. For Palm Sunday, the whole of the prayers of R. and S., with the exception of the Postcommunion, agree with the *missa* in V. The first Collect is common to the Gregorian, and the *Super Populum*, once more, is in the *missa* of the *Codex Ottobonianus*. The Postcommunion, which is not Gregorian, occurs elsewhere in V. Turning to those Sundays for which V. employs the *missae* for the 'Scrutinies,' we find that in R. and S., on the third Sunday, the first Collect agrees with the Gregorian *missa*, and the *Super Populum* with that of the

---

[1] Some of them, as also some of the non-Gregorian prayers of the *missae* for Septuagesima and Quinquagesima, appear as additional forms in Pamelius' text, but have been marked by the compiler as not belonging to the Gregorian recension.

[2] Dr. F. Probst, in his recent work on the Roman Sacramentaries, treats the presence of these *missae* on the third, fourth, and fifth Sundays of Lent as part of the original Gelasian arrangement, and supposes them to have been discarded in R. and S., in favour of new *missae* borrowed for the most part from the Gregorian Sacramentary. (Probst, *Die ältesten Römischen Sacramentarien und Ordines*, p. 163.) As against this view it may be remarked that the *missae* for the 'Scrutinies' are not of the Gelasian type, having only a single Collect: and that it is quite possible that the proper *missae* for the Sundays have been discarded in V. in order to insert in their place the *missae* for the 'Scrutinies.' In this case, we cannot tell how far the Sunday *missae* of R. and S. agreed with those of the older Gelasian Sacramentary. They are not (with one exception) in very close agreement with the *missae* for the same Sundays in the Gregorian Sacramentary.

Codex Ottobonianus: the second Collect, Secret, and Postcommunion appear in other Gregorian *missae*, while the last is also found in V., but is assigned to another day. For the fourth Sunday, all but the *Super Populum* agree with Muratori's Gregorian text, the Secret appearing elsewhere in V., while the *Super Populum* is the same as the Postcommunion of the *missa* for the 'Scrutiny.' For the fifth Sunday, all the prayers are contained in the Gregorian Sacramentary, but only the first Collect is common to the Gregorian *missa* for the Sunday: no part of the *missa* is found in V. Possibly the small proportion of agreement which the *missae* for these three Sundays show with the contents of V. may be due to the suppression in V. of the *missae* with which they might have been expected to agree: for whatever reason, the amount of their contents which can be traced in V. is much less than in the case of the *missae* for the other Sundays of Lent[1]. Each of the Sunday *missae* of R. and S. contains a proper Preface; these appear, with more or less variation, in the supplementary part of the Gregorian Sacramentary.

The *missae* for the week-days of Lent in R. and S. differ from the series in V., in the first place by the addition of a *missa* for the Thursday in each week. It was perhaps the introduction of the Thursday 'station' which gave occasion for a rearrangement of the whole of this portion of the Sacramentary. The Thursday *missae* of R. and S. are, for the most part, made up of prayers which occur elsewhere in V. The same, indeed, may be said of most of the week-day *missae*: but, in many of them, some prayers are included which do not appear in V., and which do occur, though not always in the same position, in the Gregorian Sacramentary: while others, common to V. and to the Gregorian books, are placed in R. and S. in the same position which they occupy in the Gregorian text. In some instances, however, even where this is the case, the readings of R. and S. agree with V. where the Gregorian text shows a difference from the latter manuscript. The structure, and the apparent source of the *missae* of R. and S. may perhaps be most conveniently shown by the following

---

[1] The *missa* for the fourth Sunday is now wanting in R., but from the general agreement of R. and S. in this portion of their contents it seems most likely that there was no important difference between them with regard to what was contained in the leaves which have been lost in R.

table, which includes all the week-days from Ash Wednesday to the Thursday in *Coena Domini*, with the exception of the *Sabbatum in xii Lectionibus*, which is left out of the reckoning, for obvious reasons. In this table, V. signifies that the prayer is included in the *missa* for the same day in the Vatican manuscript, Gr., that it is included in the *missa* for the same day in Muratori's Gregorian text. Prayers found elsewhere in V. are marked (V.), those found elsewhere in the first part of the Gregorian text are marked (Gr.), those found only in the supplementary part of the Gregorian text are marked [Gr.], while an asterisk added to one or other of these symbols indicates that the prayer appears in the place indicated with some variation of text. The *missae* contained in S. are the basis of the table; R. does not now contain those for the latter part of the third and the first part of the fourth weeks, while there is a slight difference of arrangement between R. and S. in regard to the Monday of the fifth week (see App. p. 331). Each of the *missae* for the first week in S. has a proper Preface; R. omits those of the Monday and Tuesday.

		1st Coll.	2nd Coll.	Secret.	Postcom.	Sup. Popul.
Ante Dom. i	Fer. iv	Gr. (V.)	Gr. (V.)	V. Gr.	Gr. (V.)	(Gr.)
	Fer. v	(V.)	(V.)	(V.)	(Gr.)	—
	Fer. vi	Gr. (V.)	V.	V.	(V.)	V.
	Sabb.	V.	V.	V.	V.	V. (Gr.*)
Hebd. i	Fer. ii	Gr. (V.)	V. (Gr.)	V.	Gr. (V.)	V.
	Fer. iii	Gr.	(V.)	Gr.	V. (Gr.)	Gr.
	Fer. iv	Gr.	Gr.	V. (Gr.)	Gr.	V. (Gr.)
	Fer. v	(V.)	(V.)	(V.)	(V.)	(V.)
	Fer. vi	Gr.	V.	V.	V.	V.
Hebd. ii	Fer. ii	Gr.	V.	Gr.	V.	V.
	Fer. iii	Gr. (V.)	V.	Gr. (V.)	V.	V.
	Fer. iv	V.	V. (Gr.)	Gr.	V. (Gr.)	Gr.
	Fer. v	(V.)	(V.)	(V.) (Gr.)	V. (Gr.*)	(V.) Gr.*
	Fer. vi	Gr.	V.	Gr.*	Gr.	Gr.
	Sabb.	Gr. (V.)	V.	Gr. (V.)	Gr.	V.
Hebd. iii	Fer. ii	(V.) Gr.*	V.	Gr.	V.	V.
	Fer. iii	(V.) Gr.*	V.	Gr. (V.)	Gr.	V.
	Fer. iv	Gr.	V.	Gr. (V.)	Gr.	V.
	Fer. v	(V.)	[Gr.]	(V.)	(V.)	(Gr.)
	Fer. vi	Gr. (V.)	(V.)	Gr.	Gr.	[Gr.]
	Sabb.	V. (Gr.)	V.	V. (Gr.)	(V.)	V. (Gr.)
Hebd. iv	Fer. ii	V. (Gr.)	(Gr.)	V. (Gr.)	V. (Gr.)	V. (Gr.)
	Fer. iii	Gr. (V.)	V.*	V. (Gr.)	V. (Gr.)	Gr.
	Fer. iv	V. Gr.	Gr.	Gr.	Gr. (V.)	Gr. (V.)
	Fer. v	(V.)	(Gr.)	(V.)	(V.)	Gr. (V.)
	Fer. vi	Gr.	?	V. (Gr.)	Gr.	V.
	Sabb.	V.	V.	Gr. (V.)	Gr. (V.)	V.

LENT 'STATIONS' IN R. AND S.

		1st Coll.	2nd Coll.	Secret.	Postcom.	Sup. Popul.
Hebd. v	Fer. ii	Gr. (V.)	Gr.	(V.) Gr.*	(Gr.)	V.
	Fer. iii	Gr.	[Gr.]	Gr.	Gr. (V.)	V. [Gr.]
	Fer. iv	Gr. (V.)	V.	Gr.	Gr. (V.)	[Gr.]
	Fer. v	(V.)	(V.)	(V.)	(V.)	[Gr.]
	Fer. vi	Gr.	V.	V.	Gr. (V.)	V.
	Sabb.	(V.)	[Gr.]	(V.)	(V.)	[Gr.]
Hebd. vi	Fer. ii	Gr.	(V.)	V.	(V.*)	(Gr.)
	Fer. iii	Gr.	V.	(V.)	V.	(V.)
	Fer. iv	1st & 2nd Coll. Gr.; 3rd & 4th Coll. V.		V.	Gr.	Gr.

It will be seen from the table that only one of the *missae* of V. appears as a whole in R. and S., that, namely, for the Saturday before the first Sunday of Lent, a day for which the Gregorian Sacramentary provided no *missa*. With regard to the other days, it would seem that, as a general rule, the first Collect is the same as the Collect of the Gregorian Sacramentary: but the rule is not by any means absolute.

In the heading of each of the Lent *missae* of R. and S. (with the exceptions of the second Sunday and of the Saturday before Palm Sunday) there is mention of the Roman church at which the 'station' for the day was held. The list, as may be seen from the Appendix (pp. 325-333), differs but slightly from that which is furnished by the Gregorian Sacramentaries of Pamelius and Muratori. It seems to differ in regard to the Thursday of the first week, where the Gregorian Sacramentaries mention the church of S. Laurence 'foris murum': but Pamelius' marginal note seems to indicate that his manuscript, or some other authority which he employed, was in practical agreement with the heading as given in R., and that 'foris murum' is an erroneous reading, arising from a misunderstanding of the title 'ad Formonsum' or 'ad Formosum.' A more important divergence is that with regard to the Monday of Holy Week, where R. and S. mention the church of SS. Nereus and Achilleus, agreeing in this point with the list in the second volume of Mabillon's *Museum Italicum*, but differing from the Sacramentaries of Muratori and Pamelius, which, like the present Roman Missal, place the 'station' at the church of S. Praxedes.

An exact comparison of the *missae* for the Ember days, and of the prayers 'in xii. Lectionibus,' is rendered difficult by the fact that in these portions of their contents there is a certain amount of difference between R. and S. Both agree in furnishing two series of *missae* for the 'Ieiunium quarti mensis,' of which one (which in S. agrees throughout with the series of the Gregorian Sacramentary of Muratori, save for the addition of a Preface to the Wednesday *missa*) stands between the *missa* for Pentecost and that for the octave. The prayers of the other series, which is placed after the *missa* for the third week after Pentecost, are very closely in agreement with those of the series for the Pentecost week in V. The presence of the two series is probably due to the usage, which existed in some places, of observing the fast in the 'fourth month,' without regard to the date of Pentecost. The prayers for the other three seasons, while not agreeing exactly either with those of V. or with those of the Gregorian Sacramentary, have, taken together as a whole, perhaps more points of agreement with the latter, while they contain in each case some elements which are found in V. and are absent from the Gregorian *missae*.

A minute comparison with regard to the *missae* for the principal festivals and for the Saints' days which are common to the *Proprium Sanctorum* of V., of R. and S., and of the Gregorian Sacramentary, cannot well be carried out within the limits of an Introduction. The means for such a comparison will, it is hoped, be considerably increased by the present volume: and it may suffice for the present purpose to say that these *missae* point, on the whole, to the same conclusion as those which have already been discussed. R. and S. show, as a general rule, more points of agreement with the Gregorian text than can be found in the *missae* of V. At the same time, they often retain prayers which are found in V., but are absent from Muratori's Gregorian text, and thus show their connexion both with the early form of the Roman Sacramentary which furnished the basis of V., and with the later form exhibited by the Gregorian books. A further point of some importance is brought to our notice by an examination of another portion of their contents.

The Sunday *missae* of V. fall into three divisions. One series is included in each book. That in the first book consists of the *missae* for the Sundays from Septuagesima to Easter, of which we have already spoken, of the *missae* for Easter and its octave, for Pentecost and its octave, and for the Sundays 'post clausum Paschae' and 'post Ascensam Domini.' The Sundays 'post clausum Paschae' are six in number, and this division, therefore, overlaps the *missae* for the Sunday after the Ascension, and for Pentecost. The second book contains the Advent *missae*. The series in the third book consists of sixteen *missae* not appropriated to any particular Sunday, but answering to the *missae Dominicales* which we find in some of the Gallican Sacramentaries. Whether the method of leaving these *missae* unappropriated was adopted in the Roman Sacramentary used by the compiler of V., or was an adaptation of the material furnished by that Sacramentary to the Gallican usage, we can hardly say with certainty. But in R. and S. we find a full arrangement of *missae* appropriated to particular Sundays. There are two for Sundays after Christmas, six for Sundays after Epiphany, the series from Septuagesima to Easter, four for the Sundays 'post Octavas Paschae,' one for the Sunday after the Ascension, and a series of twenty-seven for the Sundays after Pentecost, beginning with that for the octave: there are also, as we have seen, five *missae* for the Sundays before Christmas, answering to the five Advent *missae* of V. Those with which we are now concerned are the *missae* for the Sundays from Christmas to Septuagesima, and from Pentecost to Advent. The first of these divisions is not covered by any series in V.: it was no doubt intended that the *missa* for any of these Sundays should be taken from the series in the third book. In the supplementary portion of the Gregorian Sacramentary, we have a long series of Sunday *missae* appropriated to particular days. Those from Christmas to Septuagesima agree with the *missae* for the same Sundays in R. and S., but with certain differences of structure. The *missae* of R. and S. have in each case two Collects and a Benediction *Super Populum*, and also a proper Preface. The second Collect, the Preface, and the *Super Populum* have no place in the Gregorian *missae*. The Prefaces of R. and S. for these Sundays appear with variations in the supplementary part of Pamelius' Gregorian text. Of the eight prayers *Super Populum* all are found elsewhere in the supplementary part of Muratori's Gregorian Sacramentary, while three are found also in V. Of the eight second Collects three have not been found in Muratori's Sacramentary, or in V., while five appear elsewhere in the supplementary part of Muratori's text, two of these being found also in the first portion of that text, and two appearing also in V.

For the Octave of Pentecost R. and S. agree in adopting the

missa assigned to the same day in V., and in ignoring the totally different *missa* provided for it (as the Sunday following the Pentecost Ember days) in the first portion of the Gregorian Sacramentary. For the Sunday following, they adopt the *missa* which V. assigns to the sixth Sunday 'post clausum Paschae.' This *missa* also furnishes, in the supplementary part of Muratori's text, the Collect, Secret and Postcommunion which make up the Gregorian *missa* for what is there called the first Sunday after Pentecost[1]. But it is to be observed that R. and S. take the whole *missa*, including the *Super Populum*, as it stands in V., so that this Sunday is in R. and S. provided with a *Super Populum*, a feature which is wanting in their remaining *missae* for the Sundays after the Octave of Pentecost. The next Sunday *missa* of R. and S. agrees with that for the Sunday after the Ascension[2] in V., save for the omission of the *Super Populum*: the parallel *missa* in Muratori's text has the same Collect, Secret, and Postcommunion. Next come, in R. and S., three *missae* to which V. does not contain any parallel. The first Collect, Secret, and Postcommunion in each case agree with the corresponding *missa* in Muratori's text. One of the second Collects is found elsewhere in the supplementary part of the Gregorian Sacramentary; the two others have not been identified either in that Sacramentary or in V. A few of the prayers of these three *missae* are found in V., and three, not contained in V., are found in the first portion of the Gregorian Sacramentary.

With the seventh Sunday after Pentecost in R. and S., or the sixth Sunday after Pentecost, according to Muratori's text, we reach a set of *missae* corresponding on the whole to the first part of the series contained in the third book of V. As a general rule R. and S. take, in these *missae*, the whole *missa* given in V., adding a Preface, while the Gregorian text simply discards the second Collect of V., R. and S.; but in a few cases R. and S. substitute for the Secret or Postcommunion of V. another prayer: in these cases R., S., and the Gregorian text agree. In two cases the Gregorian text discards the *first*

---

[1] Unless 'post Pentecosten' is understood as equivalent to 'post Octavas Pentecostes,' there is a discrepancy between the first and the supplementary portions of Muratori's text in regard to the numeration of the Sundays after Pentecost.

[2] The *missa* which R. and S. assign to the Sunday after the Ascension agrees in the main with that for the fifth Sunday 'post clausum Paschae' in V.

Collect of V., R., and S., and has the second Collect instead[1]: in one case the second Collect of R. and S. differs from that of V., and is not found either in V. or in the Gregorian text of Muratori.

The *missae* for the two Sundays between the seventeenth and the twentieth after Pentecost in R. and S. are not taken from the series in V., but correspond in part to those given in the first part of the Gregorian Sacramentary for the Sundays which precede and follow the Ember days of September, having of course, in addition to the forms contained in the Gregorian text, a second Collect and a Preface in each case. The *missa* for the Sunday after the Ember days, however, agrees with the Gregorian *missa* only in respect of the first Collect: the second Collect is found elsewhere in the first part of the Gregorian text, the Secret and Postcommunion are found elsewhere in V., but not in Muratori's Gregorian Sacramentary. With the twentieth Sunday R. and S. return to the *missae* of the third book of V.[2], and continue to follow the course of that series until it is exhausted with the *missa* for the twenty-fourth Sunday. For the twentieth Sunday R. and S. discard the second Collect of the *missa* in V., and substitute for it that which is the Collect of the parallel Gregorian *missa*. For the twenty-first, twenty-third, and twenty-fourth Sundays they differ from V., and are in agreement with the Gregorian text in regard to the Postcommunion.

The last three *missae* for the Sundays after Pentecost in R. and S. are not parallel to any *missae* contained in V., though here, as in the *missae* for the fourth, fifth, and sixth Sundays, already mentioned, some of the prayers of which the *missae* are composed are found in V. in some other position. On the other hand, the last three *missae* of the Gregorian supplement are in general agreement with the corresponding *missae* of R. and S., save that the latter have, in each case, a second Collect and

[1] In one of these cases (that of the eleventh Sunday after Pentecost according to R. and S., the tenth according to the Gregorian text) the two Collects are marked by a later hand in S. for transposition by a copyist: in Gerbert's text (p. 155) we find them transposed: and Muratori's text adopts that which the corrector of S. makes the first, discarding that which is first in R. and the original text of S.

[2] The *missae* in the supplementary part of the Gregorian text continue this series without any break, so that the *missa* for the seventeenth Sunday in the Gregorian text answers to that for the twentieth Sunday in R. and S.

a proper Preface: in one instance the Gregorian *missa* has as its Collect that which stands second in R. and S., the first Collect of R. and S. not being found either in V. or in Muratori's Gregorian text[1]. As in other cases already referred to, the Prefaces assigned to the Sundays after Pentecost in R. and S. are for the most part to be found, with a certain amount of variation, in the supplement of the Gregorian Sacramentary: and several of the second Collects of R. and S., which are discarded from the Gregorian *missae*, find a place in other parts of the supplement. The variations of reading, in the matter common to the *missae* of V., R., S., and the Gregorian Sacramentary, are seldom, so far as these *missae* are concerned, of much importance; in some cases, especially in the Prefaces, R. and S[1]. show more agreement with V. than with the Gregorian form; in others, where they differ from V., the Gregorian form is in agreement with the later and not with the earlier 'Gelasian.' The general result of a comparison of the common matter of this portion seems to show that the compiler of the supplementary part of the Gregorian books drew the *missae* which he provided for these Sundays from the later, not from the earlier, form of the 'Gelasian' Sacramentary.

The main conclusions to which an examination and comparison of the contents of the three 'Gelasian' Sacramentaries which have been under consideration would seem to lead us, are these:—

1. That the Vatican manuscript, commonly called the 'Gelasian' Sacramentary, is in the main derived from an early Roman Sacramentary, but incorporates some material drawn from

---

[1] The fact that, in almost all cases where a Gregorian *missa* agrees closely with one contained in R. and S., the collect which stands second in the 'Gelasian' *missa* is that which is discarded in the Gregorian suggests the theory that the presence of two prayers before the Secret in the Gelasian *missa* is due to the retention, not of the *oratio ad collectam*, but of a prayer answering to the *oratio super sindonem* of the Ambrosian rite. If the first prayer were the *oratio ad collectam* and the second the *oratio ad missam*, we should rather expect that the Gregorian *missa* would discard the first and retain the second. It is true that in some cases, where R. and S. have an *oratio ad collectam* (the *missae* for the Festival which they call 'S. Simeonis,' and for Ash Wednesday, and that for the Festival of S. Caesarius in S.), they have but one collect *ad missam*: but the correspondence is here of such a kind as to suggest that the 'Gregorian' *missa* has been followed by R. and S., with some slight variation. In some cases, the second Collect of R. and S. actually appears as the *oratio super sindonem* in Pamelius' Ambrosian text; and an examination of early Ambrosian *missae* may perhaps furnish other evidence of the same kind.

GENERAL CONCLUSIONS.

Gallican sources, while the Sacramentary from which it was for the most part copied probably contained insertions and additions of a date later than the beginning of S. Gregory's pontificate. The Vatican manuscript itself certainly contains such Gregorian or post-Gregorian elements.

2. If we are not to regard the differences in the structure of particular *missae*, as well as in the general arrangement of the contents of the Sacramentary, which are exhibited by the common matter of R. and S., as compared with the Vatican manuscript, as being due to the compiler of V., and to departures, in his work of compilation, from the order of the Roman Sacramentary which he employed, we must consider that a revision of the Sacramentary had taken place between the date of the parent manuscript of V. and the date of the parent manuscript, or manuscripts, of R. and S. As regards particular portions of the contents of R. and S., these manuscripts may be separated from that which was the original source of V. by more than one revision. The Lent *missae*, in particular, have apparently been rearranged at some time later than the accession of Gregory II.

3. The material contained in the second book of R. was probably derived from a source closely akin to that which furnished parts of the first and third books of V. Both in the second book and in certain parts of the contents of the first book R. shows signs of Gallican influence.

4. The revised 'Liber Sacramentorum Romanae Ecclesiae' from which R. and S. are in the main derived, while for the most part preserving in its *missae* the form which is characteristic of the 'Gelasian' Sacramentaries, was in some respects more nearly allied than the parent manuscript of V. to the recension known as Gregorian, and represented by the first portion of the Gregorian Sacramentaries[1].

5. The mention of Roman churches which we find in the headings of certain *missae* in R. and S., though not sufficient evidence to warrant the supposition that the *missae* in question were actually taken from books in use at Rome, may be held to show that the revision of the 'Gelasian' Sacramentary was not entirely independent of Roman influence, and may perhaps

---

[1] What the precise relation between the later 'Gelasian' Sacramentaries and the first portion of the 'Gregorian' Sacramentaries may be, is a question which seems to require consideration, but to belong rather to the history of the 'Gregorian' than of the 'Gelasian' Sacramentary.

indicate that a Roman Sacramentary, of a date later than the accession of Gregory II, furnished part of the materials employed in the revision [1].

6. The use of the 'Gelasian' Sacramentary of the later type was not confined to the churches of Gaul, but seems to have existed also in the district of Rhaetia Curiensis. The S. Gallen Sacramentary, which furnishes evidence of such use, contains few, if any, distinct signs of Gallican influence.

7. The 'Gelasian' books of the type of R. and S. furnished to the compiler of the supplementary part of the Gregorian Sacramentary the most important portions of his text. In adopting the *missae*, prefaces and prayers which he took from them, he appears either to have made some corrections and alterations of the text, which were followed by the second hand of the S. Gallen manuscript, or to have employed a text which had been corrected and emended in the same way as the S. Gallen Sacramentary.

The later 'Gelasian' books, therefore, may be said to form a link between the recension of the Sacramentary represented by V., and the Gregorian Sacramentaries of that recension which we now possess; so far as regards the supplement, their relation to the Gregorian books seems to be clear. But before we can fully determine their importance in the history of the Sacramentary, another question remains to be solved, the question, that is to say, of their precise relation to the 'Liber Sacramentorum' sent by Adrian to Charles the Great. The question is one which seems to have an important bearing on the history of the Western Liturgy: but it probably requires, for its full solution, not only some further study of material already edited, but also some further examination and comparison of manuscripts. For such work, in both its branches, it is hoped that the present volume may prove to be a useful instrument.

---

[1] The mention of the Roman 'stations' for the Thursdays in Lent would hardly have been inserted, had this not been the case.

LIST OF AUTHORITIES AND TEXTS CITED BY ABBREVIATIONS

Manuscripts.

Place.	Press-mark.	Cited as.
Rome. Vatican Library	MS. Reginae 316	V.
Zürich. Kantonsbibliothek	MS. Rheinau 30	R.
S. Gallen. Stiftsbibliothek	MS. 348	S. (S^1, S^2).
Oxford. Bodleian Library	MS. Bodl. Add. A. 173	A.
„ „ „	MS. Liturg. Misc. 319	B.
„ Magdalen College Library	MS. Magd. 226.	

[The Zürich manuscript which furnished Gerbert's text cannot now be traced. It is referred to by the symbol T.]

Printed Liturgical Texts.

Drum. Miss. = Missale Drummondiense. 8vo. Burntisland, 1882.
Egb. = The Pontifical of Egbert. 8vo. (Surtees Society, 1853.)
Gem. = Codex Gemmeticensis, in Martène (see below).
Gell. = Codex Gellonensis, in Martène (see below).
Gerb. = Gerbert. Monumenta Veteris Liturgiae Alemannicae. 4to. S. Blasii, 1777.

[The references to Gerbert's text are to vol. i. unless vol. ii. is specified. References enclosed in square brackets are to the parts of the text printed in small type.]

Leofr. = The Leofric Missal, edited by F. E. Warren. 4to. Oxford, 1883.
Leon. = The Leonine Sacramentary. The references are to the columns of the first volume of Muratori's *Liturgia Romana Vetus*. fol. Venice, 1748.
Mart. = Martène, *De Antiquis Ecclesiae Ritibus*. The references are given by book and chapter. The edition generally used is that of 1763-4.
Men. = Sacramentarium Gregorianum, edited by Ménard. The references are to the columns of the third volume of the Benedictine edition of S. Gregory's works.
Miss. Franc. = Missale Francorum. The references are to the columns of the second volume of Muratori's *Liturgia Romana Vetus*. fol. Venice, 1748.
Miss. Gall. = Missale Gallicanum Vetus. The references are as in the last case.
Mur. = Sacramentarium Gregorianum, edited by Muratori, in the second volume of *Liturgia Romana Vetus*. fol. Venice, 1748.

Printed Liturgical Texts (*continued*).

Pam. = Sacramentarium Gregorianum, edited by Pamelius, in the second volume of *Liturgicon Latinum*. The references are to the Cologne edition of 1609.

Pam. (Amb.) = Sacramentarium Ambrosianum, in the first volume of Pamelius' *Liturgicon Latinum*. The references are to the same edition as in the last case.

Sacr. Gall. = Sacramentarium Gallicanum. The references are to the columns of the second volume of Muratori's *Liturgia Romana Vetus*. fol. Venice, 1748.

Stowe M. = The Stowe Missal, in Warren's *Liturgy and Ritual of the Celtic Church*. 8vo. Oxford, 1881.

LIST OF ABBREVIATIONS USED IN THE APPENDIX AND INDEX

aet. = aeterne.
b. = beatus.
D. = Deus.
Dne. = Domine.
ig. = igitur.
m. = misericors.
o. = omnipotens.
obl. = oblationem.
q. = quaesumus.
sacrat. = sacratissimum or sacratissimam.
s. = sempiterne (in the Appendix, s. is also used for sanctus).
VD. = Vere dignum, &c.

Prefaces are all indexed under the words 'Vere dignum,' being arranged in the order of their first distinctive words.

The letter γ at the end of a Liturgical form in the text indicates that the form to which it is appended is found, with or without variation, in the Gregorian Sacramentary of Muratori.

LIBER SACRAMENTORUM
ROMANAE ECCLESIAE

LIBER SACRAMEN[...]
ROMANAE ECCLESI[...]

LIBER I.

A + Ω

IN NOMINE DOMINI IESU CHRISTI SALVATORIS IN-
CIPIT SACRAMENTORUM ROMANAE
ORDINIS ANNI CIRCULI.

ORATIONES ET PRECES IN VIGILIIS NATALIS DOMINI.

Ad Nonam.

DA nobis, omnipotens Deus, ut sicut adoranda Filii tui
natalitia praevenimus, sic eius munera capiamus sempiterna
gaudentes. Per Dominum nostrum. ⁊

Praesta, misericors Deus, ut ad suscipiendum Filii tui
singulare nativitatis mysterium, et mentes credentium
praeparentur, et non credentium corda subdantur. Per
Dominum nostrum.

Secreta.

Tanta nos, Domine, quaesumus, promptiore servitus huius
sacrificii praecurrere concede solemnia, quanto in [...]
constare principium nostrae redemptionis ostend[...]
Dominum.

LIBER SACRAMENTORUM ROMANAE ECCLESIAE

LIBER I.

A + Ω

*IN NOMINE DOMINI IESU CHRISTI SALVATORIS INCIPIT
LIBER SACRAMENTORUM ROMANAE ECCLESIAE
ORDINIS ANNI CIRCULI.*

ORATIONES ET PRECES IN VIGILIIS NATALIS DOMINI.

Ad Nonam.

DA nobis, omnipotens Deus, ut sicut adoranda Filii tui natalitia praevenimus, sic eius munera capiamus sempiterna gaudentes. Per Dominum nostrum. γ
<small>R. S. Gerb. 1. Pam. 184. Men. 5. Leon. 471. cf. Miss. Goth. 517.</small>

Praesta, misericors Deus, ut ad suscipiendum Filii tui singulare nativitatis mysterium, et mentes credentium praeparentur, et non credentium corda subdantur. Per Dominum nostrum.
<small>S. Gerb. 1. Pam. 184. Men. 5.</small>

Secreta.

Tanto nos, Domine, quaesumus, promptiore servitio huius sacrificii[1] praecurrere concede solemnia, quanto in hoc[2] constare principium nostrae redemptionis ostendis. Per Dominum.
<small>R. S. Gerb. 2. Leon. 471.</small>

Postcommun.

R. S.
Gerb. 5.
Pam. 186.
Men. 7.

Huius nos, Domine, sacramenti semper [novitas][3] natalis instauret, cuius nobilitas[4] singularis humanam repulit vetustatem. Per Dominum. γ

[1] *haec* (for *huius sacrificii*) Leon.: *sacrificia* V.; R. S. Gerb. as text.
[2] *his* Leon; R. omits *in hoc*. [3] V. omits *novitas* which is inserted by S² Gerb. Pam. and seems to be required by the sense; Men. reads *Eius nos* ... *semper natalis*. The reading of S¹ is uncertain, but probably agreed with V.; R. has *sacramenta semper natalaes instauret*, a reading which suggests the emendation *Huius nos Domine sacramenta semper natalis instaurent*; but for the alteration of the last word there is no MS. authority. [4] *nativitas* Pam. Men.; V. R. S. Gerb. as text.

II.

ITEM DE VIGILIA DOMINI.

In Nocte.

R. S.
Gerb. 3.
Pam. 185.
Men. 5.

Deus, qui hanc sacratissimam noctem veri luminis fecisti illustratione clarescere, da, quaesumus, ut cuius lucis mysterium[1] in terra cognovimus, eius quoque gaudiis in caelo perfruamur. Per. γ

R. S.
Gerb. 6.
Pam. 186.
Men. 7.

Concede, quaesumus, omnipotens Deus, ut[2] Unigeniti 494 tui nova per carnem nativitas liberet quos sub peccati iugo vetusta servitus tenet. Per. γ

Secreta.

R. S.
Gerb. 3
(cf. 5).
Pam. 186.
Men. 7.

Munera nostra, Domine, quaesumus[3], nativitatis hodiernae mysteriis apta perveniant[4]; ut sicut homo genitus idem[5] praefulsit[6] et[7] Deus, sic nobis haec terrena substantia conferat quod divinum est. Per. γ

R. S.
Gerb. 3.
Men. 6.
Mur. 291.

VD. et iustum est aequum et salutare. Cuius divinae nativitatis potentiam ingenita virtutis tuae genuit magnitudo, quem semper Filium et ante tempora aeterna[8] generatum[9], quia tibi pleno atque perfecto aeterni Patris nomen non defuit, praedicamus, verum etiam[10] honore[11] maiestate atque virtute aequalem tibi cum sancto Spiritu confitemur, dum trino[12] vocabulo unicam credimus maiestatem. Quem[13] laudant angeli. γ

Postcommun.

R. S.
Gerb. 6.

Laeti, Domine, frequentamus salutis humanae principia, quia trina celebratio beatae competit mysterio[14] Trinitatis. Per Dominum nostrum.

[1] *mysteria* S. Gerb. Pam. Men.; V. R. as text. [2] R. S. Gerb. Pam. Men. insert *nos*; V. as text. [3] *quaesumus, Domine* S. Gerb. Pam. Men.; R. V. as text. [4] *proveniant* S. Gerb. Men. Pam.; V. R. as text; R. S.

Gerb. add *et pacem nobis semper infundant*. [5] *idest* V. [6] *refulsit* S²
Gerb. Pam. Men.; V. R. S¹ as text. [7] Pam. Men. omit *et*. [8] *aeternae*
(perh. for *aeterne*) V. [9] *genitum* S² Gerb. Men. Mur.; V. R. S¹ as text.
[10] *et* (for *verum etiam*) Men. Mur.; V. R. S. Gerb. as text. [11] S² Gerb.
insert *et*. [12] *dum in trino* S² Gerb.; *et in trino* Men. Mur.; V. R. S¹ as text.
[13] *Quam* Gerb.; S² adds (after *Quem laudant angeli*) ' Vel *Et ideo* melius.'
Gerb. gives both endings; Men. and Mur. only *Et ideo*; V. R. S¹ as text.
[14] *mysterium* V.; R. S. Gerb. as text.

III.

ITEM IN VIGILIA DOMINI.

Mane prima.

Deus, qui per beatae Mariae sacrae virginis partum sine humana concupiscentia procreatum[1], in Filii tui · membra venientes paternis fecisti praeiudiciis non teneri, praesta, quaesumus, ut huius creaturae novitate suscepta, vetustatis antiquae contagiis exuamur. Per eundem Dominum. γ

R. S.
Gerb. 7.
Pam. 187.
Men. 9.

Respice nos, omnipotens et misericors Deus, et mentibus clementer humanis nascente Christo summae veritatis lumen infunde[2]. Per. γ

R. S.
Gerb. 3.
Pam. 187.
Men. 6.

Secreta.

Da nobis, Domine[3], ut nativitatis Domini nostri Iesu Christi solemnia, quae praesentibus sacrificiis[4] praevenimus, sic nova sint nobis, ut[5] continuata permaneant, sic perpetua perseverent, ut suo miraculo[6] nova[7] semper existant. Per eundem.

R. S.
Gerb. 2.
Leon. 467.

Item alia.

Cuncta, Domine, quaesumus, his muneribus a nobis semper diabolica figmenta seclude, ut nostri Redemptoris exordia purificatis mentibus celebremus. Per.

R. S.
Gerb. 4.

VD.[8] Nos[9] sursum cordibus erectis divinum adorare mysterium[10] quo[11] humana conditio veteri terrenaque lege cessante, nova caelestisque[12] substantia mirabiliter restaurata profertur, ut[13] quod magno Dei munere geritur magnis ecclesiae gaudiis celebretur. Per. γ

R. S.
Gerb. 13.
Mur. 293.

Postcommun[14].

Concede nobis, Domine, quaesumus, ut sacramenta[15] quae sumpsimus quicquid in nostra mente vitiosum est, ipsius medicationis[16] dono curetur. Per. γ

II. viii
infra.
R.S.(*alibi.*)
Gerb. 196.
Pam. 415. cf. Men. 186. cf. Leon. 472.

Ad Populum.

Populum tuum, Domine, quaesumus, tueantur, sanctificent, et gubernent, aeternumque perficiant tam devotionibus acta

R. S.
Gerb. 5.

solemnibus, quam natalitiis agenda divinis Iesu Christi Domini nostri.

¹ *percreatum* V.; R. S. Gerb. Pam. Men. as text. ² *ostende* R. S. Gerb. Pam. Men.; V. as text. ³ *Da nobis, quaesumus, omnipotens et misericors Deus, et sempiterne Pater* Leon. ⁴ *officiis* Leon. ⁵ *et* Leon. ⁶ *pro sui miraculo* S. Gerb. Leon.; *pro suo miraculo* R.; V. as text. ⁷ *per novo* V. ⁸ This Preface is given by R. S. Gerb. Mur. to the first Sunday after Christmas. ⁹ *Et* (for *Nos*) S² Gerb. Mur.; V. R. S¹ as text. ¹⁰ Mur. inserts here *ut quod magno Dei munere geritur magnis ecclesiae gaudiis celebretur.* ¹¹ *quod* R. S. Gerb.; *quoniam* Mur.; V. as text. ¹² *caelestique* S² Gerb. Mur.; V. R (S¹?) as text. ¹³ See note 10 *supra.* ¹⁴ See note on II. viii *infra.* The Postcommunion is evidently corrupt. ¹⁵ Perhaps *sacramenta* is an accusative for ablative : or we may follow Tommasi's proposal and read *per sacramenta.* ¹⁶ *medicationes* (prob. for *medicationis*) V.; *miserationis* V. (in II. viii); Leon. reads *ipsius doni medicatione.*

IV.

Item in Natale Domini.

In Die.

R. S.
Gerb. 5.
cf. Miss.
Goth. 521.

Omnipotens sempiterne Deus qui hunc diem per incarnationem · Verbi tui, et per partum beatae virginis Mariae consecrasti, da populis tuis in hac celebritate laetitiae¹ ut et qui tua gratia sunt redempti tua adoptione sint filii². Per Dominum. γ

496

R. S.
Gerb. 6.
Pam. 187.
Leon. 474.

Praesta, misericors Deus³, ut natus hodie Salvator [mundi]⁴, sicut divinae [nobis]⁴ generationis est auctor, ita et immortalitatis sit ipse largitor. Per. γ

Secreta.

R. S.
Gerb. 6.
Leon. 473.

Oblatio tibi sit, Domine, hodiernae⁵ festivitatis accepta, qua et nostrae reconciliationis processit perfecta placatio, et divini cultus nobis est indita plenitudo⁶ Iesu Christi Domini nostri. Qui tecum vivit.

R. S.
Gerb. 6.
Leon. 470.

VD. Tuae laudis hostiam iugiter immolantes. Cuius figuram Abel iustus instituit agnus quoque legalis ostendit, celebravit Abraham, Melchisedech sacerdos exhibuit, sed verus agnus, [et]⁷ aeternus pontifex, hodie natus Christus implevit. Et ideo cum angelis.

Infra actionem.

R. S.
Gerb. 6.

Communicantes et diem sacratissimum celebrantes in quo incontaminata⁸ virginitas huic mundo edidit Salvatorem Iesum Christum Dominum nostrum. Sed et memoriam. γ

Postcommun.

Da nobis, Domine, quaesumus, ipsius[9] recensita nativitate vegetari[10] cuius caelesti mysterio et[11] pascimur et potamur, Iesu Christi Domini nostri Filii tui[12]. Qui tecum vivit. γ

R. S.
Gerb. 2.
Leon. 473.
Pam. 184.

Ad Populum.

Praesta, quaesumus, Deus noster, ut familia tua, quae Filii tui Domini nostri Iesu Christi est nativitate salvata, eius etiam sit perpetua redemptione secura. Per Dominum.

[1] *iustitiae* V.; *laetitiam* R. S. Gerb.; Miss. Goth. as text. The first part of the Collect in R. is written over an erasure. [2] *tua sint adoptione securi* S² Gerb.; V. R. S¹ as text. [3] *Praesta, quaesumus, omnipotens Deus* R. S. Gerb. Pam.; V. Leon. as text. [4] V. omits *mundi* and *nobis*, which are restored from R. S. Leon. Gerb. Pam. [5] *hodierna* V.; R. S. Gerb. Leon. as text. [6] R. S. Gerb. end the Secret at *plenitudo*; Leon. adds *et via veritatis et vita regni caelestis apparuit*, but omits *Iesu Christi Domini nostri*; V. as text. [7] V. omits *et*. [8] S² Gerb. insert *beatae Mariae*; V. R. S¹ as text. [9] *unigeniti Filii tui* (for *ipsius*) R. S. Gerb. Pam.; V. Leon. as text. [10] *respirare* R. S. Gerb. Pam.; V. Leon. as text. [11] R. S. Gerb. Pam. Leon. omit *et*. [12] R. S. Gerb. Pam. Leon. omit *Iesu* . . . . *tui* and end with *per* or *per eundem*.

V.

ITEM ORATIONES DE NATALI DOMINI.

Ad Vesp. sive Matut.

Adesto, Domine, supplicationibus nostris, et populum tuum, qui te factore[1] conditus, teque est reparatus auctore, te etiam iugiter operante salvetur. Per Dominum.

R. S.
Gerb. 6.

Largire, quaesumus, Domine, famulis tuis fidei et securitatis[2] augmentum, ut qui de[3] nativitate Domini nostri Iesu Christi glorientur et adversa mundi, te gubernante, non sentiant, et quae temporaliter celebrare desiderant, sine fine percipiant. Per Dominum. γ

R. S.
Gerb. 6.
Pam. 187.

Deus, qui populo tuo plene praestitisti redemptionis effectum, ut non solum Unigeniti tui nativitate corporea, sed etiam crucis eius patibulo[4] salvaretur, huius, quaesumus, fidei famulis tuis tribue firmitatem[5], ut usque ad promissum gloriae[6] praemium, ipso quoque gubernante, perveniant. Per.

S.
[Gerb. 6.]

Deus qui humanae substantiae dignitatem et mirabiliter condidisti et mirabilius reformasti, da, quaesumus, ut eius efficiamur in divina consortes[7], qui nostrae humanitatis fieri dignatus est particeps[8] Christus Filius tuus. Per eundem Dominum nostrum. γ

R. S.
Gerb. 6.
Pam. 188.

6 LIBER SACRAMENTORUM [I. vi.

R. S.
Gerb. 7.
Pam. 188.

Omnipotens sempiterne Deus, creator humanae reformatorque naturae, quam Unigenitus tuus in utero perpetuae virginitatis assumpsit, respice nos propitius, ut, Filii tui incarnatione suscepta, inter ipsius mereamur membra numerari. Per eundem.

R. S.
Gerb. 7.

Deus, qui nativitatis tuae exordia [9] pro nostra necessarium salvatione duxisti, respice nos propitius; et quos similes ad imaginem tuam fecisti, similiores observatione perfice mandatorum. Per.

[1] S. Gerb. insert *est*. [2] *fidei spei et caritatis* Pam.; V. R. S. Gerb. as text. [3] Gerb. Pam. omit *de*; V. R. S. as text. [4] *etiam et crucis patibulum* V. (ungrammatically); S. Gerb. as text. [5] *firmitate* V.; S as text. [6] S. Gerb. insert *tuae*. [7] *da nobis, quaesumus, eius divinitatis esse consortes* Gerb. (following S[2].), Pam.; V. R. (S[1]?) as text. [8] Gerb. inserts *Iesus*; Pam. ends the Collect at *particeps*. [9] *exordium* S[2] Gerb.; *exordio* V.; R. S[1] as text.

VI.

IN NATALI SANCTI STEPHANI MARTYRIS.

vii Kal. Ianuarias.

R. S.
Gerb. 8.
Pam. 189.
Leon. 383.
Pam.
(Amb.)306.

Omnipotens aeterne [1] Deus, qui primitias martyrum in sancti [2] levitae Stephani sanguine [3] dedicasti, tribue, ·quaesumus, ut pro nobis intercessor assistat [4], qui pro suis etiam persecutoribus supplicavit [5]. Per. γ

498

Praesta, quaesumus, omnipotens Deus, ut sicut divina laudamus in sancti Stephani passione magnalia, sic indulgentiam tuam piis eius precibus assequamur. Per.

S.
[Gerb. 8.]
Leon. 387.

Praesta, quaesumus, omnipotens Deus, ut beatus Stephanus levita magnificus, sicut ante alios imitator Dominicae passionis et pietatis enituit, ita sit fragilitatis nostrae promptus adiutor. Per.

Secreta.

R. S.
Gerb. 8.
Pam. 189.
Leon. 388.

Grata tibi sint, Domine, munera, quaesumus, devotionis hodiernae, quae beati Stephani martyris tui commemoratio gloriosa depromit. Per.

Postcommun.

R. S.
[Gerb. 8.]
Pam. 190.
Leon. 388.
Pam. (Amb.) 307.

Gratias [6] agimus, Domine, multiplicatis circa nos miserationibus tuis, qui et Filii tui nativitate nos salvas, et beati martyris Stephani [7] deprecatione sustentas. Per.

Ad Populum.

Beatus martyr Stephanus, Domine, quaesumus, pro fidelibus tuis suffragator accedat, qui dum bene sit tibi placitus⁸ pro his etiam possit audiri⁹. Per.

R. S.
[Gerb. 8.]

¹ *aeterne* so V.; the rest have *sempiterne*. ² *beati* R. S. Gerb. Pam.; V. Leon. Pam. (Amb.) as text. ³ *sanguinem* V. R. (ungrammatically); Leon. as text. ⁴ *existat* R. S² Gerb. Pam. (both forms), Leon.; V. (S¹?) as text. ⁵ *exoravit* Gerb. Pam.; V. R. S. Leon. Pam. (Amb.) as text. ⁶ Pam. and Pam. (Amb.) insert *tibi*. ⁷ *martyrum beatorum* Leon. ⁸ *beneplacitus tibi sit* S² Gerb.; V. R. S¹ as text. ⁹ *prosit auditor* V.; R. S. Gerb. as text.

VII.

IN NATALI SANCTI IOANNIS EVANGELISTAE.

vi Kal. Ianuarias.

Deus, qui per os beati apostoli tui Ioannis evangelistae¹ Verbi tui nobis arcana reserasti, praesta, quaesumus, ut quod ille nostris auribus excellenter infudit, intelligentiae competentis² eruditione capiamus. Per Dominum nostrum. γ

R. S.
Gerb. 9.
Pam. 190.
Pam. (Amb.)307.
Leon. 474.

Deus, qui beati Ioannis evangelistae praeconiis principii sempiterni secreta reserasti, da, quaesumus, ut ad intelligentiam Verbi eius per quem nobis resplendet³ suffragiis accedamus. Per Dominum.

R. S.
Gerb. 10.
Pam. 191.

499 Praesta, quaesumus, omnipotens Deus, ut excellentiam Verbi tui, quam beatus • evangelista Ioannes asseruit, et convenienter intelligere valeamus et veraciter confiteri⁴. Per.

R. S.
Gerb. 10.
Pam. 191.
Men. 12.

Secreta.

Supplicationibus apostolicis beati Ioannis evangelistae, quaesumus, ecclesiae tuae, Domine⁵, commendetur oblatio, cuius magnificis praedicationibus eruditur. Per.

[Gerb. 10.]
Pam.
(Amb.)308.
Leon. 475.
Pam. 190.

Postcommun.

Beati evangelistae Ioannis nos, Domine, quaesumus, merita prosequantur, et tuam nobis indulgentiam semper implorent. Per.

Pam. 190.

Ad Populum.

Adsit ecclesiae tuae, Domine, quaesumus⁶, beatus evangelista Ioannes, ut cuius perpetuus doctor existit, semper esse non desinat suffragator. Per.

R. S.
[Gerb. 10.]
Pam. 191.

¹ *Ioannis et evangelistae* S¹; *et evangelistae Ioannis* S² Gerb.; Pam. omits *evangelistae*; V. R. Leon. Pam. (Amb.) as text. ² *intellegentia conpetentes* V.; *intelligentiae competentes* R.; the rest as text. ³ *splendit* V.;

R. S. Gerb. Pam. as text.   ⁴ *profiteri* S. Gerb. Pam. Men.; V. as text.
⁵ *quaesumus, Domine, ecclesiae tuae* Gerb. Pam. (Amb.); Pam. omits *Domine*;
V. Leon. as text.   ⁶ *quaesumus Domine* Gerb.; Pam. omits *Domine*; V.
S. as text.

VIII.

IN NATALI INNOCENTIUM.

v Kal. Ianuarias.

R. S.
Gerb. 11.
Pam. 192.
Men. 12.

Deus, cuius hodierna die praeconium Innocentes martyres non loquendo, sed moriendo confessi sunt, omnia in nobis vitiorum mala mortifica; ut fidem tuam, quam lingua nostra loquitur, etiam moribus vita fateatur. Per Dominum. γ

R. S.
Gerb. 11.
Leon. 476.

Deus, qui bonis tuis infantium quoque nescia sacramenti corda praecedis, tribue, quaesumus, ut in nostra conscientia ¹ fiduciam ² non habentes indulgentia ³ semper copiosa praeveniat ⁴. Per.

R. S.
Gerb. 12.
Pam. 192.
Men. 13.

Adiuva nos, Domine, quaesumus, eorum deprecatione sanctorum, qui Filium tuum humana necdum voce profitentes, caelesti sunt pro eius nativitate gratia coronati. Per.

Secreta.

R. S.
Greb. 11.
Men. 12.
Leon. 477.

Adesto, Domine, muneribus Innocentium festivitate sacrandis, et praesta, quaesumus, ut eorum sinceritatem ⁵ possimus imitari, quorum tibi dicatam ⁶ veneramur infantiam ⁷. Per.

Postcommun.

R. S.
Gerb. 11.
Pam. 193.
Men. 13.

Ipsi nobis, Domine, quaesumus, postulent mentium 500 puritatem, quorum innocentiam hodie solemniter celebramus. Per Dominum.

Ad populum.

R. S.
Gerb. 11.

Discat ecclesia tua, Deus, Infantium, quos hodie veneramur, exemplo ⁸, sinceram tenere pietatem, quae prius vitam praestitit sempiternam quam posset ⁹ nosse praesentem. Per Dominum nostrum.

---

¹ *ut et nostrae conscientiae* S. Gerb.; *ut nostra conscientiae* R.; *ut nostrae conscientiae* Leon.; V. as text.   ² *fiducia* V. (ungrammatically); R. S. Leon. as text.   ³ S² Gerb. insert *nos*; V. R. S¹ Leon. as text.   ⁴ *perveniat* V.; R. S. Gerb. Leon. as text.   ⁵ *sinceritate* V. R. (ungrammatically).   ⁶ *dicanda* V. (ungrammatically); *dicandam* S.; *dicata* R.; Leon. Gerb. Men. as text.   ⁷ *infantia* V. (ungrammatically).   ⁸ *exemplum* V. (ungrammatically).   ⁹ *possit* (prob. for *posset*) V. R.; *posse* S¹; *possent* S² Gerb.

IX.

ITEM IN OCTAVAS[1] DOMINI.

Kal. Ianuarias.

Deus qui nobis[2] nati Salvatoris diem celebrare concedis octavum, fac, quaesumus, nos eius perpetua divinitate muniri cuius sumus carnali commercio reparati. Per.

R. S.
Gerb. 14.
Pam. 194.

Omnipotens sempiterne Deus, qui[3] Unigenito tuo novam creaturam nos tibi esse fecisti, custodi opera misericordiae tuae, et ab omnibus nos maculis vetustatis emunda, ut per auxilium gratiae tuae in illius inveniamur forma in quo tecum est nostra substantia. Per.

R. S.
Gerb. 14.
Pam. 194.
Men. 14.
Pam.
(Amb.)312.

Secreta.

Praesta, quaesumus, Domine, ut per haec munera, quae Domini[4] Iesu Christi arcanae nativitatis mysterio gerimus purificatae mentis intelligentiam consequamur. Per Dominum.

R. S.
Gerb. 14.
Pam. 194.
Men. 14.

VD. Per Christum Dominum nostrum. Cuius hodie octavas nati[5] celebrantes tua, Domine, mirabilia veneramur. Quia[6] quae peperit et mater et virgo est; qui natus est, et infans et Deus est[7]. Merito[8] caeli locuti sunt, angeli gratulati, pastores laetati, magi mutati, reges turbati, parvuli gloriosa passione coronati[9]. Lacta, mater, cibum nostrum; lacta panem de caelo venientem, in praesepio positum velut piorum cibaria iumentorum. Illic namque agnovit bos possessorem suum, et asinus praesepium Domini sui, circumcisio[10] scilicet et praeputium. Quod etiam Salvator et • Dominus noster a Simeone susceptus in templo plenissime dignatus est adimplere[11]. Et ideo cum angelis et archangelis. γ

R. S.
cf.Gerb.14.
cf. Men. 14.
cf.Mur.293.

Postcommun.

Praesta, quaesumus, Domine, ut quod Salvatoris nostri iterata solemnitate percipimus[12], perpetuae nobis redemptionis conferat medicinam. Per.

R. S.
Gerb. 14.
Pam. 194.
Men. 14.

Ad Populum.

Omnipotens sempiterne Deus, qui tuae mensae participes a diabolico iubes abstinere convivio, da, quaesumus, plebi tuae, ut gustu[13] mortiferae profanitatis abiecto puris mentibus ad epulas aeternae salutis accedat[14]. Per.

R. S.
Gerb. 14.
Pam.
(Amb.)312.
Leon. 301.

---

[1] *octabas* V.   [2] *bonis* V.; R. S. Gerb. Pam. as text.   [3] S. Gerb. Pam. Men. insert *in*; V. R. as text.   [4] Gerb. Pam. Men. insert *nostri*.   [5] *hodie circumcisionis diem et nativitatis octavum* (*octavam* S²) S² Gerb. Men. Mur.; V. R. (S ?) as text.   [6] *Qui quia* V.   [7] In Men. the Preface ends here.

[8] R. S² Gerb. insert *ergo*; V. S¹ Mur. as text. [9] In Gerb. Mur. the Preface ends here. In S. *Et ideo cum angelis* is added at this point by the corrector: but there is a marginal note '*si volueris totum scribe et lege.*' [10] *circumcisionem* V. S¹ wrongly; R. S² as text. [11] *manifestare* S²; V. R. S¹ as text. [12] *percepimus* Pam. Men.; V. R. S. Gerb. as text. [13] *gustum* V. (ungrammatically); R. S. Leon. as text. [14] *accedant* Leon.

X.

PROHIBENDUM AB IDOLIS[1].

S.
Gerb. 15.
Leon. 363.

Omnipotens sempiterne Deus, da nobis voluntatem tuam et fideli mente retinere, et pia conversatione depromere, ut ecclesia tua, a profanis vanitatibus expiata, non aliud profiteatur verbis aliud exerceat actione. Per Dominum.

Secreta.

S.
Gerb. 15.
Leon. 364.

Ut tibi grata sint, Domine, munera populi tui, ab omni, quaesumus, eum[2] contagione perversitatis emunda, nec falsis gaudiis inhaerere patiaris quos ad veritatis[3] tuae praemia venire promittis. Per.

Postcommun.

S.
Gerb. 15.
Leon. 479.

Mysteriis tuis veneranter[4] assumptis, quaesumus, Domine, ut contra[5] nostrae conditionis errorem et contra diabolicas[6] armemur insidias[6]. Per.

[1] *Missa Prohibendo ab Idolis* S¹; *Missa de Prohibendo ab Idolis* S² Gerb.; V. as text. [2] *nos* Leon. [3] *quos ad diversitatis* V.; S. Gerb. Leon. as text (Muratori reads *quibus* in Leon.). [4] Leon. places *Domine* before *veneranter.* [5] *ut et contra* S. Gerb.; V. Leon. as text. [6] *diabolicis . . . insidiis* V. (ungrammatically); S. Gerb. Leon. as text.

XI.

IN VIGILIIS DE THEOPHANIA.

R. S.
Gerb. 15.
Pam. 195.
Men. 15.

Corda nostra, quaesumus, Domine, venturae festivitatis splendor illustret, quo mundi huius tenebras[1] carere valeamus, et perveniamus[2] ad patriam claritatis aeternae. Per.

Secreta.

502

R. S.
Gerb. 15.
Pam. 195.
Men. 15.

Tribue, quaesumus, Domine, ut eum praesentibus[3] immolemus sacrificiis et sumamus, quem venturae solemnitatis pia munera praeloquuntur. Per.

R.S.(*alibi.*)
Gerb. 18.
Pam. 196.
Men.16,17.

VD. Quia[4] quum Unigenitus tuus in substantia nostrae mortalitatis [apparuit, in novam nos immortalitatis suae[5]] lucem reparavit. Per quem laudant angeli. γ

Postcommun.

R. S.
Gerb. 16.
Men. 16.

Illumina, quaesumus, Domine, populum tuum, et[6] splendore gratiae tuae cor eius semper accende; ut

Salvatoris mundi, stella famulante, manifestata nativitas mentibus eorum et⁷ reveletur semper et crescat. Per. γ

¹ *tenebris* S² Gerb. Pam.; V. S¹ as text (ungrammatically). ² *carere et pervenire valeamus* S² Gerb.; *carere valeamus et pervenire* R.; V. S¹ Pam. Men. as text. ³ *ut ei praesentibus* Pam.; *ut praesentibus illi* Men. (both altering what follows); V. R. S. Gerb. as text. ⁴ R. S. Gerb. assign this Preface to the Sunday after Epiphany, Pam. to the Epiphany itself, Men. to the Epiphany and also to the Sunday. ⁵ V. omits the words in brackets, which are restored from the other texts, where they appear with a variation. R. S. Pam. read *in nova... luce*; S² Gerb. *nova... luce*. The *lucem* of V. points to the reading of the text, with which Men. agrees. ⁶ S¹ omits *et*. ⁷ Gerb. omits *et*.

XII.

ITEM IN THEOPHANIA.

In Die.

Omnipotens sempiterne Deus, qui Verbi tui incarnationem praeclari testimonio sideris indicasti, quod videntes magi oblatis maiestatem tuam muneribus adorarunt¹, concede ut semper in mentibus nostris tuae appareat stella iustitiae, et² noster in tua sit confessione thesaurus. Per.

R. S.
Gerb. 16.
Pam.
(Amb.) 313.
Miss.
Goth. 538.

Deus, cuius Unigenitus in substantia nostrae carnis apparuit, praesta, quaesumus, ut per eum quem similem nobis foras³ agnovimus intus reformari mereamur. Per Dominum nostrum. γ

R. S.
(*in Oct.*)
Gerb. 18.
Pam. 197.
Men. 18.

Deus illuminator omnium gentium, da populis tuis perpetua pace gaudere, et illud lumen splendidum infunde cordibus nostris, quod trium magorum mentibus aspersisti⁴. Per. γ

R. S.
Gerb. 17.
Pam. 196.
Men. 17.
Miss. Goth. 541.

Secreta.

Hostias tibi, Domine, pro nati tui Filii⁵ apparitione deferimus, suppliciter exorantes, ut sicut ipse nostrorum auctor est munerum⁶, ipse sit misericors et susceptor Iesus Christus⁷ Dominus noster. Qui tecum vivit.

R. S.
(*in Oct.*)
Gerb. 18.
Pam. 198.
Men. 18.

VD. Te laudare⁸ mirabilem Deum⁹ in omnibus operibus tuis¹⁰ quibus¹¹ regni tui mysteria revelasti. Hanc enim¹² festivitatem¹³ index puerperae¹⁴ · virginalis stella praecessit, quae natum in terra caeli Dominum magis stupentibus nuntiaret, ut manifestandus mundo Deus et caelesti denuntiaretur indicio, et temporaliter procreatus signorum temporalium ministerio panderetur. Et ideo. γ

R. S.
(*in Vig.*)
Gerb. 15.
Pam. 552.
Men. 15.
Mur. 293.

Infra actionem.

Communicantes, et diem sacratissimum celebrantes¹⁵, quo Unigenitus tuus in tua tecum gloria sempiternus¹⁶ in

R. S.
Gerb. 16.

veritate nostrae carnis natus, magis de longinquo venientibus visibilis et corporalis apparuit. Sed et memoriam. γ

Postcommun.

R. S.
(*in Oct.*)
Gerb. 19.
Pam. 198.
Men. 18.

Caelesti lumine, quaesumus, Domine, semper et ubique nos praeveni, ut mysterium cuius nos participes esse voluisti et puro cernamus intuitu et digno percipiamus effectu. Per. γ

Ad Populum.

R. S.
Gerb. 17.

Deus, qui per huius celebritatis mysterium aeternitatis tuae lumen cunctis gentibus suscitasti, da plebi tuae Redemptoris sui plenum cognoscere [17] fulgorem, ut ad perpetuam claritatem per eius incrementa perveniat [18]. Per.

[1] *adorarent* V.; *adoraverunt* S² Gerb. Pam. (Amb.); R. (S¹?) Miss. Goth. as text.   [2] *ac* Miss. Goth.   [3] *foris* R. S² Gerb. Pam. Men.; V. S¹ as text.   [4] *aspersisti*, so V. R.; the other texts cited have *aspirasti*.   [5] *nati Filii tui* S. Gerb.; V. R. Pam. Men. as text.   [6] S² Gerb. Pam. Men. insert *ita*; Pam. omits *ipse*; V. R. S¹ as text.   [7] Pam. inserts *Filius tuus*.   [8] *Et te laudare* S² Gerb. Pam. Men. Mur.; V. R. S¹ as text.   [9] S² Gerb. omit *Deum*; Men. has *Dominum*; V. R. S Pam. Mur. as text.   [10] *suis* Pam.   [11] *sacratissima* should perhaps be inserted here: it is absent from V., but appears in all the other texts cited.   [12] *etenim* S² Gerb. Pam. Men. Mur.; V. S¹ as text.   [13] S² Gerb. Pam. Men. Mur. insert *Dominicae apparitionis*.   [14] *puerpera* V. S¹; *puerperii* S² Gerb.; Pam. Men. Mur. omit *puerperae virginalis*; R. as text.   [15] R. S. Gerb. insert *in*.   [16] *coaeternus* R. Gerb.   [17] *agnoscere* S. Gerb.; V. R. as text.   [18] After *perveniat* R. S¹ continue *per quem eadem (eandem* R.) *sumpsit exordium. Per Dominum nostrum (exordia. Per eundem* R.); S² alters *eadem* to *eiusdem* and adds in the margin *fulgoris scilicet sive claritatis*. Gerb. adopts the reading *eiusdem* and subjoins the marginal gloss as part of the text before *sumpsit exordia*.

XIII.

IN SEPTUAGESIMA.

R. S.
Gerb. 32.
Pam. 212.

Deus, qui per ineffabilem observantiam sacramenti famulorum tuorum praeparas voluntates, donis gratiae tuae corda nostra purifica, ut quod [1] sancta est devotione tractandum [2], sinceris mentibus exequamur. Per Dominum.

R. S.
Gerb. 32.
Pam. 212.
Men. 32.
xxvi *infra*.

Concede, quaesumus, omnipotens Deus, fragilitati nostrae sufficientiam competentem, ut suae reparationis effectum [3] et pia conversatione recenseat, et cum exultatione suscipiat. Per.

Secreta.

R. S.
Gerb. 32.
Men. 32.

Concede nobis, misericors Deus, et digne tuis servire semper altaribus, et eorum perpetua participatione salvari. Per.

Postcommun.

504 Sacrae nobis, quaesumus, Domine, ·mensae libatio et piae conversationis augmentum et tuae protectionis[4] continuum praestet auxilium[5]. Per.

R. S.
Gerb. 32.
xxv *infra.*

[1] *quo* V.; R. S. Gerb. Pam. as text. [2] *devotione est tractandum* S.; *devotione tractandum est* Gerb.; V. R. Pam. as text. [3] *in sui reparationis affectum* V. (here); *sui reparationis affectum* S. Gerb.; *et suae rep. aff.* R.; Pam. Men. V. (in xxvi *infra*) as text. [4] *propitiationis* R. S. Gerb. V. (in xxv *infra*); V. here as text. [5] *continuo praestet auxilio* V. (but in xxv *infra*, *continuum auxilium*); R. has *continuo praestet auxilium*; S. Gerb. as text.

XIV.

In Sexagesima.

Tuere, quaesumus, Domine, plebem tuam, et sacram solemnitatem[1] recolentem gratiae caelestis largitate prosequere, ut visibilibus adiuta solatiis ad invisibilia bona promptius[2] incitetur. Per Dominum nostrum.

R. S.
Gerb. 33.
Pam. 213.
Men. 34.
Leon. 481.

Adiuva nos, Deus salutaris noster, et ad beneficia recolenda quibus nos instaurare dignatus es, tribue venire gaudentes. Per. γ

Pam. 247.

Secreta.

Intende, quaesumus, Domine, hostias[3] familiae tuae, et[4] quam sacris muneribus[5] facis esse participem[6] tribuas ad eam[7] plenitudinem venire. Per.

R. S.
Gerb. 33.
Pam. 213.
Men. 33.
xxxvii *infra.*

Postcommun.

Sit[8] nobis, quaesumus, Domine[9], cibus sacer potusque salutaris, qui et temporalem vitam muniat et praestet aeternam. Per.

R. S.
Gerb. 33.
Pam. 213.
Men. 34.
Leon. 413.

Ad Populum.

Rege, quaesumus[10], Domine, populum tuum, et gratiae tuae in eo dona multiplica, ut ab[11] omnibus liber offensis, et temporalibus non destituatur auxiliis, et sempiternis gaudeat institutis. Per.

R. S.
Gerb 33.
Pam. 213.
Leon. 417.

[1] *sacra solemnia* Leon. [2] *prumptior* V.; R. S. Leon. as text. [3] *hostiam* S. Gerb.; V. R. Pam. Men. as text. [4] V. omits *et* here, but inserts it in xxxvii *infra*. [5] *sacri muneris* S² Gerb. Men.; V. R. (S¹?) Pam. as text. [6] *participes* V. [7] *ad eius* R. S. Gerb. Pam. Men. and V. (in xxxvii *infra*); V. as text. *Ad eius* is ungrammatical if we read also *hostias* and *sacris muneribus* (as in R. Pam. and in V. xxxvii *infra*); on the other hand, the meaning of *ad eam* is obscure. [8] *Adsit* Men. Pam.; V. R. S. Gerb. Leon. as text. [9] *Domine quaesumus* Leon. [10] Leon. omits *quaesumus* here and inserts it after *gratiae tuae.* [11] *ut et ab* Leon.

XV.

ORATIONES ET PRECES SUPER POENITENTES[1].

S.
Pam. 451.
Men. 213.

Exaudi, Domine, preces nostras et confitentium tibi[2] parce peccatis, ut quos conscientiae reatus accusat, indulgentiae tuae miseratio absolvat. Per. γ

S.
Pam. 451.
Men. 214.

Praeveniat hunc famulum tuum, quaesumus, Domine, misericordia tua, et[3] omnes iniquitates eius celeri indulgentia deleantur. Per Dominum nostrum. γ

S.
Pam. 451.
Men. 214.

Adesto, Domine, supplicationibus nostris, nec sit ab hoc famulo tuo clementiae tuae longinqua miseratio. Sana vulnera[4] eiusque remitte peccata, ut nullis a te ∗ iniquitatibus 505 separatus, tibi semper Domino[5] valeat adhaerere. Per. γ

S.
Pam. 451.
Men. 214.

Domine Deus noster, qui offensione nostra[6] non vinceris, sed satisfactione[6] placaris, respice, quaesumus, ad hunc famulum tuum, qui se tibi peccasse graviter confitetur. Tuum est ablutionem[7] criminum dare, et veniam praestare peccantibus, qui dixisti poenitentiam te malle peccatorum quam mortem. Concede ergo, Domine, hoc ut et[8] tibi poenitentiae[9] excubias celebret, et[10] correctis actibus suis conferri sibi a te sempiterna gaudia gratuletur[11]. Per. γ

S.
Men. 214.

Precor, Domine, clementiam tuae maiestatis ac nominis, ut huic famulo tuo peccata et facinora sua confitenti veniam[12] dare, et praeteritorum criminum [debita][13] relaxare digneris. Qui humeris tuis ovem perditam reduxisti ad caulas, qui publicani precibus vel confessione placatus es, tu etiam, Domine, et huic famulo tuo placare, tu eius[14] precibus benignus assiste; ut in confessione flebili permanens clementiam tuam celeriter exoret, et sanctis ac sacris altaribus[15] restitutus, spei rursus aeternae et caelestis gloriae[16] reformetur. Per.

---

[1] S. has these prayers *after* the direction contained in section xvi *infra*.
[2] *tibi confitentium* Pam. Men.; V. S. as text.   [3] *ut* (for *et*) Pam. Men.; V. S. as text.   [4] *vulnera sana* Pam.   [5] *tibi Domino semper* S² Pam. Men.; V. S¹ as text.   [6] *offensionem nostram . . . satisfactionem* V. (ungrammatically); S. Pam. Men. as text.   [7] *absolutionem* S.; V. Pam. Men. as text.   [8] Pam. Men. omit *et*.   [9] *poenitentiam* V. (ungrammatically); S. Pam. Men. as text.   [10] *ut* (for *et*) S¹; V. S² Pam. Men. as text.   [11] *conferre tibi ad te sempiterni gaudia celebretur* V.; *conferre sibi ante sempiterni gaudia [.....]etur* S¹; S² Pam. Men. as text.   [12] *veniam relaxari* (for *relaxare*) S¹; *veniam delictorum* S².   [13] *debita*, omitted by V. S. seems required to complete the sense, and is restored from Men.   [14] *tu eum* V.; S. Men. as text.   [15] *et sanctis altaribus* Men.; *ac sacrosanctis altaribus* S²; V. S¹ as text.   [16] *caelesti gloriae* Men.; V. S. as text.

XVI.

ORDO AGENTIBUS PUBLICAM POENITENTIAM[1].

Suscipis eum iv feria mane in capite Quadragesimae, et cooperis eum cilicio, oras pro eo, et inclaudis usque ad Coenam Domini. Qui eodem die in gremio praesentatur ecclesiae[2], *et prostrato eo omni corpore in terra, dat orationem pontifex super eum ad reconciliandum in quinta feria Coenae Domini sicut ibi continetur.*

[1] This rubric is placed in S. before the prayers contained in the last section.
[2] *praesentatur in gremio ecclesiae* S.

XVII.

ORATIONES ET PRECES A QUINQUAGESIMA USQUE AD QUADRAGESIMAM.

Aufer[1] a nobis, Domine, quaesumus, iniquitates nostras, ut ad sancta sanctorum puris mereamur sensibus[2] introire. Per. γ

R. S.
Gerb. 34.
Pam. 214.
Leon. 430.

Perfice, Domine, benignus in nobis observantiae sanctae subsidium; ut quae te auctore • facienda cognovimus te operante impleamus. Per. γ

R.S.(*alibi*).
Gerb. 45.
Pam. 226.

Secreta.

Sacrificium, Domine, observantiae paschalis offerimus[3]: praesta, quaesumus, ut tibi et mentes nostras reddat acceptas, et continentiae promptioris [nobis tribuat facultatem[4]]. Per. γ

R. S.
Gerb. 34.
Pam. 216.
Men. 36.

Postcommun.

Repleti sumus, Domine[5], donorum participatione caelestium: praesta, quaesumus, ut eadem et sumamus iugiter et incessabiliter ambiamus. Per.

R. S.
Gerb. 34.
Pam. 214.
Men. 34.

Ad Populum.

De multitudine misericordiae tuae, Domine, populum tibi protege confitentem, et corporaliter gubernatum piae mentis affectum[6], tuis muneribus assequendis effice promptiorem. Per.

R. S.
Gerb. 34.
Pam. 214.
Men. 34.

IN IEIUNIO. PRIMA STATIONE.

Feria iv.

Inchoata ieiunia, quaesumus, Domine, benigno favore prosequere, ut observantiam, quam corporaliter exercemus, mentibus valeamus implere[7] sinceris. Per. γ

R. S.
(*Fer. vi.*)
Gerb. 36.
Pam. 216.
Men. 36.

R. S. Fac nos, quaesumus, Domine, salutis nostrae causas et
(Fer. v.) devotis semper frequentare servitiis, et devotius recolere
Gerb. 35.
Pam. 216. principaliter inchoatas. Per.

Secreta.

R. S. Fac nos, quaesumus, Domine[8], his muneribus offerendis
Gerb. 35.
Pam. 215. convenienter aptari, quibus ipsius venerabilis sacramenti
Men. 35. venturum celebramus exordium. Per. γ

Postcommun.

R. S. Tribue nobis, omnipotens Deus, ut dona caelestia, quae
(Fer. vi.)
Gerb. 36. debito frequentamus obsequio, sincera professione sentiamus[9]. Per.

Ad Populum.

Pam. 215. Respice, Domine, quaesumus[10], super famulos tuos; et in tua misericordia confidentes caelesti protege benignus auxilio. Per.

Feria vi in Quinquagesima. 507

R. S. Da, quaesumus, Domine, fidelibus tuis ieiuniis paschalibus
(Fer. v.)
Gerb. 35. convenienter aptari, ut suscepta solemniter castigatio corporalis cunctis ad fructum proficiat animarum. Per.

R. S. Adiuva nos, Deus salutaris noster, ut quae collata nobis
Gerb. 36. honorabiliter recensemus, devotis mentibus assequamur. Per.

Secreta.

R. S. Praepara nos, quaesumus, Domine, huius praecipuae[11]
Gerb. 36.
cf.Pam.217. festivitatis officiis, ut haec sacrificia sobriis mentibus celecf.Men. 37. bremus. Per.

Postcommun.

R.S.(alibi.) Salutari munere, Domine[12], satiati supplices deprecamur[13]
Gerb. 38.
Pam. 219. ut cuius laetamur gustu reparemur[13] effectu. Per Dominum
Leon. 414. nostrum. γ

Ad Populum.

R. S. Praesta famulis tuis, Domine, abundantiam[14] protectionis
Gerb. 36.
Pam. 216. et gratiae; da salutem mentis et corporis; da continua
Leon. 382. prosperitatis[15] augmenta; et tibi semper fac[16] esse devotos. Per Dominum nostrum.

Feria vii in Quinquagesima.

R. S. Observationis huius annua celebritate laetantes, quaesumus,
Gerb. 36.
Pam. 217. Domine, ut paschalibus actionibus[17] inhaerentes[18], plenis
cf. Leon. eius effectibus gaudeamus. Per.
360.

ROMANAE ECCLESIAE.

Adesto, Domine, supplicationibus nostris[19], et[20] hoc solemne ieiunium, quod animis corporibusque[21] curandis salubriter institutum est, devoto servitio celebremus. Per. R. S.
Gerb. 36.
Pam. 217.
Leon. 322.

Secreta.

Suscipe, Domine, sacrificium, cuius te voluisti dignanter[22] immolatione placari ; [23] praesta, quaesumus, ut huius operatione mundati, beneplacitum tibi nostrae mentis offeramus affectum. Per. R. S.
Gerb. 36.
Pam. 217.
Leon. 479.

508

Postcommun.

Caelestis vitae munere vegetati quaesumus, Domine, ut quod est nobis in praesenti vita mysterium, fiat aeternitatis auxilium. Per. R. S.
Gerb. 37.
Pam. 217.
Leon. 382.

Ad Populum.

Fidelibus tuis, Domine, perpetua dona[24] firmentur, ut eadem percipiendo te quaerant[25], et quaerendo sine fine percipiant. Per. γ R. S.
Gerb. 37.

[1] *Aufers* V. [2] *mentibus* Pam. [3] *exerimus* V.; R. S. Gerb. Pam. as text. [4] *continentiae promptiores* V. (omitting the words in brackets). But *promptiores* may be only an error for *promptioris* (as in S¹ at this point) and it seems best to restore the bracketed words from R. S. Gerb. Pam. Men. [5] Gerb. omits *Domine*. [6] *affectu* Pam. Men. ; V. R. S. Gerb. as text (perhaps ungrammatically). [7] *exhibemus, mentibus etiam sinceris exercere* Pam. Men. Gerb.; V. R. S. as text. [8] *Domine quaesumus* Pam. Men. [9] *sentiamur* V.; S. Gerb. as text; R. has *sinceris pro confessione sentiamus*. [10] *quaesumus Domine* Pam. [11] *praecipue* V. (probably for *praecipuae*, which is apparently the reading of S¹ as well as of R. Gerb. : Pam. and Men. have the Secret in a much altered form. [12] *Salutari tuo Domine satiati* Leon.; *Salutaris tui (tuae* R.) *Domine munere* R. S. Gerb. Pam. Men.; V. as text. [13] *exoramus—renovemur* R. S. Gerb. Pam. Men. ; *deprecamur—renovemur* Leon.; V. as text. [14] S³ Gerb. insert *tuae*; V. R. S¹ Pam. Leon. as text. [15] *continentiae et prosperitatis* Pam.; *continuae prosperitatis* Leon. [16] *tibi semper eos fac* S² Gerb.; *tibi fac semper* Pam.; V. R. S¹ Leon. as text. [17] *actibus quadragesimalibus* Pam. [18] *inhaerentibus* V.; R. S. Gerb. Pam. as text, which is supported also by the Leonine with *quorum actionibus inhaeremus*. [19] *supplicibus tuis* Leon. [20] *ut* Leon.; *et concede ut* Pam.; V. R. S. Gerb. as text. [21] *corporibus* V.; R. S. Gerb. Pam. Leon. as text. [22] *dignanti* V.; R. S. Gerb. Pam. Leon. as text. [23] Leon. inserts *et*. [24] *Fideles tui Domine (Deus* Gerb.) *per tua dona* S² Gerb. (R. has *Fidelis tui ... perpetua dona*); V. as text. [25] *percipiendo requirant* R. S. Gerb.; V. as text.

XVIII.

ORATIONES ET PRECES. DOMINICA IN QUADRAGESIMA[1]. INCHOANTIS INITIUM.

Concede nobis, omnipotens Deus, ut per annua quadragesimalis exercitia sacramenti et ad intelligendum Christi R. S.
Gerb. 37.

C

proficiamus arcanum, et affectus² eius digna conversatione sectemur. Per.

Omnipotens sempiterne Deus, qui nobis in observatione ieiunii et eleemosynarum semine posuisti nostrorum remedia peccatorum, concede nos opere mentis et corporis semper tibi esse devotos. Per.

Secreta.

Sacrificium, Domine, quadragesimalis initii solemniter immolamus, te, Domine, deprecantes, ut cum epularum restrictione carnalium a noxiis quoque voluptatibus³ temperemur. Per. y

Postcommun.

Praesta nobis, omnipotens Deus, ut vivificationis tuae gratiam consequentes, in eius munere semper⁴ gloriemur. Per. y

Ad Populum.

Super populum⁵ tuum, Domine, quaesumus, benedictio copiosa descendat [indulgentia veniat⁶], consolatio tribuatur, fides sancta succrescat, redemptio sempiterna firmetur. Per Dominum nostrum. y

Feria ii in Quadragesima. 509

Sanctifica, Domine, quaesumus, nostra ieiunia, et cunctarum nobis indulgentiam propitius largire culparum. Per. y

Omnipotens sempiterne Deus, qui per continentiam salutarem et corporibus mederis et mentibus, maiestatem tuam suppliciter exoramus ut pia ieiunantium precatione placatus et praesentia nobis subsidia praebeas et aeterna. Per. y

Secreta.

Accepta tibi sit, Domine, nostrae devotionis oblatio, quae et ieiunium nostrum, te operante, sanctificet, et indulgentiam nobis tuae consolationis obtineat. Per.

Postcommun.

Quaesumus, omnipotens Deus, ut inter eius numeremur membra, cuius corpore⁷ communicamus et sanguine⁷. Per. y

Ad Populum.

Esto, Domine, propitius plebi tuae, et temporali consolatione non deseras quam vis ad aeterna contendere. Per.

Feria iii.

Da quaesumus, Domine, nostris effectum ieiuniis salutarem[8], ut castigatio carnalis[9] assumpta ad nostrarum vegetationem transeat animarum. Per Dominum. γ

R.S.(*alibi*.)
Gerb. 48.
Pam. 229.
Men. 46. Leon. 479.

Cordibus nostris quaesumus, Domine, benignus infunde ut sicut ab escis corporalibus temperamur[10], ita sensus quoque nostros a noxio[11] retrahamus excessu[11]. Per. γ

R.S.(*alibi*.)
Gerb. 50.
Pam. 230.
Men. 48.
Leon. 480.

Secreta.

Suscipe, creator omnipotens Deus, quae ieiunantes de tuae munificentiae largitate deferimus; et pro temporali nobis collata[12] praesidio ad vitam converte propitiatus aeternam. Per.

R. S.
(*Fer. v.*)
Gerb. 40.
Men. 40.

Postcommun.

Sumpsimus, Domine, celebritatis annuae votiva sacramenta: praesta, quaesumus, • ut temporalis vitae nobis remedio praeveniant[13] et aeternae. Per. γ

R. S.
Gerb. 39.
Men. 39.
Leon. 480.

Ad Populum.

Respice, Domine[14], propitius ad[14] plebem tuam, et quam divinis tribuis[15] proficere sacramentis ab omnibus absolve peccatis. Per Dominum nostrum.

R. S.
(*Fer. v.*)
Gerb. 41.
Pam. 221.
Leon. 481.

Feria iv.

Precamur, omnipotens Deus, ut de transitoriis operibus abstinentes[16], ea potius operemur, quibus ad aeterna gaudia consequenda et spes nobis suppetat et facultas. Per.

R. S.
(*Fer. v.*)
Gerb. 40.
Pam. 222.
Leon. 480.

Pacem nobis tribue, Domine, quaesumus, mentis et corporis, ut per ieiunium nostrae fragilitatis[17] et manifesti subiiciantur hostes et invisibiles excludantur. Per.

R. S.
(*Fer. iii.*)
Gerb. 39.
Pam. 220.
Leon. 480.

Secreta.

Sacrificia[18], Domine, propitius[19] ista nos salvent, quae medicinalibus sunt instituta ieiuniis. Per. γ

R. S.
Gerb. 40.
Pam. 221.

Postcommun.

Tuorum nos, Domine, largitate donorum et temporalibus attolle praesidiis, et renova sempiternis. Per. γ

R.S.(*alibi*.)
Gerb. 41.
II.lxxxv*inf.*
Pam. 221. Leon. 479.

Ad Populum.

Da, quaesumus, Domine, populis Christianis, et quod profitentur[20] agnoscere, et caeleste[21] munus diligere, quod frequentant. Per. γ

R. S.
Gerb. 40.
Pam. 221.
xxiv *infra.*

Feria vi.

Pam. 222.
II. lxxxv infra.
Leon. 480.

Huius nobis parsimoniae, quaesumus, Domine, praebe mensuram, ut quod licentiae carnis auferimus [22] salutarem nobis fructum mentis acquirat. Per.

R. S.
Gerb. 41.
Pam. (Amb.) 327.

Da, quaesumus, nobis [23], omnipotens Deus, ieiuniorum magnifici [24] sacramenti et digne semper tractare mysteria, et competenter honorare primordia. Per.

Secreta.

R. S.
Gerb. 41.
Pam. (Amb.) 326.
Leon. 476.

Suscipe, quaesumus, Domine, devotorum munera famulorum, et tuis [25] divinis purifica servientes pietate mysteriis, quibus etiam iustificas ignorantes. Per.

Postcommun.

R. S.
Gerb. 41.
Leon. 481.

Praesta, quaesumus, Domine, spiritalibus gaudiis nos repleri; ut quae actu gerimus mente sectemur. Per.

Ad Populum.

R. S.
Gerb. 41.
Leon. 372.

Plebs tua, Domine, quaesumus, benedictionis sanctae munus accipiat, per quod et noxia quaeque declinet, et optata reperiat. Per.

Feria vii.

Pam. 224.

Deus, qui nos gloriosis remediis in terris adhuc positos iam caelestium rerum facis esse consortes, tu, quaesumus, in ista qua vivimus nos vita guberna, ut ad illam in qua ipsa es lucem perducas. Per Dominum nostrum.

Pam. 225.

Reparet nos, quaesumus, Domine, semper et innovet tuae providentia pietatis, quae [26] fragilitatem nostram et inter mundi tempestates proteget et gubernet, et in portum perpetuae salutis inducat. Per.

Secreta.

R.S.(alibi.)
Gerb. 35.

Haec, quae [27] nos reparent, quaesumus, Domine, beata mysteria [28] suo munere dignos efficiant. Per Dominum.

Postcommun.

R. S.
Gerb. 42.
Leon. 416.

Perpetuo, Domine, favore prosequere quos reficis divino mysterio, et quos [29] imbuisti caelestibus institutis, salutaribus comitare solatiis. Per.

Ad Populum.

Fideles tuos, Domine, benedictio desiderata confirmet, quae eos et a tua voluntate nunquam faciat discrepare, et tuis semper indulgeat beneficiis gratulari. Per.

R. S.
Gerb. 42.
Pam. 224.
Leon. 441.
lxii *infra*.

[1] *Quadragensima* V.; Tommasi, however, notes that V. reads *quadragesimae*, and this may be the true reading, *inchoantis* being connected with *quadragesimae*, and *initium* an ungrammatical accusative. [2] *effectus* S² Gerb. Pam. Men.; *affectos* S¹; V. R. as text. [3] *voluntatibus* R. S²; V. Gerb. Pam. Men. as text. [4] *in tuo semper munere* R. S. Gerb. Pam. V. (lvii *infra*); V. here as text. [5] *In populum* Men. [6] V. here omits *indulgentia veniat*, which is restored from Leon. R. S. Gerb. Pam. Men. and xxvi *infra*. [7] *corpori* ... *sanguini* Leon. Pam. Men.; V. has *corpore* ... *sanguinem*. [8] *nostrae affectus ieiunii salutare* V.; R. S. Gerb. Pam. Men. Leon. as text. [9] *carnis* R. S. Gerb. Pam. Men. Leon.; V. as text. [10] *temperemur* S¹; *temperamus* Leon.; *abstinemus* S² Gerb. Pam. Men.; V. R. as text. [11] *noxiis* ... *excessibus* S. Gerb. Men. Pam.; V. R. Leon. as text. [12] *collato* Gerb.; V. R. S. Men. as text. [13] *remedia praebeant* S² Gerb. Leon.; *remedio proveniant* Men.; V. R. S¹ as text. [14] Gerb. omits *Domine* and *ad*. [15] *tribues* V.; R. S. Gerb. Pam. Leon. as text. [16] Leon. reads *opibus* (*operibus* in Mur.) and omits *abstinentes*. [17] *ut nostrae fragilitati* (omits *per ieiunium*) Leon.; V. R. S. Gerb. Pam. as text. [18] Pam. inserts *quaesumus*. [19] *propensius* S² Gerb.; V. R. S¹ Pam. as text. [20] *quos providentur* V.; R. S. Gerb. Pam. as text. [21] *ad caelesti munus* V; R. inserts *ad*; S. Gerb. Pam. as text. [22] *auferamus* Leon. [23] *nobis quaesumus* R. S. Gerb. Pam. (Amb.). [24] *magnifice* V.; R. S. Gerb. Pam. (Amb.) as text. [25] *tua* S² Gerb.; Pam. (Amb.) omits *tuis*; V. R. S¹ Leon. as text. [26] *providentiae pietatisque* V.; Pam. as text. [27] *Haecque* S¹; *Haec* S² Gerb.; V. R. as text. [28] S² Gerb. insert *et*. [29] V. omits *quos*.

XIX.

ISTAE ORATIONES QUAE SEQUUNTUR PRIMO SABBATO
IN MENSE PRIMO SUNT DICENDAE.

Orationes et preces in xii lectiones mense primo.

Deus qui delinquentes perire non pateris, donec convertantur[1] et vivant, debitam, quaesumus, peccatis nostris sus·pende vindictam, et praesta propitius ne dissimulatio cumulet ultionem, sed potius per ieiunium emendatio prosit ad veniam. Per Dominum nostrum.

R. S.
Gerb. 42.
Pam. 223.
Men. 42.
Leon. 410.

Omnium nostrum[2] Domine quaesumus ad te corda converte, et[3] ab his quibus offenderis abstinentes, non iram tuam sed misericordiam sentiamus. Per.

Leon. 412.

Ieiunia, quaesumus, Domine, nos sacrata laetificent, ut imbecillitati nostrae tribuatur[4] auxilium, et mentibus desideratus virtutum succedat affectus. Per Dominum.

Adesto, quaesumus, omnipotens Deus, ac[5] ieiunio corporali mentem nostram operibus tuorum reficc mandatorum. Per Dominum.

xxvi *infra*. Da nobis observantiam, Domine [6], legitima devotione perfectam, ut cum [7] refrenatione carnalis alimoniae, sancta tibi conversatione placeamus. Per.

Pam. 342.
xviii *supra*.
xxv *infra*.
xxviii *inf.*

Omnipotens sempiterne Deus, qui per continentiam salutarem corporibus mederis et mentibus, maiestatem tuam suppliciter exoramus, ut pia ieiunantium precatione placatus, et temporalia subsidia nobis tribuas [8] et [9] aeterna. Per. γ

[1] *pateris, sed expectas ut convertantur* Pam. Men.; V. R. S. Gerb. Leon. as text. [2] *nostrorum* V.; Leon. as text. [3] *ut* Leon. [4] *tribuantur* V. [5] *ad* V. (corr. by Tommasi). [6] *Domine quaesumus observantiam* V. in xxvi *infra*. [7] V. xxvi *infra* omits *cum*: here as text. [8] *praebeas* V. in xviii *supra*, xxv *infra*, Pam. [9] V. omits *et* here, but has it in xviii *supra*.

XX.

ORDO [1] QUALITER IN ROMANA SEDIS APOSTOLICAE ECCLESIA PRESBYTERI, DIACONI, VEL SUBDIACONI ELIGENDI SUNT.

Martène lib. I. cap. viii.
Gerb. ii. 40.

Mensis primi, quarti, septimi et decimi [2] *Sabbatorum die in xii lectiones* [3] *ad sanctum Petrum, ubi missas* [4] *celebrantur, posiquam antiphonam ad introitum dixerint, data oratione annuntiat* [5] *pontifex in populo* [6] *dicens:*

Auxiliante Domino Deo et Salvatore nostro Iesu Christo.

Iterum iterum [7] *dicit:*

Auxiliante Domino Deo et Salvatore nostro Iesu Christo, elegimus in ordine [8] diaconii [9] *sive* presbyterii [10] *illum* subdiaconum *sive* diaconum de titulum *illum* [11]. Si quis autem habet aliquid contra hos viros, pro Deo [12] et propter Deum [12] cum fiducia exeat et dicat. Verumtamen memor sit communionis suae. γ

Et post modicum intervallum mox incipiant [13] *omnes* Kyrie eleison [14] *cum litania.* *Hac expleta ascendunt ipsi electi ad sedem pontificis, et benedicit eos a quo* [15] *vocati sunt, et descendunt. Stant in ordine suo* [16] *benedictione percepta.* Per Dominum [17]. *Sequitur oratio de Benedictione. Require ipsam in quarto aut decimo mense.*

Ad ordinandos presbyteros [18].

Miss. Franc. 607.

Oremus, dilectissimi, Deum Patrem omnipotentem, ut super hos famulos suos, quos ad presbyterii munus elegit, caelestia dona multiplicet, et quae eius dignatione [19] suscipiunt [20] eius [21] exequantur [22] auxilio. Per [23] Dominum. γ

Martène lib. I. cap. viii.
Gerb. ii. 41.
Leon. 424.

Exaudi nos, Deus salutaris noster [24], et super hos famulos tuos benedictionem [25] sancti Spiritus et gratiae sacerdotalis effunde virtutem, ut quos tuae pietatis aspectibus [26] offerimus consecrandos perpetua muneris tui largitate prosequaris [27]. Per. γ

Consecratio.

Domine sancte, Pater omnipotens, aeterne Deus, honorum [28] omnium dignitatum quae tibi militant distributor [29], per quem [30] proficiunt universa, per quem [30] cuncta firmantur, amplificatis semper in melius naturae rationalis incrementis [31] per ordinem congrua ratione [32] dispositum: unde [33] sacerdotales [34] gradus, et officia Levitarum sacramentis mysticis instituta creverunt, ut, quum pontifices summos regendis populis praefecisses, ad eorum societatis et operis adiumentum sequentis ordinis viros et secundae dignitatis eligeres [35]. Sic in eremo per lxx virorum prudentium mentes [36] Moysi spiritum propagasti, quibus ille adiutoribus usus in populo innumeras multitudines facile gubernavit. Sic et Eleazaro et Ithamar filiis Aaron [37] paternae plenitudinis [38] abundantiam transfudisti, ut [39] ad hostias salutares [et frequentioris [40]] officii sacramenta [41] sufficeret meritum [42] sacerdotum. Hac providentia Domine apostolis Filii tui doctores fidei [43] comites addidisti, quibus illi [44] orbem totum secundis praedicatoribus impleverunt. Quapropter infirmitati quoque nostrae, Domine, quaesumus [45], • haec adiumenta largire, qui quanto [46] magis fragiliores sumus tanto his plurius [47] indigemus. Da, quaesumus, omnipotens Pater, in hos famulos tuos [48] presbyterii dignitatem: innova in visceribus eorum spiritum sanctitatis, ut [49] acceptum a te, Deus, secundum [50] meriti munus obtineant [51], censuramque morum exemplo suae conversationis insinuent [51]. Sint providi cooperatores nostri ordinis [52]; luceat in eis [53] totius forma iustitiae, ut bonam rationem dispensationis sibi creditae reddituri [54] aeternae beatitudinis praemia [55] consequantur. Per. γ

Consummatio presbyteri [56].

Sit nobis, fratres, communis oratio ut hi qui in adiutorium et utilitatem vestrae salutis eliguntur presbyteratus benedictionem divini indulgentia muneris consequantur, ut sancti Spiritus sacerdotalia [57] dona privilegio virtutum ne impares [58] loco deprehendantur obtineant. Per suum. Per.[59] γ

Item Benedictio.

Sanctificationum [60] omnium auctor, cuius vera consecratio, cuius [61] plena benedictio est, tu, Domine, super hos famulos tuos quos presbyterii honore [62] dedicamus, manum tuae benedictionis [63] infunde, ut gravitate actuum et censura vivendi [64] probent [65] se esse [66] seniores, his [67] instituti disciplinis, quas Tito et Timotheo Paulus exposuit [68], ut in lege tua die ac nocte, omnipotens [69], meditantes, quod legerint [70] credant, quod crediderint doceant, quod docuerint imitentur; iustitiam, constantiam, misericordiam, fortitudinem in se ostendant, et exemplo probent, admonitionem confirment [71], ut purum atque immaculatum ministerii tui [72] donum custodiant, et per [73] obsequium plebis tuae corpus et sanguinem Filii tui immaculata benedictione [74] transforment, et inviolabili caritate [75] in virum perfectum, in mensuram aetatis plenitudinis Christi, in die iustitiae et aeterni iudicii [76] conscientia [77] pura, fide plena, Spiritu sancto pleni persolvant [78]. Per. γ

---

[1] The forms for Ordination contained in V. are curiously broken up. See, besides this and the following sections, sections xcv, xcvi, xcix *infra*. The text of V. has been here corrected by a comparison with the following sources:—

(*a*) The text given by Gerbert (vol. ii. p. 140 sqq.) from a Zürich MS. (saec. ix circ.).

(*b*) The *Missale Francorum*. (See Muratori, *Lit. Rom. Vet.* vol. ii.)

(*c*) Three of Martène's Ordines, numbered by him ii, iii, iv (*De Ant. Eccl. Rit.* lib. I. cap. viii.). Of these the first is taken from the Pontifical of Egbert, the second from the Jumièges MS., the third in the main from the Gellone MS. In the following notes these are cited respectively as Egb., Gem., and Gell., except where Martène notes a variation among the three MSS. employed for the last *Ordo*.

(*d*) The Leonine Sacramentary. The readings of this are as a rule only noted where they differ from the text: when it is not cited, it agrees with the text, save in spelling or punctuation.

[2] Egb. has *Mensis primi hebdomada secunda, quarti hebdomada secunda, septimi hebdomada tertia, decimi hebdomada quarta*: Martène's *Ordo* iv inserts (after *decimi*) *feria quarta et sexta scrutandi sunt ipsi electi secundum canones, si digni sunt hoc onus fungi*, but these words are omitted in the Codex Gellonensis, which thus, with V. Gem. Gerb., reads as the text. [3] *lectiones*, so V. (ungrammatically); Martène's Ordines have *lectionibus*. [4] So V. Gell. (ungrammatically); *missae* Egb. Gem.; *missa celebratur* Gerb. [5] Gem. here inserts a form for the presentation of the candidates for Ordination by the archdeacon. *annuat* Egb.; *adnunciet* Gem.; V. Gell. Gerb. as text. [6] *in*

populum Egb.; *populum* Gem.; V. Gell. Gerb. as text. [7] Gem. Gell. Gerb. omit the second *iterum*; Egb. omits the repetition of the words *Auxiliante—Christo*; V. as text. [8] *in ordinem* Egb. Gem. Gell.; V. Gerb. as text (ungrammatically). [9] *diaconi* V. Egb. Gem. Gerb.; Gell. as text. [10] *presbyteri* Gem. Gerb.; V. Egb. Gell. as text. [11] So V. (ungr.); the rest have *de titulo illo*. Gem. adds *illum presbyterum ad titulum*. [12] *Domino —Dominum* Gerb. [13] *incipiunt* Egb. Gem. Gerb.; Gell. omits *mox*. [14] In one or more of the MSS. used by Martène for his Ordo iv the words *novem vicibus* are inserted here. [15] *ad quod* Egb. Gem. Mart. iv; V. Gerb. Mart. iv (marg.) as text. [16] *descendentes stant in ordine suo* [*sua* Egb.] Egb. Gem.; *discedentes stant in ordine suo* Gell.; V. Gerb. as text. [17] The words *Per Dominum* and the rubric following appear only in V. They are, as Tommasi suggests, misplaced, and should be connected, not with the preceding rubric, but with the *Orat. in xii Lect.* (see lxxxiii, and II. lxxxv, *infra*). [18] The prayers which follow in V., like those in Leon., refer to more than one ordinand; in the other texts they contemplate one only, but there are here and there indications of their being copied from forms worded in the plural. • [19] *qui eius dignationem* Gem. Gerb.; *quibus quod eius dignatione* Leon.; V. Miss. Franc. Egb. Gell. as text. [20] *suscepit* Gem.; *suscipiunt* Miss. Franc. Gerb. [21] *ipsius* Egb. Gell.; *et eius* Gerb.; V. Miss. Franc. Gem. as text. [22] *exequantur* Miss. Franc. Gerb. [23] *auxiliante Domino nostro I. C.* Egb. Gell. [24] *Domine Deus noster* Gem. Gell. Gerb.; *Domine Deus salutaris noster* Egb.; V. Miss. Franc. as text. [25] *benedictione* Miss. Franc. (ungrammatically). [26] *suspectibus* Miss. Franc. [27] *consequantur* V.; *consequaris* Gerb.; Miss. Franc. Egb. Gem. Gell. as text. [28] *honorum omnium et* Leon. (*bonorum* ed. Mur.); Egb. Gem. Gell. Gerb. insert *auctor. et distributor*; V. Miss. Franc. as text. [29] Gerb. omits *quae tibi militant distributor*; Egb. Gem. Gell. omit *distributor*; V. Miss. Franc. as text. [30] *per te* Gem. [31] *amplificantes* ... *incrementi* V. [32] *congruam rationem* Miss. Franc. (ungrammatically). [33] Egb. Gem. Gell. Gerb. insert *et*. [34] *sacerdotalis* (! for *sacerdotales*) V. Gell.; *sacerdotales* Miss. Franc. Egb. Gem. Gerb. [35] *elegeris* V. Leon. (ed. Ball.) Miss. Franc. Gem. Gerb. (prob. for *eligeres*, which Tommasi substitutes here). [36] *mentem* Gem. Gerb. [37] Gerb. omits *filiis Aaron*. [38] *beatitudinis* Gerb. [39] *et* V. Miss. Franc.; Egb. Gem. Gell. Gerb. as text. [40] V. omits *et frequentioris*, which all the other texts have. [41] *sacrum* (for *sacramenta*) Gem. [42] *ministerium* Egb. Gem. Gell. Gerb.; V. Miss. Franc. Leon. as text. [43] Gerb. inserts *presbyterii*. [44] *illis* V. [45] Egb. Gell. omit *quaesumus*. [46] *quia quanto* Egb. Gem. Gell.; *qui tanto* Miss. Franc.; V. Gerb. as text. [47] *plurius*, so V. Miss. Franc. (perhaps for *pluribus*, which is the reading of the other texts). [48] *in hoc famulo tuo illo* Miss. Franc. (ungrammatically). [49] *et* Egb. Gell.; Miss. Franc. Gerb. Leon. omit *ut*; V. Gem. as text. [50] *secundi* Miss. Franc. Egb. Gem. Gell. Leon.; V. Gerb. as text. [51] *obtineant* ... *insinuent* Gerb. [52] *sint probi cooperatores ordinis nostri* Gerb. Leon.; *sit probus cooperator ordinis nostri* Gell.; *sit providus cooperator ordinis nostri* Miss. Franc. Egb. Gem.; V. as text. [53] *eluceat in eum* Miss. Franc. Gerb.; *eluceat in eo* Egb. Gem.; *eluceat in eis* Leon.; *et luceat in eo* Gell.; V. as text. [54] *sibi credituri* Gerb. [55] Gell. omits *praemia*. [56] Gerb. Leon. do not give this form or that which follows it. Gem. inserts before them some other forms. [57] *sacerdotali* Miss. Franc. [58] *imparis* (perh. for *impares*) Gell. [59] Both V. and Miss. Franc. have this ending; Egb. Gell. have *Per*; Gem. *Per Dominum*. [60] *Deus sanctificationum* Egb. Gem. Gell.; V. Miss. Franc. as text. [61] *cuius* is found in V. only. [62] *ad presbyterii honorem* Egb. Gem. Gell.; V. Miss. Franc. as text. [63] Miss. Franc. inserts *eum*. [64] *videndi* V.; Gell. omits *et censura vivendi*. [65] *praebeat* Egb. [66] Gell. inserts *omnium*. [67] *sit* (for *his*) Gem. [68] *instituit* Gell. [69] *in lege tua omnipotens Deus die ac nocte* Gell. [70] *elegerint et* V.; *elegerit* Miss. Franc.; *legerit* Egb. Gem. Gell. [71] *exemplum probet; admonitionem confirmet* Miss. Franc.; *exemplum praebeat, admonitionem confirmet* Egb.; *exemplum praebeat, admonitione confirmet* Gem.; *ostendat, probet, admonitione confirmet* Gell.; V. as text, perh. ungrammatically. [72] Gell. omits *tui*. [73] Gell. omits *per*. [74] Egb. omits *benedictione* and reads *immaculati*. [75] *ut inviolabilem caritatem* Egb. Gell.; Gell. inserts *et*. [76] *iustitiae aeternae iudicii* V.; *iusti et aeterni iudicii* Gell.; Miss. Franc. omits *et*; Egb. Gem. as text. [77] *constantia* V. [78] *appareat* Gem.

XXI.

Capitulum sancti Gregorii Papae [1].

Gerb. ii. 40.
Martène
lib. I. cap.
viii.

Sicut qui invitatus renuit, quaesitus refugit, sacris altaribus est removendus [2], sic qui ultro ambit, vel importunus se ingerit, est procul dubio repellendus. Nam qui nititur ad altiora conscendere [3] quid agit nisi ut crescendo decrescat? Cur non perpenditur [4], quia benedictio illi [5] in maledicto [6] convertitur, qualiter [7] ad hoc ut fiat haereticus promovetur [8].

[1] This *capitulum* is found in Gerb. and in the three Ordines of Martène, cited for the last section: Gem. Gerb. continue the extract. [2] *removendus* is the reading of all the texts cited, as well as of V.; the Benedictine editors of S. Gregory propose to read (in Menard's Sacramentary) *admovendus*, which is supported by the MSS. of S. Gregory's Letters : but the reading of the text seems to have been established in the Sacramentaries. [3] Egb. inserts *indignus*. [4] *perpendit* Egb. Gem. Gell.; V. Gerb. as text. [5] *illa* Egb. [6] *in maledictum* Egb. Gem. Gerb.; *in maledictionem* Gell.; V. as text (ungrammatically). [7] *qui* Egb. Gell.; *quia* Gem. Gerb. ; V. as text, but probably erroneously. [8] V. adds *Per*.

XXII.

Ad ordinandos diaconos [1].

A.
Miss.
Franc. 664.
Gerb. ii. 40.
Martène
lib. I. cap.
viii.
Leon. 423.

Oremus [2], dilectissimi, Deum Patrem omnipotentem ut [3] super hos famulos suos quos ad officium diaconatus vocare dignatur [4], benedictionem gratiae suae [5] clementer effundat [6], et consecrationis adultae propitius dona conservet [7]. γ

Oremus.

Sequitur oratio [8].

Domine Deus [9] preces nostras clementer exaudi, et [10] quae [11] nostro gerenda sunt servitio [12] tuo [13] benignus prosequaris [13] auxilio, et quos sacris ministeriis [14] exequendis pro nostra intelligentia [15] credimus offerendos tua [13] potius electione iustifices [13]. γ

Consecratio.

Adesto, quaesumus [16], omnipotens Deus, honorum dator [17], ordinum distributor, officiorumque [18] dispositor, qui in te manens innovas omnia, et cuncta disponis [19] per Verbum, Virtutem, Sapientiamque tuam Iesum Christum Filium tuum, Dominum nostrum, sempiterna providentia [20] praeparas, et singulis quibusque temporibus [21] aptanda [22] dispensas: cuius corpus, ecclesiam tuam, caelestium gratiarum varietate distinctam [23], suorumque connexam [23] discretione [24] membrorum, per legem totius mirabilem [25] compagis [26] uni·tam, in augmentum templi tui crescere, dilatarique largiris, sacri muneris servitutem [27] trinis gradibus ministrorum nomini tuo militare [28] constituens [29]: electis [30] ab initio Levi filiis, qui [31] mysticis operationibus domus tuae fidelibus excubiis permanentes, haereditatem benedictionis aeternae sorte perpetua possiderent. Super hos quoque famulos tuos, quaesumus, Domine, placatus intende, quos tuis sacris [32] servituros in officium diaconii [33] suppliciter dedicamus. Et nos quidem tanquam homines divini sensus et summae rationis ignari [34] horum vitam quantum possumus aestimamus. Te autem Domine [35], quae a nobis sunt ignota non transeunt, te occulta [36] non fallunt. Tu cognitor peccatorum [37], tu scrutator es animarum [38]: tu [39] veraciter in eis [40] caeleste potes adhibere iudicium et velut [41] indignis donare quae poscimus. Emitte [42] in eos, quaesumus, Domine [43], Spiritum sanctum, quo [44] in opus ministerii fideliter exequendi munere septiformis tuae gratiae [45] roborentur. Abundet in eis totius forma virtutis, auctoritas modesta [46], pudor constans innocentiae et spiritalis observantia disciplinae [47]: in moribus [eorum [48]] praecepta tua fulgeant, ut suae castitatis exemplo imitationem [49] sanctae plebis [50] acquirant, et bonum conscientiae testimonium praeferentes [51] in Christo [52] firmi et stabiles perseverent, dignisque successibus [53] de inferiore gradu per gratiam tuam potiora capere [54] mereantur [55]. Per. y

---

[1] The text of V. has been here compared with the same texts cited for section xx, and also, as regards the first bidding prayer and the prayer following, with A., which contains that portion only. As in sect. xx the readings of Leon. correspond with the text where it is not cited by name. As in sect. xx, the forms in the other texts (Leon. excepted) are for the most part worded in the singular number. [2] In Miss. Franc. and in A. this form and the prayer following are combined into one longer 'bidding prayer,' and a similar combination is found in Egb. and in Codex Gellonensis. In Gem. both appear separately (with variations), the prayer *Domine Deus* being given as an alternative for one which takes its place in Egb. and Gerb. The arrangement of Martène's Ordo iv agrees with that of V. [3] Gerb. Gell. omit *ut*. [4] *quem in sacrum ordinem diaconatus officii dignatus es assumere* Egb. Gem.; *quem in sacro ordine dignatus es assumere* Gerb.; V. Miss. Franc. A. as text (so also Leon., except for the reading *Diaconii*, and Gell., except for the reading *dignatus est*). [5] *benedictionis suae gratiam* Egb. Gem. Gerb.; *benedictionem gratiae* Miss. Franc.; V. A. Gell. as text. [6] *infundat* Gem. [7] *eique donum consecrationis propitius indulgeat* Egb. Gem. and (omitting *propitius*) Gerb.; V. A. as text. Similarly Miss. Franc. (reading *adulta*), and Leon. and Gell. (reading *indultae*). After *conservet* Miss. Franc. and A.

proceed *ut preces nostras clementer exaudiat et quae*, &c.; similarly Egb. and Codex Gellonensis. The endings of the 'bidding prayer' in Egb. Gem. Gerb. differ both from V. and from one another. [7] This prayer is omitted by Egb. and Gerb.; Leon. also omits it, substituting another. [9] Gem. and Martène's Ordo iv insert *omnipotens*. [10] *et* Miss. Franc. A. [11] *quos* V. [12] *nostro sunt gerenda servitio* Miss. Franc. Gem. Mart. iv; *nostras gerenda servitio* A. [13] *suo ... prosequatur ... sua ... iustificet* Miss. Franc. A. [14] *mysteriis* A. Gem. [15] *pro nostram intelligentiam* V. (corr. by Tommasi). [16] Egb. Gell. insert *Domine*. [17] *bonorum dator* Leon. (ed. Mur.); *honorum datum* V. [18] *et officiorum* Gerb. [19] *disponens* Leon. Egb. Gem. Gell.; V. Miss. Franc. Gerb. as text. [20] *sempiternam providentiam* V.; the rest as text. [21] *temporalium* (for *temporibus*) V.; the rest as text. [22] *apta* Gem. [23] *distincta ... connexa* V.; the rest as text. [24] *distinctione* Gerb. Leon. [25] *mirabilem totius* Egb. Gem. Gell. Gerb.; V. Leon. Miss. Franc. as text. [26] *compaginis* Gem. Gerb. [27] *sacri muneris servientem* V. Miss. Franc.; *sacri muneris virtutem* Gerb.; Leon. Egb. Gem. Gell. as text. [28] *ministrare* Gem. [29] *constitues* V. [30] *electi* V. [31] Egb. Gell. insert *in*. [32] *sacrariis* Leon. (ed. Ball.) Egb. Gem. Gell. Gerb.; V. Miss. Franc. as text. [33] *diaconatus* Gem. Gerb. [34] *ignorare* V.; *signare* Miss. Franc.; Egb. Gem. Gell. Gerb. as text. [35] Egb. Gem. Gell. Gerb. insert *ea*. [36] *nota* V.; the rest as text. [37] *pectorum* Miss. Franc.; *es secretorum* Gem. Gerb.; *secretorum* Egb.; V. Gell. Leon. as text. [38] *cordium* Egb. Gem. Gerb.; *animorum* Leon.; V. Miss. Franc. Gell. as text. [39] Egb. Gem. Gerb. have (in place of *tu veraciter—poscimus*) the following:—*tu eius vitam caelesti poteris examinare iudicio, quo semper praevales et admissa purgare, et ea quae sunt agenda concedere*. [40] *in eum* Miss. Franc. Gell.; V. as text, perhaps for *eos*. [41] *velut* so V. Miss. Franc. Gell. probably for *vel*. Leon. (ed. Mur.) has *ut vel*. [42] *Et mitte* V. [43] *Domine quaesumus* Egb. Gem. Gerb. Leon. [44] Miss. Franc. omits *quo*; Gerb. has *quod*. [45] *septiformis gratiae tuae munere* Egb. Gem. Gell. Gerb. (Gem. Germ. omit *tuae*); V. Miss. Franc. as text. [46] *modestia* Miss. Franc. [47] *innocentiae puritas, et spiritalis observatio disciplinae* Egb. Gem. Gell. Gerb. Leon.; V. Miss. Franc. as text. [48] V. omits *eorum*, which is restored from Miss. Franc. and the others which read *eius* or *eorum*. [49] *imitatione* V. Miss. Franc. (ungrammatically); Leon. and the rest as text. [50] *sancta plebs* Egb. Gem. Gell.; V. Miss. Franc. Gerb. as text. [51] *perferens* Miss. Franc.; *proferens* Egb. Gem. Gell.; *proferentes* Gerb.; V. as text. [52] Gerb. omits *in Christo*. [53] *successionibus* Miss. Franc. [54] *capere potiora* Egb. Gem. Gell. Gerb. Leon.; V. Miss. Franc. as text. [55] *mereamur* Miss. Franc.

[XXIII [1].]

AD CONSUMMANDUM DIACONATUS OFFICIUM [2].

Miss. Franc. 666.
Martène lib. I. cap. viii.

Commune votum [3] communis oratio prosequatur, ut hi [4] totius ecclesiae prece qui in diaconatus ministerio [5] praeparantur Leviticae benedictionis [ordine clarescant [6]] et spiritali conversatione praefulgentes gratia [7] sanctificationis eluceant. Per. γ

Sequitur benedictio.

Domine sancte [8], spei, fidei, gratiae et [9] profectuum munerator, qui in caelestibus et terrenis angelorum ministeriis [10] ubique dispositis per omnia elementa voluntatis ✻tuae diffundis [11] affectum, hos quoque famulos tuos [*nomina*] [12] speciali dignare [illustrare] [13] aspectu [14]; ut tuis obsequiis expediti sanctis altaribus ministri puri accrescant, et indulgentia puriores [16], eorum gradu, quos apostoli tui in septenarium numerum [16], beato Stephano duce atque praevio, Spiritu sancto auctore elegerunt, digni existant, et virtutibus universis, quibus tibi servire oportet instructi complaceant [17]. Per. γ

[1] These two forms are (in V.) apparently reckoned, though not actually numbered, as a separate section, while the parallel forms for presbyters are included in sect. xx. Like those parallel forms, they are absent from Leon. and from Gerbert's MS. They have been compared with Missale Francorum, and with Martène's three Ordines (see note on sect. xx, *supra*). [2] *officia* V.; *officio* Gell.; *ad conservandum diaconatus officii* Egb.; Gem. Gell. as text: so (abbreviated) Miss. Franc. [3] Gem. inserts *permaneat*. [4] *et is* Egb. [5] *in Diaconatus ministerii* Miss. Franc.; *in diaconatus officii ministerio* Egb.; V. Gell. as text (perhaps ungrammatically); Gem. reads *ministerium*. [6] V. Miss. Franc. omit *ordine clarescant*, which is restored from Egb. Gem. Gell. [7] *per gratiam* Gem. [8] *sanctae* V.; the rest as text. [9] V. omits *et*. [10] *ministeriis angelorum* Egb. Gell. [11] *defundas* V.; *defendes* Miss. Franc.; Egb. Gem. Gell. as text. [12] V. has *tuos nostris speciali*, which Tommasi proposes to correct by the substitution of *nomina* for *nostris*. This is supported by the other texts, which indicate the mention of names at this point. [13] V. omits *illustrare* which is supplied from the other texts. [14] *affectu* Egb. Gem. [15] *indulgentiae prioris* Egb. [16] *in septenario numero* Miss. Franc. Egb.; V. Gem. Gell. as text. [17] *complcat* Miss. Franc.; *polleat* Gem.; *complaceat* Egb. Gell.; V. as text.

XXIV.

Item Orationes et Preces ad Missam.

Exaudi, Domine, supplicum preces, et devoto tibi pectore famulantes perpetua defensione custodi, ut nullis perturbationibus impediti, liberam servitutem tuis semper exhibeamus officiis. Per.

Leon. 412.
Miss.
Franc. 665.

Secreta.

Tuis Domine quaesumus operare mysteriis, ut haec tibi munera dignis mentibus offeramus. Per.

VD. Qui[1] rationabilem creaturam ne[2] temporalibus dedita bonis ad praemia sempiterna non tendat[3] ea dispensatione dignaris erudire[4], ut nec castigatione[5] deficiat[6] nec prosperitatibus insolescat[6], sed[7] hoc potius fiat ejus gloriosa devotio, quo[8] nullis adversitatibus obruta superetur[9]. Per quem maiestatem tuam. γ

R.S.(*alibi.*)
Gerb. 33.
Pam. 554.
Men. 33.
Leon. 412.

Infra actionem.

Hanc igitur oblationem, quam tibi offerimus pro famulis ✶tuis, quos ad presbyterii, vel diaconatus, gradus promovere dignatus es, quaesumus, Domine, placatus suscipias: et

Cf. Miss.
Franc. 673.

quod eis divino munere contulisti, in eis propitius tua dona
custodi. Per Christum Dominum nostrum. Quam.

Postcommun.

S. (alibi.) Hos quos reficis Domine [10] sacramentis attolle benignus
Gerb. 53. auxiliis, et tuae redemptionis effectum et mysteriis capia-
xxvi infra. mus et moribus. Per.

Ad Plebem.

R. S. Da quaesumus Domine populis Christia·nis et quod [11] 518
(Fer. iv.)
Gerb. 40. profitentur agnoscere, et caeleste munus diligere quod
Pam. 221. frequentant. Per. γ
xviii supra.

[1] R. S. Gerb. Pam. Men. give this Preface for Sexagesima: Leon. has it
among the forms for the *Ieiunium Mensis Septimi*. [2] *nec* V. R. (S¹†);
Leon. as text.   [3] *contendat* (for *non tendat*) V. R. S.; Leon. as text.
[4] *erudi* V. R, S¹; Leon. as text.   [5] *et nec castigationem* V.   [6] *deficiant
... insolescant* V.   [7] *sunt* V.   [8] *quod* Leon.   [9] *superatur* S⁸ Gerb.
[10] *Hos Domine quos reficis* S. Gerb., and V. in xxvi *infra*.   [11] *quos* V.; R.
S. Gerb. Pam. as text.

XXV.

Secunda Dominica in Quadragesima.

Praesta nobis, omnipotens Deus, ut quia vitiis subiacet
nostra mortalitas, tua nos et medicina purificet, et potentia
tueatur. Per Dominum.

R. S. Praesta nobis, misericors Deus, ut placationem tuam
Gerb. 43.
III.x infra. promptis mentibus exoremus, et peccatorum veniam con-
sequentes, a noxiis [1] liberemur incursibus. Per.

Secreta.

R. S. Ecclesiae tuae, Domine, munera placatus assume, quae
Gerb. 43.
Pam. 225. et misericors offerenda tribuisti, et in [2] nostrae salutis
Men. 43.
Leon. 478. potenter efficis transire mysterium. Per.
II. lxxxv
infra.

Postcommun.

R. S. Refecti, Domine, pane caelesti, ad vitam, quaesumus,
Gerb. 43.
Pam. 225. nutriamur aeternam. Per. γ
Men. 43.

Ad Populum.

R. S. Familiam tuam, quaesumus, Domine, propitiatus illustra,
Gerb. 43.
Pam. 225. ut beneplacitis inhaerendo, cuncta quae bona sunt mereatur
Men. 43. accipere. Per. γ

Feria ii Hebdom. Secunda.

Tuis, quaesumus, Domine, adesto supplicibus, et inter mundanae pravitatis insidias, fragilitatem nostram sempiterna pietate prosequere. Per Dominum.   R. S. Gerb. 44. Pam. 226. Men. 44. III. xiv *infra.*

Ecclesiam tuam, Domine, perpetua miseratione prosequere, ut inter saeculi turbines[3] constituta et praesenti iocunditate respiret et aeternae beatitudinis [dona][4] percipiat. Per. γ   R. S. (*Fer. v.*) Gerb. 47 [46]. Pam. 228. Leon. 359.

Secreta.

Concede nobis haec, quaesumus, Domine, frequentare mysteria, quia quoties huius hostiae celebratio commemoratur, opus nostrae redemptionis exercetur[5]. Per. γ   R.S.(*alibi.*) Gerb. 155. Pam. 408. III. v *infra.*

519
Postcommun.

Percepta[6], Domine, sancta nos adiuvent, et suis repleant institutis. Per.   R. S. Gerb. 45.

Ad Populum.

Populum tuum, Domine, quaesumus, ad te toto corde converte, quia quos defendis etiam delinquentes maiore pietate tueris sincera mente devotos. Per.   R. S. Gerb. 45. xxxvii *infra.* Pam. 247.

Feria iii Hebdom. Secunda.

Deus, qui ob[7] animarum medelam ieiunii devotione castigare[8] corpora praecepisti, concede ut corda nostra ita pietatis tuae valeant exercere mandata, quatenus ab omnibus possimus semper[9] abstinere peccatis. Per. Sacr.   R. S. Gerb. 45. see Men. 44. Miss. Goth. 570. Gall. 817.

Imploramus, Domine, clementiam tuam, ut haec divina ieiuniorum[10] subsidia a vitiis expiatos ad festa ventura nos praeparent. Per. γ   R.S.(*alibi.*) Gerb. 205. Pam. 226.

Secreta.

Praesentibus sacrificiis, Domine, ieiunia nostra santifica, ut quod observantia nostra profitetur extrinsecus, interius operetur. Per. γ   R.S.(*alibi.*) Gerb. 42. Pam. 224. Men. 42.

Postcommun.

Delicias, Domine, mirabiles mensae caelestis ambimus, quibus ieiunando copiosius saginamur. Per.   R. S. Gerb. 45.

Ad Populum.

Da, quaesumus, Domine, fidelibus tuis et sine cessatione capere paschalia sacramenta, et desideranter expectare ventura, ut[11] mysteriis quibus renati sunt, permanentes, ad novam vitam his operibus perducantur. Per.   R. S. Gerb. 45. xxxvii *infra.*

Feria iv Hebdom. Secunda.

R. S.
Gerb. 46.
Pam. 227.

Deus, qui per Verbum tuum humani generis reconciliationem mirabiliter operaris, praesta, quaesumus, ut sancto ieiunio et tibi toto simus corde subiecti, et in tua nos efficiamur [12] prece [13] concordes. Per Dominum.

R. S.
Gerb. 46.
Pam. 227.
Men. 45.

*Praesta nobis, Domine, quaesumus, auxilium gratiae 520 tuae, ut ieiuniis et orationibus convenienter intenti, liberemur ab hostibus mentis et corporis. Per. y

Secreta.

Gerb. 47.
Pam. 227.

Praesente sacrificio nomini tuo nos, Domine, ieiunia dicata sanctificent; et [14] quod observantia nostra profitetur extrinsecus, interius operetur effectus [15]. Per. y

Postcommun.

R. S.
Gerb. 46.
Pam. 228.
Men. 45.

Gratia tua nos, quaesumus, Domine, non relinquat, quae et sacrae nos deditos faciat servituti, et tuam [16] nobis opem semper acquirat. Per. y

Ad Populum.

R. S.
(*Fer. v.*)
Gerb. 47.
Pam. 228.
Men. 45.
Leon. 413.

Adesto, Domine, famulis tuis, et opem tuam largire poscentibus, ut his qui te auctore et gubernatore gloriantur et grata [17] restaures et restaurata conserves. Per.

Feria vi Hebdom. Secunda.

R. S.
Gerb. 47.
Pam. 228.
Leon. 419.

Ad hostes nostros, Domine, superandos, praesta, quaesumus, ut auxilium tuum ieiuniis tibi placitis et bonis operibus impetremus. Per Dominum.

xviii *supra.*
xix *supra.*
xxviii *inf.*
Pam. 342.

Omnipotens sempiterne Deus, qui per continentiam salutarem et [18] corporibus mederis et mentibus, maiestatem tuam suppliciter exoramus ut pia ieiunantium precatione placatus et temporalia nobis subsidia praebeas et [18] aeterna. Per. y

Secreta.

R.S.(*alibi.*)
Gerb. 57.
Men. 54.

Efficiatur haec hostia, Domine, quaesumus, solemnibus grata ieiuniis, et ut [19] tibi fiat acceptior, purificatis mentibus immoletur [20]. Per.

Postcommun.

R. S.
Gerb. 47.
Pam. 247.
Men. 61.

Praebeant [21] nobis Domine quaesumus divinum [22] tua sancta fervorem, quo eorum pariter et actu delectemur et fructu. Per. y

Ad Populum.

Adesto, Domine, propitius plebi tuae, et temporali consolatione non deseras quam vis ad aeterna contendere. Per.

521 *Feria vii Hebdom. Secunda.*

Subveni, Domine, servis tuis pro sua iugiter iniquitate gementibus, mentesque nostras terrenis affectibus praegravatas medicinalibus tribue exonerare [23] ieiuniis, et corporis afflictione corrobora [24]. Per Dominum.

R. S.
Gerb. 48.
Pam. 229.
Cf. Men. 47.

Deus, qui profundo consilio, prospiciendo mortalibus, sancta instituisti ieiunia, quibus corda languentium salubriter curarentur, tu animam nostram corpusque castifica, corporis animaeque salvator, aeternae felicitatis benigne largitor. Per Dominum.

Miss.
Goth. 570.

Secreta.

Domine Deus noster, in cuius spiritalibus castris militat laudanda sobrietas, abstinentia fructuosa et casti pectoris opulenta frugalitas, ieiunantium vota clementer assume, et fidelibus postulatis consueta pietate succurre. Per.

Postcommun.

Sacrae nobis, quaesumus, Domine, mensae libatio et piae conversationis augmentum et tuae propitiationis [25] continuum praestet auxilium. Per Dominum nostrum.

R.S.(*alibi.*)
Gerb. 32.
xiii *supra.*

Ad Populum.

Implorantes, Domine, misericordiam fideles populos propitius intuere: qui [26] praeter te alium non noverunt, tuis semper beneficiis glorientur. Per.

R. S.
Gerb. 48.
Pam. 230.

---

[1] *noxios* V. [2] Pam. omits *in.* [3] *turbidinis* V. (S[1]?); *turbinis* R.; S[2] Gerb. Pam. Leon. as text. [4] V. R. omit *dona*, which is restored from S; Gerb. has *donum*; Pam. reads *aeternam beatitudinem percipiat*; Leon. *aeternae beatitudinis percipiat claritatem.* [5] *exercitum* V. [6] *Praecepta* V.; R. S. Gerb. as text. [7] *ad* Sacr. Gall. [8] *castigari* S[2] Gerb., and so in the Preface in Men.; V. R. S[1] Miss. Goth. as text. [9] *semper possimus* Sacr. Gall. [10] R. S. Gerb. (placing the prayer as an Advent Postcommunion) omit *ieiuniorum*; V. Pam. as text. [11] S[2] Gerb. insert *in*; V. S[1] as text; R. has *ut ministeriis.* [12] *efficiamus* V. [13] *pace* Gerb.; V. S. Pam. as text; R. has *praede.* [14] *ut* Gerb. Pam.; V. as text. [15] *effectum* Gerb. Pam.; V. as text. [16] Pam. omits *quae—tuam.*; V. R. S. Gerb. Men. as text. [17] *creata* Leon.; *congregata* S[2] Gerb. Pam. Men.; V. R. S[1] as text. [18] *et* omitted by V. here, is inserted from xviii *supra.* [19] *ut et* V. S[1]; R. S[2] Gerb. Men. as text. [20] *immolemur* V.; R. S. Gerb. Men. as text. [21] *Praeveniant* V. R. S.; Gerb. Pam. Men. as text. [22] *divina* V. S.; R. Gerb. Pam. Men. as text. [23] *exonerari* Gerb. Pam., and so in the Preface in Men.; V. R. S. as text. [24] *corroborari* Pam.; V. R. S. Gerb. as text. [25] *protectionis* V. in xiii *supra.* [26] *et qui* R. Pam.; *ut qui* S[2] Gerb.; V. S[1] as text.

XXVI.

Tertia Dominica.

Quae pro scrutiniis electorum celebratur [1].

R. Gerb. 248.
Da, quaesumus, Domine, electis nostris digne [2] atque sapienter ad confessionem tuae laudis accedere, ut dignitati pristinae quam originali transgressione perdiderant, per tuam gratiam reformentur. Per.

Secreta.

R. Gerb. 248.
Miseratio tua, Deus, ad haec percipienda · mysteria 522 famulos tuos quaesumus, et praeveniat [3] competenter, et devota conversatione perducat. Per.

Infra Canonem, ubi dicit [4]

R. Gerb. 248.
Memento, Domine, famulorum, famularumque tuarum, qui electos tuos suscepturi sunt ad sanctam gratiam baptismi tui: et omnium circumadstantium [5]. *Et taces. Et recitantur* [6] *nomina virorum et* [7] *mulierum, qui ipsos infantes suscepturi sunt. Et intras* Quorum tibi fides cognita.

Item infra actionem [8].

R. Gerb. 248.
Hanc igitur oblationem, Domine, ut propitius suscipias deprecamur: quam tibi offerimus pro famulis et famulabus tuis, quos ad [9] aeternam vitam et beatum gratiae tuae donum numerare [10], eligere atque vocare dignatus es. Per Christum [11].

R. Gerb. 248.
Et recitantur nomina electorum. Postquam recensita fuerint, dicis [12] Hos, Domine, fonte baptismate innovandos, Spiritus tui munere ad sacramentorum tuorum plenitudinem [13] poscimus praeparari. Per [14].

Postcommun.

R. Gerb. 248.
xlviii *infra*.
xlix *infra*.
Adesto, Domine, quaesumus, redemptionis effectibus, ut quos sacramentis aeternitatis instituis, eosdem protegas dignanter aptandos [15]. Per.

Ad Populum.

R. Gerb. 248.
Suppliciter, Domine, sacra familia munus tuae miserationis expectat; concede, quaesumus, ut quod te iubente desiderat, te largiente percipiat. Per.

Feria ii Hebdom. Tertia.

Conserva, Domine, familiam tuam bonis semper operibus eruditam, et sic praesentibus consolare subsidiis ut ad superna [16] perducas dona propitius. Per. R. S.
Gerb. 50.
Pam. 231.
Men. 48.

Da, quaesumus, omnipotens Deus, ut abstinentiae nostrae restaurationis exordiis competentem dignis praecurramus officiis. Per [17].

523 **Secreta.**

Haec nos beata mysteria, Deus, principia sua aptos efficiant recensere. [Per.]

Infra actionem, ut supra. Sequitur

Postcommun.

Quos ieiunia votiva castigant, tua, Domine, sacramenta purificent [18]; ut, terrenis affectibus mitigatis, facilius caelestia capiamus. Per. R. S.
Gerb. 50,
134.

Ad Populum.

Gratias tibi referat, Domine, corde subiecto tua semper ecclesia, et consequenter obtineat, ut observationes antiquas iugiter recensendo proficiat in futurum. Per. R. S.
Gerb. 50.
lxxxiii
infra.

Feria iii Hebdom. tertia.

Prosequere nos omnipotens Deus; et quos ab escis carnalibus praecipis abstinere a noxiis quoque vitiis cessare concede. Per [19]. R. S.
Gerb. 50.
Cf. xxvii
infra.

Da, quaesumus, Domine, rex aeterne cunctorum, ut sacro nos purificatos ieiunio sinceris quoque [20] mentibus ad tua sancta ventura facias pervenire. Per. S. (*Fer. v.*)
Gerb. 51.
Pam. 232.

Secreta.

Ut accepta sint, Domine, nostra ieiunia, praesta nos, quaesumus, huius munere sacramenti purificatum tibi pectus offerre. Per. γ Pam. 304.

Postcommun.

Sacramenti tui, Domine, veneranda perceptio et mystico nos mundet effectu et perpetua virtute defendat. Per. S. (*Fer. v.*)
Gerb. 52.
Pam. 233.
Men. 50.

Ad Populum.

Concede, misericors Deus, ut devotus tibi populus [21] semper existat, et de tua clementia quod ei prosit indesinenter obtineat. Per. lvi *infra.* R. S.
Gerb. 51.
Pam. 231.
Men. 49.

Feria iv Hebdom. tertia.

R. S.
Gerb. 51.
Pam. 232.

Deus, qui nos formam humilitatis ieiunando et orando Unigeniti tui Domini nostri imitatione docuisti, concede, quaesumus, ut quod ille iugi ieiuniorum continuatione complevit, nos quoque [22] per partes dierum facias adimplere. Per.

xix supra.

Da nobis, Domine, quaesumus, observantiam [23] legitima devotione perfectam, ut [24] refrenatione carnalis alimoniae sancta tibi conversatione placeamus. Per.

Secreta.

S. (Fer. v.)
Gerb. 52.
Pam. 232.
Men. 49.

Deus, de cuius gratiae rore descendit, ut ad mysteria tua purgatis sensibus accedamus, praesta, quaesumus, ut in eorum traditione solemniter honoranda competens [25] deferamus obsequium. Per.

Postcommun.

R.S.(alibi.)
Gerb. 40.

Percipientes, Domine, gloriosa mysteria [26], referimus gratias, quod in terris positos iam caelestium praestas esse participes. Per.

Ad Populum.

S.
Gerb. 51.
Pam. 233.
Leon. 408.

Defende Domine familiam tuam et toto tibi corde prostratam ab hostium tuere [27] formidine : nec bona tua difficulter inveniant pro quibus [28] et sancti tui et angelicae tibi [29] supplicant potestates. Per.

Feria vi Hebdom. tertia.

R.S.(alibi.)
Gerb. 179.
Pam. 342.
Men. 132.
xxviii inf.

Praesta, quaesumus, Domine, ut observationes sacras annua devotione recolentes, et corpore tibi placeamus et mente. Per. γ

R.S.(alibi.)
Gerb. 32.
Pam. 212.
Men. 32.
xiii supra.

Concede, quaesumus, Domine [30], fragilitati nostrae sufficientiam competentem ; ut suae reparationis effectum [31] et pia conversatione recenseat, et cum exultatione suscipiat. Per.

Secreta.

R.S.(alibi.)
Gerb. 47, 179.
Pam. 342.
Men. 45.
Leon. 414.

Accepta tibi sint, Domine, quaesumus, nostri dona ieiunii, quae et [32] expiando nos tuae gratiae [33] dignos efficiant, et ad sempiterna promissa perducant. Per. γ

Postcommun.

S. (Sabb.)
Gerb. 53.
xxiv supra.

Hos, Domine, quos reficis [34] sacramentis, attolle benignus auxiliis, ut [35] tuae redemptionis effectum et mysteriis capiamus et moribus. Per.

Ad Populum.

Super populum[36] tuum, Domine, quaesumus, benedictio copiosa descendat, indulgentia veniat[37], consolatio tribuatur, fides sancta succrescat, redemptio sempiterna firmetur. Per. γ

R.S.(*alibi.*)
Gerb. 37.
Pam. 218.
Men. 38.
Leon. 482.
xviii *supra.*

Feria vii Hebdom. tertia.

Praesta, quaesumus, omnipotens Deus, ut dignitas conditionis humanae, per immoderantiam sauciata, medicinalis parsimoniae studio reformetur. Per Dominum. γ

S.
Gerb. 53.
Pam. 243.
Men. 51.
Leon. 317.

Auge fidem tuam, Domine, quaesumus, miseratus[38] in nobis, quia pietatis tuae subsidia non negabis quibus integre[39] contuleris firmitatem. Per.

S.
Gerb. 53.
Pam. 235.
Leon. 367.

Secreta.

Domine Deus noster, qui in his potius creaturis quas ad fragilitatis nostrae subsidium[40] condidisti, tuo quoque[41] nomini munera iussisti dicanda constitui, tribue, quaesumus, ut et vitae nobis praesentis auxilium et aeternitatis efficiant sacramentum. Per. γ

R.S.(*alibi.*)
Gerb. 53.
135.
Pam. 243.
Men. 107.
Leon. 415.
lxxxiii *infra.* Leofr. 3.

Postcommun.

Quod ore sumpsimus, Domine[42], mente capiamus, et de munere temporali fiat nobis remedium sempiternum. Per. γ

Pam. 243.
Leon. 366.

Ad Populum.

Esto, quaesumus, Domine, propitius plebi tuae, ut[43] quae tibi non placent respuentes, tuorum potius repleantur delectationibus mandatorum. Per Dominum. γ

S.
Gerb. 53.
Pam. 243.

---

[1] S. marks the Saturday, R. the Friday of the second week as the time of the first 'scrutiny.' The only other note of the time in V. is in sect. xxix *infra*, from which it would seem that the Monday of the third week is the time contemplated in V., as in Mabillon's *Ordo Romanus* vii. The Tuesday in the third week is mentioned (perhaps by a slip) in the Codex Gellonensis, of which the corresponding portion is to be found in Martène lib. I. cap. i. From this last source some readings are given in the following notes, where it is cited as Gell. The clauses for insertion in the Canon are, however, the only portions of this *Missa* which Martène gives at length. The *Missa* appears in R. (from which Gerbert's text of it is taken) as the first of the *Missae pro Scrutiniis* which R. gives as part of the *Ordo Baptisterii*. These *Missae* are not contained in S.
[2] *dignis* V.; R. as text. [3] *proveniat* R. [4] *Infra* R. [5] R. Gell. join the words *Et omnium circumadstantium* with *quorum tibi fides*, &c., placing both after the rubric which separates them in V. [6] *recita* Gerb.; V. R. Gell. as text. [7] *ac* R. Gell.; V. as text. [8] R. omits this heading. [9] R. omits *ad*. [10] *gratiae tuae dinumerare* V.; *gratiae tuae donum eligere* R.; Gell. as text. [11] After *Per Christum*, and before the rubric following, R. inserts *Quam oblationem*: but see note 14. [12] *dices* R.; *dicit* Gell.
[13] *plenitudine* V.; R. Gell. as text. [14] Both R. and Gell. have at this point *Per Christum. Diesque nostros.* [15] *obtados* R.; Gerb. reads *optatos.*

[16] *aeterna* S² Gerb.; V. R. S¹ Pam. Men. as text. [17] This Collect is given as it appears in V., but it is evidently corrupt: it would become intelligible if *abstinentiam* were read for *abstinentiae*. [18] *vivificent* V. in lxxxiii *infra*, R. S. Gerb.; V. here as text. [19] R. S. Gerb. follow the form of this Collect given in xxvii *infra* (omitting *quaesumus* and reading *abstinere* for *temperare*). [20] S² Gerb. omit *quoque*; V. S¹ Pam. as text. [21] S² Gerb. insert *tuus*; V. S¹ Pam. Men. as text. [22] *saltem* (for *quoque*) S² Gerb.; V. S¹ Pam. as text. [23] *Da nobis observantiam Domine* V. in xix *supra*. [24] V. in xix *supra* inserts *cum*. [25] S² Gerb. insert *tibi*; V. S¹ Pam. Men. as text. [26] S² Gerb. insert *tibi*; V. R. S¹ as text. [27] *ut toto tibi corde prostrata et ab hostium tuere* V.; S. Gerb. Leon. Pam. as text. [28] *inveniat pro qua* Leon. (ed. Mur.); *inveniat pro quibus* Pam.; V. S. Gerb. Leon. (ed. Ball.) as text. [29] Pam. omits *tibi*; V. has *angelica et tibi*; S. Gerb. Leon. as text. [30] *Concede, quaesumus, omnipotens Deus* V. in xiii *supra*; so R. S. Gerb. Pam. Men. [31] See note 3 on xiii *supra*. [32] V. omits *et*; R. S. Gerb. Pam. Men. Leon. as text. [33] *tua gratia* Leon. [34] *Hos quos reficis Domine* V. in xxiv *supra*. [35] *et* S. Gerb.; V. as text. [36] *In populum* Men. [37] See note 6 on xviii *supra*. [38] *operatus* Pam.; V. S. Gerb. Leon. as text. [39] *integre*, the reading of V. (S¹?) Pam. is perhaps a corruption of *in de credendi*, the reading of Leon.; S² Gerb. read *integram illius contuleris*. [40] *praesidium* V. in lxxxiii *infra*, R. S. (*alibi*) Gerb. (135) Men. Leon. Leofr.; V. here, S. Gerb. (53) Pam. as text. [41] *tuoque* V. here; R. S. Gerb. Pam. Leon. V. in lxxxiii *infra* as text. [42] Leon. inserts *quaesumus*. [43] *et* S¹; V. S² Gerb. Pam. as text.

XXVII.

Quarta Dominica. Pro scrutinio II [1].

R.
Gerb. 248.
Cf. xxviii
infra.
Cf.Pam.241.

Omnipoteus sempiterne Deus, ecclesiam tuam spirituali fecunditate [2] mul·tiplica, ut qui sunt generatione terreni, 526 fiant regeneratione caelestes. Per.

[Secreta.]

R.
Gerb. 248.

Remedii sempiterni munera, Domine, laetantes offerimus, suppliciter exorantes ut eadem nos et digne [3] venerari et pro salvandis congruenter exhibere [4] perficias. Per.

Infra Canonem [5] *ut supra. Sequitur*

Postcommun.

R.
S. (*sup. pop.*)
Gerb. 54,
248.
Pam. 236.

Tu semper, quaesumus, Domine, tuam attolle benignus familiam; tu dispone correctam; tu propitius tuere [6] subiectam; tu guberna perpetua bonitate [7] salvandam. Per.

Ad Populum.

R.
Gerb. 248.
III.li *infra*

Tu famulis tuis, quaesumus, Domine, bonos mores [8] placatus institue, tu in eis quod tibi placitum sit dignanter infunde, ut et digni sint, et tua valeant beneficia promereri. Per.

Feria ii Hebdom. quarta.

R. S.
(*Fer. iii.*)
Gerb. 55.
Pam. 236.

Sacrae nobis, quaesumus, Domine, observationis ieiunia, et piae conversationis augmentum, et tuae propitiationis continuum praestent auxilium. Per. γ.

Proficiat, quaesumus, Domine, plebs tibi dicata [9] piae devotionis affectu [9]; ut sacris actionibus erudita, quanto maiestati tuae fit gratior, tanto donis potioribus augeatur. Per. γ.

S.
Gerb. 55.
Pam. 244.
Men. 52.
lxxxiii
infra.

Secreta.

Cunctis nos, quaesumus [10], Domine, reatibus et periculis propitiatus absolve, quos tantis mysteriis [11] tribuis esse consortes. Per Dominum. γ.

S.
Gerb. 55.
Pam. 244.

Postcommun.

Divini satiati muneris largitate [12], quaesumus, Domine Deus noster, ut in huius semper participatione vivamus. Per. γ.

S.
Gerb. 55.
Pam. 245.
Leon. 449.

Ad Populum.

Tueatur, quaesumus, Domine, dextera tua populum deprecantem, et purificatum dignanter erudiat, ut consolatione praesenti ad futura bona proficiat. Per. γ.

S.
Gerb. 55.
Pam. 245.
Cf. Leon. 415.

Feria iii Hebdom. quarta.

Da, nostrae summe conditionis reparator [13], ut [14] semper declinemus a malis, et omne quod bonum est prompta voluntate sectemur. Per Dominum.

Pam. 237.

Exercitatio [15] veneranda, Domine, ieiunii salutaris populi tui corda disponat [15], ut et dignis mentibus suscipiat paschale mysterium, et continuatae devotionis sumat augmentum. Per.

R. S.
Gerb. 55.

Secreta.

Purifica nos, misericors Deus, ut ecclesiae tuae preces, quae tibi gratae sunt, pia munera deferentes [16], fiant expiatis mentibus gratiores. Per. γ.

R. S.
Gerb. 55.
Pam. 238.
Men. 53. Leon. 429.

Postcommun.

Caelestia dona capientibus, quaesumus, Domine, non ad iudicium pervenire [17] patiaris quod fidelibus tuis ad remedium providisti. Per. γ.

R. S.
Gerb. 56.
Pam. 238.
Men. 53. Leon. 370.

Ad Populum.

Populi tui Deus institutor et rector, peccata quibus impugnatur [18] expelle, ut semper [19] tibi placitus [20] et tuo munimine sit securus. Per. γ.

R. S.
(*Fer. v.*)
Gerb. 57.
Pam. 238. Leon. 345.

Feria iv Hebdom. quarta.

R. S.
Gerb. 56.
Pam. 237.
Men. 53.

Omnipotens sempiterne Deus, qui et iustis praemia meritorum et peccatoribus per ieiunium erroris sui veniam praebes, miserere supplicibus, parce peccantibus, ut reatus nostri confessio indulgentiam valeat percipere delictorum. Per Dominum nostrum.

Concede, misericors Deus, ut sicut nos tribuis solemne tibi deferre ieiunium, sic nobis indulgentiae tuae praebeas[21] benignus auxilium. Per.

Secreta.

R.S.(alibi.)
Gerb. 38.
Pam. 219.
Men. 39.
xviii supra.

Accepta tibi sit, Domine, nostrae devotionis oblatio, quae et ieiunium nostrum, te operante[22], sanctificet, et indulgentiam [nobis][23] tuae consolationis obtineat. Per.

·Postcommun.

Leon. 369.

Sacramentorum benedictione satiati, quaesumus, Domine, ut per haec semper mundemur[24] a vitiis[25]. Per.

Ad Populum.

Pam. 238.
III. lxiv
infra.

Da plebi tuae, Domine, piae semper devotionis affectum; ut quae prava sunt respuens, sancta conversatione firmetur, et a peccatis libera nullis adversitatibus atteratur. Per.

Feria vi Hebdom. quarta.

R. S.
(Fer. v.)
Gerb. 57.

Praesta, quaesumus, Domine, ut salutaribus ieiuniis eruditi, a noxiis etiam vitiis abstinentes, propitiationem tuam facilius impetremus. Per.

R.S.(alibi.)
Gerb. 50.
Cf. xxvi
supra.

Prosequere, quaesumus[26], omnipotens Deus, ieiuniorum sacra mysteria, et quos ab escis carnalibus praecipis temperare[27], a noxiis quoque vitiis cessare concede. Per.

Secreta.

R. S.
Gerb. 57.
Pam. 247.

Haec sacrificia nos, omnipotens Deus, potenti virtute mundatos ad suum faciant puriores venire principium. Per. γ.

Postcommun.

R. S.
(Fer. v.)
Gerb. 57.
Leon. 441. xxxvii infra.

Sancta tua nos, Domine, quaesumus, et vivificando[28] renovent, et renovando vivificent. Per.

Ad Populum.

R. S.
Gerb. 58.
Pam. 239.
Leon. 371.
III.lix infra.

Adesto, Domine, populis qui sacra mysteria[29] contigerunt, ut nullis periculis affligantur qui te protectore confidunt. Per Dominum.

Feria vii Hebdom. quarta.

Deus, omnium misericordiarum ac totius bonitatis auctor, qui peccatorum remedia ieiuniis, orationibus, et eleemosynis demonstrasti, respice propitius in hanc humilitatis nostrae confessionem, ut qui inclinamur conscientia [30] nostra tua semper misericordia erigamur. Per.

R. S.
Gerb. 58.

Tua nos, Domine, quaesumus, gratia et sanctis exerceat veneranda ieiuniis, et [31] caelestibus mysteriis efficiat aptiores. Per.

R. S.
Gerb. 58.

Secreta.

529

Offerimus tibi, Domine, munera quae dedisti, ut et creationis tuae circa mortalitatem nostram testificentur auxilium, et remedium [32] immortalitatis operentur. Per. γ.

R.S.(alibi.)
Gerb. 232.
Pam. 417.
Leon. 370.

Postcommun.

Percepta nobis, Domine, praebeant tua sacramenta subsidium, ut et [33] tibi grata sint nostra ieiunia, et nobis proficiant ad medelam. Per Dominum γ.

R.S.(alibi.)
Gerb. 35.
Pam. 215.

Ad Populum.

Plebem tuam, Domine, quaesumus [34], interius exteriusque restaura, ut quam corporeis non vis delectationibus impediri, spirituali facias vigere proposito, et sic rebus foveas transitoriis [35] ut tribuas potius inhaerere perpetuis. Per.

R. S.
Gerb. 58.
Pam. 239.
Leon. 435.

---

[1] The *Missa* for this Sunday is the second of the series '*pro scrutiniis*' as given by R.   [2] *iocunditate* V. here: R. as text, and so V. in xxviii *infra*.   [3] *digni* V. (corr. by Tommasi); R. as text.   [4] *exhiberi* R.; V. as text.   [5] *Infract.* R.   [6] Gerb. reads *intuere* (wrongly); R. has *tuaere*.   [7] *benignitate* R. S. Pam.; V. as text.   [8] *bonis moris* V. here; R. has *bonus mores*; V. in III. li as text.   [9] *plebi tibi decata ... affectus* V.; S. Gerb. Pam. Men. V. in lxxxiii *infra* as text.   [10] S. Gerb. omit *quaesumus*; Pam. has *quaesumus Domine*; V. as text.   [11] *tanti mysterii* Pam.; V. S. Gerb. as text.   [12] *muneris largitate satiati* Leon.   [13] Pam. inserts *omnipotens Deus*.   [14] Pam. inserts *et*.   [15] *Exorcitio ... dispone* R.; *Exercitatio ... dispone* S.; *Exercitatione ... dispone* Gerb.; V. as text.   [16] *deferentes* so R. S. Gerb. Pam. Leon.; V. Men. have *deferentis*.   [17] *provenire* Leon.; V. R. S. Gerb. Pam. Men. as text.   [18] *impugnantur* V.; R. S. Gerb. Pam. Leon. as text.   [19] Leon. inserts *et*.   [20] *placatus* V. R² S¹; R¹ S² Gerb. Pam. Leon. as text.   [21] *praebe* V.   [22] *cooperante* Pam.   [23] V. here omits *nobis*, which is restored from xviii *supra*, R. S. Gerb. Pam. Men.   [24] *emundemur* Leon.   [25] Leon. adds *et periculis caveamus*.   [26] The parallel collect in xxvi *supra* has a different beginning; R. S. Gerb. omit *quaesumus*; V. here as text.   [27] *abstinere* R. S. Gerb. V. in xxvi *supra*; V. here as text.   [28] V. in xxxvii *infra* inserts *semper*; V. here, R. S. Gerb. Leon. as text.   [29] *donaria* Leon.; V. R. S. Gerb. Pam. as text.   [30] *constantia* S¹; *inconstantia* S² Gerb.; V. R. as text.   [31] V. omits *et*; R. S. Gerb. as text.   [32] R. S. Gerb. Pam. Leon. insert *nobis*; V. as text.   [33] Pam. omits *et*.   [34] Pam. omits *quaesumus*.   [35] *transituriis* V.; *transituris* S. Leon.; R. Gerb. Pam. as text.

XXVIII.

Quinta Dominica. Quae pro scrutinio celebratur[1].

R.
Gerb. 249.
 Concede, Domine, electis nostris, ut sanctis edocti mysteriis et renoventur fonte baptismatis, et inter ecclesiae tuae membra numerentur. Per.

Secreta.

R.
Gerb. 249.
 Exaudi nos, omnipotens Deus, et famulos tuos, quos fidei Christiane primitiis imbuisti, huius sacrificii tribuas operatione mundari. Per.

Infra Canonem[2], *ubi supra. Sequitur*

Postcommun.

R.
Gerb. 249.
 Concurrat, Domine, quaesumus[3], populus tuus, et toto tibi corde subiectus obtineat, ut ab omni perturbatione securus, et salvationis suae gaudia promptus exerceat, et pro regenerandis[4] benignus exoret. Per.

Ad Populum.

R.
Gerb. 249.
 Deus, qui quum salutem[5] hominum semper operaris, nunc tamen populum tuum gratia abundantiore multiplicas; respice propitius ad electionem tuam, ut paternae protectionis auxilio et regenerandos munias et renatos. Per.

Feria ii Hebdom. quinta. 530

Pam. 241.
Cf. xxvii supra.
Cf. Gerb. 248.
 Deus, qui ad imaginem tuam conditis[6] ideo das temporalia ut largiaris aeterna, ecclesiam tuam spiritali fecunditate multiplica, ut qui sunt generatione terreni fiant regeneratione caelestes. Per Dominum.

R.S.(*alibi.*)
Gerb. 47.
 Adiuva nos Deus salutaris noster, et in sacrificio ieiuniorum nostras mentes purifica, ut[7] ad beneficia recolenda, quibus nos instaurare dignatus es, tribuas[7] venire gaudentes[8]. Per.

Secreta.

Domin. *supra.*
 Exaudi nos, omnipotens Deus, et famulos tuos, quos fidei Christianae primitiis imbuisti, huius sacrificii tribuas operatione mundari. Per.

Postcommun.

 Sanctificent nos, Domine, sumpta mysteria et paschalis observantiae sufficientem nobis tribuant facultatem. Per.

Ad Populum.

Benedictio, Domine, quaesumus[9], in tuos fideles copiosa descendat, et quam subiectis cordibus expetunt, largiter consequantur. Per.

R. S.
Gerb. 60.
Men. 57.

Feria iii Hebdom. quinta.

Praesta, quaesumus, Domine[10], ut observationes sacras annua devotione recolentes et corpore tibi placeamus et mente. Per. γ.

R.S.(alibi.)
Gerb. 179.
Pam. 236.
Men. 132.
xxvi supra.

Fiat, quaesumus, Domine[11], per gratiam tuam fructuosus nostrae devotionis affectus, quia tunc nobis proderunt suscepta ieiunia si tuae sint placita pietati. Per. γ.

cf. lxxxiii infra.
Men. 55.
Pam. 239.

Secreta.

Concede nobis, Domine, quaesumus, ut celebraturi sancta mysteria[12], non solum abstinentiam[13] corporalem, sed quod est potius, habeamus mentium puritatem. Per.

R. S.
(Fer. v.)
Gerb. 62.
Men. 58.
Cf. Leon. 380.

Postcommun.

Vegetet nos, Domine, semper et innovet tuae mensae libatio, quae fragilitatem nostram[14] gubernet et protegat et in portum perpetuae salutis inducat. Per. Men. 59.

R. S.
(Fer. v.)
Gerb. 62.
Leon. 415.

Ad Populum.

Libera, Domine, quaesumus[15], a peccatis et hostibus tibi populum supplicantem, ut in[16] sancta conversatione viventes nullis afficiantur adversis. Per Dominum. γ. Men. 58.

R. S.
Gerb. 61.
Pam. 377.
Leon. 462.

Feria iv Hebdom. quinta.

Ieiunia, quaesumus, Domine, quae sacris exequimur institutis, et nos a reatibus nostris semper expediant, et tuam nobis iustitiam faciant esse placatam. Per.

R. S.
Gerb. 61.

Praesta, quaesumus, omnipotens Deus, ut quos ieiunia votiva[17] castigant, ipsa quoque devotio sancta laetificet, ut terrenis affectibus mitigatis, facilius caelestia capiamus. Per. γ.

R.S.(alibi.)
Gerb. 56.
Pam. 238.
Men. 53.

Secreta.

Praesta, [quaesumus[18],] omnipotens Deus, ut ieiuniorum placatus sacrificiis, remissionis tuae nos venia prosequaris. Per.

R.S.(Sabb.)
Gerb. 63.
Pam. 243.
Men. 60.

Postcommun.

Adesto, Domine, fidelibus tuis, et quos caelestibus reficis[19] sacramentis a terrenis conserva periculis. Per Dominum.

R.S.(Sabb.)
Gerb. 63.
Men. 60.
Leon. 412.

Ad Populum.

R.S.(*alibi.*)
Gerb. 239.
Leon. 364.
xxxix *inf.*
III. xvii *inf.*

Gregem tuum, Pastor bone, placatus intende, et oves, quas pretioso sanguine Filii tui [20] redemisti, diabolica non sinas incursione lacerari. Per.

Feria vi Hebdom. quinta.

R. S.
(*Fer. v.*)
Gerb. 62.

Tribue nobis, quaesumus, Domine, indulgentiam peccatorum, ut instituta paschalia tibi placitis sensibus operemur. Per.

R. S.
Gerb. 63.
Pam. 244.

Omnipotens sempiterne Deus, clementiam tuam suppliciter exoramus ut qui mala nostra semper praevenis miserendo · facias nos [21] tibi placitos et piis actionibus et ieiuniis salubribus expiando. Per.

Secreta.

R. S.
Gerb. 63.

Sanctifica nos, quaesumus, Domine, his muneribus offerendis, et paschalis observantiae sufficientem nobis tribue facultatem. Per.

Postcommun.

cii *infra.*

Da, quaesumus, Domine, ut tanti mysterii munus indultum non condemnatio sed sit medicina sumentibus. Per.

Ad Populum.

R. S.
Gerb. 63.

Protege, Domine, populum tuum et in sanctorum tuorum patrocinio confidentem perpetua defensione guberna. Per.

Feria vii Hebdom. quinta.

xviii *supra.*
xix *supra.*
xxv *supra.*
Pam. 342.

Omnipotens sempiterne Deus, qui per abstinentiam [22] salutarem et corporibus nostris mederis et mentibus, maiestatem tuam supplices exoramus, ut pia ieiunantium prece placatus et praesentia nobis subsidia praebeas et futura [23]. Per.

R. S.
(*Fer. iv.*)
Gerb. 61.
Pam. 242.
Cf. Leon. 411.

Sanctificata ieiunio [24] tuorum corda fidelium [25], Deus miserator [26], illustra; et quibus devotionis praestas [27] affectum, praebe supplicantibus pium benignus auditum. Per. y.

Secreta.

Pam. 248.
Men. 62.

Sacrificia [28], Domine, propensius ista restaurent quae medicinalibus sunt instituta ieiuniis. Per. y.

Postcommun.

Supplices te rogamus, Domine Deus noster, ut sicut nos Filii tui corporis et sanguinis sacrosancti pascis alimonio, ita nos et divinae naturae eius facias esse consortes. Per.

Ad Populum.

Visita, quaesumus, Domine, plebem [29] tuam, et corda sacris dicata mysteriis pietate tuere pervigili [30], ut remedia salutis aeternae, quae te miserante percipit [31], te protegente custodiat [32]. Per.

Pam. 245.
Leon. 411.

[1] This *Missa* is the third of the *Missae pro Scrutiniis* in R., and has there the title '*in auris apertionem*.' [2] *Infrac*. R. [3] *quaesumus Domine* R. [4] *generandis* R. [5] *consalute* R. [6] *conditos* V.; *qui homini ... condito* Pam.; the parallel collect in Gerb. and in xxvii *supra* has a different beginning. [7] *et ... tribue* Gerb.; *ut ... tribue* R.; V. S. as text. [8] *gaudenter* V.; R. S. Gerb. as text. [9] *quaesumus Domine* Men. [10] *quaesumus omnipotens Deus* R. S. Gerb. Pam. Men.; V. as text. [11] *Domine quaesumus* Pam. Men. [12] *Domine Deus noster, ut celebraturi sanctorum solemnia* Leon.; V. R. S. Gerb. Men. as text. [13] *observantiam* Leon.; V. R. S. Gerb. Men. as text. [14] Leon. inserts *et inter mundi tempestates*; V. R. S. Gerb. Men. as text. [15] *quaesumus Domine* Men. [16] V. omits *ut*; Men. omits *in*; S. Gerb. Pam. Leon. as text. [17] *votiva ieiunia* Pam. [18] V. omits *quaesumus*, which is restored from R. S. Gerb. Pam. Men. [19] *instituis* Leon. (which also inserts a clause after *sacramentis*, see ed. Ball.); V. R. S. Gerb. Men. as text. [20] R. S. Gerb. Leon. and V. in III. xvii *infra* omit *Filii tui*; V. (here and in xxxix *infra*) as text. [21] R. S. Gerb. omit *nos*; V. Pam. as text. [22] *continentiam* in xviii, xix *supra*. [23] *praebeas et aeterna* xviii *supra*; *tribuas aeterna* xix *supra*. [24] *Sanctifica hoc ieiunium* V.; *Sanctificato hoc ieiunio* R. S. Gerb. Pam. Men.; Leon. as text. [25] *filiorum* Leon. [26] *habitator* Leon. [27] *praestas devotionis* Leon. [28] Pam. Men. insert *nos, quaesumus*. [29] *familiam* Leon. [30] *pervigili tuere pietate* Leon. [31] *percepit* Pam.; *percipiunt* Leon.; V. as text. [32] *custodiant* Leon.

XXIX.

DENUNTIATIO [1] PRO SCRUTINIO,
quod tertia hebdomada in Quadragesima,
secunda feria [2] *initiatur* [3].

Scrutinii diem, dilectissimi fratres, quo electi nostri divinitus instruantur, imminere cognoscite. Ideoque [4] sollicita devotione succedente sequente *illa* [5] feria circa horam diei sextam [6] convenire dignemini; ut caeleste mysterium quo [7] diabolus cum sua pompa destruitur [8], et [9] ianua regni caelestis aperitur, inculpabili, Deo iuvante [10], ministerio peragere valeamus. Per [11] Dominum nostrum Iesum Christum, qui cum Patre et Spiritu sancto vivit et regnat Deus per omnia saecula saeculorum. Amen.

R. (Gerb. 249.) Gerb. ii. 1. Martène, lib. I. cap. i.

Ut autem venerint [12] *ad ecclesiam* [13], *scribuntur* [14] *nomina infantum* [15] *ab acolyto, et vocantur* [16] *in ecclesiam per nomina* [17], *sicut scripti sunt. Et statuuntur masculi in dexteram partem, feminae in sinistram* [18], *et dat orationem presbyter super eos* [19].

[footnotes at top:]

¹ This notification is given in R. as part of the *Ordo Baptisterii*. It has also been compared with the form given by Gerbert (ii. 1) from a Zürich MS. (saec. ix. circ.), and with that given by Martène (*de Ant. Eccl. Rit.* lib. I. cap. i), from Codex Gellonensis. The former of these is cited as Gerb., the latter as Gell. ² *tertia feria* Gell.; V. R. Gerb. as text (but see note 1 on xxvi *supra*). ³ *initiarum* V. (corr. by Tommasi from Cardinal Santori's MS.); *initiantur* Gell.; R. Gerb. as text. ⁴ *ibidemque* Gerb.; V. R. Gell. as text. ⁵ *quarta* Gerb.; V. R. Gell. as text. ⁶ *circa horam diei tertia* Gell.; *circa horam tertiam* Gerb.; V. R. as text. ⁷ *quod* Gell. ⁸ *destruetur* V.; *distruetur* R. (probably for *destruitur*, as both have *aperitur* immediately after); Gell. Gerb. as text. ⁹ Gerb. omits *et*. ¹⁰ *Deo iubente* R. Gell.; *Domino iuvante* Gerb.; *Deo iubante* V. ¹¹ V. only has this clause at length: Gerb. omits, the others abbreviate it. ¹² *Aut aut hora quinta venerint* R. ¹³ Gell. inserts *hora tertia*; Gerb. has *sicut diximus, quarta feria hora tertia*. ¹⁴ *scribantur* R. Gerb. ¹⁵ Gell. Gerb. insert *vel eorum qui ipsos* (*eos* Gerb.) *suscepturi sunt*. ¹⁶ Gell. Gerb. insert *ipsi infantes ab acolyto*. ¹⁷ *in ecclesia per ordine per nomina* Gell.; *in ecclesia per nomina vel ordine* Gerb. ¹⁸ Gell. Gerb. have *ita dicendo*; Ille puer, *et sic per singulos eorum*: (*per singulis* Gell.) *statuuntur masculi seorsum ad dexteram partem* (*ad dexteram seorsum partem* Gell.): Ille virgo *et sic per singulas* (*singula* Gell.) *statuuntur feminae seorsum ad sinistram partem*. ¹⁹ R. directs that the *Electi* are to be bidden by the Deacon to pray before they receive the Benediction. Gell. Gerb. make no mention of this prayer by the *Electi*, but direct that the Benediction should be given after each of them has been signed with the cross.

XXX

ORATIONES SUPER ELECTOS.

Ad catechumenum faciendum ¹.

R.
Gerb. 249.
Pam. 258.
A.

Omnipotens sempiterne Deus, Pater Domini nostri Iesu Christi, respicere dignare super hos famulos tuos, quos ad rudimenta fidei vocare dignatus es. Omnem caecitatem cordis ab eis expelle: disrumpe omnes laqueos Satanae, quibus fuerant colligati: aperi eis, Domine, ianuam pietatis tuae; et signum ² sapientiae tuae imbuti, omnium cupiditatum foetoribus ³ careant, et suavi odore ⁴ praeceptorum tuorum laeti tibi in ecclesia ⁵ deserviant; et proficiant de die in diem, ut idonei efficiantur accedere ad gratiam baptismi tui, percepta medicina ⁶. Per Dominum nostrum.

Pam. 259.

Preces nostras, quaesumus, Domine, clementer exaudi, et hos electos tuos crucis Dominicae, cuius impressione signamus ⁷, • virtute custodi, ut magnitudinis gloriae rudimenta 534 servantes, per custodiam mandatorum tuorum ad regenerationis pervenire gloriam mereantur. Per. γ.

Pam. 259.

Deus, qui humani generis ita es conditor, ut sis etiam reformator, propitiare populis adoptivis, et novo testamento sobolem novae prolis ascribe, tu filii promissionis quod non potuerunt ⁸ assequi per naturam gaudeant se recepisse per gratiam. Per Dominum nostrum. γ.

[1] R. adds to this title the words *Ex his tribus orationibus unam, qualem volueris, dices.* But only the first of the three is given. In Gerbert's text (ii. 2) and in Martène's text from the Codex Gellonensis, cited for the last section, only the first prayer is mentioned, and it is not given at length. Pam. gives all three: the first is contained in A. Both in A. and in Pam. the prayers are worded for a single catechumen, and the rubrics of Gerb. and Gell. perhaps imply the use of the first of them over each of the *Electi* separately. [2] *ut signo* A. Pam.; V. R. as text (ungrammatically). [3] *foetores* R.; V. A. Pam. as text. [4] *ad suavem odorem* R. Pam.; V. A. as text. [5] R. A. Pam. insert *tua*; V. as text. [6] A. omits *ut idonei ... medicina*, substituting *signatus promissae gratiae tuae*; V. has *perceptae medicinae*; R. *percepte medicine*; Pam. as text. [7] *signamur* V; *eum signamus* Pam. [8] *potuerint* V. (corrected by Tommasi from Pam.).

XXXI.

BENEDICTIO SALIS DANDI CATECHUMENIS [1].

Exorcizo te, creatura salis, in nomine Dei Patris omnipotentis, et in caritate Domini nostri Iesu Christi, et in virtute Spiritus sancti. Exorcizo te per Deum vivum et per Deum verum, qui te ad tutelam humani generis procreavit, et populo venienti ad credulitatem per servos suos consecrari [2] praecepit [3]. Proinde rogamus te, Domine Deus noster, ut haec creatura salis in nomine [4] Trinitatis efficiatur salutare sacramentum ad effugandum inimicum; quem [5] tu, Domine, sanctificando sanctifices, benedicendo benedicas, ut fiat omnibus accipientibus perfecta medicina, permanens in visceribus eorum, in nomine Domini nostri Iesu Christi qui venturus est iudicare vivos et mortuos et saeculum per ignem. γ

R. Gerb. 250. Cf. Pam. 259.

Et post hanc orationem ponis [6] *sal in ore infantis et dicis* [6]: Accipe *Ille* [7] sal sapientiae propitiatus in vitam aeternam.

[1] *dandum caticumin* V. [2] *consecrare* V.; R. Pam. as text. [3] Pam. has *praecepit, ut in nomine sanctae Trinitatis efficiare salutare sacramentum,* &c. [4] R. inserts *sanctae.* [5] *quod* R.; *quam sanctificando sanctifices* Pam. [6] *pones ... dicis* V.; R. has *expleta autem ista oratione accepit de ipso sale et ponit in ore infantium, dicendo.* In A. this rubric is appended to the prayer *Omnipotens sempiterne Deus* (see xxx *supra*). [7] *illi* V.

XXXII.

BENEDICTIO POST DATUM SALEM [1].

Deus patrum nostrorum, Deus universae conditor veritatis, te supplices exoramus, ut hunc famulum tuum respicere digneris propitius, ut hoc primum pabulum salis gustantem non·diutius esurire permittas, quo minus cibo

R. Gerb. 250. A. Pam. 260.

expleatur caelesti; quatenus sit semper, Domine, spiritu fervens, spe gaudens, tuo semper nomini serviens. Perduc eum ad novae regenerationis lavacrum, ut cum fidelibus tuis promissionum tuarum aeterna praemia consequi mereatur². Per Dominum γ.

¹ *datam sale* V.; *datum salis* A.; R. gives no title. ² *mereamur* A.

XXXIII.

ITEM EXORCISMI SUPER ELECTOS.

*Quos acolyti*¹ *imposita manu super eos dicere*² *debent.*

R.
Gerb. 250.
Pam. 260.
A.

Deus Abraham, Deus Isaac, Deus Iacob, Deus qui Moysi famulo tuo in monte Sinai apparuisti, et filios Israel de terra Aegypti eduxisti, deputans eis angelum pietatis tuae, qui custodiret eos die ac nocte, te quaesumus, Domine, ut mittere digneris sanctum angelum tuum, ut³ similiter custodiat et hos famulos tuos, et perducat eos ad gratiam baptismi tui. γ

Ergo, maledicte diabole, recognosce sententiam tuam, et da honorem Deo vivo et vero, et⁴ da honorem Iesu Christo Filio eius, et Spiritui sancto, et recede ab his famulis Dei. Quia istos sibi Deus et Dominus noster Iesus Christus ad suam sanctam gratiam et benedictionem fontemque baptismatis donum⁵ vocare dignatus est. Per hoc signum⁶ sanctae crucis, frontibus eorum quod⁷ nos damus, tu maledicte diabole nunquam audeas violare. γ

Item super feminas.

R.
Gerb. 251.
Pam. 261.
A.

Deus caeli, Deus terrae, Deus angelorum, Deus archangelorum⁸, Deus prophetarum, Deus martyrum⁹, Deus omnium bene viventium, Deus cui omnis lingua confitetur¹⁰ caelestium¹¹, terrestrium et infernorum, te invoco Domine, ut has famulas tuas perducere et custodire digneris¹² ad gratiam baptismi tui. γ

Ergo maledicte *ut supra.*

Item super masculos.

536

R.
Gerb. 251.
Pam. 261.

Audi maledicte Satanas adiuratus¹³ per nomen aeterni Dei et Salvatoris nostri Filii Dei; cum tua victus invidia tremens gemensque discede. Nihil sit tibi commune cum servis Dei, iam caelestia cogitantibus, renuntiaturis tibi ac saeculo tuo, et beatae immortalitati victuris[14]. Da igitur honorem advenienti Spiritui sancto qui ex[15] summa caeli arce[16] descendens, perturbatis fraudibus tuis, divino fonte purgata pectora[17], id est sanctificata, Deo templum et habitum[18] perficiat, ut[19] ab omnibus penitus noxiis[20] praeteritorum criminum liberati servi Dei gratias perenni Deo referant semper, et benedicant nomen eius sanctum in saecula saeculorum. Per Dominum nostrum Iesum Christum, qui venturus est iudicare vivos et mortuos et saeculum per ignem. γ

Item super feminas.

Deus Abraham, Deus Isaac, Deus Iacob, Deus qui tribus Israel[21] monuisti et Susannam de falso crimine liberasti, te supplex deprecor, Domine, ut liberes et has famulas tuas, et perducere eas[22] digneris ad gratiam baptismi tui. γ
Ergo maledicte, *ut supra.*

Item super masculos.

Exorcizo te, immunde spiritus[23], in nomine Patris, et Filii, et Spiritus sancti, ut exeas et recedas ab his famulis Dei. Ipse enim tibi imperat, maledicte, damnate, qui pedibus super mare ambulavit, et Petro mergenti dexteram porrexit. γ
Ergo maledicte, *sicut supra.*

Item super feminas.

Exorcizo te immunde spiritus, per Patrem et Filium et Spiritum sanctum ut exeas et recedas ab his famulabus Dei[24]. Ipse enim tibi imperat maledicte, damnate, qui caeco nato oculos aperuit, et quatriduanum Lazarum de monumento suscitavit. γ
Ergo maledicte, *ut supra.*

Sequitur oratio quam sacerdos dicere debet[25].

Aeternam ac iustissimam pietatem tuam deprecor, Domine sancte, Pater omnipotens, aeterne Deus luminis et veritatis, super hos famulos[26] et famulas tuas ut digneris eos illuminare lumine intelligentiae tuae. Munda eos et sanctifica. Da eis scientiam veram, ut digni efficiantur accedere ad gratiam baptismi tui. Teneant firmam spem, consilium rectum, doctrinam sanctam, ut apti sint ad percipiendam gratiam tuam[27]. Per. γ

¹ The first rubric of this section in R. cannot easily be read, the letters being now very faint. Gerbert apparently could not read it (see his note at p. 250). It runs *Tunc primum veniens acolitus facit crucem in frontibus singulorum ponens manu su* (sic) *super eos dans orāt excelsa voce his verbis*. Gerbert understands the later rubrics as directing that the exorcisms should be said by a Deacon: but these probably refer not to the exorcisms, but to proclamations between them, such as are found in the Codex Gellonensis (Mart. lib. I. cap i.) where the Deacon makes the proclamations, and a succession of Acolytes say the exorcisms. Pam. and A. give no indication as to either Acolyte or Deacon. The latter omits the second pair of exorcisms. The forms in Pam. are for a single catechumen. ² *dici* V. ³ R. omits *ut*. ⁴ R. A. Pam. omit *et*; V. as text. ⁵ *dono* R.; Pam. omits the word; V. A. as text (ungrammatically). ⁶ *Et hoc signum* Pam.; V. R. A. as text. ⁷ *quem* V.; *quod nos fronti eius damus* Pam.; R. A. as text. ⁸ A. omits *Deus archangelorum*. ⁹ A. Pam. insert *Deus virginum*. ¹⁰ R. Pam. insert *et omne genu flectitur*. ¹¹ R. inserts *et*. ¹² *super hanc famulam tuam ut perducere eam digneris* Pam.; R. A. insert *eas* after *perducere* (otherwise as text); V. as text. ¹³ *adiuratis* R. (Gerb. reads *adiuro te*). ¹⁴ *renuntiatoribus tibi a saeculo tuo et beatae immortalitatis victoris* V. *renuntiatori* (marg. *renuntiaturo*) *tibi ac saeculo tuo et beatae immortalitatis victori* Pam.; *renuntiaturus . . . a seculo . . . immortalitatis uicturis* R. ¹⁵ R. omits *ex*. ¹⁶ *arche* R.; *archae* V.; Pam. as text. ¹⁷ *discedens pro turbatis fraudibus tuis divino purgata pectora* R. ¹⁸ Tommasi substitutes *habitaculum*, perhaps rightly: but V. R. Pam. all have *habitum*. ¹⁹ *et* V. R. Pam.; *ut* is required for the sense. ²⁰ *noxis* Pam.; V. R. as text. ²¹ Pam. inserts *de Aegypti servitute liberasti per Moysen famulum tuum, et de custodia mandatorum tuorum in deserto*; V. R. as text. ²² R. omits *eas*. ²³ *spiritus immunde* A. ²⁴ V. omits *Dei*; R. A. Pam. as text. ²⁵ This prayer has in A. the title which Pam. gives (from one MS.) in the margin of his text : ' *Oratio super infantes in Quadragesima ad quatuor Evangelia*.' ²⁶ R. inserts *tuos*. ²⁷ *gratiam baptismi tui* Pam.

XXXIV.

See Gerb.
ii. 2.

Incipit Expositio Evangeliorum¹ in Aurium Apertione ad Electos.

*Primitus enim procedunt de sacrario iv diaconi cum quatuor evangeliis*², *praecedentibus duobus candelabris*³ *cum thuribulis, et ponuntur super iv angulos altaris. Et tractat presbyter antequam aliquis eorum legat, his verbis:*

Miss. Gall.
714.
Sacr. Gall.
828.

Aperturi vobis, filii carissimi, evangelia, id est gesta⁴ divina, prius ordine⁵ insinuare debemus quid est Evangelium⁶, et unde descendat, et cuius in eo verba ponantur, et quare quatuor sint qui haec gesta scripserunt, vel qui sunt ipsi⁷ quatuor, qui divino Spiritu, annuntiante propheta⁸, signati sunt; ne forte sine hac ordinis ratione vel causa stuporem vobis⁹ in mentibus relinquamus; et, quia¹⁰ ad hoc venistis ut aures vobis aperiantur, ne incipiat sensus vester obtundi. Evangelium dicitur proprie bona annuntiatio, quae utique annuntiatio est Iesu Christi Domini nostri. Descendit autem evangelium ab eo quod annuntiet et ostendat, quod is qui per prophetas¹¹ loquebatur venit in carne, sicut scriptum est, Qui loquebar, ecce adsum. Explicantes autem [12] breviter quid sit evangelium, vel qui sint ii quatuor, qui per prophetam [13] ante monstrati sunt, nunc sua quaeque nomina singulis [14] assignemus indiciis. Ait enim propheta Ezechiel, Et similitudo vultus eorum ut [15] facies Hominis, et [16] facies Leonis a dextris il·lius ; et facies Vituli et facies Aquilae a sinistris illius. Hos [17] quatuor has figuras habentes Evangelistas esse non dubium est: sed nomina eorum, qui Evangelia scripserunt, haec sunt, Matthaeus, Marcus, Lucas, Ioannes.

Et annuntiat diaconus, dicens State cum silentio, audientes [18] intente.

[19] *Et incipiens legit initium Evangelii secundum Matthaeum, usque*: Ipse enim salvum faciet populum suum a peccatis eorum.

Postquam legerit, tractat presbyter his verbis [20] :

Filii carissimi, ne diutius ergo vos teneamus, exponamus [21] vobis quam rationem et [22] quam figuram unusquisque in se contineat, et quare Matthaeus in se [23] figuram Hominis habeat ; quia [24] in [25] initio suo nihil aliud agit, nisi nativitatem Salvatoris pleno ordine generationis enarrat. Sic [26] enim coepit : Liber generationis Iesu Christi Filii David, Filii Abraham. Videtis, quia non immerito huic Hominis assignata persona est, quando ab hominis nativitate initium comprehendit : nec immerito, ut diximus, huic mysterio assignata est Matthaei persona.

Item annuntiat diaconus, ut supra ; State cum silentio, audientes intente.

Et legit initium Evangelii secundum Marcum, usque: Ego baptizo vos aqua ; ille vero baptizabit [27] vos Spiritu sancto.

Et prosequitur [28] *presbyter his verbis :*

Marcus evangelista, Leonis gerens figuram a solitudine incipit dicens [29], Vox clamantis in deserto ; sive quia regnat invictus. Huius Leonis multifarie [30] invenimus exempla, ut non vacet [31] dictum illud, Iuda filius meus, catulus leonis, de germine mihi ascendisti : recubans dormivit [32] ut leo, et sicut catulus leonis ; quis excitabit [33] eum ?

Item annuntiat diaconus, ut supra. Et legit initium Evangelii secundum Lucam, usque: Parare Domino plebem perfectam.

Miss. Gall. 714. Cf. Sacr. Gall. 829.

Miss. Gall. 715. Cf. Sacr. Gall. 829.

Et prosequitur[34] *presbyter his verbis:*

Miss. Gall. 715. Cf. Sacr. Gall. 830.

Lucas evangelista speciem Vituli gestat, ad cuius instar Salvator noster est immolatus. Hic enim Christi evangelium locuturus, sic coepit[85] de Zacharia et Elisabeth, de quibus Ioannes Baptista in summa natus est senectute. Et ideo Lucas Vitulo comparatur, quia duo cornua, duo Testamenta, et quatuor pedum ungulas[36], quatuor Evangelia, quasi tenera firmitate[37] nascentia, in se plenissime[38] continebat.

Item annutiatur a diacono ut supra. Et legit initium Evangelii secundum Ioannem usque: Plenum gratiae et veritatis.

Iterum prosequitur presbyter his verbis.

Miss. Gall. 715. Cf. Sacr. Gall. 830.

Ioannes habet similitudinem Aquilae, eo quod nimis alta petierit; ait enim, In principio erat Verbum, et Verbum erat apud Deum, et Deus erat Verbum. Hoc erat in principio apud Deum. Et David dicit[39] de persona Christi, Renovabitur sicut aquilae iuventus tua; id est Iesu Christi Domini nostri, qui resurgens a mortuis, ascendit in coelos. Unde iam vobis conceptis praegnans[40] gloriatur ecclesia, omni festivitate[41] votorum ad nova tendere Christianae legis exordia: ut adveniente die venerabilis Paschae[42], lavacro baptismatis renascentes, sicut sancti omnes mereamini[43] fidele munus infantiae a Christo[44] Domino nostro percipere. Qui vivit et regnat in saecula saeculorum[45].

---

[1] This exposition is given at length in the Missale Gallicanum, and also (with the exception of a few lines at the beginning) by Gerbert from the Zürich MS. already cited in the notes to sect. xxix. *supra*. The Sacramentarium Gallicanum contains it in an abbreviated form. The *Ordines* published by Martène refer to the various divisions of the Exposition by their first words, but do not give it at length. [2] *Evangelia* V. (corrected by Tommasi). [3] *praecedentibus duo candilabra* V. [4] *gaudia* Miss. Gall. Sacr. Gall.; V. as text. [5] *ordinem* V.; Miss. Gall. Sacr. Gall. as text. [6] *quid Evangelium* Miss. Gall.; *quid Evangelium sit* Sacr. Gall.; V. as text. [7] Miss. Gall. Sacr. Gall. insert *ii*; V. as text. [8] Miss. Gall. Sacr. Gall. insert *ante*; V. Gerb. as text. [9] Sacr. Gall. omits *vobis*; Miss. Gall. has *vobiscum*; V. Gerb. as text. [10] *ut qui* Sacr. Gall. [11] Sacr. Gall. Miss. Gall. Gerb. insert *suos*; V. as text. [12] *ergo* Miss. Gall. Sacr. Gall.; V. Gerb. as text. [13] *prophetas* Gerb. [14] *nunc figuras atque nomina singulis* (*singula* Sacr. Gall.) Miss. Gall. Sacr. Gall.; V. Gerb. as text. [15] *et* Gerb. [16] *ut* Miss. Gall. Sacr. Gall; V. Gerb. as text. [17] *Hi* V. (corr. by Tommasi) Miss. Gall. Gerb.; Sacr. Gall. as text. [18] *audite* Gerb.; V. as text. The Gallican books do not give the form of the proclamation. [19] Gerb. inserts *et dicit* Dominus vobiscum. [20] Gerb. has here *Iterum annuntiet diaconus ut supra* State cum silentio, *et post haec tractet presbyter his verbis*. [21] *exponimus* Gerb. [22] Gerb. omits *quam rationem et*; Sacr. Gall. omits *quam rationem* and reads *ut* in place of *et*. [23] Sacr. Gall. Gerb. omit *in se*. [24] *qui* Gerb. [25] Miss. Gall. Sacr. Gall. Gerb. omit *in*; V. as text. [26] *sicut* Gerb. [27] *baptizavit* V. Gerb. (latter omitting *vos*). [28] *sequitur* V.; Gerb. as text. [29] *dicere* Miss. Gall. Sacr. Gall.; V. Gerb. as text.

[30] *multifaria* : Miss. Gall.; *multifariae* V.; Sacr. Gall. Gerb. as text. [31] *vagit* Gerb. [32] *dormisti* Miss. Gall. Sacr. Gall.; V. Gerb. as text. [33] *excitavit* V. Gerb. [34] *sequitur* Gerb. [35] *Hic Christi Evangelio locutus sic concepit* Gerb.; V. Miss. Gall. as text; Sacr. Gall. omits the clause. [36] Miss. Gall. inserts *et*. [37] *infirmitate* Miss. Gall. (perhaps for *in firmitate*); V. Gerb. as text; Sacr. Gall. omits the phrase. [38] *plenissima* V.; Miss. Gall. Gerb. as text. [39] Gerb. omits *dicit*; Miss. Gall. has *Et David ex persona Christi dicit*; Sacr. Gall. *Ait enim David ex persona Christi*; V. as text. [40] *regnans* Miss. Gall. Sacr. Gall.; V. Gerb. as text. [41] *omnem festivitatem* V. (ungrammatically); Miss Gall. Gerb. as text; Sacr. Gall. omits the phrase. [42] *ad venientem diem Paschae* Gerb.; V. Miss. Gall. as text. [43] *mereamur* Miss. Gall. [44] *Christo Iesu*, Miss. Gall. [45] *Qui vivit et regnat Deus* Miss. Gall.

XXXV [1].

INCIPIT PRAEFATIO SYMBOLI AD ELECTOS: Gerb. ii. 3.
Id est, antequam dicis Symbolum, his verbis prosequeris.

Dilectissimi nobis, accepturi sacramenta baptismatis, et in novam creaturam sancti Spiritus procreandi, fidem qua [2] credentes iustificandi estis toto corde concipite, et animis vestris veram conversationem mutatis [3], ad Deum, qui mentium nostrarum [4] est illuminator, accedite [5], suscipientes evangelici symboli sacramentum [6], a Domino inspiratum ab [7] apostolis institutum, cuius pauca quidem verba sunt sed magna mysteria. Sanctus etenim Spiritus, qui magistris ecclesiae ista dictavit tali eloquio, talique brevitate, salutiferam condidit fidem, ut quod credendum vobis [8] est, semperque profitendum [9], nec intelligentiam possit latere, nec memoriam fatigare [10]. Intentis itaque animis Symbolum discite, et quod vobis sicut accepimus [11] tradimus non alicui materiae quae [12] corrumpi potest, sed paginis vestri cordis ascribite. Confessio itaque fidei [13] quam suscepistis hoc inchoatur exordio.

Post haec, accipiens acolytus unum ex ipsis infantibus masculum, tenens eum [14] *in sinistro brachio ponens manum super caput eius* [15]. *Et interrogat ei* [16] *presbyter*. Qua lingua confitentur [17] Dominum nostrum Iesum Christum? R. Graece [18]. *Iterum dicit* [19] *presbyter*, Annuntia fidem ipsorum qualiter credunt [20]. *Et dicit acolytus Symbolum Graece decantando, tenens manum super caput infantis, in his verbis* [21]:

Credo in unum Deum Patrem omnipotentem factorem
Pisteuo his ena Theon Patera panhocratoran pyetin
caeli et terrae visibilium omnium et invisibilium Et
uranu kae gis oraton kae panton kae auraton Kae

in unum Dominum Iesum Christum Filium Dei
his ena Kyrion Ihm Xρm tonion tu theu
unigenitum de Patre natum ante omnia
ton monogenin ton ec tu patros genitenta pro panton
saecula lumen de lumine Deum verum de Deo vero
ton eonon fos ec fotos theon alithin ec theu alithinu
natum non factum consubstantialem Patris per quem
genithenta upyithenta omoysion tu patri diuta-
omnia facta sunt qui propter nos homines et propter
panta egenonton ton di himas tus antrophus kae dia tin
nostram salutem descendentem de caelis et
himeteran soterian kateltonta ec ton uranon kę
incarnatum de Spiritu sancto et Maria virgine
sarcotenta ecpneuma tos agiu kae Marias tis par tenu
et humanatum crucifixum etiam pro nobis sub 541
kae inantropisanta staurotentha de yper himon epi
Pontio Pilato et passum et sepultum et resurgentem
pontio pilatu kae pathonta kae tapenta kae anastenta
tertia die secundum scripturas et ascendentem in
titriti himera kata tas graphas kae anelthonta his tus
caelis et sedentem ad dexteram Patris et iterum
uranus kae katezomeno en dexia tu patros kae palin
venturum cum gloria iudicare vivos et mortuos cuius
ercomenon meta doxis crine zontas kae necrus vtis
regni non erit finis et in Spiritum sanctum Dominum
basilias vc estin thelos kae histo pneuma to agion ton kyrion
et vivificatorem et Patre procedentem qui cum
kae zoopyon ton ec tu patros emporegomenon ton syn
Patre et Filio simul adoratum et conglorificatum
patri kae yion synpros kynumenon kae syn doxazomen
qui locutus est per prophetas in unam sanctam catho-
tolalesas dia ton prophiton his mian agian catho-
licam et apostolicam ecclesiam confiteor unum baptisma
licin kae apostolicin eclesian omologo en baptisma
in remissionem peccatorum spero resurrectionem
his apesin amartion prosdogo anastas
mortuorum et vitam futuri saeculi Amen.
sin necron kae zoin tumellos tos aeonas Amin.

Filii carissimi, audistis Symbolum Graece, audite[22] et Latine. *Et dicis* Qua lingua confitentur Dominum nostrum Iesum Christum? *Resp.* Latine. Annuntia fidem ipsorum qualiter credunt.

Ponens manum acolytus super caput infantis, et dicit Symbolum decantando, his verbis[23] :

Credo in unum Deum, Patrem omnipotentem, factorem caeli et terrae, visibilium omnium et invisibilium. Et in unum Dominum Iesum Christum, Filium Dei unigenitum; de Patre[24] natum ante omnia saecula[25]; lumen de lumine; Deum verum de Deo vero; natum[26], non factum; consubstantialem Patris[27]; per quem omnia facta sunt; qui propter nos homines, et propter nostram salutem descendentem[28] de caelis; et incarnatum[29] de Spiritu sancto et[30] Maria virgine, et humanatum[31]; crucifixum etiam[32] pro nobis sub Pontio[33] Pilato, et[34] passum et sepultum[35]; et resurgentem[36] tertia die secundum Scripturas; et[34] ascendentem in caelos[37] et[38] sedentem ad[39] dexteram Patris; et iterum venturum[40] cum gloria iudicare vivos et mortuos; cuius regni non erit finis. Et in Spiritum sanctum Dominum[41] et vivificatorem; ex Patre procedentem[42]; qui cum Patre et Filio simul adoratum et conglorificatum[43]: qui locutus est per prophetas[44]. In unam sanctam, catholicam et apostolicam[45] ecclesiam. Confiteor unum baptisma in remissionem peccatorum. Spero resurrectionem mortuorum, et vitam futuri saeculi. Amen.

Hoc expleto sequitur presbyter his verbis.

Haec summa est[46] fidei nostrae, dilectissimi nobis, haec verba sunt Symboli, non sapientiae humano sermone[47] facta sed vera divinitus ratione disposita. Quibus comprehendendis atque servandis nemo non idoneus, nemo non[48] aptus. Hic Dei Patris et Filii una aequalis pronuntiatur potestas. Hic Unigenitus Dei de Maria virgine et Spiritu sancto secundum carnem natus ostenditur. Hic eiusdem crucifixio[49] et sepultura, ac die tertia resurrectio praedicatur. Hic ascensio ipsius super caelos et consessio in dextera paternae maiestatis agnoscitur, venturusque ad[50] iudicandos vivos et mortuos declaratur. Hic Spiritus sanctus in eadem qua Pater et Filius deitate indiscretus accipitur. Hic postremo ecclesiae vocatio, peccatorum remissio et carnis resurrectio perdocetur[51]. Vos[52] itaque, dilectissimi, ex vetere homine in novum reformamini; et de carnalibus spiritales, de terrenis incipitis esse caelestes: secura et constanti fide credite resurrectionem, quae facta est in Christo, etiam in nobis omnibus esse complendam [53], et hoc secuturum [54] in toto corpore quod praecessit in capite. Quoniam et ipsum, quod percepturi [55] estis, baptismi sacramentum huius spei [56] exprimit formam [57]. Quaedam enim ibi mors, et quaedam resurrectio celebratur. Vetus homo deponitur et novus sumitur. Peccator aquas ingreditur et iu.stificatus egreditur. Ille abiicitur qui traxit ad mortem, 543 et suscipitur ille qui reduxit ad vitam, per cuius gratiam vobis confertur, ut filii Dei sitis, non carnis voluntate editi, sed sancti Spiritus virtute generati. Et ideo hanc brevissimam plenitudinem ita debetis vestris cordibus inhaerere [58], ut omni tempore praesidio huius confessionis utamini. Invicta est enim semper talium armorum [59] potestas, contra omnes insidias inimici ad bonam Christi militiam profutura [60]. Diabolus, qui [61] hominem tentare non desinit [62], munitos vos hoc Symbolo semper inveniat [63]; ut, devicto adversario, cui renuntiatis [64], gratiam Domini incorruptam et immaculatam usque in finem, ipso quem [65] confitemini protegente, servetis, ut [66] in quo peccatorum remissionem accipitis, in eo gloriam resurrectionis habeatis [67]. Ergo dilectissimi, praefatum Symbolum fidei catholicae [68] in praesenti cognovistis, nunc euntes edocemini nullo mutato sermone. Potens est enim Dei misericordia quae et vos ad baptismi fidem currentes perducat, et nos qui vobis mysteria tradimus, una vobiscum ad regna caelestia faciat pervenire. Per eundem Dominum nostrum Iesum Christum, qui [69] vivit et regnat in saecula saeculorum. Amen.

---

[1] This section has been compared for the greater part of its extent with the parallel form given by Gerbert (ii. 3) from his Zürich MS. (saec. ix circ.), the readings of which are, as before, cited as Gerb. The form of the Creed has been compared with that contained in A. which has, after the last prayer contained in xxxiv. *supra*, the direction '*Hic exponat presbyter Pater noster qui in caelis totum. Hic exponat Credo in unum*,' followed by a Latin version of the Creed, which has originally agreed very closely with the version contained in V., but has been altered by a later hand into agreement with the more usual form. [2] *quam* V. (corrected by Tommasi as text, from Santori's MS., with which Gerb. agrees). [3] *animis bonam conversationem mutate* Gerb.; V. as text (ungrammatically: Tommasi reads *vera conversatione*). [4] *vestrarum* Gerb.; V. as text. [5] *illuminator. Accedite* Gerb. [6] *Evangelicae* V.; Tommasi retains this, but notes that Santori's MS. read *evangelicis*; Gerb. has *Evangelici symbolum sacramenti*. [7] V. omits *ab*, which Tommasi notes as being contained in Santori's MS.; Gerb. also has it. [8] *quid*

credendum nobis Gerb.; V. as text. ⁹ *providendum* V.; Gerb. has *profitendum* which seems on the whole more likely. ¹⁰ *memoria fatigari* Gerb. ¹¹ *accipimus* V.; Gerb. as text. ¹² *materie qui* V.; Gerb. as text. ¹³ *fidem* V.; Gerb. as text. ¹⁴ Gerb. omits *eum*. ¹⁵ Both V. and Gerb. give this sentence in the same ungrammatical form. ¹⁶ Gerb. omits *ei*; V. as text (ungrammatically). ¹⁷ *confitetur* Gerb. ¹⁸ *Latina* Gerb. ¹⁹ *Et dicit* Gerb. ²⁰ *credent* Gerb. ²¹ Gerb. has *Et ille cantat symbolum*, followed by the Apostles' Creed. In the bilingual Creed which is given here the readings are those of V. except that the spelling of the Latin version has been slightly altered for uniformity. ²² *audi* V. ²³ Gerb. has, after the Apostles' Creed, instead of the preceding, this rubric ' Et dum hoc cantat, semper manum super caput infantis tenet: hoc finito iterum accipiens alter acolytus ex ipsis infantibus feminam sicut supra, et interrogat presbyter sicut antea, et ipse cantat symbolum sicut supra scriptum est.' ²⁴ *et ex Patre* A²; V. A¹ as text. ²⁵ A² inserts *Deum de Deo*. ²⁶ *genitum* A²: V. (A¹?) as text. ²⁷ *Patri* A¹; V. A² as text. ²⁸ *descendit* A (but see note ³⁷). ²⁹ *incarnatus est* A²; V. A¹ as text. ³⁰ *ex* A²; V. A¹ as text. ³¹ *homo factus est* A²; V. (A¹?) as text. ³² *crucifixus etiam* A²; *crucifixum* (omitting *etiam*) A¹; V. as text. ³³ *supponcio* A. ³⁴ *et* erased by A². ³⁵ *sepultus est* A²; V. A¹ as text. ³⁶ *resurrexit* A²; V. A¹ as text. ³⁷ *ascendit in caelum* A²; *ascendentem* (?) *de caelis* A¹ (perhaps due to the presence of *descendentem de caelis* in the MS. from which A was copied) see note ²⁸; V. as text. ³⁸ A. omits *et*. ³⁹ *sedet ad* A²; V. A¹ as text. ⁴⁰ *iterum venturus est* A²; A¹ has *venturum* preceded by an erasure; V. as text. ⁴¹ *Dm̄* A¹; V. A² as text. ⁴² *vivificantem qui ex Patre Filioque procedit* A²; V. A¹ as text, save that A¹ reads *vivificantem*. ⁴³ *adoratur et conglorificatur* A.; V. as text. ⁴⁴ A² inserts *et*. ⁴⁵ A¹ omits *et apostolicam*; the words are added by A² (apparently to follow *sanctam*). ⁴⁶ Gerb. omits *est*. ⁴⁷ Gerb. inserts *sunt*. ⁴⁸ Gerb. omits *non*. ⁴⁹ *crucifixo* V. ⁵⁰ *venturus atque ad* Gerb. ⁵¹ *perducitur* V. (corrected by Tommasi from Santori's MS. to reading of text); *praedicatur* Gerb. ⁵² Gerb. omits the portion *Vos—virtute generati*. ⁵³ *est conplenda* V. (corr. by Tommasi from Santori's MS.). ⁵⁴ *secuturus* V. ⁵⁵ *precepturi* V. ⁵⁶ *huc spei* V. (corr. by Tommasi). ⁵⁷ V. has *formam ibi*. *Quaedam enim ibi* which Tommasi retains, noting that the former *ibi* is absent from Santori's MS. ⁵⁸ Gerb. (see note ¹²) has *Quae brevissima plenitudo ita debet vestris cordibus inhaerere*; V. as text. ⁵⁹ *armatorum* Gerb. ⁶⁰ *profuturis* V.; *et contra omnes vobis insidias diaboli, tanquam bonis Christi militibus profutura* Gerb. ⁶¹ *quia* Gerb. ⁶² *desistit* Gerb. ⁶³ *nos hoc symbolum inveniat* Gerb.; V. as text. ⁶⁴ *renuntiastis* Gerb. ⁶⁵ V. omits *quem* which seems needed for the sense: Gerb. has *in finem ipsum quem ... protegentem*. ⁶⁶ Gerb. omits *ut*. ⁶⁷ *habetis* Gerb. ⁶⁸ *symbolum catholice* Gerb. ⁶⁹ *Filium tuum qui tecum* Gerb.

XXXVI.

Item Praefatio Orationis Dominicae [1].

Et admonentur a diacono ut supra.

Dominus et Salvator noster Iesus Christus inter caetera salutaria [2] praecepta, discipulis suis petentibus quemadmodum orare deberent, eam formam eis orationis concessit quam etiam lectione praesenti et vos plenius cognovistis [3]. Audiat nunc dilectio vestra quemadmodum doceat discipulos suos orare Deum Patrem omnipotentem: Tu autem cum orabis, intra in cubiculum tuum, et clauso ostio, ora Patrem tuum. Cubiculum quod nominat, non occultam

Gerb. ii. 3.
Miss. Gall.
716–8.

domum ostendit, sed cordis nostri secreta[4] illi soli patere commemorat. Et clauso ostio Deum adorare debere, id est, ut a mala cogitatione[5] pectus nostrum mystica[6] clave claudamus, ac labiis clausis, incorrupta. mente Deo loqua- 544 mur. Deus autem[7] noster fidei et[8] non vocis auditor[9] est. Claudatur[10] ergo clave fidei pectus nostrum contra insidias adversarii, et soli Deo pateat cuius templum esse cognoscitur, ut quum habitat in cordibus nostris ipse sit advocatus in precibus nostris. Ergo Dei Sermo et Dei Sapientia[11], Christus Dominus noster, hanc orationem nos docuit, ut ita oremus.

Post hoc intras et dicis, PATER NOSTER QUI ES IN CAELIS.

Haec libertatis vox est et plena fiducia. Ergo his vobis[12] moribus est vivendum, ut et filii Dei et fratres Christi esse possitis[13]. Nam Patrem suum Deum qua[14] temeritate dicere praesumit, qui ab eius voluntate degenerat? Unde vos, dilectissimi, dignos exhibete adoptione divina, quoniam scriptum est, Quotquot[15] crediderunt in eum, dedit eis potestatem filios Dei fieri.

SANCTIFICETUR NOMEN TUUM.

Id est, non quod Deus nostris sanctificetur orationibus[16], qui semper est sanctus, sed petimus ut nomen eius sanctificetur in nobis, ut qui in baptismate eius sanctificamur in eo[17] quod esse coepimus[18] perseveremus[19].

ADVENIAT REGNUM TUUM.

Deus namque noster quando non regnat maxime cuius regnum est immortale? Sed quum dicimus, Veniat regnum tuum, nostrum regnum petimus advenire, a Deo nobis promissum, Christi sanguine et passione[20] quaesitum.

FIAT VOLUNTAS TUA.

Id est, in eo[21] fiat voluntas tua, ut quod tu vis in caelo hoc nos in terra positi irreprehensibiliter faciamus.

PANEM NOSTRUM QUOTIDIANUM DA NOBIS HODIE.

Hic spiritalem cibum intelligere debemus. Christus enim panis est noster, qui dixit, Ego sum panis vivus, qui de caelo descendi. Quem quotidianum dicimus, quod . ita 545 nos semper immunitatem petere debemus[22] peccati, ut digni simus caelestibus alimentis.

ET DIMITTE NOBIS DEBITA NOSTRA, SICUT ET NOS
DIMITTIMUS DEBITORIBUS NOSTRIS.

Hoc praecepto significans [23], non nos aliter peccatorum posse veniam promereri, nisi prius nos in nobis delinquentibus aliis [24] relaxemus: sicut in evangelio Dominus [25] dicit, Nisi dimiseritis peccata hominibus, nec vobis Pater vester dimittet peccata vestra.

ET NE NOS INDUCAS IN TENTATIONEM.

Id est, ne nos patiaris induci ab eo qui tentat, pravitatis auctore [26]. Nam dicit scriptura, Deus enim intentator malorum est [27]. Diabolus vero tentator [28]; ad quem evincendum [29] Dominus dicit [30], Vigilate et orate, ne intretis in tentationem.

SED LIBERA NOS A MALO.

Hoc ideo ait, quia dixit apostolus, Nescitis quid vos [31] oportet orare. Unus Deus [32] omnipotens ita a nobis orandus [33], ut quicquid humana fragilitas cavere et vitare non praevalet [34], hoc ille ut possimus [35] propitius nobis conferre dignetur Iesus Christus Dominus noster, qui vivit et regnat Deus in unitate Spiritus sancti [36], per omnia saecula saeculorum.

Item annuntiat diaconus, ut supra; State cum disciplina et cum silentio, audientes intente [37].

Audistis, dilectissimi, Dominicae orationis sancta mysteria: nunc euntes ea vestris cordibus innovate, ut ad exorandam et ad percipiendam Dei misericordiam [38] perfecti in Christo esse possitis. Potens est Dominus Deus noster, ut [39] et vos qui ad fidem curritis ad lavacrum aquae regenerationis perducat, et nos qui [40] vobis mysterium fidei catholicae tradidimus, una [41] vobiscum ad caelestia regna faciat pervenire. Qui vivit et regnat cum Deo Patre in unitate Spiritus sancti, per omnia saecula saeculorum [42].

---

[1] This form of instruction appears in a very similar shape in Missale Gallicanum, and also in Gerbert's Zürich MS. (see note [1] on xxix. *supra*). The latter is for the most part in agreement with the Missale Gallicanum, where that differs from V., but resembles V. more closely in some important points.
[2] *sacra* Gerb.; V. as text; Miss. Gall. omits the words between *noster* and *discipulis*. [3] Miss. Gall.␣Gerb. have (after *deberent*) *non solum formam orationis concessit, verum etiam qua mente et puritate precarentur ostendit, ut in praesenti sacra haec lectio demonstravit*: and proceed *Tu autem*, &c.
[4] *secretum* Miss. Gall. Gerb. which omit the words *illi soli ... debere*. [5] *ut malae cogitationi* Miss. Gall. Gerb. [6] Miss. Gall. Gerb. insert *fidei*.
[7] *enim* Miss. Gall. Gerb. [8] Miss. Gall. Gerb. omit *et*. [9] *author*

Gerb. ^{10} Miss. Gall. Gerb. omit *Claudatur ... nostris*. ^{11} *Ergo unde sermo est, id est sapientia* Miss. Gall. Gerb. ^{12} *nobis* Gerb.; Miss. Gall. omits the word. ^{13} *possimus* Miss. Gall. Gerb. ^{14} *quam* V. (corrected by Tommasi); Miss. Gall. Gerb. as text. ^{15} Gerb. inserts *autem*. ^{16} *non quod Deus nostris sanctificationibus* V.; Miss. Gall. Gerb. as text. (S. Cyprian *de Orat. Dom.* has 'Non quod optamus Deo ut sanctificetur orationibus nostris.') ^{17} *in id* V. Miss. Gall. Gerb. (ungrammatically). S. Cyprian *de Or. Dom.* as text. ^{18} *incipimus* V.; Miss. Gall. Gerb. and S. Cyprian *de Or. Dom.* as text. ^{19} *perseveremur* V. ^{20} *sanguinem et passionem* V. (corrected by Tommasi); Miss. Gall. Gerb. as text; so S. Cyprian *de Or. Dom.* ^{21} Gerb. omits *in eo*. ^{22} *quotidianum dicens ita nos semper immunes praecipit esse* Miss. Gall. Gerb. ' ^{23} *Hoc factum est significans* Miss. Gall. Gerb. ^{24} Miss. Gall. Gerb. insert *veniam*. ^{25} Miss. Gall. Gerb. insert *noster*. ^{26} *auctor est* Gerb. ^{27} *est malorum* Miss. Gall. Gerb. ^{28} *tentator est* Miss. Gall.; *est tentator* Gerb. ^{29} *vincendum* Gerb. ^{30} *dixit* Miss. Gall. ^{31} *vobis* Miss. Gall. Gerb. ^{32} *Unde Deus* Miss. Gall. Gerb. ^{33} Miss. Gall. Gerb. insert *est*. ^{34} *fragilitas capere non praevalet* Gerb. ^{35} Miss. Gall. Gerb. omit *ut possimus*. ^{36} *regnat cum Deo Patre (omnipotente* Miss. Gall.) *et Spiritu sancto* Miss. Gall. Gerb. ^{37} Gerb. has *Et dicit diaconus* State cum silentio audientes intente, *et prosequitur presbyter his verbis*. Miss. Gall. omits the proclamation of the deacon, and substitutes another form for the first part of the concluding paragraph, in which Gerb. is in general agreement with V. ^{38} *ad exoranda et praecipienda Dei misericordia* V.; Gerb. as text. ^{39} V. Miss. Gall. omit *ut*; Gerb. as text. ^{40} *et non qui* V. ^{41} *una tradimus* Miss. Gall.; *et una tradidimus* Gerb.; *una tradidimus* V.; but see end of last section. ^{42} Miss. Gall. has (after *pervenire*) *praestante Domino nostro Iesu Christo; cui est honor et imperium in saecula saeculorum. Amen*.

XXXVII.

Dominica in Palmis.

De Passione Domini.

R. S.
Gerb. 65.
Pam. 246.
Men. 60.

Deus^1, qui humano generi ad imitandum humilitatis exemplum, Salvatorem nostrum et ^{2} carnem sumere et crucem subire fecisti, concede ^{3} propitius ut et ^{4} patientiae eius ^{5} habere documentum et resurrectionis eius ^{6} consortia mereamur, Christi Domini nostri ^{7}. Qui tecum vivit et regnat Deus in unitate Spiritus sancti, per.

R. S.
Gerb. 65.
Pam. 247.

Deus, quem diligere et amare iustitia est, ineffabilis gratiae tuae in nobis dona multiplica: et ^{8} qui fecisti nos morte Filii tui sperare quod credimus, fac ^{9} nos, eodem resurgente, pervenire quo tendimus. Per.

Secreta.

R. S.
Gerb. 65.
Pam. 246.

Ipsa maiestati tuae, Domine, fideles populos commendet oblatio, quae per Filium tuum reconciliavit inimicos ^{9}, Iesum Christum Dominum nostrum. Qui tecum vivit et regnat Deus in unitate Spiritus sancti, per omnia saecula saeculorum.

Postcommun.

Sacro munere satiati, supplices te, Domine, deprecamur, ut qui debite [10] servitutis celebramus officio, salvationis tuae suscipiamus [11] augmentum. Per. γ   Pam. 284. Leon. 400.

Ad Populum.

Purifica, quaesumus, Domine [12], familiam tuam, et ab omnibus contagiis pravitatis emunda [13], ut redempta vasa sui [14] Domini passione, non spiritus immundus [15] rursus inficiat [16], sed salvatio sempiterna possideat. Per. γ   R. S. Gerb. 65. Pam. 246. Leon. 378.

Feria ii Hebdom. sexta.

Reminiscere miserationum tuarum, Domine, et famulos tuos aeterna protectione sanctifica, pro quibus [16] Christus Filius tuus per suum cruorem nobis instituit paschale mysterium. Per [17] Dominum nostrum.   R. S. (*Fer. iii.*) Gerb. 67. Patn. 248. Men. 61.

547 • Excita, Domine, tuorum corda fidelium, ut sacris intenta doctrinis et intelligant quod sequantur, et sequendo fideliter apprehendant. Per. γ   Pam. 377.

Secreta.

Respice, Domine, propitius sacra mysteria quae gerimus, et quod ad nostra evacuanda praeiudicia [18] misericors providisti [19], vitam nobis tribue fructificare perpetuam. Per.   R. S. Gerb. 66.

Postcommun.

Sancta tua nos, Domine, quaesumus, et vivificando semper [20] renovent et renovando vivificent. Per.   Leon. 441.   R.S.(*alibi.*) Gerb. 57. xxvii *supra.*

Ad Populum.

Populum tuum, Domine, quaesumus, [ad te [21]] toto corde converte; quia quos defendis etiam delinquentes, maiore pietate tueris [22] sincera mente devotos. Per.   R.S.(*alibi.*) Gerb. 45 [66]. Pam. 247. xxv *supra.*

Feria iii Hebdom. sexta.

Da, misericors Deus, ut quod in tui Filii passione mundus exercuit, salutare nobis fideliter sentiamus. Per.   Gerb. 66.   R. S. (*Fer. ii.*) Pam. 247.

Fac, omnipotens Deus, ut quae veraciter facta recolimus [23] in nostrum transire remedium gratulemur. Per.   R. S. Gerb. 67.

Secreta [24].

. Intende, quaesumus, Domine, hostias familiae tuae, et quam sacris muneribus facis esse participem tribuas ad eius plenitudinem pervenire. Per.   Men. 33.   R.S.(*alibi.*) Gerb. 33. Pam. 213. xiv *supra.*

Postcommun.

R. S.
Gerb. 67.
Pam. 248.
Men. 62.

Repleti, Domine, sacri muneris gratia, supplices exoramus, ut quae gustu corporeo dulci veneratione contigimus [25], dulciora mentibus sentiamus. Per.

Ad Populum.

R.S.(*alibi.*)
Gerb. 45.
xxv *supra.*

Da, quaesumus, Domine, fidelibus tuis et sine cessatione capere paschalia sacramenta, et desideranter expectare ventura; ut [26] mysteriis quibus renati sunt permanentes ad novam vitam his operibus perducantur [27]. Per.

Feria iv Hebdom. sexta. 548

R. S.
Gerb. 68.
Pam. 249.
Men. 62.

Omnipotens sempiterne Deus, qui Christi tui beata passione nos reparas, conserva in nobis opera misericordiae tuae, ut in huius celebritate mysterii perpetua devotione vivamus. Per.

R. S.
Gerb. 68.

Praesta, quaesumus, omnipotens et misericors Deus, ut sicut in condemnatione Filii tui, salus omnium fuit piaculum [28] perfidorum, ita et per misericordiam tuam communis sit cultus iste credentium. Per.

Secreta.

R. S.
Gerb. 68.
Men. 65.
Pam. 249.
xl *infra.*

Suscipe, quaesumus, Domine, munus oblatum, et dignanter operare, ut quod passionis mysterio gerimus, piis affectibus consequamur. Per.

Postcommun.

Leon. 327.
III. xxxi
infra.

Caelestis doni benedictione percepta [29], supplices te, Domine [30], deprecamur, ut hoc idem nobis semper et sacramenti causa sit et salutis. Per. γ

Ad Populum.

R.S.(*alibi.*)
Gerb. 20.
Pam. 379.
II. lx *infra.*

Auxiliare, Domine, populo tuo, ut sacrae devotionis [31] proficiens incrementis, et tuo semper munere gubernetur, et ad redemptionis aeternae pertineat [32], te docente [33], consortium.

---

[1] *Omnipotens sempiterne Deus* R. S. Gerb. Pam. Men.; V. as text.   [2] Gerb. Pam. Men. omit *et*; V. R. S. as text.   [3] R. S. insert *nobis*.   [4] Pam. omits *et*.   [5] *ipsius* R. S. Gerb. Pam. Men.; V. as text.   [6] Pam. Men. omit *eius*; V. R. S. Gerb. as text.   [7] R. S. Gerb. Pam. Men. omit *Christi Domini nostri*; S. Gerb. Pam. have *Per* or *Per eundem*; Men. *Qui tecum*; V. as text.   [8] *ut ... fac* V. R. S¹; *ut ... facias* S¹ Gerb.; Pam. as text.   [9] *amicus* V.; R. has *inimicus. Iesus Christus Dominus noster*; S. Gerb. Pam. omit *Iesum Christum Dominum nostrum* and end with *Per eundem*, or *Per Dominum.*   [10] *quod debitae* Pam. Leon. (so Tommasi here); V. as text (*officio* being perhaps abl. for acc.).   [11] *sentiamus* Pam. Leon.

¹² *Domine quaesumus* Leon.   ¹³ Leon. inserts a clause here.   ¹⁴ *sua* Leon.   ¹⁵ *immundi . . . inficiat* (sic) Leon. (see ed. Ball.).   ¹⁶ R. S. Gerb. Pam. Men. insert *Iesus*.   ¹⁷ *Qui tecum* Gerb. Men.   ¹⁸ *periudicia* V. (corr. by Tommasi); R. S. Gerb. as text.   ¹⁹ *praevidisti* S. Gerb.; V. R. as text.   ²⁰ R. S. Gerb. Leon. V. in xxvii *supra* omit *semper*.   ²¹ V. here omits *ad te*, which is restored from xxv *supra*, R. S. Gerb. Pam.   ²² V. here inserts *et*, which is omitted by V. in xxv *supra*, R. S. Gerb. Pam.   ²³ *recurrimus* V. S¹; *recurremus* R.; probably for *recolimus*, which is the reading of S² Gerb.   ²⁴ This *Secreta* is given here as it stands in V.; see xiv *supra* and notes 3–7 on that section.   ²⁵ *contingimus* Pam. Men.; V. R. S. Gerb. as text.   ²⁶ S. Gerb. insert *in*; R. has *ministeriis*.   ²⁷ V. here has *perducamur*; R. S. Gerb. V. in xxv *supra* as text.   ²⁸ *piaculus* V.   ²⁹ *praecepta* V.; Leon. and V. in III. xxxi *infra* as text.   ³⁰ Leon. V. in III. xxxi *infra* have *Deus omnipotens* for *Domine*, and vary slightly the order of the following words.   ³¹ *ut sacris et devotionem* V.; R. S. Gerb. Pam. and V. in II. lx *infra* as text.   ³² *pertingat* V.; R. S. Gerb. Pam. and V. in II. lx *infra* as text.   ³³ *docere* V., but in II. lx as text; R. S. Gerb. Pam. have *ducente*.

XXXVIII¹.

Orationes in Quinta Feria².

Eodem die non psallitur, nec salutat, id est non dicit Dominus vobiscum : *et Reconciliatio Poenitentis.*

Omnipotens sempiterne Deus, da, quaesumus, universis   S. Gerb. 68.
famulis tuis plenius atque perfectius omnia festi³ paschalis
introire mysteria ; ut incunctanter pia corda cognoscant
quantum debeant de confirmata in Christo renascentium
glorificatione gaudere. Per.

Concede credentibus, misericors Deus, salvum nobis⁴ de   S. Gerb. 69.
Christi passione remedium, et ⁵ humanae fragilitatis⁶ prae-
teritae · culpae laqueos aeterno suffragio plebs absolvat⁷.
Per Dominum nostrum.

Omnipotens sempiterne Deus, qui vitam humani generis,   S. Gerb. 69.
pro nobis Filio tuo moriente, salvasti, praesta, quaesumus,
ut in hac populi tui devotione fructus proveniat⁸ gaudiorum.
Per Dominum.

Ordo agentibus publicam poenitentiam.

Egreditur poenitens de loco ubi poenitentiam gessit, et in gremio praesentatur ecclesiae prostrato omni corpore in terra⁹. Et postulat in his verbis diaconus.

Adest, o venerabilis pontifex, tempus acceptum, dies   S. Gerb. 69.
propitiationis divinae et salutis humanae, qua mors interitum
et vita accepit aeterna principium, quando in vinea Domini
Sabaoth sic novorum plantatio facienda est ut purgetur
et curatio¹⁰ vetustatis. Quamvis enim a divitiis bonitatis
et pietatis Dei nihil temporis vacet, nunc tamen et largior¹¹

est per indulgentiam remissio peccatorum, et copiosior per gratiam assumptio renascentium. Augemur regenerandis, crescimus reversis. Lavant aquae, lavant lacrimae. Inde gaudium de assumptione vocatorum, hinc laetitia [12] de absolutione poenitentium. Inde est quod supplex tuus, postea quam in varias formas criminum, neglectu mandatorum caelestium, et morum probabilium [13] transgressione, cecidit, humiliatus atque prostratus, prophetica ad Deum voce clamat, dicens, Peccavi, impie egi, iniquitatem feci, miserere mei, Domine, evangelicam vocem non frustratoria aure capiens, Beati qui lugent, quoniam ipsi consolabuntur. Manducavit [14], sicut scriptum est, panem doloris, lacrimis stratum rigavit, cor suum luctu, corpus afflixit ieiuniis, ut animae suae reciperet quam perdiderat sanitatem. Unicum itaque est poenitentiae suffragium, quod et singulis prodest, et omnibus in commune succurrit. Hic ergo, dum ad poenitudinis actionem tantis excitatur exemplis, sub conspectu ingemiscentis ecclesiae, venerabilis pontifex, protestatur [15] et dicit, Iniquitates meas ego agnosco [16] . et delictum 550 meum contra me est semper. Averte faciem tuam a peccatis meis, Domine, et omnes iniquitates meas dele. Redde mihi laetitiam salutaris tui, et spiritu principali confirma me. Quo ita supplicante, et misericordiam Dei afflicto corde poscente, redintegra in eo, apostolice pontifex, quicquid diabolo scindente [17] corruptum est, et orationum tuarum patrocinantibus meritis, per divinae reconciliationis gratiam fac hominem proximum Deo, ut qui ante in suis perversitatibus displicebat, nunc iam placere se Domino in regione vivorum [18], devicto mortis suae auctore gratuletur. Per Dominum.

Post hoc admonetur ab episcopo sive ab alio sacerdote, ut quod poenitendo diluit, iterando non revocet. Inde vero has dicit orationes sacerdos super eum.

S. Gerb. 69.
Adesto Domine supplicationibus nostris, et me qui etiam misericordiam tuam [19] primus indigeo clementer exaudi, ut quem [20] non electione [21] meriti sed dono gratiae tuae constituisti operis huius ministrum; da fiduciam tui muneris exequendi, et ipse in nostro ministerio quod tuae pietatis est operare. Per. γ

S. Gerb. 69.
Praesta quaesumus Domine huic famulo tuo dignum poenitentiae fructum, ut ecclesiae tuae sanctae, a cuius

integritate deviarat [22] peccando, admissorum veniam consequendo, reddatur innoxius. Per Dominum. y

Deus humani generis conditor et benignissime reformator [23], qui hominem invidia diaboli ab aeternitate [24] deiectum unici Filii [25] tui sanguine redemisti, vivifica itaque quem [26] tibi nullatenus mori desideras, et qui non derelinquis devium [27], assume correctum [28]. Moveant pietatem tuam, quaesumus, Domine, huius famuli tui lacrimosa suspiria. Tu eius medere vulneribus. Tu iacenti manum porrige salutarem, ne ecclesia tua aliqua sui corporis portione vastetur, ne grex tuus detrimentum sustineat, ne de familiae tuae damno inimicus exultet, ne renatum lavacro salutari mors secunda possideat. Tibi ergo, Domine, supplices · preces [29], tibi fletum cordis effundimus. Tu parce confitenti ut in imminentes poenas sententiamque [30] futuri iudicii, te miserante, non incidat. Nesciat quod terret in tenebris, quod stridet in flammis, atque ab erroris via ad iter reversus iustitiae nequaquam ultra novis [31] vulneribus saucietur, sed integrum sit ei atque perpetuum et quod gratia tua contulit et quod misericordia reformavit. Per. y S. Gerb. 70.

Item ad reconciliandum poenitentem [32].

Omnipotens sempiterne Deus, confitenti tibi huic famulo tuo pro tua pietate peccata relaxa, ut non plus ei noceat conscientiae reatus ad poenam quam indulgentia tuae pietatis ad veniam. Per Dominum. S. Gerb. 70.

Omnipotens et misericors Deus, qui peccatorum indulgentiam in confessione [33] celeri posuisti, succurre lapsis, miserere confessis, ut quos delictorum catena constringit, magnitudo tuae pietatis absolvat. Per. S. Gerb. 70.

Deus [34] qui confitentium tibi corda purificas, et accusantes se [35] conscientias ab omni vinculo iniquitatis absolvis, da indulgentiam reis, et medicinam tribue vulneratis, ut percepta [36] remissione omnium peccatorum sincera deinceps devotione permaneant, et nullum redemptionis aeternae sustineant detrimentum. Per. S. Gerb. 72.

Domine sancte, Pater omnipotens, aeterne Deus, respice super hunc famulum tuum qui ab infesta saeculi tempestate demersus [37], flebili lamentatione suos accusat excessus, ut fletus ac gemitus eius pie suscipias, eumque de tenebris ad lumen revoces, et medelam confitenti, salutem poenitenti, S. Gerb. 70.

et vulnerato auxilium sanitatis indulgeas. Nec ultra inimicus in eius habeat anima potestatem, eiusque [38] confessionem libenter admittens, ecclesiae tuae purificatum restitue, ac tuo altario repraesenta, ut ad sacramentum reconciliationis admissus una nobiscum sancto nomini tuo gratias agere mereatur. Per.

RECONCILIATIO POENITENTIS AD MORTEM [39]. 552

R. Gerb. 312

Deus misericors, Deus clemens, qui secundum multitudinem miserationum [40] tuarum peccata poenitentium [41] deles, et praeteritorum criminum culpas venia remissionis evacuas, respice super hunc famulum tuum et remissionem sibi omnium peccatorum tota cordis confessione poscentem deprecatus exaudi. Renova in eo, piissime Pater, quicquid terrena fragilitate corruptum est vel quicquid diabolica fraude violatum est ; in unitatem [42] corporis ecclesiae tuae membrum perfecta remissione restitue ; miserere Domine gemituum, miserere lacrimarum, et non habentem fiduciam, nisi in tua misericordia, ad sacramentum reconciliationis admitte. Per. γ

R. Gerb. 312. Pam. 454.

Maiestatem tuam, Domine, supplices deprecamur, ut huic famulo tuo [43], longo squalore poenitentiae macerato, miserationis tuae veniam largiri digneris, ut, nuptiali veste recepta, ad regalem mensam unde eiectus fuerat mereatur intrare [44]. Per. γ

R. Gerb. 312.

Maiestatem tuam quaesumus, Domine sancte, Pater omnipotens, aeterne Deus, qui non mortem sed peccatorum vitam semper inquiris, respice flentem famulum tuum, attende prostratum, eiusque planctum in gaudium tua miseratione concede [45]. Scinde delictorum saccum, et indue eum laetitiam salutarem, ut post longam [46] peregrinationis famem [46] de sanctis altaribus tuis satietur : ingressus cubiculum Regis, in ipsius aula benedicat nomen gloriae tuae semper. Per Dominum.

[Cf. Gerb. 70.]

Deus misericors, Deus clemens, qui indulgentiam tuam [47] nulla temporum lege concludis, sed pulsanti [48] misericordiae tuae ianuam aperis, poenitentes etiam sub ipso vitae huius termino non relinquis [49]. Respice propitius super hunc famulum tuum [50], remissionem sibi omnium peccatorum tota cordis confessione poscentem. Renova in eo, piissime Pater, quod actione, quod verbo, quod ipsa denique cogi-

tatione, diabolica fraude vitiatum est, et unitati corporis
553 ecclesiae membrum tuae • redemptionis annecte. Miserere
gemituum, miserere lacrimarum, et non habentem fiduciam,
nisi in misericordia tua, ad sacramentum reconciliationis
admitte [51], quia nullius animae in hoc corpore constitutae
difficilis apud te, aut tarda curatio est. Fidelis enim es in
verbis tuis, qui conversum peccatorem non longa temporum
spatia differendum, sed mox ut in te gemuisset dixisti esse
[audiendum [52]?]. Per.

Oratio [53] *post reconciliationem, vel posteaquam communicaverit.*

Deus qui confitentium tibi corda purificas, et accusantes se conscientias ab omni vinculo iniquitatis absolvis, da indulgentiam reis [54] et medicinam tribue vulneratis, ut percepta remissione omnium peccatorum in sacramentis tuis [55] sincera deinceps devotione permaneat, et nullum redemptionis aeternae sustineat detrimentum. Per.   S. Gerb. 72.

Post haec offert plebs, et conficiuntur sacramenta [56].

Secreta.

Virtutum caelestium Deus, de cuius gratiae rore descendit ut ad mysteria tua purgatis sensibus accedamus, praesta quaesumus ut in eorum traditione solemniter honorum [57] tibi placitum deferamus obsequium. Per.   S. Gerb. 71.

Infra actionem.

Communicantes et diem sacratissimum celebrantes quo traditus est Dominus noster Iesus Christus. Sed et memoriam. γ   S. Gerb. 72.

Item infra.

Hanc igitur oblationem, Domine, cunctae familiae tuae, quam tibi offerunt ob diem ieiunii Coenae Dominicae, in qua Dominus noster Iesus Christus tradidit discipulis suis corporis et sanguinis sui mysteria celebranda, quaesumus, Domine, placatus intende, ut per multa curricula annorum salva et incolumis munera sua tibi Domine mereatur offerre; diesque nostros in tua pace d[isponas]. γ   S. Gerb. 72.

Item infra canonem [58], *ubi dicimus* Qui pridie quam
554 pateretur, *in huius diei pro•cessione dicimus* [59] Qui hac die antequam traderetur, accepit panem in suis sanctis manibus, elevatis. γ   S. Gerb. 72.

Postcommun.

373 S. Gerb. 72. xl *infra*.

Concede, quaesumus, Domine, ut percepti novi sacramenti mysterium et corpore sentiamus et mente. Per.

Ad Populum [60]

374 R.S.(*alibi*.) Gerb. 239. Leon. 364. xxviii *supra*. III. xvii *infra*.

Gregem tuum, Pastor bone, placatus intende, et oves, quas pretioso sanguine Filii tui [61] redemisti, diabolica non sinas incursione lacerari. Per.

---

[1] Two sections at least appear to be here blended together. The *Reconciliatio poenitentis ad mortem*, at all events, and possibly also the additional prayers *ad reconciliandum poenitentem* may be considered to have been joined with the form for use on the Thursday in *Coena Domini* on the principle of bringing material of the same kind together. The *Reconciliatio poenitentis ad mortem* does not appear in S., which does contain, at this point, all the rest of the section, with the exception of the *Super populum*, though with some differences of arrangement. There is no section in V. numbered as xxxix; but this may be due either to a displacement of the *Reconciliatio poenitentis ad mortem*, or to the union of the *Missa Chrismalis* and the *Missa ad Vesperum* in one section. Gerbert notes that S. *alone* contains this section: but he may merely mean that the section is not in R., for the text as he gives it is evidently not taken from S., as some of the prayers are worded in the plural, while in S. they are in the singular. His text, except in this respect, corresponds for the most part with S[2], while S[1] generally is in closer agreement with V. [2] S. gives as the title *Feria v. Coenae Domini*: and places the rubric *Egreditur poenitens . . . in terra* before the three prayers which precede it in V. To these last S. gives the title *Orationes ad Missa* (sic). [3] *festa* S[1]; V. S[2] Gerb. as text. [4] S[2] Gerb. omit *nobis*. [5] *ut* Gerb. [6] S[2] Gerb. insert *et*. [7] *laqueis aeterno suffragio absolvantur* S[2] Gerb.; V. S[1] as text. [8] *praeveniat* V.; S[1] Gerb. as text. [9] S. Gerb. place this rubric elsewhere (see note 2): they here have *Et antequam offerat postulat diaconus his verbis*. [10] *Execratio* S[2] Gerb.; V. S[1] as text. [11] *largitor* V.; S[1] Gerb. as text. [12] *laetitiae* V. [13] *improbabilium* V. S[1]; S[2] Gerb. as text. [14] *Mandavit* V.; *Manducabit* S[1]; S[2] Gerb. as text. [15] *prostratur* Gerb.; V. S. as text. [16] *cognosco* S. Gerb.; V. as text. [17] *suadente* Gerb.; V. S. as text. [18] V. S[1] insert *cum*, which S[2] Gerb. omit, no doubt rightly. [19] *misericordiam tuam* V. S[1] (ungrammatically). [20] *clementer exaudiens quem* S[2] Gerb.; V. (S[1]?) as text. [21] *electio* V. S[1]; S[2] Gerb. as text. [22] *deviaverat* S. Gerb.; V. as text. [23] *formator* V.; S[1] Gerb. as text. [24] S[2] Gerb. insert *beata*. [25] V. omits *Filii*; S. Gerb. as text. [26] *Vivifica hunc famulum tuum quem* S[2]; *vivifica eos quos* Gerb.; V. (S[1]?) as text. [27] *dereliquisti devios* Gerb. (which refers to the penitents in the plural throughout this prayer); V. S[1] as text (S[2] has *dereliquisti*). [28] *corruptum* V.; S[1] as text. [29] *supplices preces prosternimus* S[1]; *suppliciter preces prosternimus* S[2] Gerb.; V. as text. [30] Tommasi's correction is here followed: V. has *ut imminentibus paene sentenciaequae*; the reading of S[1] is uncertain; Gerb. reads practically as text. [31] Gerb. omits *novis*. [32] S. Gerb. omit *poenitentem*. Gerb. words all these prayers in the plural. [33] *ad confessione* V.; S. Gerb. as text. [34] S. and Gerb. omit this prayer here, and place it after the Postcommunion of the *Missa*. V. repeats it after the *Reconciliatio poenitentis ad mortem*. [35] *suas* V. here; V. *infra*, S. Gerb. as text. [36] *peraccepta* V. here; V. *infra*, S. Gerb. as text. [37] *emersus* S[2]; *emersi* Gerb.; V. S[1] as text. [38] *cuiusque* V.; S. as text (Gerb. has *eorumque*). [39] The part of Gerbert's text which answers to this portion of the text of V. is rightly marked by him as not found in S. or R. It does not agree with V. At a later point of his text, however, he prints from R. certain prayers with the title *Reconciliatio poenitentis ad mortem*, which agree with the first three of the series in V. more closely than those which he prints at p. 71. [40] *misericordiarum* R. [41] *poenitentiam* R.; Gerb. reads *poenitentia*; V. as text. [42] *unitate* R. [43] Pam. inserts *N*. [44] *introire* Pam.; V. R. as text. [45] *concede*, so V. R.; Gerb. proposes *converte*, which gives

a clearer sense, and is apparently supported by T. (Gerb. p. 71).   ⁴⁶ *longa*...
fame V.; *longam*...*fame* R.   ⁴⁷ *multitudine indulgentiarum*...*concluderis*
Gerb.   ⁴⁸ *pulsantis* V.; *pulsantibus* Gerb.   ⁴⁹ *termino non repellis*
Gerb.   ⁵⁰ *hos famulos tuos* Gerb. (and similarly throughout).   ⁵¹ Gerb.
ends the prayer at this point.   ⁵² Some word such as that suggested seems
required to complete the sense.   ⁵³ *Oration*. V. (see note 34). The title
of the prayer in S. is *Oratio super penitenti posteaquam commun*.   ⁵⁴ *eis* V.
here; V. *supra*, S. Gerb. as text.   ⁵⁵ *in sacramentis tuis* omitted by V.
supra, inserted here by V. S. Gerb. perhaps with reference to the special use of
the prayer.   ⁵⁶ This rubric is not in S. or Gerb., but see note 9.   ⁵⁷ *hono-*
rem S¹; S² Gerb. substitute *celebranda*; V. as text: Tommasi suggests *hono-*
randa, as in xxvi *supra*.   ⁵⁸ *canone* V.   ⁵⁹ S. Gerb. have simply *Item*
infra actionem.   ⁶⁰ S. Gerb. have no *super populum* in the corresponding
Missa.   ⁶¹ See note 20 on xxviii *supra*.

XL.

Item in Quinta Feria.

Missa Chrismatis[1].

Domine Deus, qui in regenerandis plebibus tuis minis-   S.
terium[2] uteris sacerdotum, tribue nobis perseverantem in   Gerb. 72.
tua voluntate famulatum, ut dono gratiae tuae in diebus
nostris et[3] merito et numero sacratus tibi populus augeatur.
Per Dominum.

Da nobis, omnipotens Deus, remedia conditionis humanae   S.
et sincero tractare servitio et cum profectu[4] salutis implere.   Gerb. 72.
Per.

Secreta.

Huius sacrificii potentia, Domine, quaesumus, et vetus-   S.
tatem nostram clementer abstergat et novitatem nobis   Gerb. 72.
augeat et salutem[5]. Per.

VD. Clementiam tuam suppliciter obsecrare, ut spiritalis   Leofr. 94
lavacri baptismum[6] renovandis creaturam chrismatis in   Mur. 311.
sacramentum perfectae salutis vitaeque confirmes, ut sanctificatione unctionis infusa, corruptione primae nativitatis
absorpta[7], sanctum uniuscuiusque templum acceptabilis
vitae innocens odor[8] redolescat: ut secundum constitutionis
tuae sacramentum regio et sacerdotali propheticoque honore
perfusi, vestimento incorrupti muneris induantur. Per quem
maiestatem tuam. γ

555   *Infra actionem*[9], Communicantes, *ut supra*.

Hanc igitur oblationem famulorum famularumquetuarum,   S.
quam tibi offerunt ob diem in qua Dominus noster Iesus   Gerb. 72.
Christus tradidit discipulis suis corporis et sanguinis sui[10]
mysteria celebranda, quaesumus, Domine, placatus accipias,

et tua pietate concedas, ut per multa curricula annorum salvi et incolumes munera sua tibi Domino mereantur offerre [11], diesque nostros. γ

Benedictio olei. Ad populum in his verbis, Istud oleum ad ungendos infirmos. *Ut autem veneris* Nobis quoque peccatoribus famulis tuis ; *et reliqua usque ad* Per Christum Dominum nostrum. *Et intras* [12].

S. Gerb. 74.

Emitte, quaesumus, Domine, Spiritum sanctum [13] Paraclitum de caelis in hac pinguedine olei [14] quam de viridi ligno producere dignatus es ad refectionem mentis et corporis. Et tua sancta benedictio sit omni ungenti, gustanti [15], tangenti, tutamentum corporis, animae et spiritus, ad evacuandos omnes dolores, omnem infirmitatem, omnem aegritudinem mentis et corporis, unde unxisti sacerdotes, reges, et [16] prophetas, et martyres, chrisma tuum perfectum, a te, Domine, benedictum, permanens in visceribus nostris, in nomine Domini nostri Iesu Christi. Per quem haec omnia, Domine, semper bona creas. *Et caetera* [17]. γ

Expleto enim canone dicis [18] Oremus. Praeceptis salutaribus moniti. *Sequitur oratio Dominica. Et iterum subsequitur alia oratio* Libera nos, quaesumus, Domine. *Ipsa expleta confrangis et tegis de sindone altaris munera et ascendis ad sedem. Ibique oblato a diacono alio oleo ad benedicendum et dicis* Dominus vobiscum. *Resp.* Et cum spiritu tuo. *Dicis* [18] Oremus. *Et intras*.

S. Gerb. 75.

Deus incrementorum et profectuum spiritalium munerator [19], qui virtute sancti Spiritus tui imbecillarum mentium rudimenta confirmas, te oramus, Domine, ut venturis ad beatae regenerationis lavacrum • tribuas per unctionem 556 istius creaturae purgationem mentis et corporis. Ut si quae illis adversantium spirituum inhaesere reliquiae [20] ad tactum sanctificati olei huius abscedant. Nullis [21] spiritalibus nequitiis locus, nulla refugis virtutibus sit facultas, nulla insidiantibus malis latendi licentia relinquatur, sed venientibus ad fidem servis tuis, et sancti Spiritus [22] operatione mundandis sit unctionis huius praeparatio [23] utilis ad salutem, quam etiam per caelestis regenerationis nativitatem in sacramento sunt baptismatis adepturi. Per Dominum nostrum Iesum Christum, qui venturus est iudicare [24] saeculum per ignem.

Iterum dicis [25] Dominus vobiscum.
Resp. Et cum spiritu tuo.
Sursum corda.
Resp. Habemus ad Dominum [26].
Gratias agamus Domino Deo nostro.
Resp. Dignum et iustum est.
VD. Et iustum est, aequum et salutare, nos tibi semper hic et ubique gratias agere, Domine sancte, Pater omnipotens, aeterne Deus. Qui in principio inter caetera bonitatis et pietatis [27] tuae munera terram producere fructifera ligna iussisti. Inter quae huius pinguissimi liquoris ministrae oleae nascerentur, quarum fructus sacro chrismati deserviret. Nam David prophetico spiritu gratiae tuae sacramenta praenoscens, vultus nostros in oleo exhilarandos esse cantavit. Et quum mundi crimina diluvio quondam expiarentur effuso [28] similitudinem futuri muneris columba demonstrans per olivae ramum pacem terris redditam nuntiavit. Quod in novissimis temporibus manifestis est effectibus declaratum, quum, baptismatis aquis omnium criminum commissa delentibus, haec olei unctio vultus nostros iocundos efficiat [29] ac serenos. Inde etiam Moysi famulo tuo mandata dedisti, ut Aaron fratrem suum prius aqua lotum per infusionem [30] huius unguenti constitueret [31] sacerdotem. Accessit ad hoc [32] amplior honor, quum Filius tuus, Dominus noster Iesus Christus, lavari a Ioanne undis Iordanicis exegisset, et [33] Spiritu sancto in columbae similitudine desuper misso, Unigenitum tuum, • in quo tibi optime complacuisse testimonio subsequentis vocis ostenderes [34], hoc illud esse manifestissime comprobares, quod eum oleo laetitiae prae consortibus suis ungendum David propheta cecinisset. Te igitur deprecamur, Domine sancte, Pater omnipotens, aeterne Deus, per Iesum Christum Filium tuum Dominum nostrum, ut huius creaturae pinguedinem sanctificare tua benedictione digneris et in sancti Spiritus immiscere [35] virtutem per potentiam [36] Christi tui, a cuius sancto nomine chrisma [37] nomen accepit, unde unxisti sacerdotes, reges, prophetas, et martyres tuos [38], ut sit his qui renati fuerint ex aqua et Spiritu sancto chrisma [37] salutis, eosque aeternae vitae participes et caelestis gloriae [39] facias esse consortes. Per eundem Dominum nostrum Iesum Christum Filium tuum. γ

S. Gerb. 75.

Item olei exorcizati confectio [40].

Hoc loco misces balsamum cum oleo et sequitur hic exorcismus [41].

Exorcizo te creatura olei, in nomine Dei Patris omnipotentis, et in nomine Iesu Christi Filii eius, et Spiritus sancti, ut in [42] hanc invocationem trinae potestatis, atque virtutem Deitatis, omnis nequissima virtus adversarii, omnis inveterata malitia diaboli, omnis violentiae [43] occursio, omne confusum et caecum phantasma, eradicare et effugare et discede [44] a creatura huius olei, ad utilitatem hominum constituta: ut fiat haec unctio divinis sacramentis purificata in adoptionem [45] carnis et spiritus eis qui ex eo ungueri [46] habent in remissionem omnium peccatorum; efficiatur in eis cor purum [47] ad omnem gratiam spiritalem sanctificatum. Per eundem Iesum Christum Dominum nostrum, qui venturus est in Spiritu sancto iudicare [48] vivos et mortuos et saeculum per ignem. Per Dominum.

VD. Omnipotens aeterne Deus, qui mysteriorum tuorum secreta revelans nemus ore columbae gestatum [49] Noe oculis ostendisti ut discerent habitatores arcae per Spiritum sanctum et olivae chrisma mundo liberationis gloriam [50] rever•suram. Per Dominum nostrum, Iesum Christum, 558 qui venturus est iudicare vivos et mortuos et saeculum per ignem.

Hoc autem expleto, veniens [51] *ante altare, ponis in ore calicis de ipsa hostia: non dicis* Pax Domini, *nec faciunt pacem: sed communicant, et reservant de ipso sacrificio in crastinum unde communicent* [52].

Item in Feria V.
Missa ad vesperum [53].

Secreta.

R.S.(*alibi.*)
Gerb. 68.
Men. 65.
Pam. 249.
xxxvii *supr.*

Suscipe, quaesumus, Domine, munus oblatum, et dignanter operare ut quod passionis mysterio gerimus, piis affectibus [54] consequamur. Per Dominum.

Leofr. 94.
Men. 66.
Pam. 565.

VD. Et iustum est. Per Christum Dominum nostrum. Quem in hac nocte inter sacras epulas increpantem mens sibi conscia traditoris ferre non potuit, sed apostolorum derelicto [55] consortio sanguinis pretium a Iudaeis accepit, ut vitam perderet quam distraxit. Coenavit igitur hodie proditor mortem suam, et cruentis manibus panem de manu Salvatoris exiturus accepit, ut saginatum cibo maior poena constringeret, quem nec suprema pietas [56] a scelere revocaret. Patitur itaque Dominus noster Iesus Christus Filius tuus cum hoste novissimum participare convivium, a quo se noverat continuo traditurum, ut exemplum innocentiae mundo reliqueret, et passionem suam pro saeculi redemptione suppleret. Pascit igitur mitis [57] Deus barbarum Iudam, et sustinet in mensam [58] crudelem convivam, donec se suo laqueo perderet [59] qui [60] de magistri sanguine cogitarat [61]. O Dominum per omnia patientem! O Agnum inter suas epulas mitem! adhuc cibum eius Iudas in ore ferebat, et ad lanianda membra eius Iudaeos carnifices [62] advocabat. Sed Filius tuus Dominus noster, tanquam pia hostia, et immolari se tibi pro nobis patienter permisit, et peccatum quod mundus commiserat relaxavit. Per ipsum [63] te Domine supplices deprecamur, supplici confessione dicentes. γ

559 *Infra canonem ut supra* [64].

Postcommun.

Concede, quaesumus Domine, ut percepti [65] novi sacramenti mysterium et corpore sentiamus et mente. Per.

S. (*alibi*.) Gerb. 72. xxxviii *supra*.

Ad Populum.

Praesta, quaesumus, Domine, ut sicut de praeteritis ad nova [66] transimus, ita, vetustate deposita, sanctificatis mentibus innovemur. Per.

S. (*alibi*.) [Gerb. 77.] Leon. 325.

---

[1] *Chrismatis*, so V. perhaps for *Chrismalis*. S. has '*Missa crismale*.' R. has not the *Missa*. [2] *ministerio* S² Gerb.; V. S¹ as text (ungrammatically). [3] *ut* V.; S¹ Gerb. as text. [4] *perfecto* V.; S. Gerb. as text. [5] *augeat salutem* V. (Tommasi reads *augeat salutarem*); S¹ Gerb. as text. [6] *baptismo* Leofr. Mur.; V. as text (ungrammatically). [7] *obsorbta* Leofr. [8] *odor*, so V. Leofr. Mur.; Tommasi substitutes *odore*: but perhaps the error is rather in *sanctum . . . templum*. [9] S. repeats the clauses *infra actionem* with the same variation from those in the previous *Missa* which is observed in V. They are not repeated in Gerb. [10] S. omits *sui* (at the end of a page). [11] *offerre. Per Christum. Quam oblationem* S. [12] For this direction S. has '*Item in ultimo antequam dicatur* Per quem haec omnia, Domine, *benedicis oleum pro infirmis sive pro populo his verbis*.' Gerb. varies the rubric, and inserts an exorcism before the form *Emitte* (see note 40). [13] S² Gerb. insert *tuum*. [14] *in hanc pinguedinem olivae* S² Gerb.; V. S¹ as text (ungrammatically). [15] Gerb. omits *gustanti*: there is an erasure in S. [16] S. Gerb. omit *et*. [17] S. adds *usque per omnia saecula saeculorum*, and proceeds '*Postea oblato a diacono alio oleo ad benedicendum, et sic dicis* Dominus vobiscum'; Gerb. inserts an exorcism before the Benediction. [18] *dicit* V. [19] *remunerator* S. Gerb.; V. as text. [20] *inhaerere reliquiae* V.; *illis maculae adversantium spirituum inheserunt reliquae* S.; *illis maculae adv. sp. inhaesere reliquiae* Gerb. [21] *Nullus* Gerb.; V. S¹ as

text. [29] S² Gerb. insert *tui*. [30] S¹ inserts *illis*, which S² omits. [31] S. has in the margin (original hand) *vivos et mortuos et*. [32] S. has here '*Post haec miscis balsamum cum alio oleo et benedicis crisma in his verbis.*' [33] *a Domino* V. [27] S¹ omits *et pietatis*. [34] V. inserts *in*; S. Gerb. as text. [29] *efficit* Gerb.; V. S. as text. [30] *infusione* V. (ungrammatically); S. Gerb. as text. [31] *constituerit* V. (probably for *constitueret*); S. Gerb. as text. [32] *adhuc* (for *ad hoc*) S. Gerb.; V. as text. [33] *ut* S. Gerb.; V. as text. [34] S² Gerb. insert *et*; V. S¹ as text. [35] *et sancti Spiritus ei admiscere* S. Gerb.; V. as text. [36] *cooperante potentia* S. Gerb.; V. as text. [37] *chisma* V. [38] S² Gerb. omit *tuos*. [39] *regni* S. Gerb.; V. as text. [40] S. has at this point '*Hoc expleto, veniens ante altare, dicis*, Oremus. Praeceptis salutaribus moniti. Sequitur Oratio Dominica. Postea Libera nos Domine. Et communicant.' Then follow in order the Postcommunion and *Oratio super Populum* of the *Missa* (the same which appear in V. for the *Missa ad Vesperum*). After these comes '*Item oleo exorcisato* (sic) *confectio*,' followed by the same two forms as in V. Gerb. has only the exorcism, placed before the Benediction of the Oil of the Sick (see note 12). [41] As to this direction see note 25, *supra*. V. reads *hoc exorcimum*. [42] *ad* S² Gerb.; V. S¹ as text (perhaps ungrammatically, for *in hac invocatione . . . virtute*). [43] *violenta* S. Gerb.; V. as text. [44] *eradiceris, effugeris et discedas* S² Gerb.; S¹ has *discedere*, otherwise V. S¹ as text (ungrammatically). [45] *adoptione* V.; S. Gerb. as text. [46] *eisque ex eo unguere* V.; S¹ as text: S² Gerb. correct the barbarous form *ungueri* to *unguere*. [47] *corporum* V. S¹; S² Gerb. as text. [48] *indicare in Spiritu sancto* S.; V. Gerb. as text. [49] *testatum* V.; S¹ as text; S² Gerb. alter *nemus* to *munus*. [50] *gratiam* S² Gerb.; V. S¹ as text. [51] *venies* V. [52] These directions do not, of course, appear in S. or Gerb. at this point (see note 40). [53] R. S. also recognize this late Mass, providing two Collects, Secret, clauses *infra canonem*, and Postcommunion, '*Ad Mū. Sero.*' (perhaps '*ad Missam Serotinam*'). The forms given, however, are not the same as those in V., except the clauses *infra canonem*. [54] *effectibus* V. here; V. in xxxvii *supra*, R. S. Gerb. Pam. Men. as text. [55] *relicto* Men. Pam. Leofr.; V. as text. [56] *sub praemia pietas* V.; Pam. Men. Leofr. alter to *quem nec sacrati cibi collatio*. [57] *Pascitur mitis* Men.; V. Pam. Leofr. as text. [58] *in mensam*, so V. (probably ungrammatically); *immitem Iudam et sustinet pius crudelem* Pam. Men.; *immitem et sustinet prius crudelem* Leofr. [59] *convivam, qui merito laqueo suo periturus erat* Pam. Men. Leofr.; V. as text. [60] *quod* Pam.; *quia* Men. Leofr.; V. as text. [61] *cogitaret* V. [62] *ferebat et quibus eum traderet persecutores* Pam. Men. Leofr. [63] *Per quem*, &c. Pam. Leofr.; Men. inserts some further clauses. [64] In S. the *Hanc igitur* runs '*servitutis nostrae sed et cunctae familiae tuae.*' [65] *perceptum* V. here; S. Gerb. V. in xxxviii *supra* as text. [66] *novam* V.; Leon. inserts *sacramenta*; S. Gerb. as text.

XLI.

INCIPIT ORDO DE FERIA VI, PASSIONE DOMINI.

Hora nona[1] *procedunt omnes ad ecclesiam; et ponitur sancta crux super altare. Et egreditur sacerdos de sacrario cum sacris ordinibus, cum silentio, nihil canentes, et veniunt ante altare, postulans sacerdos pro se orare, et dicit*[2]: Oremus. *Et annuntiat diaconus*: Flectamus genua. *Et post paululum dicit*: Levate. *Et dat Orationem.*

R. S.
Gerb. 78.
Pam. 250.
Men. 62.

Deus, a quo et Iudas[3] reatus sui poenam, et confessionis suae latro praemium sumpsit, concede nobis tuae propitiationis[4] effectum; ut sicut[5] passione sua Christus Dominus

noster diversa utrisque intulit stipendia meritorum, ita [6]
nobis, ablato vetustatis errore, resurrectionis suae gratiam
largiatur. Qui tecum vivit. ү
*Ista oratione expleta vadit retro altare et legitur lectio.
Deinde sequitur responsorium.*
Iterum dicit sacerdos: Oremus. *Et annuntiat diaconus
ut supra, et sequitur alia oratio* [7].

Deus, qui peccati veteris haereditariam mortem, in qua R.
posteritatis genus omne successerat, Christi tui Domini Gerb. 78.
nostri passione solvisti, dona [8] ut conformes eidem [9] facti, Pam. 253.
sicut imaginem terreni naturae necessitate portavimus, ita
imaginem caelestis gratiae sanctificatione portemus, Christi
Domini nostri. Qui tecum vivit [10]. ү

560 •*Item sequitur lectio et responsorium. Inde vero legitur
Passio Domini. Ipsa expleta, incipit sacerdos orationes
solemnes, quae sequuntur.*

Oremus, dilectissimi nobis, in primis pro ecclesia sancta R. S.
Dei ut eam [11] Deus et Dominus noster pacificare, adunare, Gerb. 79.
et custodire dignetur per universum orbem terrarum [12], Pam. 254.
subiciens ei principatus et potestates, detque nobis tran- Men. 63.
quillam et quietam vitam degentibus glorificare Deum
Patrem omnipotentem. Oremus. ү

Annuntiat diaconus: Flectamus genua. *Iterum dicit*:
Levate [13].

Omnipotens sempiterne Deus, qui gloriam tuam [14] om- R. S.
nibus in Christo gentibus revelasti, custodi opera miseri- Gerb. 79.
cordiae tuae, ut ecclesia tua [15] toto orbe diffusa stabili fide Pam. 254.
in confessione [16] tui nominis perseveret. Per. ү Men. 63.

Oremus et pro beatissimo papa nostro [17] *Ill.* et pro R. S.
antistite nostro *Ill.* [18] ut Deus omnipotens qui elegit eos [19] Gerb. 79.
in ordine [20] episcopatus salvos [19] et incolumes [19] custodiat Pam. 254.
ecclesiae suae sanctae ad regendum populum sanctum Men. 63.
Dei. ү Oremus [21].

Item annuntiat diaconus ut supra.

Omnipotens sempiterne Deus, cuius aeterno iudicio R. S.
universa fundantur, respice propitius ad preces nostras et Gerb. 79.
electos [22] a te nobis antistites tua pietate conserva, ut Pam. 254.
Christiana plebs quae talibus gubernatur auctoribus sub Men. 63.
tantos pontifices [23] credulitatis suae meritis augeatur.
Per. ү

76　　　　LIBER SACRAMENTORUM　　　　[I. xli.

R. S.
Gerb. 79.
Pam. 254.
Men. 63.

Oremus et pro omnibus episcopis, presbyteris, diaconibus, subdiaconibus, acolytis, exorcistis, lectoribus, ostiariis, confessoribus, virginibus, viduis, et pro omni populo sancto Dei. ỹ Oremus.

Item annuntiat diaconus ut supra.

R. S.
Gerb. 79.
Pam. 254.
Men. 63.

Omnipotens sempiterne Deus, cuius Spiritu totum corpus ecclesiae sanctificatur et regitur, exaudi nos pro universis ordinibus supplicantes, ut gratiae tuae munere ab omnibus [tibi gradibus] [24] fideliter serviatur. Per. ỹ

R. S.
Gerb. 79.
Pam. 254.
Men. 63.

•Oremus et pro Christianissimo imperatore vel rege 561 nostro [25] *Ill.*, ut Deus omnipotens [26] subditas illis [27] faciat omnes barbaras nationes ad nostram perpetuam pacem. ỹ Oremus.

Item annuntiat diaconus ut supra.

R. S.
Gerb. 79.
Pam. 255.
Men. 63.

Omnipotens sempiterne Deus, qui regnis omnibus aeterna potestate dominaris [28], respice propitius ad Romanum sive Francorum [29] benignum imperium, ut gentes quae in sua feritate confidunt dexterae tuae potentia [30] comprimantur. Per. ỹ

R. S.
Gerb. 79.
Pam. 255.
Men. 63.

Oremus et pro catechumenis nostris, ut Deus et Dominus noster adaperiat aures praecordiorum ipsorum [31], ianuamque misericordiae, ut per lavacrum regenerationis accepta remissione omnium peccatorum, digni [32] inveniantur in Christo Iesu Domino nostro. ỹ Oremus.

Annuntiat diaconus ut supra.

R. S.
Gerb. 79.
Pam. 255.
Men. 63.

Omnipotens sempiterne Deus, qui ecclesiam tuam nova semper prole fecundas, auge fidem et intellectum catechumenis nostris, ut renati fonte baptismatis, adoptionis tuae filiis aggregentur. Per. ỹ

R. S.
Gerb. 80.
Pam. 255.
Men. 63.

Oremus, dilectissimi nobis, Deum Patrem omnipotentem, ut cunctis mundum purget erroribus, morbos auferat, famem depellat, aperiat carceres, vincula dissolvat, peregrinantibus reditum, infirmantibus sanitatem, navigantibus portum salutis indulgeat. ỹ Oremus.

Annuntiat diaconus ut supra.

R. S.
Gerb. 80.
Pam. 255.
Men. 64.

Omnipotens sempiterne Deus, moestorum consolatio, laborantium fortitudo, perveniant ad te preces de quacumque tribulatione clamantium, ut omnes sibi in necessitatibus suis misericordiam tuam gaudeant adfuisse. Per Dominum. ỹ

Oremus et pro haereticis et schismaticis, ut Deus et [33] R. S.
Dominus noster eruat eos ab erroribus universis, et ad Gerb. 80. Pam. 255.
sanctam matrem ecclesiam catholicam atque apostolicam Men. 64.
562 revocare dignetur [34]. ℣. Oremus.
Annuntiat diaconus ut supra.

Omnipotens sempiterne Deus, qui omnes salvas [35] et R. S.
neminem vis perire, respice ad animas diabolica fraude Gerb. 80. Pam. 255.
deceptas, ut omni haeretica perversitate depulsa [36] errantium Men. 64.
corda resipiscant et ad veritatis tuae redeant firmitatem.
Per Dominum. ℣

Oremus et pro perfidis Iudaeis, ut Deus et Dominus R. S.
noster auferat velamen de cordibus eorum, ut et ipsi cog- Gerb. 80. Pam. 256.
noscant [37] Christum Iesum Dominum nostrum. ℣ Oremus. Men. 64.
Annuntiat diaconus ut supra.

Omnipotens sempiterne Deus, qui etiam Iudaicam per- R. S.
fidiam a tua misericordia non repellis, exaudi preces Gerb. 80. Pam. 256.
nostras, quas tibi [38] pro illius populi obcaecatione deferimus, Men. 64.
ut cognita veritatis tuae luce, quae Christus est, a suis
tenebris eruantur. Per Dominum. ℣

Oremus et pro paganis, ut Deus omnipotens auferat R. S.
iniquitatem [39] a cordibus eorum, et relictis idolis suis, con- Gerb. 80. Pam. 256.
vertantur ad Deum [40] verum, et unicum Filium eius Iesum Men. 64.
Christum Dominum nostrum, cum quo vivit et regnat Deus
in unitate Spiritus sancti [41]. ℣ Oremus.
Annuntiat diaconus ut supra.

Omnipotens sempiterne Deus qui non mortem pecca- R. S.
torum sed vitam semper inquiris, suscipe propitius ora- Gerb. 80. Pam. 256.
tionem nostram, et libera eos ab idolorum cultura, et Men. 64.
aggrega ecclesiae tuae sanctae ad laudem et gloriam nominis tui. Per. ℣

Istas orationes supra scriptas expletas [42], *ingrediuntur* R.
diaconi in sacrario [42]. *Procedunt cum corpore et sanguinis* [42]
Domini quod ante die remansit: et ponunt super altare.
Et venit sacerdos ante altare, adorans crucem Domini et
osculans. Et dicit Oremus. *Et sequitur* Praeceptis salutaribus moniti, *et oratio Dominica. Inde* Libera nos Domine
quaesumus. *Haec omnia expleta* [42], *adorant omnes sanctam*
crucem et communicant.

[1] R. has in place of these directions only the heading *Ff. vi. oratio quae dicende sunt maiore mane in Hierusalem.* S. has *Ōrā. quę dicende sunt sexta ff. maiore mane in Hieruī.* [2] So V. (ungrammatically, if *et* is to be retained). [3] R. S. insert *proditor.* [4] *nobis piae petitionis* R. S.; V. Gerb. as text. [5] R. S. Gerb. Pam. Men. insert *in*; V. as text. [6] S. inserts *in*; V. R. Gerb. Pam. Men. as text. [7] S. has only one Collect, after which follows the rubric ' Secuntur due lec. quas in capitulare commemora. una in oseae. alia in exodo cum respunsuriis suis. Inde sequitur Euangī. Pās. Dn̄i. Item secuntur or. solemnes.' Both R. and Gerb. recognize two lections each preceded by a Collect, and followed by a *responsorium* (called in Gerb. Gradual and Tract: they are not the same in both), before the reading of the Passion. [8] *da* R. Gerb. Pam.; V. as text. [9] *eiusdem* R. Gerb. Pam.; V. as text. [10] *portemus. Per eundem* R. Gerb. Pam.; V. as text. [11] *etiam* V. (corrected by Tommasi); R. S. Gerb. Pam. Men. as text. [12] *dignetur toto orbe terrarum* R. S. Gerb. Pam. Men.; V. as text. [13] S. has ' Oremus. *Et dicit diaconus* Flectamus genua. *Postquam oraverint dicit* Levate.' But the directions for the deacon's proclamations are not, as in R. V., repeated before each prayer. [14] V. inserts *in*; R. S. Gerb. Pam. Men. as text. [15] Pam. Gerb. omit *tua.* [16] *confessionem* V. [17] R. inserts *sedis apostolicae.* [18] S. Gerb. Pam. Men. omit *et pro antistite nostro Ill.*; V. R. as text. [19] *eum ... salvum ... incolumem* S. Gerb. Pam. Men. [20] *ordinem* Gerb. Pam. Men.; V. R. S. as text (probably ungrammatically). [21] In the margin of S. opposite this and each of the following forms of ' bidding ' is a character which appears to be the letter K (possibly intended as an abbreviation of *Cantor*). Opposite each prayer is written ' Oī.' [22] *electum* S. Gerb. Pam. Men. (which have the singular throughout). [23] *Tantos pontifices,* so V. (ungrammatically). [24] V. omits *tibi gradibus,* but the omission is probably accidental. [25] *Christianissimis imperatoribus nostris vel rege nostro Ill.* R.; *Christianissimis imperatoribus nostris* S.; *Christianissimo imperatore nostro* Pam. Gerb.; *Christianissimo rege nostro* Men.; V. as text. [26] *Deus et Dominus noster* R. S. Gerb. Pam. Men.; V. as text. [27] *illi* Gerb. Pam. Men.; V. as text (perhaps copied from a text which read *imperatoribus,* like R. S., but more likely because *vel* is conjunctive and the prayer which follows is for the Emperor *and* the King. [28] Gerb. Pam. Men. have (after *Deus*) *in cuius manu sunt omnium potestates et omnia iura regnorum*; V. R. S. as text. [29] *ad Romanorum atque Francorum* R. Men.; *ad Romanorum* S¹; *ad Romanorum* Pam.; *ad Christianum* S² Gerb.; V. as text. [30] *potentiae tuae dextera* R. S. Gerb. Pam. Men.; V. as text. [31] S¹ omits *ipsorum,* for which R. S² insert *eorum.* [32] *et ipsi* (for *digni*) Pam. Men.; V. R. S. Gerb. as text. [33] *ac* R. S. Gerb. Men.; V. Pam. as text. [34] V. adds *Per.* [35] *salvas omnes* R. S. Gerb. Pam. Men.; V. as text. [36] *pravitate deposita* Gerb. Pam. Men.; *pravitate depulsa* R.; V. S. as text. [37] *agnoscant* Gerb. Pam. Men.; V. R. S. as text. [38] S². Gerb. Pam. Men. omit *tibi*; V. R. S. as text. [39] *iniquitates* S. [40] S² Gerb. Pam. Men. insert *vivum et*; V. R. S¹ as text. [41] *regnat cum Spiritu sancto Deus, per,* &c. Gerb. Pam. Men.; V. R. S. as text, R. S. adding *per omnia,* &c. [42] So V. (ungrammatically): these directions are not in S., which passes on at once to the *Benedictio Cerei.* R. agrees with the ungrammatical readings of V. (save that it has *expleti* for *expleta*).

XLII.

SABBATORUM DIE.

Mane reddunt infantes symbolum. Prius catechizas eos, imposita super capita eorum manu, his verbis [1] :—

R.
Gerb. 252.
Martène
lib. I.
cap. i.

Nec te latet, Satanas, imminere tibi poenas, imminere tibi tormenta, imminere tibi diem iudicii, diem supplicii, diem qui venturus est velut clibanus ardens, in quo tibi atque universis angelis tuis aeternus veniet interitus. Pro-

inde, damnate, da honorem Deo vivo et vero, da honorem
Iesu Christo Filio eius, et Spiritui sancto, in cuius nomine
atque virtute praecipio tibi[2] ut exeas et recedas ab hoc
famulo Dei, quem hodie Dominus Deus noster Iesus
Christus ad suam sanctam gratiam et benedictionem fontemque baptismatis dono[3] vocare dignatus est, ut fiat eius
templum per aquam regenerationis in remissionem[4] omnium peccatorum, in nomine Domini nostri Iesu Christi,
qui venturus est iudicare vivos et mortuos et saeculum per
ignem. γ

*Inde tangis ei nares et aures de sputo, et dicis ei ad
aurem*[5]*:*

Effeta[6], quod est adaperire, in odorem suavitatis. Tu
autem effugare, diabole, appropinquavit enim iudicium Dei.

*Postea vero tangis ei pectus et inter scapulas de oleo exor-
cizato, et vocato nomine, singulis dicis*[7]*:*

Abrenuntias Satanae?

Resp. Abrenuntio.

Et omnibus operibus eius?

Resp. Abrenuntio.

Et omnibus pompis eius?

Resp. Abrenuntio.

*Inde vero dicis symbolum, imposita manu super capita
ipsorum. Postea vero dicitur eis ab archidiacono:*

Orate, electi, flectite genua. Complete orationem vestram in unum, et dicite, Amen. *Et respondent omnes,*
Amen.

Iterum admonentur ab archidiacono his verbis:

Catechumeni recedant. Omnes catechumeni exeant
foras[8].

Iterum dicit diaconus:

Filii carissimi revertimini in locis vestris[9], expectantes[10]
horam qua possit circa vos Dei gratia baptismum operare.

SEQUITUR ORDO QUALITER SABBATO SANCTO AD
VIGILIAM INGREDIANTUR[11].

*Primitus enim viii hora diei mediante procedunt ad eccle-
siam, et ingrediuntur in sacrario*[12]*, et induunt se vesti-
mentis sicut mos est. Et incipit clerus litania*[12]*, et procedit sacerdos de sacrario cum ordinibus sacris. Veniunt
ante altare stantes inclinato capite usquedum dicent*

Agnus Dei, qui tollis peccata mundi, miserere. *Deinde veniens*[12] *archidiaconus ante altare, accipiens*[12] *de lumine quod vi feria absconsum fuit, faciens*[12] *crucem super cereum, et illuminans*[12] *eum, et completur ab ipso benedictio cerei.*

Mur. ii. 145.
Gerb. ii. 205.

Deus, mundi conditor, auctor luminis, siderum fabricator, Deus qui iacentem mundum in tenebris luce perspicua retexisti, Deus per quem ineffabili potentia omnium claritas sumpsit exordium, te in tuis operibus invocantes, in hac sacratissima noctis vigilia de donis tuis cereum[13] tuae suppliciter offerimus maiestati, non adipe carnis pollutum, non[14] profana unctione vitiatum, non sacrilego igne contactum, sed cera, oleo, atque papyro[15] constructum[16], in tui nominis honore[17] succensum, obsequio religiosae devotionis offerimus. Magnum igitur mysterium, et noctis huius mirabile sacramentum, dignis necesse est laudibus cumulari[18]. In quo Dominicae resurrectionis miraculo diem sibi introductum tenebrae inveteratae senserunt, et mors quae olim fuerat aeterna nocte damnata, inserto veri fulgoris lumine[19], captivam se trahi Dominicis triumphis obstupuit, et[20] quod praevaricante primoplasto[21] tenebrosa praesumptione fuerat in servitute[22] damnatum, huius noctis miraculo splendore libertatis[23] irradiat. Ad huius ergo festivitatis reverentiam fervore spiritus • descendentes, 565 quantum devotio humana exigit, tibi Deo fulgore flammarum placita[24] luminaria exhibemus, ut dum haec fide integra persolvuntur, creaturae tuae etiam praeconia extollantur[25]. Flammae lux quippe dicenda est per quam[26] potestas Deitatis Moysi apparere dignata est, quae de terra servitutis populo exeunti salutifero lumine ducatum exhibuit, quae tribus pueris in camino sententia tyranni depositis vitam blandimentis mollioribus reservavit. Nam ut[27], praecedente huius luminis gratia[28], tenebrarum horror excluditur, ita, Domine, lucescente maiestatis tuae imperio, peccatorum sarcinae diluuntur[29]. Quum igitur huius substantiae miramur exordium, apum necesse est laudemus originem. Apes vero sunt frugales in sumptibus, in procreatione castissimae. Aedificant cellulas cereo[30] liquore fundatas quarum[31] humanae peritiae ars magistra non coaequat[31]. Legunt pedibus flores, et nullum damnum in[32] floribus invenitur. Partus non edunt, sed ore legentes concepti fetus reddunt examina, sicut exemplo mirabili Christus ore paterno processit. Fecunda est in his sine partu virginitas, quam utique Dominus sequi [33] dignatus carnalem se matrem habere virginitatis amore constituit. Talia igitur, Domine, digne [34] sacris altaribus tuis munera offeruntur, quibus te laetari religio Christiana non ambigit.

Benedictio super incensum [35].

Veniat ergo, omnipotens Deus, super hunc incensum larga tuae benedictionis infusio, et hunc nocturnum splendorem, invisibilis regnator, intende; ut non solum sacrificium quod hac nocte litatum est arcana luminis tui admixtione refulgeat, sed quocumque loco ex huius aliquid sanctificationis fuerit mysterio deportatum, expulsa diabolica fraudis nequitia, virtus tuae maiestatis [36] assistat. Per Dominum nostrum Iesum Christum Filium tuum, qui tecum vivit et regnat Deus in unitate Spiritus sancti per omnia saecula saeculorum. Amen. γ

Post hoc surgens sacerdos a sede sua, dicit orationes de vigilia Paschae, sicut in Sacramentorum [37] *continetur.*

Mur. ii. 146.

---

[1] S. has not any form for the *Redditio Symboli*: but it has a trace of the ceremony in the rubric *Sabbato sancto postquam reddunt symbolum et catechizantur infantes impletur cerei benedictio*. R. contains the form as part of the *Ordo Baptisterii* (see Gerb. p. 252), but unfortunately some liquid has been spilt on this part of the MS., which has rendered the rubrics almost entirely illegible, except that at the beginning of the section, which is not correctly reproduced by Gerb. It runs *Sabbatorum diae mane reddentes symbolū prius cathacizas eos Inposita super caput eorum manu his verbis.* The form given by Martène (*de Ant. Eccl. Rit.* lib. I. cap. i.) from the Codex Gellonensis is in pretty close agreement with V. and R. Its readings are occasionally noted below (cited as Gell.). [2] R. inserts *quicumque es spiritus immunde.* [3] Gerb. inserts *Spiritus sancti*, but the words are not in R. [4] *remissione* R. [5] This rubric is illegible in R.; Gell. has *Deinde tangit eos presbyter per singulos nares et aures de sputo oris sui dicens* [? *ad*] *unumquemque aurem.* [6] *Effecta* V.; Gell. has *Effeta* twice; R. as text. [7] This rubric also is illegible in R.: in Gell. the unction and interrogatories are concurrent. After the conclusion of the latter R. inserts '*Dicit presbyter Ego te linio de oleo salutis in Christo Iesu Domino nostro in vitam aeternam. Amen.*' After the recitation of the Creed R. inserts interrogations as to the belief of the catechumens similar to those in the Baptismal Order of V. (xliv *inf.*) and after the response to the last of these proceeds, '*Complete orationem vestram*,' &c. [8] *foris* V. [9] *locis vestris* R.; V. Gell. as text (all ungrammatically). [10] *et expectantes* V. R.; Gell. as text: but perhaps *expectantes = expectantes estote.* [11] The rubrics of this *Ordo* are not in R. S. or Gerb., which give the more ordinary form for the *Benedictio cerei*. The form given in V. has been compared with the text given by Gerbert, vol. ii. p. 205, from a twelfth cent. Vienna MS. (cited as Gerb.) and with that given in Muratori's Gregorian Sacramentary (*Lit. Rom. Vet.* ii. 145). The latter is cited as Mur. [12] So V. (ungrammatically). [13] Gerb. omits *cereum*. [14] *nec* Mur.; V. Gerb. as text. [15] *sed cera atque stuppa* Gerb. [16] *constrictum* V. [17] *honorem* Mur. [18] *cumulare* Mur. [19] *in fonte veri fulgoris et lumine* Gerb.; V. Mur. as text. [20] *at* Mur. [21] *primo plaustro* V.; *protoplasto* Gerb.; Mur. as text. [22] *servitutem* Gerb. (and so

Tommasi): V. Mur. as text, not necessarily ungrammatically. ⁹³ *liberatis* V.; Mur. Gerb. as text. ⁹⁴ *placida* V. Mur.; Gerb. as text. ⁹⁵ *extolluntur* V. ⁹⁶ *per quem* V. ⁹⁷ *et* Gerb. ⁹⁸ *huius gratia luminis* Gerb. ⁹⁹ *deluantur* V. ⁵⁰ *caere* V.; Mur. Gerb. as text. ⁵¹ *fundatus quarum* V.; *fundatas; quarum . . . coaequat* Mur.; *fundatas, quibus . . . coaequatur* Gerb.; Tommasi reads *fundatas, quas . . . coaequat*: but it seems just possible that *fundatas* may be a substantival form. ⁵² Gerb. omits *in*. ⁵³ Mur. omits *sequi*. ⁵⁴ *dignae* V.; *digna* Mur. Gerb. ⁵⁵ Gerb. does not contain this Benediction. ⁵⁶ *virtutis tuae majestas* Mur. ⁵⁷ Probably the word *libro* should be inserted. This reference to a *liber Sacramentorum* suggests that the form has been copied in V. from a MS. of another kind, to which this name would not apply, the final rubric having been copied as well as the rest, without regard to the fact that the prayers in question follow immediately in V.

XLIII.

ORATIONES PER SINGULAS LECTIONES IN SABBATO SANCTO¹. 566

R. S. (1)
Gerb. 83.
Mur. ii.
147.

Deus, qui divitias misericordiae tuae in hac praecipue nocte largiris, propitiare universo ordini sacerdotalis officii, et omnes gradus famulatus nostri perfecta delictorum remissione sanctifica, ut ministraturos regeneratrici² gratiae tuae nulli esse obnoxios patiaris offensae³. Per. y

Sequitur lectio: In principio fecit Deus.

R. S. (3)
Gerb. 83.
Mur. ii.
147.

Deus, incommutabilis virtus, lumen aeternum, respice propitius ad totius⁴ ecclesiae tuae mirabile sacramentum, et opus salutis humanae perpetuae dispositionis affectu tranquillus⁵ operare, totusque mundus experiatur et videat deiecta erigi, inveterata novari, et per ipsum redire omnia in integrum, a quo sumpsere principium. Per. y

Sequitur de Noe.

R. S. (10)
Gerb. 84.
Mur. ii.
149.

Omnipotens sempiterne Deus, qui in omnium operum tuorum dispensatione mirabilis es, intelligant redempti tui non fuisse excellentius quod initio factus est mundus, quam quod in fine⁶ saeculorum Pascha nostrum immolatus est Christus. Per eundem Dominum⁷. y

De Abraham tertia.

R. S. (4)
Gerb. 83.
Mur. ii.
148.

Deus, fidelium Pater summe, qui in toto orbe terrarum promissionis tuae filios diffusa adoptione⁸ multiplicas et per paschale sacramentum Abraham puerum tuum universarum, sicut iurasti, gentium efficis patrem, da populis tuis digne ad gratiam tuae vocationis intrare. Per. y

In Exodo quarta, cum cantico Cantemus Domino.

R. S. (5)
Cf. Gerb.
83.

Deus⁹, cuius antiqua miracula etiam nostris saeculis coruscare sentimus, dum quod uni populo a persecutione

Aegyptia liberando dexterae tuae potentia contulisti, id in salutem gentium per aquam regenerationis operaris, praesta
567 ut et in • Abrahae filios et in Israeliticam dignitatem totius mundi transeat plenitudo. Per. y

In Esaia v.

Omnipotens sempiterne Deus, multiplica in honore[10] nominis tui quod patrum fidei spopondisti[11] et promissionis filios sacra adoptione dilata, ut quod priores sancti non dubitaverunt futurum, ecclesia tua magna iam parte cognoscat impletum. Per. y

In Ezechiel vi.

Deus, qui nos ad celebrandum paschale sacramentum utriusque[12] testamenti paginis imbuisti, da nobis intelligere misericordias tuas[13], ut ex perceptione praesentium munerum firma sit expectatio futurorum. Per. y

vii in Esaia cum cantico Vinea Domini.

Deus, qui in omnibus ecclesiae tuae filiis sanctorum prophetarum voce manifestasti in omni loco dominationis tuae satorem te bonorum seminum, et electorum palmitum esse cultorem[14], tribue populis tuis, qui et vinearum apud te nomine censentur et segetum, ut[15] spinarum et tribulorum squalore resecato digni[16] efficiantur fruge fecundi. Per. y

Item in Exodo viii.

Deus, qui diversitatem omnium gentium in confessione tui nominis unum esse fecisti[17], da nobis et velle et posse quod[18] praecipis, ut populo ad aeternitatem vocato una sit fides mentium et pietas actionum. Per. y

ix In Deuteronomio, cum cantico.

Deus celsitudo humilium, et fortitudo rectorum; qui per sanctum Moysen puerum tuum ita erudire populos tuos sacri carminis tui decantatione voluisti, ut illa legis iteratio fieret etiam nostra directio, excita in omnem iustificatarum gentium plenitudinem potentiam tuam, et [da[19]] laetitiam mitigando terrorem, ut, omnium peccatis tua remissione deletis, quod denuntiatum est in ultionem[20] transeat in salutem. Per. y

568 *In Daniele x.*

Omnipotens sempiterne Deus, spes unica mundi, qui prophetarum tuorum praeconio praesentium temporum declarasti mysteria, auge populi tui vota placatus, quia in nullo fidelium, nisi ex tua inspiratione, proveniunt quarumlibet incrementa virtutum. Per. γ

Oratio post psalmum xli.

R. S. (14)
Gerb. 84.
Mur. ii.
150.

Omnipotens sempiterne Deus, respice propitius ad devotionem populi renascentis, qui sicut cervus aquarum expectat[21] fontem; et concede propitius ut fidei ipsius sitis baptismatis mysterio animam corpusque sanctificet. [Per.] γ

Inde procedunt ad fontes cum litania ad baptizandum[22]. *Baptismum expletum*[23], *consignantur ipsi infantes ab episcopo, dum accipiunt septem dona gratiae Spiritus sancti, et mittit chrisma in frontibus eorum. Postea vero ipse sacerdos revertit*[23] *cum omnibus ordinibus in sacrario*[23]; *et post paululum incipiunt tertiam litaniam; et ingrediuntur ad missas in vigilia, ut stella in caelo apparuerit. Et sic temperent, ut in trinitate numero*[23] *ipsae litaniae fiant.*

[1] R. S. and Gerb. give the same series of prayers and lections which appears in the supplemental portion of Muratori's Gregorian Sacramentary (including the prayer there appended to the *Benedictio cerei*, which in R. S. Gerb. as in V. is the first of the series), and in the same order. V. lacks two prayers (the second and seventh of the series in R. S. Gerb.) and two lections, as compared with the others, and it seems possible that this is due to accident: but the prayers are also arranged somewhat differently in V. [2] *regenerati* V.; R. S. Gerb. Mur. as text. [3] *offendi* V.; R. S. Gerb. Mur. as text. [4] S. Gerb. omit *ad totius*; V. R. Mur. as text. [5] *tranquillius* Mur.; V. R. S. Gerb. as text. [6] *finem* V. [7] R. ends with *Per dominum*; S[1] with *Qui cum patre*, &c.; S[2] Gerb. Mur. with *Qui tecum*, &c. [8] *diffusa adoptionis gratia* S. Gerb.; R. has *diffusa adoptionis*; V. Mur. as text. [9] Gerb. has this prayer in a different recension (as in Mur. ii. 62); V. R. S. Mur. (148) agree. [10] *honorem* Mur.; V. R. S. Gerb. as text. [11] *spondisti* V., and perhaps S[1]. [12] *utrisque* V. S[1]. [13] *misericordiam tuam* S[2] Gerb.; V. R. (S[1]?) Mur. as text. [14] *cultore* V. [15] S[1] omits *ut*. [16] *digna* S[2] Gerb.; V. R. S[1] Mur. as text. [17] *nominis effecisti* S[1]; *nominis adunasti* S[2] Gerb. Mur.; V. R. as text (except that R. reads *effecisti*). [18] *quae* Gerb. [19] V. omits *da*; R. S. Gerb. Mur. as text. [20] *ultione* R. S[1]; V. Gerb. Mur. as text. [21] *aquarum expetit* Mur. Gerb.; *aquarum tuarum expetit* S[2] Gerb. (marg.); V. R. (S[1]?) as text. [22] R. S. have *Inde descendis cum letania ad Fontem*: and have nothing corresponding to the rubric following. [23] So V. (ungrammatically).

XLIV.

Inde Descendis cum Litania ad Fontem.
Benedictio Fontis[1].

R.
Gerb. 85.
Pam. 266.
Mur. ii. 63.
Sacr. Gall.
A.

Omnipotens sempiterne Deus, adesto magnae pietatis tuae mysteriis, adesto sacramentis, et ad creandos novos populos[2] quos tibi fons baptismatis parturit, spiritum adoptionis emitte; et[3] quod humilitatis nostrae gerendum est ministerio tuae virtutis compleatur effectu. Per. γ

Item Consecratio Fontis.

Deus[4], qui invisibili potentia tua sacramentorum tuorum mirabiliter operaris effectum[5], et licet nos tantis mysteriis exequendis simus indigni, tu tamen gratiae tuae dona non deserens[6] etiam ad no‹stras preces aures tuae pietatis inclina. Deus cuius Spiritus super aquas inter ipsa mundi primordia ferebatur, ut iam tunc virtutem sanctificationis aquarum natura conciperet; Deus qui nocentis mundi crimina per aquas abluens, regenerationis speciem in ipsa diluvii effusione signasti, [ut][7] unius eiusdemque elementi mysterio et finis esset vitiis et origo virtutum[8]; respice, Domine, in faciem ecclesiae tuae et multiplica in ea generationes tuas, qui gratiae tuae[9] effluentis[10] impetu[11] laetificas civitatem tuam, fontemque baptismatis aperis toto orbe terrarum gentibus innovandis, ut tuae maiestatis imperio sumat Unigeniti tui gratiam de Spiritu sancto, qui hanc aquam regenerandis hominibus praeparatam arcana sui luminis admixtione fecundet, ut, sanctificatione concepta, ab immaculato divini fontis utero in novam renata[12] creaturam progenies caelestis emergat, et quos aut sexus in corpore aut aetas discernit in tempore omnes in una[13] pariat gratia mater infantia[13]. Procul ergo hinc iubente te, Domine, omnis spiritus immundus abscedat, procul tota nequitia diabolicae fraudis absistat, non insidiando circumvolet, non latendo subripiat, non inficiendo corrumpat. Sit haec sancta et innocens creatura libera ab omni impugnatoris incursu, et totius nequitiae purgata discessu. Sit fons vivus, aqua[14] regenerans, unda purificans, ut omnes hoc lavacro salutifero diluendi, operante in eis Spiritu sancto, perfectae[15] purgationis indulgentiam consequantur[16].

Hic signas.

Unde benedico te, creatura aquae, per Deum vivum, per Deum sanctum, per Deum[17] qui te in principio verbo separavit ab arida[18] et in quatuor fluminibus totam terram rigare praecepit, qui te in deserto amaram suavitate indita[19] fecit esse potabilem et sitienti populo de petra produxit. Benedico te et per Iesum Christum Filium eius unicum, Dominum nostrum, qui te in Cana Galileae signo admirabili sua potentia convertit in vinum; qui pedibus super te ambulavit, · et a Ioanne in Iordane in te baptizatus est; qui te una cum sanguine de latere suo produxit, et discipulis suis iussit ut credentes baptizarentur in te, dicens, Ite, docete omnes gentes, baptizantes eos in nomine Patris, et Filii, et Spiritus sancti.

Hic sensum mutabis.

Haec nobis praecepta servantibus, tu Deus omnipotens clemens adesto, tu benignus aspira. Tu has simplices aquas tuo ore benedicito, ut praeter naturalem emundationem, quam lavandis possunt adhibere corporibus, sint etiam purificandis mentibus efficaces.

Descendat in hanc plenitudinem fontis virtus Spiritus tui, et totam [20] huius aquae substantiam regenerandi [21] fecundet effectu. Hic omnium peccatorum maculae deleantur. Hic natura ad imaginem tuam condita, et ad honorem sui reformata principii, cunctis vetustatis squaloribus emundetur, ut omnis homo hoc sacramentum regenerationis ingressus in vera innocentia, nova infantia [22], renascatur. Per [23] Dominum nostrum Iesum Christum Filium tuum, qui venturus est in Spiritu sancto [24] iudicare vivos et mortuos et saeculum per ignem. γ

Inde benedicto fonte baptizas unumquemque in ordine suo, sub has interrogationes [25] :

Credis in Deum Patrem omnipotentem [26] ?

Resp. Credo.

Credis et in Iesum Christum Filium eius unicum Dominum nostrum, natum et passum?

Resp. Credo.

Credis et in Spiritum sanctum; sanctam ecclesiam [27]; remissionem peccatorum; carnis resurrectionem [28] ?

Resp. Credo.

Deinde per singulas vices mergis eum tertio in aqua.

Postea cum ascenderit a fonte infans signatur a presbytero in cerebro de chrismate, his verbis:

Deus omnipotens, Pater Domini nostri Iesu Christi, qui te regeneravit ex aqua et Spiritu sancto, quique dedit tibi remissionem omnium peccatorum, ipse te linit [29] chrismate [30] salutis in Christo Iesu Domino nostro [31] in vitam aeternam. γ

Resp. Amen.

Deinde ab episcopo datur eis Spiritus septiformis. Ad consignandum imponit eis manum in his verbis [32] :

Deus omnipotens, Pater Domini nostri Iesu Christi, qui regenerasti famulos tuos ex aqua et Spiritu sancto, quique dedisti eis remissionem omnium peccatorum, tu Domine immitte in eos Spiritum sanctum tuum Paraclitum, et da eis spiritum sapientiae et intellectus, spiritum consilii et fortitudinis, spiritum scientiae et pietatis; adimple eos spiritum [33] timoris Dei in nomine Domini [34] nostri Iesu Christi [35], cum quo vivis et regnas Deus semper cum Spiritu sancto, per omnia saecula saeculorum. Amen. γ

Cf. lxxv *infra*.

Postea signat eos in fronte de chrismate dicens:
Signum Christi in vitam aeternam.
Resp. Amen.
Pax tecum.
Resp. Et cum spiritu tuo.
Inde vero cum litania ascendit ad sedem suam, et dicit [36] :
Gloria in excelsis Deo.

---

[1] The form for the Benediction of the Font is not in S.; R. places it in the *Ordo Baptisterii*: and Gerbert, while he gives some details as to R., has chosen, apparently, rather to follow T. and to omit the corresponding portion of the *Ordo Baptisterii*. The forms in Pam., in Muratori's Gregorian Sacramentary, in A., and the partly parallel form in the Sacramentarium Gallicanum, have been employed for comparison, as well as R. and Gerbert's text. [2] *et creandis novis populis* Sacr. Gall. [3] *ut* Gerb. Pam. Mur. A. and Sacr. Gall.; V. R. as text. [4] Gerb. A. Pam. insert here the formula *Sursum corda* ... *VD. ... aeterne*. R. has, as a title before *D. qui invisibili*, what appears to be *Consecr. Fontis*, and places the heading *Coll.* (=*Collecta*) before *D. cuius Spiritus*. [5] *affectum* V. [6] *deseres* V.; *deseris* R.; Gerb. Pam. Mur. A. Sacr. Gall. as text. [7] V. omits *ut*. [8] *vitii et origo virtutis* Mur.; *vitiis ... virtutis* R.; *vitiis ... virtutibus* Gerb. Pam. A.; V. as text. [9] *tuas, quae gratiae tuae* V.; *tuas. Gratiae tuae* A.; Gerb. omits *tuae*; R. Pam. Mur. as text. [10] *affluentis* Gerb. Pam. A.; *affluente* R.; V. Mur. as text. [11] *impetum* V. (ungrammatically). [12] *renatam* V. A.; R. Gerb. Pam. Mur. as text. [13] *in unam ... infantiam* Gerb. Pam. Mur.; *una ... infantia* A.; V. R. as text (perhaps ungrammatically). [14] *aquae* V.; R. Gerb. Pam. Mur. A. as text, and Sacr. Gall. has *Sit vivis aqua*, &c. [15] *perfecti* V.; *perfecte* A.; R. Gerb. Pam. Mur. as text. [16] A. adds *Per*. [17] Gerb. Pam. Mur. A. omit *per Deum*. [18] R. inserts here *cuius spiritus super te ferebatur, qui te de Paradiso manare*. So also Pam. Mur.: but these differ from R. in omitting *verbo* before *separavit* in the clause preceding. [19] *suavitatem inditam* V. (ungrammatically); R. has *suavitatem indita*. [20] *tui, totamque* Pam. Mur. Gerb. A.; V. R. as text. [21] *regenerandis* V. [22] *verae innocentiae novam infantiam* Pam. Mur. Gerb. A.; *vere innocentiam novam infantiam* R.; V. as text. [23] R. has only *Per*; Pam. ends with *Qui tecum*. [24] Gerb. Mur. A. omit *in Spiritu sancto*. [25] R. has here 'In ordine suo inde benedicto [fonte] *baptizas unumquemque*,' followed by the form *Deus omnipotens ... qui te regeneravit*. The interrogations in R. are written at an earlier point of the *Ordo Baptisterii* and not repeated here (see note 7 on xlii *supra*). Pam. similarly refers to an earlier point. *sub has interrogationes*, so V. (probably ungrammatically). [26] R. A. Pam. add *creatorem caeli et terrae*; V. Gerb. as text. [27] R. Gerb. add *catholicam*; A. Pam. add *catholicam, sanctorum communionem*; V. as text. [28] R. adds *vitam aeternam*; A. Pam. *et vitam aeternam*; V. as text. [29] *liniat* Pam.;

lineat V. in lxxv *infra*; *linet* R. A.; V. Gerb. Mur. as text. [30] *chrisma* V. R. A. (ungrammatically); V. in lxxv *infra*, Gerb. Mur. Pam. as text. [31] Gerb. Pam. Mur. omit *in Christo . . . nostro*; A. places the same words after *in vitam aeternam*; V. R. as text. [32] R. does not contain this form; and Gerb. (87) Mur. Pam. A. all have it in another recension. [33] *spiritum*, so V. (ungrammatically) both here and in lxxv *infra*. [34] V. in lxxv *infra* has *Dei et Domini* (omitting *in nomine*). [35] V. in lxxv *infra* inserts *et iube eum consignari signum crucis in vitam aeternam Per eundem*, &c. [36] R. has the corresponding rubric immediately after the form *Deus omnipotens . . . qui te regeneravit*.

XLV.

Orationes et Preces ad Missam in Nocte.

Miss. Gall. 742.
Sacr. Gall. 854.

Omnipotens sempiterne Deus, qui hanc sacratissimam noctem per universa mundi spatia gloria[1] Dominicae resurrectionis illustras, conserva in nova[2] familiae tuae progenie[2] sanctificationis spiritum quem dedisti; ut corpore et mente renovati puram tibi animam et purum pectus semper exhibeant. Per Dominum.

R. S.
Gerb. 89.
Pam. 272.
Men. 74.
Cf. Miss.
Gall. 742.
Sacr. Gall. 854.

Deus qui hanc sacratissimam noctem gloria[3] Dominicae resurrectionis illustras, conserva in nova[4] familiae tuae progenie[4] adoptionis spiritum quem dedisti, ut corpore et mente renovati[5] puram tibi exhibeant servitutem. Per Dominum. γ

Secreta.

R. S.
Gerb. 89.
Men. 74.

Suscipe, quaesumus, Domine, et plebis tuae et tuorum hostias renatorum, ut et confessione tui nominis et baptismate renovati sempiternam beatitudinem consequantur. Per Dominum.

Item alia.

R.S.(*Dom*.)
Gerb. 91.
Pam. 272.
Men. 75.
Miss. Gall. 742. Sacr. Gall. 854.

Suscipe, Domine, preces populi tui cum oblationibus hostiarum ut paschalibus initiata[6] mysteriis ad aeternitatis nobis medelam, te operante, proficiant[7]. Per Dominum. γ

R. S.
Gerb. 89.

VD. Et iustum est aequum et salutare. Adest enim nobis optatissimum tempus, et desideratae noctis lumen advenit. Quid enim maius vel melius inveniri poterit quam Domini resurgentis praedicare virtutem? Hic namque inferorum claustra disrumpens, clarissima[8] nobis hodie suae resurrectionis vexilla[8] suscepit[9], atque hominem, remeans[10], invidia inimici deiectum mirantibus intulit astris. O noctis istius mystica et veneranda commercia! O sanctae matris ecclesiae pia sempiterna[11] beneficia! Non vult habere[12] quod perimat, sed cupit invenire quod redimat. Exultavit Maria in sacratissimo puerperio [13]. Exultat ecclesia in filiorum suorum generationis [14] specie [15]. Sic fons ille beatus qui Dominico lateri circumfluxit [16] moles excepit [17] vitiorum ut his sacris altaribus vitales escas perpetua vita [18] conferat renatorum. Et ideo cum angelis.

458   VD. [19] Te quidem omni tempore sed in hac potissimum nocte [20] gloriosius praedicare, quum Pascha nostrum immolatus est Christus. Ipse enim verus est Agnus qui abstulit peccata mundi; qui mortem nostram moriendo destruxit, et vitam resurgendo reparavit. Propterea profusis paschalibus gaudiis totus in orbe terrarum mundus exultat. Sed et supernae virtutes atque angelicae concinunt potestates, hymnum gloriae tuae sine fine dicentes [21]. γ

S. Miss. Gall. 743. Sacr. Gall. 854. Gerb. 90. Pam. 272. Men. 75.

Infra actionem.

459   Communicantes, et noctem sacratissimam celebrantes resurrectionis Domini nostri Iesu Christi secundum carnem. γ

R. S. Gerb. 90.

Item infra actionem.

460   Hanc igitur oblationem servitutis nostrae, sed et cunctae familiae tuae quam tibi offerimus pro his quoque, quos 573 regenerare dignatus es ex aqua et Spiritu sancto, • tribuens eis remissionem omnium peccatorum, ut invenires [22] eos in Christo Iesu Domino nostro, quaesumus, Domine, placatus accipias. Pro quibus [22] maiestati tuae supplices fundimus preces, ut nomina eorum ascribi iubeas in libro viventium: diesque nostros. γ [23]

R. S. Gerb. 90. Pam. 272. Men. 74.

Postcommun.

461   Praesta, quaesumus, omnipotens Deus, ut divino munere satiati et sacris mysteriis innovemur et moribus. [Per.]

R. S. Gerb. 90. III. xiii *infra*.

Item alia.

462   Concede, quaesumus, omnipotens Deus, ut paschalis perceptio sacramenti continuata [24] in nostris mentibus perseveret. Per. γ   Miss. Gall. 745. Pam. 275. Men. 77.

R. S. (*Fer. iii.*) Gerb. 95. See lxxviii *infra*.

---

[1] *gloriae* V.; *gloriosae* Sacr. Gall.; Miss. Gall. as text.   [2] *novam* ... *progeniem* V. (ungrammatically); Miss. Gall. Sacr. Gall. as text.   [3] *gloriosae* V. Sacr. Gall. Miss. Gall.; R. S. Gerb. Pam. as text.   [4] *novam* ... *progenie* V.; *novam progeniem* R. S. Gerb.; Sacr. Gall. Pam. Men. as text.   [5] Sacr. Gall. omits *renovati*.   [6] *initiatae* Pam. Gerb.; V. R. S. Men. Miss. Gall. Sacr. Gall. as text.   [7] Miss. Gall. inserts a clause with reference to the position of the prayer as *Coll. ad Pacem*.   [8] *carissimam* ... *vixillam* V.; R. S. Gerb. as text.   [9] *reportavit* S² Gerb.; V. R. S¹ as text.

At this point S² inserts in margin '*et triumphato diabolo victor inclytus caelorum regna conscendit*'; adding the note '*Potes quidem et usque ad finem canere sed tamen aliam in ultimo libri perquire.*' ¹⁰ *reparans* S² Gerb.; V. R. S¹ as text. ¹¹ *sempiternaque* S² Gerb.; V. R. S¹ as text. ¹² *quia non vult Deus noster habere* S² Gerb.; V. R. S¹ as text. ¹³ *sacratissimam puerperi* V.; *sacratissima puerperi* R. S¹; S² Gerb. as text. ¹⁴ *regenerationis* S² Gerb.; V. R. S¹ as text. ¹⁵ *sacramento* S² Gerb.; V. as text (word erased in S¹); R. has *speciae*. ¹⁶ *latere circumfulxit* V.; R. S. Gerb. as text. ¹⁷ *expulit* S² Gerb.; V. R. (S¹¹) as text, ¹⁸ *vitalis esse perpetuam vitam* S² Gerb.; V. R. as text; reading of S¹ doubtful. ¹⁹ S. Gerb. Pam. Men. have this Preface in a shortened form, ending at *reparavit* with the clause *Et ideo cum angelis*. The Gallican books agree with V. ²⁰ *hanc potentissimam noctem* V. S¹; *hac potentissimum nocte* S²; Miss. Gall. Sacr. Gall. Gerb. Pam. Men. as text. ²¹ *gloriam sine cessatione dicentes* Sacr. Gall. ²² R. S. Gerb. Pam. Men. omit *ut invenires . . . nostro*, and also the clause *Pro quibus . . . viventium*. ²³ S. inserts, after the *Hanc igitur* the *Benedictio Agni*, ending with the clause *Per quem haec omnia*. ²⁴ *continua* R. Gerb. Pam. Men. Miss. Gall.; V. S. as text.

XLVI.

Dominicum¹ Paschae.

R. S.
(*in nocte.*)
Gerb. 89.
Miss. Gall.
744, 750.
Cf. Sacr.
Gall. 858.

Deus², qui per Unigenitum tuum aeternitatis nobis aditum, devicta morte, reserasti, da nobis, quaesumus, ut qui resurrectionis Dominicae solemnia colimus, per innovationem³ tui Spiritus a morte animae resurgamus. Per Dominum. γ

R. S.
(*Fer. iv.*)
Gerb. 96.
Miss. Gall.
744, 752.
Cf. Sacr.
Gall. 858.

Deus, qui nos resurrectionis Dominicae annua⁴ solemnitate laetificas, concede propitius, ut per temporalia festa quae agimus pervenire ad gaudia aeterna mereamur. Per Dominum. γ

Pam. 276. Men. 78.   **Secreta.**

Sacr. Gall.
860.
Cf. xlv
supra.

Suscipe, Domine, propitius, munera famulorum tuorum, ut⁵ confessione tui nominis et baptismate renovati, sempiternam beatitudinem consequantur. Per Dominum.

S.
Gerb. 92.
Miss. Gall.
745.
Sacr. Gall.
861.
Pam. 567.

VD. Te quidem omni tempore, sed in hoc praecipue die laudare, benedicere, et praedicare, quod⁶ Pascha nostrum immolatus est Christus; per quem in⁷ aeternam vitam filii lucis oriuntur, fidelibus regni caelestis atria reserantur, et beati⁸ lege commercii divinis humana mutantur. Quia nostrorum⁹ omnium mors cruce Christi redempta¹⁰ est, et in resurrectione eius omnium vita resurrexit. Quem in susceptione mortalitatis Deum agnoscimus; et in divinitatis 574 gloria¹¹ Deum et hominem confitemur. Qui mortem nostram moriendo destruxit et vitam resurgendo restituit¹², Iesus Christus Dominus noster. Et ideo cum angelis. γ

Infra actionem, ut supra in nocte sancta. Sequitur

Postcommun.[13]

Omnipotens sempiterne Deus, qui ad aeternam vitam in Christi resurrectione nos reparas, custodi opera misericordiae tuae, et suavitatem corporis et sanguinis Domini nostri Iesu Christi unigeniti Filii tui nostris infunde pectoribus. Per Dominum.

R. S.
Gerb. 92.

[1] *Dominicum*, so V. (probably ungrammatically for *Dominico*). [2] Sacr. Gall., by a blunder of the scribe, joins the beginning of this collect with the end of the next. [3] *innovatione* V.; *invocationem* Miss. Gall. 750; R. S. Miss. Gall. 744, Gerb. as text. [4] Miss. Gall. 752 omits *annua*. [5] *munera et vota famulorum ut* Sacr. Gall. [6] *quo* Sacr. Gall. Pam.; *quia* R.; *quando* S[2] Gerb.; V. S[1] Miss. Gall. as text. [7] *ad* S[2] Gerb. Pam.; Sacr. Gall. omits *in*; V. R. S[1] Miss. Gall. as text. [8] *beatae* Miss. Gall. (Mabillon reads *beatae legis commercio*); V. R. S. Sacr. Gall. Gerb. Pam. as text. [9] *nostrum* S[2] Gerb.; the rest as text (ungrammatically). [10] *perempta* R. S[2] Gerb. Pam.; V. S[1] Miss. Gall. Sacr. Gall. as text. [11] *gloriam* V. S[1] Sacr. Gall.; R. S[2] Miss. Gall. Gerb. Pam. as text. [12] *reparavit. Et ideo cum*, &c. S[2] Gerb. Pam.; V. R. S[1] Sacr. Gall. as text. (Miss. Gall. has *restituit Iesus Christus. Per Dominum*). [13] This heading is misplaced in V. before the line which precedes it in the text.

XLVII.

INCIPIUNT TOTIUS ALBAE ORATIONES ET PRECES.

FERIA SECUNDA.

Paschale mysterium recensentes, apostolorum, Domine, beatorum precibus foveamur, quorum magisterio[1] cognovimus exequendum. Per.

R. S.
Gerb. 93.

Deus, ecclesiae tuae redemptor atque perfector, fac, quaesumus, ut apostolorum precibus paschalis sacramenti dona capiamus, quorum nobis ea tribuisti magisterio praedicari. Per.

R. S.
(*Fer. iii.*)
Gerb. 95.

Secreta.

Sacrificia, Domine, paschalibus gaudiis immolamus[2], quibus ecclesia tua mirabiliter renascitur[3] et nutritur. [Per.] γ   Pam. 276. Men. 78. Pam. (Amb.) 358.

R. S.
(*Fer. iv.*)
Gerb. 96
Miss. Gall. 745.

VD. Nos[4] precari clementiam tuam ut ad celebrandum digne paschale mysterium, beatorum apostolorum precibus adiuvemur; et quorum praedicatione haec credenda suscepimus, eorum patrociniis fideliter exequamur. Per Christum Dominum.

R. S.
Gerb. 94.

575 *Infra actionem, ut supra in nocte sancta. Sequitur*

Postcommun.

Impleatur in nobis, quaesumus, Domine, sacramenti paschalis sancta libatio nosque de[5] terrenis affectibus ad caeleste[6] transferat institutum. Per.

R. S.
Gerb. 94.
Men. 76.
Miss. Gall. 743.

¹ *magisterium* V.; *mysterio* R.; S. Gerb. as text.   ² *immolata dignanter assume* R.   ³ *et renascitur* Miss. Gall.; *et nascitur* S. Men.; *et pascitur* R. Pam.; *pascitur* Gerb. (Amb.) and Pam. (Amb.); V. as text.   ⁴ *Et* (for *Nos*) S⁹ Gerb.; V. S¹ as text; R. has *nos praedicare*.   ⁵ *a* S⁹ Gerb.; V. R. S¹ Miss. Gall. Men. as text.   ⁶ *caelestem* V. R. S¹; Miss. Gall. S⁹ Gerb. Men. as text.

XLVIII.

Feria Tertia.

R. S.
(*Domin.*)
Gerb. 91.
Pam. 274.
Men. 76.
Miss. Gall. 745.   Sacr. Gall. 860.

Deus, qui paschalia nobis remedia¹ contulisti, populum tuum caelesti dono prosequere; ut inde post in perpetuum gaudeat unde nunc temporaliter exultat. Per.

R. S.
(*Fer. iv.*)
Gerb. 96.

Deus, qui solemnitate paschali caelestia mundo remedia benignus operaris, annua festivitatis huius dona prosequere, ut observantia temporalis ad vitam² proficiat sempiternam. Per. γ

Secreta.

R. S.
(*Fer. vi.*)
Gerb. 98.
Pam. 277.
Men. 79.

Hostias, Domine, quaesumus³, placatus assume quas et pro renatorum expiatione peccati deferimus, et [pro]⁴ acceleratione caelestis auxilii. Per. γ

R. S.
Gerb. 95.
Pam.
(Amb.)
361.
Cf. Leon. 304.
Cf. Men.77.

VD. Per Christum Dominum nostrum. Qui oblatione sui [corporis]⁵ remotis sacrificiis carnalium victimarum, seipsum tibi pro salute nostra offerens, idem Sacerdos et sacer Agnus exhibuit. Quem laudant. γ

Infra actionem, ut supra in nocte sancta. Sequitur

Postcommun.

xxvi *supra*.
xlix *infra*.
Miss. Gall. 746.

Adesto, Domine, quaesumus, nostrae redemptionis effectibus⁶; ut quos sacramentis aeternitatis instituis, iisdem protegas dignanter aptandos. [Per.]

R. S. (*Sabb. in nocte.*)
Gerb. 90.
Miss. Gall. 745.
Pam.
(Amb.)354.

Digne⁷ nos tuo nomini, quaesumus, Domine, famulari, salutaris cibus et sacer potus instituat, et⁸ renovationem⁹ conditionis humanae, quam¹⁰ mysterio continet in nostris iugiter sensibus operetur¹¹. [Per.]

---

¹ *paschale nobis remedium* R. S. Gerb. Pam. Men.; *paschalium nobis remedia* Miss. Gall. Sacr. Gall.; V. as text.   ² S⁹ Gerb. insert *nobis*.   ³ *Hostias quaesumus Domine* R. S. Gerb. Pam. Men.; V. as text.   ⁴ V. omits *pro*; S. Gerb. Pam. Men. as text; R. has *pro hac celebratione*.   ⁵ V. omits *corporis*, which is restored from R. S. Gerb. Pam. (Amb.); Leon. omits the phrase.   ⁶ V. varies between *affectibus* and *effectibus* in the three places where this Postcommunion occurs: Miss. Gall. has (apparently) *affectibus*.   ⁷ *Digni* Miss. Gall.   ⁸ *ut* V.; R. S. Gerb. Pam. (Amb.) Miss. Gall. as text.   ⁹ *renovationibus* Miss. Gall.   ¹⁰ *que* V.; R. S. Gerb. Pam. (Amb.) Miss. Gall. as text.   ¹¹ *operentur* V.; S. Gerb. Pam. (Amb.) Miss. Gall. as text; R. has *aperetur*.

XLIX.

Feria Quarta.

576   Deus, qui pro salute mundi sacrificium paschale fecisti, propitiare supplicationibus nostris, ut interpellans pro nobis Pontifex summus, quos per id quod nostri est similis, reconciliatur[1], per id quod[2] tibi est aequalis, absolvat, Iesus Christus[3] Dominus noster, Qui tecum vivit et regnat. γ   R.S.(*alibi.*) Gerb. 101. Pam. 280. Men. 82.

Deus, qui omnes[4] in Christo renatos genus regium[5] et sacerdotale fecisti, da nobis et[6] velle et posse quod praecipis, ut populo ad aeternitatem vocato una sit fides cordium et pietas actionum. Per. γ   R.S.(*alibi.*) Gerb. 101. Pam. 279. Miss. Gall. 745. Miss. Goth. 599.

Secreta.

Suscipe, quaesumus, Domine, hostias[7] redemptionis humanae, et salutem nobis mentis et corporis operare placatus[8]. Per Dominum nostrum. γ   S. (*alibi.*) Gerb. 231. Pam. 416. III. xx *infra.*

VD. Circumdantes altaria tua, [Domine][9] virtutum, et in ipsius Agni immaculati agnitione gloriantes, qui seipsum pro nobis obtulit immolandum, ut corpore eius et[10] sanguine quo a peccatis redempti sumus, ad aeternam vitam sacrificiis[11] caelestibus[12] pascamur[13]. Per Christum Dominum.   R. S. Gerb. 96. Pam. (Amb.) 359.

Infra actionem, ut supra in nocte sancta. Sequitur

Postcommun.

Adesto, Domine, quaesumus, nostrae redemptionis effectibus[14], ut quos sacramentis aeternitatis instituis iisdem protegas dignanter aptandos. Per Dominum nostrum.   xxvi *supra* xlviii *supra.* Miss. Gall. 746.

---

[1] *summus quos per id quod dei* (?) *est similis reconciliat* R. ; *summus, per id quod nostri est similis reconciliat* S¹ ; *summus, nos per id quod [quo* Pam.] *nostri est similis reconciliet* S² Gerb. Pam. Men. ; V. as text (ungrammatically or corruptly).   [2] *quo* Pam.   [3] Pam. Men. insert *Filius tuus*; S. Gerb. omit *Iesus Christus Dominus noster*; (S¹ ends with *Per Dominum*; S² Gerb. with *Qui tecum*).   [4] V. transposes *omnes* and *qui*.   [5] V. has *regnum*.   [6] Miss. Goth. omits *et*.   [7] *hostiam* R. S. Gerb. Pam. V. in III. xx *infra* ; V. here as text.   [8] *placatus operare* S² Gerb.; V. S¹ Pam. as text.   [9] V. omits *Domine*, which is restored from R. S. Gerb. Pam. (Amb.).   [10] *in* (for *et*) V.   [11] S² Gerb. insert *utique.*   [12] *paschalibus* Pam. (Amb.) [13] *nutriamur* S² Gerb.; *pasceremur* Pam. (Amb.); *paschamur* R.; word erased in S¹; V. as text.   [14] See note 6 on xlviii *supra.*

L.

Feria Quinta.

R. S¹. Deus, qui multiplicas sobolem¹ renascentium, fac eos gaudere propitius de suorum venia peccatorum. Per. γ

S.
[Gerb. 101.]
Pam. (Amb.) 353.
Deus², qui humanam naturam supra primae originis reparas³ dignitatem, respice ad pietatis tuae ineffabile sacramentum, et⁴ quos regenerationis mysterio⁵ dignatus es innovare, in his dona tuae perpetuae gra·tiae benedic- 577 tionisque⁶ conserva. Per Dominum nostrum.

Secreta.

R.S.(Sabb.)
Gerb. 99.
Pam. 278.
Men. 80.
Concede, quaesumus, Domine, semper nos per haec mysteria paschalia gratulari, ut continua nostrae reparationis operatio perpetua⁷ nobis fiat causa laetitiae. Per Dominum nostrum. γ

R. S.
Gerb. 97.
VD. Quia vetustate destructa renovantur universa deiecta; et vitae nobis in Christo reparatur integritas. Quem laudant angeli.

Infra actionem, ut supra in nocte sancta. Sequitur

Postcommun.

R.S.(alibi.)
Gerb. 184.
Pam. 411.
Men. 181.
III. xii infra.
Miss. Gall. 746.
Purifica⁸, Domine, quaesumus, mentes nostras benignus et renova caelestibus sacramentis, ut consequenter et corporum praesens pariter et futurum capiamus auxilium. Per. γ

¹ *sobole* S¹; V. R. as text; S² Gerb. Pam. Men. read *multiplicas ecclesiam tuam in sobole* and alter the end of the collect. ² *Omnipotens sempiterne Deus* S. Gerb.; V. Pam. (Amb.) as text. ³ *praeparas* V.; S. Gerb. Pam. (Amb.) as text. ⁴ *ut* V. S¹ Pam. (Amb.); S² Gerb. as text: but it seems possible that *ut* is an older ungrammatical reading. ⁵ *mysterii* V.; S. Gerb. Pam. (Amb.) as text. ⁶ *perpetua gratiae protectione* Gerb.; *perpetis gratiae benedictionisque* Pam. (Amb.); S. is defective after *dignatus es*; V. as text. ⁷ *perpetuae* S² Gerb. Pam. Men.; V. R. S¹ as text. ⁸ *Purificatio* V.; (Tommasi reads *Purificato*). V. in III. xii *infra*, R. S. Gerb. Pam. Men. Miss. Gall. all have *Purifica*.

LI.

Feria Sexta.

R. S.
Gerb. 98.
Cf. Pam. 281.
Deus¹, qui ad caeleste regnum nonnisi renatis ex aqua et Spiritu sancto pandis introitum, auge semper super famulos tuos gratiae tuae dona, ut qui ab omnibus sunt purgati peccatis a nullis fraudentur promissis. Per Dominum. γ

Deus qui credentes in te fonte baptismatis innovasti, hanc renatis in Christo concede custodiam, ut nullo erroris incursu gratiam tuae benedictionis amittant. Per. γ

R.S.(*alibi*.)
Pam. 280.
Men. 80.

Secreta.

Paschales hostias recensentes² quaesumus, Domine, ut quod frequentamus actu comprehendamus effectu³. Per.

Miss. Gall. 745.

VD. Per Christum Dominum nostrum. Qui secundum promissionis suae incommutabilem veritatem⁴ caelestis Pontifex factus in aeternum solus omnium sacerdotum peccati remissione non eguit, sed potius peccatum mundi idem verus Agnus abstersit. Et ideo cum angelis⁵. γ

R. S.
Gerb. 98.
Pam.
(Amb.)
362.
Men. 80.

578 *Infra actionem ut supra in nocte sancta. Sequitur*

Postcommun.

Immortalitatis alimoniam⁶ consecuti, quaesumus, Domine, ut quod ore percipimus⁷ mente sectemur. Per. γ

R.S.(*alibi*.)
Gerb. 191.
Pam. 414.
Men. 185.
Miss. Gall. 747.

¹ Pam. has a variation of this collect which also appears in Gerb. and in V. in lvi *infra*; R. S. Gerb. here agree with the text. ² *immolantes* Miss. Gall. ³ *effectum* V. (ungrammatically); Miss. Gall. as text. ⁴ S² Gerb. omit *secundum ... veritatem*. V. has *veritate* (ungrammatically); R. S¹ Pam. (Amb.) Men. as text. ⁵ S. Gerb. Pam. (Amb.) Men. all have the ending *Per quem*, &c.; R. has *per Christum*; V. as text. ⁶ *alimonia* V. (ungrammatically); R. S. Miss. Gall. Gerb. Pam. Men. as text. ⁷ *percepimus* S. Gerb. Pam. Men.; V. R. Miss. Gall. as text.

LII.

FERIA SEPTIMA.

Deus, qui nos exultantibus animis pascha tuum celebrare tribuisti, fac, quaesumus, nos¹ et temporalibus gaudere subsidiis, et aeternitatis effectibus² gratulari. Per Dominum. γ

S. (*alibi*.)
Gerb. 101.
Pam. 279.
Men. 81.

Deus³, innocentiae restitutor et amator, dirige ad te tuorum corda famulorum, ut quos⁴ de infidelitatis tenebris liberasti⁴, nunquam a tuae veritatis luce discedant. Per. γ

R. S.
Gerb. 99.
Cf. Pam.
280.
Cf. Men. 82.

Secreta.

Suscipe munera, quaesumus, Domine, exultantis ecclesiae, et cui causam tanti gaudii praestitisti, perpetuum fructum concede laetitiae. [Per.] γ

R.S.(*alibi*.)
Gerb. 100.
Pam. 279.
Men. 81.

VD. Nos te suppliciter obsecrare, ut Iesu Christi Domini nostri⁵, cuius muneris⁶ pignus accepimus, manifesta dona comprehendere valeamus, et⁷ quae nobis feliciter⁸

S.
Gerb. 99.
Pam.
(Amb.)
363. Men. 80.

speranda paschale[9] contulit sacramentum[9], attingere mereamur resurrectionis Dominicae firmitate[10]. Et ideo cum angelis[11]. γ

Infra actionem, ut supra in nocte sancta. Sequitur

Postcommun.

S. (*alibi.*)
Gerb. 100.
Pam.
(Amb.)
365.

Exuberet, quaesumus, Domine, mentibus nostris paschalis gratia sacramenti, ut donis suis ipsa nos dignos efficiat[12]. [Per.]

[1] *fac nos quaesumus* S. Gerb. Pam. Men.; V. as text.   [2] *affectibus* Men.
[3] R. S¹ insert *qui*.   [4] S² Gerb. omit *quos*, and read *liberati*; V. R. S¹ as text.   [5] *et Iesum Christum Dominum nostrum ut* R. S¹; (S² Gerb. substitute *per* for *et*; Pam. (Amb.) has VD.... *aeterne Deus. Poscentes ut cuius*, &c.; Men. VD.... *aeterne Deus. Per quem supplices exposcimus ut cuius*, &c.; V. as text.   [6] Pam. (Amb.) inserts *mysticum*.   [7] *ut* Pam. (Amb.)
[8] *fideliter* R. S. Gerb. Pam. (Amb.) Men.; V. as text.   [9] *paschali*... *sacramento* S. Gerb.; V. R. Pam. (Amb.) Men. as text.   [10] *resurrectionis eius attingere mereamur exemplo* S² Gerb.; *per resurrectionis eius attingere mereamur ineffabile mysterium* Men. Pam. (marg.); V. R. Pam. (Amb.) and probably S¹ as text. (V. R. have *firmitatem*, ungrammatically.)   [11] *Per quem* S. Gerb. Men.; *Per eundem* Pam. (Amb.); *Per Christum* R.
[12] *donis suis ipsi nos efficiat* V.; Pam. (Amb.) reads *donis tuis*, otherwise as text, with S. Gerb.

LIII.

Octavas[1] Paschae.

Die Dominico.

R. S.
Gerb. 100.
Pam. 279.

Deus, qui renatis baptismate mortem adimis et vitam tribuis sempiternam, concede, quaesumus, ut quorum nunc regenerationis sacrae diem celebramus octavum, ita corpora eorum animasque custodias, ut gratiam se catholicae fidei percepisse pietatis tuae defensione cognoscant. Per.

579

R.S.(*alibi.*)
[Gerb. 99.]
Pam. 280.
Men. 82.

Deus, qui credentes in te populos gratiae tuae largitate multiplicas, respice propitius ad electionem tuam; ut qui sacramento baptismatis sunt renati, regni caelestis mereantur introitum. Per. γ

Secreta.

S. (*alibi.*)
Gerb. 95.

Suscipe, quaesumus, Domine[2], oblationes familiae tuae, ut sub tuae protectionis auxilio et[3] collata[4] non perdant et ad aeterna dona perveniant[5]. Per.

R.S.(*alibi.*)
Gerb. 188.
Pam. 578.
Men. 183.

VD. Nos clementiam[6] tuam suppliciter exorare, ut Filius tuus Dominus noster Iesus Christus, qui se usque in finem saeculi suis promisit fidelibus adfuturum, et prae-

sentiae corporalis mysteriis non deserat quos redemit, et⁷
maiestatis suae beneficiis non relinquat.   Et ideo cum⁸. γ

Infra actionem, ut supra.   *Sequitur*

Postcommun.⁹

Maiestatem tuam, Domine, supplices exoramus, ut quos   R. S.
viam fecisti perpetuae salutis intrare nullis permittas errorum   Gerb. 101.
laqueis implicari.   Per.

¹ *Octabas* V.; R. S. have *Die Dom. post Albas*.   ² *Domine quaesumus*
S. Gerb.   ³ S¹ omits *et*.   ⁴ *consolata* V. (corr. by Tommasi); R. S.
Gerb. as text.   ⁵ *perveniamus* Gerb.   ⁶ *VD. Et clementiam* S² Gerb.
Pam.; V. R. S¹ Men. as text.   ⁷ V. omits *et* which is restored from R. S.
Gerb. Pam. Men.   ⁸ S¹ has the ending *Per Christum*; S² Gerb. Pam. Men.
have *Per quem*.   ⁹ V. gives the heading *Commū*.

LIV.

ORATIONES ET PRECES DE PASCHA ANNOTINA.

Deus, per¹ cuius providentiam nec praeteritorum mo-   R. S.
menta deficiunt, nec ulla superest² expectatio futurorum,   Gerb. 102.
tribue permanentem peractae, quam recolimus³, solem-   Pam. 283.
nitatis effectum⁴; ut quod recordatione percurrimus,
semper in opere teneamus.   Per.

Deus, qui renatis fonte baptismatis delictorum indul-   S.
gentiam⁵ tribuisti, praesta misericors ut recolentibus huius   Gerb. 102.
nativitatis insignia, plenam adoptionis gratiam largiaris.   Pam. 283.
580 Per.

Secreta.

Clementiam tuam, Domine, suppliciter exoramus, ut   R. S.
paschalis muneris sacramentum, quod fide recolimus, et   Gerb. 103.
spe desideramus intenti, perpetua dilectione capiamus.   Per   Pam. 283.
Dominum.

VD. Per Christum Dominum nostrum⁶ redemptionis   R. S.
nostrae festa recolere quibus humana substantia vinculis   Gerb. 103.
praevaricationis exuta spem resurrectionis [accepit]⁷ per   Pam. 568.
renovatam originis dignitatem.   Per quem maiestatem. γ

Infra actionem.

Hanc igitur oblationem famulorum famularumque tuarum,   R. S.
quam tibi offerunt, annua recolentes mysteria, quibus eos   Gerb. 103.
tuis adoptasti regalibus institutis, quaesumus, Domine,
placatus intende.   Pro quibus supplices preces effundimus,
ut in eis et collata custodias, et⁸ promissae beatitudinis
praemia largiaris, diesque nostros.

H

Postcommun.

R. S.
Gerb. 103.
Pam. 283.

Tua nos, quaesumus, Domine, quae sumpsimus, sancta purificent, et operationis suae remedio nos perficiant esse placatos⁹. Per Dominum. γ

¹ *apud* S² Gerb.; V. (S¹?) Pam. as text; R. has *D. qui per cuius*.   ² *ulla est* Pam.   ³ *quam colimus* S. Gerb.; *quae recolimus* V.; R. has *peracte quere colimus*.   ⁴ *affectum* S¹; V. R. S² Gerb. Pam. as text.   ⁵ *indulgentia* V. (ungrammatically); S. Gerb. Pam. as text.   ⁶ S² Gerb. Pam. insert *et*; V. R. S¹ as text.   ⁷ *accepit* is restored from R.; S¹ like V. has no verb; Pam. has *assumpsit*, which Tommasi gives as a marginal reading; S² Gerb. read *percepit*, both verbs being placed after *dignitatem*.   ⁸ *ut* V. S.; R. Gerb. as text.   ⁹ *placatus* (prob. for *placatos*) V.; *purgatos* Pam.; R. S. Gerb. as text.

LV.
ORATIONES ET PRECES IN PAROCHIA¹.

S.
Gerb. 103.

Deus, qui humani generis es et² reparator et rector, da, quaesumus, ecclesiam tuam et nova prole semper augeri et devotione cunctorum³ crescere filiorum. Per.

S.
Gerb. 103.

Renovatos, Domine, fontis⁴ ac Spiritus tui potentia in hereditarium populum clementer adnumera, ut qui a multitudine purgati sunt criminum, invisibilium etiam mereantur copiam praemiorum. Per.

[Secreta.]

S.
Gerb. 103.

Offerimus tibi, Domine, laudes et munera; et pro concessis beneficiis exhibentes gratias, pro concedendis suppliciter deprecamur. Per. γ

S.
Gerb. 103.
Pam.
(Amb.)
363.
Men. 76.

•VD. Nos te⁵ suppliciter exorare ut fidelibus tuis dig- 581 nanter impendas quo et paschalia capiant sacramenta, et desideranter expectent ventura⁶; ut in mysteriis quibus renati sunt permanentes, ad novam vitam his operantibus⁷ perducantur⁸. Et ideo cum angelis⁹. γ

Postcommun.

S.
Gerb. 103.

Adiuvet nos, quaesumus, Domine, sanctum istud paschale mysterium, et ut devotis hoc mentibus exequamur obtineat. Per.

Ad Populum.

S.
Gerb. 103.
Pam. 283.

Populus tuus, quaesumus, Domine, renovata semper exultet animae¹⁰ iuventute, ut qui antea¹¹ peccatorum veternoso in mortis venerat senio¹², nunc laetetur in pristinam se gloriam¹³ restitutum. Per.

[1] This *Missa* is not contained in R.   [2] S[1] omits *es et*; S[2] Gerb. omit *et*;
V. as text.   [3] *suorum* (for *cunctorum*) S[2] Gerb.; V. S[1] as text.   [4] *Renovatur Domine fontes* V.; Tommasi reads *Renovatum Domine fonte*; S. Gerb.
as text.   [5] *VD. Et te* S[2] Gerb. Men.; V. S[1] Pam. (Amb.) as text.   [6] *venturum* V.; S. Gerb. Pam. (Amb.) Men. as text.   [7] *operibus* S. Gerb.; V.
Pam. (Amb.) Men. as text.   [8] *perducant* V.   [9] S. Gerb. Men. have
the ending *Per Christum*; V. Pam. (Amb.) as text.   [10] *animi* Pam.
[11] *ante* V.; S. Gerb. Pam. as text.   [12] *veterno in morbi venerat senium*
Pam.; *veternoso in morte venerat senio* S[1]; S[2] Gerb. correct *morte* to *mortem*.
The reading in the text is that of V., *verternoso.. senio* being an ungrammatical ablative.   Tommasi suggests *veterno in mortis venerat senium*.
[13] *in pristinae se novitatis gloriam* S[2] Gerb.; V. (S[1]?) Pam. as text.

LVI.

INCIPIUNT ORATIONES PASCHALES VESPERTINALES [1].

Deus, qui ad aeternam vitam in Christi resurrectione nos reparas, imple pietatis tuae ineffabile sacramentum; ut quum in maiestate sua Salvator noster advenerit, quos fecisti baptismo regenerari, facias beata immortalitate vestiri. Per Dominum. γ

R.
Gerb. 101.
Pam. 281.
Men. 82.

Paschalibus nobis, quaesumus, Domine, remediis [2] dignanter impende, ut terrena desideria respuentes, discamus inhiare [3] caelestia. Per.

R.
Gerb. 102.
Pam. 282.

Quaesumus, omnipotens Deus [4], iam non teneamur obnoxii [5] sententiae damnationis humanae, cuius nos vinculis [6] haec redemptio paschalis absolvit. Per Dominum.

R.
Gerb. 102.
Pam. 282.
Cf. Miss.
Gall. 744.

Concede [7], misericors Deus, ut quod paschalibus exequimur institutis, fructiferum nobis omni tempore sentiamus. Per.

S.
[Gerb. 102.]
Pam. 282.

Multiplica fidem, quaesumus, Domine [8], populi tui, ut cuius per te sumpsit initium, per te consequatur augmentum. Per. γ

R.S.(*alibi*.)
Gerb. 97.
Pam. 277.
Men. 79.

Praesta nobis, omnipotens [9] Deus, ut percipientes paschali munere veniam pecca•torum, deinceps peccata vitemus. Per Dominum.

S.
[Gerb. 102.]
Pam. 282.

Deus, per quem nobis et redemptio venit et praestatur adoptio, respice in opera misericordiae tuae, ut in Christo renatis et aeterna tribuatur hereditas et vera libertas. Per. γ

S. (*alibi*.)
Gerb. 98.
Pam. 278.
Men. 80.

Deus, qui per Unigenitum tuum, devicta morte, aeternitatis nobis aditum reserasti, erige ad te tuorum corda credentium, ut omnis generatio apprehendat meritis quod suscipit [10] mysteriis. Per.

S.
[Gerb. 102.]

R.S.(*alibi.*)
Gerb. 127.
Pam. 280.
Men. 82.
lxxxi *infra.*

Omnipotens sempiterne Deus, deduc nos ad societatem caelestium gaudiorum; ut Spiritu sancto renatos regnum tuum tribuas introire, atque eo [11] perveniat humilitas gregis, quo processit fortitudo [12] Pastoris. Per. γ

R.
Gerb. 102.
Pam. 281.
Men. 83.

Deus, qui renatis per aquam et Spiritu sancto [13] caelestis regni pandis introitum, auge super famulos tuos gratiam quam dedisti; ut qui ab omnibus sunt purgati peccatis, a nullis priventur promissis. Per. γ

R.
[Gerb. 101.]
Pam. 281.

Dele [14], quaesumus, Domine, conscriptum peccati lege chirographum, quod in nobis paschali mysterio per resurrectionem tui Filii vacuasti. Per. γ

R.
Pam. 281.

Fac, omnipotens Deus, ut qui, paschalibus remediis innovati [15], similitudinem terreni parentis evasimus, ad formam caelestis transferamur [16] auctoris. Per. γ

R. S.
Gerb. 102.
Pam. 281.
Men. 82.

Da [17], misericors Deus, ut in resurrectione [18] Domini nostri Iesu Christi inveniamus et nos veraciter [19] portionem. Per Dominum. γ

S.
[Gerb. 102.]
Pam. 278.
Men. 80.

Adesto, quaesumus, Domine, tuae adesto familiae [20], et dignanter impende, ut quibus fidei gratiam contulisti et coronam largiaris aeternam. Per.

S.
[Gerb. 102.]

Exaudi nos, omnipotens Deus, et familiae tuae corda, cui perfectam baptismi gratiam contulisti, ad promerendam beatitudinem aptes aeternam. [Per.]

S.
[Gerb. 102.]
Pam. 282.
Men. 83.

Conserva in [21] nobis, quaesumus, Domine, misericordiam tuam, et [22] quos ab erroris liberasti caligine veritatis tuae firmius inhaerere facias documento [23]. Per.

S.
[Gerb. 102.]
Pam. 282.
Men. 83.

Sollicita [24], quaesumus, Domine, quos lavasti [25] pietate custodi; ut quia [26] tua [27] sunt [28] passione redempti tua [29] resurrectione laetentur [28]. Per Dominum nostrum [30].

S.
[Gerb. 102.]
Pam. 282.

•Christianam, quaesumus, Domine, respice plebem, et 583 quam aeternis dignatus es renovare mysteriis, a temporalibus culpis dignanter absolve. Per.

S. (*alibi.*)
Gerb. 60.
Pam. 242.
Men. 58.

Da, quaesumus, omnipotens Deus, ut quae divina sunt iugiter ambientes [31] donis semper [32] mereamur caelestibus propinquare [33]. Per. γ

S.
[Gerb. 102.]
Pam. 282.
Men. 83.

Omnipotens sempiterne Deus, propensius his diebus tuam misericordiam consequamur, quibus eam plenius, te largiente, cognovimus. Per Dominum.

Concede, misericors Deus, ut devotus tibi populus tuus [34] existat et de tua clementia quod ei prosit indesinenter obtineat. Per.

S. (*alibi*.)
Gerb. 51.
Pam. 231.
Men. 49. xxvi *supra*.

Deus, qui sensus nostros terrenis actionibus perspicis retardari, concede, quaesumus, ut tuo potius munere tuis aptemur remediis. Per.

S. [Gerb. 102.]

Tribue, quaesumus, Domine, ut illuc semper [35] tendat Christianae devotionis affectus, quo tecum est nostra substantia [36]. Per. γ

R.S.(*alibi*.)
Gerb. 96.
Pam. 276.
Men. 78. Leon. 316.

Concede [37], quaesumus, omnipotens Deus, ut ecclesia tua et in suorum firmitate [38] membrorum, et in nova semper fecunditate laetetur. Per.

R.S.(*alibi*.
Gerb. 97.
Pam. 277.
Men. 79.

Largire, quaesumus, ecclesiae tuae, Deus, et a suis semper et ab alienis abstinere delictis; ut pura tibi mente deserviens, pietatis tuae remedia sine cessatione percipiat. Per Dominum.

S. [Gerb. 102.]

---

[1] Answering to this series in R. S. Gerb. Pam. Men. are collections of '*Aliae Orationes Paschales*,' having a good deal in common with this collection, and with each other. Gerbert by some error employs for many of the prayers which are actually contained in S. or R. the type which indicates matter absent from those MSS. In the series contained in S. something is wanting, as one of the prayers stops short in the middle: probably a leaf is missing (between the pages numbered 180 and 181). A good many prayers of the series are found (in whole or in part) in the Gallican books. [2] *Paschalia nobis, Domine, quaesumus, remedia* Pam.; R. has *Paschalibus nos ... remediis*; V. Gerb. as text (probably ungrammatically). [3] *amare* Pam.; V. R. Gerb. as text. [4] R. Gerb. insert *ut*. [5] *obnoxiis* V. R. [6] *vinculi* V.; R. Gerb. Pam. Miss. Gall. as text (but *vinculi* may be ungrammatical). [7] Pam. inserts *quaesumus*. [8] *quaesumus, Domine, fidem* R. S. Gerb. Pam. Men.; V. as text. [9] *Praesta quaesumus omnipotens* Pam. [10] *omnes regenerati apprehendant meritis quod suscepere* S. Gerb.; V. as text. [11] *atque in ea* V. here and in lxxxi *infra*; R. S. Gerb. Pam. Men. as text. [12] *praecessit celsitudo* V. in lxxxi *infra* and S. Gerb. Pam. Men. (R. has *processit celsitudo*); V. here as text. [13] *ex aqua et Spiritu sancto* R. Gerb. Men.; *aqua et Spiritu sancto* Pam.; V. as text, perhaps ungrammatically. [14] *Depelle* R. Pam.; *Repelle* Gerb.; V. as text. [15] *innovasti* V.; end of word erased in R. [16] *transferamus* V.; *transferantur* R. [17] *Praesta nobis omnipotens et* Pam. Men.; V. S. Gerb. as text. [18] *resurrectionem* V. (ungrammatically); R. S. Gerb. Pam. Men. as text. [19] *percipiamus veraciter* Pam. Men.; V. S. Gerb. as text. [20] *Domine, familiae tuae* S. Gerb. Pam. Men.; V. as text. [21] S. Gerb. omit *in*. [22] *ut* Pam. Men. [23] *docimentum* V. [24] *solita* S. Gerb. Pam. Men.; V. as text. [25] *quos salvasti* S. Gerb.; *nos* Pam. Men.; V. as text. [26] *qui* S² Gerb. Pam. Men.; V. S¹ as text. [27] *Unigeniti tui* Pam. Men. [28] *sumus ... laetemur* Pam.; S. Gerb. Men. have *passione sunt*. [29] *eius* Pam. Men. [30] So V. S¹ (wrongly); S² Gerb. have *Qui cum*, &c.; Pam. Men. (see notes [27], [29]) have *Per eundem*. [31] *exequentes* S. Gerb. Pam. Men.; V. as text. [32] Pam. Men. omit *semper*. [33] *appropinquare* Men. [34] V. omits *tuus* in xxvi *supra*. [35] S. Gerb. Pam. Men. Leon. omit *semper*; V. as text. [36] Pam. adds *Iesus Christus Filius tuus Dominus noster*. [37] *Da* R. S. Gerb. Pam. Men.; V. as text. [38] *et suorum infirmitate* V.; R. S. Gerb. Pam. Men. omit *in* at this point, and also before *nova*.

LVII.

Orationes et Preces Dominicum[1] post octavas Paschae.

R. S.
Gerb. 103.
Miss. Gall.
755.
Pam. 400.
Men. 88.

Deus, qui in Filii tui humilitate iacentem mundum erexisti, laetitiam concede fidelibus tuis[2]; ut quos perpetuae [mortis][3] eripuisti casibus, gaudiis facias sempiternis perfrui[4]. Per. γ

R. S.
Gerb. 104.
Miss. Gall.
755.

Deus, in cuius praecipuis mirabilibus est humana reparatio, solve opera diaboli, et mortifera peccati vincula disrumpe; ut destructa malignitate quae nocuit, vincat misericordia quae redemit. Per.

Secreta. 584

R. S.
Gerb. 104.
Miss. Gall.
755.
Pam. 400.

Benedictionem[5], Domine, nobis conferat salutarem[6] sacra semper oblatio, ut quod agit mysterio virtute perficiat. Per. γ

R.S.(alibi.)
Gerb. 185.
Pam. 577.
Men. 182.

VD[7]. Nos tibi semper et ubique gratias agere, et suppliciter exorare[8] sic nos bonis tuis[9] instrui[10] sempiternis ut temporalibus consoleris[11]; sic praesentibus refoveri[12], ut ad gaudia nos mansura perducas. Per Christum Dominum nostrum. γ

Postcommun.

R. S.
Gerb. 104.
Pam. 400.

Praesta nobis, omnipotens Deus, ut vivificationem tuae gratiae[13] consequentes in tuo semper munere[14] gloriemur. Per. γ

[1] *Dominicum* so V. (ungrammatically).   [2] *fidelibus tuis perpetuam concede laetitiam* S² Gerb. Pam. Men.; R. S¹ similarly, but have *perpetuam laetitiam concede*; V. Miss. Gall. as text.   [3] V. omits *mortis*; restored from Miss. Gall. R. S. Gerb. Pam. Men.   [4] *perfrui sempiternis* S² Gerb. Men.; R. S¹ as text; V. has *perfruere*.   [5] Pam. inserts *tuam*.   [6] *salutares* V.   [7] R. S. Gerb. Pam. Men. assign this Preface to the twenty-first Sunday after Pentecost (after the Octave in Pam.), beginning the Preface proper with *Et suppliciter* (*Et te suppliciter* Men.).   [8] S² Gerb. Pam. insert *ut*.   [9] S² Gerb. omit *tuis*.   [10] *instruas* R. S. Gerb. Pam. Men.; V. as text.   [11] *temporalibus quoque consolari digneris* Pam. Men.; V. R. S. Gerb. as text.   [12] *refovere* R. S¹ Men.; *refove* Pam.; *refoveas* S² Gerb.; V. as text.   [13] *vivificationis tuae gratiae* V.; *vivificationis tuae gratiam* S. Gerb. Pam.; R. as text.   [14] *munere semper* S¹.

LVIII.

Item secunda Dominica post clausum Paschae[1].

R. S.
Gerb. 106.
Pam. 401.
Men. 89.
Leon. 301.

Deus, qui errantes ut in via[2] possint redire, veritatis tuae[3] lumen ostendis, da cunctis, qui Christiana professione censentur, et illa respuere quae huic inimica sunt nomini, et ea quae sunt apta sectari. Per Dominum. γ

Tibi placitam, Deus noster, populo tuo tribue voluntatem, quia tunc illi prospera cuncta praestabis, quum tuis aptum feceris institutis. Per Dominum.

R. S.
Gerb. 106.
Leon. 413.

Secreta.

His nobis, Domine⁴, mysteriis conferatur⁵, quo terrena desideria mitigantes⁶, discamus habere⁷ caelestia. Per. γ

R. S.
Gerb. 106.
Pam. 401.

VD. Per Christum Dominum nostrum. Qui humanis⁸ miseratus erroribus⁸, per virginem nasci dignatus est; et per passionem mortis a perpetua nos morte liberavit; ac⁹ resurrectione sua aeternam nobis contulit vitam¹⁰. Quem laudant angeli.¹¹

S.
[Gerb. 106.]
Pam. 568.
Men. 89.

Postcommun.

Sacramenta quae sumpsimus, quaesumus, Domine, et spiritalibus nos expient¹² alimentis, et corporalibus tueantur auxiliis. Per Dominum nostrum Iesum Christum. γ

S.
Gerb. 106.
Pam. 401.

¹ *Post octavas Paschae* in R. S. Gerb. Pam. Men.   ² *errantibus ut in viam* S² Gerb. Pam. Men.; V. as text (ungrammatically); R. has *errantes . . . viam*, and so probably S¹; while Leon. has *Deus errantes in via posse.* ³ *redire iustitiae, veritatis tuae* R. Gerb. Men.; *redire, iustitiae tuae* Pam.; V. S¹ Leon. as text.   ⁴ Pam. omits *Domine.*   ⁵ *conferat* V.; R. S. Gerb. Pam. as text.   ⁶ *devitantes* S²; *vitantes* Gerb.; V. R. S¹ Pam. as text.   ⁷ *amare* Pam.   ⁸ *humanos . . . errores* S² Gerb.; V. S¹ as text; so apparently R. which is here mutilated; Pam. Men. omit the phrase, having *Qui de virgine nasci dignatus, per passionem et mortem.*   ⁹ *et* Pam. Men.   ¹⁰ *vitam donavit* S¹ Gerb.; *vitam contulit* Pam.; V. R. S¹ Men. as text.   ¹¹ S. Gerb. Pam. Men. have *Per quem maiestatem, &c.*; V. as text.   ¹² *excipiant* R. S¹; *instruant* Pam.; V. S² Gerb. as text.

LIX.

585 TERTIA DOMINICA POST CLAUSUM PASCHAE¹.

Deus, qui fidelium mentes unius efficis voluntatis², da populis tuis, id amare quod praecipis, id desiderare quod promittis, ut inter mundanas varietates ibi nostra fixa sint corda ubi vera sunt gaudia. Per. γ

R. S.
Gerb. 110.
Pam. 401.
Men. 90.

Exaudi, Domine, preces nostras, ut quod tui Verbi santificatione³ promissum est evangelico ubique compleatur effectu, et⁴ plenitudo adoptionis obtineat quod praedixit testificatio veritatis. Per Dominum.

R. S.
Gerb. 110.
Cf. Leon. 411.

Secreta.

Deus, qui nos per huius sacrificii veneranda commercia unius summae⁵ divinitatis participes effecisti, praesta,

R. S.
Gerb. 110.
Pam. 401.

III. xiv *infra*.	quaesumus, ut sicut tuam cognovimus⁶ veritatem sic eam dignis moribus⁷ assequamur. Per. ү
R. S. Gerb. 110. Pam. 568. Men. 90.	VD. De tuo munere postulantes⁸ ut tempora quibus post resurrectionem⁹ Dominus noster Iesus Christus cum discipulis corporaliter habitavit¹⁰, pia devotione tractemus¹¹. Per Dominum. ү

Postcommun.

R. S. Gerb. 110. Pam. 401.	Adesto¹², Domine Deus noster, ut per haēc quae fideliter sumpsimus et purgemur a vitiis et a periculis omnibus exuamur¹³. Per Dominum nostrum. ү

¹ *Post octavas Paschae* in R. S. Gerb. Pam. Men. ² *voluntati* V. ³ *sanctione* S² Gerb. ; *sanctificationem* V. ; R. S¹ as text. ⁴ Leon. has *ut in omni natione quod Verbi tui promissum est evangelio compleatur, et*. ⁵ *summaeque* V. in III. xiv *infra*. ⁶ *cognoscimus* R. Pam. Gerb. V. in III. xiv *infra*. ⁷ *moribus et mentibus* V. in III. xiv *infra*. ⁸ *Et tui misericordiam muneris* (*mun. mis.* Gerb.) *postulare* Gerb. Pam. Men. ; V. R. S. as text (the end of the Preface in R. is mutilated). ⁹ S² Gerb. Pam. Men. insert *suam*. ¹⁰ *apparuit sic ipso opitulante* Men. ; *conversatus est ita* (*sic* Gerb.) *ipso opitulante* S² Gerb. ; Pam. inserts *sic ipso opitulante* ; V. S¹ as text (so apparently R.). ¹¹ *transigamus* S² Gerb. ; S² Gerb. Pam. Men. add *quatenus in his omnium vitiorum sordibus careamus*. ¹² S² Gerb. insert *nobis*. ¹³ Tommasi suggests *eruamur*; but V. R. S. Gerb. Pam. as text.

LX.

Quarta Dominica post Clausum Paschae¹.

R. S. Gerb. 113. Pam. 402. Men. 90.	Deus, a quo bona cuncta procedunt, largire supplicibus² ut cogitemus, te inspirante, quae recta sunt, et, te gubernante, eadem faciamus. Per. ү
S. Gerb. 113.	Deus, qui misericordiae ianuam fidelibus patere voluisti, respice in nos et miserere nostri; ut qui voluntatis tuae viam, te donante³, sequimur, a vitae nunquam semitis deviemus. Per.

Secreta.

Miss. Gall. 756.	Praesta, Domine, quaesumus⁴, ut illius salutis capiamus effectum⁵, cuius per haec mysteria pignus accipimus⁶. Per Dominum.
R.S.(*alibi*.) Gerb. 122.	VD.⁷ Ut quia primum tuae pietatis indicium⁸ est, si tibi nos facias toto corde subiectos, tu spiritum nobis tantae devotionis infundas, ut propitius largiaris consequenter auxilium. Per.

Postcommun.

S. Gerb. 113. Pam. 402. Leon. 368.	Tribue nobis, Domine, caelestis mensae virtute satiatis⁹, et desiderare quae recta sunt, et desiderata percipere. Per Dominum. ү

[I. lxi.] ROMANAE ECCLESIAE. 105

[1] *Post Octavas Paschae* in R. S. Gerb. Pam. Men. There is a leaf wanting in R. at this point. [2] S² Gerb. Men. insert *tuis*; V. R. S¹ Pam. as text. [3] *donante te* S. Gerb.; V. as text. [4] Miss. Gall. inserts *veritati* (*sic*). [5] *affectum* Miss. Gall. [6] *accepimur* V. [7] S. and Gerb. assign this Preface to the Sunday after the Ascension, and insert *Et clementiam tuam suppliciter obsecrare*. [8] *iudicium* Gerb.; V. S. as text. [9] *satietatis* V.; erasure in S¹; *caelestes mensae satietate* Pam. (marg.); S² Gerb. Pam. Leon. as text.

LXI.

Quinta Dominica post clausum Paschae[1].

Omnipotens sempiterne Deus, fac nos[2] tibi semper et devotam gerere voluntatem, et maiestati tuae sincero corde servire. Per. γ

R. S.
Gerb. 122.
Pam. 402.
Men. 95. III. ix *infra*.

Deus, vita fidelium, gloria humilium[3], beatitudo iustorum, propitius suscipe supplicum preces, ut animae quae promissiones tuas sitiunt de tua semper abundantia repleantur. Per Dominum nostrum.

R. S.
Gerb. 122.
Pam. 402.
Men. 96.

Secreta.

Oblatio nos[4], Domine, tuo nomini dicata[5] purificet, et de die in diem ad caelestis vitae transferat actionem. Per Dominum. γ

R.S.(*alibi.*)
Gerb. 133.
Pam. 403.
Men. 169. lxv and III. ix *infra*.

VD. Tu mentes[6] nostras bonis operibus semper informes, quia sic erimus praeclari muneris prompta sinceritate[7] cultores, si ad meliora iugiter transeuntes, paschale mysterium studeamus habere perpetuum. Per quem maiestatem[8]. γ

S. (*alibi.*)
Gerb. 113.
Pam.
(Amb.)
372.
Men. 91.

Postcommun.

Repleti, Domine, muneribus sacris, da, quaesumus, ut in gratiarum[9] semper actione maneamus. Per. γ

R. S.
Gerb. 122.
Men. 96.
Pam. 402. Leon. 436.

[1] The Collects and the Postcommunion of this *Missa* are assigned in R. S. Gerb. Pam. Men. to the Sunday after the Ascension (their series of Sundays '*post Octavas Paschae*' ending with the fourth). Pam. makes the second Collect a '*super populum*,' and Men. an additional '*ad complendum*.' Pam. assigns the Secret to the second, R. S. Gerb. Men. to the third, Sunday after Pentecost: the Preface is given by all these but R., which is there defective, to the fourth Sunday '*post Oct. Paschae*.' [2] *nobis* Pam. [3] R. S¹ Pam. Men. insert *et*. [4] V. in lxv *infra* omits *nos*. [5] *dicanda* R. S. Gerb. Pam. Men. V. lxv *infra*; V. here and in III. ix *infra* as text. [6] *Et clementiam tuam humiliter implorare ut tu mentes* S² Gerb.; *Et maiestatem tuam indefessis precibus exorare ut mentes* Pam. Men.; V. S¹ as text. [7] *securitate* Gerb. [8] *Per Christum*, &c. S. Gerb. Pam. Men.; V. as text. [9] S² Gerb. insert *tuarum*.

LXII.

SEXTA DOMINICA POST CLAUSUM PASCHAE [1].   587

R. S.
Gerb. 132.
Pam. 403.
Men. 168.

Deus, in te sperantium fortitudo, adesto propitius invocationibus nostris; et quia sine te nihil potest mortalis infirmitas, praesta auxilium gratiae tuae, ut in exequendis [2] mandatis tuis et voluntate tibi et actione placeamus. Per Dominum. γ

R. S.,
Gerb. 132.

Deus spei luminis sincerum [3] mentium, luxque perfecta beatorum, qui vere es lumen ecclesiae tuae, da cordibus nostris et dignam tibi orationem persolvere, et te semper praeconiorum munere collaudare. Per.

Secreta.

R. S.
Gerb. 133.
Pam. 403.

Hostias nostras, Domine, tibi dicatas placatus assume, et ad perpetuum nobis tribue pervenire [4] subsidium. Per. γ

R. S.
Gerb. 133.
Pam. 573.
Men. 169.

VD. Qui ecclesiae tuae filios sicut erudire non cessas ita non desinas [5] adiuvare, ut recte faciendi [voluntatem] [6] cognoscant, et possibilitatem capiant exequendi. Per Christum. γ

Postcommun.

R. S.
Gerb. 133.
Pam. 403.
Men. 169.
Cf. Leon. 377.

Tantis, Domine, repleti muneribus, praesta [7], quaesumus, ut [8] salutaria dona capiamus, et [9] a tua nunquam laude cessemus. Per. γ

Ad Populum.

R. S.
Gerb. 133.
Pam. 403.
Men. 169.
xviii *supra.*
Leon. 441.

Fideles tuos, Domine, benedictio desiderata confirmet, quae eos et a tua voluntate nunquam faciat [10] discrepare, et tuis semper indulgeat beneficiis gratulari. Per.

---

[1] This *Missa* is assigned as a whole by R. S. Gerb. to the second Sunday after Pentecost, to which Men. also assigns the first Collect, Preface, Postcommunion and '*Ad Populum*.' Pam. assigns the first Collect, Secret, Postcommunion and '*Ad Populum*' to the first Sunday after Pentecost, and the Preface to the second Sunday after the Octave.   [2] *sequendis* Men.; R. omits *in*.   [3] So V. R. and apparently S¹; S² Gerb. correct *spei* to *spes*, but leave *luminis sincerum* unaltered; Gerbert suggests *sincerarum*: but perhaps the simplest emendation is that of *lumen* for *luminis*, which is furnished by the marginal note of Tommasi.   [4] *provenire* R. S. Gerb. Pam.; V. as text.   [5] *desinis* S² Gerb. Pam. Men.; V. R. S¹ as text.   [6] V. R. omit *voluntatem*, which is restored from S.; Gerb. has *ut et scientiam recte faciendi* and omits *cognoscant*; and with this Pam. Men. agree to some extent, having *ut* (*ut et* Pam.) *scientiam, te miserante, recta faciendi, et possibilitatem.*   [7] Men. omits *praesta.*   [8] R. Gerb. Pam. Men. insert *et*; V. S. as text.   [9] *ut* Leon. (which places *praesta quaesumus* after *capiamus*).   [10] *faciat nunquam* Pam. Men.; V. R. S. Gerb. Leon. as text.

LXIII.

ORATIONES ET PRECES IN ASCENSA DOMINI[1].

Deus, qui ad declaranda tua[2] miracula maiestatis post resurrectionem a mortuis hodie in caelos, apostolis adstantibus, ascendisti, concede nobis tuae pietatis auxilium, ut secundum tuam • promissionem et tu nobiscum semper[3] in terris, et nos tecum in caelo vivere mereamur. Per[4].

R. S.
Gerb. 121.
Pam. 294.

Praesta, quaesumus, omnipotens Pater[5], ut nostrae mentis intentio quo solemnitatis hodiernae gloriosus auctor ingressus est, semper intendat, et quo fide pergit, conversatione perveniat. Per.

R. S.
Gerb. 120.
Leon. 315.

Secreta.

Sacrificium, Domine, pro Filii tui supplices venerabili nunc ascensione deferimus; praesta, quaesumus, ut et[6] nos per ipsum his commerciis sacrosanctis ad caelestia consurgamus. Per.

R. S.
Gerb. 121.
Pam.
(Amb.)
374.

VD. Per Christum Dominum nostrum. Qui saluti humanae subvenire dignatus est: nascendo etenim nobis donavit gloriam, patiendo diabolum vicit, resurgendo[7] a mortuis vitae aeternae aditus praestitit, ascendendo ad Patrem caelestes ianuas reseravit[8]. Quem laudant angeli.

Infra actionem.

Communicantes et diem sacratissimum celebrantes, quo Dominus noster unigenitus Filius tuus unitum sibi hominem nostrae substantiae in gloriae tuae dextera collocavit. Sed et memoriam. γ

Leon. 316.

Inde vero modicum ante expleto canone[9] benedices fruges novas. Sequitur benedictio.

Benedic, Domine, et has[10] fruges novas[10] fabae quas[10] tu, Domine, rore caelesti et inundantia pluviarum ad maturitatem perducere dignatus es, ad percipiendum nobis cum gratiarum actione in nomine Domini nostri Iesu Christi. Per quem haec omnia, Domine, semper bona *usque*[11] *expleto canone*[9]. γ

See III.
lxxxviii
infra.

Postcommun.

Deus, cuius Filius, in alta caelorum potenter ascendens, captivitatem nostram sua duxit virtute captivam, tribue,

R.S.(*alibi.*)
Gerb. 122.
Pam. 294.
Men. 95.

quaesumus, ut dona quae suis participibus contulit, largiatur [12] et nobis [13]. Per Dominum nostrum. γ

Ad Populum. 589

R.S.(*alibi.*)
Gerb. 122.

Erectis sensibus, et oculis cordis ad sublimia elevantes, quaesumus ut quae in precum vota detulimus, ad impetrandi fiduciam referamus. Per [14].

[1] R. S. Gerb. also have two *Missae* for this Festival, of which the former is in R. and Gerb. assigned to the Vigil. Their contents are to some extent the same as those of the two *Missae* in V. but they do not agree as to order. In S. the former has the heading *In Ascensa Domini*, the latter *Item in Ascensa Domini ad S Pe* (i.e. ad *S. Petrum*). Pam. and Men. have but one *Missa*. [2] *tuae* R. S² Gerb. Pam.; V. S¹ as text. [3] *nobis cum semper sis* Gerb.; V. R. S. Pam. as text. [4] So V. S¹ (wrongly); R. S² Gerb. Pam. have *Qui cum*, &c. [5] *omnipotens Deus* Leon.; R. has *omnipotens Deus Pater*. [6] Pam. (Amb.) omits *et*. [7] *regendo* V. [8] *reparavit* V. [9] *expleto canone*. So V. (ungrammatically). [10] *hos ... novos ... quos* V. (probably from a form which read *fructus*). [11] *bonusque* V. [12] *largiat* V. [13] Pam. inserts *Iesus Christus Dominus noster*, Men. *Iesus Christus Filius tuus*. [14] S² Gerb. have *elevatis*, but otherwise leave the grammar of this passage uncorrected. V. S¹ as text. R is mutilated at the point where the prayer occurs.

LXIV.

Item alia Missa.

R.S.(*alibi.*)
Gerb. 122.
Pam. 294.
Men. 95.
Leon. 313.

Adesto, Domine, supplicationibus nostris, ut sicut humani generis Salvatorem consedere tecum in tua maiestate confidimus, ita usque ad consummationem saeculi manere nobiscum, quemadmodum est[1] pollicitus, sentiamus[2]. Per. γ

R. S.
Gerb. 121.
Pam. 295.
Men. 95.

Tribue, quaesumus, omnipotens Deus, ut munere festivitatis hodiernae illuc filiorum tuorum dirigatur intentio, quo[3] in tuo Unigenito tecum est nostra substantia. Per.

Secreta.

R.S.(*alibi.*)
Gerb. 122.
Pam. 402.
Men. 95.

Sacrificia nos, Domine, immaculata purificent, et mentibus nostris supernae gratiae dent vigorem. Per Dominum. γ

R. S.
Gerb. 121.
Pam. 569.
Leon. 315.

VD. In hac praecipue[4] die, qua[5] Iesus Christus Filius tuus Dominus noster, divini[6] consummato fine mysterii, dispositionis antiquae munus explevit[7], ut scilicet et diabolum, caelestis operis inimicum[8], per hominem quem subiugarat elideret, et humanam reduceret ad superna dona substantiam[9]. Et ideo cum angelis. γ

Infra actionem, ut supra. Sequitur

Postcommun.

Tribue, quaesumus, Domine, ut per haec sacra quae sumpsimus, illuc tendat nostrae devotionis affectus, quo tecum est nostra substantia. Per Dominum [10]. Cf. Leon. 316. R. S. Gerb. 121. Men. 94. Cf. lvi *supra*.

Ad Populum.

Da, quaesumus, omnipotens Deus, illuc subsequi tuorum membra fidelium quo caput nostrum principium[que] [11] praecessit. Per Dominum [12]. R. S. Gerb. 121. Men. 95. Leon. 315.

[1] *es* Leon. [2] Men. adds *Iesum Christum Dominum nostrum*, and ends *Qui tecum*. [3] *quod* V.; *ubi* Pam. (marg.); R. S. Gerb. Men. as text. [4] Leon. omits *praecipue*. [5] *quo* V. S¹. [6] *divino* V. S¹; R. Leon. S³ Gerb. Pam. as text. [7] *manus explevit* V.; *munus explicuit* Leon.; R. S. Gerb. Pam. as text. [8] *inimicus* V. [9] *substantiae* V.; *substantiam ad superna dona reduceret* Pam.; Pam. Leon. end with *Per quem*. [10] *Qui tecum* Men. [11] V. R. S. omit *que* which is restored from Leon. Men.; S¹ Gerb. have *principio*. [12] R. Men. add *Iesus Christus Dominus noster*, and end *Qui tecum*.

LXV.

590 ORATIONES ET PRECES [1] DOMINICA POST ASCENSA [2] DOMINI.

Sancti nominis tui, Domine, timorem pariter et amorem fac nos habere perpetuum; quia nunquam tua gubernatione [3] destituis quos in soliditate tuae dilectionis instituis. Per. γ R. S. Gerb. 133. Pam. 403. Men. 169.

Deus qui te [4] rectis ac sinceris manere pectoribus asseris, da nobis tua gratia tales existere in quibus habitare digneris. Per Dominum. R. S. Gerb. 133 [131]. Pam. 404. Men. 170.

Secreta.

Oblatio [nos] [5], Domine, tuo nomini dicanda purificet, et de die in diem ad caelestis vitae transferat actionem. Per Dominum nostrum. γ R. S. Gerb. 133. Pam. 403. Men. 169. lxi *supra*.

VD. Cuius hoc mirificum opus ac salutare [6] mysterium fuit, ut perditi dudum atque prostrati de [7] diabolo et mortis aculeo ad hanc gloriam vocaremur, quia [8] nunc genus electum, sacerdotiumque [9] regale [10], populus acquisitionis et sancta gens [11] vocaremur [12]. Agentes igitur indefessas gratias, sanctamque munificentiam praedicantes, maiestati tuae haec sacra deferimus, quae nobis ipse salutis nostrae auctor Christus instituit. Quem laudant angeli [13]. γ R. S. Gerb. 134. Pam. 573. Men. 170.

110   LIBER SACRAMENTORUM   [I. lxvi.

Postcommun.

R. S.
Gerb. 134.
Pam. 403.
Men. 170.
II. lxxxi
infra.

Sumptis muneribus, Domine, quaesumus, ut cum frequentatione [14] mysterii crescat nostrae salutis affectus. Per Dominum nostrum. γ

Ad Populum.

S. (*alibi.*)
Gerb. 239.
III. xvii
infra.

Benedic, Domine [15], familiam tuam' in caelestibus et reple eam donis tuis spiritalibus: concede eis [16] caritatem, gaudium, pacem, patientiam, bonitatem, mansuetudinem, spem, fidem, continentiam [17], ut repleti omnibus castitatem [18] donis tuis desiderantes ad te pervenire mereantur. Per Dominum nostrum.

[1] R. S. Gerb. give this *Missa* (omitting the '*Ad Populum*') for the third Sunday after Pentecost. Pam. gives for the second Sunday the two Collects (the second as an '*Ad Populum*'), Secret and Postcommunion, assigning the Preface to the third Sunday after the Octave; so also Men. None of the four has the '*Ad Populum*' of this *Missa* in conjunction with the other portions. [2] *post Ascensa* so V., and S¹ in the corresponding *Missa* (ungrammatically). [3] *tuam gubernationem* V. (ungrammatically). [4] S² Gerb. Pam. Men. insert *in*; V. R. S¹ as text. [5] V. here omits *nos*, which is restored from R. S. Gerb. Pam. Men. and V. in lxi *supra*. [6] *singulare* Pam. [7] *a* S² Gerb. [8] *qua* Gerb. Pam. Men.; V. R. S. as text. [9] *sacerdotumque* V. [10] S² Gerb. insert *ac*. [11] *gens sancta* S¹ Gerb. Pam. Men.; V. R. S¹ as text. [12] *vocemur* S², *vocamur* Gerb.; V. R. S¹ Pam. Men. as text. [13] *Per quem maiestatem* S. Gerb. Pam. Men.; *per Christum* R.; V. as text. [14] *quaesumus tuam frequentationem* V. here; V. in II. lxxxi *infra* as text, and so R. S. Gerb. Pam. Men.; Tommasi reads *tua frequentatione*. [15] V. in III. xvii *infra*, S. Gerb. insert *hanc*. [16] *eius* V. [17] *continentia* V. here; but in III. xvii. as text, so S. Gerb. [18] Tommasi remarks that *castitatem* is superfluous; but something more than its elimination seems to be wanted to emend the text, in which V. (here and in III. xvii) S. and Gerb. agree. But for this agreement it might be supposed that the word was misplaced in repairing its omission, and should be placed after *continentiam* as Tommasi seems to suggest: but this would still leave *desiderantes* to be accounted for.

LXVI [1].

Sabbato Pentecosten [2] *celebrabis baptismum sicut in nocte* 591 *sancta* [3] *Paschae.*

AEGROTANTI CATECHUMENO IMPOSITA MANUUM [4].

R.
Gerb. 253.
Mart. lib. I.
cap. i.

Innumeras medelae tuae curas deprecamur [5], Domine sancte, Pater omnipotens, aeterne Deus, quas distribuit [6] humanis infirmitatibus Christus: erige famulum tuum [7] aegritudinis languore [8] depressum; et omnem sensum eius [9] dignare tuis visitationibus refovere, quatenus adoptionem tuam possit [10] cum gaudio [11] sanitatis percipere. Expelle itaque ab eo cuncta valetudinis tela, ut ad gratiam tuam gradanter occurrat [12]. Releva quem redimere gloriaris, ut

baptismi sit in illo palma non mortis, et gloriosum semper
baiulet quod accipit signaculum crucis[13]. Per Christum
Dominum nostrum, qui venturus est iudicare vivos et
mortuos.

[1] This section, and those which follow it to lxxv inclusive, are to be found in nearly the same order as part of the *Ordo Baptisterii* in R. They appear in V. at a point where they seem to have no special connexion with their context, except such as is furnished by the rubric at the beginning of this section. These sections have been compared with the text of R., and also with the parallel portions of the *Ordo* from the Codex Gellonensis, given by Martène (*de Ant. Eccl. Rit.* lib. I. cap. i) (cited as Gell.): but this *Ordo* does not contain all the forms which appear in V., or in R.   [2] *Sabbato sancto Pentecost.* R.; V. as text, ungrammatically.   [3] *sanctae* V.   [4] *impoñ. manu his verbis* R.; V. as text.   [5] *Medellam tuam deprecor* R.; V. Gell. as text.   [6] *tribuit* R.; *distribuet* Gell.; V. as text.   [7] *hunc famulum tuum* Gell.; *famulum tuum Ill.* R.   [8] *languoris* Gell.   [9] *est* V.; *ei* Gell.; R. as text.   [10] *adoptionis tuam possit* Gell. (Mart. suggests *gratiam* for *tuam*); *adoptionem tuis expossit* (sic) R.; V. as text.   [11] *gaudium* Gell. (ungrammatically).   [12] Gell. omits *ut . . . occurrat*: *gradanter* is the reading of both V. and R., but Gerbert's suggestion of *gratanter* seems probable.   [13] *crucis Christi. Per Dominum* Gell.; V. as text; R. has *signaculus crucis* (perhaps for *signaculum sanctae crucis*).

LXVII[1].

ITEM IMPOSITIO MANUS, ENERGUMENUM CATECHU-
MENUM[2].

Omnipotens sempiterne Deus, a cuius facie caeli distillant, R. (*bis*.)
montes sicut cera[3] liquescunt, terra tremuit[4], cui patent Gerb. 253.
abyssi, quem infernus pavescit, quem omnis[5] irarum motus Leofr. 233.
aspiciens humiliatur, te supplex deprecor, dominator[6]
Domine, ut invocatione nominis tui ab huius[7] famuli tui
vexatione[8] inimicus confusus abscedat, et ab huius posses-
sione anima liberata ad auctorem[9] suae salutis recurrat,
liberatoremque suum[10], diabolico foetore depulso, et odore
suavissimo Spiritus sancti percepto, sequatur. Per. γ

[1] This and the next section are not contained in the *Ordo* of the Codex Gellonensis; but they are to be found in Pam. and Leofr., as well as in R. In R. they occur twice, once in the *Ordo Baptisterii*, and again near the end of the MS.   [2] Tommasi (marg.) supplies *super* before *energumenum catechumenum*: but it is omitted in R. as well as in V., and the accusative is probably an accusative absolute. R. has *inposita manu*.   [3] *cerae* R. in *Ord. Bapt.*   [4] *tremit* Pam. Leofr.; V. R. as text.   [5] *omnipotens* R. (in *Ord. Bapt.*).   [6] Pam. omits *dominator*.   [7] *ut ab eius* Leofr.; (V. marg. has *ut*).   [8] *vexationibus* Gerb. (R. has *vexatioñ.* and *vexatione*).   [9] *ab auctore* V.; *ad aurē* R. in *Ord. Bapt.*; R. (*alibi*) Pam. Leofr. as text.   [10] *suo* V.; R. Pam. Leofr. as text.

LXVIII.

ITEM ALIA, PRO PARVULO ENERGUMENO [1].

R.
Gerb. 253.
Pam. 475.
Leofr. 233.

Domine sancte, Pater omnipotens, aeterne Deus, virtutem tuam [2] totis exoro gemitibus pro huius a diabolo oppressa infantia [3]. Qui etiam indignis inter [4] pressuras donas praesidium, exurge pro [5] infantia debellata, et noli diu retinere vindictam : nec ante conspectum tuum veniant parentum delicta, qui nec [6] pro filio patrem nec pro patre [7] promisisti filium iudicare [8] : auxiliare, quaesumus, inimici furore vexato ; ne sine baptismate facias eius animam a diabolo possideri ; sed potius tenera aetas, malignis [9] oppressionibus libera, tibi referat [10] gratias sempiternas. Per Dominum nostrum Iesum Christum. Qui venturus est iudicare vivos et mortuos et saeculum. γ

[1] *parvulo energuminum* V.   [2] R. omits *tuam*.   [3] *huius famuli tui oppressa infantia* Pam.; *hoc famulo tuo* Ill., *a diabolo oppresso* Leofr.; V. R. as text.   [4] R. (in *Ord. Bapt.*) omits *inter*; but elsewhere as text.   [5] Pam. Leofr. insert *huius*.   [6] *quin et* Gerb.; but R. as text.   [7] *patrem* V.   [8] *iudicari* R. Pam.; V. Leofr. as text.   [9] *maligni* R.   [10] *liberatib' referat* R. (in *Ord. Bapt.*); *liberata tibi referat* Pam. Leofr.; V. R. (*alibi*) as text.

LXIX.

ORATIO SUPER CATECHUMENUM INFIRMUM.

R.
Gerb. 254.
Mart. lib. I.
cap. i.

Famulum tuum, Domine, ad tui [1] baptismi gratiam recurrentem respicere et conservare dignare [2], ut in tui nominis signo, quicquid in eo [3] per originalis peccati transgressionem [4] poenae obnoxium diabolus detinebat [5] sacri [6] fontis indulgentia [7] resolvatur, veteris hominis exuvias [8] deponat [9], et novae vitae indutus amictu resurgat. Omnis [10] nequissimi spiritus ab eo venena depelle, et salutari baptismi tui gratia adimple, ut tui muneris perceptione [11] in aeternam vitam [12] valeat exultare. Per Dominum.

[1] *a tui* V.   [2] Gell. omits *dignare*.   [3] *eum* R. Gell.; V. as text.   [4] *transgressione* V. Gell. (ungrammatically); R. as text.   [5] *obtinebat* Gell.   [6] *sacris* V.   [7] *indulgentiam* V. (ungrammatically); R. Gell. as text.   [8] *excubias* V. Gell.; *exsubias* R.   [9] *deponatur* Gell.   [10] *omnes* V.; R. Gell. as text.   [11] *praeceptione* V.; *perceptionem* R. Gell.   [12] *in aeternam vitam.* So V. R. Gell. (probably ungrammatically).

LXX.

Si fuerit baptizandus, accedens sacerdos dicit ei[1] *Orationem et Symbolum, et catechizat eum his verbis, imposita manu capiti eius: deinde dicit hanc orationem super eum:* Nec te lateat[2] Satanas, *sicut scriptum est in Sabbato.*

Te, Domine, supplices exoramus ut visitatione tua sancta erigas ad te • hunc famulum tuum, ne adversario liceat usque ad tentationem animae[3] pervenire: sed[4] sicut in Iob terminum pone, ne inimicus de anima huius sine redemptione baptismatis incipiat triumphare. Differ, Domine, exitum mortis[5], et spatium vitae distende. Releva[6] quem perducas ad baptismi sacramentum[7], ne redemptioni tuae inferas damnum. Tolle occasionem diabolo triumphandi, et reserva quem triumphis compares[8] Christi, ut sanus tibi in ecclesia tua gratia baptismatis renascatur, facturus cuncta quae petimus. Per.

[1] Gerb. omits *ei* which in R. is very faint, but can still be read. [2] *latet* R.; V. as text here and in lxxii *infra*. R. places 'Nec te latet Satanas *sicut scriptum est in Sabb. Sco.*' (sic) after the words *capiti eius* and before *deinde• dicit,* &c. Gell. does not contain the direction in this form, but places the prayer *Te, Domine, supplices* before the recital of the Lord's Prayer and the Creed, which are followed by the exorcism *Nec te latet.* The order in the repetition of the rubric in V. R. (see lxxii *infra*) is the same in both texts, agreeing with that of V. here. [3] Gell. omits *animae.* [4] R. inserts *in*; Gerb. reads *in eo*; V. Gell. as text. [5] R. inserts *qui iudicas de futuris*; V. Gell. as text. [6] *distendere. Leva* Gell.; R. has *extendere. releva.* [7] *sacramenti* V. [8] *in quem triumphes cumpares* R.; *quem triumphis comparare* Gell.; V. as text.

LXXI.

ITEM AD CATECHUMENUM EX PAGANO FACIENDUM[1].

Gentilem hominem cum susceperis, in primis[2] *catechizas eum divinis sermonibus, et das ei monita*[3]*, quemadmodum post cognitam veritatem vivere debeat. Post haec facis eum catechumenum: exsufflas in faciem eius, et facis ei crucem in fronte*[4]*: imponis manum super caput eius his verbis.*

Accipe signum crucis tam in fronte quam in corde[4]: sume fidem caelestium praeceptorum: talis esto moribus, ut templum Dei esse iam possis: ingressusque ecclesiam Dei, evasisse te laqueos mortis[5] laetus agnosce. Horresce idola: respue simulacra: cole[6] Deum Patrem omnipotentem, et Iesum Christum Filium eius, qui vivit cum Patre et Spiritu sancto [7], per omnia saecula saeculorum.

Sequitur oratio [8].

Te deprecor, Domine sancte, Pater omnipotens, aeterne Deus, ut [9] huic famulo tuo, qui in saeculi huius nocte vagatur [10] incertus et dubius, viam veritatis et agnitionis tuae [11] iubeas demonstrari [12]; quatenus reseratis oculis cordis sui [13] te unum Deum Patrem in Filio et Filium in Patre cum sancto Spiritu [14] recognoscat, atque huius confessionis fructum et hic et in futuro saeculo percipere mereatur [15]. Per.

Inde [16] *vero, postquam gustaverit medicinam salis, et ipse se* [17] *signaverit, benedicis* [18] *eum his verbis:*

R.
Gerb. 255.

•Domine sancte, Pater omnipotens, aeterne Deus, qui es, et [19] eras, et permanes usque in finem, cuius origo nescitur, nec finis comprehendi potest; te, Domine, supplices invocamus super hunc famulum tuum, quem liberasti de errore gentilium et conversatione turpissima. Dignare exaudire eum qui tibi cervices suas humiliat; perveniat ad lavacri fontem, ut renatus ex aqua et Spiritu sancto [20], expoliatus veterem hominem induatur novum, qui secundum te creatus est; accipiat vestem incorruptam et immaculatam, tibique Domino nostro servire mereatur [15]. Per.

594

[1] This section does not appear in the *Ordo* from Codex Gellonensis. [2] R. omits *in primis*. [3] *da ei monita* R. [4] R. inserts *et*. [5] R. omits *mortis*. [6] *respice simul agricolam* Gerb.; but R. has really the reading of the text. [7] *sancto Spiritu* R. [8] R. omits this rubric. [9] R. omits *Deus, ut*. [10] *vacatur* V.; *vocatur* R.; Tommasi emends as text. [11] R. omits *tuae*. [12] *demonstrare* V. R. [13] *tui* R. [14] *Spiritu sancto* R. [15] *mereantur* V.; R. as text. [16] *Deinde* R. [17] Gerb. omits *se*; there is perhaps a trace of the word in R. [18] *benedices* R. [19] R. inserts *qui*. [20] R. omits *sancto*.

LXXII.

ITEM AD SUCCURRENDUM CATECHUMENUM INFIRMUM [1].

R.
Gerb. 255.
Cf. Mart.
lib. I.
cap. i.

Si baptizandus [2] *fuerit, accedens sacerdos dicit super eum orationes quae supra scriptae sunt; et tradit ei Symbolum et Orationem; et catechizat eum his verbis* [3]*:* Nec te lateat [4] Satanas: *et reliqua sicut supra* [5] *in nocte sancta scriptum est. Inde saliva* [6] *oris sui* [7] *cum digito tangit* [8] *nares et aures, et dicit ei* [9]*:*

Effeta, quod est adaperire, in odorem¹⁰ suavitatis. Tu autem effugare, diabole, appropinquavit¹¹ enim iudicium Dei.

*Deinde tangit*⁸ *ei pectus et inter scapulas de oleo exorcizato sub has interrogationes*¹²*:*

Abrenuntias Satanae?
Resp. Abrenuntio.
Et omnibus operibus eius?
Resp. Abrenuntio.
Et omnibus pompis eius?
Resp. Abrenuntio.

¹ So both R. and V. (ungrammatically). Both agree in giving at this point the recapitulation of a former rubric in a slightly different shape (see note ² on lxx *supra*). ² *baptizatus* R. ³ *verbibus* V. ⁴ *latet* R. Gell. ⁵ *super* V.; R. as text. ⁶ *salivo* V. ⁷ *tui* R. ⁸ *tangis* R. ⁹ *dices ei* R.; *dicit ad aure* Gell.; V. as text. ¹⁰ *odore* R. ¹¹ *adpropinquabit* V.; R. Gell. and V. in xlii *supra* as text.· ¹² *has orationes* R.; V. as text (both ungrammatically). Gell. gives more precise directions, making the Unction and the Interrogations concurrent.

LXXIII.

Quum autem expoliatur infirmus, benedicit fontem.

*Incipit oratio*¹.

Exaudi nos, omnipotens Deus, et in huius aquae substantiam tuam² immitte³ virtutem, ut abluendus per eam et sanitatem simul et vitam mereatur aeternam. Per.

R.
Gerb. 255.
Cf. Mart.
lib. I.
cap. i.

Item Benedictio aquae ad succurrendum.

Exorcizo te, creatura aquae, per Deum vivum, per Deum sanctum, per Deum totius dulcedinis creatorem, qui te in principio verbo separavit a terra, et in quatuor fluminibus dividens totam terram rigare praecepit. Adiuro te per Iesum Christum Filium eius unicum, Dominum nostrum, ut efficiaris in eo qui in te baptizandus erit fons aquae salientis in vitam aeternam, regenerans eum Deo Patri et Filio et Spiritui sancto: qui venturus est iudicare vivos et mortuos et saeculum per ignem.

¹ *benedicit fontem incip. Oral.* R.; *benedicit aqua dicens: Dominus vobiscum. R. Et cum spiritu tuo. Deinde dicit: Oremus. Et dicit* Gell. The prayers and Benedictions which follow in this and the two succeeding sections of V. are only indicated by their first words in the *Ordo* from Cod. Gellonensis. ² *tua* V. ³ *immisce* R.

LXXIV.

Item alia ad succurrendum[1].

Adesto, Domine, tuis adesto muneribus, ut quod nostro est gerendum servitio tuo impleatur auxilio. Per Dominum.

Sequitur benedictio.

Domine sancte, Pater omnipotens, aeterne Deus, aquarum spiritalium sanctificator, te suppliciter deprecamur, ut ad hoc ministerium humilitatis nostrae respicere digneris, et super has abluendis aquas[2] et vivificandis hominibus praeparatas angelum sanctitatis emittas, quo peccatis vitae prioris ablutis[3], reatuque deterso, purum sancto Spiritui habitaculum in regeneratis procuret. Per Dominum nostrum.

[1] *cuccurrendum* V. This Collect and Benediction are omitted in R. and only indicated by their first words in Martène. [2] *aquis* V. [3] *abluti* V.

LXXV.

Item alia Benedictio[1].

R. Gerb. 255. Mur. ii. 263.

Exorcizo te, creatura aquae, in nomine Dei Patris omnipotentis et in nomine Iesu Christi Filii eius, et Spiritus sancti. Omnis virtus adversarii, omnis incursio diaboli, omne phantasma eradicare et effugare ab hac creatura aquae, ut fiat fons salientis[2] in vitam aeternam: et[3] quum baptizatus fuerit[4] fiat templum Dei vivi in remissione[5] peccato-rum. Per Dominum nostrum Iesum Christum Filium tuum, qui venturus est iudicare vivos [et mortuos[6]] et saeculum per ignem. γ

R. Gerb. 256.

Et[7] antequam perfundas eum aqua interrogas ei[8] verba Symboli et dicis[9]:

Credis in Deum Patrem omnipotentem?
Resp. Credo.

Credis et in Iesum Christum, Filium eius unicum, Dominum nostrum, natum et passum?
Resp. Credo.

Credis et in Spiritum sanctum, sanctam ecclesiam[10], remissionem peccatorum, carnis resurrectionem[11]?
Resp. Credo.

Et quum interrogas, per singulas vices mergis eum tertio in aqua[12]. *Postea, quum ascenderit a fonte, infans signatur a presbytero in cerebro*[13] *de chrismate, his verbis:*

Deus omnipotens, Pater Domini nostri Iesu Christi, qui te regeneravit ex aqua et Spiritu sancto[14], quique dedit tibi remissionem omnium peccatorum, ipse te liniat[15] chrismate salutis in Christo Iesu in vitam aeternam[16]. ℣

Resp. Amen.

Postea, si fuerit oblata, agendae sunt missae[17], *et communicat*[18]; *sin autem, dabis ei tantum sacramenta corporis et sanguinis Christi, dicens:*

Corpus Domini nostri Iesu Christi sit tibi in vitam aeternam[19].

Et das[20] *ei orationem ita dicens:*

Omnipotens sempiterne Deus, qui regenerasti famulum tuum ex aqua et Spiritu sancto, quique dedisti ei remissionem omnium peccatorum, tribue ei continuam sanitatem ad agnoscendam unitatis tuae[21] veritatem. Per Dominum nostrum.

Omnipotens[22] et misericors Deus, maiestatem tuam supplices deprecamur, ut famulum tuum digneris serenis aspectibus praesentari[23]: et cui donasti baptismi sacramentum, longaevam tribuas sanitatem. Per Dominum nostrum.

Deinde consignatur ab episcopo, in his verbis: Cf. xliv supra.

Deus omnipotens, Pater Domini nostri Iesu Christi, qui regenerasti famulum tuum ex aqua et Spiritu sancto, quique dedisti ei remissionem omnium peccatorum, tu, Domine, emitte[24] in eum Spiritum • sanctum tuum Paraclitum, et da ei spiritum sapientiae et intellectus, spiritum consilii et fortitudinis, spiritum scientiae et pietatis; adimple eum spiritum[25] timoris Dei et Domini[26] nostri Iesu Christi; et iube eum consignari signum[27] crucis in vitam aeternam. Per eundem Dominum nostrum Iesum Christum, cum quo vivis et regnas in unitate Spiritus sancti. ℣

Postea signat eum in fronte de chrismate, dicens:

Signum Christi in vitam aeternam.

Resp. Amen.

Pax tecum.

Resp. Et cum spiritu tuo.

118   LIBER SACRAMENTORUM   [I. lxxvi, lxxvii.

¹ This Benediction appears (with the same title) in R., and (with the rubric *Benedicis aquam his verbis*) in Muratori's Gregorian Sacramentary; the latter form (cited as Mur.) shows one or two variations, the text of R. corresponding closely with that of V.   ² *fons salientis* so V. R.; *fons saliens* Mur. Perhaps *fons aquae salientis* is the true reading.   ³ *ut* R.; V. Mur. as text. Tommasi suggests in a marginal note the reading *qui ex ea* (for *quum*). ⁴ Something seems to be wanting here in the text of V., with which R. agrees. Mur. inserts *hic famulus Domini*.   ⁵ *remissione* so V.; R. Mur. Gerb. have *remissionem*.   ⁶ V. omits *et mortuos*. R. stops at *venturus est*. The ending does not fit with the clause preceding.   ⁷ The remainder of the section is not found in Muratori's Gregorian text, but the greater part of it appears in R., agreeing closely with V.   ⁸ *eum* Gerb.; V. R. as text.   ⁹ *Symboli, dicens* R.   ¹⁰ *sancta ecclesia* V. (ungrammatically); *sanctam ecclesiam catholicam* R.   ¹¹ R. adds *et vitam aeternam?*   ¹² *tertio in aqua, et cum interrogas ei per singulas vices mergis eum* R.   ¹³ R. omits *in cerebro*.   ¹⁴ R. at this point abbreviates the form with *Et reliqua*. ¹⁵ *lineat* V. (see note ²⁰ on xliv *supra*).   ¹⁶ *vita aeterna* V. here (ungrammatically); in xliv *supra* as text.   ¹⁷ *agenda est missa* R.   ¹⁸ *communicant* R.   ¹⁹ R. adds *Et R. Amen*.   ²⁰ *dat* V.; R. as text.   ²¹ R. omits *tuae*.   ²² R. omits this prayer, and also (as in the *Ordo* for Easter Even) the form of Confirmation.   ²³ So V.; the addition of *tuis* before *praesentari*, suggested by Tommasi, does not seem to be all the alteration required to make the text run smoothly.   ²⁴ *immitte* V. in xliv *supra*. ²⁵ *spiritum* so V. (ungrammatically) both here and in xliv *supra*.   ²⁶ *Dei in nomine Domini* V. in xliv *supra*.   ²⁷ *signum*, so V. (ungrammatically); the clause is omitted in xliv *supra*.

LXXVI.

AD SUCCURRENDUM. BENEDICTIO OLEI EXORCIZATI ¹.

Cf. Leofr. 259.

Exorcizo te, creatura olei, per Deum Patrem omnipotentem, qui fecit caelum et terram, mare et omnia quae in eis sunt. Omnis virtus adversarii, omnis exercitus diaboli, omnis incursus, omne ² phantasma Satanae eradicare et effugare ab hac creatura olei, ut fiat omnibus qui ex eo ungendi sunt in adoptione ³ filiorum per Spiritum sanctum, in nomine Dei Patris omnipotentis, et in caritate Iesu Christi Domini nostri, qui venturus est in Spiritu sancto iudicare vivos et mortuos et saeculum per ignem.

¹ This form appears, with some alteration, as the 'Exorcismus olei' in the Order for consecrating the Chrism in the 'Leofric Missal.'   ² *omnes* V. ⁴ So V. (probably ungrammatically).

LXXVII.

ORATIONES ¹ PER SINGULAS LECTIONES IN SABBATO PENTECOSTEN ².

R. S. (1)
Gerb. 124.
Leon. 319.
Pam.
(Amb.)
378.
Pam. 297.

Da nobis, quaesumus, Domine, per gratiam Spiritus sancti novam tui Parocliti spiritalis observantiae disciplinam, ut mentes nostrae, sacro purgatae ³ ieiunio, cunctis reddantur eius muneribus aptiores. Per Dominum nostrum. γ

Leofr. 110. lxxix *infra*.

598 *Sequitur lectio in Genesis.*

Omnipotens sempiterne Deus, indeficiens lumen, qui Spiritum tuum sanctum, quum super aquas in mundi⁴ creationis exordio ferretur⁵, humanae declarasti salutis auctorem, praesta quaesumus, ut idem Spiritus veritatis ecclesiae tuae dona multiplicet. Per Dominum. γ
R. S. (2) Gerb. 124. Pam. (Amb.) 378. Pam. 298. Leofr. 110.

Item de cantico Exodi.

Deus, qui primis temporibus impleta miracula novi testamenti luce reserasti, quod mare⁶ rubrum forma sacri fontis existeret, et liberata plebs ab Aegyptia servitute Christiani populi sacramenta praeferret, da ut omnes gentes Israelis privilegium meritum⁷ fidei consecutae, Spiritus tui participatione regenerentur⁸. Per. γ
R. S. (4) Gerb. 124. Pam. (Amb.) 379. Pam. 299. Leofr. 110.

Item de cantico Deuteronomii [*cum*]⁹ *lectione.*

Deus, gloriatio fidelium et vita¹⁰ iustorum, qui per Moysen famulum tuum nos quoque modulatione¹¹ sacri carminis erudisti, in universis gentibus misericordiae tuae munus operare, tribuendo beatitudinem auferendo¹² terrorem, ut quod praenuntiatum est ad supplicium in remedium transferatur aeternum. Per Dominum. γ
R. S. (5) Gerb. 124. Pam. 299. Leofr. 110.

Item de cantico Esaiae cum lectione.

Omnipotens sempiterne Deus, qui per unicum Filium tuum ecclesiae tuae demonstrasti te esse cultorem, ut¹³ omnem palmitis¹⁴ fructum in eodem Christo tuo, qui vera vitis est, efferentem¹⁵ clementer excolens, fructus afferat ampliores¹⁶, fidelibus tuis, quos velut vineam ex Aegypto per fontem baptismi pertulisti¹⁷, nullae peccatorum spinae praevaleant; ut Spiritus tui sanctificatione muniti¹⁸ perpetua fruge ditentur. Per. γ
R. S. (6). Gerb. 124. Pam. 299. Leofr. 110.

Domine¹⁹ Deus virtutum, qui collapsa reparas et reparata conservas, auge populos in tui nominis sanctificatione renovandos; ut omnes qui diluuntur sacro baptismate, ²⁰ tua semper inspiratione dirigantur. Per. γ
R. S. (alt. Ps. xli). Gerb. 124. Pam. 299.

---

¹ *Oratio* V. ² *Pentecosten*, so V., ungrammatically, unless *Pentecosten* is regarded as indeclinable. The series of Collects in R. S. Gerb. Leofr. agrees with that in the supplementary portion of Muratori's Gregorian Sacramentary (*Lit. Rom. Vet.* ii. 150–152), except that Leofr. omits one Collect, which S. Gerb. Mur. give as an alternative to the last in the series of Leofr. All the Collects of the series in the text are included in R. S. Gerb. Mur., all but the last in Leofr. But V. omits the Collect which in R. S. Gerb. Mur. is alternative with the last, and also two Collects (and the corresponding lections) from the earlier part of the series. Pam. (Amb.) has the first three Collects of V. in the same

order as the first three of its own series. ⁹ *purificatae* V. in lxxix *infra*; *purificante* Gerb. Pam.; V. R. S. Leon. Pam. (Amb.) Leofr. as text. ⁴ *mundanae* Pam. ⁵ *fereretur* V. (S¹!); *ferreretur* R. ⁶ *ut et mare* Pam. (Amb.). ⁷ *merito* S² Gerb. Pam. (both texts) Leofr.; V. R. (S¹!) as text (ungrammatically). ⁸ *regnentur* V.; R. S. Gerb. Pam. (both texts) Leofr. as text. ⁹ V. omits *cum* which is restored from the next rubric. ¹⁰ *vitae* V. ¹¹ *modulationem* Leofr. ¹² *offerendo* V. ¹³ Tommasi proposes to omit *ut* here, and insert it before *fructus afferat*. But V. R. S. Gerb. Pam. Leofr. agree in the order. Either the grammar or the text of the Collect is corrupt, and it is not clear how it should be emended. ¹⁴ *palmitem* S² Gerb. Pam. *palmitum* Leofr.; V. R. S¹ as text (ungrammatically). ¹⁵ *afferentem* R. S. Gerb. Pam.; V. Leofr. as text. ¹⁶ *fructus conferens ampliores* Pam.; *fructus afferre facias ampliores* S² Gerb.; V. R. Leofr. as text; an erasure in S¹. ¹⁷ *transtulisti* R. S. Gerb. Pam.; V. Leofr. as text. ¹⁸ *mundati* S²; *mundique* Gerb.; V. R. S¹ Pam. Leofr. as text. ¹⁹ It appears from R. S. Gerb. Pam. that this Collect was preceded by Ps. xli. ²⁰ Pam. inserts *in*.

LXXVIII[1].
ITEM IN VIGILIA DE PENTECOSTEN[2]. 599
Ad Missa[3].

R. S.
(*alibi*.)
Gerb. 94.
Pam. 275.
Men. 77.

Deus, qui ecclesiam tuam novo semper fetu multiplicas, concede famulis tuis ut sacramentum tuum[4] vivendo teneant, quod fide perceperunt[5]. Per. y

R. S.
Gerb. 125.
Pam. 298.
Men. 98.
Pam.
(Amb.)
379.
Miss.
Goth. 617.

Deus[6], cuius Spiritu totum corpus ecclesiae multiplicatur et regitur, conserva in novam[7] familiae tuae progeniem[7] sanctificationis gratiam quam dedisti, ut corpore et[8] mente renovati[9], in unitate fidei ferventes tibi, Domine, servire mereantur[10]. Per.

Secreta.

R. S.
Gerb. 125.
Pam.
(Amb.)
379. Sacr. Gall. 874.

Virtute sancti Spiritus, Domine, munera nostra continge, ut quod solemnitate praesenti[11] suo nomini[12] dedicavit, et intelligibile nobis faciat et aeternum. Per.

Leon. 318.
Cf. R. S.
Gerb. 125.
Pam. 298.
Men. 98.

VD. Per Christum Dominum nostrum. Qui ascendens[13] super omnes caelos sedensque ad dexteram tuam, promissum Spiritum sanctum in filios adoptionis effudit[14]. Unde laetantes inter altaria tua, Domine virtutum, hostias tibi laudis offerimus per Christum Dominum. Quem laudant. y

Infra actionem.

R. S.
Gerb. 125.
Men. 97.
Leon. 318.

Communicantes et diem sacratissimum Pentecosten[15] praevenientes, quo Spiritus sanctus apostolos[16] plebemque credentium praesentia[17] suae maiestatis implevit. Sed et memoriam. y

See Leon. 318.

Item infra actionem Hanc igitur *dicis sicut et in nocte sancta, et de creaturis benedicendis.*

Postcommun.

Concede [quaesumus][18], omnipotens Deus, ut paschalis perceptio[19] sacramenti mentibus nostris continua[20] perseveret[21]. Per Dominum. γ. Miss. Gall. 275. Men. 77. Pam. (Amb.) 380. Cf. xlv *supra*.

R.S.(*alibi*.)
Pam. 275.
Gerb. 95.

---

[1] Two *Missae* for the Vigil appear also in S., the contents of which correspond to some extent with those of this section and that which follows it. The former of the two *Missae* in S. has the heading 'Orā. ad Miā. P'. Ascensum Foñ. Stacio ad Lateranis' (*sic*). The second is headed simply 'Item alia Missa,' but the reviser has added 'Infra Ebd.', and this addition appears also in Gerbert's text. R. has not this second *Missa*.   [2] *Pentecosten*. So V., perhaps ungrammatically, but see note [2] on lxxvii.   [3] *Ad Missa*. So V. ungrammatically.   [4] R. S. Gerb. Pam. Men. omit *tuum*; V. as text.   [5] *perciperint* V.; R. has *percipebant*.   [6] *Domine sancte Pater omnipotens aeterne Deus* Miss. Goth.   [7] *nova ... progenie* Pam. (both texts) Men.; R. S. Gerb. Miss. Goth. as text (ungrammatically).   [8] Pam. omits *corpore et*; R. S. Gerb. Miss. Goth. Pam. (Amb.) Men. as text.   [9] Miss. Goth. alters the ending to suit the position of the prayer as *Collectio ad Pacem*.   [10] *mereamur* Pam. (both texts).   [11] *solemnitate Quinquaginsimae* Sacr. Gall.   [12] *tuo nomini* R. S. Gerb.; *suo nomine* V.; Sacr. Gall. Pam. (Amb.) as text.   [13] *ascendit* Leon.; V. R. S. Gerb. Pam. Men. as text.   [14] *effundet* R. The parallel preface in R. S. Gerb. Pam. Men. does not agree with the text after this point.   [15] *Pentecosten sacratissimum* Leon.; *sacratissimum Pentecostes* S[2] Gerb. Men.; V. R. S[1] as text.   [16] *apostolis* V.   [17] *presenciae* V.   [18] *quaesumus*, omitted here by V., is restored from xlv *supra*, R. S. Gerb. Pam. (Amb.).   [19] *perfeccio* V.; R. S. Gerb. Miss. Gall. Pam. (both texts) V. in xlv *supra* as text.   [20] *continua in nostris mentibus* R. Gerb. Pam. Men. Miss. Gall.; *continuata in nostris mentibus* V. in xlv *supra*, S.; V. here, Pam. (Amb.) as text.   [21] *perseverent* V.

LXXIX.

600   ITEM ALITER IN VIGILIA PENTECOSTEN[1].

Concede nobis, Domine, praesidia militiae Christianae sanctis inchoare ieiuniis; ut contra spiritales nequitias pugnaturi[2], continentiae muniamur auxiliis. Per. γ Leon. 319. lxxxiii *infra*.

R.S.(*alibi*.)
Gerb. 35
[34].

Da nobis, quaesumus, Domine, per gratiam sancti Spiritus novam tui Parscliti spiritalis observantiae disciplinam, ut mentes nostrae sacro purificatae[3] ieiunio, cunctis reddantur eius muneribus aptiores. Per Dominum. γ Pam. (Amb.) 378. lxxvii *supra*.

R.S.(*alibi*.)
Gerb. 124.
Leon. 319.
Pam. 297.
Leofr. 110.

Secreta.

Hostias populi tui, quaesumus, Domine, miseratus intende, et ut tibi reddantur acceptae, conscientias nostras sancti Spiritus salutaris emundet adventus[4]. Per. Men. 97.

S.
Gerb. 125.
Pam. 297.
Leon. 320.

VD. Qui sacramentum paschale[5] consummans, quibus per[6] Unigeniti tui consortium filios adoptionis esse tribuisti, per sanctum Spiritum[7] largiris dona gratiarum, et sui coheredibus Redemptoris iam nunc supernae pignus hereditatis impendis, ut tanto se certius[8] ad eam[9] confi-

S.
Gerb. 126.
Pam. 570.
Men. 97.

dant¹⁰ esse venturos, quanto in eius participationem profecerint. Propterea¹¹. γ

Infra actionem, ut supra.

Item Postcommun.

S.
Gerb. 126.
Leon. 317.
lxxx *infra.*

Sacris caelestibus, Domine, vitia nostra purgentur, ut muneribus tuis possimus semper aptari. Per.

R. S.
Gerb. 125.
Pam. 298,
299.
Men. 97.

Praesta, quaesumus, omnipotens Deus, ut Spiritus¹² adveniens maiestatem nobis Filii tui manifestando clarificet. Per¹³ eundem. γ

¹ See notes ¹ and ² on lxxviii *supra.* ² *pugnari* V. here, *pugnare* V. in lxxxiii *infra*; R. S. Gerb. Leon. as text. ³ *purgatae* V. in lxxvii *supra*, R. S. Leon. Pam. (Amb.) Leofr.; *purificante* Gerb. Pam.; V. here as text. ⁴ *adventus emundet* Leon.; V. S. Gerb. Pam. Men. as text. ⁵ *sacramenta paschalia* S² Gerb.; V. S¹ Pam. Men. as text. ⁶ *eis quos per* S² Gerb.; V. S¹ Pam. Men. as text. ⁷ *spiritum sanctum* Pam. Men.; V. S. Gerb. as text. ⁸ *tanto secretius* V. (S¹ †); S² Gerb. Pam. Men. as text. ⁹ *eum* Gerb. Pam. Men.; V. S. as text. ¹⁰ S¹ inserts *se*. ¹¹ *quanto se sciunt ab eo redemptos et (eiusdem* Pam.*) sancti Spiritus infusione ditatos. Et ideo* S² Gerb. Pam. Men.; V. as text (probably ungrammatically); an erasure in S¹. ¹² *Spiritus sanctus* S² Gerb. Pam. (299) Men.; *sanctus Spiritus* Pam. (298); V. R. S¹ as text. ¹³ R. ends with *Qui tecum et cum domino*, &c.

LXXX.

ORATIONES ET PRECES DOMINICA PENTECOSTEN¹.

R. S.
Gerb. 126.
Leon. 316.
Pam.
(Amb.)
381.
Men. 98.

Omnipotens sempiterne Deus, qui paschale sacramentum quinquaginta dierum voluisti mysterio contineri, praesta ut gentium facta dispersio divisione² linguarum ad unam confessionem³ tui · nominis caelesti munere congregetur⁴. 601 Per. γ

R. S.
Gerb. 127.
Pam. 300.
Men. 99.
[Cf. Gerb. 128.]

Deus, qui sacramento festivitatis hodiernae universam ecclesiam tuam in omni gente et natione sanctificas, in totam mundi latitudinem Spiritus tui sancti⁵ dona defunde⁶, ut⁷ quod inter ipsa evangelicae praedicationis exordia operata est divina dignatio nunc quoque per credentium corda defunde⁸. Per. γ

Secreta.

S. (*alibi.*)
Gerb. 128.
Pam. 301.
Men. 100.
Leon. 321.

Mentes nostras, quaesumus, Domine, Spiritus sanctus⁹ divinis praeparet¹⁰ sacramentis, quia ipse est omnium remissio¹¹ peccatorum. Per Dominum nostrum. γ

S. (*alibi.*)
Gerb. 128.
Pam. 301.
Men. 99.
Leon. 321.

Purificet nos, quaesumus, Domine¹², muneris praesentis oblatio, et¹³ dignos sacra participatione perficiat. Per Dominum. γ

[I. xxx.] ROMANAE ECCLESIAE. 123

VD. Quia hodie sancti Spiritus celebramus adventum. Qui [14] principiis nascentis ecclesiae [15] cunctis gentibus imbuendis et Deitatis scientiam indidit et loquelam, in diversitate donorum mirabilis operator unitatis [16], variarumque gratiarum tributor [17] idem et unus effector [18] et [19] praedicantium dispensator ipse linguarum. Quem laudant angeli [20].

R. S.
Gerb. 126.
Pam.
(Amb.)
380.

Infra actionem.

Communicantes, et diem Pentecosten sacratissimum celebrantes, quo Spiritus sanctus apostolos plebemque credentium praesentia suae maiestatis implevit. Sed et memoriam.

R. S.
(in Vig.)
Gerb. 125.
Men. 97.
Leon. 318.

Hanc igitur oblationem. *Dicis sicut in nocte sancta.*

Postcommun.

Sacris caelestibus, Domine, vitia nostra purgentur, ut muneribus tuis possimus semper aptari. Per.

S.
Gerb. 126.
Leon. 317. lxxix *supra*.

Ad Populum.

Praesta, quaesumus, Domine, ut a nostris mentibus et [21] carnales amoveat Spiritus sanctus [22] affectus, et spiritalia nobis dona [23] potenter infundat. Per Dominum.

R. S.
Gerb. 127.
Pam. 302.
Men. 101.

Adesto, Domine, quaesumus, populo tuo, et quem mysteriis caelestibus satiasti [24], ab hostium incursione [25] defende. Per Dominum. γ

S. (*alibi*.)
Gerb. 128.
Pam. 301.
Men. 99.
Leon. 320.

---

[1] *Pentecosten*. So V. R.   [2] *divisiones* V.; *divisio* (preceded by erasure of perhaps two letters) S[1]; R. Leon. S[2] Gerb. Pam. (Amb.) Men. as text.   [3] *ad unae confessione* V.; *ad une confessionem* R.; S. Leon. &c. as text.   [4] *congregentur* V.; R. S. Gerb. Leon. Pam. (Amb.) Men. as text.   [5] Pam. Men. omit *sancti*.   [6] *diffunde* R. Gerb. Pam. Men.; V. S. as text. S. Gerb. Men. end the Collect at this point. Pam. gives the clause following, from a single MS. R. also contains the clause, which may have come from a confusion with another Collect (see Gerb. p. 128).   [7] *et* Pam.; V. R. as text.   [8] *diffunde* R. Pam.; V. as text.   [9] *sanctus Spiritus* Leon.   [10] *reparet* S. Gerb. Pam. Men. (all making the prayer a Postcom.); V. Leon. as text.   [11] *remissio omnium* S. Gerb. Pam. Men.; V. Leon. as text.   [12] *Domine quaesumus* S. Gerb. Pam.; V. Leon. Men. as text.   [13] *ut* Leon.   [14] S[2] Gerb. insert *in*; V. R. S[1] Pam. (Amb.) as text.   [15] S[2] Gerb. insert *principibus eiusdem ecclesiae*; V. R. S[1] Pam. (Amb.) as text.   [16] Gerb. inserts *donavit*.   [17] *distributor* R. S. Gerb. Pam. (Amb.); V. as text.   [18] *idem et fidei unius effector* Pam. (Amb.); V. R. S. Gerb. as text.   [19] *in ore* (omitting *et*) S[2] Gerb.; V. R. S[1] Pam. (Amb.) as text.   [20] *Per Christum Dominum* R. S[1]. *Et ideo cum* S[2] Gerb. *Propterea profusis* &c. Pam. (Amb.).   [21] S. Gerb. Pam. Men. omit *et*; R. also omits *mentibus*; V. as text.   [22] Men. omits *sanctus*.   [23] *dona nobis* Gerb.   [24] *imbuisti* R. S. Gerb. Pam. Men. Leon.; V. as text.   [25] *furore* R. S. Gerb. Pam. Men. Leon.; V. as text.

LXXXI.

Item Orationes ad Vesperos infra Octavas Pentecosten[1].

S.
[Gerb. 127.]
Pam. (Amb.) 381.
Pam. 300.
Men. 99.

Deus, qui discipulis tuis[2] Spiritum sanctum Paraclitum in ignis fervore tui amoris[3] mittere dignatus es, da populis tuis in unitate fidei esse ferventes, ut in tua semper dilectione permanentes[4] et in fide inveniantur stabiles et in opere efficaces. Per.

R. S.
Gerb. 127.
Pam. 280.
Men. 82.
lvi *supra*.

Omnipotens sempiterne Deus, deduc nos ad societatem caelestium gaudiorum, ut Spiritu sancto renatos regnum tuum facias[5] introire, atque eo[6] perveniat humilitas gregis quo praecessit celsitudo[7] Pastoris. Per. y

S.
(*Fer. iii.*)
Gerb. 128.
Pam. 301.
Men. 99.
Leon. 321.

Adsit nobis, quaesumus, Domine[8], virtus Spiritus sancti, quae[9] et corda nostra clementer expurget, et ab omnibus tueatur[10] adversis. Per Dominum. y

R. S.
(*Fer. iv.*)
Gerb. 128.
Pam. 301.
Men. 100.

Mentes nostras[11], Domine, Spiritus[12] Paraclitus qui a te procedit illuminet et inducat in omnem, sicut tuus promisit Filius, veritatem. Per. y

R. S.
(*Dom.*)
Gerb. 127.
Pam. 298.

Sancti Spiritus, Domine, corda nostra mundet infusio, et sui roris ubertate[13] fecundet. Per Dominum nostrum. y
Men. 98.

R. S.
Gerb. 127.
Pam. 300.

Concede nobis, misericors Deus, ut sicut[14] nomine Patris et Filii divini[15] generis intelligimus veritatem, sic in Spiritu sancto totius cognoscamus substantiam Trinitatis. Per.

[1] So V. The corresponding section of S. is headed simply 'Alias Orat.' (*sic*). So also in R., which omits one prayer included in S. [2] *discipulis Christi Filii tui* S[2] Gerb.; V. S[1] Pam. (both texts) Men. as text. [3] *tui amore* Pam.; in Pam. (Amb.) *specie* is inserted (conjecturally) after *ignis*; Men. omits *tui amoris*; V. S. Gerb. as text (S[1] has *fervorem*). [4] *ut in tua se permanentes* V.; *ut permanentes* Pam.; S. Gerb. Pam. (Amb.) Men. as text. [5] *tribuas* V. in lvi *supra*. [6] See note [11] on lvi *supra*. [7] *processit fortitudo* V. in lvi *supra*; R. has *processit*. [8] *Domine quaesumus* S. Gerb. Pam. Men. Leon.; V. as text. [9] *qui* V.; S. Gerb. Pam. Men. Leon. as text. [10] *tueantur* V. [11] S. Gerb. Pam. Men. insert *quaesumus*. [12] Gerb. Pam. Men. omit *Spiritus*. [13] *sui roris intima aspersione* R. S. Gerb. Pam. Men.; V. as text. [14] S[2] Gerb. Pam. insert *in*; V. R. S[1] as text. [15] *devino* V.

LXXXII.

Denuntiatio Ieiuniorum[1] Quarti, Septimi, et Decimi Mensis.

R. S.
Gerb. 134.
Men. 105.

Anniversarii[2], fratres carissimi[3], ieiunii puritatem, qua et corporis acquiritur et animae sanctitas, nos commonet *illius* mensis instaurata devotio. Quarta igitur et sexta feria, sollicite[4] convenientes occursu, offeramus Deo spiritale ieiunium; die vero sabbati[5] apud beatum Petrum[6], cuius nos intercessionibus credimus adiuvandos, sanctas vigilias Christiana pietate celebremus; ut per hanc institutionem salutiferam peccatorum • sordes, quas corporis fragilitate contrahimus[7], ieiuniis et eleemosynis abluamus, auxiliante Domino nostro Iesu Christo, qui cum Patre et Spiritu sancto vivit et regnat Deus, per omnia saecula saeculorum[8].

Item aliter[9].

Illius[10] mensis ieiunia in hac nobis sunt hebdomada[11] tenenda: ideoque hortamur sanctam fidem vestram, ut quarta[12] sexta vel septima feria[13] ieiunemus; quatenus divinis inhaerendo mandatis, propitiationem Dei nostri perseverantia debitae[14] servitutis obtineat. Per[15].

S. Gerb. 134. Men. 106.

[1] R. S. Gerb. Men. insert *Primi*. [2] *anniversaria* V. R.; *anniversariam* Men.; S. Gerb. as text. [3] *dilectissimi* R. S. Gerb.; V. Men. as text. [4] *solliciti* V.; *sollicitate* R.; *sollicito* S. Gerb. Men. [5] *sabbato* R. S¹. [6] Men. inserts *apostolum*. [7] *contraimus* V.; *contrahemus* R. S¹; *contraximus* S² Gerb.; Men. as text. [8] S. Gerb. add *Amen*. [9] In Gerbert's text (following T. ?), this form is headed '*Item alia Gelas.*'; it is not contained in R. [10] *Illi* V. [11] *in hac hebdomada nobis sunt* S. Gerb. Men.; V. as text. [12] S. Gerb. insert *et*. [13] *vel sabbato* S² Gerb.; V. S¹ Men. as text. [14] *perseverantiam devitą* V. [15] Men. has the ending *Auxiliante*, &c.

LXXXIII.
Incipiunt Orationes et Preces Mensis Quarti[1].

Feria Quarta.

Concede nobis, Domine, praesidia militiae Christianae sanctis inchoare ieiuniis, ut contra spiritales nequitias pugnaturi continentiae[2] muniamur auxiliis. Per. γ

R.S.(*alibi*.) Gerb. 35 [34.] Leon. 319. lxxix *supra*.

Omnipotens et misericors Deus, apta nos tuae propitius voluntati, quoniam[3] sicut eius praetereuntes tramitem deviamus, sic integro tenore[4] dirigamur[5], ad illius semper ordinem recurrentes. Per.

S. Gerb. 134. Men. 106. Leofr. 3.

Da nobis mentem, Domine, quae tibi sit placita, quia talibus iugiter quidquid est prosperum ministrabis. Per.

S. Gerb. 134. Men. 106.

Secreta.

Solemnibus ieiuniis expiatos[5] suo[6] nos, Domine, mysterio congruentes hoc sacrum munus efficiat[7]; quia tanto nobis salubrius aderit[8], quanto id[9] devotius sumpserimus. Per.

S. Gerb. 134. Men. 106. Leofr. 3.

S.
[Gerb.
129.]
Men. 106.
Pam. 572.
Leon. 322.

VD. Post illos enim laetitiae dies quos in honore[10] Domini a mortuis resurgentis, et in caelos ascendentis exegimus, postque[11] perceptum sancti Spiritus donum, necessaria etenim[12] nobis[13] ieiunia sancta provisa sunt, ut pura conversatione viventibus quae divinitus sunt ecclesiae collata permaneant[14]. Per Christum Dominum nostrum. γ

Postcommun. 604

S.(R.*alibi*.)
Gerb. 134,
50.
Leofr. 3.
xxvi *supra*.

Quos ieiunia votiva castigant tua, Domine, sacramenta vivificent[15], ut terrenis affectibus mitigatis facilius caelestia capiamus. Per.

Ad Populum.

R.S.(*alibi*.)
Gerb. 50.
xxvi *supra*.

Gratias tibi referat, Domine, corde subiecto tua semper ecclesia, et consequenter obtineat, ut[16] observationes antiquas iugiter recensendo[16] proficiat in futurum. Per.

Feria sexta.

R. S.
Gerb. 135.
Men. 106.
Leofr. 3.

Ut nobis, Domine, terrenorum[17] frugum tribuas[18] ubertatem, fac mentes nostras caelesti fertilitate fecundas. Per.

S.
[Gerb.
135.]
Leofr. 3.
xxviii
supra.

Fiat[19] tua gratia, Domine, fructuosus[19] nostrae devotionis affectus, quia tunc[20] nobis proderunt suscepta ieiunia si tuae sint placita[21] pietati. Per Dominum. γ

Secreta.

R. S.
Gerb. 135.
Men. 102.
Leofr. 3.

Omnipotens sempiterne Deus, qui non sacrificiorum ambitione placaris, sed studio piae devotionis intendis, da familiae tuae spiritum rectum et habere cor mundum, ut fides eorum haec dona tibi conciliet [et][22] humilitas oblata[23] commendet. Per.

Postcommun.

R. S.
Gerb. 135.
Men. 107.
Leofr. 3.
Leon. 379.

Annue, quaesumus, omnipotens Deus, ut sacramentorum tuorum gesta recolentes, et temporali securitate relevemur, et erudiamur legalibus institutis. Per.

Ad Populum.

R. S.
Gerb. 135.
Men. 107.

Fideli populo, Domine, misericordiam tuam placatus impende, et praesidia corporis copiosa tribue supplicanti. Per.

Sabbato in xii Lect.

Praesta, Domine, quaesumus, famulis tuis, talesque nos concede fieri [24] tuae gratiae largitate, ut bona tua et fiducialiter imploremus [25], et sine difficultate sumamus. Per.
R. S.
Gerb. 135.
Men. 107.
Leofr. 3.

Da, nobis, Domine, quaesumus [26], regnum tuum iustitiamque semper inquirere, ut quibus indigere nos perspicis [27] clementer facias abundare. Per.
R. S.
Gerb. 135.
Men. 107.
Leofr. 3.

605 •Deus, qui nos de praesentibus adiumentis esse vetuisti [28] sollicitos, tribue, quaesumus, ut pie sectando [29] quae tua sunt universa nobis salutaria condonentur. Per.
R. S.
Gerb. 135.
Men. 107.
Leofr. 3.

Deus, qui misericordiam tuam [30] praevenis non petentes, da nobis affectum maiestatem tuam iugiter deprecandi, ut pietate perpetua supplicibus potiora defendas [31]. Per.
R. S.
Gerb. 135.
Men. 107.
Leofr. 3.

Deus, qui non [32] despicis corde contritos et afflictos miseriis, populum tuum ieiunii ad te devotione [33] clamantem propitiatus [34] exaudi, ut quos humiliavit adversitas attollat reparationis tuae prosperitas. Per.
S.
[Gerb. 135.]
Men. 107.
Leofr. 3.

Item post Benedictionem [35].

Deus cuius adorandae potentia [36] maiestatis flammae saevientis incendium sanctis tribus pueris in splendore [37] demutatum est animarum [38], ecclesiae tuae similibus adesto remediis, ut de gravioribus mundi huius adversitatibus propitiatione caelesti populus tuus ereptus exultet. Per.
R.S.(alibi.)
Gerb. 179.
Leofr. 3.

Secreta.

Domine Deus noster, qui in his potius creaturis, quas ad fragilitatis nostrae praesidium [39] condidisti, tuo quoque nomini [40] munera iussisti dedicanda [41] constitui, tribue, quaesumus, ut et vitae nobis praesentis auxilium, et aeternitatis efficiant sacramentum. Per.
R. S.
Gerb. 135,
53.
Pam. 243.
Men. 107.
Leofr. 3.
Leon. 415.
xxvi supra.

VD. [42] Tibi sanctificare ieiunium quod nos ad [43] aedificationem animarum et castigationem [44] corporum servare docuisti; quia strictis [45] corporibus animae saginantur [46]; in quo exterior homo noster affligitur, dilatatur interior. Memento [47], Domine, ieiunii nostri [48] et misericordiarum tuarum, quas peccatoribus pie semper ieiunantibus contulisti, ut non solum a cibis, sed a peccatis omnibus abstinentes, devotionis tibi ieiunio placeamus. Et ideo cum angelis. γ
S. (alibi.)
[Gerb. 180.]
Pam. 577.
Men. 133.

128   *LIBER SACRAMENTORUM*   [I. lxxxiii.

Postcommun.

R. S.
Gerb. 135.
Men. 107.
Leofr. 3.

Sumptum, quaesumus, Domine, venerabile sacramentum et praesentis vitae subsidiis nos foveat et aeternae. Per.

Ad Populum.   606

R. S.
Gerb. 135.
Men. 108,
52.
Pam. 244.
xxvii
supra.

Proficiat, Domine, quaesumus, plebs tibi dicáta [49] piae devotionis affectu [49]; ut sacris actibus erudita [50], quanto maiestati tuae fit gratior, tanto donis potioribus augeatur. Per. γ

---

[1] R. and S. have after Pentecost another series of *Missae* for the Pentecost Ember Days: but at a point a little later, after the *Missa* for the third week after Pentecost, they have a series for the *Ieiunium Mensis Quarti*, which in S. agrees almost exactly with the Pentecost series of V.; R. omits part of the series; Men. also has two series of *Missae* for this season, the second of which is in close agreement with the text of V., and has a heading showing that it was to be employed if the *Ieiunium Mensis Quarti* fell after Pentecost. Leofr. also has (in the *latest* portion of its contents) a series of *Missae* for a *Legitimum Ieiunium*, the contents of which are to a great extent in agreement with this section. [2] *pugnare continentiam* V.; *pugnari continenciae* V. in lxxix *supra*; R. S. Gerb. Leon. as text. [3] *quo . . . dirigamur* Men. Leofr.; *quoniam . . . dirigimur* S² Gerb.; V. S¹ as text. [4] *tellore* V.; S. Gerb. Men. Leofr. as text. [5] *expiandos* Leofr. [6] *suos* V.; *tuo* S² Gerb. Men.; (S¹ ?) Leofr. as text. [7] *hoc sacro munus efficiat* V.; *hoc sacro munere efficiant* S¹; *haec sacrosancta munera efficiant* S² Gerb.; *hoc sacro munere effice* Men.; Leofr. as text. [8] *aderis* Men.; *adherit* (?) S¹; *adhęrent* S² Gerb.; V. Leofr. as text. [9] *ea* S² Gerb. [10] *honorem* Leon. (and so Tommasi here); V. S. Gerb. Pam. Men. as text, perhaps ungrammatically. [11] *postquam* V. (? S¹) Pam.; Leon. S² Gerb. Men. as text. [12] *necessarie* Leon.; *necessario* S² Gerb. Men.; *necessaria* Pam. (all omitting *etenim*); V. S¹ as text. [13] Leon. inserts *haec*. [14] S² Gerb. add *incorrupta*. [15] *purificent* V. in xxvi *supra*. [16] *et . . . recensendum* V.; V. in xxxvi *supra* R. S. Gerb. as text. [17] *terrenorum* so V. R. S¹ (ungrammatically). [18] *des* Leofr. [19] *Fiant . . . fructuosius* V. (S¹ ?); *Fiat . . . fructuosior* Leofr.; S² Gerb. as text, and so V. in xxviii *supra*. [20] *qui actu* V.; S. Gerb. Leofr. V. in xxviii *supra* as text. [21] *beneplacita* S. Gerb. [22] V. omits *et*, which is restored from R. S. Gerb. Men. Leofr. [23] *optata* S. Gerb.; V. R. Men. Leofr. as text. [24] *Praesta Domine quaesumus tales nos fieri* S² Gerb. Men.; V. S¹ as text, and so Leofr. (which inserts *nobis* before *famulis tuis*); R. as text, omitting *que* after *tales*. [25] *impetremus* S. Gerb. Men. Leofr.; V. R. as text. [26] Men. omits *quaesumus*. [27] *prospicis* Leofr. [28] *voluisti* V.; R. S. Gerb. Men. Leofr. as text. [29] *piis sectando* V. R.; *pie sectantibus* S² Gerb. Men.; S¹ Leofr. as text. [30] *misericordiam tuam* so V. R. (ungrammatically); *misericordia tua* S. Gerb. Men. Leofr. [31] *dependas* S² Gerb. [32] *nos* Leofr. [33] *devotitione* V. [34] *propitius* Men.; V. S. Gerb. Leofr. as text. [35] S. has not this Collect at this point, substituting '*Deus qui tribus pueris*,' which Leofr. also gives (the latter with the heading '*Ad Missam*'). Men. gives another Collect with the heading '*Post Benedictiones*.' But Leofr. adds (after the Postcommunion) the Collect in the text with the heading '*Oratio post ymnum trium puerorum*.' R. S. and Gerb. also have the Collect in another place, with the heading '*Post Benedictionem*.' [36] *adorandae potentiam* V. (ungrammatically); *adoranda potentia* S. Gerb.; *adoranda potentiae* R.; Leofr. as text. [37] *splendorem* Leofr.; V. R. S. Gerb. as text (ungrammatically). [38] Tommasi proposes *animabus*, connecting the word with *ecclesiae*: but V. R. S. Gerb. Leofr. agree in reading *animarum*, which the punctuation of S. shows to be dependent on *splendorem*. [39] *subsidium* V. in xxvi *supra* (where see note [10]). [40] *nomine* V. here; V. in xxvi *supra*, R. S. Gerb. Leon. Pam. Men. Leofr. as text. [41] *dicanda* S. Gerb. Leon. Pam. Men. Leofr.; *decanda* V. in xxvi *supra*; V. here, R. as text. [42] S. Gerb.

Pam. Men. insert *Et.*   ⁴⁸ *ob* Gerb. Pam. Men.   ⁴⁴ *castigatione* V. S.;
Gerb. Pam. Men. as text.   ⁴⁵ *restrictis* S² Gerb. Pam. Men.; V. S¹ as text.
⁴⁶ S³ Gerb. insert *et.*   ⁴⁷ S. Gerb. Pam. Men. insert *quaesumus*; V. as text.
⁴⁸ *ieiuniorum nostrorum* S. Gerb. Pam. Men.; V. as text.   ⁴⁹ See note ⁹ on xxvii *supra*.   ⁵⁰ *eruditi* V.

LXXXIV.

Orationes et Preces in Dominica Octavorum Pentecosten [1].

Timentium [te][2], Domine, salvator et custos, averte ab ecclesia tua mundanae sapientiae oblectamenta[3] fallaciae[4]; ut Spiritus tui eruditione formandos[5] prophetica et apostolica potius instituta quam philosophiae verba delectent, ne[6] vanitas mendaciorum decipiat quos eruditio veritatis illuminat. Per.
R. S.
Gerb. 130.
Pam. 305.

Sensibus nostris, Domine, Spiritum tuum sanctum[7] benignus infunde, ut tibi semper simus devoti, cuius sapientia creati sumus et providentia gubernamur. Per.
Cf. Pam. 473.
Cf. III.
lxxxiv *infra*.

Omnipotens et misericors Deus, ad cuius beatitudinem esmpiternam non fragilitate carnis sed alacritate mentis ascenditur, fac nos atria supernae civitatis et te inspirante semper ambire, et tua indulgentia fideliter introire[8]. Per.
R. S.
Gerb. 130.
Pam. 305.
Leon. 368.

Secreta.

Remotis obumbrationibus carnalium victimarum, spiritalem tibi, summe Pater, hostiam supplici servitute deferimus, quae miro[9] ineffabilique mysterio et immolatur semper, et eadem semper offertur, pariterque et devotorum munus et remunerantis est praemium. Per.
R. S.
Gerb. 130.
Pam. 305.
Leon. 327.

VD. Qui cum unigenito Filio tuo et sancto Spiritu unus es Deus, unus es Dominus, non in unius singularitate personae, sed in unius trinitate[10] substantiae; quod enim de tua gloria, revelante te, credimus, hoc de Filio tuo, hoc de Spiritu sancto, sine differentia [et][11] discretione sentimus, ut in confessione verae sempiternaeque Deitatis, et in personis proprietas et in essentia[12] unitas, et in maiestate adoretur aequalitas. Quem laudant angeli[13]. γ
R. S.
Gerb. 130.
Pam. 572.
Men. 103.

607
Postcommun.

Laetificet nos, quaesumus, Domine, sacramenti veneranda solemnitas; pariterque mentes nostras et corpora[14]
R. S.
Gerb. 131.
Pam. 305.

K

Leon. 378. spiritali[16] sanctificatione fecundet, et castis gaudiis semper exerceat. Per.

Ad Populum.

R. S.
Gerb. 131.
Pam. 305.
Leon. 360.

Ecclesia tua, Domine, caelesti gratia[16] repleatur et crescat; atque ab omnibus vitiis expiata percipiat sempiternae redemptionis augmentum[17], ut[18] quod in membris suis copiosa[19] temporum prorogatione[20] veneratur, spiritalium[21] capiat largitate donorum[22]. Per Dominum nostrum.

[1] So V. [2] V. omits *te*, which is restored from R. S. Gerb. Pam. [3] *delectamenta* Pam. [4] *fallacia* S[2] Gerb. Pam.; V. R. S[1] as text. [5] *forma nobis* V.; R. S. Gerb. Pam. as text. [6] *nec* S[2] Gerb.; V. R. S[1] Pam. as text. [7] *sensibus nostris quaesumus Domine lumen sanctum tuum* V. in III. lxxxiv *infra* and Pam. [8] *fidenter intrare* Leon.; V. R. S. Gerb. Pam. as text. [9] V. inserts *et*; R. S. Gerb. Pam. Leon. as text. [10] *trinitatis* V. [11] V. omits *et*, which is restored from R.; *differentiae discretione* Men.; *differentia discretionis* S. Gerb. Pam. [12] *et essentiae* V.; R. S. Gerb. Pam. Men. as text. [13] S[1] has *Per Christum Dominum*; S[2] adds *vel quam laudant angeli*; Gerb. has *Per Christum. Quam laudant angeli*; Pam. Men. *Quam laudant angeli*; V. R. as text. [14] Leon. inserts *et*. [15] Pam. omits *spiritali*. [16] *gratiae* V.; R. S. Gerb. Pam. Leon. as text. [17] *augmentu* V. [18] *et* R. Gerb. Pam. [19] *copiosas* V.; *copiose* S[1] Pam.; R. Leon. S[2] Gerb. as text. [20] *prorogatione* V. and so R. S[1]; S[2] Gerb. Leon. Pam. as text. [21] *spiritali* V. S[1] Pam.; *spiritalia* R.; Leon. S[2] Gerb. as text. [22] *bonorum* Pam.

LXXXV.

BENEDICTIO SUPER EOS QUI DE ARIANA AD CATHOLICAM REDEUNT UNITATEM [1].

Leofr. 229.
Cf. xliv
supra.
Cf. lxxv
supra.

Domine Deus omnipotens, Pater Domini nostri Iesu Christi, qui dignatus es famulos et famulas tuas[2] ab errore et mendacio haereseos Arianae eruere[3], et ad ecclesiam tuam sanctam catholicam eos perducere, tu, Domine, mitte in eos Spiritum Paraclitum sanctum[4] sapientiae et intellectus, spiritum consilii et fortitudinis[5], spiritum scientiae et pietatis, et adimple eos[6], Domine, spiritum[7] timoris Dei, in nomine Iesu Christi salvatoris nostri[8]. Per quem[9] et cum quo est tibi honor et gloria in saecula saeculorum. Amen.

[1] A parallel form appears in Leofr. with the title '*Reconciliatio hereticorum*.' The form in the text may be compared with the forms for Confirmation in xliv and lxxv *supra*. [2] *hunc famulum tuum Ill.* Leofr. [3] *mendatio hereticę pravitatis eruere* Leofr. [4] *tu, Domine, Spiritum tuum paraclitum in eum emittere dignare, spiritum* Leofr. [5] *virtutis* Leofr. [6] *eum* Leofr. [7] *spiritu* Leofr.; V. as text, ungrammatically, as in xliv and lxxv *supra*. [8] *timoris tui, ut in nomine Domini nostri Iesu Christi signo crucis signetur in vitam aeternam* Leofr. But V. in xliv *supra* agrees with the text. [9] Leofr. has the more normal ending *Per eundem*, &c.

LXXXVI[1].

ITEM PRO EOS[2] QUI DE DIVERSIS HAERESIBUS REDEUNT.

Sancte Pater, omnipotens Deus, qui famulum tuum ab errore haereseorum[3] dignatus es eruere, et ad sanctam ecclesiam catholicam revocare, quaesumus te, Domine, immitte in eum Paraclitum Spiritum tuum sanctum septiformem, Spiritum sapientiae et intellectus, consilii et fortitudinis, scientiae et pietatis: adimple famulum tuum spiritum[4] timoris Dei. Per Dominum nostrum Iesum Christum.

[1] This form may be compared with that immediately preceding, which it closely resembles. [2] *eos*, so V. (ungrammatically). [3] *haereseorum*, so V. [4] *spiritum*, so V. here and in the parallel forms: see note [7] on lxxxv.

LXXXVII.

RECONCILIATIO REBAPTIZATI AB HAERETICIS.

Omnipotens Pater misericordiarum et Deus consolationis, qui per Unigenitum tuum Dominum nostrum Iesum Christum ita regenerationis humanae consecrasti mysterium ut nec in eis qui fraude diabolicae malignitatis a baptismi unitate discedunt nulla possit iteratione recensendi[1], quia cum geminatura[2] sacrae legis non virtus inditae consecrationis excluditur, sed iniuria fidei sacramentis manentibus irrogatur, ideo quum ad veram matrem ecclesiam catholicam tui muneris aspiratione resipiscentes apostatae redeunt, non quod amiserunt baptismum recipiunt, sed quod in se permanenti fecerunt contumeliam, veracis poenitentiae satisfactione reparantur. Hinc tuam misericordiam, Pater sancte, supplices exoramus, ut hunc famulum tuum ad sancta tua, quae reliquerat, atria revertentem, immensa benignitate suscipias, et piissima propitiatione salvifices, ut qui ruinae suae lapsum, anathematizando[3] nunc Arium, iugi lamentatione castigat, dignae[4] poenitentiae fructus, te miserante, perficiat. Tuo quippe respectu satisfactionis sumpsit initium, tuo[5] munere de perditionis se iam sentiat longinquitatem[6] regressum; longius enim a te[7] tam collatae fidei negatione, quam operum pravitate disceditur. Unde quaesumus, ut secundum multitudinem miserationum tuarum immanissima supplicis tui remittatur impietas, et aberrantem longius ab itinere salutis aeternae [6] tua dignetur revocare maiestas. Nos autem sicut in exequendis mysteriis tuis probamur indigni, ita de tua sumus miseratione certissimi; et ob hoc non audemus revertenti atque pulsanti reconciliationis ianuam claudere, cui ad revertendum cordis oculos te confidimus revelasse; et licet actione [9] poenitentiae metas temporum praeficiamus, tamen quia non solum diem mortis, sed et qua·litatem 609 pectoris ignoramus, sic eum ad spem reconciliationis admittimus [10], ut affectum iugis poenitudinis non omittat, sed perenni timore, continua lamentatione redivivus, et sacramentorum caelestium communione mereatur esse perpetuus. Per.

Alia [11] minore aetate.

Deus, qui hominem ad imaginem tuam conditum in id reparas quod creasti, respice propitius super hunc famulum tuum, et quidquid ignorantiae ipsius haeretica pravitas irrepsit, indulgentia [12] tuae pietatis ignosce; ut quod in eo diaboli fraude commissum est, et nequitia Arianae perfidiae nocuit, non ei reputetur ad culpam, sed membrum ecclesiae catholicae remissionis tuae [13] clementia reformetur [14], ut ad [15] altaribus sacris, recepta veritatis tuae communione, reddatur. Per.

Item alia [11] minore aetate.

Deus humani generis conditor et redemptor, Deus qui facturam similitudinis et imaginis tuae secundum divitias bonitatis in id reparas quod creasti, respice propitius super hunc famulum tuum; ut [16] quidquid ignorantiae ipsius necessitas hostilitatis influxit, indulgentiae tuae pietatis ignosce [16]; ut in eo cui adhuc intelligentia integra non suppetit, nihil reputetur ad culpam, sed ecclesiae membrum remissionis tuae benignitate reputetur [17]. Per.

---

[1] So V.; Tommasi suggests *rescindi* or *recenseri*; the former seems to give the better sense: probably *nulla* should be *ulla*.   [2] Tommasi proposes to read *geminatur*: but the reading of the text seems to give an intelligible sense, and the alteration would require some further emendation of the text.   [3] *anathemando* V.   [4] *digne* V.; Tommasi suggests *dignos*.   [5] *tuum* V.; Tommasi corrects as text.   [6] *longinquitatem*, so V. (ungrammatically).   [7] *ante* V.; the correction in the text is suggested by Tommasi.   [8] *aeterna* V.; Tommasi corrects as text.   [9] *accione* is the reading of V.; Tommasi's text has *actioni*, but the ablative seems to give a possible sense.   [10] *amittimus* V.   [11] Tommasi suggests the insertion of *pro*: but *minore aetate*

may conceivably be an ablative absolute, or the result of a misspelling for *minori aetati*. [13] *indulgentiam* V. here: but *indulgentia* in the parallel clause of the prayer immediately following. [13] *remissiones tua* V. [14] *reformetur*, so V. here; *reputetur* in the prayer following. [15] *ad*, so V.; Tommasi suggests *et*. [16] *ut ... ignosce* so V.; Tommasi proposes to correct to *et ... ignosce*, but the same grammatical error appears elsewhere. [17] *reformetur*, as in the prayer preceding, is perhaps the true reading here.

LXXXVIII[1].

Oratio in Dedicatione Basilicae Novae.

Deus, qui loca nomini tuo dicata sanctificas, effunde super hanc orationis domum[2] gratiam tuam, ut ab omnibus hic[3] invocantibus te auxilium tuae misericordiae sentiatur. Per. ɣ

Mart. lib. II. cap. xiii.
Egb. 38.
Men. 148.

Consecratio Basilicae.

Deus, sanctificationum omnipotens dominator, cuius pietas sine fine sentitur, Deus, qui caelestia simul et terrena complecte·ris, servans misericordiam tuam populo tuo ambulanti ante conspectum gloriae tuae, exaudi preces servorum [tuorum][4], ut sint oculi tui aperti super domum istam die ac nocte; hancque basilicam, in honorem[5] sancti[6] *Illius* sacris mysteriis institutam, clementissimus[7] dedica, miserator[8] illustra, proprio splendore clarifica, omnemque hominem venientem adorare in hoc loco[9] placatus admitte, propitius dignare respicere: et propter nomen tuum magnum et manum fortem[10] et brachium excelsum, in hoc habitaculo[11] supplicantes libens protege, dignanter exaudi, aeterna defensione conserva: ut semper felices, semperque[12] tua religione laetantes, constanter in sanctae Trinitatis fide catholica[13] perseverent. Per. ɣ

Mart. *u. s.*
Egb. 38.
Men. 149.
Leofr. 219.

Oratio super aquam et vinum ad consecrationem altaris.

Creator et conservator humani generis, dator gratiae[14] spiritalis, largitor aeternae salutis, tu permitte[15] Spiritum tuum super vinum cum aqua mixtum, ut armata[16] virtute caelestis defensionis ad consecrationem huius ecclesiae *vel* altaris proficiat[17]. Per.

Miss. Franc. 677.
Mart. *u. s.*
Egb. 36.
Men. 148.

Sequitur praefatio consecrationis altaris.

Primitus enim ponis[18] super cornu altaris digito tuo vinum cum aqua mixtum; et asperges[18] altare septem vicibus: reliquum autem fundes[18] ad basem, et offeres[18] incensum super altare, odorem suavissimum Domino.

Miss. Franc. 677.

Benedictio altaris [19].

Miss.
Franc. 677.
Mart. u. s.
Egb. 40.
Men. 149.
Leofr. 220.

Dei Patris omnipotentis misericordiam, dilectissimi fratres, deprecemur, ut hoc altare [20] sacrificiis spiritalibus consecrandum, vocis nostrae exorandus [21] officio praesenti benedictione sanctificet; [ut in eo semper oblationes famulorum suorum] [22] studio suae devotionis [23] impositas benedicere et sanctificare dignetur, et spiritali placatus incenso, precanti familiae suae promptus [24] exauditor assistat. Per. γ

Benedictio altaris, sive consecratio [25].

Miss.
Franc. 678.
Mart. u. s.
Egb. 40.
Men. 149.
Pam. 424.

Deus omnipotens, in cuius honore [26] altare [27] sub invocatione tui [nominis] [28] consecramus, clemens et propitius preces nostrae humilitatis exaudi et praesta ut in hac mensa sint tibi libamina accepta, sint grata, sint pinguia, et Spiritus sancti tui semper rore perfusa; ut omni tempore in hoc loco supplicantis tibi familiae tuae anxietates [29] releves, aegritudines cures, preces audias, vota suscipias, desiderata confirmes, postulata concedas. Per. γ

Praefatio linteaminum [30].

Miss.
Franc. 678.
Mart. u. s.
Egb. 43.
Leofr. 221.

Domine Deus omnipotens, sicut ab initio hominibus vitalia [31] et necessaria creasti, et quemadmodum vestimenta pontificalia sacerdotibus et Levitis, ornamenta [que et linteamina fieri famulo tuo Moysi per quadraginta dies docuisti, sive etiam ea] [32] quae Maria texuit et fecit in usum ministerii tabernaculi foederis, sanctificare, benedicere, consecrareque digneris haec linteamina [33] in usum altaris tui ad tegendum involvendumque [34] corpus et sanguinem Filii tui Domini nostri Iesu Christi, qui tecum vivit et regnat Deus. γ

Ad consecrandam patenam.

Miss.
Franc. 678.
Mart. u. s.
Egb. 47.
Men. 151.
Pam. 425.
Leofr. 221.

Consecramus et sanctificamus hanc patenam ad conficiendum in ea corpus Domini nostri Iesu Christi patientis crucem pro salute nostra omnium [35]. Qui cum Patre [36] et Spiritu sancto [37] vivit et regnat Deus per omnia saecula saeculorum. γ

Inde facis signum crucis de oleo sancto super patenam, et dicis hanc orationem:

Miss.
Franc. 678.
Mart. u. s.
Egb. 47.
Men. 151.

Consecrare et sanctificare digneris, Domine [38], patenam hanc per istam unctionem et nostram benedictionem, in Christo Iesu Domino nostro. Qui vivit [39] et regnat. γ

Pam. 425. Leofr. 221.

Ad calicem benedicendum.

Oremus, dilectissimi fratres, ut Dominus Deus noster calicem suum in ministerio[40] consecrandum [41] caelestis gratiae inspiratione sanctificet, et [42] ad humanam benedictionem plenitudinem divini favoris accommodet. Per Dominum. γ

Item alia.

Dignare, Domine, calicem istum, in usum ministerii tui pia famuli tui[43] devotione formatum, ea sanctificatione perfundere, qua Melchisedech famuli tui sacratum [44] calicem perfudisti, et quod arte [45] vel metallo effici non potest [46] altaribus tuis dignum fiat [47] tua benedictione pretiosum [48]. Per. γ

Item benedictio ad omnia in usum basilicae [49].

Dignare, Domine, Deus omnipotens, Rex regum, et Dominus dominantium, Sacerdos omnium, Pontifex universorum, per quem una cum Patre sanctoque Spiritu facta sunt universa, Christe Iesu, benedicere, consecrare, et sanctificare digneris [50] vasa haec cum hoc altari [51], linteaminibus, caeterisque vasis: et quemadmodum sanctificasti officia tabernaculi testimonii olim cum arca, oraculo, cherubin alosis [52], velis, columnis, candelabro, altari [53], argenteis basibus [54], tabulis deauratis, holocaustis, hostiis, aereo altari [55] cum aeneis vasis, tentoriis, funibus, oleo unctionis, et caeteris aliis in figura nostri, per manus sanctorum sanctificasti sacerdotum, ita nunc manens in aeternum summus [56] Sacerdos sacerdotum secundum ordinem Melchisedech, ut diximus, patenam hanc, et calicem hunc, et [57] omnia instrumenta altaris huius ecclesiae, sive basilicae, quae inter nostras palmas habentur, corde precamur [ut] [58] benedicas, purifices, consecres, et consummes, quibus inter nos et [59] aeternam unitatem in supremo meatu sine fine constare credimus. Per.

Praefatio chrismalis.

Oremus [60], fratres carissimi, ut Deus omnipotens hoc ministerium corporis [61] Filii sui Domini nostri Iesu Christi gerulum benedictione, sanctificationis tutamine, defensionis donatione [62] implere dignetur orantibus nobis. Per Dominum.

Item alia.

Miss. Franc. 680.
Mart. *u. s.*
Egb. 48.
Leofr. 222.

Omnipotens [Deus,][63] Trinitas inseparabilis, manibus nostris [64] opem tuae benedictionis infunde ; ut per nostram benedictionem hoc vasculum sanctificetur, et corporis Christi novum sepulcrum Spiritus sancti gratia perficiatur. Per Dominum. γ

[1] All the prayers which make up this section appear, though in different order, and with different headings, in the *Ordo* for the Dedication of a Church given by Martène (*de Ant. Eccl. Rit.* lib. II. cap. xiii) from the Codex Gellonensis: they also occur, though with more variation, in the corresponding part of the Pontifical of Egbert. This *Ordo* is also given by Martène, but in an abridged form: hence the edition of Egbert's Pontifical, published by the Surtees Society, has been here employed for comparison (Egbert's Pontifical, pp. 36 sqq.). These two *ordines* are cited as Gell. and Egb. respectively. All but the first two prayers appear (in the same order as in V. and with a close agreement in readings) in the Missale Francorum (Muratori ii. 677-80); while some of the prayers are also to be found in the corresponding portions of Menard's Gregorian Sacramentary, and of the Leofric Missal, and also (as separate forms of Benediction) in Pamelius' Gregorian text. [2] *desuper hanc sanctificationis domum* Men.; V. Gell. Egb. as text. [3] *hinc* Gell.; V. Egb. Men. as text. [4] V. omits *tuorum* which is restored from Gell. Egb. Men. Leofr. [5] *honore* Gell. Egb. Men. Leofr.; V. as text (perhaps ungrammatically). [6] Egb. Leofr. insert *tui*. [7] *clementissime* Egb. [8] *miseratus* Gell. Men.; V. Egb. Leofr. as text. [9] *loco hoc* Men. [10] *manu forte* V.; perhaps for *manu forti* which is the ungrammatical reading of Gell. Leofr.; Egb. Men. as text. [11] *habitaculum* Gell.; *habitaculo hoc* Men.; V. Egb. Leofr. as text. [12] Egb. inserts *in*. [13] *fidei catholicae* Gell. [14] Miss. Franc. inserts *et*. [15] *tu Domine mitte* Egb.; *tu Domine permitte* Men.; *tu Domine permittis* Gell.; V. Miss. Franc. as text. [16] *arma* V.; *armatum* Egb.; Miss. Franc. Gell. Men as text. [17] *proficiat*, so V. Miss. Franc. Gell.; Men. reads *proficiant*; Egb. *armatum . . . proficiat*. [18] These verbs are given as they appear in V., except the last, which appears as *offeris*; Miss. Franc. reads *ponis . . . aspergis . . . fundes . . . offeres*. [19] This title is omitted in Miss. Franc. but appears in Gell. [20] *altarium* Miss. Franc. Leofr. [21] *exoratus* Men.; *exorandum* Gell.; *exornandum* Egb.; V. Miss. Franc. Leofr. as text. [22] V. omits the words in brackets, which are restored from Miss. Franc. Men. Leofr.; Egb. has *famulorum famularumque suarum*; Gell. omits *famulorum . . . devotionis*. [23] *studiosa devotione* Egb. [24] *propitiatus* Leofr. [25] *consecrationem* V. This prayer appears in Leofr. with some alteration (see Leofr. 220). [26] *honorem* Miss. Franc.; V. Gell. Egb. Men. Pam. as text. [27] *hoc altare* Pam.; *altare hoc* Men.; *altarium* Miss. Franc. [28] V. Miss. Franc. omit *nominis*, which is restored from the other texts; Men. inserts *indigni* before *consecramus*. [29] *auxilietates* V. [30] This prayer in Leofr. has the heading '*Consecratio corporalis*,' and begins *Domine, sancte Pater, omnipotens aeterne Deus, misericordiam tuam supplices deprecamur ut sicut*. [31] *utilia* Gell. Egb. Leofr.; V. Miss. Franc. as text. [32] V. omits the words in brackets, which are restored from Miss. Franc. with a slight correction, the substitution of *que* for *quae*. Gell. has *ornamenta et linteamina fieri*; Egb. *ornamenta quoque fieri*; Leofr. omits *fieri* and *sive etiam ea*, otherwise as text. The archetype of V. probably had *quae*; the occurrence of the same word just after the omitted words accounts for the omission. [33] *hoc linteamen* Leofr. [34] *velandumque* Leofr. [35] *pro omnium nostra salute* Egb. Pam. [36] *Qui vivis*, &c. Leofr. [37] V. inserts *qui*, wrongly. [38] Egb. inserts *Deus omnipotens*. [39] *Qui vivis*, &c. Men. [40] *calicem suum in usum ministerii* Egb.; *calicem in usum sui ministerii* Men.; V. Miss. Franc. Gell. Leofr. as text (perhaps ungrammatically). [41] *consecratum* V.; Miss. Franc. Gell. Egb. Men. Leofr. as text. [42] *ut* Egb. Leofr. [43] *famuli tui* Ill. Men.; Egb. Pam. omit *famuli tui*. [44] *sacramentum* V.; *sacramento* Leofr.; Miss. Franc. Gell. Egb. Men. Pam. as text. [45] *ante* Egb. [46] *officii non potest* V.; *officii*

compositum est Gell.; Tommasi corrects as text, and so Miss. Franc.(?) Egb. Leofr. Pam. Men.   [47] Leofr. inserts *ad omnia*.   [48] Gell. Egb. add *atque sanctificatum*.   [49] Egb. has this Benediction in a shorter form, omitting the passage *et quemadmodum ... ut diximus*.   [50] Gell. Leofr. omit *digneris*, which is superfluous; V. Miss. Franc. Egb. as text.   [51] *altario* Miss. Franc. Leofr. (Leofr. omits *hoc*).   [52] *ansulis* Leofr.; V. Miss. Franc. Gell. as text. [53] *candelabra, altare* V. Gell.; *candelabro, altaribus* Miss. Franc. Leofr.; Tommasi reads *candelabris, altari*; but the reading of V. Gell. may be merely a misspelling.   [54] *vasibus* Gell.; V. Miss. Franc. Leofr. as text.   [55] *ac sacrum altare* Leofr.   [56] *summe* Leofr.; Gell. omits *ita ... sacerdotum*. [57] *vel* Egb.   [58] V. Leofr. omit *ut*, which is restored from Miss. Franc. Gell. Egb.   [59] Gell. omits *et*; V. Miss. Franc. Leofr. as text; Egb. omits all after *consummes*.   [60] Egb. inserts *dilectissimi et*.   [61] *corporum* Egb.; Leofr. omits *corporis*.   [62] *donaciones* V.; *et donationis* Leofr.; *donationis* Egb. Gell.; *dominatione* Miss. Franc.   [63] V. omits *Deus*, which is restored from Miss. Franc. Gell. Egb.; Leofr. has *Omnipotens sancta Trinitas, Deus*. [64] Gell. inserts *Christi*.

LXXXIX[1].

Orationes et Preces ad Missas in Dedicatione Basilicae Novae.

Deus, qui sacrandorum tibi auctor es munerum, ad sanctificationem loci huius propitius adesse dignare: ut qui haec in honorem tui nominis [2] condiderunt protectorem te habere in omnibus [3] mereantur [4]. Per. [Gerb. 227.] Egb. 51. Mart. lib. II. c. xiii.

Magnificare, Domine Deus noster, in sanctis tuis, et hoc in [5] templo aedificationis appare, ut qui omnia in filiis adoptionis operaris, ipse semper in tua hereditate lauderis [6]. Per. γ [Egb. 33. Men. 145.]

Secreta.

Omnipotens sempiterne Deus, qui gregalium [7] differentias hostiarum in unius huius sacrificii perfectione [8] sanxisti, respice propitius de throno gloriae tuae, et super hoc altare benedictionis tuae munus effunde; ut in eo sic temporales hostiae consecrentur, ut perpetuae vitae sumentibus procurent [9] substantiam [10]. Per Dominum nostrum Iesum Christum. γ [Gerb. 227.] Egb. 51. Mart. u. s.

VD. Qui quum ubique sis [11] totus, et universa tua maiestate contineas, sacrari tamen tibi loca [12] tuis mysteriis apta [12] voluisti, ut ipsae orationum domus supplicum mentes [13] ad invocationem tui nominis incitarent [14]. Effunde super hunc locum gratiam tuam, et omnibus in te sperantibus auxilii tui munus [15] ostende; ut hic et sacramentorum virtus et votorum obtineatur effectus [16]. Per. [Gerb. 227.] Men. 154. Egb. 51. Mart. u. s.

Infra actionem.

[Gerb. 227.]
Mart. *u. s.*

Hanc igitur oblationem famuli [tui] [17] vel famulae tuae *Illius* quam tibi offerunt hanc de‧dicantes [18] ecclesiam, 614 quaesumus, Domine [19], placatus accipias, nostrasque preces dignanter exaudias, ut sint oculi tui aperti super domum istam die ac nocte: templumque hoc in honore beatorum martyrum tuorum *Illorum vel Illarum* sanctarum, et confessorum [20], sacris mysteriis institutum clementissimus dedica, miserator [21] illustra, propitius [22] splendore clarifica; cunctam[que] [23] familiam tuam ad aulae huius suffragia concurrentem benignus exaudi; eiusque [24] conditorum omnia desideria cordis complacita tibi pius adimple, votisque responde; augmenta eis annos vitae et temporum [25] felicitatem; ut per spatia longaeva viventes [26] melioribus ornamentis studio eorum locus iste refulgeat: diesque nostros.

Postcommun.

[Gerb. 228.]
Egb. 50.
Men. 154.
Mart. *u. s.*

Copiosa beneficia, quaesumus, Domine, Christianus populus assequatur, ut qui in honore [27] sanctorum sacrandis tibi liminibus [28] [devotus occurrit, et vitae subsidia] [29] praesentis accipiat, et gratiam sempiternae redemptionis inveniat. Per.

---

[1] The greater part of this section corresponds with the '*Missa Dedicationis*' given by Martène from the Codex Gellonensis at the end of the *Ordo* referred to for the last section. All but the second Collect is to be found in the Ambrosian portion of Gerbert's text, and all but the *Hanc igitur* in the Pontifical of Egbert. [2] *haec in tui nominis honore* Gerb.; V. Gell. Egb. as text. [3] *in omnibus habere* Gerb.; V. Gell. Egb. as text. [4] Egb. adds *atque custodem*. [5] *in hoc* Men.; V. Egb. as text. [6] *laudaris* V. [7] *legalium* Egb. Gerb. (so V. in II. iii *infra*); V. Gell. as text. [8] *perfectiones* V.; *perfectionis* Gell.; *protectione* Egb.; Gerb. as text. [9] *procurrant* Gell. [10] *substantia* V. (ungrammatically); Gell. Egb. Gerb. as text. [11] *sit* V. [12] *locum ... aptum* Egb. [13] *supplimentes* V. [14] In Gerb. the Preface ends at this point. [15] *auxilium tui munus* V.; *auxilium tui muneris* Egb.; Gell. Men. as text. [16] *ut hic sacramentorum virtus omnium fidelium corda confirmet* Men.; V. Gell. Egb. as text (Gell. has *in* for *et* in Martène's text). [17] V. omits *tui*; Gerb. has *oblationem famulorum tuorum quam*; Gell. as text. [18] *ob hanc dedicandam* Gerb.; V. Gell. as text. [19] Gerb. inserts *ut*. [20] *in honore sanctorum tuorum* Gerb.; *in honorem beatorum martyrum tuorum* Illorum vel Illarum, *sanctorum confessorum* Gell.; V. as text. [21] *miseratus* Gell.; V. Gerb. as text. [22] *propitio* Gell. Gerb.; V. as text; but perhaps *proprio* (as in the *Consecratio Basilicae* in the preceding section) is the true reading. [23] From this point to *annos vitae* the text of Gell. is in confusion, the words *pius adimple votisque responde augmenta eis* being placed between *familiam tuam* and *ad aulae huius*. V. omits *que* which is supplied from Gell. (*cunctaque*) and Gerb. [24] *eiusdemque* Gell. [25] *tempora felicitate* Gell.; V. Gerb. as text. [26] *ut eis per spatia longaeva viventibus* Gerb.; V. Gell. as text (ungrammatically). [27] *in odore* V.; *in honorem* Gell.; Egb. Gerb. Men. as text. [28] *luminibus* V. [29] V. omits the words in brackets, which are restored from Gell. Egb. Men. (Gerb. has *et praesentis vitae subsidia*).

XC.

ITEM ALIA MISSA[1].

Deus, qui sacrandorum tibi auctor es munerum, effunde super hanc orationis domum benedictionem tuam; ut ab omnibus[2] invocantibus nomen tuum defensionis [tuae][3] auxilium sentiatur. Per Dominum. ℣

Deus, qui ex omni coaptatione sanctorum aeternum tibi condis habitaculum, da aedificationis[4] tuae incrementa caelestia, et[5] quorum hic reliquias pio amore[6] complectimur eorum semper meritis adiuvemur. Per. ℣

Secreta.

Omnipotens sempiterne Deus, effunde super hunc locum gratiam tuam, et omnibus te invocantibus[7] auxilii tui munus ostende[8], ut hic sacramentorum virtus omnium fidelium corda confirmet. Per Dominum.

•VD. Per Christum Dominum nostrum. Per quem te supplices deprecamur ut altare hoc sanctis usibus praeparatum caelesti dedicatione sanctifices, et[9] sicut Melchisedech sacerdotis praecipui oblationem dignatione mirabili suscepisti, ita imposita novo huic altari munera semper accepta ferre[10] digneris, ut populus tuus[11] in hanc ecclesiae domum sanctam conveniens[11], per haec pura[12] libamina caelesti sanctificatione salvatus, animarum quoque suarum salutem perpetuam[13] consequatur. Per quem maiestatem. ℣

Infra actionem.

Hanc igitur oblationem famuli *vel* famulae tuae *Illi vel Illae*[14] quam tibi in huius templi sanctificationem offerunt immolandam[15], quaesumus, Domine, dignanter intende, ut aulam, quae beati martyris tui *Illius* meritis aequipetere[16] non possit, tuae claritatis vultus illustret, fiatque tua propitiatione tuis sacris sanctisque digna mysteriis. Sit aeternae lucis habitaculum temporale[17]: nihil hic mundanae sordes obscuritatisque possideant, ut veniens hic populus tuus suae consequatur orationis effectum, dignumque[18] locum hunc tua[19] sentiat maiestate, dum a te[20] postulata fuerit[21] consecutus: sitque aedificantibus in pretio[22] delictorum, dum a te[20] non pro sui operis quantitate, sed pro offerentum fuerit [23] devotione suscepta: diesque nostros.

Postcommun.

[Gerb. 228.]
Men. 154.
Leon. 305.

Sanctorum tuorum, Domine, precibus confidentes, quaesumus ut per [24] ea quae sumpsimus aeterna remedia capiamus. Per.

[1] The greater part of this *Missa* appears from the type of Gerbert's text to be contained in R. and S.; but this is not so. [2] Leofr. inserts *hic*. [3] V. Leofr. omit *tuae* which is inserted from Gerb. Egb. Men. [4] *aedificationi* Leofr. Men.; V. Gerb. as text (V. has *de* for *da*). [5] *ut* Gerb. Men. Leofr.; V. as text. [6] *pio more* V.; Gerb. Men. Leofr. as text. [7] *invocantibus te* Gerb. [8] The parallel Postcommunion in Gerb. ends at this point. [9] *ut* Gerb. Egb. Leofr.; V. Men. as text. [10] *super accepto ferre* V.; *semper acceptabilia habere* Gerb.; Egb. Men. Leofr. as text. [11] *populus qui . . . convenit* Gerb. Egb.; *populus qui . . . convenerit* Men.; V. Leofr. as text. [12] Gerb. Egb. Men. omit *pura*; V. Leofr. as text. [13] *salute perpetua* V. (ungrammatically). [14] *Illi vel Illae* so V. [15] *immolandas* V. [16] *aequipetere*, so V.; Tommasi suggests *aequiparare*. [17] *temporalem* V. [18] *dignaque* V. [19] *tuae* V. [20] *ad te* V. [21] *fuerint* V. [22] *in pretio*, so V. (ungrammatically). [23] *fuerat* V. [24] *Sanctorum precibus, Domine, confidentes, quaesumus, per* Leon.; V. Gerb. Men. as text (save that V. has *confitentes*).

XCI.

ORATIONES ET PRECES IN DEDICATIONE BASILICAE QUAM [1] CONDITOR NON DEDICATAM RELIQUIT [1].

Deus qui loca nomini tuo dedicata sanctificas, et benedictionibus tuis dicanda praecedis, praesta, quaesumus, ut quod beato apostolo tuo *Illi* [2] et sanctis martyribus *Illis* famulus tuus *Ille* in hoc aedificio deputavit, digno praeparetur officio. Per.

•Omnipotentiam tuam, quaesumus, Domine, sanctus tuus 616 *Ille* interventor exoret, ut eius meritis hanc ecclesiam deputatam clementer illustres; quoniam quidquid sanctis honoris impenditur tuae respicit insignia maiestatis. Per Dominum.

Secreta.

Concede, quaesumus, Domine, ut sicut famulus tuus *Ille* oblatis optavit muneribus, beatorum martyrum tuorum *Illorum* hic semper merita celebrentur. Per.

VD. Qui tribuis ut [3] tibi fideles tui quod te inspirante devoverunt impleant [4]. Ideoque huius basilicae dedicatione [5], quam beato apostolo tuo *Illi* et sanctis martyribus tuis *Illis* famulus tuus offerre instituit, pio praevenientes officio [5], dignas maiestati tuae laudes offerimus. Per quem [6] maiestatem tuam.

Postcommun[7].

Da, quaesumus, omnipotens Deus, ut divino muneri satiati, et sicut famulus tuus *Ille* pro suae animae requie deputavit in huius consummationis requiem beati apostoli tui *Illius*[8] et sanctorum martyrum *Illorum* gloriam tuam plebs devota veneretur. Per.

[1] *quę . . . dedicata reliquid* V.   [2] *illo* V.   [3] *et* V.   [4] *impleantur* V.   [5] *dedicatione*, so V., ungrammatically; but perhaps the words *pio praevenientes officio* are an insertion only intended for occasional use.   [6] The clause *Per Christum* is required before this termination.   [7] This Postcommunion is evidently corrupt: one emendation which seems possible is the omission of *ut* before *divino*, and another the substitution of *ut* for *et* before *sicut*: but some further correction seems to be necessary.   [8] *illi* V.

XCII.

IN EIUSDEM CONDITORIS AGENDIS.

Deus fidelium receptor animarum, praesta, quaesumus, ut famulus tuus *Ille* et in perpetua luce quiescat, et quod de hoc loco desideravit, obtineat. Per Dominum nostrum.

Secreta.

Pro anima famuli tui *Illius*, Domine, tibi sacrificium [deferentes?][1] supplices exoramus, ut ad tuam misericordiam conferendam perpetuam dignanter eius vota perficias. Per.

Infra actionem.

Hanc igitur oblationem, quam tibi offerimus pro anima famuli tui *Illius*[2], Domine, quaesumus, placatus intendas, et, ut fructum boni operis consequatur, quae in his locis Christiana promisit mente perficias: diesque nostros.

Postcommun.

Largire, quaesumus, omnipotens Deus, ut anima famuli tui *Illius*[2] plenam capiat de huius ecclesiae perfectione mercedem. Per Dominum nostrum.

[1] Some word such as that supplied in brackets seems required to complete the sense of the *Secreta*.   [2] *Illi* V.

XCIII.

ORATIONES ET PRECES IN DEDICATIONE LOCI ILLIUS UBI PRIUS FUIT SYNAGOGA.

Deus qui absque ulla temporis mutabilitate cuncta disponis, et ad meliorandum[1] perducis quae eligis esse mutanda, respice super hanc basilicam in honore beati *Illius*[2] nomini tuo dicatam; ut vetustate Iudaici erroris expulsa, huic loco sancti Spiritus novitatem[3] ecclesiae conferas veritatem[3]. Per Dominum nostrum.

Omnipotens sempiterne Deus, qui hunc locum, Iudaicae superstitionis foeditate detersa, in honore beati *Illius*[2] ecclesiae tuae dignatus es pulchritudinem[4] decorare[5]. Per Dominum.

Praesta, quaesumus, Domine, ut illa fides hic fulgeat, quae, signo crucis erecto[6], mortem subegit, et salutem nobis contulit et triumphum. Per.

Secreta.

Deus, vita credentium, et origo virtutum, reple, quaesumus, hoc templum tuae gloria maiestatis[7]: in honore beati *Illius* fiat domus orationis quod perditum[8] fuerat ante latibulum: et quia infidelium turba in isto loco conveniebat adversa, populus tuus oblationibus suis te hic semper mereatur invenire propitium. Per.

Postcommun.

III. xiv *infra*.

Gratias tibi referimus, Domine, sacro munere vegetati, tuam misericordiam deprecantes, ut dignos eius nos participatione perficias. Per. γ

Ad Populum[9].

A plebe tua, quaesumus, Domine, spiritales nequitiae repellantur, et aeriarum discedat malignitas potestatum. Per Dominum.

[1] *meliorandam* V.; Tommasi suggests *meliora* or *melioranda*.   [2] *Illi* V.
[3] *novitatem ... veritatem*, so V.; one of the accusatives is ungrammatical; Tommasi reads *novitate*, and this seems the more probable correction.
[4] *pulchritudinem*, so V. (ungrammatically).   [5] The Collect is incomplete. Possibly that which follows it should form part of it, and *Per Dominum* be omitted here.   [6] *erecta* V.   [7] Perhaps *ut* should be inserted here: Tommasi reads *gloria maiestatis in honore*, &c.   [8] Perhaps *perditorum* is the true reading.   [9] This prayer appears in another form in III. xlvii *infra*.

XCIV.

Orationes et preces in Dedicatione Fontis[1].

Egb. 53.
Pam. 425.
Gerb. ii. 59.

Omnipotens sempiterne Deus, hoc baptisterium caelesti visitatione dedicatum Spiritus tui illustratione sanctifica, ut quoscumque fons iste lavaturus est, trina ablutione purgati, indulgentiam omnium delictorum tuo munere consequantur. Per. γ

Omnipotens sempiterne Deus, fons omnium virtutum et plenitudo gratiarum, dignare eadem[2] sacro baptismati praeparata[2] maiestatis tuae praesentia consecrare, ut qui ubique totus es[3], etiam hic adesse te in nostris precibus sentiamus. Per. *Egb. 53. Gerb. ii. 59.*

Secreta.

Suscipe, quaesumus, Domine, preces nostras cum oblationibus supplicantum: et concede propitius, ut quidquid hic novum regenerandi per Spiritum sanctum acceperint, tua gratia fiat aeternum. Per. *Egb. 53.*

VD. Per Christum Dominum nostrum. Per quem nobis regenerationis exortus est[4], ut qui per carnalem originem mortales in hoc saeculo[5] veneramus, ad spem vitae aeternae ex aqua et Spiritu sancto renasceremur. Quod sacramentum pietatis tuae, Domine, ut [hoc][6] loco tota gratiae tuae potentia celebretur, supplices tibi hoc sacrificium laudis offerimus, obsecrantes misericordiam tuam, ut huic fonti virtutem Spiritus tui indesinenter praesidere concedas; quo operante, omnes qui in haec fluenta descenderint, ab universorum criminum contagiis emundati, et perpetua sanctificatione purgati, libro beatae vitae mereantur ascribi. Per.

Infra actionem.

Hanc igitur oblationem, quam tibi offerimus in huius consecratione baptisterii, quaesumus, Domine, placatus accipias; et tua pietate concedas, ut quoscumque fons iste lavaturus est, omnium criminum abolitione purgentur; atque famulis tuis conditoribus mercedem tan·ti operis promissae retributionis impendas. Quam oblationem tu Deus.

Postcommun.

Multiplica, Domine, benedictionem tuam, et per Spiritum tui muneris[7] fidem nostram corrobora; ut qui in haec fluenta descenderint[8], eos in libro vitae ascribi iubeas[9], in regno tibi Deo Patri in resurrectione tradendos. Per. γ *Egb. 53. Pam. 425. Gerb. ii. 59.*

Ad Populum.

Propitiare, Domine, familiae tuae, et benignus humilitatis nostrae vota sanctifica; et[10] omnes in hoc fonte regenerandos universali adoptione custodi. Per. *Egb. 54. Gerb. ii. 59.*

[1] The contents of this section, except the Preface and *Hanc igitur*, appear (with slight variations) in the Pontifical of Egbert. Some of the prayers are given also by Gerbert from two Vienna MSS. in which they form part of the *Ordo in Dedicatione Baptisterii* (Gerb. ii. 59). [2] *dignare hoc fasciculum* (sic) ... *praeparatum* Gerb.; *eadem* (v.l. *eundem*) ... *praeparatum* Egb.; V. as text. [3] *est* V.; Egb. Gerb. as text. [4] Some substantive should probably be supplied here: *exortus* may of course be taken as the subject: but if so, *renasceremur* is ungrammatical. [5] *saeculo*, so V. (ungrammatically). [6] *hoc* is not in V. but seems to be required by the sense. [7] *et Spiritus tui munere* Gerb. Pam.; V. Egb. as text. [8] *descenderunt* Gerb. [9] Egb. Pam. Gerb. have *in libro vitae ascribi mereantur* (omitting *eos*); Egb. Pam. also omit *in regno ... tradendos*; V. as text. [10] *ut* V.; Egb. Gerb. as text.

XCV.

INCIPIT ORDO DE SACRIS ORDINIBUS BENEDICENDIS [1].

Martène, lib. l. cap. viii.

Haec autem singulis gradibus obseranda sunt tempora. Si ab infantia ecclesiasticis ministris [2] nomen dederit, inter lectores usque in vicesimum aetatis annum continuata observatione perduret [3]. Si maiori aetati [4] iam accesserit, ita tamen ut post baptismum statim se divinae militiae desiderat mancipari [5], sive inter lectores sive inter [6] exorcistas quinquennio [7] teneatur, et exinde acolytus [8] vel subdiaconus quatuor annis stet [9], et sic ad benedictionem diaconatus, si meretur, accedat. In quo ordine quinque annis, si inculpate se gesserit, haerere debet [10] : exinde [11] suffragantibus meritis stipendiis [12] per tot gradus, datis propriae fidei documentis, presbyterii sacerdotium poterit promereri. De quo loco [13] si illum exactior ad bonos mores vita perduxerit [14], summum pontificatum sperare debebit. Hac tamen lege servata, ut neque bigamus [15] neque poenitens [16] ad hos gradus possit admitti : sane ut etiam defensores [17] ecclesiae, qui ex laicis fiunt [18], supradicta observatione teneantur, si meruerint esse in ordine clericatus [19].

Martène, lib. I. cap. viii.
Miss. Franc. 661.

Episcopus quum ordinatur, duo episcopi ponant [20] et teneant [21] Evangeliorum codicem [22] super caput [23] eius : et uno super eum fundente [24] benedictionem, reliqui omnes episcopi qui adsunt [25] manibus suis caput eius tangant [26].

Presbyter quum ordinatur, episcopo eum be·nedicente [27], etiam omnes presbyteri qui praesentes sunt [manus suas iuxta manum episcopi super caput illius teneant] [28].

Diaconus quum ordinatur, solus episcopus qui eum benedicit, manum super caput eius ponat : [reliqui vero sacerdotes iuxta manum episcopi caput illius ponant :] [29] quia non ad sacerdotium sed ad ministerium consecratur [30].

Subdiaconus quum ordinatur, quia manuum [31] *impositionem non accipit, patenam de manu episcopi accipiat vacuam et calicem vacuum: de manu vero archidiaconi accipiat urceolum cum aqua, et* [32] *aquamanili, ac manutergio* [33].

Acolytus quum ordinatur, ab episcopo quidem doceatur [34] *qualiter se in officio* [35] *suo agere debeat: sed ab archidiacono* [36] *accipiat ceroferarium cum cereo, ut sciat se ad accendenda luminaria ecclesiae mancipari: accipiat et urceolum vacuum ad suggerendum vinum in eucharistia corporis Christi.*

Exorcista quum ordinatur, accipiat de manu episcopi libellum in quo scripti sunt exorcismi, dicente sibi episcopo:

Accipe et commenda [37], et habeto potestatem imponendi manum [38] super energumenum, sive baptizatum sive catechumenum. γ

Lector quum ordinatur, faciat de illo [39] *verbum episcopus ad plebem, indicans eius fidem* [40] *atque ingenium. Post haec, spectante* [41] *plebe, tradat ei codicem de quo lecturus est* [42], *dicens ad eum* [43]:

Accipe et esto verbi Dei relator, habiturus [44], si fideliter et utiliter impleveris officium, partem cum his qui verbum Dei ministraverunt [45]. γ

Ostiarius quum ordinatur, postquam ab archidiacono instructus fuerit qualiter in domo Dei debeat conversari, ad suggestionem [46] *archidiaconi tradat ei episcopus claves ecclesiae de altari, dicens ei* [47]:

Sic age quasi redditurus Deo rationem pro his rebus quae [48] istis clavibus recluduntur. γ

Psalmista, id est cantor, [49] *potest absque scientia* [50] *episcopi, sola iussione presbyteri, officium suscipere cantandi, dicente sibi presbytero:*

Vide ut quod ore cantas, corde credas, et quod corde credis operibus probes. γ

Sanctimonialis [51] *virgo quum ad consecrationem sui episcopo* [52] *offertur, in talibus vestibus applicetur, qualibus semper usura est, professioni et sanctimoniae aptis.*

---

[1] This section contains certain canonical regulations on the subject of Ordination, extracted from two documents, viz. (*a*) the letter of Pope Zosimus to Hesychius of Salona; (*b*) the canons known as *Statuta Ecclesiae antiqua*, sometimes called those of the Fourth Council of Carthage. The former docu-

ment is also cited in three of Martène's Ordines, already referred to for the forms of Ordination of Priests and Deacons (xx-xxiii *supra*). In one of these (that taken from Egbert's Pontifical), the extract appears under the name of Innocent. It also appears, in a somewhat different form, in the Decretum of Gratian (Dist. lxxvii. c. 2). The Codex Gellonensis does not contain it; but it is found, apparently, in both the other MSS. which Martène employed, together with that codex, for his fourth *Ordo*. The Missale Francorum contains some of the canons cited here from the second document, and, like V., brings them together, as a preface to the liturgical formulae which follow: but they are not given in the same order as in V., the regulation as to the Ostiarius being placed first, that as to the Bishop last, while V. follows the order of the canons. In Martène's *Ordines* the canonical regulations and the liturgical formulae are blended together, so that the canon as to each order precedes immediately the forms of admission to that order. In V., as has already been noted on xx *supra*, the forms of Ordination for Bishops, Priests, and Deacons are separated from those for the minor orders. Otherwise it may be said that this section and that which follows it are, taken together, parallel to the corresponding portion of the Missale Francorum, and to the three *Ordines* of Martène. These last will be cited (as before) as Egb. Gem. Gell. [2] *ministeriis* Egb. Gem.; V., and Mart. *Ordo* iv, as text. [3] For *nomen dederit—perduret* Egb. Gem. substitute *nostra didicerit exempla et inter lectores usque in vicesimum annum continuata observatione perduraverit. Exinde* ... [4] *aetati*, so V. Egb. Gem.; *aetate* Mart. *Ordo* iv; Tommasi reads *aetate*, and it seems not unlikely that this is the true reading. [5] *divino cultui mancipare desiderat* Egb. Gem.; V. *aetatem* for *statim*, otherwise as text: Mart. *Ordo* iv has *desideret*. [6] *in* Egb. [7] *quinque annis* Egb. Gem. [8] *et tunc catholicus* (sic) Egb. Gem. [9] *fit* Egb. Gem. [10] Egb. Gem. insert *ut melius inveniat*. [11] *Ex* V.; all Martène's *Ordines* as text. [12] Egb. Gem. omit *stipendiis*. [13] Egb. Gem. omit *presbyterii—loco*. [14] *si acutior vita illum (illius* Gem.) *ad bonos mores perduxerit* Egb. Gem. [15] *digamus* Mart. *Ordo* iv. [16] *neque revertens neque* (*sive* Gem.) *poenitens a maximis criminibus* Egb. Gem. [17] *Alioquin defensores* Egb. Gem. [18] Egb. Gem. insert *unius uxoris viri, si*. [19] *teneantur, et si vita, et moribus, et scientia scripturarum meruerint, in ordine clericatus admitti debent* Egb. Gem. [20] *duo episcopi manus eorum super caput eius ponant* Miss. Franc. [21] Gem. omits *et teneant*. [22] *librum* Egb. Gem. [23] *cervicem* Miss. Franc. Egb. Gem. [24] *et unus fundat super eum* Egb. Gem.; Miss. Franc. has *infundente*. [25] *adstant* Egb. [26] *super caput eius teneant* Miss. Franc.; *super capud eius tangant* Gem.; Egb. alters the end of the canon: V. Gell. as text. [27] *episcopum eum benedicentem* V. (ungrammatically); Gell. as text: Egb. Gem. Miss. Franc. have variations and insertions. [28] The words in brackets, omitted by V., are supplied from Miss. Franc. Gell. Egb.; Gem. adds *et componant*. [29] The words in brackets appear in V. and (with slight variation) in Martène's *Ordo* iv: they are not in Codex Gellonensis, or in the Missale Francorum: nor do they appear in Egb. Gem. which break up the canon into separate rubrical directions. They have probably been inserted in error through some confusion between this canon and such a form of that preceding, as appears in Miss. Franc. [30] Miss. Franc. omits *quia—consecratur*. [31] *manus* Egb. Gell. (*qui manus impositionem accipit* Gem.); Miss. Franc. omits the canon. [32] Egb. Gem. Gell. (?) omit *aqua et*. [33] *manutergium* Egb. Gem.; *aquimanile ac manutergio* V. [34] *ab archidiacono quidem doceatur* Miss. Franc.; *ab episcopis* (sic) *quidem doceatur* V.; *primum ab episcopo doceatur* Egb. Gem. Gell. [35] Miss. Franc. omits *se in*; Egb. Gem. Gell. omit *se*; V. as text. [36] *sed ab ipso archidiacono* Miss. Franc.; *et ab archidiacono* Gem. [37] Egb. Gem. Gell. insert *memorias*; V. Miss. Franc. as text. [38] *manus* Miss. Franc. [39] *de illum* V. (ungrammatically); Egb. Gem. Gell. as text; Miss. Franc. omits the canon. [40] Egb. Gem. Gell. insert *ac vitam*; V. as text. [41] *expectante* Gem. Gell.; V. Egb. as text. [42] *sit* Egb. [43] Egb. Gem. omit *ad eum*. [44] *habitaturus* V. (corrected by Tommasi); Egb. Gem. Gell. as text. [45] *ministraverint* Gell. [46] *a suggescione* V.; Miss. Franc. Egb. Gem. Gell. as text. [47] Miss. Franc. Egb. Gem. Gell. omit *ei*. [48] *quaeque* V.; Miss. Franc. Egb. Gem. Gell. as text. [49] Egb. Gem. insert *posteaquam* (*postquam* Gem.) *ab archidiacono instructus fuerit*; Miss. Franc. Gell. omit the canon. [50] *conscientia* Egb. Gem. [51] This canon is probably inserted here in view of the fact that the form for benediction of virgins follows (in ciii *infra*) after the forms relating to ordinations. It appears in the matter prefatory to the form cited below from Gerb. ii. 95 (see notes on ciii *infra*). [88] *sui episcopi* V. Gerb. ii. 95 ; Bruns (*Canones*, p. 142) reads *suo episcopo*. The correction adopted in the text is that of Tommasi's note.

XCVI.

621 ITEM BENEDICTIONES SUPER EOS QUI SACRIS ORDINIBUS BENEDICENDI SUNT[1].

PRAEFATIO OSTIARII.

Deum Patrem omnipotentem suppliciter deprecemur[2], ut hunc famulum suum, nomine *Illum*[3], benedicere dignetur, quem in officium ostiarii eligere dignatus est[4]; ut sit ei fidelissima cura[5] in diebus ac noctibus ad distinctionem horarum certarum ad invocandum nomen Domini. Per Dominum[6]. γ

Miss. Franc. 661. Martène, lib. I. cap. viii.

Item Benedictio eiusdem.

Domine sancte, Pater omnipotens, aeterne Deus, benedicere digneris hunc famulum tuum ostiarium, nomine *Illum*[7], ut inter ianitores ecclesiae paret obsequia, et inter electos tuos partem[8] mereatur habere mercedis. Per. γ

PRAEFATIO LECTORIS.

Eligunt te fratres tui, ut sis lector in domo Dei tui : et agnoscas[9] officium tuum ut impleas illud : potens est enim Deus, ut augeat tibi gratiam. Per. γ

Benedictio Lectoris[10].

Domine sancte, Pater omnipotens, aeterne Deus, benedicere digneris hunc famulum tuum nomine *Illum* in officio[11] lectoris, ut assiduitate lectionum distinctus atque ornatus[12], curis modulis[13] spiritali devotione[14] resonet ecclesiae. Per Dominum. γ

PRAEFATIO EXORCISTAE.

Deum Patrem omnipotentem supplices deprecemur[15], ut hunc famulum suum, nomine *Illum*[16], benedicere dignetur in officium[17] exorcistae, ut sit spiritalis imperator ad abiciendos daemones de corporibus obsessis cum omni nequitia eorum multiformi. Per[6]. γ

Benedictio Exorcistae.

Domine sancte, Pater omnipotens, aeterne Deus, benedicere digneris famulum tuum hunc, nomine *Illum*, in officio [18] exorcistae [19], ut per impositiones [20] manuum et oris [21] officium eum eligere digneris, et imperium habeat spirituum immundorum coercendo [22], et probabilis sit medicus ecclesiae tuae, gratiae curationum virtute [23] confirmatus. Per Dominum. γ

PRAEFATIO ORDINANDI SUBDIACONI.

Oremus Deum ac Dominum nostrum, ut super servum suum, nomine *Illum* [7], quem ad subdiaconatus officium evocare [24] dignatus est, infundat benedictionem et gratiam suam : [ut [25]] in conspectu suo fideliter serviens, destinata [26] sanctis praemia consequatur. Per [27]. γ

Benedictio Subdiaconi.

Domine sancte, Pater omnipotens, aeterne Deus, benedicere digneris famulum tuum hunc [28], nomine *Illum*, quem ad subdiaconatus officium dignatus es eligere [29], ut eum sacrario tuo sancto strenuum sollicitumque caelesti militiae instituas ; et sanctis altaribus fideliter subministret, et requiescat super eum spiritus sapientiae et intellectus, spiritus consilii et fortitudinis, spiritus scientiae et pietatis ; repleas eum spiritu [30] timoris tui, ut eum ministerio divino [31] confirmes, ut obediens [32] atque dicto parens tuam gratiam consequatur. Per. γ

Consecratio manuum [33].

Consecrentur manus istae per istam unctionem et nostram benedictionem, ut quaecumque benedixerint, benedicta sint, et quaecumque sanctificaverint, sanctificentur. Per Dominum nostrum. γ

---

¹ The forms contained in this section are compared with the parallel portion of the Missale Francorum, and with the three *Ordines* of Martène cited for the last section. It may be noted that V. altogether omits the forms for Acolytes. ² *deprecamur* Gem. Gell. ³ *nomine* Ille V. ⁴ *dignatus es* V. ⁵ Gem. inserts *in domu Dei*. ⁶ Egb. Gem. have (instead of *Per Dominum*, &c.) *adiuvante Domino*, &c. ⁷ *nomine* Illi V. ⁸ *partem tuam* Miss. Franc. ; *partem tuae* Egb. Gell. ; *partem suae* Gem. ; V. as text. ⁹ *cognoscas* Gell. ¹⁰ Egb. Gem. have before this benediction a bidding of prayers, which does not appear in V. Miss. Franc. Gell. ¹¹ *officium* Miss. Franc. Egb. Gem. ; V. Gell. as text (perhaps ungrammatically). ¹² *ordinatus* Miss. Franc. Egb. ; V. Gem. Gell. as text. Egb. Gem. proceed *et agenda dicat et dicta opere compleat et utroque* (*in utroque* Egb.) *sanctae ecclesiae consulat* (*contuceat* Gem.). *Per*. ¹³ Martène notes the reading *cuius modulis* as appearing in some of

the MSS. used for his fourth *Ordo*. ¹⁴ Miss. Franc. inserts *lingua*; Gell. inserts *gratiae*; V. as text. ¹⁵ *deprecamur* Miss. Franc. Egb. Gem. Gell. ¹⁶ *nomine* Illo V. ¹⁷ *officio* Miss. Franc.; V. Egb. Gem. Gell. as text. ¹⁸ *officium* Egb. Gem. Gell.; V. Miss. Franc. as text (perhaps ungrammatically). ¹⁹ *exorcistam* V. ²⁰ *et ad impositionem* Egb.; *ut per impositionem* Gem. Gell.; V. Miss. Franc. have *ut per impositionis*. ²¹ V. inserts *in*. ²² *coercendum* Miss. Franc.; *coercendorum* Egb. Gell.; V. Gem. as text. ²³ *virtutis* Gem. ²⁴ *vocare* Egb. Gem. Gell.; V. Miss. Franc. as text. ²⁵ V. omits *ut*. ²⁶ *praedestinata* Egb. Gem. Gell.; V. Miss. Franc. as text. ²⁷ Egb. Gem. Gell. have *Auxiliante Domino*, &c. ²⁸ *huic* V. ²⁹ *eligere dignatus es* Miss. Franc. Egb. Gem. Gell.; V. as text. ³⁰ *spiritum* V. ³¹ *ut eum in ministerio divino* Miss. Franc.; *et eum ministerio tuo* Egb.; *et eum mysterio divino* Gem.; *et eum ministerio divino* Gell.; V. as text. ³² Egb. Gem. Gell. insert *facto*; V. Miss. Franc. as text. ³³ Tommasi notes that this form is misplaced, belonging to the ordination of a priest. It appears in Miss. Franc. Gem. Gell. among the forms relating to priests: but in Egb. it is attached to the forms for deacons, with the title *Consecratio manuum diaconi de oleo sancto et chrisma* (*de oleo ad chrisma* Mart.). Its wording is slightly varied in the different texts.

XCVII.

IN NATALE[1] CONSECRATIONIS DIACONI.

Ad preces nostras, quaesumus, Domine[2], propitiatus intende, ut Levitae tui[3] sacris altaribus servientes, et fidei veritate fundati, et mente sint spirituali[4] conspicui. Per Dominum. *Leon.* 421.

Secreta[5].

Suscipe, quaesumus, Domine, hostias famuli et Levitae tui *Illius*, quibus mentium nos tui nomine devotarum, et a terrenis contagiis expiari et caelestibus contulisti propinquare consortes[6]. Per Dominum nostrum. See *Leon.* 450.

Infra actionem.

Hanc igitur oblationem famuli tui *Illius*, quam tibi offerimus ob diem quo eum in Levitarum sacrarii ministeriis constituisti, quaesumus, Domine, placatus accipias, eique propitiatus concedas, ut cui donasti Levitae ministerii facultatem, tribuas sufficientem gratiam ministrandi. Quam oblationem.

Postcommun.

Praesta quaesumus Domine ut [et de[7]] nostrae gaudeamus provectionis[8] augmento, et de congruo sacramenti paschalis obsequio. Per Dominum. *Leon.* 430.

[1] *Natale* so V. [2] *Domine, quaesumus* Leon. [3] Leon. omits *Levitae tui*. [4] *et mentis sint puritate* Leon. [5] This secret is given in the text in the form in which it stands in V., the result of an unskilful adaptation of the form in Leon.; the latter has *Suscipe, Domine, quaesumus, hostias mentium tuo nomini devotarum, quibus nos et a terrenis*, &c. [6] *consortiis* Leon. [7] V. omits the words in brackets, which are restored from Leon. [8] *profeccionis* V.; Leon. as text.

XCVIII.

IN NATALE CONSECRATIONIS PRESBYTERI QUALITER SIBI MISSAM DEBEAT CELEBRARE [1].

R.
Gerb. 257.
Leon. 431.
    Deus cuius arbitrio omnium saeculorum [2] ordo decurrit, respice propitius ad nostri temporis aetatem [3]; ut tibi servitus nostra complaceat, et misericordiae tuae in nobis dona concedas [4]. Per Dominum.

Secreta.

R.
Gerb. 257.
Leon. 449.
    Muneribus nostris, Domine, precibusque susceptis, et caelestibus [nos [5]] munda mysteriis et clementer exaudi. Per Dominum. γ

    .V.D. Aequum et salutare. Quia in saeculorum saecula, Domine, permanet laudatio tua. Vox haec populi tui fideliter concinentis ut maiestati tuae placens atque iocunda sit deprecamur: simul etiam illud supplex quaeso ut haec sacrificia quae [6] tibi indignus offerre praesumo ob diem, quo me sacris altaribus sacerdotem consecrari iussisti, de excelso [7] throni tui respicere digneris, benedictione tua benedicas, sanctificatione tua sanctifices. Per Christum Dominum.

Infra actionem.

R.
Gerb. 257.
    Hanc igitur oblationem, quam tibi offero ego tuus famulus hodie ob diem quo me nullis [8] dignum meritis, sed solo tuae misericordiae dono, ad hunc locum perducere dignatus es presbyterii, quaeso placatus accipias; maiestatem tuam suppliciter deprecans, ut sicut me sacris altaribus tua dignatio sacerdotali servire praecepit officio, ita et dignum praestet et meritum [9]. Quam oblationem.

Postcommun.

R.
Gerb. 257.
Leon. 437.
    Purificet nos, Domine, caelestis executio sacramenti, et ad tuam magnificentiam capiendam divinis affectibus [10] semper instauret. Per.

---

[1] This Missa agrees for the most part with that given by Gerb. (from R.) with the title '*Consecratio Presbyteri*.' Another *Missa* for the same use is given in III. xxvii *infra*.   [2] *caelorum* V.; R. Leon. as text, and so V. in the similar collect III. xxvii *infra*.   [3] *nostrae tempus aetatis* Leon.; V. Gerb. as text (R. has *temporibus* for *temporis*); Leon. inserts *et* before *ut tibi*.   [4] *complaceat, tua in nobis dona conserva* Leon.; V. R. Gerb. as text.   [5] V. omits *nos* which seems required for the sense, and is restored from R. Leon.   [6] *quam* V.   [7] *excelsa* V.   [8] *nullius* V.; R. as text.   [9] *meritum*, so V. R.; Tommasi suggests *merito*.   [10] *effectibus* Leon.; V. R. as text.

XCIX.

Orationes de Episcopis Ordinandis[1].

Oremus, dilectissimi nobis, ut his viris ad utilitatem ecclesiae provehendis[2] benignitas omnipotentis Dei gratiae suae tribuat largitatem. Per. γ   *Miss. Franc. 670.*

Exaudi, Domine, supplicum preces, ut quod nostro gerendum est ministerio tua potius[3] virtute firmetur. Per.   *Leon. 421. Miss. Franc.*

Propitiare, Domine, supplicationibus nostris, et inclinato super hos famulos tuos cornu gratiae sacerdotalis benedictionis tuae in eos effunde virtutem. Per Dominum. γ   *670. Leon. 422. Miss. Franc. 670.*

625   **Consecratio.**

Deus honorum omnium, Deus omnium dignitatum quae gloriae tuae sacris famulantur ordinibus ; Deus qui Moysen famulum tuum secreti familiaris affatu[4] inter caetera caelestis documenta culturae[5] de habitu quoque indumenti sacerdotalis instituens, electum Aaron mystico amictu vestiri[6] inter sacra iussisti, ut intelligentiae sensum de exemplis priorum[7] caperet secutura posteritas, ne eruditio doctrinae tuae ulli deesset aetati, quum et apud veteres reverentiam ipsa[8] significationum species obtineret, et apud nos certiora essent experimenta rerum quam aenigmata figurarum. Illius namque sacerdotii anterioris habitus nostrae mentis ornatus est, et pontificalem gloriam[9] non iam nobis honor[10] commendat vestium sed splendor[11] animarum, quia et illa quae tunc carnalibus blandiebantur obtutibus, ea potius quae in ipsis erant intelligenda poscebant. Et idcirco [his[12]] famulis tuis, quos ad summi sacerdotii ministerium elegisti[13], hanc, quaesumus, Domine, gratiam largiaris, ut quidquid illa velamina in fulgore auri, in nitore gemmarum, in[14] multimodi operis varietate signabant, hoc in horum moribus actibusque clarescat. Comple, Domine[15], in sacerdotibus tuis mysterii[16] tui summam, et ornamentis totius glorificationis instructos caelestis unguenti fluore[17] sanctifica. Hoc, Domine, copiose in eorum caput influat, hoc in oris subiecta decurrat, hoc in totius corporis extrema descendat, ut tui Spiritus virtus et interiora horum[18] repleat et exteriora circumtegat. Abundet in his constantia fidei, puritas dilectionis, sinceritas pacis. Sint speciosi[19] munere tuo pedes horum ad evangelizandum

Leon. 422. Miss. Franc. 671. Martène, lib. I. cap. viii.

pacem [20], ad evangelizandum bona tua. Da eis, Domine, ministerium reconciliationis in verbo, et in factis, et in virtute [21] signorum et prodigiorum. Sit sermo eorum et praedicatio non in persuasibilibus humanae sapientiae verbis, sed in ostensione Spiritus et virtutis. Da eis, Domine, claves regni caelorum : utantur [22], nec [23] glorientur potestate [24], quam · tribuis in aedificationem, non in destructionem. Quodcumque ligaverint super terram sit ligatum [25] et in caelis, et quodcumque solverint super terram sit solutum [25] et in caelis. Quorum detinuerint [26] peccata, detenta sint; et quorum dimiserint, tu dimittas. Qui benedixerit [eis [27]], sit benedictus; et qui maledixerit eis, maledictionibus repleatur. Sint fideles servi [et] prudentes [28], quos constituas tu, Domine, super familiam tuam, ut dent illis cibum in tempore necessario ; ut exhibeant omnem hominem perfectum. Sint sollicitudine [29] impigri, sint spiritu ferventes. Odiant superbiam ; diligant veritatem, nec eam unquam deserant aut lassitudine aut timore superati. Non ponant lucem tenebras, nec tenebras lucem [30]; non dicant malum bonum, nec bonum malum. Sint sapientibus [et insipientibus [31]] debitores, et fructum de profectu omnium consequantur. Tribuas eis, Domine, cathedram episcopalem ad regendam ecclesiam tuam et plebem universam. Sis eis auctoritas [sis eis potestas, sis eis firmitas [32]]; multiplices super eos benedictionem et gratiam tuam, ut ad exorandam semper misericordiam tuam tuo munere idonei, tua gratia possint esse devoti. Per. γ

626

Secreta.

Miss. Franc. 673.

Suscipe, Domine, munera quae tibi offerimus pro famulo tuo *Illo*, et propitius in eodem tua dona custodi. Per Dominum. γ

Postcommun.

Mart. *u. s.*

Plenum, quaesumus, Domine, in nobis remedium tuae miserationis operare, et tales nos esse perfice, [ut] propitius fovere digneris [33]. Per. γ

---

[1] This section has been compared with the parallel forms in the Leonine Sacramentary, and in the Missale Francorum : and also with the following *Ordines* in Martène and Gerbert; (*a*) Martène's *Ordo* ii (Pontifical of Egbert, cited as Egb.); (*b*) Martène's *Ordo* iii (Missal of Robert of Jumièges, cited as Gem.); (*c*) Martène's *Ordo* iv, taken from Codex Gellonensis and two others (cited as Gell.) ; (*d*) Gerbert's *Ordo* from a Vienna MS. saec. ix ('olim Augiensis monasterii') in *Mon. Vet. Lit. Aleman.* ii. 42 (cited as Gerb.). The readings of these four *Ordines* are not given in all cases. Some of them are

intended for the consecration of one bishop only. ² *providendis* V. Miss. Franc. Gell.; *provehendo* Egb. Gem. (Duchesne, *Or. du Culte Chrétien* makes the correction here adopted). ³ *propitius* V.; Leon. Miss. Franc. Gell. as text; Egb. Gem. Gerb. have *tuae virtutis impleatur effectu*. ⁴ *affectu* V. Miss. Franc.; *afflatu* Gerb.; Leon. as text. ⁵ *culturem* V. ⁶ *vestire* V. Miss. Franc.; Leon. Gell. Egb. Gem. Gerb. as text. ⁷ *piorum* Gerb. ⁸ *ipsam* V. ⁹ *pontificalis gloriae* V. Gell.; *pontificalis gloria* Miss. Franc.; Leon. Egb. Gem. Gerb. as text. ¹⁰⁻¹¹ *honorem . . . splendorem* V. Miss. Franc. Gell.; Leon. Egb. Gem. Gerb. as text (Leon. has *animorum*). ¹² V. Miss. Franc. omit *his*, which is restored from Leon. ¹³ *delegisti* Leon. ¹⁴ *et* V. Miss. Franc. Gell.; Leon. Egb. Gem. Gerb. as text. ¹⁵ Leon. Egb. Gem. Gerb. omit *Domine*. ¹⁶ *ministerii* V. Gell. Egb. Gem.; Leon. Miss. Franc. Gerb. as text. ¹⁷ *flore* V. Miss. Franc. Gell. Egb. Gem. Gerb.; Leon. as text. ¹⁸ *interiorum ora* V. Miss. Franc.; Leon. as text (similarly Gell. Egb. Gem. Gerb.). ¹⁹ Leon. Gerb. omit the whole passage from *Sint speciosi* to *profectu omnium consequantur*: while Egb. Gem. have it with omissions and variations. ²⁰ *speciosi pedes eius ad evangelizandum verbum tuum* Egb. Gem., which omit what follows immediately in the text, and proceed *non in persuasibilibus*, &c. ²¹ Miss. Franc. inserts *et*; V. Gell. as text. ²² Egb. Gem. omit *utantur . . , destructionem*, and read *claves regni caelorum, ut quodcumque*, &c. ²³ *ne* V.; Miss. Franc. Gell. as text. ²⁴ *potestatem* V. (ungrammatically); Miss. Franc. Gell. as text. ²⁵ *sint ligata . . . sint soluta* V.; Miss. Franc. Gell. as text. ²⁶ *retinuerint* V.; Miss. Franc. Gell. as text. ²⁷ V. omits *eis*, which is restored from Miss. Franc. Gell. ²⁸ *servi fideles et prudentes* Miss. Franc.; V. omits *et*; Gell. as text. ²⁹ *sollicitudinem* V. (ungrammatically); Miss. Franc. Gell. as text. ³⁰ *lucem ad tenebras nec tenebras lucem* V. Miss. Franc.; Gell. as text. ³¹ V. omits *et insipientibus*, which is restored from Miss. Franc. Gell. ³² V. omits the words in brackets, which are restored from Leon. Miss. Franc. Gell.: Egb. Gem. Gerb. have them with slight variation. ³³ *perficere propitius fovere digneris* V.; Egb. has *perfice ut nos ubique fovere digneris*, which suggests the correction in the text. The other *Ordines* cited do not contain the prayer.

C.

ITEM MISSA QUAM PRO SE EPISCOPUS DIE ORDINATIONIS SUAE CANTAT [1].

Deus, qui non propriis suffragantibus meritis, sed sola ineffabili gratiae largitate, me familiae tuae praeesse iussisti, tribue tibi digne persolvere ministerium sacerdotalis officii, et ecclesiasticis convenienter servire ministeriis, plebemque commissam, te in omnibus protegente, gubernare concede. Per.   Men. 227.

Deus, mundi creator et rector, ad humilitatis meae preces placatus attende [2], et me famulum tuum, quem [3] nullis suffragantibus meritis, sed immensa largitate clementiae tuae [4], caelestibus mysteriis servire tribuisti, dignum sacris altaribus fac ministrum; ut quod mea celebrandum [5] voce depromitur, tua sanctificatione firmetur. Per.   Leon. 427. Men. 227.

Secreta.

Ad gloriam, Domine, tui nominis, annua festa repetentes sacerdotalis exordii, hostiam tibi laudis offerimus, suppli-   Leon. 432. Men. 227.

citer exorantes, ut cuius ministerii vice tibi servimus immeriti, suffragiis eius reddamur [6] accepti [7]. Per.

Infra actionem.

Men. 227. Hanc quoque [8] oblationem, quam offero ego tuus famulus et sacerdos ob diem in quo me dignatus es ministerio sacro constituere sacerdotem, obsecro, Domine, placatus accipias. Unde maiestatem tuam supplex exoro [9] ut quod in me [10] largiri dignatus es, propitius custodire digneris [11]. Per Christum Dominum nostrum. Quam oblationem.

Postcommun.

Men. 228.
Cf. Leon.
433.

Repleantur consolationibus tuis, Domine, quaesumus, tuorum corda fidelium, pariterque etiam et de ecclesiae praesule, et de suorum votorum plenitudine gratiarum referant actiones [12]. Per.

[1] This Missa corresponds very closely with the *Missa propria in die ordinationis suae* in Menard's Sacramentary. [2] *intende* Men.; V. Leon. as text. [3] *quae* V. [4] Leon. omits *tuae*. [5] *celebranda* V. [6] *reddantur* Leon. (wrongly). [7] *acceptis* V. [8] *Hanc quoque*, so V.; Men. has *Hanc igitur*. [9] *suscipias; maiestatem tuam supplex exorans* Men. [10] *ut in me quod* Men. [11] Men. like V. seems to ignore the clause *Diesque nostros*. [12] *actionem* Men.; V. as text. The parallel collect in Leon. only agrees with that in the text as regards its first clauses.

CI.

Item in Natalitio Episcopi, si infirmus aut absens fuerit, qualiter Presbyter debeat celebrare Missam.

Leon. 426. Praesta, quaesumus, omnipotens sempiterne Deus, ut fidelibus tuis ordinatum praebeamus affectum, eisque nos similiter spiritum sanctum diligendi [1] benignus infunde [2]. Per.

Secreta.
628

Da, quaesumus, omnipotens Deus, ut in tua spe et caritate sincera sacrificium tibi placatum deferamus et plebis [3] et praesulis. Per.

Infra actionem.

Hanc igitur oblationem sancti patris nostri *Illius* episcopi, quam tibi offerimus ob diem quo eum pontificali benedictione ditasti [quaesumus, Domine, placatus accipias [4]]. Praebe ei, quaesumus, aetatis spatia prolixiora, cuius sacerdotii nobis tempora dignatus es donare praecipua. Quam oblationem.

Postcommun.

Deus, qui nos sacramentis tuis pascere non desistis, tribue, quaesumus, ut eorum nobis indulta refectio vitam conferat sempiternam. Per. Leon. 428.

[1] *eisque nos similiter diligendi spiritum* Leon. (omitting *sanctum*); V. as text. [2] The collect in the text forms the first part of that in Leon. [3] *plebi* V. [4] The words in brackets are not in V., but this, or some equivalent form, is required for the completion of the clause.

CII.
Item Missa pro alio sacerdote.

Deus, qui dierum nostrorum numeros, mensurasque temporum[1] maiestatis tuae potestate dispensas, ad humilitatis nostrae propitius[2] respice servitutem, et[3] tuae pacis abundantia tempora nostra et episcopi nostri tua gratia benignus accumula[4]. Per. Leon. 428.

Secreta.

Respice, quaesumus, Domine, nostram propitius servitutem; et haec oblatio nostra sit[5] tibi munus acceptum, sit fragilitatis nostrae subsidium sempiternum. Per[6]. γ Leon. 448.

Infra actionem.

Hanc igitur oblationem famuli tui et antistitis tui *Illius*, quam tibi offert ob devotionem mentis suae, quaesumus, Domine, placatus accipias, tuaque in eo munera ipse custodias; donesque ei annorum spatia, ut ecclesiae tuae feliciter praesidendo, te omnia in omnibus operante, sic utatur temporalia[7] ut praemia mereatur aeterna. Diesque nostros.

Postcommun.

Da, quaesumus, Domine, ut tanti mysterii munus indultum non condemnatio, sed sit medicina sumentibus. Per. xxviii supra.

[1] *temporumque mensuras* Leon. [2] *propitius ad humilitatis nostrae* Leon. [3] *ut* Leon. [4] *tempora nostra cumulentur* Leon. [5] *ut quod offerimus sit* Leon. [6] *sit nostrae fragilitati subsidium*. Per. Leon. [7] *temporalia*, so V. ungrammatically.

CIII.

CONSECRATIO SACRAE VIRGINIS, QUAE IN EPIPHANIA, VEL SECUNDA FERIA PASCHAE, AUT IN APOSTOLORUM NATALITIO CELEBRATUR.[1]

Sequitur oratio.

Leon. 444. Respice propitius, Domine, super hanc famulam tuam, ut virginitatis sanctae propositum, quod te inspirante suscipit[2], te gubernante custodiat. Per. γ

Item Benedictio.

Leon. 444.
Miss.
Franc. 674.
Egb. 108.
Gerb. ii. 95.

Deus, castorum corporum benignus habitator, et incorruptarum Deus[3] amator animarum, Deus qui humanam substantiam, in primis hominibus diabolica fraude vitiatam, ita in Verbo tuo, per quod omnia facta sunt, reparas, ut eam non solum ad primae originis innocentiam revoces, sed etiam ad experientiam quorumdam bonorum[4] quae in novo saeculo sunt[5] habenda, perducas, et obstrictos adhuc conditione mortalium, iam ad similitudinem provehas angelorum; respice, Domine, super hanc famulam tuam, quae in manu tua continentiae suae propositum collocans, tibi devotionem suam offert, a quo ipsa vota[6] assumpsit[7]. Quando enim animus, mortali carne circumdatus, legem naturae, libertatem licentiae, vim consuetudinis, et stimulos aetatis evinceret, nisi tu per liberum arbitrium hunc amorem virginitatis clementer[8] accenderes, tu hanc cupiditatem in earum[9] corde benignus aleres, tu fortitudinem ministrares? Effusa namque in omnes gentes gratia tua, ex omni natione quae est sub caelo[10] in stellarum innumerabilem numerum novi testamenti heredibus adoptatis, inter caeteras virtutes quae filiis tuis, non ex sanguinibus, neque ex vo‧luntate[11] 630 carnis, sed de tuo Spiritu genitis, indidisti; etiam hoc[12] donum in quasdam[13] mentes de largitatis tuae fonte defluxit, ut quum honorem[14] nuptiarum nulla interdicta minuissent, ac super sanctum coniugium initialis[15] benedictio permaneret, existerent tamen sublimiores animae, quae in viri[16] ac mulieris copula fastidirent connubium, concupiscerent sacramentum[17], nec imitarentur quod nuptiis agitur, sed diligerent quod nuptiis praenotatur. Agnovit auctorem suum beata virginitas, et aemula integritatis angelicae, illius thalamo, illius cubiculo se devovit qui sic perpetuae virginitatis est [sponsus,quemadmodum perpetuae virginitatis est][18] filius. Imploranti ergo auxilium tuum, Domine, et confirmari se benedictionis [19] tuae consecratione cupienti, da protectionis tuae munimen et regimen [20], ne hostis antiquus qui excellentiora studia subtilioribus infestat insidiis, ad obscurandam perfectae continentiae palmam per aliquam mentis serpat [21] incuriam, et rapiat de proposito virginum, quod etiam moribus decet inesse nuptarum [22]. Sit in ea, Domine, per donum Spiritus tui prudens modestia, sapiens benignitas [23], gravis lenitas, casta libertas: in caritate ferveat, et nihil extra te diligat, laudabiliter vivat, laudarique non appetat.' [Te] in sanctitate corporis, te in animi sui puri[tate glori]ficet [24]; amore te timeat, amore tibi serviat. Tu ei honor sis, tu gaudium, tu voluntas, tu in moerore consola[tio], tu [25] in ambiguitate consilium, tu in iniuria defensio, in tribulatione patientia, in paupertate abundantia, in ieiunio cibus, in infirmitate medicina. In te habeat omnia quem diligere appetit [26] super omnia, et quod est professa custodiat, scrutatori pectorum non corpore placitura sed mente. Transeat in numerum sapientium puellarum, ut caelestem sponsum accensis [27] lampadibus cum oleo praeparationis expectet; nec turbata [28] improvisi regis adventu, secutura cum lumine [ut] praecedentium choro iungatur occurrat [29], nec excludatur cum stultis. Regalem [30] ianuam cum sapientibus virginibus licenter introeat, et in Agni · tui perpetuo comitatu probabilis mansura castitate permaneat. Per Dominum. γ

Benedictio vestimentorum virginum [31].

Deus, aeternorum bonorum fidelissime [32] promissor, certissime [32] persolutor [33], qui vestimentum salutare, et indumentum iocunditatis tuis fidelibus promisisti, clementiam tuam suppliciter exoramus, ut haec indumenta, humilitatem cordis et contemptum mundi significantia, quibus famulae tuae sancto visibiliter sunt informandae proposito, propitius [34] benedicas; ut [35] beatae castitatis habitum, quem te aspirante [36] suscipiunt, te protegente custodiant; et quas vestibus venerandae promissionis induis temporaliter, beata facias immortalitate vestiri. Per Dominum nostrum. γ

Egb. 107.
Gerb. ii.
93, 95.

---

[1] The heading of the parallel form in Gerb. ii. 95 (from a Vienna MS. saec. x) agrees with that here given, except in reading *natalitiis* for *natalitio*. The offices in Leon. Miss. Franc. Egb. are for more than one person:

the variations due to this difference from V. are not noted. ² *suscepit* V.; *suscipiunt* Leon. ³ Egb. Gerb. omit *Deus*; V. Leon. Miss. Franc. as text. ⁴ *experientiam horum bonorum* Egb.; *experientiam bonorum* Miss. Franc.; V. Leon. Gerb. as text. ⁵ *sunt saeculo* Egb. ⁶ *et ipsa idem votum* Gerb. ⁷ *sumpserunt* Leon. Miss. Franc. Egb. ⁸ *nisi tu hanc flammam clementer* Leon.; *nisi tu hanc flammam virginitatis clementer* Egb.; V. Miss. Franc. Gerb. as text. ⁹ *eius* Gerb.; V. Miss. Franc. Egb. as text: Leon. omits *in earum corde*. ¹⁰ *sub caelo est* Gerb. ¹¹ *sanguinibus, ne voluptate* Miss. Franc. ¹² *et iam hoc* Gerb. ¹³ *quorumdam* Miss. Franc. Egb.; V. Leon. Gerb. as text. ¹⁴ *cum honore* V. Miss. Franc. Egb.; *quamvis honorem* Gerb.; Leon. as text. ¹⁵ *super \coniugalem* Egb.) *copulam tua* Miss. Franc. Egb.; V. Leon. Gerb. as text. ¹⁶ For *quae in viri . . . praenotatur* Miss. Franc. and Egb. have *quae non concupiscerent quod habet mortale connubium, sed hoc eligerent quod promisit* (*praemittit* Miss. Franc.) *divinum Christi ecclesiaeque* (*divinum ecclesiae Christi* Egb.) *sacramentum*. ¹⁷ *sacramento* V. (ungrammatically); Leon. Gerb. as text. ¹⁸ V. omits the words in brackets, which are supplied from Leon. Miss. Franc. Egb. Gerb. ¹⁹ *confirmari ex benedictionis* Miss. Franc. ²⁰ Miss. Franc. omits *et regimen*. ²¹ *serpat mentis* Miss. Franc. Egb.; V. Leon. Gerb. as text. ²² *nupciarum* V., and so Miss. Franc. Egb. Gerb.; Leon. as text. ²³ Miss. Franc. Egb. omit *sapiens benignitas . . . appetit super omnia*. ²⁴ *In sanctitate corporis te in animi sui purificet* V.; the portions in brackets are restored from Leon. Gerb. (the latter has *animae suae*). ²⁵ *in merore consolatu* V.; *in moerore solatium, tu* Leon. Gerb. ²⁶ *appetat* V.; Gerb. as text: Leon. has *quem elegere super omnia*, and so ends the benediction. ²⁷ *aversis* Gerb. ²⁸ *perturbatae* Egb. ²⁹ *adventu, sed secura cum lumine et praecedentium virginum choro iuncta occurrat* Gerb. *sed securae cum lumine praecedentium choro virginum occurrant* Egb.; V. (Miss. Franc. agreeing) as text, save that V. omits *ut*. ³⁰ *stultis, sed regalem* Egb. ³¹ Gerb. gives this benediction in full from one Vienna MS., and its opening words from another. ³² *fidelissimi . . . certissimi* V.; Egb. Gerb. (ii. 95) as text. ³³ *consolator* Egb.; Gerb. (ii. 93) omits *certissime persolutor . . . ut*. ³⁴ *informandae propitius propositum* V.; Egb. Gerb. as text. ³⁵ *et* Egb. Gerb.; V. as text. ³⁶ *spirante* V.; Egb. Gerb. as text.

CIV.

ITEM ORATIO SUPER ANCILLAS DEI, QUIBUS CONVERSIS VESTIMENTA MUTANTUR [1].

Egb. 108.
Gerb. ii.
97.

Te invocamus Domine sancte, Pater omnipotens, aeterne Deus, super has famulas tuas, quae tibi voluerunt [2] servire puris mentibus mundoque corde, ut eas sociare digneris inter illa centum quadraginta quatuor millia infantium, [qui] [3] virgines permanserunt [4] et se [5] cum mulieribus non coniquinaverunt, in quorum ore dolus inventus non est: ita et [6] has famulas tuas facias permanere immaculatas usque ad finem. Per immaculatum Iesum Christum Dominum nostrum, cum quo vivis [7] et regnas Deus in unitate Spiritus sancti per omnia saecula. γ

[1] This benediction appears in Egbert's Pontifical, and in one of Gerbert's Vienna MSS. (the same to which reference has been made for the form *Deus castorum corporum*). In Egbert's Pontifical, the benediction is apparently a prelude to *Deus castorum corporum*: in Gerbert's MS. it is part of a separate form. [2] *hanc famulam tuam, quae tibi vovit* Gerb. [3] *qui* omitted by V. is supplied from Gerb.; Egb. has *quae*. [4] *promanserunt* V.; Egb. Gerb. as text. [5] Gerb. omits *se*. [6] *Etita* Gerb. [7] *qui vivit* Egb.; V. Gerb. as text.

CV.

Item Orationes ad Missas eiusdem.

Da, quaesumus, Domine, famulae tuae, quam virginitatis honore dignatus es decorare, inchoati operis consummatum effectum; et ut perfectam tibi offerat plenitudinem, initia sua perducere mereatur ad finem. Per. γ

Secreta.

Oblatis hostiis, Domine, quaesumus, praesenti famulae tuae perseverantiam perpetuae virginitatis accommoda; ut apertis ianuis summi Regis adventu cum laetitia mereatur intrare. Per. γ

Infra actionem.

Hanc igitur oblationem famulae tuae *Illius*, quam tibi offert ob diem natalis sui, in quo eam tibi socians, sacro velamine protegere dignatus es, quaesumus, Domine, propitiatus sanctifica, ut tibi Domino ac Sponso suo venienti cum lampade suo[1] inextinguibili placitura occurrere mereatur. Per.

Postcommun.

Respice, Domine, famulae tuae tibi debitam servitutem; ut inter humanae fragilitatis incerta, nullis adversitatibus opprimatur, quae de tua protectione confidit. Per. γ

Cf. Leon. 405.

[1] *suo*, so V. (ungrammatically, as in cvi *infra*).

CVI.

Item alia eiusdem.

Deus, castitatis amator et continentiae conservator, supplicationem nostram benignus exaudi, et hanc famulam tuam propitius intuere; et quae pro timore tuo continentiae pudicitiam vovit tuo auxilio conservetur, ut sexagesimum fructum continentiae vitam aeternam, te largiente, percipiat. Per.

Secreta.

Munera, quaesumus, Domine, famulae et sacratae tuae *Illius*, quae tibi ob consecratione[1] sui corporis offert[2], simul ad eius animae medela[1] proficiant. Per Dominum nostrum.

Postcommun.

Bonorum, Deus, operum institutor, famulae tuae *Illius*[3] corda purifica, ut nihil in ea quod punire, sed quod coronare possis, invenias. Per.

ITEM ALIA EIUSDEM. 633

Preces famulae tuae *Illius*, quaesumus, Domine, benignus exaudi; ut assumptam castitatis gratiam, te auxiliante, custodiat. Per.

Secreta.

Votivis, quaesumus, Domine, famulae tuae *Illius*[3] adesto muneribus; ut te custode servata hereditatem benedictionis aeternae percipiat. Per.

Infra actionem.

Hanc igitur oblationem famulae tuae *Illius*, quam tibi offerimus ob diem natalis eius[2], quo eam sacro velamine 634 protegere dignatus es, quaesumus, Domine, placatus accipias. Pro qua maiestati tuae supplices fundimus preces, ut in numero[4] eam sanctarum virginum transire praecipias ut tibi Sponso veniente cum lampade suo[5] inextinguibili possit occurrere, atque intra regni caelestis[6] claustra gratias tibi referat, choris sanctarum virginum sociata. Quam oblationem.

Postcommun.

Deus, qui habitaculum tuum in corde pudico fundasti, respice super famulam tuam; et quae castigationibus assiduis postulat, tua consolatione percipiat. Per. γ

---

[1] *consecracione . . . medilla* V. (ungrammatically).   [2] *offeret*, the reading of V., is retained by Tommasi, but is a mere mis-spelling, which occurs elsewhere in the MS.   [3] *Illi* V.   [4] *numero*, so V. (ungrammatically).
[5] *suo*, so V. (ungrammatically, as in cv *supra*).   [6] *regna caelestia* V.; Tommasi corrects as text.

LIBER II.

A + Ω

INCIPIT LIBER SECUNDUS.
ORATIONES ET PRECES DE NATALITIIS SANCTORUM.

I.

DENUNTIATIO NATALITII UNIUS MARTYRIS.

Noverit vestra devotio, sanctissimi fratres, quod beati martyris *Illius* anniversarius dies intrat, quo[1] diaboli tentationes exsuperans universitatis Creatori gloriosa passione [coniunctus[2] est. (*Item pluraliter* Quo[3] diaboli tentamenta vincentes universitatis Creatori gloriosa passione] coniuncti sunt.) Ideoque Dominum collaudemus[4], qui est mirabilis in sanctis suis : ut qui illis victoriae coronam contulit nobis eorum meritis delictorum indulgentiam largiatur. In *illo* igitur loco (vel in *illa* via[5]) *illa* feria hanc eandem[6] festivitatem solita[7] devotione celebremus.

R. S.
Gerb. 214.
see Men.
note 588.

DENUNTIATIO QUUM RELIQUIAE PONENDAE SUNT MARTYRUM.

Dilectissimi fratres, inter caetera uirtutum solemnia, quae ad gloriam pertinent Christi Domini nostri hoc quoque[8] praestitit martyribus, qui pro nominis[9] eius confessione morte suscepta caelestia praemia meruerunt ; ut fidelium votis eorum praeclaris reliquiis collocatis integritas sancti corporis esse credatur. Et ideo commonemus[10] dilectionem vestram, quoniam *illa* feria *illo* loco reliquiae sunt[11] sancti *Illius* martyris collocandae[11] : quaesumus ut vestram praesentiam nobis admonentibus non negetis.

See Gerb.
ii. 49
(from a
Zürich MS.
saec. ix.).

[1] *quod* V. R. S¹ Men. ; S² as text.   [2] The words within square brackets, printed by Tommasi and retained by Vezzosi, are marked by the collator as

absent from V. They are found in R. and S. [2] *quod* S¹ Men.; R. S² as text. [4] *collaudamus* S. [5] *villa* Men. [6] *eadem* V. R. S¹; R. S² Men. as text. [7] *sollicita* R. S. Men. [8] Gerb. inserts *suis*. [9] *martiribus pro nomine* V. [10] *monemus* Gerb. [11] Gerb. places *sunt* after *collocandae*.

II.

IN NATALI SANCTI FELICIS[1] CONFESSORIS.

xviii Kal. Februarias.

Sancti Felicis, Domine, confessio recensita conferat nobis piae devotionis augmentum, qui in confessione tui nominis perseverans meruit honorari. Per.

R. S.
Gerb. 19.
Pam. 199.

Da, quaesumus, omnipotens [Deus][2], ut qui beatus Felix[3] donis tuis extitit gloriosus, apud te nostris existat nominibus idoneus interventor. Per.

Secreta.

R. S.
Gerb. 19.
Men. 18.

Hostias tibi, Domine, pro commemoratione sancti Felicis tui[4] confessoris offerimus, suppliciter deprecantes ut sicut illi praebuisti sacrae fidei largitatem sic nobis largiaris et pacem. Per Dominum.

Postcommun.

S.
Gerb. 19.
Leon. 305.

Sanctorum precibus confidentes quaesumus, Domine, ut per ea quae sumpsimus aeterna remedia capiamus. Per.

[1] *Natale sancti Filicis* V.; *Natl. Sce Felicis in pensis* R. [2] V. omits *Deus*. [3] *ut beatus Felix qui* Pam.; *ut qui beatus Felix qui* R.; *ut quia beatus Felix* S² Gerb.; V. S¹ as text. [4] Men. omits *tui*.

III.

IN NATALI SANCTI MARCELLI CONFESSORIS[1].

xvii Kal. Februarias.

Exaudi, Domine, preces nostras, quas in sancti confessoris tui atque pontificis Marcelli solemnitate deferimus, ut qui[2] tibi digne meruit famulari, eius intercedentibus meritis ab omnibus nos absolve peccatis. Per Dominum nostrum Iesum Christum.

Praesta, quaesumus, omnipotens Deus, ut beatus Marcellus tibi placito[3] fulgeat sorte pontificatus, et pietati tuae nos pia supplicatione commendet. Per.

S.
[Gerb. 20.]

·Da, quaesumus, omnipotens Deus, ut qui beati Marcelli confessoris[4] tui atque pontificis solemnia colimus, eius apud te intercessionibus adiuvemur. Per.

Secreta.

Sancti Marcelli confessoris tui atque pontificis, quaesumus, Domine, annua solemnitas pietati tuae nos reddat acceptos: per haec piae oblationis officia et illum retributio comitetur et nobis gratiae tuae dona conciliet. Per Dominum.

Postcommun.

Deus, fidelium remunerator animarum, praesta ut beati Marcelli confessoris tui atque pontificis, cuius venerandam celebramus festivitatem, precibus indulgentiam consequamur. Per Dominum.

[1] *Papae* in R. S. Gerb. Men. Pam. [2] So V.; possibly *et quia* is the true reading. [3] So V., perhaps for *placiti* or *placita*. [4] *martyris* S. Gerb.

IV.

IN NATALI SANCTORUM MARTYRUM SEBASTIANI, MARIAE, MARTAE, AUDIFAX ET ABACUC.

xiii Kal. Februarias[1].

Concede, quaesumus, omnipotens Deus, ut sanctorum martyrum tuorum, quorum celebramus victorias, participemur et praemiis. Per Dominum.

Praesta, quaesumus, Domine, ut, intercedente beato Sebastiano martyre tuo, et a cunctis adversitatibus muniamur in corpore, et a pravis cogitationibus mundemur in corde[2]. Per.   S. Gerb. 21.

Secreta.

Sancto Sebastiano interveniente[3], Domine, tibi servitus nostra[4] complaceat; et obsequia munerum fiant praesidia devotorum. Per.   R. S. Gerb. 21. Cf. Leon. 307, 349.

Postcommun.

Caelesti munere satiati quaesumus, Domine Deus noster, ut haec nos dona, martyris tui Sebastiani deprecatione, sanctificent. Per.   Cf. Leon. 348.

[1] R. places this Festival on xiv Kal. Feb.; S. Gerb. also have the festival of SS. Mary and Martha on xiv Kal. Feb., placing next the *Missa in Nat. S. Fabiani* (xiii Kal. Feb.), and then (on the same day), the *Missa in Nat. S. Sebastiani*, which in R. follows that for SS. Mary and Martha. Men. and Pam. make no mention of SS. Mary and Martha, but give separate *Missae* for the festivals of S. Fabian and S. Sebastian, both on xiii Kal. Feb. V. stands alone in the mention of SS. Audifax and Abacuc.   [2] *mente* Ger b.; V.S as text.   [3] V. has *Sanctum Sebastianum intervenientem* (ungrammatically); R. S. as text.   [4] *noster* V. R.; S. as text.

V.

In Natali Sancti Fabiani[1].
Item xiii Kal. Februarias.

S. Gerb. 21.

Adsit nobis, Domine, quaesumus, sancta precatio beati pontificis et martyris tui Fabiani; quae nos et a terrenis affectibus incessanter expediat et caelestia desiderare[2] perficiat. Per Dominum.

Secreta.

S. Gerb. 21. (See l. infra.)

Intercessio, quaesumus, Domine, [3] pontificis et martyris tui Fabiani munera nostra commendet; nosque eius veneratio tuae maiestati reddat acceptos. Per.

Postcommun.

Cf. Leon. 305.

Sumpsimus, Domine, sancti Fabiani solemnitate caelestia sacramenta; cuius suffragiis, quaesumus, largiaris[4], ut quod temporaliter gerimus aeternis gaudiis consequamur. Per.

[1] S. and Gerb. add *martyris*. [2] *desideria* V.; S¹ Gerb. as text. [3] Gerb. inserts *sancti*. [4] *largitatis* V. (corrected by Tommasi).

VI.

In Natali sanctae Agnetis virginis de passione sua[1].
xii Kal. Februarias.

R. S. Gerb. 21. Pam. 202.

Crescat, Domine, semper in nobis sanctae iocunditatis affectus; et beatae Agnae[2] virginis atque martyrae[3] tuae veneranda festivitas augeatur. Per.

S. Gerb. 21. Pam. 202.

Praesta, quaesumus, Domine, mentibus nostris cum exultatione profectum[4]; ut beatae Agnes[5] martyris[6] tuae, cuius diem passionis annua devotione recolimus, etiam fidei constantiam subsequamur. Per. γ

Secreta.

R. S. Gerb. 22.

Hodiernum, Domine, sacrificium laetantes exequimur[7], quo beatae Agnes[8] caelestem victoriam recensentes, et tua magnalia praedicamus, et nos adquisisse gaudemus suffragia gloriosa. Per.

Postcommun.

S. Gerb. 22. Pam. 202.

Sumentes, Domine, gaudia sempiterna de participatione sacramenti festivitatis[9] sanctae martyris[6] Agnes[10], suppliciter deprecamur, ut quae sedula servitute, donante te, gerimus, dignis sensibus tuo munere capiamus. Per.

Men. 21.
(See l. infra.)

[1] S. Gerb. have *Natl. Sanctae Agnae virginis*: R. has *Natl. See Agne.* [2] *ut beatae Agnetis* Pam.; V. R. S. Gerb. as text. [3] *martyris* S² Gerb. Pam.; V. R. S¹ as text. [4] *pervectu* V. [5] *Agnis* S¹: *Agnetis* Pam.; V. as text. [6] *martyrae* S¹. [7] *offerimus* S² Gerb.; *obsequimur* R.; erasure in S¹; V. as text. [8] *Agnis* S¹. [9] In l. (*infra*) *et festivitate*. [10] *Agnis* S. Gerb.; *Agnetis* R. Pam. Men.

VII.

639 ITEM IN NATALI EIUSDEM DE NATIVITATE[1].

v Kal. Februarias.

28 janv.

Adesto nobis, omnipotens Deus, beatae Agnes[2] festa repetentibus, quam hodiernae festivitatis prolatam[3] exortu ineffabili munere sublevasti. Per.

S. Gerb. 25.
Pam. 204.
Men. 23.

Secreta.

Grata tibi sint, quaesumus, Domine, munera, quibus sanctae Agnetis magnifica solemnitas recensetur: sic enim ab exordio sui usque in finem beati certaminis extitit gloriosa, ut eius nec initium debeamus praeterire nec finem. Per.

S. Gerb. 25.
Pam. 204.

Postcommun.

Adiuvent nos, quaesumus, Domine, [et][4] haec mysteria sancta quae sumpsimus, et beatae Agnae intercessio veneranda. Per.

S. Gerb. 25.
Pam. 204.

[1] S. Gerb. Men. have *Natl. sanctae Agnae* (*Agnetis* Men.) *de nativitate*; Pam. *Natale sanctae Agnetis virginis secundo*. [2] *Agnae* Gerb.; *Agnetis* Men.; V. S. as text. [3] *proratam* V. (corr. by Tommasi). [4] V. omits *et*.

VIII.

ORAT. IN PURIFICATIONE SANCTAE MARIAE[1].

iv Nonas Februarias.

2 fev.

Deus, cui[2] in hodierna die Unigenitus tuus in nostra carne, quam assumpsit pro nobis, in templo est praesentatus, praesta ut quem redemptorem nostrum laeti suscipimus venientem quoque iudicem securi videamus. Per eundem Dominum nostrum.

Pam. 206.

Secreta.

Accepta tibi sit, Domine, quaesumus, hodiernae festivitatis oblatio; et[3] tua gratia largiente, [per[4]] haec sacrosancta

R.S.(*alibi.*)
Gerb. 3.
Men. 6.

commercia in illa⁵ inveniamur forma in qua⁶ tecum est nostra substantia. Per. γ

Postcommun⁷.

S. (*alibi.*)
Gerb. 196.
Pam. 415.
See I. iii *supra.*
Cf. Leon. 472.
Cf. Men. 186.

Concede nobis, Domine, quaesumus, ut sacramenta quae sumpsimus quidquid in nostra mente vitiosum est ipsius miserationis⁸ dono curetur. Per Dominum nostrum. γ

¹ R. and S. give to this festival the title *Sancti Simonis* (R.) or *Sancti Simeonis* (S.). Gerb. (from T. 1) gives *Yppapanti*; Pam. *Hypanti*. ² *qui* V.; Pam. reads *cuius* (omitting *tuus*). ³ *ut* R. S. Gerb. Men. ⁴ V. omits *per*, which is restored from R. S. ⁵ *illius* R. S. Gerb. Men.; V. as text. ⁶ *quo* R. S. Gerb. Men.; V. as text. ⁷ The Postcommunion is apparently either corrupt or ungrammatical: see note on I. iii *supra*. ⁸ *medicationis* R. S¹ Gerb. Pam.; *medicationes* V. in I. iii. *supra*; Leon. has *ipsius doni medicatione*; V. here as text.

IX.

IN NATALI SANCTAE AGATHAE.

Nonas Februarias¹.

R. S.
Gerb. 26.
Pam. 207.
Men. 25.

Indulgentiam nobis, Domine, beata Agatha martyra tua² imploret, quae tibi grata extitit virtute martyrii et merito castitatis³. Per Dominum. γ

Secreta.

R. S.
Gerb. 26.
Leon. 457.

Fiant, Domine, tuo⁴ grata conspectui munera supplicantis ecclesiae; et ut nostrae saluti⁵ proficiant, adsit intercessio beatae tuae martyrae⁶ Agathae. Per.

Postcommun.

R. S.
Gerb. 26.
Pam. (Amb.) 323.
Leon. 456.

Exultamus⁷ pariter et de percepto pane iustitiae, et de tuae, Domine, festivitate martyrae Agathae: quia⁸ interventionibus tibi placentium confidimus nobis ad perpetuam vitam profutura quae sumpsimus⁹. Per.

¹ *Nonas Februar.* so V. ² *beatae Agathae martyrae tuae* V.; R. S. Gerb. Pam. Men. omit *tua*; R. S. have *Agathe*; S. Gerb. Pam. Men. have *martyr*. ³ S¹ Gerb. Pam. Men. have a different ending; V. R. S¹ as text. ⁴ *tua* V. ⁵ *salutis* V. ⁶ *martyris* S¹ Gerb. ⁷ *exultemus* R. Pam. (Amb.). ⁸ *qualiter* V.; R. S. Gerb. Leon. Pam. (Amb.) as text. ⁹ V. adds *proficiant*.

X.

IN NATALI SANCTAE SOTERIS¹.

iv Id. Februarias.

S.
Gerb. 28.

Praesta, quaesumus, omnipotens Deus, ut sanctae Soteris, cuius humanitatis celebramus exordia, martyris beneficia sentiamus. Per.

Secreta.

Preces nostras, quaesumus, Domine, propitiatus admitte, et dicatum tibi sacrificium beata Soteris[2] commendet. Per. S. Gerb. 28.

Postcommun.

Sanctae Soteris precibus confidentes quaesumus, Domine, ut per ea quae sumpsimus aeterna remedia capiamus. Per. S. Gerb. 28.

[1] S. and Gerb. have the form *Sotheris* throughout. *beata Sotheris martyr* S. Gerb.   [2] *beatae Soteris* V.;

XI.

ORAT. IN NATALI VALENTINI, VITALIS, ET FELICULAE[1].

xvi Kal. Martias.

Tuorum nos, Domine, quaesumus, precibus tuere sanctorum: ut festa • martyrum tuorum Valentini, Vitalis, et Feliculae[1] sine cessatione venerantes, et fideli muniamur auxilio, et magnifico proficiamus exemplo. Per. S. Gerb. 29.

Secreta.

Ad martyrum tuorum Valentini, Vitalis, et Feliculae[1], Domine, festa venientes, cum muneribus nomini tuo dicatis occurrimus[2]: ut illis reverentiam deferentes[3] nobis veniam impetremus[4]. Per Dominum. S. Gerb. 29. Leon. 306.

Postcommun.

Protege, Domine, plebem tuam, et festivitate[5] martyrum tuorum Valentini, Vitalis, et Feliculae[1], quam nobis tradis[6], assidue debita tibi persolvi[7] precibus concede sanctorum[8]. Per Dominum. S. Gerb. 29. Cf. Leon. 462. Cf. xxviii *infra*.

[1] V. has the form *Feliculae* in the Collect, *Filiculae* in the heading and in the other prayers of the *Missa*. S. and Gerb. have throughout *Valentini, Vitalis, Feliculae* [*Feliculi* S[1]], *et Zenonis*. In the Postcommun. the *Feliculi* of S[1] has been left uncorrected.   [2] *offerimus* S[1]; S[2] has altered *cum muneribus ... dicatis* to *munera ... dicata*; so also in Gerb.; V. Leon. as text.   [3] *impendentes* S[2] Gerb.; V. S[1] Leon. as text.   [4] *consequamur* Leon.   [5] *festivitatem* V.; *in festivitate* S[2] Gerb.; S[1] as text.   [6] *qua nobis tribuis* S[2] Gerb.; V. (and app. S[1]) as text.   [7] *persolvere* S[2] Gerb.; V. S[1] as text.   [8] S[2] Gerb. omit *sanctorum*, and read *concedas eorum nostrarum absolutionem culparum*; V. as text. There is an erasure in S[1]. Perhaps the original form of the prayer may be traced in the Leonine Sacramentary or in the Postcommunion for the Festival of SS. John and Paul in V. (see xxviii *infra*). The reading of V., even when corrected, is rather obscure; while the attempt shown in S. to produce a better sense is not altogether satisfactory.

XII.

In Natali Sanctae Iulianae.
xiii Kal. Martias.

S.
Gerb. 29.
Leon. 456.
See lxiv
infra.

Omnipotens sempiterne Deus, qui eligis infirma mundi[1], ut fortia quaeque confundas; da nobis in festivitate sanctae martyrae[2] tuae Iulianae congrua devotione gaudere; ut et potentiam tuam in eius passione laudemus, et provisum nobis percipiamus auxilium. Per. γ

Secreta.

S.
Gerb. 29.
Leon. 463.

In sanctae martyrae[2] tuae Iulianae passione pretiosa te, Domine, mirabilem praedicantes, munera votiva deferimus: praesta, quaesumus, ut sicut eius tibi grata sunt merita, sic nostrae servitutis accepta reddantur officia. Per.

Postcommun.

S.
Gerb. 29.
Leon. 462.
xxiii infra.
See lxiii
infra.

Libantes, Domine, mensae tuae beata mysteria, quaesumus ut sanctae Iulianae martyrae[2] tuae interventionibus temporalem[3] et praesentem nobis misericordiam conferant et aeternam. Per.

[1] *Infirma mundi eligis* S¹ Gerb.   [2] *martyris* S² Gerb.   [3] *temporalem* seems superfluous, and is omitted in lxiii *infra*. It appears in the Leonine Sacramentary as well as in V. (though apparently only as an alternative reading), and was perhaps also the reading of S¹, where S² has *gloriosis* over an erasure; Gerb. agrees with S².

XIII.

In Natali Sanctae[1] Perpetuae et Felicitatis.
Non. Martias[2].

S.
Gerb. 30.
Leon. 462.

Da nobis, Domine Deus noster, sanctorum martyrum palmas incessabili veneratione[3] venerari: ut quos digna mente non possumus celebrare, humilibus saltem frequentemus obsequiis[4]. Per.

Secreta.

S.
Gerb. 30.
Leon. 461.

Intende, Domine, munera, quaesumus, altaribus tuis pro sanctarum tuarum Felicitatis[5], Perpetuae, commemoratione proposita: ut sicut per haec beata mysteria illis gloriam contulisti, nobis indulgentiam largiaris. Per.

Postcommun.

S.
Gerb. 30.
Leon. 462.

Praesta nobis, Domine, quaesumus, intercedentibus sanctis[5], ut quae ore contingimus pura mente capiamus. Per. γ

[II. xiv.] ROMANAE ECCLESIAE. 169

¹ *sanctorum* S¹; *sanctarum* S² Gerb.   ² *Non. Martias*, so V. (ungrammatically).   ³ *devotione* Leon.; V, S. Gerb. as text.   ⁴ *humilibus saltem frequentibus obsequiis veneremur* V.; S. Gerb. Leon. as text.   ⁵ S² and Gerb. insert *et*. The Leonine form contains only the name of S. Felicitas.
⁶ Leon. inserts *tuis*.

XIV.

IN ANNUNTIATIONE SANCTAE MARIAE MATRIS DOMINI NOSTRI IESU CHRISTI[1].

viii Kal. Apriles.

25 mars

Exaudi nos, Domine sancte, Pater omnipotens, aeterne Deus, qui per beatae Mariae sacri uteri[2] divinae gratiae obumbrationem universum mundum illuminare dignatus es; maiestatem tuam supplices exoramus[3], ut quod nostris meritis non valemus obtinere, eius adipisci praesidiis mereamur. Per.

S. Gerb. 31.
Cf. Men.
31.
Cf. Sacr.
Gall. 809.

[4] Te quaesumus, Domine, famulantes, prece humili auxilium implorantes, ut[5] beatae semper virginis Mariae nos gaudia comitentur solemniis; cuius praeconia ac meritis nostra deleantur chirographa peccatorum: atque rubiginem scelerum moliviciorum igne compunctionis tui amore mundemur incursu. Per.

Cf. Sacr.
Gall. 809.

Secreta.

Oblationes nostras, quaesumus, Domine, propitiatus intende, quas in honore beatae et gloriosae semper virginis Dei genitricis Mariae annua solemnitate deferimus: et coaeternus Spiritus Sanctus tuus, qui illius viscera splendore suae gratiae veritatis[6] replevit, nos ab omni facinore delictorum emundet benignus. Per.

S. Gerb. 31.

Postcommun.

Quos caelesti, Domine, alimento satiasti, intercedente beata et gloriosa semperque virgine Dei genitrice Maria, ab omni nos, quaesumus, adversitate custodi. Per Dominum. γ

See Mur. ii. 102, 103.

Orationes ad vesperum.

Beatae et gloriosae semperque virginis Dei genitricis Mariae nos, Domine, quaesumus, merita prosequantur[7], et tuam nobis indulgentiam semper implorent. Per Dominum.

S. Gerb. 32.
Men. 32.

Beatae et gloriosae semperque[8] virginis Dei genitricis Mariae, quaesumus, omnipotens Deus, intercessio nos

S. Gerb. 32.

170   LIBER SACRAMENTORUM   [II. xv.

gloriosa⁹ protegat, et ad vitam perducat aeternam. Per Dominum.

S. Gerb. 32. Men. 32. Cf. Mur. 262.

Porrige nobis, Deus, dexteram tuam; et per intercessionem beatae et gloriosae semperque virginis Dei genitricis Mariae auxilium nobis supernae virtutis impende. Per. γ

---

[1] The title of this festival in R. S. and Gerb. is *Annuntiatio S. Mariae*; in Men. it is *Annuntiatio Angeli ad B. Mariam*. The 'Gelasian' *Missa* of Gerbert's triple sacramentary appears to have been taken from S.; the prayers of R. are different from those of either S. or V. These two MSS. agree, in part, as to the prayers included, and both show a close relation with the corresponding portion of Mabillon's *Sacramentarium Gallicanum*. The *Collectio* of the *Sacr. Gall.* is closely parallel to the first and part of the second of the Collects in V. In S. the first place is given to a collect not included in V., while the second collect of V. is omitted in S. But on the other hand the Preface contained in S. (which has been very largely altered by the corrector) seems to have been written by the original scribe in a form resembling very closely the *Contestatio* of the Gallican Sacramentary.   ² S² and Gerb. insert *foetum et*; V. S¹ Men. as text.   ³ S² and Gerb. read *exorantes*: Men. alters the phrase to *praesta ut*: V. and app. S¹ as text.   ⁴ This Secret appears in part in the *Sacramentarium Gallicanum*: it is omitted by S., possibly on account of the obscurity or corruption of its wording. The form in which it appears in V. is evidently corrupt: the latter portion is characterized by Tommasi as 'locus valde mendosus, et nonnisi ex aliis codicibus emendandus,' and it has at least one instance of the interchange of cases, of which the Gallican books show proportionately more examples than V. R. or S. Possibly the doubtful clauses may be corrected as follows:—'cuius praeconio ac meritis nostra deleantur chirographa peccatorum; atque rubigine scelerum, mole vitiorum, igne compunctionis tui amoris mundemur incursu.'   ⁵ *et* V.; Sacr. Gall. as text.   ⁶ S² Gerb. omit *veritatis*.   ⁷ *consequantur* Men.   ⁸ *semper* S. Gerb.   ⁹ *gloriosa nos* S² Gerb.; V. S¹ as text.

XV.

13 avril

IN NATALI¹ SANCTAE EUPHEMIAE².

*Id. Aprilis*³.

S. Gerb. 105.

Concede nobis, omnipotens Deus⁴, sanctae martyris Euphemiae et exultare meritis et beneficia referre suffragiis. Per Dominum nostrum.

S. Gerb. 105.

Annue, quaesumus, Domine, ut sanctae martyris Euphemiae tibi placitis deprecationibus adiuvemur. [Per.]

Foveat nos, Domine, sanctae martyris Euphemiae iocunda solemnitas, et pietati tuae commendare non desinat. Per.

Secreta.   644

S. Gerb. 105.

Muneribus, Domine, te magnificamus oblatis, quibus⁵ in sanctae nobis solemnitatibus Euphemiae et gaudia superna concilies⁶ et patrocinia sempiterna largiaris⁷. Per.

Item alia.

Benedictio tua, Domine, larga descendat, quae munera nostra, deprecante beata Euphemia, tibi reddat accepta, et nobis sacramentum redemptionis efficiat. Per. γ

Cf. Mur. ii. 127.

Postcommun.

Sanctae nos martyris Euphemiae precatio tibi, Domine, grata comitetur, et tuam nobis indulgentiam poscere non desistat. Per.

S. Gerb. 105.

---

[1] *Nativitate* (?) V. [2] *Eufimiae* V. S¹; *Eufemiae* S² Gerb. (throughout). [3] *Aprilis*, so V., perhaps for *Apriles*. [4] *Concede quaesumus omnipotens Deus* S. Gerb. [5] *quibus* S²; some letters have been erased in S¹. [6] *conciliae* V.; S² Gerb. as text; an erasure in S¹ (perhaps *conciliabis*). [7] *largiaris* V. S². Gerb.; S¹ perhaps *largieris*.

XVI.

IN NATALI PHILIPPI ET IACOBI APOSTOLORUM [1].

Kalend. Madias [2].

Deus, qui es omnium sanctorum tuorum splendor mirabilis, quique [3] hunc diem beatorum apostolorum Philippi et Iacobi martyrio coronasti, da ecclesiae tuae de natalitia [4] tantae festivitatis laetari: ut apud misericordiam tuam et exemplis eorum [5] et meritis adiuvemur. Per. γ

R. S. Gerb. 110. Pam. 288.

[Quaesumus [6]], omnipotens Deus, ut sancti nos Iacobi laetificet ac Philippi festiva solemnitas: et quorum suffragiis nitimur natalitiis gloriemur. Per.

Secreta.

Respice, Domine, munera quae in sanctorum apostolorum tuorum Philippi et Iacobi commemoratione deferimus; ut quorum honore sunt grata eorum nobis fiant intercessione perpetua. Per.

Leon. 298.

Praefatio.

VD. Quia tui est [7] operis tuaeque virtutis ut beatorum apostolorum Iacobi et Philippi gloriosa confessio usque in finem saeculi nobis capiat [8] regni caelestis augmentum. Per Christum.

R. S. Gerb. 110. Pam. (Amb.) 370.

Postcommun.

Beatorum apostolorum, Domine, quaesumus, intercessione nos adiuva, pro quorum solemnitate percepimus [9] tua sancta [10] laetantes. Per.

Leon. 338. Pam. 288.

¹ *apostolis* V.   ² *Kalend. Madias* so V. (ungrammatically).   ³ *quibusque* R. S¹.   ⁴ *natalitio* Pam.; V. R. S. Gerb. as text.   ⁵ S¹ omits *et exemplis eorum*; S² Gerb. insert *eorum* but omit *et exemplis*; Pam omits *et*.   ⁶ Some word such as this seems required for the sense.   ⁷ *Quia tibi et* V. (corrected by Tommasi from Pam. (Amb.) with which R. S. and Gerb. agree).   ⁸ *tribuat* S² Gerb.; V. R. S¹ Pam. (Amb.) as text.   ⁹ *percipimus* V.; Leon. Pam. as text.   ¹⁰ *dona* Pam.; V. Leon. as text.

XVII.

In Natali sancti Iuvenalis.

v Nonas Madias.

3 mai

S. Gerb. 111.   Beati nobis¹, quaesumus, Domine, Iuvenalis et confessio semper prosit et meritum. Per.

S. Gerb. 111.   Annue, quaesumus, Domine, ut merita tibi placita sancti confessoris et episcopi tui² Iuvenalis pro gregibus quos sincero ministerio³ gubernavit pietatem tuam semper exorent⁴. Per.

Secreta.

S. Gerb. 111.   Hostias nostras, quaesumus, Domine, sanctus pontifex Iuvenalis nomini tuo reddat acceptas, qui eas tibi digne complacuit offerendas⁵. Per.

Postcommun.

S. Gerb. 111.   Laeti, Domine, sumpsimus sacramenta caelestia, quae nobis intercedente beato Iuvenale confessore tuo atque pontifice uberius confidimus profutura. Per.

¹ *nos* V.; S. Gerb. as text.   ² *confessoris tui et episcopi* S. Gerb.   ³ *sincero misterio* V.; *sincero tibi ministerio* S. Gerb.   ⁴ *exoret* V. S¹; S² Gerb. as text.   ⁵ So V. S. Gerb. (for *eis . . . offerendis*).

XVIII.

De Inventione sanctae Crucis.

Item v Nonas Madias.

3 mai

R. S. Gerb. 112. Pam. 289. Men. 86. Leofr. 141.   Deus, qui in praeclara salutiferae Crucis inventione passionis tuae miracula suscitasti, concede ut vitalis ligni pretio aeternae vitae suffragia consequamur. Per¹.

R. S. Gerb. 112. Pam. 289. Men. 87. Leofr. 142.   Deus², cui cunctae obediunt creaturae et³ omnia in⁴ Verbo tuo fecisti in sapientia⁵, supplices quaesumus ineffabilem clementiam tuam, ut quos per lignum sanctae Crucis Filii tui pio cruore es dignatus redimere, tu qui es⁶ lignum vitae, Paradisi[que] reparator⁷, omnibus in te credentibus⁸ dira serpentis venena extingue⁹, et per gratiam Spiritus sancti poculum salutis semper infunde¹⁰. Per.

Secreta.

Sacrificium, Domine, quod immolamus placatus intende, ut ab omni nos exuat bellorum nequitia, et per vexillum sanctae Crucis Filii tui ad conterendas potestatis adversariorum¹¹ insidias nos in tuae protectionis securitate constituat. Per.

R. S.
Gerb. 112.
Pam. 289.
Men. 86.
Leofr. 141.

Postcommun.

Repleti alimonia caelesti et spiritali poculo recreati quaesumus, omnipotens Deus, ut ab hoste maligno defendas quos per lignum sanctae Crucis Filii tui, arma¹² iustitiae pro salute mundi, triumphare iussisti. Per.

R. S.
Gerb. 112.
Pam. 289.
Men. 87.
Leofr. 142.

---

¹ *Qui cum*, &c. S² Gerb.; *Qui vivis* Pam. Men. Leofr.²; V. R. S¹ Leofr.¹ as text.   ² This Collect occupies the same place in R. and S. as in V., but is marked in the margin of S. for use as a Postcommunion, and is placed accordingly in Gerb.; it is a Postcommunion also in Men. Pam. Leofr.   ³ Men. omits *cui cunctae—et*; Pam. encloses the same words in brackets: both insert *qui* before *omnia*; V. R. S. Gerb. Leofr. as text (spelling excepted).   ⁴ Pam. Men. Leofr. omit *in*.   ⁵ *in Verbi tui fecisti sapientia* S² Gerb.; Men. omits, and Pam. brackets, *in sapientia*; V. R. S¹ as text.   ⁶ *per eum qui est* S² Gerb.   ⁷ Men. omits, and Pam. brackets, *tu qui . . . reparator* (Pam. has *quo reparetur vita*); V. omits *que*, which is restored from R. S. Leofr.   ⁸ *intercedentibus* V.; S² Gerb. omit *omnibus . . . credentibus* and insert *ab eis*; R. S¹ as text.   ⁹ *extinguas* Men. Leofr.; *excludas* S² Gerb.; V. R. S¹ Pam. as text (ungrammatically).   ¹⁰ *infundas* S² Gerb. Men. Leofr.; V. R. S¹ Pam. as text (ungrammatically).   ¹¹ *adversae* R. Pam. Men.; *potestates adversariorum vel* S² Gerb.; V. S¹ Leofr. as text.   ¹² S² Gerb. have (for *arma . . . iussisti*) *etiam contra spiritales nequitias armare non cessas*; V. R. S¹ Pam. Men. Leofr.¹ as text; Leofr.² has *armis*.

XIX.

IN NATALI SANCTORUM NEREI ET ACHILLEI FRATRUM ET SANCTI PANCRATI¹.

iv Id. Madias.

Semper nos, Domine, martyrum tuorum Nerei et Achillei² foveat, quaesumus, beata solemnitas, et tuo dignos reddat obsequio. Per.

S.
Gerb. 115.
Pam. 292.

Secreta.

Sanctorum tuorum, Domine, Nerei et Achillei² tibi grata confessio et munera nostra commendet, et tuam nobis indulgentiam semper imploret. Per.

S.
Gerb. 115.
Pam. 292.

Postcommun.

S.
Gerb. 115.
Pam. 292.

Quaesumus, Domine, ut beatorum martyrum tuorum Nerei et Achillei[3] deprecationibus sacramenta sancta quae sumpsimus ad tuae nobis proficiant placationis augmentum. Per.

[1] *Nerei, Achillei, et Pancratii* S. Gerb.; *Nerei et Achillei et Pancratii* Pam. [2] *Nerei Achillei et (atque* Pam.) *Pancratii* S. Gerb. Pam. [3] *Nerei Achillei vel (atque* Pam.) *Pancratii* S. Gerb. Pam.

XX.

IN NATALI SANCTORUM PETRI ET MARCELLINI[1].

iv Non. Iunias.

S.
Gerb. 132.

Laetetur ecclesia tua, Deus, martyrum tuorum Petri et Marcellini[2] confisa suffragiis, atque eorum precibus gloriosis et devota permaneat[3] et secura consistat. Per.

Secreta.

S.
Gerb. 132.
Pam. 306.
Men. 104.

Votiva, Domine, munera deferentes in tuorum Petri et Marcellini[4] martyrum[5] passione, et[6] tuam magnificentiam veneramur, et per eam nobis imploramus tuae pietatis auxilium. Per.

Postcommun.

S.
Gerb. 132.

Quaesumus, Domine, ut salutaribus repleti mysteriis[7], quorum solemnia celebramus orationibus adiuvemur. Per Dominum. γ

S.
Gerb. 132.
Pam. 307.
Men. 104.

Intercedentibus sanctis tuis, Domine[8], plebi tuae praesta subsidium: ut ab omnibus noxiis expedita, cuncta sibi profutura percipiat. Per.

[1] *Marcellini et Petri* S. Gerb. Pam. Men. [2] *Marcellini et Petri* S. Gerb. [3] *maneat* S¹. [4] *Marcellini et Petri* S² Gerb.; V. S¹ Pam. as text. [5] V. inserts *et*. [6] S¹ Gerb. Men. Pam. omit *et*. [7] *Q. Dne. salutaribus repleti mysteriis ut* S² Gerb.; V. S¹ as text. [8] Men. inserts *Marcillino et Petro*.

XXI.

ITEM IN [NATALI[1]] SANCTORUM[2] CYRINI NABORIS ET NAZARI[3].

Pridie Id. Iunias.

S.
Gerb. 133.
Pam. 307.
Men. 105.
Leofr. 144.

Sanctorum[2] Cyrini, Naboris, et Nazari quaesumus, Domine, natalitia nobis vota[4] resplendeant: et quod illis contulit excellentiam sempiternam[5] fructibus nostrae devotionis crescat[6]. Per Dominum.

Secreta.

Pro sanctorum[2] Cyrini, Naboris, et Nazari sanguine venerando hostias tibi, Domine, solemniter immolamus, tua mirabilia pertractantes, per quem[7] talis est perfecta victoria. Per.

S. Gerb. 133.
Pam. 308.
Men. 105.
Leofr. 144.

Postcommun.

Semper[8], Domine, sanctorum martyrum[2] Cyrini, Naboris, et Nazari solemnia celebremus[9], et[10] eorum patrocinia iugiter sentiamus. Per.

S. Gerb. 133
Pam. 308.
Men. 105.
Leofr. 144.

[1] V. omits *natali*. [2] S. Gerb. Pam. Men. Leofr. insert *Basilidis*.
[3] V. S¹ both have the form *Nazari* throughout. [4] *votiva* S² Gerb. Men. Pam. Leofr.; V. S¹ as text. [5] *excellentia sempiterna* Men. Pam. Leofr.; V. S. Gerb. as text. [6] all but V. have *adcrescat*. [7] *quam* V. (S¹?) Men.; *quae* Leofr.; S² Gerb. Pam. as text. [8] *Laeti* (for *Semper*) S² Gerb. [9] *celebramus* V. [10] *ut* Men. Leofr.

XXII.

IN NATALI SANCTI VITI.
xvii Kal. Iulias.

Da ecclesiae tuae, Domine, quaesumus, sancto Vito intercedente, superbe non sapere[1], sed tibi placita humilitate proficere: ut proterva despiciens quaecumque matura sunt libera exerceat caritate. Per. Cf. Leon. 353. Cf. III. xxvii *infra*.

S. Gerb. 136.
Pam.
(Amb.)
388.

Secreta.

Sicut gloriam[2] divinae potentiae munera pro sanctis oblata testantur sic nobis effectum, Domine, tuae salvationis impendant. Per.

S. Gerb. 136.
Pam.
(Amb.)
388.

Postcommun.

Refecti, Domine, benedictione solemni, quaesumus ut per intercessionem sancti Viti medicina sacramenti[3] et corporibus nostris prosit et mentibus. Per.

S. Gerb. 136.
Pam.
(Amb.)
388.

[1] *saperet* V. [2] *gloriae* V (S¹?); S² Gerb. Pam. (Amb.) as text. The Ambrosian form of the *Secreta* (both in Gerb. and Pam.) differs from the Gelasian, reading *Maiestatem tuam suppliciter imploramus O. D. ut sicut*, and adding *Domine* at a later point. [3] S² Gerb. insert *caelestis*.

XXIII.

IN NATALI SANCTORUM MARCI ET MARCELLIANI.
xiv Kal. Iulias.

Sanctorum tuorum nos, Domine, Marci et Marcelliani natalitia tueantur, quia tanto fiducialius tuo nomini suppli-

S. Gerb. 137.
Pam. 309.

camus, quanto frequentius martyrum benedictionibus confovemur. Per.

Secreta.

S.
Gerb. 137.
Pam. 309.
Leon. 304.

Suscipe, Domine, munera tuorum populorum votiva; et sanctorum Marci et Marcelliani tibi precibus grata esse concede, pro quorum solemnitatibus offeruntur[1]. Per.

Postcommun.

Cf. xii *supr.*
Pam. 309.
Cf. Leon.
462.

Libantes, Domine, mensae tuae beata mysteria, quaesumus ut beatorum interventione sanctorum Marci et Marcelliani et temporalem[2] nobis misericordiam conferant et aeternam. Per.

[1] Pam. omits the clause *pro quorum ... offeruntur.*   [2] *corporalem* Pam.

XXIV.

IN VIGIL. SANCTORUM MARTYRUM GERBASI ET PROTASI[1].

Item xiv Kal. Iulias.

18 juin

S.
Gerb. 137.
Pam. 310.
Pam.
(Amb.) 390.

Martyrum tuorum, Domine, Gerbasi et Protasi natalitia praeeuntes[2] supplices te rogamus, ut quos caelesti gloria sublimasti tuis adesse concedas[3] fidelibus. Per.

Pam. 310.

Sanctorum Gerbasi et Protasi suffragiis imploramus[4] ut a cunctis, Domine, liberemur offensis. Per.

Secreta.

S.
Gerb. 137.
Pam.
(Amb.)
390.

Sacrificium, Domine, quod pro sanctis martyribus Gerbasio et Protasio[5] praevenit nostra devotio, eorum merito[6] nobis augeat, te donante, suffragium. Per.

Postcommun.

S.
Gerb. 137.
Leon. 437.

Sumpti sacrificii, Domine, perpetua nos tuitio non relinquat et noxia semper a nobis cuncta depellat. Per. γ

ITEM IN NATALI UT SUPRA.

xiii Kal. Iulias[7].

19 juin

S.
Gerb. 137.
Pam. 309.
Pam.
(Amb. 390).
Men. 108.

Sanctorum martyrum[8] nos, Domine, Gerbasi et Protasi confessio beata communiat, et fragilitatis[9] nostrae subsidium dignanter exoret. Per.

Secreta.

Concede nobis, omnipotens[10] Deus, ut his muneribus, quae pro sanctorum martyrum Gerbasi et Protasi honore deferimus, et te placemus exhibitis, et nos vivificemur acceptis. Per.

S. Gerb. 137.
Pam. 310.
Men. 108.

Postcommun[11].

Da, quaesumus, omnipotens Deus, ut mysteriorum virtute sanctorum Gerbasi et Protasi vita nostra firmetur. Per. γ

S. Gerb. 138.
Pam. 310.
Pam. (Amb.)
390.
Men. 108.
Leon. 440.

[1] In the Ambrosian form given by Pam. the name of S. Protasius precedes that of S. Gervasius throughout. S. Gerb. use the form *Gervasius*, S[1] like V. generally making the genitives *Gervasi*, *Protasi*. [2] Pam. (making this the *orat. sup. pop.* of the Festival) has *celebrantes* for *praeeuntes*; Pam. (Amb.) as text. [3] *adesse concede* V. S[1]; *concedas adesse* S[2] Gerb.; Pam. (both forms) as text. [4] *imploremus* V. [5] *Gerbasi et Protasi* V.; similarly S[1]; Pam. (Amb.) inserts *tuis* after *martyribus*. [6] *merita* (perh. for *meritis*) V. S[1]; S[2] Gerb. Pam. (Amb.) as text. [7] *iii Kal. Iulias* V. [8] Gerb. Pam. (Amb.) insert *tuorum*. [9] *fragilitati* Pam. (both forms) Men.; V. S. Gerb. as text. [10] *misericors* (for *omnipotens*) Pam. [11] This Postcommunion is given as it stands in V., but something is evidently wanting to complete the sense, and the other authorities are at variance. S[1] had ... *mysteriorum virtute satiati sanctorum quoque Gervasii et Protasii vita nostra firmetur*: this is corrected by S[2] so as to read ... *mysteriorum tuorum virtute satiati sanctorum Gervasii et Protasii intercessione firmemur*. Gerbert's text agrees with the corrections of S[2], except as to the last word, for which it retains the ungrammatical ending *vita nostra firmetur* (see Mur. ii. 177). Pam. reads ... *sanctorum, et beatorum martyrum Gervasii et Protasii orationibus vita nostra firmetur*. Pam. (Ambros.) has ... *sanctorum, Protasio et Gervasio martyribus intercedentibus vita nostra firmetur*. Men. has ... *sanctorum et intercessione beatorum Gervasii et Protasii martyrum tuorum, vita nostra fulciatur*. It seems most likely that the confusion has resulted from the careless insertion of the names of SS. Gervasius and Protasius in the form found in the Leonine Sacramentary, which only differs from that in V. in respect of the words *Gerbasi et Protasi*.

XXV.

IN VIGILIA[1] SANCTI IOANNIS BAPTISTAE.

ix Kal. Iulias[2].

Praesta, quaesumus, Domine, ut populus tuus ad plenae devotionis effectum[3] beati Baptistae Ioannis natalitiis praeparetur[4], quem praemisisti Filio tuo parare plebem perfectam, Iesu Christo[5].

R. S.
Gerb. 139.
Pam. 311.
Men. 109.
Sacr. Gall.
878.

Beati Ioannis Baptistae nos, Domine, praeclara comitetur oratio, et quem venturum esse praedixit poscat nobis favere[6] placatum. Per[7]. γ

S.[2]
Gerb. 140.
Pam. 311.
Leon. 325.

Pam. (Amb.) 392. Men. 108.

Secreta.

Munera populi tui, Domine placatus intende, et beati Baptistae Ioannis, cuius nos tribuis praeire solemnia, fac gaudere suffragiis. Per.

R. S.
Gerb. 139.

Postcommun.

S.
Gerb. 141.

Da, quaesumus, misericors Deus, ut mysticis ecclesia tua⁸ beati Ioannis Baptistae exordiis et sacris erudita praeconiis ad iram venturi iudicii declinandam, dignos salutis fructus iugiter operetur. Per.

R. S.
Gerb. 140.
Men. 109.

Beati nos, Domine, Baptistae Ioannis oratio et intelligere Christi tui mysterium postulet et mereri. Per.

¹ *Ieiunio* R. S. ² *viii Kal. Iulii* V. ³ *affectum* R. S. Gerb. ⁴ *imbuatur* Sacr. Gall. ⁵ *Iesum Christum* V.; *Iesu Christo Domino nostro*, &c. R. S. Gerb. Pam. ⁶ *facere* V.; *fieri* Pam.; *habere* (*pacatum*) Pam. (Amb.); S² Gerb. Men. Leon. as text. ⁷ Gerb. Pam. (both forms) omit *per*, Pam. (Amb.) has *Qui vivit*, the others *Dominum nostrum*, etc.; V. S² Leon. as text. ⁸ *ecclesiae tuae* V. S.; Gerb. as text.

XXVI.

ITEM IN NATALI UNDE SUPRA.

R. S.
Gerb. 140.
Pam. 312.
Pam.
(Amb.)
393.
Men. 109.

Deus, qui praesentem diem honorabilem nobis in beati Ioannis nativitate¹ fecisti, da populis tuis spiritalium gratiam gaudiorum, et omnium fidelium mentes dirige in viam salutis et pacis². Per Dominum. γ

Miss. Goth. 621. Leon. 326.

R. S.
Gerb. 141.
Leon. 326.

Omnipotens sempiterne Deus, qui instituta legalia et sanctorum praeconia prophetarum in diebus beati Baptistae³ Ioannis implesti, praesta, quaesumus⁴, ut cessantibus significationum figuris ipsa sui manifestatione⁵ veritas eloquatur⁶, Iesus Christus Dominus noster. Qui tecum.

Secreta.

R. S.
Gerb. 141 (140).
Pam. 312.
Pam.
(Amb.)
392. Men. 109. Sacr. Gall. 878. Leon. 324.

Tua, Domine, muneribus altaria⁷ cumulamus, sancti Ioannis⁸ nativitatem⁹ honore debito celebrantes, qui Salvatorem mundi et cecinit adfuturum et adesse monstravit¹⁰, Iesum Christum. γ

Postcommun.

R. S.
Gerb. 141.
Pam. 312.
Men. 110.

Sumat ecclesia tua, Deus, beati Ioannis Baptistae generatione¹¹ laetitiam, per quem suae regenerationis cognovit auctorem. Per¹². γ

Sancti Ioannis natalitia celebrantes, supplices te, Domine, deprecamur, ut hoc idem nobis semper et indulgentiae causa sit et salutis. Per.

Ista in vigilia sancti Ioannis[13].

Beati Ioannis Baptistae nos, quaesumus, Domine, prae- R. S.[1]
clara comitetur oratio, et quem venturum esse praedixit,
poscat nobis ab eo sempiternum remedium. Per.

[1] *nativitatem* V.; R. S. Leon. as text.   [2] *salutis aeternae* R. S. Gerb.
Pam. (Gr.), Men.; V. Leon. Pam. (Amb.) Miss. Goth. as text.   [3] *beati
famuli tui Ioannis* Leon.   [4] Leon. omits *quaesumus*.   [5] *manifestationem*
S[1] Gerb.   [6] *eloquatur. Per.* Leon.   [7] *salutaria* (for *altaria*) Sacr. Gall.
[8] *illius* (for *sancti Ioannis*) Leon. Pam. (both forms), Gerb. 140; *illius nobis
per haec opem adesse poscentes et* Men.; *beati Ioannis Baptistae* Sacr. Gall.; V.
R. S. Gerb. 141 as text.   [9] *nativitate* V. R. S[1]; Leon. as text.   [10] After
monstravit Leon. has *Per*; Pam. (Gr.) Men. have *Dominum*; Pam. (Amb.)
Qui tecum; Gerb. 140 *Dominum vel Qui tecum*; Sacr. Gall. ends with *cecinit
ad salutem* (sic); V. S. as text.   [11] *generationis* V.; R. S. as text.
[12] *Dominum.* (for *Per.*) Pam. Men.; *per eundem* S[2] Gerb.; V. S[1] as text.
[13] This Postcommunion is evidently misplaced in V. It appears in R. S[1] as
the Postcommunion for the Vigil, and has been altered by S[2] into the form
given above as the second Collect for the Vigil.

XXVII.

IN VIGILIA MARTYRUM IOANNIS ET PAULI.

vii Kal. Iulias.

Beatorum martyrum Ioannis et Pauli natalitia veneranda, R. S.
quaesumus, Domine, ecclesia tua devota suscipiat, et fiat Gerb. 142.
magnae glorificationis amore devotior. Per. Cf. Leon. 460.

Beatorum martyrum tuorum Ioannis et Pauli nos Domine Pam. 313.
merita prosequantur, et tuam nobis indulgentiam semper
implorent. Per.

Secreta.

Sint tibi, quaesumus, Domine, nostri munera grata R. S.
ieiunii, quia[1] tunc eadem in sanctorum tuorum Ioannis et Gerb. 142.
Pauli digna[2] commemoratione deferimus, si [et[3]] actus Leon. 346.
eorum pariter subsequamur. Per Dominum.

Postcommun.

Protege, Domine, plebem tuam, et quam martyrum R. S.
tuorum Ioannis et Pauli adsidua tribuis festivitate[4] devo- Gerb. 142.
tam, tibi semper placitam fieri precibus concede iustorum. Leon. 462.
Per.

[1] *qualiter* V.; R. S. Gerb. Leon. as text.   [2] *digne* S. Gerb.; V. R. Leon.
as text.   [3] V. om. *et.*   [4] *festivitatem* V.; R. S. Leon. as text.

XXVIII.

Item in Natali eorumdem[1].

vi Kal. Iulias.

R. S.
Gerb. 142.
Men. 110.
Pam. 313.
Leon. 328.

Quaesumus, omnipotens Deus, ut nos geminata laetitia hodiernae festivitatis excipiat, quae [de[2]] beatorum Ioannis et Pauli glorificatione procedit, quos eadem fides et passio[3] fecit esse germanos. Per. γ

Secreta.

R. S.
Gerb. 142.
Leon. 329.
Men. 110.

Hostias altaribus tuis, Domine, placationis imponimus[4], potentiam tuam in sanctorum tuorum passionibus honorando, et per eos nobis implorando veniam peccatorum. Per Dominum.

Postcommun.

R. S.
Gerb. 143.

Sumpta munera, Domine, nostra sanctificatione tuorum precibus concede sanctorum. Per[5].

Pam. 313.
Leon. 348.

Caelesti munere satiati quaesumus, Domine, ut haec [nos][6] dona martyrum tuorum Ioannis et Pauli deprecatione sanctificent. Per Dominum.

[1] *eiusdem* V. [2] V. om. *de*. [3] Pam. Men. insert *vere*. [4] *placationum imponemus* V.; R. S. Leon. as text. [5] V. R. S¹ give this Post-communion in the same form: *sumpta munera* is apparently an accusative for the ablative, *nostra sanctificatione* an ablative for the accusative. S¹ Gerb. read *nostrae sanctificationi*. [6] V. omits *nos*; Leon. as text; Pam. has *ut nos haec*.

XXIX.

In Vigilia Apostolorum Petri et Pauli.

iv Kal. Iulias[1].

R. S.
Gerb. 143.
Pam. 315.
Men. 111.

Deus, qui nobis apostolorum beatorum[2] Petri et Pauli natalitia gloriosa praeire concedis; tribue, quaesumus, eorum nos semper et beneficiis praeveniri et orationibus adiuvari. Per.

Secreta.

R. S.
Gerb. 143.
Men. 111.
Leon. 341.

Munera, Domine, tuae glorificationis offerimus; quae tibi pro nostris grata ieiuniis sanctorum apostolorum, quaesumus, deprecatio[3] quorum solemnia praevenimus efficiat. Per.

Postcommun.

Beatorum Petri et Pauli honore continuo plebs tua semper exultet, et his praesulibus gubernetur, quorum doctrinis gaudet et meritis. Per.

[1] *iii Kal. Iulias* V. [2] *beatorum apostolorum* S¹ Gerb. [3] *deprecatione* S¹; R. has q̄s dn̄e precatio.

XXX.

Item in Natali Sancti Petri proprie[1].
iii Kal. Iulias.

Deus, qui beato apostolo tuo Petro, collatis clavibus regni caelestis, animas ligandi atque solvendi pontificium tradidisti; concede ut intercessionis eius auxilio a peccatorum nostrorum nexibus liberemur. Per[2]. γ Cf. Pam. 316.   R.S.(*alibi.*) Gerb. 30. Pam. 208. Men. 29. Leofr. 138. Cf. Men 113. Cf. Gerb. 145.

Secreta.

Ecclesiae tuae, quaesumus, Domine, preces et hostias beati Petri apostoli[3] commendet oratio; ut quod pro illius gloria celebramus nobis prosit ad veniam. Per. γ
    Leofr. 138.   Cf. Leon. 337.   Cf. Pam. 316.   Cf. Men. 113.   Cf. Gerb. 146.

R.S.(*alibi.*) Gerb. 30. Pam. 208. Men. 29.

Postcommun.

Laetificet nos Domine, munus oblatum; ut sicut in apostolo tuo Petro te mirabilem praedicamus, sic per illum tuae sumamus indulgentiae[4] largitatem. Per.   R.S.(*alibi.*) Gerb. 30. Pam. 208. Men. 29. Leofr. 138.

[1] R. Pam. and Leofr. give to the festival of iii Kal. Iul. the title of *Natale S. Petri Ap.*, but even in them the Missa for that day is not the same as that given in V. Pam. 316, Men. 113, Gerb. 145 have the Collect (in a revised form) among the additional prayers for the Festival: and the Secret, in the same form in which it appears in Leon. (where it is not specially adapted for S. Peter's day) in the Missa for the Festival of S. Paul. But the Collect, Secret, and Postcommunion of the *Missa* here assigned to iii Kal. Iul. appear in R. S. Gerb. Pam. Men. Leofr. as those of the *Missa* for the Festival of the Chair of S. Peter, in the same form in which they have in the text.   [2] For *Per.* Pam. Men. have the ending *Qui vivis.*   [3] S[2] Gerb. insert *tibi.*   [4] *sumamus indulgentiae tuae* Pam.

XXXI.

In Natali Apostolorum Petri et Pauli.
iii Kal. Iulias.

Deus, qui hunc diem beatorum apostolorum Petri et Pauli martyrio consecrasti, da ecclesiae tuae toto terrarum orbe diffusae eorum semper magisterio gubernari per quos sumpsit religionis exordium. Per[1].   Leon. 330. Miss. Goth. 621. Cf. Gerb. 144.

Largiente te[2] Domine beati Petri et Pauli natalitium nobis [lumen[3]] effulsit: concede quaesumus ut hodierna[4] gloria passionis sicut illis magnificentiam tribuit sempiternam, ita nobis munimen operetur perpetuum[5]. Per.   R. S. Gerb. 144. Leon. 343. Sacr. Gall. 881. Cf. Miss. Goth. 622.

182   LIBER SACRAMENTORUM   [II. xxxii.

Secreta.

Leon. 332.   Oblationes populi tui, Domine, quaesumus, beatorum apostolorum Petri et Pauli passio beata conciliet; et quae nostris non apta[6] sunt meritis fiant tibi placita[6] tuorum deprecatione iustorum. Per.

Praefatio.

R. S. (*in Vigil.*)
Gerb. 143.
Leon. 338.
Pam.
(Amb.)
395.
Cf. Men.
112.

VD. Apud quem quum[7] beatorum apostolorum continuata festivitas et aeterna celebritas atque triumphi[8] caelestis perpetuus sit natalis, nos[9] tamen beatae confessionis[10] initia recolentes[9] frequenti[11] tribuis devotione gaudere[12], ut crebrior[13] honor sacratissimae[14] passioni repensus maiorem nobis retributionis gratiam largiatur[15]. Per. y

Postcommun.

R. S.
Gerb. 145
Pam. 315.
Men. 112.

Sumptis, Domine, remediis sempiternis tuorum mundentur corda fidelium, ut apostolici[16] Petri et Pauli natalis insignia, quae corporalibus[17] officiis exsequuntur, pia cordis intelligentia comprehendant. Per.

Item alia[18].   654

Sumpsimus, Domine, pignus salutis aeternae[19] celebrantes Apostolorum Petri et Pauli votiva solemnia et perpetua merita venerantes. Per.

[1] This Collect has in V. the same form as in Leon. That in Miss. Goth. is almost identical. In R. S. Gerb. Men. Pam. it has undergone some revision.
[2] V. omits *te*.   [3] V. R. S. Gerb. omit *lumen*, which seems required for the sense, and is restored from Leon. and Sacr. Gall.   [4] *hodiernae* S² Gerb.
[5] Sacr. Gall. and Miss. Goth. alter the ending of this Collect.   [6] *apta . . . placitae* Leon.   [7] *licet* (for *quum*) Pam. (Amb.); *licet quum* Gerb.; R. omits *quum*.   [8] *festivitas, aeterna celebritas et triumphi* Leon.   [9] *nobis . . . recolentibus* Pam. (Amb.).   [10] S² Gerb. insert *eorum*.   [11] *annua* S² Gerb.; *celebriori* Pam. (Amb.).   [12] *venerari* Leon.   [13] *annuus* Pam. (Amb.).   [14] *sacramentissimae* V.   [15] *impensus sacratissimae passioni maiorem nobis prosit ad gratiam* Leon.   [16] *apostolice* V. R.; *apostolorum* Pam.; S. Gerb. Men. as text.   [17] *corporalis* V.   [18] This second Postcommunion appears to be incomplete, containing no petition.
[19] *aeterna* V.

XXXII.

ITEM IN NATALI SANCTI PAULI PROPRIE.

iii Kal. Iulias[1].

R. S.
Gerb. 146.
Pam. 317.
Men. 113.

Deus, qui multitudinem gentium beati Pauli apostoli praedicatione[2] docuisti, da nobis, quaesumus, ut cuius[3] natalitia colimus eius apud te patrocinia sentiamus. Per. y

Maiestatem tuam, Domine, supplices exoramus, ut sicut ecclesiae tuae sanctus apostolus Paulus extitit praedicator ita sit [pro]⁴ nobis perpetuus suffragator. Per. γ

*See lxix infra.
Leon. 466.*

Secreta.

Praeveniant nobis⁵, Domine, quaesumus, apostoli tui⁶ desiderata commercia, ut quorum perpetuam dignitatem sacro mysterio frequentamus in terris et praesentia nobis subsidia postulent et aeterna. Per.

*R. S.
Gerb. 146.*

Postcommun.

Perceptis, Domine, sacramentis, subdito corde rogamus et petimus ut intercedente beato Paulo apostolo tuo, nobis proficiant ad medelam quae pro illius gesta sunt passione. Per. γ

*R. S.
Gerb. 146.
Leon. 332.*

¹ R. S. Men. assign this *Missa* to the last day of June: so possibly Gerb. Pam. Leofr. which have *ii Kal. Iul.* ² *praedicacionis* V. ³ *qui eius* V. ⁴ V. omits *pro*, which is found in lxix *infra*: Leon. omits *nobis* also. ⁵ *nos* S² Gerb.; V. R. S¹. as text. ⁶ *apostolorum tuorum* S²; V. R. S¹ Gerb. as text.

XXXIII.

Orationes ad Vesperum¹.

Deus qui ligandi solvendique licentiam tuis apostolis contulisti; da, quaesumus, ut per ipsos a terrenis vitiis expediti², liberi possimus³ caelestibus interesse mysteriis. Per.

*R. S.
Gerb. 144.
Pam. 315.
Men. 112.*

Omnipotens sempiterne Deus, qui nos beatorum apostolorum Petri et Pauli multiplici facis celebritate gaudere; da, quaesumus, ut eorum saepius iterata solemnitas nostrae sit tuitionis augmentum. Per.

R. S.

655 Apostolicis nos, Domine, quaesumus, beatorum Petri et Pauli attolle praesidiis; ut quanto fragiliores sumus tanto validioribus auxiliis foveamur. Per Dominum.

*R. S.
Gerb. 144.
Pam. 315.
Men. 112.*

Concede, quaesumus, Domine, apostolos tuos⁴ intervenire pro nobis: quia tunc nos⁵ salvari posse confidimus⁶ si eorum precibus tua gubernetur ecclesia⁷ quibus utitur te constituente principibus. Per Dominum.

*S.
Gerb. 145.
Leon. 340.*

Omnipotens sempiterne Deus, qui nos omnium apostolorum merita sub una tribuisti celebritate venerari, quaesumus ut celeriter⁸ nobis tuae propitiationis abundantiam multiplicatis⁹ intercessoribus largiaris. Per.

*S.
Gerb. 146.
Leon. 341.*

Leon. 339.
Pam. 317.
Men. 113.
Gerb. 144.

Exaudi nos, Deus salutaris noster, et apostolorum [10] tuere praesidiis quorum donasti fideles esse doctrinis. Per. γ

Leon. 345.

Solemnitatis apostolicae multiplicatione gaudentes, clementiam tuam deprecamur, omnipotens Deus, ut tribuas iugiter nos eorum et [11] confessione benedici et patrociniis confoveri. Per.

Praesta, quaesumus, omnipotens Deus, ut qui iugiter apostolica defensione [12] munimur nec succumbamus vitiis nec opprimamur adversis. Per.

---

[1] The collects entitled *Orationes ad Vesperum* in V. are for the most part to be found in either R. S. Gerb. Pam. or Men. though in various positions. Thus the first of the series appears in all five among the prayers for the Vigil: in Pam. and Men. it is an *Oratio super Populum*, in R. S. and Gerb. an *Oratio ad Matutinum*. The second is apparently in R. S. only: it is there the first of the *aliae Orationes* for iii Kal Iul. The third, again, is assigned in all five to the Vigil: in Pam. it is an additional *Or. sup. Pop.* in the rest an *Or. ad Vesperas*. The fourth in S. comes next to the second: it was in the same position, apparently, in T., since it appears in Gerbert: but it is not in R. The fifth is in S. and Gerb. the last of the *aliae Orationes* for the festival. The sixth is among the parallel series of prayers in Gerbert (though not in S. or R.); so also in Men. Pam. The seventh and eighth do not seem to have found their way into any of the five Sacramentaries.   [2] *expeditique* V.
[3] *possumus* V.   [4] *apostolis tuis* V.; S. Gerb. Leon. as text   [5] *ita enim nos* Leon.   [6] *credimus* Gerb.   [7] *precibus ecclesia gubernetur* Leon.
[8] *celerem* Leon.; *desideratam* S² Gerb.; V. S¹ as text.   [9] *multiplicas* V.
[10] Leon. Pam. Men. Gerb. insert *tuorum nos*.   [11] Leon. omits *et*.   [12] *defensionum* V.

XXXIV.

Item de Vigilia omnium Apostolorum [1].

R.S.(*alibi.*)
Gerb. 188.
Men. 136.
Leofr. 164.

Concede, quaesumus, omnipotens Deus, ut sicut apostolorum tuorum *illorum* gloriae natalitia praevenimus, sic ad tua beneficia promerenda maiestatem tuam pro nobis ipsi praeveniant. Per.

Secreta.

R.S.(*alibi.*)
Gerb. 188.
Men. 136.
Leofr. 164.
Cf. Leon. 398.

Muneribus nostris, Domine, apostolorum [2] *illorum* festa praecedimus, ut quae conscientiae nostrae praepediuntur obstaculis [3], illorum [2] meritis grata reddantur. Per.

Postcommun.

R.S.(*alibi.*)
Gerb. 189.
Men. 136.
Leofr. 164.
Cf. Leon. 340.

Sumpto, Domine, sacramento, suppliciter deprecamur ut, intercedentibus beatis apostolis [4], quod temporaliter gerimus ad vitam [5] capiamus aeternam [6]. Per.

---

[1] The *Natale Omnium Apostolorum* does not appear as a Festival in the other Sacramentaries here cited. The Collect, Secret, and Postcommunion here assigned to the Vigil appear in R. S. Gerb. Men. Leofr. for the Vigil of

SS. Simon and Jude: while the corresponding parts of the *Missa* for the Festival are employed for the Festival of the same two Apostles. The Collect and Secret of this *Missa* are apparently intended to be employed on the vigil of any feast of Apostles: R. S. Gerb. and Men. insert the names of the two Saints: Leofr. omits all names in these two prayers, but inserts them in the prayers of the *Missa* for the Festival. ³ In the Leonine Sacramentary this is a *Secreta* for the Festival of S. Laurence, and this phrase is varied accordingly.   ³. *obstaculo* Leon..   ⁴ *sacramento, beatis apostolis intervenientibus, suppliciter deprecamur ut quod* Leon.   ⁵ Leon. omits *ad vitam*.   ⁶ *aeternum* Leon.

XXXV.

Item in Natali omnium Apostolorum[1].

Deus, qui nos per beatos apostolos[2] ad cognitionem tui nominis venire tribuisti; da nobis eorum[3] gloriam sempiternam et proficiendo[4] celebrare et celebrando proficere. Per.

R.S.(*alibi.*)
Gerb. 189.
Pam. 348.
Men. 137.
Leofr. 164.

Secreta.

Gloriam, Domine, sanctorum apostolorum perpetuam praecurrentes[5] quaesumus ut eandem[6] sacris mysteriis expiati dignius celebremus. Per Dominum.

R.S.(*alibi.*)
Gerb. 189.
Pam. 348.
Men. 137.
Leofr. 164.

Praefatio.

VD. Qui ecclesiam tuam sempiterna pietate non deserens[7], per apostolos tuos iugiter eam et[8] erudis et protegis[9]. Et ideo cum angelis[10]. γ

R.S.(*alibi.*)
Leon. 334.
Gerb. 169.
Men. 124. Leofr. 156.

Postcommun.

Perceptis, Domine, sacramentis, suppliciter[11] rogamus ut intercedentibus beatis apostolis tuis quae pro illorum veneranda gerimus passione nobis proficiant ad medelam. Per. γ

R.S.(*alibi.*)
Gerb. 189.
Pam. 348.
Men. 137.
Leofr. 164.

[1] See note 1 on xxxiv *supra*. The Collect, Secret, and Postcommunion of this *Missa* appear also in Pam. for SS. Simon and Jude's Day. The Preface is found in R. S. for S. Bartholomew's Day, and appears also for that day in Gerb. Men. Leofr., with variations.   [2] R. S. Gerb. Men. insert *tuos*; Pam. Leofr. insert *tuos Simonem et Iudam*.   [3] Gerb. inserts *sequi*.   [4] *perficiendo* V. (corr. by Tommasi).   [5] *recurrentes* S¹; *percurrentes* Pam.; *recensentes* S³ Gerb.; *venerantes* Men. Leofr.; V. R. as text.   [6] *eadem* R. S¹; *eam* Pam. Men. Leofr.; V. S³ Gerb. as text.   [7] *deseres* V. (corr. by Tommasi); *deseris* Men. Leofr.; R. S. Gerb. Leon. as text.   [8] Men. Leofr. omit *eam et*; S¹ Gerb. omit *et*; V. R. S² Leon. as text.   [9] S³ Gerb. add *et sine fine custodis*, which Pam. Men. Leofr. substitute for *et protegis*.   [10] All but V. R. have *Per Christum* for *Et ideo*.   [11] Men. Leofr. insert *te*.

XXXVI.

In Octav. Apostolorum.

Pridie Nonas Iulias[1].

S. Gerb. 147.
Pam. 318.
Men. 114.

Deus cuius dextera Petrum apostolum ambulantem in fluctibus ne mergeretur[2] erexit, et coapostolum eius Paulum tertio naufragantem de profundo pelago liberavit, concede propitius[3] ut amborum meritis aeternam Trinitatis gratiam[4] consequamur. Per. γ

Secreta.

Leon. 338.

Offerimus sacrificium, Domine, quod pro reverentia apostolorum Petri et Pauli maiestati tuae iugiter et reddimus et debemus. Per Dominum nostrum.

R. S.
Gerb. 143.
Pam. 315.
Men. 112.
Leon. 345.

VD. Suppliciter exorantes[5] ut gregem tuum Pastor aeterne non deseras, et[6] per beatos apostolos[7] continua protectione custodias, ut iisdem rectoribus dirigantur[8] quos operis tui vicarios iisdem[9] contulisti praesse pastores. Per[10]. γ

Postcommun.

S.
Gerb. 148.
Leon. 339.

Pignus aeternae vitae[11] capientes, humiles[12] imploramus ut apostolicis fulti patrociniis quod imagine contingimus[13] sacramenti manifesta perceptione sumamus. Per.

[1] *Iulii* V. [2] *mergeret* V. [3] *exaudi nos propitius et concede* Gerb. Pam. Men.; V. S. as text. [4] *aeternitatis gloriam* S¹ Gerb. Pam. Men.; S¹ possibly *aeternae Trinitatis gloriam*; V. as text. [5] *Te Domine suppliciter exorare* R. S. Gerb. Pam.; *Et te suppliciter exorare* Men.; V. Leon. as text. [6] *sed* R. S. Gerb. Pam. Men.; V. Leon. as text. [7] R. S. Gerb. Pam. Men. insert *tuos*. [8] *dirigatur* Leon.; *gubernetur* S. Gerb. Pam. Men.; there is an omission in R. at this point, probably due to the repetition of *eisdem*. [9] *eidem* S. Gerb. Pam. Men.; Leon. omits *iisdem*. [10] *Et ideo* S. Gerb. Pam. Men.; V. Leon. as text. [11] *Aeternae pignus vitae* Leon. [12] *humiliter* Leon. Gerb. [13] *quod in imagine gerimus* Leon.

XXXVII.

In Natali Sanctorum Simplici[1] Faustini et Viatricis[2].

v Kal. seu potius iv Kal. Augustas[3].

S.
Gerb. 153.
Pam. 321.
Cf. Leon. 455.

Praesta, Domine, quaesumus, ut sicut populus Christianus martyrum tuorum Simplici[1], Faustini, et Viatricis[2] temporali solemnitate congaudet, ita perfruatur aeterna: et quod votis celebrat comprehendat effectu. Per Dominum.

Secreta.

Hostias tibi, Domine, pro sanctorum martyrum Simplici[1], Faustini, et Viatricis[2] commemoratione deferimus, suppliciter[4] obsecrantes ut et indulgentiam nobis pariter conferant et salutem. Per.

S.
Gerb. 153.
Pam. 321.
Cf. Leon. 455.

Postcommun.

Praesta, quaesumus, omnipotens Deus, ut sanctorum tuorum Simplici[1], Faustini, et Viatricis[2] caelestibus mysteriis celebrata solemnitas indulgentiam nobis tuae propitiationis acquirat. Per Dominum.

S.
Gerb. 153.
Pam. 321.

[1] S¹ has this form in the title, corrected to *Simplicii* by S². Otherwise S. Gerb. Pam. all have *Simplicii* throughout. [2] *Beatricis* S. Gerb. Pam. (throughout). [3] V. gives the date as in text (using the form *Agust.*); S. puts the Festival on v Kal. Aug.; Gerb. Pam. on iv Kal. Aug. [4] *simpliciter* V.

XXXVIII.

IN NATALI ABDO ET SENIS[1].

iii Kal. Augustas.

30 juil.

Sancti tui nos, Domine, Abdo et Senis piis orationibus prosequantur, et ab huius vitae periculis iugiter postulent expediri. Per.

Praesta, quaesumus, Domine, ut ecclesia tua et martyrum tuorum Abdo et Senis confisa suffragiis devota permaneat, et eorum precibus gloriosis secura consistat. Per.

Secreta.

Munera tibi, Domine, pro sanctorum martyrum Abdo et Senis[1] occisione[2] deferi·mus, qui dum finiuntur in terris facti sunt caelesti luce perpetui[3]. Per.

S.
Gerb. 155.
Men. 116.
See xlviii *infra*.

Postcommun.

Populum tuum, Domine, perpetua munitione defende: nec difficulter[4] quod pie, quod[5] iuste, postulat consequatur, cui sanctorum tuorum merita suffragantur. Per.

S.
Gerb. 155.
Men. 117.

[1] *Abdo et Sennis* S.; *Abdon et Sennen* Gerb. Men. [2] *passione* Men. (so in xlviii). [3] Men. adds *humiliter postulantes, ut eorum semper meritis muniamur*. [4] *deficultas* V. (corr. by Tommasi); S. Gerb. Men. as text. [5] *et* Men.

XXXIX.

IN NATAL. MACHABAEORUM.

Kal. Augustas[1].

Deus, qui in sanctis habitas, et pia corda non deseris, suscipe propitius orationem nostram; et tribue misericordiam tuam[2], ut te custode servati ab omnibus vitae huius periculis liberemur. Per Dominum.

Secreta.

Leon. 457. Fiant, Domine, tuo grata conspectui munera supplicantis ecclesiae, et, ut nostrae proficiant saluti, adsit intercessio beatorum[3] sanctorum tuorum[4]. Per.

Postcommun.

Pam. 323. Caelesti munere satiati quaesumus, Domine Deus noster,
Leon. 348. ut haec nos dona, martyrum tuorum deprecatione, sanctificent. Per.

[1] *Agustas* V. (ungrammatically). [2] So V. (perhaps ungrammatically for *misericordia tua*). [3] *beata* Leon. [4] Leon. omits *tuorum*.

XL.

IN NATALI SANCTI SIXTI[1].

viii Id. Augustas.

S. Gerb. 157. Beati Sixti, Domine, tui sacerdotis et martyris annua festa recolentes, quaesumus ut quae tuarum[2] nobis sunt instrumenta praesentium fiant aeternarum[2] patrocinia gratiarum. Per.

S. Gerb. 157. Sancti Sixti, Domine, frequentata solemnitas et de sacerdotalibus nos instruat, te miserante, doctrinis, et de gloria[3] martyrii foveat ubique suffragiis. Per Dominum.

Secreta.

S. Gerb. 157.
Pam. 324. Suscipe, Domine, munera propitiatus oblata, quae maiestati tuae beatus Sixtus sacerdos commendat[4] et martyr.
Men. 118. Per. γ

Postcommun.

S. Gerb. 158. Repleti sumus[5] Domine munere solemnitatis optatae qua beati Sixti et celebritate iuvamur et precibus[6]. Per.

XLI.

IN NATALI SANCTI DONATI.

vii Id. Augustas.

Adesto, Domine, precibus nostris, quas in sancti confessoris et episcopi tui Donati[1] commemoratione deferimus; ut qui nostrae iustitiae fiduciam non habemus [eius][2] qui tibi placuit meritis adiuvemur. Per. Leon. 300.

Deus, tuorum gloria sacerdotum, praesta, quaesumus, ut sancti confessoris et episcopi tui Donati, cuius festa gerimus[3], sentiamus auxilium[4]. Per. S. Gerb. 159.

Secreta.

Praesta, quaesumus, Domine, ut[5] sancti confessoris et episcopi tui Donati, quem ad laudem nominis tui dicatis muneribus honoramus, piae nobis devotionis fructus adcrescat. Per. S. Gerb. 159.

Postcommun.

Votiva, Domine, pro beati confessoris tui et episcopi [commemoratione dona][6] percepimus[7]: quaesumus ut eius precibus et praesentis vitae nobis pariter et aeternae tribuas conferre[8] praesidium. Per Dominum. See xliii *infra.* Cf. Leon. 403.

[1] *in sanctorum tuorum* Leon. [2] V. omits *eius*; Leon. has *eorum*. [3] *celebramus* S³ Gerb. [4] *auxilium sentiamus* S³ Gerb. [5] S³ Gerb. insert *intercessione*. [6] Something seems to be wanting in V.; *dona* appears from Leon. and from the similar Postcommunion in xliii, to be one missing word: the other is perhaps *commemoratione*. [7] *percipimus* V. [8] So V. (perhaps for *conferri*); Leon. has *quae ... tribue conferre*.

XLII.

IN VIGILIA SANCTI LAURENTI[1].

v Id. Augustas.

Da, quaesumus, omnipotens Deus, ut beati Laurenti martyris tui, quam praevenimus, veneranda solemnitas et devotionem nobis augeat et salutem. Per.

Quaesumus, omnipotens Deus, ut nostra devotio quae natalitia beati Laurenti martyris antecedit, patrocinia nobis eius accumulet. Per. R.S.(*alibi.*) Gerb. 214. Men. 155.

R. S.
Gerb. 160.

Beati Laurenti martyris tui, Domine, geminata gratia nos refoveat², quam glorificationis eius³ et optatis praeimus of·ficiis et desideranter expectamus adventuram⁴. Per. 660

Secreta.

R.S.(*alibi*.)
Gerb. 214.
Men. 156.

Magnifica Domine beati Laurenti solemnia recensemus, quae promptis cordibus ambientes, oblatis muneribus et suscipimus et praeimus. Per.

S. (*alibi*.)
Gerb. 214.
Men. 156.

VD. Gloriosi Laurenti martyris pia certamina praecurrendo: cuius honorabilis annua recursione solemnitas et perpetua semper et nova est: quia et in conspectu tuae maiestatis permanet mors tuorum pretiosa iustorum, et restaurantur incrementa laetitiae, quum felicitatis aeternae⁵ recoluntur exordia. Et ideo cum angelis⁶.

Postcommun.

R.S.(*alibi*.)
Gerb. 215.
Men. 156.

Sancta tua, Domine⁷, beati Laurenti martyris pretiosa passione, et solemnia⁸ quae praeimus nos refovent⁹, quibus et iugiter satiamur¹⁰ et semper desideramus expleri. Per.

¹ V. uses the form *Laurenti* throughout; S. Gerb. Men. have *Laurentii*. The greater part of the contents of this *Missa* appear in R. S. Gerb. Men. in the *Missa* for a Saint (R. S. Gerb.) or a Martyr (Men.). The third of the collects is the only portion which R. S. and Gerb. assign to the Vigil of S. Laurence. ² *refovet* S¹. ³ *pro glorificationis eius honore* S² Gerb.; V. R. S¹ as text (R. has *glorificationes*). ⁴ *expectemus adventum* V. R. (S¹?); S² Gerb. as text. ⁵ *restaurata incrementa laeticiae confelicitatis aeterna* V. (corrected by Tommasi); S. Gerb. Men. as text. ⁶ *Per Christum* (for *Et ideo*) S. Gerb. Men. ⁷ S. inserts *de*; Men. inserts *in*. ⁸ *solemnitate* S²; Men. omits *et solemnia* and has *quam praeimus*. ⁹ *refoveant* S² Men.; V. R. S¹ Gerb. as text. ¹⁰ *sociamur* V.; R. S. Gerb. Men. as text.

XLIII.

Item in Natali Eiusdem.

iv Id. Augustas.

S.
[Gerb. 161.]
Pam. 327.
Pam. (Amb.) 411.
Men. 120.

Deus, cuius caritatis ardore beatus Laurentius edaces incendii flammas contempto persecutore devicit, concede propitius, ut omnes qui martyrii eius merita veneramur protectionis tuae auxilio muniamur. Per. γ

R. S.
Gerb. 161.
Pam. 327.
Men. 119.

Deus, qui mundi creator et rector es, et qui¹ hunc diem in Levitae tui Laurenti martyrio consecrasti; concede propitius ut omnes qui martyrii eius merita veneramur intercessionibus eius ab aeternis gehennae incendiis liberemur. Per.

Secreta.

Praesta, quaesumus, Domine, ut beati sancti[2] Laurenti suffragiis in nobis tua munera tuearis, pro cuius[3] honoranda confessione hostias tibi laudis offerimus. Per. R. S. Gerb. 162.

661 VD.[4] In die[5] solemnitatis hodiernae: qua beati Laurenti hostiam tibi placitam et castam corporis glorioso certa∘mine[6] suscepisti : prunis namque superposita stridebant membra viventia: nec tamen erat poena patientis[7], sed piae confessionis incensum[8] : neque terreno liberari cruciatu[9] martyr optabat, sed coronari deprecabatur in caelis. Per Christum. γ R. S. Gerb. 162. Leon. 398.

Postcommun.

Votiva, Domine, pro beati martyris tui Laurenti passione dona percepimus[10]: quaesumus ut eius precibus et praesentis vitae nobis pariter et aeternae tribuas conferre[11] praesidium. Per. xli *supra*. Leon. 403.

Orationes ad Vesperum.

Sancti Laurenti nos, Domine, sancta precatio[12] tueatur : et quod nostra conscientia non meretur[13] eius nobis qui tibi placuit oratione donetur. Per. S. Gerb. 162. Pam. 328. Men. 120. Leon. 397.

Adsit nobis, Domine, quaesumus, sancti Laurenti martyris[14] in tua[15] glorificatione benedictio, cuius nobis est hodie facta suffragium in tua virtute confessio. Per. R. S. Gerb. 162. Pam. 328. Men. 120. Leon. 399.

Praesta, quaesumus, Domine, ut semper nos[16] beati Laurenti laetificent votiva[17] mysteria, quae semper esse non desinunt admiranda. Per Dominum. R. S. Gerb. 163. Men. 120.

---

[1] *Deus mundi creator et rector qui* R. S. Gerb. Pam. Men.; V. as text.
[2] R. S² Gerb. omit *sancti*. [3] *propitius* (for *pro cuius*) V. (corrected by Tommasi); R. S. Gerb. as text. [4] This Preface in S. shows many erasures; the original readings seem to have agreed more closely with those of V. and R. than do the readings of S² and Gerb. [5] *Et in die* S² Gerb. [6] *placitam et castam corpore glorioso certamine* V.; *placitam casti corporis glorioso certamine* Leon.; *placitam pro casti corporis glorioso certamine* S² Gerb.; R. (S¹ ?) as text.
[7] *nec tantum erat poena passionis quam* S² Gerb.; V. Leon. (S¹ ?) as text; and so R., reading *plena* for *poena*. [8] *piae confessionis incessus* V. R.; an erasure in S¹; *piae confessionis igne succensus* S² Gerb.; Leon. as text.
[9] *terreno liberato cruciatum* V. (corrected by Tommasi). [10] *percipimus* V.
[11] See note 8 on xli *supra*. [12] *precatio iusta* Leon. [13] *praesumit* Leon.
[14] R. Men. insert *tui*. [15] *sua* Pam. [16] *nobis* V. (ungrammatically); R. S¹ as text. [17] *divina* R. S. Gerb.; V. Men. as text.

XLIV.
IN NATALI SANCTI TIBURTI[1].
iii Id. Augustas.

Cf. Leon. 404.

Omnipotens sempiterne Deus, qui nos sancti martyris tui Tiburti festivitate laetificas, praesta ut cuius commemoratione gaudemus praesidio muniamur. Per.

Secreta.

xvi *supra*.
Cf. Leon. 298.

Respice, Domine, munera quae in sancti Tiburti commemoratione deferimus; ut cuius honore sunt grata, eius nobis fiant intercessione perpetua. Per.

Postcommun.

S. (*alibi*.)
Gerb. 162.
Cf. Leon. 306.

Prosit nobis, Domine, sancti Tiburti celebrata solemnitas quia quanto fragiliores sumus tanto placentium tibi praesidiis indigemus. Per.

[1] The *Missa* for this festival in S. and Gerb. is entirely different from that in the text. The Postcommunion of this *Missa* is, however, found in S. and Gerb. (with the necessary variation) in the *Missa* for S. Laurence's Day.

XLV.
IN NATALI SANCTI YPOLITI[1].
Id. Augustas.

S.
Gerb. 163.
Men. 121.
Pam. (Amb.) 413.

Sancti Ypoliti martyris[2], Domine, quaesumus, veneranda festivitas salutaris auxilii nobis praestet augmentum. Per.

Secreta.

Leon. 402.

Praesta nobis, quaesumus, omnipotens Deus, ut nostrae humilitatis oblatio et pro tuorum grata sit honore sanctorum, et nos corpore pariter et mente purificet. Per.

Postcommun.

See liv *infra*.

Sumptis, Domine, sacramentis, quaesumus ut intercedente beato martyre tuo Ypolito ad redemptionis aeternae proficiamus augmentum. Per. γ

[1] So V.; in S¹ the name appears as *Ippolitus*, corrected by S² to *Yppolitus*.
[2] *Sancti martyris tui Hippolyti* Men. Pam. (Amb.).

XLVI.
IN OCTAV. SANCTI LAURENTI.
xvi Kal. Septemb.

S.
Gerb. 166.
Pam. 331.

Beati Laurenti nos faciat, Domine, passio veneranda laetantes et ut eam sufficienter recolamus efficiat[1]. Per.

Iterata festivitate beati Laurenti natalitia veneramur quae in caelesti beatitudine fulgere novimus sempiterna. Per.

Secreta.

Beati Laurenti martyris honorabilem passionem muneribus, Domine[2], geminatis exequimur; quae licet propriis sit memoranda principiis indesinenter tamen permanet gloriosa. Per.

VD. Quoniam tanto iocunda sunt, Domine, beati Laurenti martyris crebrius repetita solemnia quanto nobis eius sine cessatione praedicanda sunt merita. Et ideo cum angelis[3]. γ

Postcommun.

Solemnis[4] nobis intercessio beati Laurenti martyris, quaesumus, Domine, praestet auxilium: ut celestis mensae participatio quam[5] sumpsimus tribuat ecclesiae tuae recensita laetitiam[6]. Per.

[1] S² Gerb. Pam. add *promptiores*. [2] *Domino* Pam. [3] *Per Christum* (for *Et ideo*) Mur. [4] *Solempne* V. [5] *quae* V. S¹; S² Gerb. Pam. as text. [6] *recensita laeticia* V.; *recensitam laetitiam* S. Gerb.; Pam. as text.

XLVII.

In Assumpt. Sanctae Mariae.
xviii Kal. Septembres.

Deus, qui spe[1] salutis aeternae beatae Mariae virginitate foecunda humano generi praemia praestitisti, tribue, quaesumus, ut ipsam pro nobis intercedere sentiamus per quam meruimus auctorem vitae nostrae[2] suscipere. Per Dominum. γ

Omnipotens sempiterne Deus, qui terrenis corporibus Verbi tui veritatis[3] Filii unigeniti[4] per venerabilem ac gloriosam semper[5] virginem Mariam ineffabile mysterium coniungere[6] voluisti, petimus immensam clementiam tuam, ut quod in eius veneratione deposcimus, te propitiante consequi mereamur[7]. Per.

Secreta.

Accipe munera, Domine, quae in beatae Mariae iterata solemnitate deferimus: quia ad tua praeconia recurrit ad laudem quod vel talis assumpta est. Per.

Postcommun.

R. S.
Gerb. 166.
Pam.
(Amb.)
415.

Caelesti munere satiati [quaesumus], omnipotens Deus[1], tua [nos[2]] protectione custodi, et[10] castimoniae pacem[11] mentibus nostris atque corporibus intercedente sancta Maria propitiatus indulge[10]: ut[12] veniente sponso Filio tuo unigenito accensis lampadibus eius digni praestolemur occursum. Per.

[1] R. S. Gerb. Pam. omit *spe*. [2] R. S. Gerb. Pam. omit *nostrae*. [3] *veritatem* Sacr. Gall. [4] *Verbi tui et veritatis Filii tui scilicet unigeniti* S[2] Gerb.; Sacr. Gall. omits *Filii unigeniti*; V. R. S[1] Pam. (Amb.) as text. [5] *semperque* S. Gerb. Pam. (Amb.); V. R. as text; Sacr. Gall. omits *ac* ... *virginem*. [6] *coniungi* Sacr. Gall. [7] *mereamur consequi* Sacr. Gall. [8] *satiati omnipotens Deus* V. R. (S[1]!); *satiatos omnipotens Deus* S[2] Gerb.; *satiatos quaesumus omnipotens Deus* Pam. (Amb.). [The accidental omission of *quaesumus* accounts for the ungrammatical reading of V. R., of which the reading of S[2] and Gerb. is probably an emendation.] [9] V. omits *nos*. [10] *ut* ... *indulge* V.; *ut indulgeas* S[2] Gerb. Pam. (Amb.); *et* ... *indulge* S[1]. [11] *castimoniam et pacem* S[2] Gerb. Pam. (Amb.); V. S[1] as text. [12] *et* S[2] Gerb.; V. S[1] Pam. (Amb.) as text.

XLVIII.

IN NATALI SANCTI AGAPITI.

xv Kal. Septembres.

S.
Gerb. 167.
Men. 123.
Pam. 332.

Sancti martyris Agapiti merita nos, Domine, pretiosa tueantur, in quibus tuae maiestatis opera praedicantes, et praesens capiamus adiutorium et futurum. Per.

Secreta.

xxxviii
supra.

Munera tibi, Domine, pro sancti martyris Agapiti passione[1] deferimus; qui dum finitur in terris factus est caelesti sede[2] perpetuus. Per.

Postcommun.

xxiv *supra.*

Sumpti sacrificii, Domine, perpetua nos tuitio non relinquat, et noxia semper a nobis cuncta depellat. Per. γ

[1] *occisione* in xxxviii *supra*. [2] *luce* in xxxviii *supra*.

XLIX.

IN NATALI SANCTI MAGNI.

xiv Kal. Septembres.

S.
Gerb. 167.

Adesto, Domine, supplicationibus nostris, et intercedente beato martyre tuo Magno ab hostium nos defende propitiatus incursu. Per.

Secreta.

Grata tibî sint munera nostra, Domine, quae et tuis sunt[1] instituta praeceptis et beati Magni festivitas gloriosa commendat[2]. Per.

Leon. 302, 310, 337.

Postcommun.

Tua sancta sumentes, quaesumus, Domine, ut beati Magni nos foveant continuata praesidia. Per.

S. Gerb. 168.

[1] *sint* V.; Leon. as text (Leon. 302 omits *et* before *tuis*). [2] *commendet* V. Leon. 302; Leon. 310, 337 as text.

L.
IN NATALI SANCTI RUFFI[1].
vi Kal. Septembres.

Adesto, Domine, supplicationibus nostris, et beati Ruffi intercessionibus confidentes nec minis adversantium nec ullo conturbemur[2] incursu. Per.

S. Gerb. 169. Leon. 359.

Secreta.

Intercessio, quaesumus, Domine, sancti tui Ruffi munera nostra commendet, nosque in eius veneratione[3] tuae maiestati reddat acceptos. Per.

v *supra.*

Postcommun.

Sumentes gaudia sempiterna de participatione sacramenti et festivitate[4] beati martyris tui Ruffi, suppliciter deprecamur ut quae sedula servitute donante te gerimus dignis sensibus tuo munere capiamus. Per Dominum.

vi *supra.*

[1] S. Gerb. have the form *Rufi.* [2] *perturbemur* Leon. [3] V. in v *supra* has *nosque eius veneratio.* [4] V. in vi *supra* has *sacramenti festivitatis.*

LI.
IN NATALI SANCTI HERMIS[1].
v Kal. Septembres.

Sancti nos, quaesumus, Domine, Hermis natalitia votiva laetificent, et suae beneficiis intercessionis attollant. Per Dominum.

Secreta.

Munera nostra, quaesumus, Domine[2], propitiatus assume; et ut digne tuis famulemur altaribus sancti tui nos Hermis intercessione custodi. Per.

S. Gerb. 170. Pam. 334. Men. 125.

Postcommun.

Cf. Leon. 399.

Exultet, quaesumus, Domine, populus tuus[3] in sancti tui commemoratione Hermis: et cuius votivo[4] laetatur officio, suffragio relevetur optato. Per.

[1] S. Gerb. Pam. Men. have *Hermetis* throughout. [2] *nostra, Domine, quaesumus* S. Gerb.; *Domine, nostra, quaesumus* Men.; V. Pam. as text. [3] *populus tuus, Domine, quaesumus* Leon. [4] *votiva* V.

LII.

IN DIE PASSIONIS SANCTI IOANNIS BAPTISTAE[1].
iv Kal. Septembres.

R. S. Gerb. 171. Pam. 335. Men. 126.

Sancti Ioannis Baptistae et martyris tui, Domine, quaesumus, veneranda festivitas salutaris auxilii nobis praestet effectum[2]. Per.

R. S. Gerb. 171. Pam. 335. Men. 127. Leon. 400.

Perpetuis nos, Domine, sancti Ioannis Baptistae tuere praesidiis: et quanto fragiliores sumus, tanto magis necessariis attolle suffragiis. Per.

Secreta.

R. S. Gerb. 171. Men. 126. xxxviii *supra*. xlviii *supra*.

Munera[3] tibi, Domine, pro sancti martyris Ioannis Baptistae passione deferimus[4] qui dum finitur in terris factus est caelesti sede perpetuus. Per.

Postcommun.

R. S. Gerb. 172. Pam. 335. Men. 126.

Conferat nobis, Domine, sancti Ioannis utrumque[5] solemnitas, ut magnifica sacramenta quae sumpsimus significata[6] veneremur et in nobis potius edita gaudeamus. Per Dominum.

[1] The Collects, Secret, and Postcommunion of this *Missa* occupy the same position in V. R. S. Gerb. Pam. In Pam. (Amb.) the second collect of this *Missa* is the *Orat. super Sindonem*: in Men. it is an additional Postcommunion. [2] *affectum* S. [3] Pam. inserts *quae*. [4] Pam. has (after *deferimus*) *quaesumus ut eius obtentu nobis proficiant ad salutem*, and omits the clause *qui ... perpetuus*. R. S. Gerb. Men. retain this clause and insert the same addition which appears in Pam. after the word *perpetuus*. V. has *quia dum* (but see xxxviii and xlviii *supra*). [5] *sancti Ioannis Baptistae beata solemnitas* Pam. [6] *quae sumpsimus digne veneremur et nobis salutaria sentiamus* Men.; R. S. Gerb. agree with V. throughout.

LIII.

IN NATALI SANCTI PRISCI[1].
Kal. Septembres.

R. S. Gerb. 172.

Omnipotens sempiterne Deus, fortitudo certantium et martyrum palma, solemnitatem hodierni[2] diei propitius intuere, et ecclesiam tuam continua fac celebritate laetari³ et intercessione beati martyris Prisci omnium intercedentium⁴ vota perficias⁵. Per.

Secreta.

Eius tibi precibus, Domine, quaesumus,⁶ grata reddatur oblatio pro cuius est festivitate immolanda. Per. R. S. Gerb. 172.

Postcommun.

Praesta, quaesumus, Domine, ut sacramenti tui participatione vegetati sancti quoque martyris Prisci precibus adiuvemur. Per. R. S. Gerb. 172. See lxvi infra.

¹ *Priscę* V. There is no *Missa* for this festival in Pam. or Men. That in R. S. and Gerb. agrees throughout with V., except in the minor variations of reading here noted.   ² *hodiernae* R. S. Gerb.   ³ *laetare* V. R. S¹.   ⁴ *in te credentium* Gerb.; V. R. S. as text.   ⁵ *proficias* V.; R. S. Gerb. as text.   ⁶ R. S² Gerb. insert *haec*.

LIV.
IN NATIVIT. SANCTAE MARIAE.
vi Id. Septembres.

8 sept.

Adiuvet nos, quaesumus, Domine, sanctae Mariae gloriosa intercessio¹, cuius etiam diem, quo felix eius est inchoata nativitas, meminimus². Per. R. S. Gerb. 173. Pam. 337. Men. 128.

Secreta.

Suscipe, Domine, quaesumus, hostias placationis et laudis, quas tibi offerimus pro nativitate beatae et gloriosae semperque virginis Dei genitricis Mariae; et sanctis eius³ intercessionibus cunctis nobis proficiant ad salutem. Per. S. [Gerb. 173.]

Postcommun.

Adesto, quaesumus, Domine, fidelibus tuis⁴ ut quae sumpserunt⁴ fideliter et mente sibi⁵ et corpore, beatae Mariae intercessione, custodiant⁶. Per. Cf. Leon. 369.

Item alia.

Sumptis, Domine, sacramentis, intercedente beata et gloriosa semperque virgine Dei genitricis Maria, ad redemptionis aeternae, quaesumus, proficiamus augmentum. Per. γ S. Gerb. 174.

¹ *sanctae Mariae intercessio veneranda* R. S. Gerb. Men.; V. Pam. as text.
² *celebramus* R. S¹ Pam. Men.; *devotissime celebramus* S² Gerb.; V. as text.
³ *ut sanctis eius* S.; *ut sanctis eiusque* Gerb.   ⁴ *plebi tuae ... sumpsit* Leon.   ⁵ *simul* (for *sibi*) Leon.   ⁶ *custodiat* V. Leon.

LV.

IN NATALI SANCTI GURGONI[1].

v Id. Septembres.

S.
Gerb. 174.
Leofr. 158.

Sanctus, Domine, Gurgonius sua nos intercessione laetificet, et pia faciat solemnitate gaudere. Per Dominum.

Secreta.

S.
Gerb. 174.
Leofr. 158.

Grata sit tibi, Domine, nostrae servitutis oblatio, [pro[2]] qua sanctus Gurgonius martyr intervenit[3]. Per.

Postcommun.

S.
Gerb. 174.
Leofr. 158.

Familiam tuam, Deus, suavitas illa contingat et vegetet qua in martyre tuo Gurgonio Christi tui bono iugiter odore pascatur[4]. Per Dominum.

[1] S¹, like V., uses the form *Gurgonius*: S² Gerb. Leofr. have *Gorgonius*. There is no *Missa* for this Festival in Pam. or Men.; the Collect, Secret, and Postcommunion are the same in S. Gerb. Leofr. as in V.   [2] V. omits *pro*.
[3] *interveniat* Leofr.   [4] *poscatur* V.

LVI.

IN EXALTATIONE SANCTAE CRUCIS.

xviii Kal. Octobres.

R. S.
Gerb. 175.
Pam. 338.

Deus, qui nos hodierna die exaltatione[1] sanctae Crucis annua solemnitate laetificas, praesta ut cuius mysterium in terris cognovimus eius redemptionis praemia consequamur[2]. Per.

Secreta.

R. S.
Gerb. 175.
Pam. 338.
Men. 129.

Devotas, Domine, humilitatis nostrae preces et hostias misericordiae tuae praecedat[3] auxilium : et salutem quam per[4] Adam in Paradiso ligni clauserat temerata praesumptio, ligni rursum fides aperiat. Per Dominum.

Postcommun.

R. S.
Gerb. 175.
Pam. 339.
Men. 129.

Adesto familiae tuae, quaesumus, clemens et misericors Deus : [5] in adversis et prosperis[6] preces exaudias : et nefas adversariorum per auxilium sanctae Crucis digneris conterere : ut portum salutis tuae valeant[7] apprehendere[8]. Per.

[1] *Exaltationis* S² Gerb.; *hodiernae exaltatione* R.; V. S¹ Pam. as text.
[2] *praemia mereamur* R. (S¹?); *praemia in caelo consequi mereamur* S² Gerb.; *praemia consequi mereamur* Pam.; V. as text.   [3] *comitetur* Pam.   [4] Pam. iuserts [*protoplastum*].   [5] R. S² Gerb. Pam. Men. insert *ut*.   [6] Pam. Men. insert *eius*.   [7] *valeat* Pam. Men.   [8] *adprehendi* V.

LVII.

IN NATALI SANCTORUM CORNELI ET CYPRIANI [1].

Item xviii Kal. Octobres.

Beatorum martyrum pariterque pontificum Corneli et Cypriani nos, Domine, quaesumus, festa tueantur, et eorum commendet oratio veneranda [2]. Per.

S. Gerb. 175. Pam. 338. Men. 129. Leon. 405.

Secreta.

Plebis tuae, Domine, munera benignus intende, quae maiestati tuae pro sanctorum martyrum Corneli et Cypriani solemnitatibus [3] sunt dicata. Per.

S. Gerb. 176. Pam. 338. Men. 129. Leon. 405.

Postcommun.

Sacro munere vegetatos [4] sanctorum martyrum Corneli et Cypriani natalitia nos tibi Domine quaesumus [3] commendet oratio. Per Dominum.

S. Gerb. 176. Leon. 405.

[1] *Cibriani* V.; S¹ has throughout *Cornilii et Cibriani* (corrected by S² to *Cornelii et Cypriani*). [2] Leon. adds *atque laetificet*. [3] *solemnitate* Pam. [4] S² Gerb. insert *in*; V. S¹ Leon. as text. [5] S² Gerb. insert *eorum*.

LVIII.

IN NATALI SANCTORUM COSMAE ET DAMIANI [1].

v Kal. Octobres.

Magnificet te, Domine, sanctorum Cosmae et Damiani beata solemnitas; quia [2] et illis gloriam sempiternam [et [3]] opem nobis ineffabili providentia contulisti. Per. ȣ

S. Gerb. 182. Pam. 345. Mur. ii. 41.

Secreta.

In tuorum, Domine, pretiosa morte iustorum [4] sacrificium illud offerimus de quo martyrium [5] sumpsit omne principium [6]. Per. ȣ

S. Gerb. 182. Pam. 345. Mur. ii. 41.

Postcommun.

Sit nobis, Domine, sacramenti tui certa salvatio quae [7] beatorum martyrum Cosmae et Damiani meritis imploratur [8]. Per Dominum. ȣ

S. Gerb. 183. Pam. 345. Men. 134. Mur. ii. 41.

[1] The Collect, Secret, and Postcommunion of this *Missa* are assigned in Muratori's Gregorian Sacramentary to the Thursday of the third week in Lent (*ad SS. Cosmam et Damianum*). [2] *qua* S. Gerb. Pam.; V. Mur. as text. [3] V. omits *et*. [4] *sanctorum* Pam. Gerb. [5] *martyrum* S. Gerb. Mur. [6] Pam. adds *quod, quaesumus, propitiationis tuae nobis munus obtineat*. [7] S. Gerb. Pam. Men. Mur. insert *cum*. [8] *imploramus* S. Gerb.

LIX.

ORATIONES IN SANCTI ARCHANGELI MICHAELIS[1].

iii Kal. Octobres.

R. S.
Gerb. 183.
Pam. 346.

Da nobis, omnipotens Deus, beati Archangeli Michaelis eo[2] tenus honore proficere ut cuius in terra[3] gloriam praedicamus[4], precibus adiuvemur in caelis. Per.

R. S.
Gerb. 183.
Pam. 346.
Men. 135.
Leon. 409.

Beati Archangeli[5] Michaelis interventione suffulti, supplices te, Domine, deprecamur, ut quos[6] honore prosequimur contingamus et mente. Per.

R. S.
Gerb. 183.
Mur. 386.

Perpetuum nobis, Domine, tuae miserationis praesta subsidium, quibus et angelica praestitisti suffragia non deesse. Per. γ

Secreta.

S.
[Gerb. 183.]
Pam. 345.
Leon. 408.

Munus populi tui, Domine, quaesumus, dignanter assume; quod non nostris meritis, sed sancti Archangeli tui Michaelis deprecatione sit gratum. Per.

Postcommun.

R. S.
Gerb. 183.
Pam. 346.
Men. 135.

Adesto plebi tuae, misericors Deus; et ut gratiae tuae[7] beneficia potiora percipiat, beati Michaelis Archangeli fac supplicem deprecationibus sublevari. Per.

[1] So V.; R. and S. have *Dedicatio Basilicae Angeli Michaelis*. [2] *ea* S[2] Gerb. Pam.; V. R. S[1] as text. [3] *terris* R. S. Gerb. Pam.; *terram* V. (ungrammatically). [4] R. S. Gerb. Pam. insert *eius*. [5] R. S. Gerb. Pam. Men. insert *tui*; V. Leon. as text. [6] *quod* Pam. (marg.). [7] R. omits *tuae*.

LX.

ORATIONES IN IEIUNIO MENSIS SEPTIMI[1].

R.S.(*alibi.*)
Gerb. 35.

Praesta, quaesumus, Domine, fidelibus tuis ut ieiuniorum veneranda solemnia et congrua pietate suscipiant et secura devotione percurrant[2]. Per. γ

I. lxv
supra.

Deus, qui te sinceris asseris manere pectoribus, da nobis tua gratia tales existere in quibus habitare digneris. Per.

Secreta.

R. S.
Gerb. 178.

Deus, qui de his terrae fructibus tua sacramenta constare voluisti, praesta quaesumus, ut opem nobis et praesentis vitae conferas[3] et futurae. Per.

670 **Postcommun.**

Salutari tuo⁴ munere, Domine, satiati, supplices te deprecamur ut cuius laetamur gustu, renovemur effectu. Per Dominum. γ

R.S.(*alibi.*)
Gerb. 38.
I. xvii.
supr.
Leon. 414.

IN SEXTA FERIA MENSIS SEPTIMI.

Inchoata ieiunia⁵, Domine, quaesumus, benigno favore prosequere; et⁶ sicut ab alimentis in corpore, ita a vitiis ieiunemus in mente. Per. γ

S. (*alibi.*)
Gerb. 53.

Secreta.

Huius te, Domine, muneris oblatione placemus, et perpetuae vitae participes huius operatione reddamur. Per.

R. S.
(*Domin.*)
Gerb. 180.

Postcommun.

Caelestis mensae, quaesumus, Domine, sacrosancta⁷ libatio corda nostra purget semper et pascat⁸. Per.

R. S.
(*Domin.*)
Gerb. 180.

IN XII LECTIONES. DIE SABBATI.

Tribue, quaesumus, Domine, fidelibus tuis, ut⁹ ieiunio mensis septimi convenienter aptentur, et suscepta solemniter castigatio corporalis ad fructum cunctarum transeat animarum. Per.

R. S.
Gerb. 179.
Cf. Leon.
430.

Praesta, quaesumus, omnipotens Deus, ut qui se affligendo carnem ab alimentis abstinet¹⁰, sectando iustitiam, culpa ieiunet¹⁰. Per Dominum nostrum. γ

Gerb. 53.

Deus, humanae salutis operator, da nobis exercere ieiunia congruenter, quibus nostrae substantiae sempiterna¹¹ remedia providisti. Per.

R. S.
Gerb. 179.

Suscipe, Domine, preces populi supplicantis; et nostri vota ieiunii salutaris tui perfice sacramentum. Per.

R. S.
Gerb. 180.

Omnipotentiam tuam¹², Domine, prompta mente laudantes ieiunia tibi sacrata deferimus, ut dum grati¹³ de perceptis existimus, efficiamur percipiendis fructibus gratiores. Per Dominum.

S.
Gerb. 179.

Deus, qui tribus pueris mitigasti flammas igneas¹⁴, concede, quaesumus, ut nos famulos tuos non exurat flamma vitiorum. Per. γ

lxxxv
infra.

Secreta.

R. S.
Gerb. 180.
Haec hostia, Domine, quaesumus, et vincula nostrae iniquitatis absolvat, et tuae nobis misericordiae dona conciliet. Per. ỳ

Postcommun.

R. S.
Gerb. 180.
Perficiant in nobis, Domine, quaesumus, tua sacramenta quod continent, ut quae nunc specie gerimus rerum veritate capiamus. Per. γ

Super Populum.

Pam. 379.
I. xxxvii
supra.
Auxiliare, Domine, populo tuo, ut sacrae devotionis proficiens incrementis et tuo semper munere gubernetur et ad redemptionis aeternae pertineat [15] te docente [16] consortium. Per Dominum. γ

---

[1] The *Missae* included in this section do not agree in the order of their parts with the corresponding *Missae* in R. S. and Gerb.; several of the prayers are common to the four texts, but they are differently arranged, even the series '*in xii Lectiones*' varying in order, and to some extent in matter. [2] *procurant* V.; R. S. Gerb. as text. [3] *conferant* S² Gerb.; V. R. S¹ as text. [4] *salutaris tuae* R.; *salutaris tui* S. Gerb.; *salutari tuo* (omitting *munere*) Leon.; V. as text, here (and in I. xvii *salutari munere*). [5] *Ieiunia nostra* S. Gerb. [6] *ut* S. Gerb.; V. as text. [7] *sacra sancta* V. [8] *pascat semper et purget* S² Gerb.; V. R. S¹ as text. [9] *et* S¹; *ut et* R. S² Gerb.; V. Leon. as text (Leon. has *ut ieiuniis Paschalibus*). [10] *abstinent . . . ieiunent* Gerb. [11] *sempiterne* V. [12] *Omnipotens tua* V.; S. Gerb. as text. [13] *dum ingrati* V.; S. Gerb. as text. [14] *ignium* V. in lxxxv *infra*. [15] *pertingat* V. in I. xxxvii *supra*. [16] *ducente* Pam.; V. here as text (in I. xxxvii V. has *docere*).

LXI.

IN NATALI SANCTORUM MARCELLI ET APULEI [1].

Non. Octobres.

S.
Gerb. 185.
Sanctorum tuorum [2] nos, Domine, Marcelli et Apulei beata merita prosequantur, et suo [3] semper perficiant amore ferventes. Per.

Secreta.

S.
Gerb. 185.
Maiestatem tuam nobis, Domine, quaesumus, haec hostia reddat immolanda placatam, tuorum digna postulatione sanctorum. Per.

Postcommun.

S.
Gerb. 185.
Sacramentis [4], Domine, muniamur acceptis, et sanctorum tuorum Marcelli et Apulei [5] contra omnes nequitias irruentes armis caelestibus protegamur. Per Dominum nostrum.

---

[1] There is no *Missa* for this festival in Pam. or Men. [2] S. Gerb. omit *tuorum*. [3] *tuo* S² Gerb.; V. (S¹?) as text. [4] *sacramenti* V. [5] S² Gerb. insert *meritis intervenientibus*.

LXII.

IN NATALI SANCTORUM QUATUOR CORONATORUM,
COSTIANI, CLAUDI, CASTORI, SIMPRONIANI [1].

vi Id. Novembres.

8 nov.

Annua martyrum tuorum, Domine, vota recurrimus [2], maiestatem tuam • suppliciter deprecantes, ut cum temporalibus incrementis prosperitatis, aeterna Coronatorum capiamus augmenta [3]. Per.

S. Gerb. 191.
Leon. 455.

Secreta.

Hostias tibi, Domine, pro martyrum tuorum Coronatorum [4] commemoratione deferimus, supplicantes ut indulgentiam nobis pariter conferant et salutem. Per.

S. Gerb. 191.
Leon. 455.

Postcommun.

Sanctorum tuorum Coronatorum, quaesumus, Domine, semper nos laetificent festa [5] et maiestati tuae perpetua placatione commendent. Per.

S. Gerb. 192.
Leon. 455.

[1] S. and Gerb. give to this festival the title *Natal. Scorum iv Coronatorum*, without the addition of any proper names. From the note prefixed to the *Missa* for the festival in Men. it appears that five other saints (Claudius, Nicostratus, Simpronianus or Symphorianus, Castorius, and Simplicius) were commemorated with the Four Crowned Martyrs. These five are mentioned by name in the first collect of the Missa in S. and Gerb., which is the same as the Collect in Men. 139 and in Mur. 127. It seems most likely that *Costiani* in V. is a corrupt reading for *Nicostrati*, and that four of the five saints are thus represented in the title. [2] *recurremus* V. [3] *ut cum temporalibus incrementis, prosperitatis aeternae capiamus augmentum* Leon. (perhaps the original form). *ut cum temporalibus incrementis prosperitati aeternae Coronatorum capiamus augmentis* V.; S[1] (apparently) as text, but *temporalibus incrementis* has been altered by the corrector to *temporalis incremento*, and *et gaudia* substituted for *augmenta*. Gerb. (apparently from T.) agrees with the corrections of S[2]. [4] Leon. omits *Coronatorum*. [5] *Sanctorum tuorum nos q. Dne semper festa laetificent* Leon.

LXIII.

IN [VIGILIA [1]] SANCTAE CAECILIAE.

xi Kal. Decembres.

22 Nov.

Sanctae martyrae [2] tuae Caeciliae [Domine] [3], supplicationibus tribue nos foveri: ut cuius venerabilem solemnitatem praevenimus [4] obsequio [5], eius intercessionibus commendemur [6]. Per Dominum.

R. S.
Gerb. 196.
Pam.
(Amb.)433.

Secreta.

Suscipe, Domine, sacrificium placationis et laudis, quod nos, interveniente sancta tua Caecilia, cuius festivitatem

Cf. Leon. 297.

praevenimus⁴, et perducat ad veniam et in perpetua gratiarum constituat actione⁷. Per.

Postcommun.

Cf. xii *supr.*
Cf. Leon. 462.

Libantes, Domine, mensae tuae beata mysteria, quaesumus, ut martyrae interventione sanctae Caeciliae et praesentem⁸ nobis misericordiam conferant et aeternam. Per.

¹ *Natal.* V.; Tommasi suggests *Vigilia*, having the support of R. S. Gerb. (which agree in giving a *Missa* for the Vigil) and of the contents of the Collect and Secret. ² *martyris* S² Gerb. Pam. (Amb.); V. R. (S¹ f) as text. ³ V. omits *Domine*. ⁴ *pervenimus* V. ⁵ *obsequiis* R. Gerb. ⁶ R. S. Gerb. Pam. (Amb.) add *et meritis*. ⁷ *perpetua ... actionem* V. ⁸ *praesentis* V.; *praesentem* in xii *supra* (q. v.) and Leon.

LXIV.

[23 nov.]

ITEM IN NATALI EIUSDEM.

x Kal. [*Decembres*]¹.

S (*alibi*.)
Gerb. 29.
Cf. Leon. 456.
xii *supra*.

Omnipotens sempiterne Deus, qui eligis infirma mundi ut fortia quaeque confundas, da nobis in festivitate sanctae martyrae tuae Caeciliae congrua devotione gaudere; ut et potentiam tuam in eiusdem passione [laudemus, et provisum nobis]² percipiamus auxilium. Per. γ

Leon. 459.

Exaudi nos, Deus salutaris noster, ut sicut ⋅ de sanctae 673 Caeciliae festivitate gaudemus, ita piae devotionis erudiamur effectu. Per Dominum.

R.S.(*alibi*.)
Gerb. 21.
vi *supra*.

Crescat, Domine, semper in nobis sanctae iocunditatis affectus; et beatae Caeciliae martyrae tuae veneranda festivitas augeatur. Per Dominum.

Secreta.

Leon. 458.
Pam.
(Amb.)
433.

Quaesumus³, virtutum caelestium Domine, ut sacrificia pro sanctae Caeciliae commemoratione delata desiderium nos temporalium⁴ doceant habere contemptum, et ambire dona faciant caelestium gaudiorum. Per.

Postcommun.

R. S.
Gerb. 197.
Men. 141.
Pam. 353.
Pam.
(Amb.)
434.

Haec nos⁵, Domine, gratia tua, quaesumus, semper exerceat; ut⁶ divinis instauret nostra corda mysteriis, et sanctae Caeciliae martyrae tuae commemoratione laetificet. Per.

[II. lxv, lxvi.] ROMANAE ECCLESIAE. 205

[1] *Octob.* V. [2] The words in brackets are omitted here in V.; they are restored from the similar Collect in xii *supra* (q. v.). [3] *Tribue, quaesumus* Pam. (Amb.); V. Leon. as text. [4] *temporalem* V.; *temporale* Pam. (Amb.); *desideriorum nos temporalium* Leon. [5] *Sic nos* S¹ Gerb. Pam. Men.; V. R. S¹ Pam. (Amb.) as text. [6] *ut et* S¹ Gerb. Pam. (Amb.) Men.; V. R. S¹ Pam. as text.

LXV.

IN NATALI SANCTI CLEMENTIS.

ix Kal. Decembres.

Beati[1] Clementis sacerdotis et martyris tui[2] natalitia veneranda, quaesumus, Domine, ecclesia tua devota suscipiat, et fiat magnae glorificationis[3] amore devotior. Per.

Leon. 460. [Gerb. 198.]

Secreta.

Sacrificium tibi, Domine, laudis offerimus pro sancti celebritate Clementis; ut propitiationem tuam, quam nostris operibus non meremur, pii[4] suffragatoris intercessionibus assequamur. Per.

R. S. Gerb. 198. Pam. 354. Men. 141.

Postcommun.

Beati Clementis, Domine, natalitio[5] fidelibus tuis munere suffragetur[5]; et qui tibi placuit nobis imploret auxilium. Per Dominum nostrum.

R. S. Gerb. 198. Pam. 354.

[1] V. has *Natalem* before *Beati*, reading afterwards *natalitia veneranda*; Leon. as text. [2] *sacerdotis et martyris tui Clementis* Gerb. [3] *et magnae glorificationis efficiatur* Gerb. [4] S¹ app. had *piis*. [5] *natalitia ... munera suffragentur* Pam.; *natalitio ... caelestia munera suffragentur* S¹ Gerb.; V. R. S¹ as text (ungrammatically).

LXVI.

IN NATALI SANCTAE FELICITATIS.

Item ix Kal. Decembres.

Intercessio nos, quaesumus, Domine, sanctae Felicitatis martyrae tuae votiva • confoveat: ut eius sacrata natalitia et temporaliter frequentemus, et conspiciamus aeterna. Per.

Secreta.

Munera tibi, Domine, pro sanctae Felicitatis gloriosa commemoratione deferimus,[1] quae nobis huius solemnitatis effectum[2] et confessione dedicavit et sanguine[3]. Per.

S. Gerb. 198. Pam. 355.

206 LIBER SACRAMENTORUM [II. lxvii, lxviii.

Postcommun.

S. (alibi.)
Gerb. 172.
liii *supr.*
Pam. 355.

Praesta, Domine, quaesumus, ut sacramenti tui participatione vegetati sanctae Felicitatis quoque martyris precibus adiuvemur. Per.

[1] Pam. inserts *obsecrantes ut.*   [2] *solemnitas effectu* V.; Gerb. Pam. as text; S. *effectū.*   [3] *confessionem dedicavit et sanguinem* V.; S. Gerb. Pam. as text. After *sanguinem* Pam. adds *miserationis quoque tuae continuum imploret auxilium.*

LXVII.

IN NATALI SANCTORUM MARTYRUM SATURNINI, CRISANTI, MAURI, DARIAE, ET ALIORUM [1].

iii Kal. Decembres.

S.
Gerb. 200.

Beatorum martyrum, Domine, Saturnini et Crisanti adsit oratio, ut quos obsequio veneramur pio iugiter experiamur auxilio. Per.

Secreta.

S.
Gerb. 200.

Populi tui, Domine, quaesumus, tibi grata sit hostia, quae [2] natalitiis sanctorum martyrum tuorum Saturnini et Crisanti solemnitatibus [3] immolatur. Per.

Postcommun.

S.
Gerb. 200.
Pam. 356.

Mysteriis [4], Domine, repleti sumus, votis et gaudiis; praesta, quaesumus, ut per intercessionem sanctorum martyrum tuorum Saturnini et Crisanti [5], quae corporaliter agimus spiritaliter consequamur. Per Dominum.

[1.] S. Gerb. omit *et aliorum* from the title, while Pam. and Men. only mention S. Saturninus. The contents of the *Missae* in Men. and (except as regards the Postcommunion) in Pam., are different from what is to be found in V. S. and Gerb.   [2] S² Gerb. insert *in.*   [3] The termination of this word has been marked for omission by S², apparently for a change to *solemniter*; Gerb., however, agrees with V. and S¹.   [4] *Mysticis* Pam.   [5] *intercessionem beati Saturnini martyris tui* Pam.

LXVIII.

IN VIGILIA SANCTI ANDREAE.

iii Kal. Decembres.

R. S.
Gerb. 200.
Pam. 357.
Men. 143.

Tuere nos, misericors Deus, et beati Andreae apostoli tui cuius natalitia praevenimus, semper guberna praesidiis. Per.

Secreta [1].

R.S.(*alibi.*)
Gerb. 181.

Apostolicae reverentiae culmen offerimus, sacris mysteriis imbuendum; praesta, Domine, quaesumus [2], ut beati

Andreae suffragiis, cuius natalitia praeimus, hic³ plebs tua⁴ semper et sua vota depromat et desiderata percipiat. Per Dominum.

Leofr. 160, 219. Men. 130.

VD. Reverentiae tuae dicato ieiunio gratulantes, quo⁵ apostolica beati Andreae merita desideratis praevenimus⁶ officiis, ut ad eadem celebranda⁷ solemniter praeparemur⁸. Per.

R. S. Gerb. 201. See Men. note 505.

Postcommun.

Purificent semper et muniant tua sacramenta nos, Domine, et beati Andreae apostoli tui intercessione ad perpetuae ducant salvationis effectum. Per. γ

See III. xvii. Mur. 172.

¹ This Secret appears (with variations) for the Vigil of S. Matthew in R. S. Gerb. Men. Leofr. ² *Apostolici reverentia culminis offerentes tibi sacra mysteria Domine quaesumus* Men.; V. R. S¹ Gerb. Leofr. and MSS. cited by Menard as text. S² (marg.) has '*t cultum mirabiliter*' (the last word being probably a reflexion upon the Latinity of the original reading, not a part of the proposed alteration). ³ *haec* Leofr. ⁴ Leofr. 160 omits *tua*.
⁵ *quod* R. S¹ Gerb.; V. S² as text. ⁶ *praeveniamus* S¹. ⁷ *et ad eandem celebrandam* V.; *et eadem celebranda* R. Gerb.; *et ad eadem celebranda* S¹; S² as text. ⁸ *praeparemus* V.; R. S. Gerb. as text.

LXIX.

Item in Natali eiusdem.

Prid. Kal. Decembres.

[30 nov.]

Maiestatem tuam, Domine, suppliciter exoramus, ut sicut ecclesiae tuae sanctus Andreas apostolus extitit praedicator et rector ita¹ sit pro nobis² perpetuus suffragator³. Per Dominum nostrum. γ

R. S. Gerb. 201. Men. 143. Pam. 357. xxxii *supra*. Leon. 466.

Beatus Andreas pro nobis, Domine, quaesumus, imploret apostolus; ut et nostris reatibus absoluti, cunctis etiam periculis eruamur. Per.

Secreta.

Sacrificium nostrum tibi, Domine, quaesumus, beati Andreae precatio⁴ conciliet ut⁵ cuius honore⁶ solemniter exhibetur meritis efficiatur acceptum. Per. γ

R. S. Gerb. 201. Pam. 357. Men. 143.

VD. Qui⁷ ecclesiam tuam in apostolicis⁸ tribuisti consistere fundamentis: de quorum collegio beati Andreae solemnia celebrantes tua, Domine, praeconia non tacemus⁹. Et ideo cum¹⁰. γ

R.S.(*alibi*). Gerb. 208. Men. 145. Leon. 464.

Postcommun.

Beati Andreae apostoli tui, Domine, quaesumus, intercessione nos adiuva, pro cuius solemnitate percepimus¹¹ tua sancta laetantes. Per Dominum.   Cf. Leon. 338.

R. S. Gerb. 201. xvi *supra*. Pam. 289.

[II. lxx, lxxi.

¹ R. S. Gerb. Men. Pam. insert *apud te*; V. Leon. as text. ² Leon. omits *pro nobis*. ³ *intercessor* R. S. Gerb. Men. Pam.; V. Leon. as text. ⁴ *praedicatio* Pam. ⁵ *et ut* V. ⁶ *honorem* V. (ungrammatically); R. S. Gerb. Pam. Men. as text. ⁷ *Quia* R. ⁸ *apostolis* V. ⁹ *taceamus* Men. ¹⁰ S. Gerb. Men. Leon. have *Per Christum*. ¹¹ *percipimus* V. R.; S. Gerb. Leon. Pam. as text.

LXX.

7 déc.

IN OCTAVAS¹ SANCTI ANDREAE APOSTOLI².

vii Id. Decembres.

S. Gerb. 203. Leofr. 268.

Protegat nos, Domine, saepius beati Andreae apostoli repetita solemnitas; ut cuius patrocinia sine intermissione recolimus perpetuam defensionem³ sentiamus. Per.

Secreta.

S. Gerb. 203. Leofr. 268.

Indulgentiam nobis praebeant haec munera, quaesumus, Domine, largiorem, quae venerabilis Andreae suffragiis offeruntur. Per.

Postcommun.

S. Gerb. 203. Leofr. 268. Pam. 357. Men. 143.

Adiuvet familiam⁴ tuam, tibi, Domine, supplicando, venerandus Andreas apostolus tuus, et pius interventor efficiatur qui⁵ tui nominis extitit praedicator. Per Dominum. γ

¹ *Octabas* V. ² There is no *Missa* for the Octave in Pam. or Men.; nor is this Missa contained in R. ³ *perpetua defensione* V. (ungrammatically); S. Gerb. Leofr. as text. ⁴ *ecclesiam* Pam. Men. ⁵ *efficiat qui* V. S¹; *efficiat quod* S²; Gerb. Pam. Men. Leofr. as text.

LXXI.

21 déc.

IN NATALI SANCTI THOMAE APOSTOLI¹.

xii Kal. Ianuarias.

R. S. Gerb. 208. Pam. 364. Men. 144.

Da nobis, quaesumus, Domine, beati apostoli² Thomae solemnitatibus gloriari: ut eius semper et patrociniis sublevemur, et fidem congrua devotione sectemur. Per.

Secreta.

R. S. Gerb. 208. Pam. 364. Men. 145. Cf. Leon. 397.

Debitum, Domine, nostrae reddimus servitutis, suppliciter exorantes³ ut suffragiis beati apostoli Thomae⁴ in nobis tua munera tuearis, cuius honorando confessionem laudis tuae⁵ hostiam immolamus. Per.

Postcommun.

Conserva, Domine, populum tuum, et quem sanctorum tuorum praesidiis non desinis adiuvare, perpetuis tribue gaudere remediis. Per.

R. S.
Gerb. 208.
Pam. 365.
Men. 145.

[1] This *Missa* is marked by Gerbert as not contained in R., but is found there. [2] R. Gerb. Pam. Men. insert *tui*. [3] *exoranter* V. [4] *beati Thomae apostoli* R. S. Gerb. Pam. Men. [5] *tui* V.

LXXII[1].
ORATIONES IN NATALI PLURIMORUM SANCTORUM[2].

Exaudi, Domine, populum[3] cum sanctorum tuorum tibi patrocinio supplicantem; ut[4] temporalis vitae nos tribuas[4] pace gaudere, et aeternae reperire subsidia[5]. Per.

R.S.(*alibi.*)
Gerb. 20.
Leofr. 135.
Leon. 294.

Secreta.

Preces, Domine, tuorum respice oblationesque fidelium; ut et tibi gratae[6] sint pro tuorum[7] festivitate sanctorum[8], et nobis conferant tuae propitiationis auxilium. Per.

R.S.(*alibi.*)
Gerb. 20.
Leofr. 135.

Postcommun.

Sanctorum[8] tuorum, Domine, intercessione placatus, praesta, quaesumus, ut quae temporali celebramus actione, perpetua salvatione capiamus. Per.

R.S.(*alibi.*)
Gerb. 20.
Leofr. 135.

[1] This *Missa* and those which follow it (to lxxix inclusive) represent the 'Commune Sanctorum' of V. Gerbert, in the corresponding section of his work, ceases to employ T. as the basis of his text, and follows R. instead (T. being, as he states, defective in some leaves), but does not either limit himself to the contents or keep absolutely to the order of R. The section in V. contains many prayers which are to be found in R. and S. and in other MSS. from which Gerbert extracts his material, but differs much as regards arrangement, order, and contents from the corresponding portions of R. and S., and still more from those of Pam. Men. Mur.; while it has also a large portion of matter in common with the Leonine Sacramentary. [2] In R. S. Gerb. and also in Leofr. this *Missa* is assigned to a particular day, the Festival of SS. Mary and Martha, xiii Kal. Feb. (see iv *supra*). But in R. S. and in Gerb. the masculine form is used throughout, a fact which seems to indicate the appropriation to that day of a common form: while in Leofr. the common character of the form is made more evident by the appearance of alternative readings. [3] R. S. Gerb. Leofr. Leon. all insert *tuum*. [4] *et . . . tribue* Leon.; *ut et . . . tribuas* S. Gerb.; V. R. Leofr. as text. [5] *subsidiis* V. (ungrammatically); *subsidium* R. S. Gerb. Leon.; *aeterne subsidium reperire* Leofr. [6] *grata* V. [7] *perpetuo* V.; *perpetuorum* R.; *pro tua(o)rum* Leofr.; S. Gerb. as text. [8] *sancta(o)rum* Leofr.

LXXIII.
ITEM ALIA MISSA[1].

Praesta, Domine, quaesumus, ut sicut sanctorum tuorum nos natalitia celebranda non deserunt, ita iugiter suffragiis[2] comitentur. Per.

R. S.
Gerb. 225.
Men. 163.
Leofr. 174. Leon. 406.

S.
Gerb. 225.
Men. 164.
Leofr. 174.
Leon. 311,
338.

Adesto, Domine, populo tuo, cum sanctorum patrocinio supplicanti; ut quod propria fiducia non praesumit, suffragantium meritis consequatur³. Per Dominum.

Secreta.

R. S.
Gerb. 217.
Leofr. 163.
Leon. 402.

Salutari⁴ sacrificio, Domine, populus tuus semper exultet, quo⁵ et debitus⁶ honor sacris martyribus exhibetur, et sanctificationis tuae munus acquiritur. Per.

Postcommun.

R. S.
Gerb. 225.
Men. 164.
Leon. 313.

Et natalitiis sanctorum, Domine, et sacramenti⁷ munere vegetati, quaesumus, ut bonis, quibus per tuam⁸ gratiam nunc fovemur, perfruamur aeternis. Per.

¹ Three of the four prayers of this *Missa* appear together in S. Men. The first collect has the same position in R. S. ('*in Nat. plur. sanctorum*') and in Men. ('*in Nat. plur. confessorum*'). The second appears in S. Men. in conjunction with the first, being one of the '*aliae orationes*' in S., and the '*super Populum*' in Men. This last is also its position in the two *Missae* in which it appears in Leon. In Leofr. the two Collects appear as the Collects of a *Missa* '*in Nat. plur. sanctorum*.' The Postcommunion is in R. S. Men., in each case in the same *Missa* which contains the first Collect. In R. S. the Secret appears '*in Nat. Plur. Martyrum*,' while in Leofr. it is appropriated to the Festival of SS. Dionysius, Rusticus, and Eleutherius, and in Leon. (apparently) to that of SS. Felix and Adauctus. Gerbert marks it as being contained in Men.   ² *suffragia* S².   ³ *consequamur* V. (corrected by Tommasi); S. Gerb., &c. as text.   ⁴ *Salutaris* V.   ⁵ *quod* V.   ⁶ *debitis* S¹.   ⁷ *sacramenta* V.; *sacramenti tui* S².   ⁸ *perpetuum* (for *per tuam*) R. (corrected by Gerbert).

LXXIV.

Item alia Missa.

R. S.
Gerb. 225.

Sancti tui, quaesumus, Domine, iugiter nobis a te et veniam postulent et profectum¹. Per.

•Deus, qui nos et sanctorum martyrum solemnitatibus et confessorum gloria circumdas et protegis, praesta nobis eorum semper et imitatione proficere et emundatione fulgere. Per.

Secreta.

Haec hostia, Domine, quaesumus, solemniter immolanda pro tuorum commemoratione iustorum, conscientias nostras semper et mundet et protegat. Per.

Postcommun.

Leon. 403.

Votiva, Domine, dona percepimus²; quae³ sanctorum nobis precibus et praesentis, quaesumus, vitae pariter et aeternae tribue conferre praesidium. Per Dominum nostrum. γ

¹ *profectu* V. (ungrammatically); R. S. Gerb. as text. ² *percipimus* V.;
Leon as text.   ³ *quia* V.; Leon. as text.

LXXV.

ITEM ALIA MISSA[1].

Fac nos, Domine, quaesumus, sanctorum tuorum semper festa sectari, quorum suffragiis protectionis tuae dona sentiamus[2]. Per.

S (*alibi.*)
Gerb. 133.
Men. 104.
Leon. 392. Leofr. 144.

Secreta.

Fiat, Domine, quaesumus, hostia sacranda placabilis pretiosi celebritate martyrii; quae et peccata[3] nostra purificet, et [tuorum[4]] tibi vota conciliet famulorum[5]. Per.

S. (*alibi.*)
Gerb. 133.
Men. 104.
Leon. 307.
Leofr. 144.

Postcommun.

Quaesumus, omnipotens Deus, ut sanctorum tuorum caelestibus mysteriis celebrata solemnitas indulgentiam nobis tuae propitiationis acquirat. Per Dominum.

S. (*alibi.*)
Gerb. 133.
Men. 105.
Leon. 400.
Leofr. 144.

[1] In S. Gerb. Men. Leofr. this *Missa* is appropriated to the Festival of SS. Primus and Felicianus (v Id. Iun.). In Leon. the prayers are found apart from one another, the Collect being assigned to a *Missa* for the Festival of SS. Sixtus and others (viii Id. Aug.) and the Postcommunion to the Festival of SS. Hippolytus and Pontianus (Id. Aug.).   [2] *sentimus* V.; all the others as text.   [3] *corda* Leon. (man. sec.); Leon. (man. prim.) V. and the rest as text.   [4] *sanctorum* (for *tuorum*) V.; the epithet seems misplaced, and all the other texts cited read *tuorum*.   [5] Leon. omits *famulorum*.

LXXVI.

ITEM ALIA MISSA[1].

Maiestati tuae nos, Domine, martyrum supplicatio beata conciliet, ut qui incessabiliter[2] actibus nostris offendimus, istorum precibus expiemur. Per.

S. (*alibi.*)
[Gerb. 24.]
Leofr. 136.
Leon. 302.

Martyrum tuorum nos, Domine, semper festa laetificent: et quorum celebramus meritum experiamur[3] auxilium. Per.

S. (*alibi.*)
[Gerb. 24.]
Leofr. 136.
Leon. 302.

Secreta.

Accepta tibi sit, Domine, sacratae plebis oblatio pro tuorum honore sanctorum, quorum meritis se percepisse[4] in tribulatione agnoscit auxilium. Per. γ

S. (*alibi.*)
[Gerb. 24.]
Leofr. 136.
Leon. 393.

Postcommun.

S. (alibi.)
[Gerb. 24.]
(see Leofr.
136 note.)

Iugiter nos, Domine, sanctorum tuorum vota laetificent, et patrocinia nobis martyrum ipsae semper festivitates exhibeant. Per.

[1] This *Missa* as a whole is appropriated in S. and in Gerb. (where it is wrongly marked as not included in R. or S.) to the Festival of SS. Emerentiana and Macarius (x Kal. Feb.). Three of the four prayers form the *Missa* for the same Festival in Leofr., where the Postcommunion is discarded and the second of the Collects transferred to the vacant place. The two Collects and the Secret appear in different sections in Leon., where the Secret is assigned to the Festival of SS. Felicissimus and Agapitus (viii Id. Aug.). [2] *incessanter* Leofr. [3] *expiemur* V. [4] So Leofr.; Leon. S² Gerb. have *se meritis percepisse*; V. and perhaps S¹ *meritis semper coepisse* (probably by corruption of the reading in the text).

LXXVII.

Item alia Missa [1].

S. Gerb. 225.
Men. 164.
Leofr. 174.
Leon. 393.

Magnificantes, Domine, clementiam tuam, suppliciter [2] exoramus, ut qui nos sanctorum tuorum frequentibus facis natalitiis interesse perpetuis tribuas gaudere consortiis [3]. Per Dominum.

S. Gerb. 225.
Men. 164.
Leofr. 174.
Leon. 393.

Da nobis, omnipotens Deus, in sanctorum tuorum te semper commemoratione laudare: quia refovere curabis quos in honore tuo perseverare concedis [4]. Per.

Secreta.

Accepta tibi sit in conspectu tuo, Domine, nostrae devotionis oblatio: et eorum nobis fiat supplicatione salutaris, pro quorum solemnitate defertur. Per.

Postcommun.

S. Gerb. 218.
Men. 160.
Leon. 405.

Ad defensionem fidelium, Domine, quaesumus, dexteram [5] tuae maiestatis extende: et ut perpetua pietatis [tuae] [6] protectione muniantur, intercessio pro his non desit martyrum continuata sanctorum. Per.

[1] The two Collects of this *Missa* appear together in S. Gerb. Men. as '*aliae orationes*' ('*in Natal. plur. sanctorum*' S. Gerb.; '*in Natal. plur. confessorum*' Men.). In Leofr. the first is the '*ad complendum*,' the second the '*ad Populum*' of a *Missa* '*in Nat. plur. sanctorum*.' In Leon. they are the first and second Collects for the Festival of SS. Felicissimus and Agapitus. The Postcommunion is assigned by S. Gerb. and Men. to a Festival '*plurimorum martyrum*,' in each case among the additional prayers; Leon. gives it a place (perhaps as a '*super Populum*') in a *Missa* for the Festival of SS. Cornelius and Cyprian. [2] *supplices* Leon. [3] *consortes* V.; all the rest as text. [4] *concesseris* Leon. [5] *dextera* V. (ungrammatically); S. Leon as text. [6] V. omits *tuae*, which is restored from S. Leon.

LXXVIII.

Item alia Missa[1].

Fraterna nos, Domine, martyrum tuorum corona laeti-   S. (*alibi.*)
ficet, quae et fidei nostrae praebeat[2] incitamenta virtutum,   Gerb. 156.
et multiplici nos suffragio consoletur[2]. Per.   Leofr. 151.

Praesta, quaesumus, Domine, ut sicut nobis indiscreta   S. (*alibi.*)
pietas horum martyrum beatorum individuae caritatis   Gerb. 156.
praebet exemplum, sic spiritum gratiae tuae, quo iugiter
muniamur, semper imploret. Per.

Secreta.

680

Iterata[3] mysteria, Domine, pro sanctorum martyrum[4]   S. (*alibi.*)
devota mente tractamus, quibus nobis et praesidium crescit   Gerb. 156.
et gaudium. Per.   Leofr. 151.

Postcommun.

Caelesti munere saginati quaesumus, Domine Deus   Leon. 348.
noster, ut haec nos dona martyrum tuorum deprecatione   Cf. xxxviii
beata sanctificent[5]. Per.   *supra.*

[1] The two Collects and the Secret of this *Missa* are assigned in S. and Gerb. to the Festival of the Maccabees (Kal. Aug.), where Gerbert wrongly marks the Secret as not contained in either R. or S.; Leofr. has the first Collect and a variation of the Secret in its *Missa* for the same day; while the Postcommunion appears to be closely related to that which is assigned to the same festival in V. (xxxviii *supra*).   [2] *praebeant ... consolentur* V.; S. Gerb. Leofr. as text.   [3] *Iterata,* so V. (S¹?); S³ Gerb. have *intemerata*; Leofr. has a different beginning reading *Votiva, Domine, mysteria, sanctorum tuorum solemnia celebrantes.*   [4] S² Gerb. insert *tuorum commemoratione*; V. S¹ as text (perhaps ungrammatically: the difficulty of such a reading may have occasioned the variation in Leofr., already noted).   [5] The reading of V. is apparently corrupt:—*ut haec nobis dona martyrum tuorum duplicacio beata sanctificet.* The text has been emended by a comparison with xxxviii *supra,* and with Leon.

LXXIX.

Item alia Missa[1].

Domine Deus noster, multiplica super nos gratiam tuam;   S. (*alibi.*)
et quorum celebramus gloriosa certamina, tribue subsequi   Gerb. 28.
in sancta professione victoriam[2]. Per.   Leon. 347.

Secreta.

Suscipe, Domine, quaesumus, munera populi tui pro   S. (*alibi.*)
martyrum festivitate sanctorum, et sincero nos corde fac   Gerb. 28.
eorum natalitiis interesse. Per.

Postcommun.

S. (*alibi*.)
Gerb. 28.
Sacramenti tui, Domine, quaesumus, sumpta benedictio corpora nostra mentesque sanctificet, et perpetuae misericordiae nos praeparet adscribendos. Per Dominum.

[1] This *Missa* appears in S. and Gerb. for the Festival of S. Zoticus and others. [2] *victoria* V. (ungrammatically); S. Gerb. Leon. as text. [3] *quaesumus Domine* S. Gerb.

LXXX[1].
ORATIONES DE ADVENTUM DOMINI[2].

R. S.
Gerb. 199.
Men. 186.
Sacr. Gall. 785.
Miss. Gall. 702.
Excita, Domine, potentiam tuam, et veni, et quod ecclesiae tuae usque in finem saeculi promisisti[3] clementer operare. Per. y

R.S.(*alibi*.)
Gerb. 207.
Men. 191.
Sacr Gall. 785.
Excita, Domine, potentiam tuam, [et veni[4]], et magna nobis virtute succurre, ut per auxilium gloriae[5] tuae quod nostra peccata praepediunt, indulgentia tuae propitiationis acceleret. Per. y

Secreta.

R.S.(*alibi*.)
Gerb. 204.
Men. 188.
Miss. Gall. 702.
Placare, Domine, quaesumus, humilitatis nostrae precibus et hostiis; et ubi nulla suppetunt suffragia meritorum tuae nobis indulgentiae succurre praesidiis[6]. Per. y

R.S.(*alibi*.)
Gerb. 202.
Men. 187.
Sacr. Gall. 786.
Miss. Gall. 702.
V.D. ... Deus[7]. Cui proprium est ac singulare quod bonus es[8], et nulla unquam a te es commutatione[9] diversus[10]. Propitiare supplicationibus nostris et eccles-iae tuae misericordiam tuam quam confitentur[11] ostende, manifestans plebi tuae Unigeniti tui[12] mirabile sacramentum, ut[13] in universitate nationum perficiatur quod[14] per Verbi tui evangelium promisisti, et habeat plenitudo adoptionis quod pertulit[15] testificatio veritatis. Per Christum Dominum. y

681

Postcommun.

R.S.(*alibi*.)
Gerb. 204.
Men. 188.
Miss. Gall. 703.
Repleti cibo spiritalis[16] alimoniae supplices te deprecamur, omnipotens Deus, ut huius participatione mysterii doceas nos terrena despicere et amare caelestia, atque[17] omni nexu mortiferae cupiditatis exutos regno perpetuae libertatis consortes efficias. Per Dominum. y

[1] This *Missa* and the four which follow it apparently correspond to the five *Missae* provided by R. and S. for the five Sundays before Christmas Day. Men. likewise has five *Missae* for these weeks, reckoning backward from Christmas. S. has also a series of three *Missae* and R. has two *Missae* for the weekdays of Advent, while R. S. and Men. have each a series of '*Aliae Orationes de Adventu*,' with which, probably, the prayers contained in the latter part of

lxxxiv were intended to correspond, though they have not in V. any separate title, and appear (most likely by accident) as if they were additional Post-communions for the last of the five Advent *Missae*. Gerbert's triple text fails for the greater part of the Advent section, T. being defective at this point, and Gerbert tells us that he used S. and R. for the portion lacking in T. His text, however, shows a few variations from the readings both of R. and S., and he includes some things which are not contained in R. The contents and arrangement of the five *Missae* differ to some extent. R. S. and Gerb. show two Collects for each *Missa*, while Men. has only one: Men. has a '*super Populum*' in each *Missa*, which R. S. and Gerb. have not; and there are some variations in the text of the special Prefaces which S. Gerb. Men. agree in assigning to each of the five *Missae*. In the majority of the five, however, R. S. and Gerb. are in agreement with Men. as to one Collect, the Secret, and the Postcommunion. Four out of the five *Missae* of V. show a marked correspondence with the Advent *Missae* of the Sacramentarium Gallicanum and of the Missale Gallicanum Vetus. ² *de adventum Domini*, so V. The contents of this *Missa* appear in different positions in the other books referred to. (*a*) The first Collect has the same position in R. S. Gerb. Men. and appears in the two Gallican books as the first prayer of the first *Missa de Adventu*. (*b*) The second Collect is in the Sacramentarium Gallicanum the second prayer of the first Advent *Missa*: in R. S. Gerb. Men. it is the first Collect of the *Missa* for the Sunday next before Christmas. (*c*) The Secret in R. S. Gerb. Men. belongs to the third Sunday before Christmas. In Miss. Gall. it is the '*Post Nomina*' of the first Advent *Missa*. (*d*) The Preface is assigned by R. S. Gerb. Men. to the fourth Sunday before Christmas: in both the Gallican books it forms part of the first Advent *Missa*. (*e*) The Postcommunion is that of the third Sunday before Christmas in R. S. Gerb. Men. and appears in Miss. Gall. as the final '*Collectio*' of the first Advent *Missa*. ⁵ *promisisti usque in finem saeculi* R. S. Gerb. Men.; V. and both Gallican books, as text. ⁶ V. omits *et veni*, which is restored from the other texts. ⁸ *gratiae* R. S. Gerb. Men.; V. and Sacr. Gall. as text. ⁶ Miss. Gall. adds a clause in reference to the persons whose names had preceded the '*Collectio*.' ⁷ Miss. Gall. has this word in the same isolated position, which led Mabillon to suspect an omission ; Sacr. Gall. has *omnipotens Deus, per Christum Dominum nostrum. Cui* ...; R. has *VD. Cui* ...; S. Gerb. Men. have the normal introduction ending with *aeterne Deus*. ⁸ *est* Sacr. Gall. ⁹ *nullam umquam ad te est communicatione* V.; *communicatione* R. ¹⁰ *divisus* Sacr. Gall. ¹¹ *confitetur* R. Gerb.; *deprecatur* Men. ¹² Sacr. Gall. inserts *adventum Domini nostri Iesu Christi*; Men. inserts *et incarnationis mysterium et adventus* and after *sacramentum* proceeds in a totally different way. ¹³ *et* Miss. Gall. ¹⁴ Sacr. Gall. omits *quod*. ¹⁵ *praetulit* Miss. Gall.; *protulit* S²; V. R. S¹ Gerb. Sacr. Gall. as text. ¹⁶ *spiritali* V. ¹⁷ R. S. Gerb. Men. omit *atque ... efficias*.

LXXXI.

Item alia Missa [1].

Excita, Domine, quaesumus, corda nostra ad praeparandas Unigeniti tui vias; ut per eius adventum purificatis tibi servire mentibus [2] mereamur. Per. y
R.S.(*alibi*.) Gerb. 204. Men. 188. Miss. Gall. 703. Sacr. Gall. 785.

Praeveniat nos, quaesumus, omnipotens Deus, tua gratia semper et subsequatur; ut cum adventu [3] Unigeniti tui, quem summo cordis desiderio sustimenus, et praesentis vitae subsidia et futurae etiam consequamur. Per.
R. S. Gerb. 202. Men. 193. Sacr. Gall. 785.

Conscientias nostras, quaesumus, omnipotens Deus, quotidie visitando purifica, ut veniente Domino Filio tuo [4], paratam sibi in nobis inveniat mansionem. Per. y
R.S.(*alibi*.) Gerb. 200. Men. 192. Sacr. Gall. 785. Miss. Gall. 703.

R.S.(*alibi*.)
Gerb. 205.
Men. 194.
Miss. Gall.
704.
Sacr. Gall.
785.

Fac nos, quaesumus, Domine Deus noster, pervigiles atque sollicitos adventum expectare Christi Filii tui Domini nostri: ut dum venerit pulsans, non dormientes peccatis, sed vigilantes et in suis inveniat laudibus exultantes [5]. Per.

Secreta.

R.S.(*alibi*).
Gerb. 200.
Men. 186.
Miss. Gall.
704.
Sacr. Gall. 791. Leon. 364.

Sacrificium tibi, Domine, celebrandum placatus intende; quod et nos a vitiis nostrae conditionis emundet, et tuo nomini reddat acceptos [6]. Per.

Postcommun.

R.S.(*alibi*.)
Gerb. 208.
Miss. Gall.
706.

Sumptis muneribus, Domine, quaesumus ut cum frequentatione mysterii crescat nostrae salutis effectus. Per. γ

[1] The contents of this *Missa* appear as follows in the other books referred to:—(*a*) The first Collect is assigned by R. S. Gerb. Men. to the third Sunday before Christmas. It is a *Collectio* in the second Advent *Missa* of Miss. Gall., and in the first Advent *Missa* of Sacr. Gall. (*b*) The second Collect is in R. S. Gerb. the second Coll. for the fourth Sunday before Christmas, and follows (*a*) in Sacr. Gall.; in Men. it is one of the '*Aliae orationes quotidianis diebus.*' (*c*) The third Collect is in R. S. Gerb. the second Collect for the fifth Sunday before Christmas, and in Miss. Gall. follows (*a*). In Sacr. Gall. it is the *Post nomina* of the first Advent *Missa*. In Men. it is among the '*Orat quot. dieb.*' (*d*) The fourth Collect is in R. S. Gerb., the second for the second Sunday before Christmas. In Miss. Gall. it is the *Post nomina* of the second *Missa*: in Sacr. Gall. it is the *ad pacem* of the first. In Men. it is among the '*Orat. quot. dieb.*' (*e*) The Secret is assigned by R. S. Gerb. Men. to the fifth Sunday before Christmas. In Miss. Gall. it is the *ad pacem* of the second Advent *Missa*: in Sacr. Gall. it is the *ad pacem* of the third. (*f*) The Postcommunion is assigned by R. S. Gerb. to the Sunday before Christmas (for which Men. gives another form). In Miss. Gall. it is the last *Collectio* of the second *Missa*, which thus contains five out of the six prayers which compose this *Missa* in V. [2] *mentibus servire* R. S. Gerb. Men.; *purificati tibi servire mereamur* Sacr. Gall.; V. Miss. Gall. as text. [3] *cum adventum* V. (ungrammatically); *per adventum* R. S. Gerb. Men.; Sacr. Gall. as text. [4] *veniente Filio tuo Domino nostro* R. S¹ Gerb.; *veniens Filius tuus Dominus noster* S²; *veniens Iesus Christus Filius tuus Dominus noster* Men.; V. and Gallican books as text. [5] Miss. Gall. adds a clause referring to those whose names had preceded. [6] Miss. Gall. adds a clause referring to the Kiss of Peace.

LXXXII. 682

Item alia Missa [1].

R.S.(*alibi*.)
Gerb. 204.
Men. 194.
Sacr. Gall.
790.

Praecinge, quaesumus, Domine Deus noster, lumbos mentis nostrae divina virtute tua potenter [2], ut veniente Domino nostro Iesu Christo Filio tuo [3] digni inveniamur aeternae vitae convivio, et vota [4] caelestium dignitatum ab ipso percipere mereamur. Per.

R.S.(*alibi*.)
Gerb. 207.
Men. 192.

Adiuva, Domine, fragilitatem plebis tuae; ut ad votivum [5] magnae festivitatis effectum [5] et corporaliter gubernata percurrat⁶ et ad perpetuam gratiam devota mente perveniat. Per.

Secreta.

Grata tibi sint, Domine, munera, quibus mysteria celebrantur nostrae libertatis et vitae⁷. Per.

R.S.(*alibi.*)
Gerb. 202.
Men. 189. Miss. Gall. 702.

Postcommun.

Animae nostrae, quaesumus, omnipotens Deus, hoc potiantur⁸ desiderio, ut a tuo Spiritu inflammentur; ut sicut lampades⁹ divino munere satiati, ante conspectum venientis Christi Filii tui velut clara lumina fulgeamus. Per.

R.S.(*alibi.*)
Gerb. 200.
Men. 187.
Miss. Gall. 703.

¹ The prayers of this Missa appear in the other books referred to as follows:—(*a*) The first Collect is in R. S. Gerb. the second for the third Sunday before Christmas: in Sacr. Gall. it is a *Collectio* in the third Advent *Missa*; in Men. one of the '*Orat quot. dieb.*' (*b*) The second Collect is assigned by R. S. Gerb. Men. to the Sunday before Christmas: in the three former it is the second Collect, in the fourth it is the *super Populum*. (*c*) The Secret in R. S. Gerb. belongs to a *Missa* '*in quotidianis diebus*': Men. assigns it to the Wednesday of the Embertide: in Miss. Gall. it is the *ad pacem* of the first Advent *Missa*. (*d*) The Postcommunion in R. S. Gerb. Men. belongs to the fifth Sunday before Christmas; in Miss. Gall. it is a *Collectio post Communionem* in the first Advent *Missa*. ² *potencium* V.
³ *venientem Dominum nostrum Iesum Christum Filium tuum* V. R. S¹ Gerb. (ungrammatically); S² Sacr. Gall. as text. ⁴ *dota* S¹; *dona* S².
⁵ *votivo . . . effectu* V. R. ⁶ *recurrat* R. S. Gerb. Men.: V. as text.
⁷ Miss. Gall. adds a clause relating to the Kiss of Peace, ⁸ *pocientur* V.
⁹ *lampadas* V. R.

LXXXIII.

ITEM ALIA MISSA¹.

Festina, quaesumus, ne tardaveris, Domine², et praesidium nobis tuae pietatis impende: ut opportunis³ consolationibus subleventur qui in tua miseratione confidunt. Per.

R.S.(*alibi.*)
Gerb. 205.
Men. 189.
Sacr. Gall. 790.

Concede, quaesumus, omipotens Deus, hanc gratiam plebi tuae, adventum Unigeniti tui cum summa vigilantia expectare; ut sicut ipse auctor nostrae⁴ salutis docuit⁵, velut fulgentes lampadas⁶ in eius occursum⁷ nostras animas praeparemus. Per.

S. (*alibi.*)
Gerb. 209.
Men. 192.
Sacr. Gall. 790.

Voci nostrae, quaesumus, Domine, aures tuae pietatis accommoda: et cordis nostri tenebras lumine tuae visitationis illustra. Per.

S. (*alibi.*)
Gerb. 209.
Men. 193.

Secreta.

Sacrificiis praesentibus, Domine, quaesumus, intende placatus, ut et devotioni nostrae proficiant et saluti. Per. γ

R.S.(*alibi.*)
Gerb. 207.
Men.
(*alibi.*)

Postcommun.

R.S.(*alibi.*)
Gerb. 202.
Men. 108.
Miss. Gall. 703.

Da, quaesumus, omnipotens Deus, cunctae familiae tuae hanc voluntatem in [8] Christo Filio tuo, Domino nostro venienti [9] in operibus iustis aptos occurrere: et [10] eius dexterae sociati regnum mereantur possidere caeleste. Per.

[1] The prayers of this Missa appear in the following positions in the other Sacramentaries referred to:—(*a*) The first Collect is in R. S. Gerb. Men. the second Collect for the Wednesday of the Advent Embertide. In Sacr. Gall. it is a Collectio in the third Advent *Missa*. (*b*) The second Collect is in S. Gerb. Men. among the general Advent prayers but does not appear in R.; in Sacr. Gall. it is the '*Coll. post Prophetiam*' of the third *Missa* of Advent. (*c*) The third collect is also absent from R. but is among the general Advent prayers in S. Gerb. Men. (*d*) The Secret in R. S. Gerb. is assigned to the Sunday before Christmas. It is a form of frequent occurrence and appears elsewhere in V. (*e*) The Postcommunion is in R. S. Gerb. as that of a *Missa* '*in quot. dieb.*' In Men. it appears as the *super Populum* for the third Sunday before Christmas: and in Miss. Gall. it is a *Benedictio populi* in the first Advent *Missa*. [2] *Domine ne tardaveris* Gerb. Men. Sacr. Gall.; V. R. S. as text. [3] *adventus tui* (for *opportunis*) R. S. Gerb. Men.; V. Sacr. Gall. as text. [4] *noster* V. [5] Sacr. Gall. omits *docuit*. [6] *lampades* Gerb. [7] *occurso* (=*occursu*) Sacr. Gall. [8] Men. omits *in*. [9] *veniente* Gerb. [10] *ut* R. Gerb. Men. Miss. Gall.; V. S. as text.

LXXXIV.

Item alia Missa [1].

R.S.(*alibi.*)
Gerb. 205.
Men. 189.

Praesta, quaesumus, omnipotens Deus, ut redemptionis nostrae ventura solemnitas et praesentis nobis vitae subsidia conferat et aeternae vitae beatitudinis praemia largiatur. Per Dominum. ⁊

R.S.(*alibi.*)
Gerb. 206.
Men. 190.

Excita, quaesumus, Domine, potentiam tuam, et veni; ut hi [2] qui in tua pietate confidunt ab omni citius adversitate liberentur. Per. ⁊

S. (*alibi.*)
Gerb. 203.
Men. 194.

Exultemus, quaesumus, Domine Deus noster, omnes recti corde in unitate fidei congregati; ut veniente [3] Salvatore nostro Filio tuo immaculati occurramus illi in eius sanctorum comitatu. Per eundem Dominum.

S. (*alibi.*)
Gerb. 203.
Men. 194.

Fac nos, Domine, quaesumus [4], mala nostra toto corde respuere; ut, veniente Filio tuo Domino nostro, bona eius capere valeamus. Per. ⁊

Secreta.

S. (*alibi.*)
Gerb. 205.
Men. 189.
Sacr. Gall. 791.

Devotionis nostrae tibi, Domine, quaesumus [5], hostia iugiter immoletur, quae et sacri peragat instituta mysterii, et salutare tuum nobis mirabiliter operetur. Per Dominum. ⁊

Postcommun.

Preces populi tui, quaesumus, Domine, clementer exaudi; ut qui de adventu Unigeniti tui secundum carnem laetantur, in secundo, cum venerit in maiestate sua, praemium aeternae vitae percipiant [6]. Per. y   S.¶(*alibi.*)
Gerb. 209.
Men. 187.

[7] Indignos [8], quaesumus, Domine, famulos tuos, quia [9] actionis propriae culpa contristat, Unigeniti tui nos [10] adventu laetifica. Per Dominum. y   R. S.
Gerb. 206.
Men. 191.

Quaesumus, omnipotens Deus, preces nostras respice, et tuae super nos viscera pietatis impende: ut qui ex nostra culpa affligimur, Salvatore nostro adveniente respiremus [11]. Per.   S.
Gerb. 209.
Men. 193.

684   Concede, quaesumus, omnipotens Deus, ut qui [12] sub peccati iugo ex debito [13] deprimimur expectata Unigeniti tui nova nativitate liberemur. Per. y   R. S.
Gerb. 209.
Men. 190.

Excita, Domine, potentiam tuam et veni, ut tua propitiatione salvemur. Per.   R. S.
Gerb. 203.
Men. 194.

Festina [14], ne tardaveris, Domine Deus noster, et a diabolico furore [15] nos potenter elibera [16]. Per.   R. S.
Gerb. 203.
Men. 194.

Porrige nobis, Domine, dexteram tuae venerationis [17], et veni, et peccata nostra propitiatus absolve. Per.   S.
Gerb. 209.
Men. 193.

Deus, qui prospicis [18] quia ex nostra pravitate [19] affligimur, concede propitius ut ex tua visitatione consolemur. Per Dominum. y   R. S.
Gerb. 206.
Men. 190.

Festinantes, omnipotens Deus, in occursum Filii tui Domini nostri nulla impediant opera actus terreni [20]; sed caelestis sapientiae eruditio faciat nos eius esse consortes. Per Dominum.   S.
Gerb. 209.
Men. 193.

Praesta, quaesumus, omnipotens Deus, ut Filii tui ventura solemnitas et praesentis nobis vitae [21] remedia conferat et praemia aeterna concedat. Per. y   R. S.
Gerb. 209.
Men. 193.

Praesta, quaesumus, omnipotens Deus, ut quia [22] pro peccatis nostris meremur affligi, per adventum Filii tui a cunctis adversitatibus liberemur [23]. Per.   S.
Gerb. 209.
Men. 193.

Deus, qui nos redemptionis nostrae annua expectatione laetificas, praesta ut unigenitum Filium [24] tuum, quem redemptorem laeti suscipimus [25], venientem quoque iudicem securi videamus. Per. y   R.S.(*alibi.*)
Gerb. 1.
Men. 5.

220   LIBER SACRAMENTORUM   [II. lxxxv.

¹ The prayers included under this head may be divided into two subsections : (i) Those which make up the *Missa*, or the first six prayers: (ii) the last eleven prayers, which should probably form a section by themselves, corresponding to the general Advent prayers of R. S. Gerb. Men. The first and second Collects of (i) are in R. S. Gerb. Men. the Collects for the Wednesday and the Friday of the Embertide: the third and fourth appear in S. Gerb. as the Collects of a *Missa quotidiana* (not contained in R.), and in Men. among the '*Orationes de Adventu quotidianis diebus.*' The Secret in R. S. Gerb. Men. belongs to the second Sunday before Christmas; and it appears in Sacr. Gall. as the '*Ad pacem*' of the third Advent *Missa*. The Postcommunion is among the general '*Orationes de Adventu*' in R. S. Gerb., while in Men. it is the '*super Populum*' of the fifth Sunday before Christmas. ² *hii* V.; *hi* R. S. Gerb. Men.   ³ *veniente te* V.   ⁴ *quaesumus Domine* Men.   ⁵ *quaesumus Domine* R. Gerb. Men.   ⁶ *percipiat* V.   ⁷ Here begins the second subsection. The eleven prayers which it contains are all found in S. Gerb. Men. with slight variations. Men. includes all but the first, third, seventh, and last of the series in the '*Orationes de Adv. quotidianis diebus*' : S. Gerb. agree with Men. in placing the first and seventh among the prayers '*in xii Lect.*,' and the last as a Christmas Eve Collect, but divide the rest between the series which are arranged in three *Missae* for daily use, and the series of '*aliae orationes de Adventu.*' R. contains rather fewer of these prayers than S. but agrees with S. as to the position of those which it does contain. ⁸ R. Gerb. Men. insert *nos*; V. S. as text.   ⁹ *quos* R. S. Gerb. Mon.; V. as text.   ¹⁰ Men. omits *nos*.   ¹¹ *respiremur* V.   ¹² *quia* R. S. Gerb. Men.; V. as text.   ¹³ *ex vetusta servitute* (for *ex debito*) R. S. Gerb. Men.; V. as text.   ¹⁴ S² inserts *quaesumus*.   ¹⁵ *diabolicos furores* V. R.; S. Gerb. Men. as text.   ¹⁶ *libera* S² Men.; V. R. S. Gerb. as text.   ¹⁷ *propitiationis* S² Gerb.; V. S¹ Men. as text.   ¹⁸ *conspicis* R. S. Gerb. Men.; V. as text.   ¹⁹ *ex nostram pravitatem* V.   ²⁰ *nulli impediant actus terreni* S. Gerb.; V. Men. as text.   ²¹ *vitae nobis* Men.   ²² *qui* S² Gerb.; V. S¹ Men. as text.   ²³ *mereamur adversitatibus liberari* S² Gerb.; V. S¹ Men. as text.   ²⁴ R. S. Gerb. Men. omit *Filium*.   ²⁵ *suscepimus* R. Gerb. Men.; V. S. as text.

LXXXV.

Orationes et Preces Mensis Decimi¹.

Feria iv.

R.S.(*alibi*.)   Deus, qui conspicis quia in tua pietate confidimus,
Gerb. 202.
Men. 194.   concede propitius ut de caelesti semper protectione gaudeamus. Per.

R.S.(*alibi*.)   Subveniat nobis, Domine, misericordia tua : et ² ab imminentibus peccatorum nostrorum periculis te mereamur
Gerb. 202.
Men. 194.   veniente salvari. Per. γ

Secreta.

R. S.   Ecclesiae tuae, Domine, munera placatus assume, quae
Gerb. 205.
I. xxv   et misericors offerenda tribuisti, et in nostrae salutis potenter
supra.
Leon. 478.   efficis³ transire mysterium. Per.
R.S.(*alibi*.)   •VD. Referentes gratiarum de praeteritis [muneribus⁴] 685
Gerb. 205.   devotionem, promptius quae ventura sunt praestanda confidimus; nec est nobis seminum desperanda fecunditas

quum pro⁵ supplicationibus nostris annua devotione venerandus etiam matris virginis⁶ fructus salutaris intervenit Christus Dominus noster. Quem laudant⁷.

Postcommun.

Tuorum nos, Domine, largitate donorum et temporalibus attolle praesidiis et renova sempiternis⁸. Per. γ

<small>R. S.
Gerb. 206.
I. xviii *supra*. Leon. 479.</small>

Ad Populum.

Esto, Domine, plebi tuae sanctificator et custos: ut beatae Mariae munita praesidiis et conversatione⁹ tibi placeat et secura deserviat. Per Dominum. γ

<small>Cf. Leon. 343.</small>

In sexta Feria.

Huius nobis parsimoniae, quaesumus, Domine, praebe mensuram; ut quod licentiae carnis auferimus salutarem nobis fructum [mentis] acquirat¹⁰. Per.

<small>I. xviii *supra*. Leon. 480.</small>

Deus, qui nostram conspicis semper infirmitatem¹¹ destitui, adventus tui nos visitatione¹² custodi. Per.

<small>S. (*alibi*.) (Gerb.210.) Men. 193.</small>

Adesto¹³, quaesumus, omnipotens Deus, atque in cunctis actionibus nostris et aspirando nos praeveni et adiuvando custodi. Per.

<small>S. (*alibi*.) (Gerb. 210.) Men. 193.</small>

Secreta.

Praesta, Domine, quaesumus, ut dicato muneri congruentem¹⁴ devotionis offeramus affectum¹⁵. Per.

<small>R. S. Gerb. 206. Men. 190.</small>

Postcommun.

Refecti vitalibus alimentis quaesumus, Domine, ut¹⁶ quod tempore nostrae mortalitatis exequimur, immortalitatis tuae munere consequamur. Per. γ

<small>Leon. 482.</small>

Ad Populum.

Respice, Domine, quaesumus¹⁷, propitius ad plebem tuam, et quam divinis tribuis proficere sacramentis, ab omnibus absolve peccatis. Per Dominum nostrum.

<small>Leon. 481.</small>

Sabbato in xii Lectiones.

Adesto, Domine, supplicationibus nostris, et praesentis vota ieiunii placita tibi devotione exhibere concede. Per.

<small>R. S. Gerb. 206.</small>

Converte nos, Deus salutaris noster, et ut nobis ieiunium corporale proficiat, mentes nostras caelestibus institue disciplinis. Per. γ

<small>Cf. Mur. 30.</small>

S.
Gerb. 206.

Deus, qui pro animarum expiatione nostrarum sacri ieiunii instituta mandasti, fragilitati nostrae adiumenta concede; et effectum caelestium mandatorum benignus inspira. Per Dominum.

S.
Gerb. 206.

Miserationum tuarum, Domine, quaesumus, praeveniamur auxilio et in huius solemnitate ieiunii omnium tibi sit devotio grata fidelium. Per.

S. (*alibi.*)
Gerb. 203.
Men. 191.

Preces populi tui, quaesumus, Deus [18], clementer exaudi; ut qui iuste pro peccatis nostris affligimur pietatis tuae visitatione [19] consolemur. Per. γ

Post Benedictionem.

R. S.
Gerb. 207.
Men. 191.

Deus, qui tribus pueris mitigasti flammas ignium, concede, quaesumus, ut nos famulos tuos non exurat flamma vitiorum. Per. γ

Secreta.

R. S.
Gerb. 207.
Men. 191.

Ecclesiae tuae, Domine, munera sanctifica; et concede ut per haec veneranda mysteria pane caelesti refici mereamur. Per.

Postcommun.

R.S.(*alibi.*)
Gerb. 206.
Men. 190.
Leon. 420.

Prosint [20] nobis, Domine, sumpta mysteria, pariterque nos et a peccatis exuant et praesidiis tuae propitiationis attollant. Per.

Ad Populum.

R. S.
Gerb. 207.

Veniat, Domine, quaesumus, populo tuo supplicanti tuae benedictionis infusio, quae diabolicas ab eodem repellat insidias, quae fragilitatem mundet et protegat, quae inopem sustentet et foveat. Per Dominum nostrum Iesum Christum.

Explicit Liber Secundus de Natalitiis Sanctorum Martyrum.

---

[1] The contents of the three *Missae* included in this section correspond pretty closely with the parallel section of R. S. and Gerb. and less exactly with that of Men.; but there are some differences of arrangement. (i) The Collects of the first *Missa* are in R. S. and Gerb. those of a *Missa in quotid. diebus*; in Men. they are among the general Advent prayers. The Secret and Postcommunion are also assigned by R. S. and Gerb. to the same day as in V.; neither of them appears at this point in Men. The preface appears in R. S. and Gerb. for the second Sunday before Christmas. The '*Ad Populum*' is not in R. S. Gerb. or Men. but is found, with a variation, in the Leonine Sacramentary, for the Feast of SS. Peter and Paul. (ii) The first of the three Collects of the Friday *Missa* is found in a *Missa* for this season in the Leonine Sacramentary: it does not appear at this point in R. S. Gerb. or Men.; S. Gerb. Men. place the second and third Collects of the *Missa* among the general Advent prayers, and they, and also R., give to the Secret the same place which it holds in V. The Postcommunion and '*Ad Populum*' occur in separate *Missae* for this season in the Leonine Sacramentary, but are not in the corresponding sections of R. S. Gerb.

or Men. (iii) Of the first five Collects for the Saturday the first, third and fourth are found in the corresponding series in S. and Gerb. (the third and fourth are not contained in R.), and the fifth (which S. and Gerb. place in one of the daily Advent *Missae*) is in the corresponding series in Men. The Collect '*Post Benedictionem*' appears (with the same title) in R. S. and Gerb. (who from this point again follows T. as his principal authority) and also (with the title '*ad Missam*') in Men. The Secret is the same in all: while R. S. and Gerb. also have the same '*Ad Populum*' which appears in V. This does not occur in Men., which agrees with R. S. and Gerb. in assigning the Postcommunion to the Friday of the Embertide, and in giving another for the Saturday. [2] *ut* S² Men.; V. R. S¹ as text. [3] *efficias* V.; R. S. Leon. V. in I. xxv *supra* as text. [4] *muneribus* omitted by V. is restored from R. S. [5] *per* V.; S. omits *pro*. [6] *matri virgine* V.; *matri virginis* R. [7] R. S. have the ending *Per quem maiestatem*. [8] V. has in place of *et renova sempiternis* the last clause of the '*Ad Populum*' which follows (*et conversatione...deserviat*). The true reading is restored from R. S. Leon. and I. xviii above. [9] *conversacio* V. [10] *salvatorem nobis fructum acquirat* V.; Leon. and V. in I. xviii as text. [11] *nos conspicis ex nostra infirmitate* S²; *nostra nos conspicis semper infirmitate* Men. (and apparently S¹); V. as text. [12] *propitiatione* S²; V. S¹ Men. as text. [13] S² Gerb. insert *nobis*; V. S¹ Men. as text. [14] *munere congruentem* V. S.; *munere congruente* R. Gerb.; Men. as text. [15] *effectum* Men. [16] Leon. omits *ut*. [17] Leon. omits *quaesumus*. [18] *Domine* Men.; *omnipotens Deus* S. Gerb. [19] *visitacionis* V. [20] *Prosit* V.

LIBER III.

A + Ω

INCIPIT LIBER TERTIUS.
ORATIONES ET PRECES CUM CANONE PER DOMINICIS DIEBUS*.

I [1].

R. S.
Gerb. 148.
Pam. 405.
Men. 172.

Deus, qui diligentibus te bona invisibilia praeparasti, infunde cordibus nostris tui amoris affectum, ut te in omnibus et super omnia diligentes, promissiones tuas, quae omne desiderium [2] superant, consequamur. Per Dominum nostrum. γ

R. S.
Gerb. 148.

Deus, qui in sanctis habitas, et pia corda non deseris, libera nos a terrenis desideriis et cupiditate carnali; ut, nullo in nobis regnante peccato, tibi soli Domino liberis mentibus serviamus. Per.

Secreta.

R. S.
Gerb. 148.
Pam. 406.
Men. 172.

Propitiare, Domine, supplicationibus nostris, et has oblationes famulorum famularumque tuarum benignus assume; ut quod singuli obtulerunt ad honorem nominis tui, cunctis proficiat ad salutem. Per. γ

Postcommun.

R. S.
Gerb. 148.
Pam. 406.
Men. 172.

Quos caelesti, Domine, dono [3] satiasti, praesta, quaesumus, ut a nostris mundemur occultis, et ab hostium liberemur insidiis. Per Dominum. γ

---

[1] This *Missa* is assigned by R. S. Gerb. to the seventh Sunday after Pentecost, for which Sunday also the first Collect, Secret, and Postcommunion are given in Men. The parallel *Missa* in Pam. is for the sixth Sunday after Pentecost.
[2] *omni desiderio* V. ungrammatically. S¹ Gerb. Pam. Men. as text; R. has *omne desiderio*.   [3] *dona* V.; R. S. Gerb. Pam. Men. as text.

* So V.; Tommasi reads *pro*; but it seems most likely that *Dominicis diebus* is an ungrammatical ablative.

II.

Item alia Missa[1].

Deus virtutum, cuius est totum quod est optimum, insere pectoribus nostris amorem tui nominis, et praesta ut in nobis religionis augmento[2] quae sunt bona[3] nutrias, ac vigilanti studio quae sunt[4] nutrita custodias. Per. ỹ   R. S. Gerb. 149. Pam. 406. Men. 173.

Da nobis, Domine, quaesumus, ut in tua gratia veraciter confidentes et quae digna[5] sunt postulemus et iugiter postulata sumamus. Per.   R. S. Gerb. 149. Leon. 435.

Secreta.

Propitiare, Domine, supplicationibus nostris, et has populi tui oblationes benignus assume[6], ut nullius sit irritum votum et[7] nullius vacua postulatio : [et[8]] praesta, ut quod fideliter petimus, efficaciter consequamur. Per. ỹ   R. S. Gerb. 149. Pam. 406. Men. 173.

Postcommun.

Repleti sumus Domine muneribus tuis; tribue, quaesumus, ut eorum et mundemur effectu[9], et muniamur auxilio. Per. ỹ   R. S. Gerb. 149 Pam. 406. Men. 173. Leon. 379.

[1] In R. S. Gerb. this *Missa* is assigned to the eighth Sunday after Pentecost. The parallel *Missa* in Pam. is that for the seventh, in Men. that for the eighth Sunday. [2] *ut et nobis religionis augmentum* V. (ungrammatically) ; R. S. Gerb. as text ; Pam. Men. have *et praesta in nobis religionis augmentum, ut.* [3] *quae bona sunt* S² Gerb. Pam. Men. ; V. R. S¹ as text. [4] *ac vigilantia studium quaesumus* V.; *ac pietatis gratia quae sunt* S² Gerb. ; *ac pietatis studio quae sunt* Men. ; R. S¹ Pam. as text. [5] *quae te digna* Leon.; V. R. S. Gerb. as text. [6] Pam. Men. insert *et*. [7] S. Gerb. omit *et*. [8] V. Pam. Men. omit *et*, which is restored from R. S. Gerb. [9] *affectu* V. S¹; Leon. S² Gerb. Pam. Men. as text ; R. has *inmundemur effectu.*

III.

Item alia Missa[1].

Deus, cuius providentia in sui[2] dispositione non fallitur, te supplices exoramus, ut noxia cuncta submoveas, et omnia nobis profutura concedas. Per. ỹ   R. S. Gerb. 150. Pam. 407. Men. 173.

Custodi nos, Domine, quaesumus, in tuo servitio constitutos, ut[3] quibus famulatum esse vis sincere[4] propitius largire quod praecepisti. Per.   R. S. Gerb. 150.

Secreta.

Deus, qui legalium differentias hostiarum[5] unius sacrificii perfectione sanxisti, accipe sacrificium [a[6]] devotis tibi   R. S. Gerb. 150. Pam. 407. Men. 174.

famulis, et pari benedictione sicut munera Abel iusti[7] sanctifica; ut quod singuli obtulerunt ad maiestatis tuae honorem, cunctis proficiat ad salutem. Per. γ

Postcommun.

S. (*alibi*.)
Gerb. 232.
Pam. 417.

Quotidiani[8], Domine, quaesumus, munere sacramenti perpetuae nobis tribue salutis augmentum. Per Dominum. γ

[1] This *Missa* (except the Postcommunion) is assigned by R. S. Gerb. to the ninth Sunday after Pentecost: see the *Missa* for the eighth Sunday in Pam., and that for the ninth in Men. [2] *sua* R. (originally) S[2] Gerb.; V. S[1] Pam. Men. as text. [3] *et* S. Gerb; V. R. as text (ungrammatically). [4] *sencerē* S; *sincerum* Gerb.; V. R. as text (*famulatum esse* being used as a passive impersonal). [5] S[2] Gerb. insert *in*. [6] V. omits *a*; R. S. Gerb. Pam. Men. as text. [7] R. S. Gerb. Pam. Men. omit *iusti*. [8] *Cotidianis* V.

IV.   689

Item alia Missa[1].

R. S.
Gerb. 151.
Pam. 407.
Men. 174.
Leon. 434.

Largire nobis, Domine, quaesumus, semper[2] spiritum cogitandi quae recta sunt propitius[3] et agendi; ut qui sine te esse non possumus, secundum te vivere[4] valeamus. Per. γ

R. S.
Gerb. 151.
Pam. 379.
Leon. 437.

Concede, quaesumus, omnipotens Deus, ut viam tuam devota mente currentes, subripientium delictorum laqueos evadamus. Per. γ

Secreta.

R. S.
Gerb. 151.
Pam. 407.
Men. 174.

Suscipe munera, quaesumus, Domine, quae tibi de tua largitate deferimus; ut[5] haec sacrosancta mysteria, gratiae tuae operante virtute, [6] praesentis vitae nos conversatione sanctificent, et ad gaudia sempiterna perducant. Per. γ

Postcommun.

R. S.
Gerb. 151.
Pam. 407.
Leon. 372.

Sit nobis, Domine, reparatio mentis et corporis caeleste mysterium; ut[7] cuius exequimur actionem sentiamus effectum[8]. Per. γ

[1] This *Missa* is given in R. S. Gerb. for the tenth Sunday after Pentecost: see the *Missa* for the ninth Sunday in Pam. and that for the tenth Sunday in Men. [2] Leon. omits *semper*. [3] *promptius* Leon. [4] *quaerere* V.; R. S. Gerb. Pam. Men. as text. [5] *et* Pam. [6] S[2] Gerb. insert *in*; Men. inserts *et*; V. R. S[1] Pam. as text. [7] *et* Leon. [8] *affectum* V. R. S[1]; Leon. S[2] Gerb. Pam. as text.

V.

Item alia Missa[1].

R. S.
Gerb. 155.
Men. 175.

Praesta, quaesumus, omnipotens et misericors Deus, ut inter huius vitae caligines nec[2] ignorantia fallente mergamur, nec praecipiti studeamus voluntate peccare; sed cui³ fiduciam⁴ sperandae pietatis indulges, optatae⁵ misericordiae praesta benignus effectum. Per.

Pateant aures misericordiae, Domine, precibus supplicantium; et ut⁶ petentibus desiderata concedas, fac tibi eos, quaesumus, placita⁷ postulare. Per. γ

R. S.
Gerb. 155.
Pam. 408.

Secreta.

Concede nobis haec, quaesumus, Domine, frequentare mysteria; quia quoties huius hostiae commemoratio celebratur⁸, opus nostrae redemptionis exercetur⁸. Per. γ

R. S.
Gerb. 155.
Pam. 408.
Men. 175.

Postcommun.

Quaesumus, Domine Deus noster, ut quos divinis reparare non desinis sacramentis, tuis non destituas benignus auxiliis. Per. γ

R S.(*alibi.*)
Gerb. 160.
Pam. 408.
Men. 176.
vi *infra*.

¹ The two Collects and the Secret of this *Missa* are assigned by R. S. Gerb. to the eleventh Sunday after Pentecost. See the *Missa* for the tenth Sunday in Pam., and that for the eleventh Sunday in Men. The Postcommunion appears again in the next *Missa*, and has probably been inserted here by a mistake of the scribe. A marginal note in S. appears to direct the transposition of the two Collects: and in Gerb. they are transposed. Men. has as the Collect that which stands first, Pam. that which stands second, in V. R. and S. ² *non* V.; *ne* S¹; R. S² Gerb. Men. as text. ³ *quibus* Gerb. Men. ⁴ *fiducia* V. R.; S. as text. ⁵ *optatuae* V. ⁶ *ut et* V. S¹; R. S² Gerb. Pam. as text. ⁷ *fac eos quaesumus tibi placita* S² Gerb.; V. R. (S¹?) Pam. as text (*fac eos tibi quae sunt placita* S. marg.). ⁸ *caelebratum ... exercitum* V.

VI.

ITEM ALIA MISSA¹.

Deus, qui omnipotentiam tuam parcendo maxime et miserando² manifestas, multiplica super nos gratiam tuam; ut ad tua promissa currentes caelestium honorum facias esse consortes. Per. γ

R. S.
Gerb. 159.
Pam. 408.
Men. 175.

Secreta.

Tibi, Domine, sacrificia dicata reddantur, quae sic ad honorem nominis tui deferenda tribuisti, ut eadem remedia fieri nostra praestares. Per. γ

R. S.
Gerb. 160.
Pam. 408.
Men. 176.

Postcommun.

Quaesumus, Domine Deus noster, ut quos divinis reparare non desinis sacramentis, tuis non destituas benignus auxiliis. Per. γ

R. S.
Gerb. 160.
Pam. 408.
Men. 176.
v *supra*.

¹ This *Missa* (with a second Collect, omitted by V.) is given by R. S. Gerb., for the twelfth Sunday after Pentecost: see the *Missa* for the eleventh Sunday in Pam., and that for the twelfth Sunday in Men. ² *miserendo* S² Gerb.; V. R. S¹ Pam. Men. as text.

VII.

ITEM ALIA MISSA[1].

R. S.
Gerb. 164.
Pam. 409.
Men. 176.

Omnipotens sempiterne Deus, qui abundantia[2] pietatis tuae et merita supplicum excedis et vota, effunde super nos misericordiam tuam, ut dimittas quae conscientia metuit, et adiicias quod oratio[3] non praesumit. Per. y

R. S.
Gerb. 164.
cf. lvi *infra*.

Omnipotens sempiterne Deus[4] a quo sola[5] sancta desideria, recta consilia, et iusta sunt opera, da servis tuis illam, quam mundus dare non potest, pacem; ut et corda nostra mandatis tuis dedita, et tempora sint tua protectione tranquilla. Per. y

Secreta.

R. S.
Gerb. 164.
Pam. 409.
Men. 176.
Leon. 448.

Respice, Domine, quaesumus[6], nostram propitius servitutem; ut quod offerimus sit tibi munus acceptum, sit nostrae fragilitatis[7] subsidium. Per. y

Postcommun.

R. S.
Gerb. 164.
Pam. 409.
Men. 177.
Leon. 378.

Sentiamus, Domine, quaesumus, tui perceptione[8] sacramenti subsidium mentis et corporis, ut in utroque salvati[9] caelestis remedii plenitudine gloriemur. Per. y

[1] This *Missa* is assigned by R. S. Gerb. to the thirteenth Sunday after Pentecost: see the *Missa* for the twelfth Sunday in Pam., and that for the thirteenth Sunday in Men. [2] *habundantiam* V. [3] *oratione* Pam. [4] This Collect occurs in a somewhat different form in the *Missa pro Pace* (lvi *infra*). [5] *solo* S² Gerb.; V. R. S¹ as text. [6] *quaesumus Domine* Leon. [7] *fragilitati* Leon. Pam.; V. R. S. Gerb. Men. as text. [8] *perceptionem* V.; R. S. Gerb. Pam. Men. Leon. as text. [9] Leon. inserts *de*.

VIII.   691

ITEM ALIA MISSA[1].

R. S.
Gerb. 168.
Men. 177.

Omnipotens sempiterne Deus, per quem coepit esse quod non erat, et factum est visibile quod latebat, stultitiam[2] nostri cordis emunda, et quae in nobis sunt vitiorum secreta purifica: ut possimus tibi Domino[3] pura mente servire. Per.

R. S.
Gerb. 168.
Pam. 409.
Men. 177.
Leon. 371.

Omnipotens et misericors Deus, de cuius munere venit, ut tibi a fidelibus tuis digne et laudabiliter serviatur, tribue, quaesumus, nobis[4], ut ad promissiones tuas[5] sine offensione curramus. Per. y

Secreta.

Hostias, quaesumus, Domine, propitius intende⁶, quas sacris altaribus exhibemus: ut nobis indulgentiam largiaris⁷, tuo nomini dent honorem. Per. y

R. S.
Gerb, 168.
Pam. 409.

Postcommun.

Vivificet nos, quaesumus, Domine, huius participatio⁸ sancta mysterii, et pariter nobis expiationem tribuat et munimen. Per. y

R. S.
Gerb. 168.
Pam. 409.
Men. 177.
Leon. 356.

¹ This *Missa* is assigned in R. S. Gerb. to the fourteenth Sunday after Pentecost: see the *Missa* for the thirteenth Sunday in Pam. and that for the fourteenth Sunday in Men.   ² *stulticia* V.   ³ *Domine* V.; *Deo* R.; S. Gerb. Men. as text.   ⁴ Leon. omits *quaesumus nobis*.   ⁵ *a promissionibus tuis* V.   ⁶ *inte* V.   ⁷ *largiendo* R. S. Gerb. Pam.; V. as text.   ⁸ *Domine participatio tui* Leon.

IX.

ITEM ALIA MISSA¹.

Omnipotens sempiterne Deus, da nobis fidei, spei, et caritatis augmentum; et ut mereamur assequi quod promittis, fac nos amare quod praecipis. Per. y

R. S.
Gerb. 170.
Pam. 410.
Men. 170.
Leon. 374.

Omnipotens sempiterne Deus, fac nos tibi semper et devotam gerere voluntatem, et maiestati tuae² sincero corde servire. Per. y

R. S.
Gerb. 170.
I. lxi *supra*.

Secreta.

Oblatio nos, Domine, tuo nomini dicata purificet, et de die in diem ad caelestis vitae transferat actionem. Per. y

I. lxi *supra*.

Postcommun.

Sumptis, Domine, caelestibus sacramentis, ad redemptionis aeternae, quaesumus, proficiant³ augmentum. Per. y

R. S.
Gerb. 171.
Pam. 410.
II. xlv, liv *supra*.

¹ This *Missa* (except the Secret) is assigned in R. S. Gerb. to the fifteenth Sunday after Pentecost: see the *Missa* for the fourteenth Sunday in Pam., and that for the fifteenth Sunday in Men.   ² *maiestatem tuam* V. here; R. S. Gerb. V. in lxi *supra* as text.   ³ *proficiat* V. S¹; R. as text; Sᵗ Gerb. Pam. have *proficiamus*, which gives a clearer sense; V. also has *proficiamus* in II. xlv *supra*, and in II. liv *supra*, being supported in the latter case by S¹.

X.

ITEM ALIA MISSA¹.

Custodi, Domine, quaesumus, ecclesiam tuam propitiatione perpetua; et, quia sine te labitur humana² mortalitas, tuis semper auxiliis et³ abstrahatur a noxiis et ad salutaria dirigatur. Per. y

R. S.
Gerb. 173.
Pam. 410.
Men. 178.

R. S.
Gerb. 173.
I. xxv
supra.

Praesta nobis, misericors Deus, ut placationem tuam promptis mentibus exoremus, et peccatorum veniam consequentes, a noxiis liberemur incursibus. Per.

Secreta.

R. S.
Gerb. 173.
Fam. 410.
xli infra.

Concede nobis, Domine, quaesumus, ut haec hostia salutaris et nostrorum fiat purgatio delictorum, et tuae propitiatio potestatis. Per. γ

[Postcommun.⁴]

xxxvi
infra.

Purificent nos, Domine, sacramenta quae sumpsimus, et a cunctis efficiant vitiis absolutos. Per. γ

Postcommun.

R.S.(alibi.)
Gerb. 139.
Pam. 405.
Men. 171.
xl infra.

Sancta tua nos, Domine, sumpta vivificent, et misericordiae sempiternae praeparent⁵ expiatos. Per. γ

¹ The Collects and Secret of this *Missa* are assigned by R. S. Gerb. to the sixteenth Sunday after Pentecost: see the *Missa* for the fifteenth Sunday in Pam., and that for the sixteenth Sunday in Men.   ² *universa* Pam.   ³ Pam. omits *et*.   ⁴ V. gives to this prayer the title *Secreta*, but its contents show that this is an error of the scribe.   ⁵ *reparent* R.

XI.

Item alia Missa¹.

R. S.
Gerb. 175.
Pam. 411.
Men. 179.

Ecclesiam tuam, Domine, miseratio continuata mundet et muniat; et quia sine te non potest salva consistere, tuo semper munere gubernetur. Per. γ

R. S.
Gerb. 175.

Da, quaesumus, Domine, hanc mentem populo tuo, ut quia² ad te placandum necessitate concurrit, maiestati tuae fiat etiam voluntate devotus. Per.

Secreta.

R. S.
Gerb. 175.
Pam. 411.
Men. 179.

Tua nos, Domine, sacramenta custodiant, et contra diabolicos tueantur semper incursus. Per. γ

Postcommun.

R. S.
Gerb. 175.
Pam. 411.
Men. 179.

Mentes nostras et corpora possideat, Domine, quaesumus, doni caelestis operatio; ut non noster sensus in nobis, sed³ iugiter eius praeveniat⁴ effectus. Per. γ

¹ This *Missa* is assigned by R. S. Gerb. to the seventeenth Sunday after Pentecost: see the *Missa* for the sixteenth Sunday in Pam., and that for the seventeenth Sunday in Men.   ² *qui* S¹ Gerb.; V. R. S¹ as text.   ³ *sunt* V. (corrected by Tommasi); R. S. Gerb. Pam. Men. as text.   ⁴ *iugiter aevi praeveniat* Pam.; *iugiter eius proveniat* S¹ Gerb.; V. R. S¹ Men. as text.

XII.

Item alia Missa[1].

Fac nos[2], Domine, quaesumus, prompta voluntate subiectos, et ad supplicandum tibi[3] nostras semper excita voluntates. Per.

R. S.
Gerb. 184.
Men. 181.

Fac nos, Domine, quaesumus, tuis[4] obedire mandatis, quia tunc nobis prospera cuncta provenient[5], si[6] totius vitae sequamur auctorem. Per. γ

Pam. 383.
Men. 200.

Secreta.

Munda nos, Domine, sacrificii[7] praesentis effectu, et perfice miseratus in nobis, ut eius mereamur esse participes. Per. γ

R. S.
Gerb. 184.
Pam. 411.
Men. 181.

Postcommun.

Purifica, Domine, quaesumus, mentes nostras benignus, et renova caelestibus sacramentis, ut consequenter et corporum praesens pariter et futurum capiamus auxilium. Per. γ

R. S.
Gerb. 184.
Pam. 411.
Men. 181.
l. l. *supra*.

[1] The first Collect, Secret, and Postcommunion of this *Missa* are assigned by R. S. Gerb. Men. to the twentieth Sunday after Pentecost. In Pam. the Secret and Postcommunion, with the second Collect given by R. S. Gerb. for the twentieth Sunday, form parts of the *Missa* for the seventeenth Sunday. R. S. and Gerb. place between the *Missa* cited for the last section and that for the twentieth Sunday a *Missa* for the Sunday of the September Embertide, and one for the 'Vacant' Sunday, which partly agree with those for the eighteenth and nineteenth Sundays in Men. [2] S² Gerb. Men. insert *tibi*; V. R. S¹ as text. [3] *maiestati tuae* S² Gerb.; V. R. (S¹ ?), Men. as text. [4] *Domine Deus noster tuis* Pam. Men. [5] *prǫveniant* V.; *proveniunt* Pam.; Men. as text. [6] Pam. Men. insert *te*. [7] *sacrificiis* V. (S¹ ?); R. has *sacrificiis presentis affectum*; S² Gerb. Pam. Men. as text.

XIII.

Item alia Missa[1].

Da, quaesumus, Domine, populo tuo diabolica vitare contagia, et te solum Dominum[2] puro corde[3] sectari. Per. γ

R. S.
Gerb. 185.
Pam. 412.
Men. 182.

Custodi nos, omnipotens Deus, ut tua dextera gubernante nec nostra nobis praevaleant nec aliena peccata. Per.

R. S.
Gerb. 185.

Secreta.

Maiestatem tuam, Domine, suppliciter deprecamur, ut haec sancta quae gerimus et[4] praeteritis nos delictis exuant et futuris. Per. γ

R. S.
Gerb. 185.
Pam. 412.
Men. 182.

Postcommun.

R.S.(*alibi.*)
Gerb. 90.
I. xlv
supra.

Praesta, quaesumus, omnipotens Deus, ut divino munere satiati et sacris mysteriis innovemur et moribus. Per.

[1] The two Collects and Secret of this *Missa* are assigned by R. S. Gerb. to the twenty-first Sunday after Pentecost, for which Men. also gives the first Collect and the Secret: see the *Missa* for the eighteenth Sunday in Pam. [2] *Deum* S¹ Gerb.; V. R. S¹ Pam. Men. as text. [3] *pura mente* Pam. [4] Pam. inserts *a*, which R. has in place of *et*.

XIV.

ITEM ALIA MISSA[1].

R. S.
Gerb. 186.
Pam. 412.
Men. 182.

Dirigat corda nostra, Domine, quaesumus, tua miserationis operatio, quia tibi sine te placere non possumus. Per. γ

R. S.
Gerb. 186.
I. xxv
supra.

Tuis, Domine, quaesumus, adesto supplici·bus; et inter mundanae pravitatis insidias fragilitatem nostram sempiterna pietate[2] prosequere. Per.

694

Secreta.

R. S.
Gerb. 186.
Pam. 412.
Men. 182.
I. lix *supra.*

Deus, qui nos per huius sacrificii veneranda commercia unius summaeque divinitatis participes effecisti[3], praesta, quaesumus, ut sicut tuam cognoscimus[4] veritatem, sic eam[4] dignis moribus et mentibus[5] assequamur. Per. γ

Postcommun.

R. S.
Gerb. 186.
Pam. 412.
Men. 183.
I. xciii
supra.

Gratias tibi referimus, Domine[6], sacro munere vegetati, tuam misericordiam deprecantes, ut dignos eius nos[7] participatione perficias. Per. γ

[1] This *Missa* is assigned by R. S. Gerb. to the twenty-second Sunday after Pentecost: see the *Missa* for that Sunday in Men., and that for the nineteenth Sunday in Pam. [2] *sempiternam pietatem* V. here; R. S. Gerb. V. in I. xxv *supra* as text. [3] *efficis* R. S. Gerb. Pam. Men.; V. here and in I. lix *supra*, as text. [4] *ut et tuam cognoscamus . . . et eam* Men.; V. R. S. Gerb. Pam. as text (V. in I. lix *supra* has *cognovimus*). [5] *mentibus ac moribus* Pam. Men.; V. in I. lix omits *et mentibus*; V. here, R. S. Gerb. as text. [6] *Domine referimus* R. Pam. [7] *nos eius* Gerb. Pam. Men.; R. omits *nos*; V. S. as text.

XV.

ITEM ALIA MISSA[1].

R. S.
Gerb. 188.
Pam. 413.
Men. 183.

Omnipotens et misericors Deus, universa nobis adversantia propitiatus[2] exclude; ut, mente et corpore pariter expediti, quae tua sunt liberis mentibus exequamur. Per. γ

Da, quaesumus, omnipotens Deus, sic nos tuam³ veniam⁴ promereri ut nostros corrigamus excessus; sic fatentibus⁵ relaxare delictum ut coerceamus in suis pravitatibus obstinatos. Per.

R. S.
Gerb. 188.
Men. 183.

Secreta.

Haec munera, quaesumus, Domine, quae oculis tuae maiestatis offerimus, salutaria nobis esse concede. Per. γ

R. S.
Gerb. 188.
Pam. 413.

Postcommun.

Quaesumus, omnipotens Deus, ut munere divino⁶ quod sumpsimus salutari nobis prosit effectu. Per.

R. (*alibi.*)
Gerb. 238.

> ¹ The two Collects and the Secret of this *Missa* are assigned by R. S. Gerb. to the twenty-third Sunday after Pentecost: Men. gives for the same Sunday the first Collect, converting the second into the Secret: Pam. has the first Collect and the Secret in the *Missa* for the twentieth Sunday. The Postcommunion appears below in the series of collected Postcommunions, and has the same position in R.: S. does not now contain this series. ² *propriationis* V.; R. S. Gerb. Pam. Men. as text. ³ *sic nostram* V. S.; R. Gerb. as text, supported by Men. which has *sic nos sacris muneribus tuam*. ⁴ *indulgentiam* S² Gerb.; V. R. S¹ Men. as text. ⁵ *confitentibus* S² Gerb.; V. R. S¹ Men. as text. ⁶ *munere divino*, so V. (here and in the Postcommunions which follow the *Canon Actionis*) and R.: Tommasi reads *munus divinum*, but the reading of V. and R. is not necessarily ungrammatical.

XVI.

Item alia Missa¹.

Largire, quaesumus, Domine, fidelibus tuis indulgentiam placatus et pacem; ut pariter ab omnibus mundentur offensis, [et secura]² tibi mente deserviant. Per. γ

R. S.
Gerb. 190.
Pam. 413.
Men. 184.

Delicta nostra, Domine, quibus adversa³ dominantur absterge, et tua nos ubique miseratione custodi. Per. γ

R. S.
Gerb. 190.

Secreta.

Caelestem nobis praebeant haec mysteria, quaesumus, Domine, medicinam, et vitia nostri cordis expurgent. Per. γ

R. S.
Gerb. 190.
Pam. 413.
Men. 184.

Postcommun.

Auxilientur nobis, Domine, sumpta mysteria, et sempiterna protectione confirment. Per. γ

R.S.(*alibi.*)
Gerb. 8.
Pam. 189.
Men. 10.

> ¹ The two Collects and the Secret of this *Missa* are assigned by R. S. Gerb. to the twenty-fourth Sunday after Pentecost, for which Men. gives the first Collect and the Secret. Pam. has the first Collect and the Secret for the twenty-first Sunday. The Postcommunion appears, with an inserted clause, in the *Missa* for S. Stephen's Day in R. S. Gerb. Pam. Men. ² V. omits *et secura* which is restored from R. S. Gerb. Pam. Men. ³ S² Gerb. insert *nobis*; V. R. S¹ as text.

INCIPIT CANON ACTIONIS[1].

Sursum corda[2].

Resp. Habemus ad Dominum.

Gratias agamus Domino Deo nostro.

Resp. Dignum et iustum est.

R. S.
Miss. Franc.
Sacr. Gall.
VD. et iustum est[3] aequum et salutare[4], nos tibi semper et ubique gratias agere, Domine sancte, Pater omnipotens, aeterne Deus, per Christum Dominum nostrum. Per quem maiestatem tuam laudant angeli, adorant dominationes, tremunt[5] potestates, caeli caelorumque virtutes, ac beata Seraphin socia exultatione concelebrant: cum quibus et nostras voces ut admitti iubeas deprecamur, supplici confessione dicentes: Sanctus, Sanctus, Sanctus[6], Dominus Deus Sabaoth. Pleni sunt caeli et terra gloria tua. Osanna in excelsis. Benedictus qui venit in nomine Domini. Osanna in excelsis. Te igitur clementissime Pater per Iesum Christum Filium tuum Dominum nostrum supplices rogamus et[7] petimus uti accepta habeas et benedicas ✠ haec ✠ dona, haec ✠ munera, haec ✠ sancta sacrificia illi✠bata[8]. Inprimis quae tibi offerimus pro ecclesia tua sancta catholica[9], quam pacificare, custodire, adunare et regere digneris toto orbe[10] terrarum, una cum famulo tuo papa nostro *Illo* et antistite nostro *Illo* episcopo[11]. Memento[12], Domine, famulorum famularumque tuarum, et omnium circumadstantium, quorum tibi fides cog·nita est, et nota devotio, qui tibi offerunt hoc sacrificium laudis pro se suisque omnibus, pro redemptione animarum suarum, pro spe salutis et incolumitatis suae[13], tibi reddunt vota sua aeterno Deo vero et vivo. Communicantes[14] et memoriam venerantes inprimis gloriosae semperque[15] virginis Mariae genitricis Dei et Domini nostri Iesu Christi, sed et beatorum[16] apostolorum ac martyrum tuorum Petri et[17] Pauli, Andreae, Iacobi, Ioannis, Thomae[18], Iacobi, Philippi, Bartholomaei, Matthaei, Simonis et Thaddaei, Lini, Cleti[19], Clementis, Xysti[20], Cornelii, Cypriani, Laurentii, Chrysogoni, Ioannis et Pauli, Cosmae et Damiani, [Dionysii, Rustici], et Eleutherii, [Hilarii, Martini, Augustini, Gregorii, Hieronymi, Benedicti][21] et omnium sanctorum tuorum[22], quorum meritis precibusque concedas ut in omnibus protectionis tuae muniamur auxilio[23]. Per Christum Do-

minum nostrum. Hanc igitur oblationem servitutis nostrae, sed et cunctae familiae tuae [24], quaesumus, Domine, ut [25] placatus accipias [26], diesque nostros in tua pace disponas [27], atque ab aeterna damnatione nos eripi [28] et in electorum tuorum iubeas grege numerari. Per Christum Dominum nostrum. Quam oblationem [29] tu, Deus, in omnibus, quaesumus, benedictam, adscriptam, ratam, rationabilem, acceptabilemque facere digneris, ut [30] nobis corpus et sanguis fiat dilectissimi Filii tui Domini Dei nostri [31] Iesu Christi. Qui pridie quam pateretur accepit [32] panem in sanctas [33] ac venerabiles manus suas [34], elevatis oculis [35] in caelum [36] ad te Deum Patrem suum omnipotentem, tibi gratias agens [37], benedixit, fregit, dedit discipulis [38] suis, dicens, Accipite et manducate ex hoc omnes. Hoc est enim [39] corpus meum. Simili modo, posteaquam [40] coenatum est, accipiens [32] et hunc praeclarum calicem in sanctas ac [41] venerabiles manus suas, item tibi gratias agens, benedixit, dedit discipulis suis [42], dicens, Accipite et bibite ex eo [43] omnes : hic est enim calix sanguinis mei novi et [44] aeterni testamenti, mysterium fidei, qui pro vobis et pro multis effundetur [45] in remissionem [46] peccatorum. Haec quotiescumque feceritis in mei memoriam facietis [47]. Unde [48] et memores sumus [49], Domine, nos tui servi, sed et plebs tua sancta, Christi Filii tui Domini Dei [50] nostri tam beatae passionis necnon et ab inferis resurrectionis, sed et in caelis gloriosae [51] ascensionis: offerimus praeclarae maiestati [52] tuae de tuis donis ac datis hostiam puram, hostiam sanctam, hostiam immaculatam, panem sanctum vitae aeternae et calicem salutis perpetuae [53]. Supra quae propitio ac sereno vultu respicere [54] digneris [55], et accepta [56] habere, sicuti accepta [56] habere dignatus es munera pueri tui iusti Abel, et sacrificium patriarchae nostri Abrahae, et quod tibi obtulit summus sacerdos tuus Melchisedech, sanctum sacrificium, immaculatam hostiam. Supplices te rogamus, omnipotens Deus, iube haec perferri per manus [57] angeli tui in sublime altare tuum [58] in conspectu divinae maiestatis tuae, ut quotquot ex hac [59] altaris participatione sacrosanctum Filii tui corpus et sanguinem sumpserimus omni benedictione [60] caelesti et [61] gratia repleamur. Per Christum Dominum nostrum. Amen [62].

Nobis quoque peccatoribus, famulis tuis, de multitudine

miserationum tuarum sperantibus, partem aliquam societatis [63] donare digneris [64] cum tuis sanctis apostolis et martyribus, cum Ioanne, Stephano, Matthia [65], Barnaba [66], Ignatio, Alexandro, Marcellino, Petro, Felicitate, Perpetua, Agathe, Lucia, Agne [67], Caecilia, Anastasia [68] et cum omnibus sanctis tuis, intra quorum nos consortium [69] non aestimator meriti, sed veniae, quaesumus, largitor [70] admitte. Per Christum Dominum nostrum. Per quem haec omnia, Domine, semper bona creas, sanctificas, vivificas, benedicis, et praestas nobis. Per ipsum, et cum ipso, et in ipso est tibi Deo Patri omnipotenti in unitate Spiritus sancti omnis honor et gloria, per omnia saecula saeculorum. Amen [71].

OREMUS.

Praeceptis salutaribus moniti et divina institutione formati, audemus dicere [72]:

Pater noster qui es in caelis. Sed libera nos a malo [73].

Libera nos, quaesumus, Domine, ab omnibus malis praeteritis, praesentibus, et futuris [74], et intercedente pro nobis [75] beata et gloriosa semperque [76] virgine Dei genitrice [77] Maria, et sanctis apostolis tuis [78] Petro et Paulo, atque Andrea [79], da propitius pacem in diebus nostris, ut ope [80] misericordiae tuae adiuti, et a peccatis [81] simus liberi semper [82], et ab omni perturbatione securi. Per.

Pax Domini sit semper vobiscum [83].

Resp. Et cum Spiritu tuo.

R. S.
Gerb. 238.   *Post haec* [84] *commonenda est* [85] *plebs pro ieiunii* [86] *quarti septimi et decimi mensis temporibus suis, sive pro scrutiniis* [87], *vel aurium apertionum, sive orandum pro infirmis vel ad nuntiandum* [88] *natalitia sanctorum. Post haec communicat sacerdos cum ordinibus sacris,* [89] *cum omni populo.*

Postcommun.

R.
Gerb. 238.   Quos caelesti, Domine, alimento satiasti, apostolicis intercessionibus ab omni nos, quaesumus, adversitate custodi. Per Dominum. y

R.
Gerb. 238.   Laeti, Domine, sumpsimus sacramenta caelestia: [90] intercedente pro nobis beata et gloriosa semperque virgine Dei genitrice Maria, ad vitam nobis [91] proficiant sempiternam. Per.

Augeatur in nobis, Domine, quaesumus, tuae virtutis R.
operatio; ut, divinis vegetati sacramentis, ad eorum promissa Gerb. 238.
capienda tuo munere praeparemur. Per. γ

Omnipotens Deus, fac nos [92] tibi semper devotam gerere R.
voluntatem, [et] [93] maiestati tuae sincero corde famulari. Gerb. 238.
Per. γ

Mysteria nos, Domine, sancta purificent, et suo munere R.
tueantur. Per. γ Gerb. 238.

Quos tantis, Domine, largiris uti mysteriis, quaesumus ut R.
effectibus nos eorum veraciter aptare digneris. Per. γ Gerb. 238.

Mensa tua nos, Deus [94], a delectationibus terrenis expe- R.
diat, et caelestibus semper instruat [95] alimentis. Per. γ Gerb. 238.

Tui nobis, Domine, communio sacramenti et purifica- R.
tionem conferat, et tribuat unitatem. Per. γ Gerb. 238.

Tua sancta nobis, omnipotens Deus, et indulgentiam R.
praebeant, et auxilium perpetuae defensionis impendant. Gerb. 238.
Per. γ

699 •Tua nos, Domine, medicinalis operatio et a nostris R.
perversitatibus clementer expediat, et tuis faciat semper Gerb. 238.
inhaerere mandatis. Per. γ xxii *infra*.

Purificent semper et muniant tua sacramenta nos, Deus [94], R.
et ad perpetuae ducant salvationis effectum. Per. γ Gerb. 238.

Quaesumus, omnipotens Deus, ut munere divino [96] quod R.
sumpsimus salutari nobis prosit effectu. Per. Gerb. 238.
  xv *supra*.

---

[1] The *Canon Actionis* and the appended series of Postcommunions seem to stand, in V., outside the numbered sections, being placed between xvi, which is the last of the series of Sunday *Missae*, and the series of Benedictions, which forms a kind of additional appendage to the Canon. In R. and S. the *Canon Actionis* is inserted after the Secret of a *Missa in quotidianis diebus* (the last of a series corresponding to that which in V. follows after the Canon, in the sections numbered xviii-xxiii); but while S, after the close of the Canon, completes the *Missa* by the addition of two forms of Postcommunion, R. gives the series of Postcommunions which in V. follow the Canon, but which S. omits. At the end of this series, in Gerbert's text, appear the two Postcommunions from S., which are not contained in R. The text of the Canon as it appears in V. has here been compared with R. and S. and also with two other texts of a date certainly earlier than 800, those contained in the Sacramentarium Gallicanum and the Missale Francorum. Gerbert's text, while professing to follow R., shows some differences from the readings of that MS., and still more from those of S[1]. He has perhaps been influenced by other authorities. The text here given follows V. throughout, except in the matter of spelling, and a few corrections which are noted below.   [2] Gerb. prints before *Sursum corda* the salutation *Dominus vobiscum* and the response *Et cum spiritu tuo*, but notes the fact that they are not contained in R.: they are also omitted by S., and by Miss. Franc., while Sacr. Gall. omits all before *Vere dignum*.   [3] R. omits *et iustum est*.   [4] Miss. Franc. inserts *est*.
[5] *tremenl* S[1].   [6] Sacr. Gall. and Miss. Franc. both abbreviate the *Sanctus*.

In the former it is not written beyond *Sanctus, Sanctus*; in the latter not beyond *Deus Sabaoth*. [7] *ac* Sacr. Gall. [8] No crosses are marked at this point in R., or in Miss. Franc.; S. has *three* (over the words *dona, munera, sacrificia*); but they are perhaps a later addition. Sacr. Gall. has *one*, between the words *benedicas* and *haec*. [9] *pro tua sancta catholica ecclesia* Miss. Franc. [10] *totum orbem* Sacr. Gall. [11] R. S. omit *episcopo*. In S. there is a mark referring to the margin, after the words *antistite nostro Illo*. This has been supposed to refer to some words written at the bottom of the page, but these are not preceded by any mark corresponding to that in the body of the text. It seems clear that the additional words added for insertion at this point, to which the mark refers, were written at the top of the page, where the lower part of the letters, preceded by the reference mark, can still be traced, though the upper part has been trimmed away. The words seem to have been *et omnibus orthodoxi atque apostolicę fidei cultoribus*. A similar addition may be seen in V. where above *papa nostro illo* in one line, and above the Memento which follows *antistite nostro illo episcopo* in the next, certain *notae Tironianae* have been written between the lines of the original scribe. These have been interpreted by M. Julien Havet, who considers the first of the additions to represent the word *superscribenda*, and reads the second as follows: ' *Et omnibus orthodoxis atque catholici fide cultoribus. Memento, Deus, rege nostro cum omni populo.*' (See the third of the Plates accompanying M. Léopold Delisle's *Mémoire sur d'Anciens Sacramentaires*, and the explanatory note, p. 5.) As M. Delisle remarks, the Latinity of this insertion belongs to the Merovingian period: it might be paralleled from other parts of the MS., but is exceptional in this portion, for in the Canon the proportion of grammatical blunders is smaller than in the rest of the MS. Sacr. Gall. and Miss. Franc. show more variation: the former has *una cum devotissimo* (this word has been elided) *famulo tuo ill. papa nostro sedis apostolicae, et antistite nostro ill. et omnibus orthodoxis atque catholicae et apostolicae fidei cultoribus*. In Miss. Franc. there is no mention of the Pope or the Bishop, and the clause runs *una cum omnibus orthodoxis atque apostolicae fidei cultoribus*. [12] At this point would be inserted the additional words which appear, as already stated, at the bottom of the page in S. The words in question are written in red, in uncial character,—*Memento Domine famuli tui Remedii episcopi et*; if they are not actually by the original hand, they are by one almost of the same date. The Remedius referred to is no doubt the Bishop who occupied the see of Chur in the first years of the ninth century: he is perhaps mentioned here in his character of a temporal governor, in which case the insertion will be closely parallel to the latter part of the insertion, already noted, in V. [13] R. inserts *Memento etiam Domine et animabus famulorum famularumque tuarum fidelium catholicorum in Christo quiescentium, qui nos praecesserunt, illorum et illarum, qui per eleemosynam et confessionem*. The clause is evidently not an addition by a later hand, but (at least as it now stands) apparently an integral part of the Canon. It may, of course, have been a marginal addition to the MS. from which R. was copied. [14] Sacr. Gall. inserts at this point the variants for the seasons of Christmas and Easter, and proceeds *Sed et*: Miss. Franc. inserts *sed*. [15] *semper* S. Gerb. Sacr. Gall. Miss. Franc.; R. as text. [16] *beatissimorum* Sacr. Gall. [17] R. S. Sacr. Gall. Miss. Franc. omit *et*. [18] A line has been erased at this point in V., probably because the same words had been written twice over. [19] *Anacleti* Miss. Franc. [20] *Systi* Miss. Franc.; *Syxti* R.; *Sixti* S. Sacr. Gall. [21] The names in brackets have been erased in V., but can still be read there. R. S. Sacr. Gall. Miss. Franc. omit *Dionysii, Rustici, et Eleutherii*; in the margin of S. the words *et sanctorum confessorum tuorum* are marked by a later hand for insertion before *Hilarii*; Sacr. Gall. inserts *Ambrosii* before *Augustini*; Miss. Franc. omits *Augustini, Gregorii, Hieronymi, Benedicti*. [22] Sacr. Gall. inserts *qui per universo mundo passi sunt prop*[*ter*] *nom*[*en tuum*] *Dñ*[*e*] ... *confessoribus sunt* [? *sanctis*] *tuis*. [23] *auxilium* Sacr. Gall. [24] Sacr. Gall. inserts *quam tibi offerimus in honorem nominis tui Deus*; but Mabillon notes that the words are cancelled, the cancelling including also the words *sed et cunctae familiae tuae*; Miss. Franc. inserts *quam tibi offerimus in honore Domini beati martyris tui itti et pro peccatis atque offensionibus nostris ut omnium delictorum nostrorum remissionem consequi mereamur*. [25] R. omits *ut*. [26] *suscipias* Miss. Franc.; Mabillon notes that *accipias* has been corrected to *suscipias* in Sacr. Gall. [27] *dispone* R. [28] *eripias* R. Miss. Franc. (S¹?). [29] In

Sacr. Gall. a red cross is marked in the margin before *Quam oblationem*: V. R. and Miss. Franc. mark no crosses in this section; S. Gerb. marks *five* (at the words *benedictam, adscriptam, ratam, corpus, sanguis*); Sacr. Gall. marks *three*, one after *adscriptam* and one before and one after the word *corpus*. [30] *quae* (for *ut*) Miss. Franc.; *quae* has been corrected into *ut* in Sacr. Gall. [31] *Domini autem Dei nostri* Sacr. Gall. Miss. Franc.; *Domini nostri* R. S. [32] *accipit* Miss. Franc. (Sacr. Gall. has *accepit* for *accipiens*). [33] The words *accepit . . . sanctas* are written in red in Sacr. Gall. [34] Sacr. Gall. S² Gerb. insert *et*; R. S¹ Miss. Franc. agree with V. [35] Miss. Franc. inserts *suis*, which has been added between the lines in Sacr. Gall. [36] *ad caelum* Miss. Franc.; *in caelos* Sacr. Gall. [37] *egit* Miss. Franc. [38] *fregit, dedit discipulis* are written in red in Sacr. Gall.; in S. the word *fregit* has a red initial of larger size than the other letters. [39] Gerb. places *enim* in brackets; but the word is actually in R. [40] *post quam* Miss. Franc.; V. R. S. as text. [41] *et* Miss. Franc. [42] *dedit discipulis suis* are in red in Sacr. Gall.; S. gives to *dedit* an initial of larger size. [43] *hoc* Miss. Franc. [44] R. S¹ omit *et*. [45] *effunditur* Sacr. Gall. [46] *remissione* V. R. Sacr. Gall.; S. Gerb. Miss. Franc. as text. [47] *faciatis* R. Sacr. Gall.; V. has *faciaetis*. No crosses are marked in the *Qui pridie* in V. R. Miss. Franc. or Gerb.; S. marks one *at*, and Sacr. Gall. one *after*, the word *benedixit*, in each of the two places where it occurs. [48] *Inde* Miss. Franc. [49] *sumus* is expunged by S². [50] R. Sacr. Gall. Miss. Franc. omit *Dei*; S¹ agrees with V. [51] Gerb. places *gloriosae* in brackets. [52] *maiestatis* Sacr. Gall. [53] V. R. and Miss. Franc. mark no crosses in the *Unde et memores*. Gerb. marks *three*, one after each occurrence of the word *hostiam*: S. marks *five*, at *puram, sanctam, immaculatam, panem, calicem*: the first four are green (as are the crosses in the earlier part of the Canon), the last is only outlined in ink: Sacr. Gall. marks *two*, one after *sanctam* and one after *immaculatam*. It may be noted that R. has the variant *panem scāē vitae aeternae* probably by an error of the scribe. [54] *aspicere* corrected to *respicere* in Sacr. Gall. [55] *dignare* R. Miss. Franc. and Sacr. Gall. (corrected to *digneris* in Sacr. Gall.); S¹ agrees with V. [56] *acceptu* Miss. Franc.; Mabillon gives *acceptum* as the reading of Sacr. Gall. in both places. [57] Sacr. Gall. Miss. Franc. insert *sancti*, which Gerb. adds in brackets; R. S¹ agree with V. [58] *sublimi altari tuo* Miss. Franc.; *sublime altario tuum* Sacr. Gall. (Mabillon reads *sublimi . . . tuo*). [59] *hoc* Sacr. Gall. S¹, corrected to *hac* in each case: Miss. Franc. has *hoc altari sanctificationis*, omitting *participatione*. [60] *omnem* (?) *benedictionem* S¹; *omni benedictionem* is the present reading of S. [61] *et* elided in Sacr. Gall. [62] R. Sacr. Gall. Miss. Franc. insert *Memento etiam Domine et eorum nomina, qui nos praecesserunt cum signo* (*signum* Sacr. Gall.) *fidei et dormiunt in somno* (*somnom* R. originally) *pacis. Ipsis, Domine, et omnibus in Christo quiescentibus locum refrigerii, lucis et pacis ut indulgeas, deprecamur. Per Christum Dominum nostrum*. [63] *partem aliquam et societatem* R. Miss. Franc. S²; *partem aliquam societates* Sacr. Gall.; S¹ apparently agreed with V. [64] The *Missale Francorum* ends at this point. [65] *Matthiam* Sacr. Gall. [66] *Barnaban* V. R. Sacr. Gall.; S. as text. [67] *Agathae, Lucia, Agnem* V.; R. S. as text; Gerb. has *Agatha*. [68] The list of saints in Sacr. Gall. originally ran thus (after *Petro*): *Perpetua, Agne, Cicilia, Felicitate, Anastasia, Agathe, Lucia, Eogenia*; this has been altered to *Felicitate, Perpetua, Agatha, Agne, Cicilia, Anastasia, Eogenia*, the names of SS. Felicitas and Agatha being written over those of SS. Perpetua and Agnes, and that of S. Lucia omitted by the second hand. [69] *consortio* R. Sacr. Gall.; V. now has *consortia*, but apparently *consortium* was first written; S. Gerb. have *consortium*. [70] *non stimamur meritis, sed veniam q̃s largitor* V.; *non stimatur meriti sed veniam quaesumus largitur* Sacr. Gall.; R. S. Gerb. as text. (In S. the last syllable of *estimator* is written over an erasure). [71] V. R. Gerb. mark no crosses in the *Per quem haec omnia*. S. has three gold crosses at *sanctificas, vivificas, benedicis*, and Sacr. Gall. marks crosses before the same words, and an additional cross at the word *saeculorum*. In this clause R. reads *benedices et praestes*. [72] Sacr. Gall. originally had *Divino magisterio edocti et divina instructione, audemus dicere*. These words have been elided and the form in the text added. [73] S. gives the Lord's Prayer at length, and then inserts the heading *Item sequitur oratio*. Sacr. Gall. gives the heading *Post pater noster* to the *Libera nos*. R. has *Orat.* before the first words of the Lord's Prayer. [74] *omni malo, praeterito,*

240   *LIBER SACRAMENTORUM*   [III. xvii.

praesenti, et futuro Sacr. Gall. (corrected to reading of text).   [75] R. omits *pro nobis*: the words have been erased in S.; Sacr. Gall. agrees with V. [76] *que* erased in S.   [77] *Dei genetrice* added above the line in Sacr. Gall. [78] *et beatis apostolis* Sacr. Gall.; S. has *et beatis* over an erasure and omits *apostolis tuis*.   [79] Sacr. Gall. omits *atque Andrea*; so S. originally (*atque Andrea cum omnibus sanctis* has been added in the margin); R. has *atque Andrea et beatis confessoribus tuis illis*; V. reads *atque Andreas*.   [80] *opem* Sacr. Gall.   [81] *peccato* Sacr. Gall. S. (last letter in S. is over an erasure). [82] *semper liberi* Sacr. Gall. S²; R. S¹ agree with V.   [83] A later hand (apparently) has marked in S., after *vobiscum*, a cross, with the word *ter*. [84] This rubric occurs with slight variation in R. and S.   [85] *p* or *p̄* (for *est*) V.; R. S. as text.   [86] *ieiuniis* S²; V. R. S¹ as text.   [87] *per scrutinis* R.; V. S. as text.   [88] *adnuntiandum* V.; R. S. as text.   [89] S² inserts *et*.   [90] Gerb. inserts *ut*; V. R. as text.   [91] R. omits *nobis*. [92] *nobis* V.; R. as text.   [93] V. omits *et*, which is restored from R. [94] *Domine* (for *Deus*) R.   [95] *instituat* R.; V. as text.   [96] Tommasi reads, and Gerb. proposes to read, *munus divinum*, but the reading of the text, which is that of R. as well as V., is not necessarily ungrammatical.

[XVII.]

ITEM BENEDICTIONES SUPER POPULUM POST COMMUNIONEM [1].

R. S.
Gerb. 238.

Domine sancte, Pater omnipotens, aeterne Deus, de abundantia misericordiarum tuarum famulos [2] et famulas tuas praesta locupletes, praesta securos; ut confirmati benedictionibus tuis, abundent in omni gratiarum actione, teque perpetua exultatione benedicant. Per.

R. S.
Gerb. 239.
Leon. 364.
cf. I. xxviii
I. xxxix *sup.*

Gregem tuum, Pastor bone, placatus intende, et oves, quas pretioso sanguine [3] redemisti, diabolica non sinas incursu lacerari. Per.

R. S.
Gerb. 239.
I. lxv
supra.

Benedic, Domine, hanc familiam tuam in caelestibus, et reple eam donis tuis spiritalibus; concede eis caritatem, gaudium, pacem, patientiam, bonitatem, mansuetudinem, spem, fidem, continentiam; et [4] repleti omnibus castitatem [5] donis tuis desiderantes ad te pervenire mereantur. Per.

R. S.
Gerb. 239.

Benedicat vos Deus omni benedictione caelesti sanctosque [6] puros efficiat in conspectu suo: superabundent in vos divitiae gloriae eius: verbo veritatis instruat, et [7] evangelio salutis erudiat, omniumque sanctorum caritate [8] locupletet. Per.

R. S.
Gerb. 239.

Plebis [9] tuae, quaesumus, Domine, ad te semper corda converte, et quam tantis facis patrociniis adiuvari, perpetuis non desinas gubernare praesidiis [10]. Per.

R. S.
Gerb. 239.

Propitiare populo tuo, Deus, ut a suis pravitatibus liberatus, et toto tibi corde deserviat, et sub tua semper protectione consistat. Per.

Tuere, quaesumus, Domine [11], familiam tuam, et spiritalibus instrue disciplinis. Per Dominum nostrum. R. S.
Gerb. 239.

700 Familia tua [12], Deus, et ad celebranda prin•cipia suae redemptionis desideranter occurrat [13], et eius dona perseveranter acquirat. Per. S.
Gerb. 239.

Fideles tuos, Domine, quaesumus, corpore pariter et mente purifica, ut tua inspiratione compuncti, noxias delectationes vitare praevaleant; atque [14] ut earum non capiantur illecebris, tua semper suavitate pascantur. Per. γ S.
Gerb. 239.
Pam. 37.

Propitiare, Domine, populo tuo, et ab omnibus absolve peccatis, ut quod nostris offensionibus promeremur, tua indulgentia repellatur. Per. S.
Gerb. 239.

Adesto, Domine, supplicibus tuis [15], et nihil de sua conscientia praesumentibus, ineffabili miseratione succurre; ut quod non habet fiducia meritorum, tua [16] consecret [17] largitas invicta donorum. Per Dominum nostrum. Gerb. 239.
lxviii *infra*.

Da, quaesumus, Domine, populo tuo et mentem qua tibi devotus existat, et intellectum quo iusta deposcat, et propitiationem tuam, qua pie desiderantibus quae sint profutura perficias [18]. Per. S.
Gerb. 239.

Plebem nomini tuo subditam, Domine, propitius intuere, eique consolationes tuas [19] iugiter per caelestem gratiam dignanter operare. Per [20]. S.
Gerb. 239.
xli *infra*.
Men. 209.

Familiam tuam, Domine, pervigili protectione conserva, et perpetuis defende praesidiis; ut omni semper inordinatione seclusa, tua iugiter providentia dirigatur. Per. R.
Gerb. 231.
239.
S. (*alibi*.)

Respice, Domine, propitius plebem tuam, et toto tibi corde subiectam praesidiis invictae pietatis attolle. Per. γ S. (*alibi*.)
Gerb. 232.
Pam. 377.

---

[1] R. S. Gerb. omit *post communionem*. [2] R. S. Gerb. insert *tuos*. [3] V. in I. xxviii, xxxix *supra* inserts *Filii tui*; V. here, R. S. Gerb. Leon. as text. [4] *ut* R. Gerb., V. in I. lxv *supra*; V. here, S. as text. [5] See note [14] on I. lxv *supra*. [6] S² inserts *ac* before *puros* and *ut* before *superabundent*; V. R. S¹ as text in both cases. [7] R. S. omit *et*. [8] *caritatem* R. S¹ Gerb.; V. S² as text. [9] *Plebi* V. [10] *praesidiis gubernare* S.; V. R. Gerb. as text. [11] *Tuere Domine quaesumus* R. Gerb.; *Tuere Domine* S.; V. as text. [12] This and the five following benedictions are not included in R., which has next that beginning *Familiam tuam*, and makes it the last of the series. Gerbert marks the six as included in S., but he may have taken his text from T. [13] *accurrat* Gerb.; the first syllable is now wanting in S, where the corner of the leaf has perished; V. as text. [14] Pam. omits *atque ut . . . pascantur*. [15] *supplicationibus nostris* Gerb. V. in lxviii *infra*; V. here, S. as text. [16] *tuorum* S² Gerb.; V. S¹ as text. [17] *con-*

ferat Gerb. V. in lxviii *infra*; V. here, S. as text.   [18] *proficiat* V. ; S. has (apparently) *perficiat*; Gerb. as text.   [19] *tuas consolationes* V. in xli *infra*, Men.; V. here, S. Gerb. as text.   [20] This benediction is the last now contained in S, which ends with it: possibly the series at one time extended further and included the next at least of those in V.

XVIII.

ORATIONES QUOTIDIANIS DIEBUS AD MISSAS [1].

R. S.
Gerb. 230.
Pam. 415.
Men. 197.

Perpetua [2], quaesumus, Domine, pace custodi quos in te sperare donasti. Per. y

R. S.
Gerb. 230.
Pam. 415.
Men. 197.

Adesto nobis, misericors Deus, et tuae pietatis in [3] nobis propitius [4] dona concede. Per. y

Secreta.

cf. Pam. 309.

Munera, Domine, tibi dicata, quaesumus, sanctifica, et per eadem nos placatus intende. Per. y

[Postcommun.]

R. S.
Gerb. 230.
Pam. 415.

Mysteria sancta nos, Domine, et spiritalibus expleant alimentis, et corporalibus [5] tueantur auxiliis. Per. y

[1] This and the four following *Missae* are found with slight variations in S. Gerb. (the latter professedly following R. which does not however contain all the *Missae*).   The Canon in these texts is inserted after the Secret of the last *Missa* of the series, which is not the same with the sixth of the series in V. (xxiii *infra*). See the parallel series of *Missae* in Pam. (415-417) and in Muratori's Gregorian text (Mur. ii. 176-179). Some of the prayers appear in Men. in the series of *Orationes quotidianae* (196-200).   [2] *Perpetuum* R.
[3] Men. omits *in*.   [4] *pro cuius* (for *propitius*) R.   [5] *corporibus* V. ;
R. S. Gerb. Pam. as text.

XIX.

ITEM ALIA MISSA.

R. S.
Gerb. 230.
Pam. 415.

Exaudi nos, miserator et misericors Deus, et continentiae salutaris propitius nobis dona concede. Per. y

R. S.
Gerb. 230.

Plebis tuae, Deus, ad te corda converte; ut tuo munere talis existat cui tu perpetua beneficia largiaris. Per.

Secreta.

S. (*alibi*.)
Gerb. 185.
Pam. 347.
Men. 135.

Mystica nobis, Domine, prosit oblatio, quae nos et a reatibus nostris expediat, et perpetua salvatione confirmet. Per Dominum. y

Postcommun.

R. S.
Gerb. 230.
Pam. 416.

Sancta tua nos, Domine, quaesumus, et a peccatis exuant, et caelestis [1] vitae vigore [2] confirment. Per. y

[1] *et a caelestis* V.; R. S. Gerb. Pam. as text.   [2] *vigorem* Gerb. ; V. R. S. Pam. as text.

XX.

ITEM ALIA MISSA[1].

Quaesumus, omnipotens Deus, ut plebs tua toto tibi corde deserviens et beneficia tua iugiter mereatur et pacem. Per. γ   S. Gerb. 231. Pam. 416.

Miserere nostri, Deus, et tuae nobis pietatis effectus potenti bonitate largire. Per.   S. Gerb. 231.

Secreta.

Suscipe, Domine, quaesumus[2], hostiam redemptionis humanae, et salutem nobis mentis et corporis operare placatus[3]. Per. γ   S. Gerb. 231. Pam. 416.

Postcommun.

Tui nobis, Domine, communio sacramenti et purificationem conferat et tribuat unitatem. Per. γ   R. (alibi.) xvii supra. Gerb. 238.

[1] The two Collects and Secret of this *Missa* are contained in one of the *Missae* in S. which R. omits.   [2] *quaesumus Domine* Gerb. Pam.   [3] *placatus operare* S² Gerb.; V. S¹ Pam. as text.

XXI.

ITEM ALIA MISSA[1].

Rege nostras, Domine, propitius voluntates, ut nec propriis iniquitatibus implicentur nec subdantur alienis. Per. γ   S. Gerb. 231. Pam. 416. Men. 197.

Da famulis tuis, Deus, indulgentiam peccatorum, consolationem vitae, gubernationemque perpetuam, qua tibi fideliter servientes, ad tuam iugiter misericordiam pervenire mereantur. Per.   S. Gerb. 231.

Secreta.

Tua sacramenta nos, Deus, circumtegant et reforment, simulque nobis temporale[2] remedium conferant et aeternum. Per. γ   S. Gerb. 231. Pam. 416.

Postcommun.

Tua sancta nobis, omnipotens Deus, quae sumpsimus, et indulgentiam praebeant, et auxilium perpetuae defensionis impendant. Per Dominum. γ   S. Gerb. 231. Pam. 416.

[1] This *Missa* is absent from R. and is marked accordingly by Gerb.: but he does not state whether he employs S. or T. to furnish his text.   [2] *temporalem* V.

XXII.
Item alia Missa[1].

S. Gerb. 231.
Pam. 416.
Men. 197.

Comprime, Domine, quaesumus, noxios semper incursus, et salutarem[2] temporibus nostris propitius da quietem. Per. γ

S. Gerb. 231.

Tu, Domine, semper a nobis omnem remove pravitatem, et ad tuam nos propitius converte iustitiam. Per.

Secreta.

S. Gerb. 231.
Pam. 417.

In tuo conspectu, Domine, quaesumus, talia nostra munera efficiant[ur[3]], quae et placare[4] te valeant, et nos tibi placere perficiant. Per. γ

Postcommun.

R. (alibi.)
Gerb. 238.
V. (alibi.)

Tua nos[5], Domine, medicinalis operatio et a nostris perversitatibus clementer expediat, et ad ea quae sunt recta perducat. Per. γ

[1] This *Missa* is also omitted by R. and marked accordingly by Gerb. [2] *salutare* V. [3] *efficiant* V. S. (ungrammatically); Gerb. Pam. have *talia nostra sint munera quae.* [4] *placere* V. S[1]; Gerb. Pam. as text. [5] *nobis* V. (ungrammatically); V. (in Postcom. after Canon), R. Gerb. as text.

XXIII.
Item alia Missa[1].

S. Gerb. 232.
Pam. 417.

Ab omnibus nos defende, quaesumus, Domine, semper adversis, et continuis tuere praesidiis. Per. γ

R.S.(alibi.)
Gerb. 28.
Pam. 400.

Conserva populum tuum, Deus, et tuo nomini fac devotum, ut divinis subiectus[2] officiis temporalia utiliter et aeterna dona percipiat[3]. Per. γ

Secreta.

R.S.(alibi.)
Gerb. 28.
Pam. 400.

Haec nos oblatio, Deus, mundet[4] et renovet, gubernet et protegat. Per. γ

Postcommun.

R.S.(alibi.)
Gerb. 28.
Pam. 400.

Caelestibus, Domine, pasti deliciis, quaesumus, ut semper eadem, quo[5] veraciter vivimus, appetamus. Per. γ

S. Gerb. 231.

Adsit, Domine, fidelibus tuis sacrae benedictionis effectus, qui mentes omnium spiritali vegetatione disponat; ut pro opera[6] pietatis[7] tuae muneribus impleantur. Per.

[1] This *Missa*, as a whole, differs from that which forms the last of the series in R. S. Gerb.; but all the prayers which it contains are found in these texts at this point or elsewhere. The second Collect, Secret, and Postcommunion are in

them assigned to the sixth Sunday after Epiphany, while the last prayer is the *super populum* of one of the earlier *Missae* of this series in S. ² *subiectis* V.; R. S. Gerb. Pam. as text. ³ *temporalis viriliter et aeternae donae perficiat* V.; *temporalia utiliter et aeterna dona feliciter accipiat* S⁹ Gerb.; S¹ (apparently) as text; but the first syllable of *percipiat* is erased. Pam. has *viriliter* for *utiliter*; R. has *temporaris viriliter*; otherwise as text. ⁴ Pam. inserts *quaesumus*; S. Gerb. have *Haec oblatio Deus mundet nos a crimine*; V. R. as text. ⁵ *per quae* R. S. Gerb. Pam.; V. as text. ⁶ *per opera* Gerb.; V. S. as text. ⁷ S⁹ Gerb. insert *gratiae*; V. S¹ as text.

XXIV.

ORATIONES AD PROFICISCENDUM IN ITINERE[1].

Adesto, Domine, supplicationibus nostris, et viam famuli tui *Illius*[2] in salutis tuae prosperitate[3] dispone; ut inter omnes vitae huius[4] varietates tuo semper protegatur auxilio. Per. γ

R. Pam. 441. Men. 212. Leofr. 16.

Deus qui diligentibus te misericordiam tuam semper impendis, et a servientibus tibi in nulla es regione longinquus, dirige viam famuli tui *Illius*[2] in voluntate[5] tua, ut[6] te protectore, et[7] te praeduce[8], per iustitiae semitas sine offensione gradiatur. Per. γ

Pam. 440. Men. 211. Leofr. 16.

Exaudi, Domine, preces nostras, et profectioni famuli tui *Illius* misericordiam tuam, qui semper es ubique, praetende[9]; ut ab omnibus adversitatibus tua opitulatione defensus, iustorum desideriorum potiatur effectibus. Per. γ

cf. Sacr. Gall. 903.

Secreta.

Propitiare, Domine, supplicationibus nostris, et has oblationes, quas tibi offerimus pro famulo tuo *Illo*[10], benignus as·sume, ut viam illius et praecedente gratia tua dirigas, et subsequente comitare[11] digneris, ut de actu atque incolumitate [eius][12] secundum misericordiae tuae praesidia gaudeamus. Per. γ

Pam. 441. Men. 212. Leofr. 16.

Infra actionem.

Hanc igitur oblationem[13], Domine, famuli tui Illius, quam tibi offert ob desiderium animae suae, commendans tibi Deo iter suum,[14] placatus suscipias deprecamur: cui tu, Domine, angelum pacis mittere digneris, angelum tuum sanctum[15], sicut misisti famulo tuo Tobiae Raphael angelum, qui eum salvum atque incolumem perducat usque ad loca destinata, [et][16] iterato tempore opportuno, omnibusque rite perfectis[17], reduci eum faciat[18] in tua sancta ecclesia[19]; et laetus tibi [serviat][20], et nomini tuo gratias referat. Per.

[Gerb. 289.]

Item infra actionem.

[Gerb. 288.]

Hanc igitur oblationem, Domine, famuli tui *Illius*, quam tibi offert pro salute famuli tui *Illius*, [14] placatus suscipias deprecamur. Pro quo maiestati tuae fundimus preces, ut eum, confirmato pacis foedere [21], cum omni gaudio ad nos quantocius facias remeare. Per. Quam oblationem.

Postcommun.

B.
Pam. 442.
Men. 213.
[Gerb. 289.]

Deus infinitae misericordiae et maiestatis immensae, quem nec spatia locorum, nec intervalla temporum, ab his quos tueris abiungunt [22], adesto famulis tuis [23] in te ubique fidentibus [24], et per omnem quam acturi [25] sunt viam dux eis et comes esse dignare: nihil illis adversitatis noceat, nihil difficultatis obsistat: cuncta eis salubria, cuncta sint prospera, ut [26] sub ope dexterae tuae quidquid iusto [27] expetierunt [28] desiderio celeri consequantur effectu. Per. γ

Item alia.

Men. 212.

Deus, qui ad vitam ducis, et confidentes in te paterna protectione custodis, quaesumus ut praesenti famulo tuo a nobis egredienti angelicum tribuas comitatum, ut eius auxilio protectus, nulla mali concutiatur formidine, nullo comprimatur adversitatis angore, nullis [29] irruentis inimici molestetur insidiis; sed spatiis necessa•rii itineris prospero gressu peractis, propriisque locis feliciter restitutus, universos reperiat sospites, ac debitas exsolvat tuo nomini grates [30]. Per.

---

[1] This *Missa* does not appear as a whole in any of the texts referred to, and there are considerable variations in the wording of the separate prayers in different texts. [2] Leofr. inserts *omniumque sibi adherentium*. [3] *prosperitatis* V. [4] *viae huius* B.; *viae et vitae huius* Pam. Men.; *viae vel huius vitae* Leofr.; V. as text. [5] *veritate* Leofr. [6] *et* Pam. [7] Leofr. omits *et*. [8] *perduci* V.; Pam. Men. Leofr. as text. [9] *misericordiam semper et ubique praetende* Sacr. Gall. (in which the ending of the Collect differs considerably from the text). [10] Leofr. inserts *omnibusque secum comitantibus*. [11] *comitari* Leofr. Men.; V. Pam. as text. [12] V. omits *eius*, which seems to be required for the sense, and is found in Pam. Men. Leofr. [13] This form is given as Ambrosian in Gerb. [14] Gerb. inserts *ut*. [15] *angelum tuum sanctum mittere digneris* (om. *angelum pacis*) Gerb. [16] *et*, omitted by V. is inserted from Gerb. [17] *peractis* Gerb. [18] *facias* Gerb. [19] *tuam sanctam ecclesiam* Gerb.; V. as text (ungrammatically). [20] V. omits *serviat* which is inserted from Gerb. [21] *confirmata pacis foedera* V.; Gerb. as text. [22] *adiungunt* Pam.; *disiungunt* Men.; V. B. Gerb. as text. [23] *famulo tuo* (so throughout) B. Men. [24] *confidenti* B. [25] *ituri* Pam. Gerb.; similarly B. Men.; V. as text. [26] *et* Men. Gerb. [27] *iuste* B. [28] *expetierint* Pam. Gerb.; similarly B. Men.; V. as text. [29] *nullus* V.; Men. as text. [30] *gratias* Men.; V. has *gratis*.

XXV.

ITEM ORATIONES AD ITER AGENTIBUS[1].

Deus, verae beatitudinis auctor atque largitor, dirige nos in eam quam immaculati ambulant viam, ut testimonia legis tuae piis cordibus exquirentes, perseveremus et diligere quod praecipiunt, et desiderare quo ducunt. Per.

Deus qui sanctorum tuorum dirigis gressus, [amove][2] a nobis iniquitatis viam, et nostri tua lege[3] miserere; ut non obliti iudicia tua, viam mandatorum dilatato corde curramus. Per.

[1] So V. (ungrammatically).   [2] *amove*, required by the sense, is restored from Ps. cxviii.   [3] *de tua lege* Ps. cxviii (Vulg.).

XXVI.

ORATIONES PRO CARITATE.

Deus, qui diligentibus te facis cuncta prodesse, da cordibus nostris inviolabilem caritatis affectum[1], ut desideria de tua inspiratione concepta nulla possint tentatione mutari. Per.   B. Pam. 528.

Deus[2], qui iustitiam tuae legis[3] in cordibus credentium digito tuo scribis, da nobis fidei et spei caritatisque[4] augmentum, et ut mereamur assequi quod promittis fac nos amare quod praecepisti[5]. Per.   Pam. 528. Gerb. 262. Leofr. 176.

Secreta.

Deus, qui nos ad imaginem tuam sacramentis[6] renovas et praeceptis, perfice gressus nostros in semitis tuis, ut caritatis donum, quod fecisti a nobis sperari[7], per haec quae offerimus facias sacrificia apprehendi. Per.   B. Pam. 529.

Postcommun.

Libera nos, Domine[8], ab omni malo, propitiusque concede ut quae nobis poscimus relaxari, ipsi quoque proximis remittamus. Per.   Leon. 359.

[1] *effectum* V.   [2] *Omnipotens sempiterne Deus* Pam. Gerb. Leofr.; V. as text.   [3] *iustitiam tuam elegis* V.; Pam. Gerb. Leofr. as text.   [4] *fidei spei et caritatis* Pam. Gerb. Leofr.; V. as text.   [5] *quae praecipis* Pam.; *quod praecipis* Gerb. Leofr.; V. as text.   [6] *tuam tuam sacramenti* V.; B. Pam. as text.   [7] *fecisti nobis spirari* B.; V. Pam. as text.   [8] Leon. omits *Domine*.

XXVII.

Item alia Missa.

Leofr. 19. Deus, largitor pacis et amator caritatis, da servis tuis veram cum tua voluntate concordiam, ut ab omnibus quae nos pulsant tentationibus liberemur. Per.

Deus, qui quum omnes creaturas diligens feceris, in eam indulgentiam hominem[1], ut etiam illum ab impietatibus redimeres[2], condidisti, da servis tuis hunc[3] caritatis affectum, ut bona pro malis rependere tuo incitentur exemplo. Per.

Secreta.

Leofr. 19. His, Domine, sacrificiis, quaesumus, concede placatus, ut qui propriis oramus absolvi delictis non gravemur externis[4]. Per. γ

Postcommun.

Pam. 529.
Gerb. 263.
Leofr. 177.
Leon. 438.

Spiritum nobis, Domine, tuae caritatis infunde: ut quos uno caelesti pane satiasti, una facias pietate concordes. Per. γ

Ad populum.

Leon. 353.
cf. II. xxii
supra.

Da ecclesiae tuae, Domine, non superbe sapere, [sed][5] tibi placita humilitate proficere, ut proterva despiciens[6], et matura quaeque desiderans, exerceat liberam caritatem. Per.

Leon. 438.
Leofr. 19.

Confirma, Domine, quaesumus, tuorum corda fidelium[7], et gratiae tuae virtute corrobora; ut et[8] in tua sint supplicatione devoti, et mutua dilectione sinceri. Per.

[1] *hominum* V.   [2] *redemeris* V. (Tommasi corrects as text).   [3] *hanc* V.   [4] *aeternis* Leofr.[2]; V. Leofr.[1] as text.   [5] V. here omits *sed*, which is restored from Leon. and II. xxii *supra*.   [6] *despiciens, quaecumque matura sunt libera exerceat caritate* V. in II. xxii *supra*; *exerceat libera caritate* V. here (ungrammatically); Leon as text.   [7] *filiorum* Leon.; V. Leofr. as text.   [8] Leofr. omits *et*; V. Leon. as text.

XXVIII.

Orationes in Tribulatione.

R. B.
Pam. 446.
Gerb. 275.

Ineffabilem misericordiam tuam, Domine, nobis clementer ostende, ut simul nos et a peccatis exuas, et a poenis, quas pro his meremur, eripias. Per. γ

R. B.
Gerb. 275.
Leon. 316.

Parce, Domine, parce peccantibus[1]; et ut ad propitiationem tuam possimus accedere, spiritum nobis tribue corrigendi. Per.

Secreta.

Quaesumus, Domine, nostris placare muneribus: quo- R.
niam² tu eadem tribuis ut placeris. Per. Gerb. 275.

707 ### Postcommun.

Sumpti sacrificii, Domine, perpetua nos tuitio non relin- B.
quat, et noxia semper a nobis cuncta depellat. Per. y Gerb. 274.
Leon. 316.
¹ B. inserts *nobis.* ² *quo* V.; R. as text. II. xxiv,
xlviii
supra.

XXIX.
ITEM ALIA MISSA.

Adesto, Domine, fidelibus tuis, et quibus supplicandi R.S.(*alibi.*)
tribuis miseratus affectum, concede benignissime consola- Gerb. 29.
tionis auxilium. Per. y Pam. 380.

Da nobis, quaesumus, Domine, de tribulatione laetitiam: Pam. 373.
ut qui diu pro nostris peccatis afficimur¹, intercedentibus Gerb. 244.
sanctis tuis², celerius in tua misericordia respiremus.
Per. y

Secreta.

Suscipe, quaesumus, Domine, preces populi tui cum S. (*alibi.*)
oblationibus hostiarum, et tua mysteria celebrantes ab Gerb. 51.
omnibus defende periculis. Per. y

Postcommun.

Vivificet nos, Domine, sacra participationis infusio, et perpetua protectione defendat. Per Dominum nostrum.

¹ *affligimur* Pam. Gerb.; V. as text. ² *intercedente beato* Illo *martyre
tuo* Pam. Gerb.; V. as text.

XXX.
ITEM ALIA MISSA.

Parce, Domine, parce peccatis nostris; et quamvis inces- B.
sabiliter delinquentibus continua poena debeatur, praesta,
quaesumus, ut quod ad perpetuum meremur exitium, transeat ad correptionis¹ auxilium. Per.

Memor esto, Domine, fragilitatis humanae; et qui iuste Leofr. 187.
verberas peccatores, parce propitiatus afflictis. Per. y

Secreta.

Propitiare, Domine, populi tui propitiatus² muneribus; R.S.(*alibi.*)
ut hac oblatione placatus et indulgentiam nobis tribuas et Gerb. 171.
postulata concedas. Per. y Pam. 410.

Postcommun.

B. Vitia cordis humani haec, Domine, quaesumus, medicina compescat, quae mortalitatis nostrae venit curare languores. Per Dominum nostrum.

¹ *correctionis* B.; V. as text.   ² *populo tuo, propitiare* R. S¹ Pam.; *precibus populi tui, propitiare* S¹ Gerb.; V. as text.

XXXI.

Item alia Missa.

Leofr. 184.   Domine Deus, qui ad hoc irasceris, ut subvenias, ad hoc minaris, ut parcas, ¹ lapsis manum porrige, et laborantibus multiplici miseratione succurre : et ² qui per te redempti sunt ad spem vitae aeternae tua moderatione serventur. Per.

cf. I. xv supra.   Adesto, Domine, invocationibus nostris, et non sit a nobis clementiae tuae longinqua misericordia : sana vulnera, remitte peccata, ut nullis iniquitatibus a te separati, tibi semper adhaerere possimus. Per.

Secreta.

Leofr. 108. Leofr. 184.   Sacrificia, Domine, tibi ³ cum ecclesiae precibus immolanda, quaesumus, corda nostra purificent, et ⁴ indulgentiae tuae nobis dona concilient, et de adversis prospera sentire perficiant ⁵. Per.

Postcommun.

I. xxxvii supra. Leon. 327. Pam. 215.   Caelestis doni benedictione percepta, supplices te, Deus omnipotens ⁶, deprecamur, ut hoc idem et sacramenti nobis ⁷ causa sit et salutis. Per. γ

¹ Leofr. inserts *intercedentibus omnibus sanctis tuis*.   ² *ut* Leofr.; V. as text.   ³ Leofr. (184) omits *tibi*.   ⁴ Leofr. (184) inserts *intercedentibus omnibus sanctis tuis*; *ut et* Leofr. 108.   ⁵ *faciant* Leofr. 184.   ⁶ *Domine* (for *D. omnip.*) V. in I. xxxvii *supra*; V. here, Leon. Pam. as text.   ⁷ *hoc idem nobis semper et sacramenti* V. in I. xxxvii *supra*, Leon.; Pam. similarly, but omitting *semper*.

XXXII.

Item alia Missa.

Leofr. 107. Pam. 374. Men. 195.   Omnipotens et misericors ¹ Deus, qui peccantium non vis animas perire sed culpas, contine quam meremur iram, et quam precamur ² effunde ³ clementiam ; ut [de] maerore in gaudium per tuam misericordiam transferamur ⁴. Per.

Deus, refugium pauperum, spes humilium, salusque miserorum, supplicationes populi tui clementer exaudi; ut quos iustitia verberum fecit afflictos, abundantia remediorum faciat consolatos. Per. γ

Secreta.

Suscipe, Domine, propitiatus [5] hostias quibus et te placari [6] voluisti et nobis salutem potenti pietate restitui. Per. γ

Postcommun.

Quos munere, Domine, caelesti reficis [7], divino tuere praesidio; ut tuis mysteriis perfruentes, nullis subdamur adversis. Per.

[1] Pam. Men. omit *Omnipotens et misericors*; V. Leofr. as text. [2] Pam. Men. Leofr. insert *super nos*. [3] *infunde* Pam. [4] *ut de maerore (merito* Pam.) *gaudium tuae misericordiae consequi mereamur* Pam. Men.; V. omits *de* and has *transferamus*; Leofr. as text. [5] *propitius* S² Gerb. Pam.; V. R. S¹ Men. as text. [6] *placare* V. [7] *caelesti reficis Domine intercedentibus omnibus sanctis tuis* Leofr.

XXXIII.
ITEM ALIA MISSA.

Deus, qui offensionibus servorum tuorum et iuste irasceris, et clementer ignoscis, praesta supplicibus indulgentiam peccatorum; ut, reparato statu tibi subditae libertatis, et correptio ab iniquitate, et cessatio fiat a verbere. Per.

Parce, Domine, parce supplicibus; da propitiationis auxilium, qui praestas etiam per ipsa flagella remedium; nec haec tua correptio, Domine, sit negligentibus maior causa poenarum, sed fiat eruditio paterna correptis. Per.

Secreta.

Oblationibus [1], Domine, placare susceptis, et ad te nostras etiam rebelles compelle propitius voluntates. Per. γ

Postcommun.

Sit nobis, quaesumus, Domine [2], medicina mentibus et corporibus [3], quod de sancti [4] altaris tui benedictione percepimus [5]; ut nullis adversitatibus perfruamur [6], qui tanti remedii participatione munimur [7]. Per.

[1] R. S. Gerb. Pam. Men. insert *quaesumus*. [2] *Domine quaesumus* Leofr. [3] *mentes et corporibus* V.; *mentis et corporis* Leofr. [4] *sanctis* V.; Leofr. as text. [5] *percipimus* V. [6] *turbemur* Leofr.; V. as text. [7] *muniamur* V.; Leofr. as text.

XXXIV.
Item alia Missa.

Men. 206. Deus infinitae misericordiae et bonitatis immensae, propitiare iniquitatibus nostris, et omnibus animarum nostrarum medere languoribus, ut miserationum[1] remissione percepta, semper in tua benedictione laetemur. Per.

Secreta.

Men. 206. Tuere nos, Domine, divinis propitius sacramentis; et ut his congrue famulemur, eorum praesta potenter effectu[2]. Per.

Postcommun.

Men. 206. Muniat, quaesumus, Domine, fideles tuos sumpti[3] vivificatio sacramenti, et a vitiis omnibus expeditos in sancta faciat[4] devotione currentes. Per.

[1] *miserationum.* So V.; Men. has *peccatorum nostrorum.* [2] *effectu*, so V. Men. Tommasi reads *effectum*, but the correction seems superfluous. [3] *sumpta* V.; Men. as text. [4] Men. inserts *esse*.

XXXV.
Item alia Missa.

Men. 206. Deus sub cuius oculis omne cor trepidat[1], et omnes conscientiae pavescunt, propitiare omnium gemituum[2] et cunctorum medere vulneribus; ut sicut nemo nostrum liber a culpa est, ita nemo sit alienus a venia. Per.

Men. 207. Omnipotens sempiterne Deus, qui timore sentiris, dilectione coleris, confessione placaris, misericordiam tuam effunde supplicibus; ut qui de meritorum qualitate diffidimus, non iudicium tuum sed indulgentiam sentiamus. Per.

Secreta.

Sacrificia nos, Domine, celebranda purificent, et caelestibus imbuant institutis. Per.

Postcommun.

R. Pam. 446. Gerb. 276. Praesta, Domine, quaesumus, ut terrenis affectibus expiatis[3] ad[4] superni plenitudinem sacramenti, cuius libavimus sancta, tendamus. Per. γ

[1] *contrepitat* V.; Men. as text. [2] *omnium doloribus gementium* Men.; V. as text; the reading of Men. is perhaps an emendation of this ungrammatical form. [3] *effectibus expiati* Pam.; V. R. as text. [4] *a* V.; R. as text.

XXXVI.

Item alia Missa.

Deus, humilium consolator, et fidelium fortitudo, propitius esto supplicibus; ¹ ut humana fragilitas, quae per se proclivis est ad labendum², per te semper muniatur³ ad standum; et quae per se prona est ad offensam, per te semper³ reparetur ad veniam. Per.

Men. 207.

Suscipe, misericors Domine, supplicum preces, et secundum multitudinem indulgentiarum tuarum ab omnibus nos absolve peccatis; ut ad omnia pietatis opera te parcente⁴ reparemur; et quos venia feceris innocentes, auxilio facias efficaces. Per Dominum nostrum Iesum Christum.

Men. 207.

Secreta.

Haec hostia, Domine, quaesumus, et ab occultis ecclesiam tuam reatibus semper expediat, et manifestis convenienter expurget. Per Dominum nostrum Iesum Christum.

Men. 207.

Postcommun.

Purificent nos, Domine, sacramenta quae sumpsimus, et a cunctis efficiant⁵ vitiis absolutos. Per Dominum nostrum Iesum Christum. ỹ

Men. 207.
x supra.

¹ Men. inserts *et da*. ² *labem* Men. ³ Men. omits *muniatur* ... *semper*. ⁴ *opera re parcende* V.; Men. as text. ⁵ *efficiat* V.

XXXVII.

Item alia Missa.

Si iniquitates nostras observaveris, Domine, quis sustinebit? Precamur ergo clementiam tuam¹ ut ubi nulla fiducia suppetit actionum, gratia tua copiosa resplendeat, et quum delicta remittit indignis, et quum beneficia praestat immeritis. Per Dominum nostrum Iesum Christum.

Men. 207.

Misericors et miserator Domine, qui nos parcendo sustentas et ignoscendo sanctificas, da² veniam peccatis nostris, et sacramentis caelestibus servientes ab omni culpa liberos esse concede. Per Dominum nostrum Iesum Christum.

Men. 207.

Secreta.

Hostias tibi, Domine, placationis offerimus, ut et delicta nostra miseratus absolvas, et nutantia corda tu dirigas. Per Dominum nostrum Iesum Christum. ỹ

Men. 207.

Postcommun.

Men. 207.   Supplices te rogamus, [3] Deus, ut quos tuis reficis sacramentis, et [4] tibi placitis moribus dignanter informes. Per Dominum nostrum Iesum Christum. γ

ORATIONES IN NATALI PRESBYTERI QUALITER SIBI MISSAM DEBEAT CELEBRARE [5].

Pam. 430.
cf. I. xcviii
supra.
cf. Leon.
431.

Deus, cuius arbitrio omnium saeculorum ordo decurrit, respice propitius ad me famulum tuum, quem ad ordinem presbyterii [6] promovere dignatus es; et ut tibi mea servitus [7] placeat, tua in me misericorditer dona conserva. Per.

Domine Deus noster, verax promissor, propitiare operi tuo, et mihi famulo tuo servienti tibi tribuas perseverantem in tua voluntate famulatum, ut diebus nostris et [8] merito et numero populus tibi serviens augeatur. Per.

Super oblata [9].

Pam. 431.
Leon. 435.

Perfice, Domine, quaesumus, benignus in nobis, ut quae sacris mysteriis profitemur, piis actionibus exequamur. Per.

Pam. 431.

Hanc igitur oblationem, Domine, servitutis meae, quam tibi offero ego famulus tuus et sacerdos, pro eo quod me eligere dignatus es in ordinem presbyterii, ut sacrificiis tuis ac divinis altaribus deservirem [10]: pro hoc reddo tibi vota mea Deo vero et vivo, maiestatem tuam suppliciter implorans, ut opera manuum tuarum in me ipso custodias et idoneum me per [11] omnia ministrum tuae voluntatis efficias. Per.

Postcommun.

Pam. 431.
cf. Leon.
429.

Munerum tuorum, Domine, largitate [12] sumentes, supplices deprecamur ut quibus donasti huius ministerii servitutem exequendi, gratiae tuae tribuas facultatem. Per Dominum.

---

[1] Men. substitutes for this beginning the more ordinary form *Quaesumus clementiam tuam, omnipotens Deus.*   [2] *dona* Men.   [3] Men. inserts *omnipotens.*   [4] Men. omits *et.*   [5] This *Missa* is perhaps intentionally included in the same section with that preceding, the Collects of which seem to fit it for a similar purpose.   [6] *presbyteratus* Pam.   [7] *servitutis* V.; Pam. as text.   [8] *ut* V.   [9] The use of this heading for the *Secreta* is exceptional in V.; the absence of any heading for the *Hanc igitur* may be due to the same cause.   [10] Some words such as *placatus accipias* seem to be required here for the completion of the sense: but both in V. and in Pam. the sentence is left incomplete.   [11] *pro* V.; Pam. as text.   [12] *largitatem* Pam.; V. as text (ungrammatically); the similar Collect in Leon. has *largitate gaudentes.*

XXXVIII.

ORATIONES TEMPORE, QUOD ABSIT, MORTALITATIS.

Deus, qui non[1] mortem, sed poenitentiam desideras peccatorum, populum tuum, quaesumus, ad te converte propitius; ut dum tibi devotus extiterit, iracundiae flagella[2] amoveas. Per. γ R. Gerb. 304. Men. 209. Leofr. 186.

Populum tuum, quaesumus, omnipotens Deus, ab ira tua ad te confugientem paterna recipe pietate; ut qui tuae maiestatis flagella formidant, de tua mereantur[3] venia gratulari[4]. Per. γ [Gerb. 304 n.] Men. 209. Leofr. 187.

Secreta.

Subveniat nobis, Domine, quaesumus[5], sacrificii praesentis operatio, quae nos et ab[6] erroribus universis potenter absolvat, et a totius eripiat perditionis incursu. Per. γ R. Gerb. 305. Men. 209. Leofr. 187.

Postcommun.

Tuere[7] nos, Domine, quaesumus[5], tua sancta sumentes, et ab omni propitius iniquitate defende. Per. Men. 209. Leofr. 187.

[1] R. inserts *vis* but omits *mortem*; V. Men. Leofr. as text. [2] *tuae ab eo iracundiae flagella* R.; *iracundiae tuae ab eo flagella* Men.; *iracundiae tuae flagella ab eo* Leofr.; V. as text. [3] Leofr. inserts *semper*. [4] *gratulare* V. [5] *quaesumus Domine* Leofr. [6] R. omits *ab*. [7] *Tui* V.; Men. Leofr. as text. The Postcommunion of the *Missa* in R. is now lost: that which Gerbert gives as the Postcommunion belongs to another *Missa* (probably a *Missa pro navigantibus*), the earlier prayers of which are also wanting in R. in consequence of the loss of a leaf.

XXXIX.

ITEM ALIA MISSA.

Ecclesiae tuae, quaesumus, omnipotens Deus, placatus intende conventum; et misericordia tua nos potius quam ira praeveniat; quia si iniquitates nostras observare volueris, nulla poterit creatura subsistere; sed admirabili pietate, qua nos fecisti, ignosce peccantibus, ut opera manuum tuarum non facias interire. Per. Men. 207.

Exaudi, Domine, preces nostras, et ne velis cum servis tuis adire iudicium; quia sicut in nobis nulla iustitia reperitur, de qua praesumere valeamus, ita te fontem pietatis agnoscimus, a quo et a peccatis nostris nos ablui[1] et a necessitatibus liberari confidimus. Per. Men. 208.

Secreta.

Men. 208.
R.S.(*alibi.*)
Gerb. 50.
Pam. 231.
Men. 48.

Per haec, quaesumus, veniat, Domine [2], sacramenta nostrae redemptionis effectus, qui nos et ab humanis retrahat semper excessibus, et ad salutaria cuncta perducat. Per. γ

Postcommun.

Men. 208.

Huius operatio nos, Domine, sacramenti, quaesumus, purificet semper et muniat. Per.

[1] *absolvi* Men.; *ablue* V. [2] *veniat quaesumus Domine* S. Gerb. Pam. Men. (48); *veniat sacramenta quaesumus Domine* R.; V. Men. (208) as text.

XL.

ITEM ALIA MISSA.

Men. 208.

Deus, cuius misericordiam [1] caelestium quoque virtutum indigent potestates, et in cuius conspectu nullus est hominum absque sorde et poena peccati, delicta populi tui, quaesumus, averte propitiatus; ut quos propriae conscientiae reatus accusat, bonitatis tuae patientia faciat venia [2] promereri. Per Dominum nostrum.

Men. 208.

Deus cuius tanta est excellentia pietatis, ut, uno peccatore converso, maximum gaudium facias in caelis haberi [3], respice in exigua [4] populi portione [4]; ut, omni vexatione depulsa, hereditas tua et [5] numero augeatur, et devotione proficiat [6]. Per.

Secreta.

Men. 208.

Protegat nos, Domine, quaesumus, hostia salutaris; et quae ad honorem tui • nominis immolatur, nobis prosit ad 714 veniam. Per.

Postcommun.

Men. 208.
x *supra.*
R.S.(*alibi.*)
Gerb. 139.
Pam. 405.
Men. 171.

Sancta tua nos, Domine, sumpta vivificent, et misericordiae sempiternae praeparent [7] expiatos. Per Dominum nostrum. γ

[1] *misericordia* Men.; V. as text (ungrammatically). [2] *veniam* Men.; V. as text (ungrammatically). [3] *habere* V.; Men. as text. [4] *exiguam ...portionem* Men.; V. as text (ungrammatically). [5] *in* (for *et*) V.; Men. as text. [6] *perficiat* V.; Men. as text. [7] *reparent* R.

XLI.

ITEM ALIA MISSA.

Men. 208.

Exaudi, Domine, quaesumus, populum tuum de tua misericordia malorum suorum veniam supplicantem; et quia potens es peccata dimittere[1], supplicia quae nostris meremur operibus, potentia tuae pietatis averte. Per.

Iram tuam, quaesumus, Domine, a populo tuo miseratus averte, quam nostris quidem meremur operibus, sed humana fragilitate sustinere non possumus; illa nos itaque contine pietate, qua[2] praestare soles indignis. Per.

<small>Men. 208.</small>

Secreta.

Concede nobis, Domine, quaesumus, ut haec hostia salutaris et nostrorum fiat purgatio delictorum, et tuae propitiatio potestatis. Per. γ

<small>Men. 208.
R.S.(alibi.)
Gerb. 173.
Pam. 410.
x supra.</small>

Postcommun.

Plebem nomini tuo subditam, Domine, propitius intuere, eique[3] tuas consolationes[4] iugiter per caelestem gratiam dignanter operare. Per.

<small>Men. 209.
S. (alibi.)
Gerb. 239.
xvii supra.</small>

[1] dimittere peccata Men.; V. as text. [2] quam Men.; V. as text (ungrammatically). [3] et ei Men.; V. S. Gerb. as text. [4] consolationes tuas V. in xvii supra, S. Gerb.; V. here, Men. as text.

XLII.

ORATIONES PRO MORTALITATE ANIMALIUM.

Deus, qui laboribus hominum etiam de mutis animalibus solatia subrogasti, supplices te rogamus, ut sine quibus non alitur humana conditio, nostris facias usibus non perire. Per Dominum. γ

<small>Pam. 447.
[Gerb. 305 n.]</small>

Deus, qui humanae fragilitati necessaria providisti misericors adminicula iumentorum, quaesumus,[1] eadem miseris consulendo non subtrahas; et quorum[2] nostris meritis saevit interitus, tua, nobis parcendo, clementia cessare iubeas[3] vastitatem. Per.

<small>B.
[Gerb. 305 n.]</small>

Secreta.

Sacrificiis, Domine, placatus[4] oblatis, opem tuam nostris temporibus clementer impende. Per. γ

<small>B.
[Gerb. 305 n.]
Pam. 447.</small>

Postcommun.

Benedictionem tuam, Domine, populus fidelis accipiat, qua corpore salvatus ac mente et congruam tibi semper exhibeat servitutem, et propitiationis tuae beneficia semper inveniat. Per. γ

<small>[Gerb. 305 n.]
Pam. 447.</small>

Averte, Domine, quaesumus, a fidelibus tuis cunctos⁵ miseratus errores, et saevientium morborum depelle perniciem; ut quos merito flagellas devios, foveas tua miseratione correctos. Per. γ

¹ Gerb. inserts *ut*; V. B. as text.   ² B. inserts *pro*; V. Gerb. as text.
³ *iubeat* B.; V. Gerb. as text.   ⁴ *placare* B.; V. Gerb. Pam. as text.
⁵ *cunctis* V.; B. Gerb. Pam. as text.

XLIII.
Orationes de Sterilitate.

R.
Gerb. 300.

Sempiternae pietatis tuae abundantiam, Domine, supplices imploramus ut nos beneficiis, quibus non meremur, anticipans, benefacere cognoscaris indignis. Per.

Leofr. 187.

Da nobis, quaesumus, Domine, piae supplicationis effectum, et pestilentiam famemque propitiatus averte; ut mortalium corda cognoscant et te indignante talia flagella producere¹, et te miserante cessare. Per.

Secreta.

R.
Leon. 417.
Gerb. 301.
Leofr. 187.

Deus, qui humani generis utramque substantiam praesentium munerum et alimento² vegetas, et renovas sacramento³, tribue, quaesumus, ut⁴ eorum et corporibus nostris subsidium non desit et mentibus. Per.

Postcommun.

R.
Leon. 417.
Gerb. 301.
Leofr. 187.

Guberna, quaesumus, Domine,⁵ temporalibus adiumentis quos dignaris aeternis informare mysteriis. Per Dominum nostrum.

¹ *producere* so V., perhaps ungrammatically for *produci*: Leofr. has *prodire*.
² *alimentum* V.; R. Leon. Leofr. as text.   ³ *sacramentum* R.; V. Leon. Leofr. as text.   ⁴ *in* (for *ut*) R.; V. Leon. Leofr. as text.   ⁵ R. Leofr. insert *et*; V. Leon. as text.

XLIV.
Orationes ad Pluviam Postulandam.

R.
Leon. 448.
Pam. 449.
Gerb. 301.
Men. 210.

Deus, in quo vivimus, movemur et sumus, pluviam nobis tribue congruentem; ut praesentibus subsidiis sufficienter adiuti sempiterna fiducialius appetamus. Per. γ

[Gerb. 301 n.]
Men. 209.
Pam. 448.

Terram tuam, Domine, quam videmus¹ nostris iniquitatibus tabescentem, caelestibus aquis infunde, atque irriga beneficiis gratiae sempiternae. Per. γ

Delicta[2], Domine, quaesumus, miseratus absolve, et aquarum subsidia praebe caelestium, quibus terrena conditio vegetata subsistat. Per Dominum nostrum. γ

R.
Pam. 449.
Gerb. 301.
Men. 210.

Secreta.

Oblatis, Domine, placare muneribus, et opportunum tribue nobis[3] pluviae sufficientis auxilium. Per. γ

R.
Pam. 449.
Gerb. 301.
Men. 210.

Postcommun.

Tuere nos[4], Domine, quaesumus, tua sancta sumentes, et ab omnibus propitius absolve peccatis. Per. γ

R.
Pam. 449.
Gerb. 301.
Men. 210.

[1] *vidimus* Pam.; V. Gerb. Men. as text.   [2] R. Pam. Men. insert *fragilitatis nostrae*; V. as text.   [3] *nobis tribue* Pam. Men.; V. R. as text.
[4] R. omits *nos*; V. Pam. Men. as text.

XLV.
Item Alia Missa.

Omnipotens sempiterne Deus, cuius munere elementa omnia recreantur, reminiscere miserationum tuarum, et salutiferos imbres humano generi concede propitius, quatenus fecunditatis tuae alimoniis omnis terra laetetur. Per.

Gerb. 301.
Men. 210.

Omnipotens sempiterne Deus, petimus divinam clementiam tuam ut faciem totius terrae largioribus[1] imbribus irrigare digneris, aurasque[2] salubres tribuas, atque aegris restitue pristinam sanitatem; et animae quae promissiones tuas sitiunt de tua semper caritate abundantia repleantur. Per.

Deus qui ad mutandam aeris qualitatem operis caelum nubibus, et paras terrae pluviam, aperi fontem benignitatis tuae, et terram squalidam et ariditatem pulveream laeto imbre fecunda, ut recepisse nos venia[3] peccatorum, cessante iam correptione, laetemur. Per.

Secreta.

Placare, Domine, muneribus semper acceptis, et diuturnam tempera[4] diffusis nubibus siccitatem. Per.

Gerb. 302.
Men. 210.

Postcommun.

Precibus populi tui, Domine, quaesumus, placatus aspira, ut veniam tribuas hu·manis excessibus; et opem miseris benignus impende[5]. Per Dominum nostrum.

Gerb. 302.
Men. 210.

R.
Gerb. 301.
Pam. 449.
Men. 209.
Da nobis, Domine, quaesumus, pluviam salutarem, et aridam terrae faciem fluentis caelestibus dignanter infunde. Per. ỹ

¹ *largioris* V.   ² *auresque* V.   ³ *venia* so V. (ungrammatically).
⁴ *diuturna tempora* V.; Gerb. Men. as text.   ⁵ *impendas* Gerb. Men.; V. as text.

XLVI.

Orationes ad poscendam serenitatem.

R.
Gerb. 302.
Pam. 450.
Men. 211.
Ad te nos, Domine, clamantes exaudi, et aeris serenitatem nobis tribue supplicantibus¹; ut qui pro peccatis nostris iuste affligimur, misericordia tua praeveniente, clementiam sentiamus. Per. ỹ

[Gerb. 302 n.]
Deus, qui fidelium precibus flecteris, et humilium confessione placaris, conversis ad² te propitiare supplicibus; et quos fecisti iram intelligere castigantis³ fac misericordiam sentire parcentis. Per.

Gerb. 302.
Men. 211.
Leofr. 188.
Deus, qui omnium rerum tibi servientium naturam per ipsos motus⁴ aeris ad cultum tuae maiestatis instituis, tranquillitatem nobis misericordiae tuae remotis largire terroribus; ut cuius iram expavimus, clementiam sentiamus. Per. ỹ

Secreta.

R.
Gerb. 302.
Pam. 450.
Men. 211.
Leofr. 188.
Praeveniat nos, quaesumus, Domine, gratia tua semper et subsequatur, et has oblationes, quas pro peccatis nostris nomini tuo consecrandas deferimus⁵, benignus assume; ut per intercessionem⁶ sanctorum tuorum cunctis nobis proficiant⁷ ad salutem. Per. ỹ

Postcommun.

R.
Gerb. 302.
Pam. 450.
Men. 211.
Leofr. 188.
Plebs tua, Domine, capiat sacrae benedictionis augmentum, et copiosis beneficiorum tuorum sublevetur auxiliis, quae tantis⁸ intercessionem deprecationibus adiuvatur⁸. Per. ỹ

¹ *supplicantes* V.; *supplicantis* R.; Gerb. Pam. Men. as text.   ² *a* V.; Gerb. as text.   ³ *castigantes* V.; Gerb. as text.   ⁴ *natura per ipsos modos* V.; Gerb. Men. Leofr. as text.   ⁵ *deferemus* V.; R. Pam. Men. Leofr. as text.   ⁶ *intercessione* V.; R. Pam. Men. Leofr. as text.   ⁷ *perficiant* V.; R. Pam. Men. Leofr. as text.   ⁸ *tangis ... adiuvantur* R.

XLVII.

ORATIONES POST TEMPESTATEM ET FULGURA[1].

Magnificentiam tuam, Domine, praedicamus[2], suppliciter implorantes, ut quia[3] nos imminentibus[4] periculis exuisti, a peccatis quoque benignus absolvas; ut • et[5] beneficia nobis maiora concedas, et tuis nos facias parere mandatis. Per.

R. Leon. 371. Gerb. 303.

A domo tua, quaesumus, Domine, spiritales nequitiae pellantur, et aeriarum discedat malignitas potestatum[6]. Per. γ

Pam. 450. Gerb. 304. see I. xciii supra.

[Secreta].

Offerimus, Domine, laudes et munera, pro concessis[7] beneficiis gratias referentes[8], et pro concedendis semper[9] suppliciter deprecantes. Per. γ

R. Leon. 444. Gerb. 304. Pam. 451. Leofr. 188. see I. lv supra.

Postcommun.

Omnipotens sempiterne Deus, qui nos et castigando sanas, et ignoscendo conservas, praesta supplicibus tuis ut et tranquillitatis[10] huius optatae[11] consolatione[12] laetemur, et[13] dono[14] tuae pietatis semper utamur. Per. γ

R. Leon. 372. Gerb. 304. Pam. 451. Leofr. 188.

[1] The corresponding *Missa* in R. has the title *Pro tempest. et fulgora*; V. reads *post tempestate et fulgura*: and the wording of the first Collect, Secret and Postcommunion suggests that the *Missa* was intended for use after, and not during, a storm. [2] *praeiamus* V. (Tommasi reads *precamur*); *praecedamus* R.; Leon. as text. [3] *qui* Leon.; V. Gerb. as text. [4] *eminentibus* V. R.; Leon. as text. [5] Leon. R. omit *et*; V. as text. [6] *tempestatum* Pam. Gerb.; V. as text. [7] *consensis* R. [8] *exhibentes gratias* Leon. [9] Leon. omits *semper*. [10] *tranquillitatibus* R. Gerb. Pam. [11] *oblatae* Gerb., but R. has *oblate*. [12] *consolationis* V. R. Gerb. Pam. Leofr.; Leon. as text. [13] Leon. inserts *ad correctionis effectum*. [14] *dona* V. R.; Leon. Pam. Leofr. as text.

XLVIII.

ORATIONES PRO HIS QUI AGAPE[1] FACIUNT.

Oremus[2], dilectissimi nobis, omnipotenti Deo pro filio nostro *Illo*, qui recolens divina mandata de iustis laboribus suis victum indigentibus subministrat, quatenus haec devotio ipsius, sicut nobis est necessaria, ita sit Deo semper accepta. Per.

B. [Gerb. 284 n.]

Oremus.

Sanctum[3] ac venerabilem retributorem bonorum operum Dominum deprecamur[4] pro filio nostro *Illo*, qui de suis

[Gerb. 283 n.]

iustis laboribus victum indigentibus administrat, ut Dominus caelestis[5] sua misericordia terrenam eleemosynam compenset[6], et spiritales divitias largiatur; tribuat ei magna pro parvis, pro terrenis caelestia, pro temporalibus sempiterna. Per.

[1] *Agape*, so V. Perhaps the word is treated as indeclinable. [2] This form is adapted in B., and in the parallel *Missa* in Gerb., to serve as a Postcommunion in a *Missa pro eleemosynas facientibus*. The Postcommunion begins *Omnipotens et misericors Deus, famulos tuos placatus intende, qui recolentes*. [3] This Prayer appears in Gerb. as a 'bidding-prayer' prefixed to the *Missa pro eleemosynas facientibus*. [4] *deprecemur* Gerb.; V. as text. [5] *caelestis* so V.; Tommasi reads *caelesti*, but the reading of the text is supported by Gerb. where *ei* is inserted before *sua*. [6] *complenset* V.; Gerb. has *recompenset terrenam eleemosynam*.

XLIX.

Item Orationes ad Missas.

[Gerb. 283 n.]
B.

Deus, qui post baptismi sacramentum secundam[1] ablutionem[2] peccatorum eleemosynis indidisti, respice propitius super famulum tuum[3] *Illum*, cuius operibus tibi gratiae referuntur; fac eum praemio beatum, quem fecisti pietate devotum[4]. Per.

[Gerb. 283 n.]

»Deus, qui homini[5] ad tuam imaginem facto[5] etiam spiritalem alimoniam praeparasti, concede filio nostro famulo tuo *Illi*[6], qui in pauperes tuos tua seminat dona, ut verius[7] metat suorum operum fructus, et largitatis hodiernae compensatio istius[8] perpetua conferatur, recipiatque pro parvis magna, pro terrenis caelestia, pro temporalibus sempiterna. [Per.]

Secreta.

B.
[Gerb. 284 n.]

Deus, qui tuorum corda fidelium per eleemosynam dixisti posse mundari, praesta, quaesumus, ut huius consortiis sacramenti ut[9] ad conscientiae suae fructum non gravare studeant miseros, sed iuvare. Per.

Infra actionem.

[Gerb. 284 n.]

Hanc igitur oblationem, Domine, famuli tui *Illius*, quam tibi offert ob[10] iustis eleemosynis suis, quod[11] in pauperes tuos operatur, [12] placatus suscipias deprecamur. Pro quo maiestati tuae supplices fundimus preces, ut adiicias ei tempora vitae, ut per multa curricula annorum laetus tibi in pauperes tuos haec operetur, atque annua tibi vota[13] persolvat. Per Christum. Quam oblationem.

Postcommun.

Omnipotens sempiterne Deus, respice propitius super hunc famulum tuum *Illum*, qui in pauperes tuos [14] operatur : virtute custodi [15], potestate tuearis ; ut per multa curricula annorum laetus tibi in pauperes tuos haec operetur. Per Dominum nostrum. [Gerb. 284 n.]

[1] *secundum* V.; B. Gerb. as text. [2] *abolitionem* B. Gerb. [3] *famulos tuos* B. (and so throughout). [4] After *devotos*, B. has *recipiant pro parvis magna* &c. (see end of second Collect in text). [5] *hominem . . . facto* V. ; Gerb. as text. [6] *Illo* V. [7] *veros* Gerb. ; V. as text. [8] *ipsi* Gerb.; V. as text. [9] *ut huius consortes sacramenti* Gerb. ; *huius consortibus sacramenti ut* B. ; V. as text: perhaps the true reading is *et huius consortibus sacramenti ut*. [10] *de* Gerb.; V. as text, ungrammatically. [11] *quas* Gerb. ; V. as text (ungrammatically). [12] Gerb. inserts *ut*. [13] *vota tibi* Gerb. [14] Gerb. inserts *haec*. [15] *custodias* Gerb.; V. as text.

L.

Missa in Monasterio.

Omnipotens sempiterne Deus, qui facis mirabilia magna solus, praetende super [1] famulos tuos spiritum gratiae salutaris; et ut in veritate tibi complaceant [2], perpetuum eis [3] rorem tuae benedictionis infunde. Per. γ   B. Gerb. 278. cf. Pam. 439. cf. Men. 237.

Fac, quaesumus, Domine, famulos tuos toto semper ad te corde concurrere, tibi subdita mente servire, tua misericordia [4] suppliciter implorare, et tuis iugiter beneficiis gratulari. Per.

720 •Famulos tuos, quaesumus, Domine, placatus intende, pariterque eos et a peccatis absolve propitius, et a cunctis eripe benignus adversis. Per Dominum nostrum.

Secreta.

Hostias Domine famulorum tuorum placatus intende, et quas in honore [5] nominis tui devota mente celebrant [6], proficere sibi sentiant ad medelam. Per. γ   B. Gerb. 278. Pam. 440. cf. Men. 237. cf. Leon. 295.

V.D. Per Christum Dominum nostrum. Qui dum confessores tuos tanta pietate glorificas, ut nullum apud te sanctum propositum doceas esse sine praemio, quanto magis duriora certamina sustinentes ad tuae quoque retributionis munus invitas. Et ideo.

Infra actionem.

Hanc igitur oblationem, Domine, famulorum tuorum, quam tibi offerunt ob devotionem mentis suae, pius ac   B. Gerb. 278.

propitius clementi vultu suscipias, tibique supplicantes libens protege, dignanter exaudi [7], et aeterna eos protectione conserva [8]; ut semper in tua religione laetantes, instanter in sanctae Trinitatis fide catholica perseverent: nobis haec quoque unanimiter et crebro [9] petentibus ipse praestabis omnipotens Deus. Per Christum. γ

Postcommun.

B.
Gerb. 278.
Pam. 440.

Quos caelesti recreas munere, perpetuo, Domine, comitare praesidio; et quos fovere non desinis, dignos fieri sempiterna redemptione concede. Per. γ

[1] Gerb. inserts *nos*. Pam. Men. have special mention of the Abbat or Bishop and of those committed to his charge.   [2] *complaceamus* Gerb. [3] *nobis* Gerb.   [4] *tua misericordia* so V. (ungrammatically).   [5] *honorem* Pam. Men.; V. B. Gerb. as text.   [6] *pro eis celebramus* Pam. Men.; *pro nobis celebramus* Gerb.; V. B. as text.   [7] *protege et clementer exaudi* Gerb.; V. B. as text.   [8] B. ends the *Hanc igitur* at this point, proceeding with *Diesque*.   [9] *crebrae* V.

LI.

ITEM ORATIONES MONACHORUM [1].

B.
Gerb. 279.

Tu famulis tuis, quaesumus, Domine, bonos mores placatus institue, tu in eis quod tibi placitum sit dignanter infunde, ut et digni sint, et tua valeant beneficia promereri. Per.

Respice, quaesumus, Domine, famulos tuos, et in tua misericordia confidentes caelesti protege benignus auxilio. Per.

R.
Gerb. 270.
Pam. 438.
Men. 239.
cvi *infra*.

Da famulis [2] tuis, quaesumus, Domine, in tua fide et sinceritate constantiam, ut in caritate divina firmati [3] nullis tentationibus ab eius integritate vellantur. Per. γ

*Famulos tuos, quaesumus, Domine, tua semper gratia 721 benedicat, et inculpabiles ad vitam perducat aeternam. Per.

B.
Gerb. 279.

Famulos tuos, quaesumus, Domine, benignus intende, et eis dignanter pietatis tuae impende custodiam. Per.

Famulis tuis, quaesumus, Domine, sperata concede, et ab omnibus eos culpis excusa. Per.

Adesto, Domine, supplicationibus nostris, et famulos tuos assidua protectione conserva; ut qui tibi iugiter famulantur, continua remuneratione ditentur [4]. Per.

[1] Two of the Prayers of this series appear in B. and Gerb. as additional Postcommunions for the *Missa in Monasterio*. The third is the Postcommunion of a *Missa pro salute vivorum* in cvi *infra*, and in Gerb. Pam. Men.
[2] R. Pam. Men. and V. in cvi *infra* insert *et famulabus*.   [3] *formati* Pam.
[4] *ditentum* V.

LII.

Incipit Actio Nuptialis[1].

Adesto, Domine, supplicationibus nostris, et institutis tuis, quibus propagationem[2] humani generis ordinasti, benignus assiste; ut quod te auctore iungitur, te auxiliante servetur. [Per.]

<small>Mart. lib. I. cap. ix. Men. 263. Leon. 446. Gerb. 258.</small>

Quaesumus, omnipotens Deus, instituta providentiae tuae pio favore comitare, et quos legitima societate connectis, longaeva pace custodi. Per. γ

<small>Mart. lib. I. cap. ix. Men. 263. Leon. 446. Gerb. 258.</small>

Secreta.

Adesto, Domine, supplicationibus nostris, et hanc oblationem famularum tuarum *Illarum*[3], quam tibi offerunt pro famula tua *Illa*, quam ad statum maturitatis et ad diem nuptiarum perducere dignatus es, placidus ac benignus assume; ut quod tua dispositione expeditur[4], tua gratia compleatur. Per.

<small>Mart. lib. I. cap. ix. Men. 263. Gerb. 258.</small>

V.D. Qui foedera nuptiarum blando concordiae iugo et insolubili pacis vinculo nexuisti, ut multiplicandis adoptionum filiis sanctorum connubiorum fecunditas pudica serviret. Tua enim, Domine, providentia, tuaque gratia ineffabilibus modis utrumque dispensat, ut quod generatio ad mundi edidit ornatum, regeneratio[5] ad ecclesiae perducat augmentum[6].

<small>Mart. lib. I. cap. ix. Men. 263.</small>

Infra actionem.

Hanc igitur oblationem famularum tuarum *Illius* et *Illius*[7], quam tibi offerunt pro fa‧mula tua *Illa*[8], quaesumus, Domine, placatus accipias: pro qua maiestatem tuam supplices[9] exoramus, ut sicut eam ad aetatem nuptiis congruentem pervenire tribuisti, sic eam consortio maritali tuo munere copulatam desiderata sobole gaudere perficias[10] atque ad optatam seriem[11] cum suo coniuge provehas benignus annorum: diesque nostros[12].

<small>Mart. lib. I. cap. ix. Men. 264. Leon. 446.</small>

Infra actionem ad tricesimum vel annualem nuptiarum.

Hanc igitur oblationem, Domine, famulorum tuorum *Illius* et *Illius*[13] quam tibi offerunt ob diem tricesimum

<small>Mart. lib. I. cap. ix. Men. 264.</small>

coniunctionis suae, *vel* annualem, quo die eos iugali vinculo sociare dignatus es, placatus suscipias deprecamur: ob hoc igitur reddunt [14] tibi vota sua Deo vero et vivo, pro quibus tremendae pietati tuae supplices fundimus preces, ut pariter bene et pacifice [15] senescant, et videant filios filiorum suorum usque in [16] tertiam et quartam progeniem, et te benedicant omnibus diebus vitae suae. Per Christum Dominum nostrum. Quam oblationem tu, Deus.

Percomples canonem plenariam, et dicis orationem Dominicam, et sic eam benedicis his verbis [17].

Incipit oratio.

Mart. lib. I.
cap. ix.
Men. 265.

Deus qui mundi crescentis exordio [18] multiplicata prole benedicis, propitiare supplicationibus nostris, et super hanc famulam tuam opem tuae benedictionis infunde; ut in iugali consortio affectu compari, mente consimili, sanctitate mutua copulentur. Per.

Incipit benedictio [19].

Mart. lib. I.
cap. ix.
Men. 265.
Leon. 447.

Pater mundi conditor, nascentium genitor, multiplicandae originis institutor, qui Adae comitem tuis manibus addidisti, cuius ex ossibus ossa crescentia parem formam admirabili diversitate signarent; hinc ad totius multitudinis incrementum coniugalis thori iussa consortia, quo [20] totum inter se [21] saeculum colligarent, humani generis foedera nexuerunt. Sic enim tibi, Domine, placitum, sic necessa·rium fuit; ut [22], quia longe esset infirmius [23] quod homini simile [24], quam quod tibi Deo [25] feceras, additus [26] fortiori [27] sexus infirmior, unum efficeret [28] ex duobus, et pari pignore soboles mixta manaret [29], dum per ordinem flueret digesta [30] posteritas, et priores ventura [31] sequerentur, nec ullum sibi finem in tam brevi termino, quamvis essent caduca, proponerent [32]. Ad haec igitur [datae sint leges instituta [33]] venturae. [Quapropter [33]] huius famulae tuae, Pater, rudimenta sanctifica [33], ut bono et prospero sociata consortio, legis aeternae iussa [34] custodiat, memineritque [35], Domine, non tantum ad licentiam coniugalem, sed ad observantiam fidei sanctorum pignorum delegatam [36]. Fidelis et casta nubat in Christo, imitatrixque sanctarum permaneat feminarum. Sit amabilis ut Rachel viro suo, sapiens ut Rebecca, longaeva et fidelis ut Sarra. Nihil ex hac subsitivus [37] ille

723

auctor praevaricationis usurpet: nixa [38] fidei mandatisque permaneat [39]; serviens Deo vero devota [40], muniat infirmitatem suam robore disciplinae; uni thoro iuncta, contactus vitae illicitos fugiat [41]. Sit verecundia [42] gravis, pudore venerabilis, doctrinis caelestibus erudita: sit fecunda in sobole, sit probata et innocens, et ad beatorum requiem atque [43] ad caelestia regna perveniat. Per.

Post haec dicis: Pax vobiscum: *Et sic eos communicas. Deinde postquam communicaverint, dicis super eos benedictionem his verbis*:

Domine sancte, Pater omnipotens, aeterne Deus [44], iteratis precibus [45] te supplices exoramus pro quibus apud te supplicator [46] est Christus, coniunctiones famulorum tuorum fovere digneris: benedictiones tuas excipere mereantur, ut [47] filiorum successibus fecundentur: nuptias eorum sicut primi hominis [48] confirmare dignare: avertantur ab eis inimici omnes insidiae [49], ut sanctitatem patrum [50] etiam in ipso coniugio imitentur, qui providentia tua, Domine, coniungi meruerunt. Per.

Mart. lib. 1. cap. ix. Men. 266.

Item Postcommun.

Exaudi nos, Domine sancte, Pater omnipotens, aeterne Deus, ut quod nostro ministratur [51] officio tua benedictione potius impleatur. Per. γ

Mart. lib. 1. cap. ix. Men. 264. Leon. 446.

---

[1] This section has been compared with the parallel portion of the Leonine Sacramentary, with the text of the Codex Remensis, as given by Menard, and with the *Ordo* given by Martène (*de Ant. Eccl. Rit.* lib. 1. cap. ix) from V., Codex Remensis, and Codex Gellonensis. The two Collects and *Secreta* are also to be found in Gerbert's text. In Leon. the section is headed *Incipit velatio nuptialis*: the Secret is different from that of the later texts, and the Collects and Postcommunion occupy different positions. The Preface, the clause *infra actionem* for the commemoration of a past marriage, and the benediction after Communion are not contained in Leon. Nor has it the Collect which in the text precedes the benediction of the bride, for which it substitutes the first collect of the text. [2] *propagacione* V.; Leon. Mart. Men. Gerb. as text. [3] *famulorum tuorum* Mart.; V. Gerb. Men. as text. [4] *expetitur* Men. Gerb.; V. Mart. as text. [5] *generatio* Men.; V. Mart. as text. [6] Men. adds *Per Christum*. [7] *Illi et illas* V.; *Illorum et Illarum* Mart.; *Illarum* Men. [8] *Illi* V.; Men. omits the clause *quam tibi ... Illa*; Mart. as text. [9] *suppliciter* Mart. [10] *proficias* V.; Men. Mart. as text. [11] *atque oblatam seriem* Men. [12] Men. omits *diesque nostros*, and goes on *Per Christum Dominum nostrum*. *Quam oblationem*. [13] *Illi et Illas* V.; *Illorum et Illarum* Men. Mart. [14] *reddant* Men. [15] *pacifici* V. Mart.; Men. as text. [16] *ad* Men. [17] For *et sic eam*, &c., Mart. has *et sic cantas benedictionis orationem his verbis*. [18] *exordium* Men. [19] This benediction is called by Tommasi '*oratio mendosissima*': while the Ballerini remark that this character attaches to it '*in omnibus MSS. Sacramentariis*.' In its original form, it most probably followed the model of the Eucharistic Preface, beginning with *Vere dignum et iustum est*: the sequence of its opening clauses is clearer if such an opening is

supplied: but it does not appear in any of the texts. [20] Men. omits *quo*. [21] Men. omits *se*. [22] *Sic enim tibi placitum necessario, ut* Leon.; *Sic enim tibi Domine placitum fuit sic enim necessarium fuit ut* Men.; V. Mart. as text. [23] *quia longe est et infirmus* V. Men.; *quia longe est et infirmius* Mart.; Leon. as text. [24] *quod homine similem* V. Mart.; *quod homini silem* Men.; Leon. as text. [25] Mart. omits *Deo*; V. has *quem* for *quam*. [26] *additur* Men. [27] *forciorae* V.; *fortiore* Mart. Men.; Leon. as text. [28] *ut unum efficeris* V. Mart.; *ut unum efficeras* Men.; Leon. as text. [29] *maneret* V. Mart. Men.; Leon. as text. [30] *tunc per ordinem flueret egesta* Mart. Men.; *tunc per ordinem flueret deiesta* V.; Leon. as text. [31] *ut in prioris ventura* Men.; V. Mart. Leon. as text (Leon. *ac* for *et*). [32] *posteritas* (for *postponerent*) Leon.; V. Men. Mart. as text. [33] Leon. omits the words in brackets, which are found with some variation in V. Men. Mart. In V. they appear as in the text, save that *datae* is written *date*. Men. Mart. have *legis*, and Men. has *ventura*. As it stands in any of these texts, the passage seems to need emendation: and it is not quite clear how it should be corrected. Menard proposes to read *data sunt legis instituta venturae*, and this gives an intelligible sense. But it seems improbable that the scribe of Leon. should have omitted not only the words which the other texts insert before *venturae*, but also the *quapropter* which follows it: and the additional words may be due to an attempt to emend an obscure passage. If there is an omission in the text of Leon., it seems possible that the original form was *Ad haec igitur datae sibi legis instituta venturae huius famulae tuae, Pater, rudimenta sanctifica*. The change of *sibi* into *sint* is not in itself impossible, and would have given some occasion for the insertion of *quapropter* by a later hand. [34] *iura* Leon. Men.; V. Mart. as text. [35] Leon. inserts *se*; V. Men. Mart. as text. [36] *observantiam Dei sanctorumque pignorum custodiae delegatam* Leon.; V. Mart. have *diligatam*, Men. *diligata*, otherwise as text. [37] *subsicivus* Leon.; *subdolus* Men. Mart.; V. as text. [38] *nexa* V. Men. Mart.; Leon. as text. [39] V. Men. Mart. insert *foeminarum* (wrongly following a previous clause); Leon. as text. [40] Leon. omits *serviens Deo vero devota*; the words are in V. Men. Mart., but it is not clear whether they should be connected with *permaneat* or with *muniat*. [41] Muratori in his edition of Leon. reads *contactus vitet illicitos* (omitting *fugiat*). In this he was following a suggestion of Bianchini, afterwards withdrawn by that editor. Leon. actually agrees with the other MSS. in the reading of the text. [42] *verecunda* V. Men.; Leon. Mart. as text. [43] *usque* V. Men. Mart.; Leon. as text. [44] Men. omits *aeterne Deus*. [45] *ritibus* Men. [46] *supplicatus* Men. [47] *et* Mart.; V. Men. as text. [48] *fecundentur, sicut plurimi omnes* Men.; V. Mart. as text. [49] *inimici insidiae omnipotens* Men.; V. Mart. as text. [50] *Patrem* Men. [51] *ut quod non ministrentur* Men.; V. Mart. as text.

LIII.

Oratio in Natale Genuinum.

Omnipotens sempiterne Deus, totius conditor creaturae, preces nostras clementer exaudi, et annos famuli tui *Illius*, quem de maternis visceribus in hac vita [1] prodire [2] iussisti, prosperos plurimosque largire, ut omni [3] tibi exigat placiturus aetate [3]. Per Dominum nostrum.

Deus qui saeculorum omnium cursum ac momenta temporum regis, exaudi nos propitius, et concede ut famuli tui *Illius* cuius hodie natalem divini [4] celebramus consecratione mysterii, longaevam ei largiaris aetatem, quatenus fidei eius augmentum [5]. multisque annorum curriculis haec solemnitatis devotio perseveret. Per.

Secreta.

Adesto, Domine, supplicationibus nostris, et hanc oblationem famuli tui *Illius*, quam tibi offert ob diem natalis sui genuinum, quo die eum [6] de maternis visceribus in hunc mundum nasci iussisti, placidus ac benignus assume. Per.

Infra actionem.

Hanc igitur oblationem, Domine, famuli tui *Illius*, quam tibi offert ob [7] diem natalis sui [8] celebrans genuinum, quo die eum [6] de maternis visceribus in hunc mundum nasci iussisti, ad te cognoscendum Deum verum et vivum, placatus suscipias deprecamur: ob hoc igitur reddit tibi vota sua Deo vivo et vero: pro quo maiestati tuae supplices fundimus preces, ut adiicias ei annos et tempora vitae, ut per multa curricula annorum laetus tibi haec sua vota persolvat, atque ad optatam perveniat senectutem, et te benedicat omnibus diebus vitae suae. Per.

Postcommun.

Deus, vita fidelium, timentium te salvator et custos, qui famulum tuum *Illum* ad hanc diem natalis sui genuini, exemto anno, perducere dignatus es, gratiam in eo vitae protectoris augmenta, et dies eius annorum numerositate multiplica, • ut te annuente, per felicem provectus aetatem, ad principatum caelestium gaudiorum pervenire mereatur. Per.

[1] *in hac vita*, so V. (ungrammatically).   [2] *prodere* V.   [3] *omne* . . . *aetate* V. (probably abl. for acc.).   [4] *divinae* V.   [5] *augmentum* so V., perhaps ungrammatically; Tommasi reads *augmento*.   [6] *cum* V.   [7] *ob* seems superfluous.   [8] *suis* V.

LIV.

ORATIONES AD MISSAM PRO STERILITATE MULIERUM.

Deus, qui emortuam vulvam Sarrae ita per Abrahae semen fecundare dignatus es, ut ei etiam contra spem soboles nasceretur, preces famulae tuae *Illius*, pro suae sterilitate deprecantis [1], propitius respice, et ei [2] iuxta tenorem praecedentium patrum et fecunditatem tribuas, et filium quem donaveris benedicas. Per.

Deus, qui famulum tuum Isaac pro sterilitate coniugii sui te deprecantem exaudire, et conceptum Rebeccae donare dignatus es, preces famulae tuae *Illius* pro percipienda prole benignus exaudi; ut firmamentum spei, quod in tua misericordia posuit, ei [2] ex percepto [3] munere quod postulat confirmetur. Per.

Deus, qui opprobrium sterilitatis a Rachel auferens, dum anxietate prolem quaereret meruit fecundare [4], concede propitius, ut famula tua *Illa* in earum feminarum [5] quae tibi placuerunt sortem fecunditatis accipiat, et quod fideliter a tua pietate deposcit obtineat. Per.

Omnipotens sempiterne Deus, qui continuum etiam post futuram [6] ad te precem gemitum Annae, dum eam fecundares, in gaudium convertisti, desiderium famulae tuae *Illius*, ut fecundetur, propitius perfice, et ad laudem gloriae tuae ab ea opprobrium sterilitatis benignus averte. Per.

Deus, cuius occulto consilio ideo Helisabeth sterilis uterus extitit, ut quandoque angelica potius voce fecundaretur, concede propitius ut sicut illa in Iudaico populo praecursorem Domini, ita famula tua *Illa* in filio, qui ad credulitatem tibi huius populi pure deserviat, fecundetur. Per.

Leofr. 229. Deus, qui anxietate [7] sterilium pie respiciens, in eis fecunditatem etiam in sua desperatione mirabiliter operaris, concede propitius ut famula tua illa de percipienda sobole, quod per se non valet, • servi tui Gregorii mereatur precibus obtinere. Per.

Leofr. 229. Omnipotens sempiterne Deus, qui maternum affectum nec in ipsa sacra semper virgine Maria, quae Redemptorem nostrum genuit, denegasti, concede propitius ut eiusdem Dei genitricis precibus [8] famula tua *Illa* esse genitrix mereatur. Per.

Secreta.

Suscipe, Domine, preces nostras cum muneribus hostiarum, quas pro famula tua *Illa* clementiae tuae supplici mente deferimus; ut quia affectum filiorum maxime in matrum visceribus indidisti, maerorem infecunditatis ab ea submoveas, et ad concipiendam sobolem misericorditer benedicas. Per.

Infra actionem.

Hanc igitur oblationem servitutis nostrae, sed et cunctae familiae [tuae] [9], quam tibi offerimus pro famula tua *Illa*, quaesumus, Domine, ut placatus suscipias: pro qua maiestati tuae supplices fundimus preces, ut orationem eius exaudias, et eius uterum vinculum sterilitatis absolvens [10], et prolem in qua nomen tuum benedicatur, concedas: diesque nostros.

Postcommun.

Caelestis vitae munus accipientes, quaesumus, omnipotens Deus, quod pro famula tua *Illa* deprecati sumus, clementer a tua pietate exaudiri mereatur. Per.

[1] *deprecantes* V.   [2] *ea* V.   [3] *praecepto* V.; Tommasi corrects as text.   [4] *meruit fecundare*, so V.; perhaps *quae* should be inserted after *auferens*, and *fecundari* be substituted for *fecundare*.   [5] *in earum feminarum* so V.; perhaps the simplest emendation would be the substitution of *instar* for *in*.   [6] *continuum etiam post futuram*, so V.; perhaps for *continuo etiam post factam*.   [7] *anxietatem* Leofr.; V. as text (ungrammatically).   [8] *genetris praecis* V.   [9] V. omits *tuae*.   [10] *vinculum sterilitatis absolvens*, so V.; *vinculum* is apparently acc. for abl.; *absolvens* may be used ungrammatically for *absolvas*, or the *et* following may be wrongly inserted, or a clerical error for *ei*.

LV.

BENEDICTIO VIDUAE QUAE FUERIT CASTITATEM PROFESSA.

Consolare, Domine, hanc famulam tuam viduitatis languoribus[1] constrictam, sicut consolare dignatus es Sarapthenam viduam per Heliam[2] prophetam: concede ei pudicitiae fructum, ut antiquarum non meminerit voluptatum: nesciat etiam[3] incentiva desideria ut soli tibi subdat propria colla[4], quo possit pro laboribus tantis sexagesimum granum[5] percipere munus delectabile sanctitatis. Per. γ

Gerb. ii. 93.
Leofr. 227.

[1] *laboribus* Gerb.; *merore* Leofr.; V. as text.   [2] *Helisea* Gerb.; V. Leofr. as text.   [3] *enim* Gerb.; V. Leofr. as text.   [4] *proprium collum* Leofr.; V. Gerb. as text.   [5] *sexagisimum gradum* V.; *sexagesimo gradu* Gerb.; Leofr. as text.

LVI.

ORATIONES PRO PACE.

Deus, a quo sancta desideria, et[1] recta consilia et iusta sunt[1] opera, da servis tuis illam, quam mundus dare non potest, pacem; ut et corda[2] mandatis tuis dedita, et, hostium sublata formidine, tempora sint tua protectione tranquilla. Per. γ

B.
Pam. 445.
Men. 205.
cf. III. vii.
supra.

Deus, conditor mundi, sub cuius arbitrio omnium[3] saeculorum ordo decurrit, adesto propitius[3] invocationibus nostris, et tranquillitatem pacis praesentibus concede

[Gerb. 276 *n*.]
Men. 206.

temporibus; ut in laudibus misericordiae tuae incessabili exultatione laetemur. Per. γ

Mur. II.
203 n.

Deus, in te sperantium fortitudo, conserva in populis tuis quod es dignatus operare : [4]potentis misericordiae tuae ostende virtutem; ut qui superbe impetimur hostium feritate, tua mereamur pace gaudere. Per. γ

Secreta.

B.
Pam. 445.
Men. 206.

Deus, qui credentes in te populos nullis sinis noceri[5] terroribus, dignare precibus et hostiis[6] dicatae tibi plebis suscipere, ut pax a[7] tua pietate concessa Romanos[8] fines ab omni hoste faciat esse securos. Per. γ

Postcommun.

B.
Pam. 446.
Men. 206.

Deus, auctor pacis et amator, quem nosse vivere, cui servire regnare est, protege ab omnibus impugnationibus supplices tuos; ut qui defensione tua fidimus[9], nullius hostilitatis arma timeamus. Per. γ

[Gerb. 276 n.]
Men. 206.

Deus, qui misericordiae tuae potentis auxilium[10] et prospera tribuis et adversa depellis, universa obstacula, quae servis tuis adversantur, expugna; ut, remoto terrore bellorum, et libertas[11] secura, [et][12] religio sit quieta. Per. γ

---

[1] B. Pam. Men. omit *et* and *sunt*; V. as text.   [2] B. Pam. Men. insert *nostra*.   [3] Men. omits *omnium* and *propitius*; V. Gerb. as text.   [4] Mur. inserts *et*.   [5] *populis nullis sinis nocere* V.; *populos nullis sinis nocere* B.; *populos nullis sinis concuti* Pam. Men.; *nocere* in V. B. seems to be an error for the ungrammatical reading of the text.   [6] *preces et hostias* B. Pam. Men.; V. as text (ungrammatically).   [7] B¹ Pam. Men. omit *a*; V. B² as text.   [8] *Christianorum* B¹ Pam. Men.; *Christianos* B²; V. as text.   [9] *in defensione tua confidimus* B. Pam.; *in defensione tua fidimus* Men.; *defensione tua fidemus* V.   [10] *potenti auxilio* Gerb.; *potentis auxilio* Men.; V. as text (ungrammatically).   [11] Gerb. inserts *sit*; V. Men. as text.   [12] V. omits *et*, which is inserted from Gerb. Men.

LVII.

Orationes Tempore Belli[1].

Men. 204.

Deus, qui conteris bella, et impugnatores in te sperantium potentia[2] tuae defensionis expugnas, auxiliare implorantibus misericordiam tuam; ut omnium gentium feritate compressa, indefessa te gratiarum actione laudemus[3]. Per. γ

B.
Pam. 444.
Men. 204.

• Deus, regnorum omnium regumque dominator, qui nos et[4] percutiendo sanas, et ignoscendo conservas, praetende nobis[5] misericordiam tuam; ut tranquillitatem[6] pacis tua potestate firmati [7] ad remedia correctionis utamur. Per Dominum nostrum. γ

Deus, cuius regnum [8] est omnium saeculorum, supplicationes nostras clementer exaudi, et Romanorum [9] regnum tibi subditum protege principatum [10]; ut in tua virtute fidentes, et tibi placeant, et super omnia regna praecellant. Per. γ   Men. 204.

Secreta.

Sacrificium, Domine, quod immolamus [11] intende; ut ab omni nos exuat bellorum nequitia, et in tuae protectionis securitate constituat. Per. γ   B. Pam. 444. Men. 204.

Postcommun.

Sacrosancti corporis et sanguinis Domini nostri Iesu Christi refectione vegetati, supplices te rogamus, omnipotens Deus, ut hoc remedio singulari ab omnium peccatorum nos contagione purifices, et a periculorum munias incursione cunctorum. Per. γ   Pam. 444. Men. 204.

[1] *bellis* V.   [2] *potentiae* V.; Men. as text.   [3] *laudemur* V.   [4] B. omits *et*.   [5] B. omits *nobis*.   [6] *tranquillitate* B. Pam. Men.; V. as text (ungrammatically).   [7] *firmata* B. Pam. Men.; V. as text.   [8] Men. repeats *regnum*.   [9] *Christianorum* Men.   [10] So V.; Men. omits *principatum* which seems superfluous: Tommasi read *Romanorum regum*; V. Men. however agree in favour of *regnum*, for which *principatum* may have been an alternative reading. But the word *principatum* occurs twice again in lx *infra*, once in the same context as here, and once where it is clearly equivalent to *principum*. It seems possible that in all three passages the word is to be explained as the genitive of *principates=principes*.   [11] *immolamur* V.

LVIII.

Item alia Missa.

Contere, quaesumus, Domine, hostes populi tui, et delicta nostra, quorum merito nobis dominantur, emunda; ut quum, te placito, puritatem [1] mentibus nostris infunderis, largiaris et pacem. Per.   Leon. 357.

Hostium nostrorum, quaesumus, Domine, elide superbiam, et dexterae tuae virtute prosterne. Per Dominum nostrum. γ   Men. 205.

Omnipotens Deus, Romani [2] nominis inimicos virtute, quaesumus, tuae comprime maiestatis; ut populus tuus et fidei integritate laetetur, et temporum tranquillitate semper exultet. Per. γ   Pam. 444.

274 LIBER SACRAMENTORUM [III. lix.

Secreta.

Pam. 445.
Men. 205.

Huius, Domine, quaesumus, virtute mysterii et a nostris mundemur occultis, et ab inimicorum liberemur insidiis. Per. γ

Postcommun. 729

Pam. 445.
Men. 205.
Leon. 356.

Vivificet nos, quaesumus, Domine, participatio tui sancta mysterii[3], et pariter nobis expiationem tribuat et munimen. Per. γ

[1] *tibi placitam puritatem* Leon.; *te placito puritate* V. [2] *Christiani* Pam. [3] *tui sancta misteriis* V.; Leon. Pam. Men. as text.

LIX.
ITEM ALIA MISSA.

Deus, qui regnis omnibus aeternis[1] dominaris imperio, inclina ad preces humilitatis nostrae aures misericordiae tuae, et Romani regni adesto principibus; ut tua tranquillitatem clementer[2] tua sint semper virtute victores. Per.

Leon. 450.

Propitiare, Domine, in te sperantibus[3] populis, et ad custodiam[4] Romani nominis dexteram tuae protectionis ostende[5]; ut regnum maiestati tuae deditum tua semper sit virtute defensum. Per.

cf.
Men. 205.

Deus, qui sub tuae maiestatis arbitrio omnium regnorum contines potestatem, Romani imperii propitiare principibus; ut qui tua expectant protectione defendi omnibus sint hostibus fortiores. Per.

Secreta.

R.S.(*alibi.*)
Gerb. 191.
Pam. 414.
Men. 185.
xxxii *supra.*

Suscipe, Domine, propitius[6] hostias, quibus et te placari[7] voluisti, et nobis salutem potenti[8] pietate restitui. Per. γ

Postcommun.

Leon. 371.
R.S.(*alibi.*)
Gerb. 58,
278.
Pam. 239.
I. xxvii
supra.

Adesto, Domine, populis qui sacra mysteria[9] contigerunt; ut nullis periculis affligantur qui te protectore[10] confidunt. Per.

[1] *aeternis* so V., probably for *aeterno.* [2] *tua tranquillitatem clementer* so V., perhaps for *tua tranquillitate clementes.* [3] *confidentibus* Leon. [4] *a custodia.* V.; Leon. as text. [5] *extende* Leon.; V. as text. [6] *propitiatus* V. in xxxii *supra*, R. [7] *placare* V. [8] *potentie* V. [9] *donaria* Leon. [10] *in te protectorem* Gerb. 278.

LX.

ITEM ALIA MISSA.

Deus, qui providentia tua caelestia simul et terrena moderaris, propitiare Romanis[1] rebus et regibus; ut omnis hostium fortitudo, te pro nobis pugnante, frangatur. Per. γ   Pam. 445.
Men. 205.

Deus, servientium tibi fortitudo regnorum, propitius Romani nominis esto[2] principibus; ut quorum tibi subiecta est humilitas, eorum ubique excellentior sit potestas. Per. γ   Men. 205.

Deus, cuius regnum nulla saecula praevenerunt, nulla conclaudunt, supplicationes nostras clementer exaudi, et Rom•anorum regnum tibi subditum protege principatum[3]; ut in tua virtute fidentes omnibus sint hostibus fortiores. Per.

Secreta.

Propitiare, Domine, preces et hostias[4] famulorum tuorum, et propter nomen tuum Romani imperii[5] defende rectores; ut salus servientium tibi principatum[6] pax tuorum possit esse populorum. Per. γ   Pam. 445.
Men. 205.

Postcommun.

Protege, Domine, famulos tuos subsidiis pacis, et corporis[7] et spiritalibus enutriens alimentis, a cunctis hostibus redde securos. Per. γ   Pam. 445.
Men. 205.
Leon. 370.

[1] *Christianorum* Pam. Men.   [2] *propitius Christianorum adesto* Men.
[3] See note [10] on lvii *supra*.   [4] *precibus et hostiis* Pam. Men.; V. as text (ungrammatically).   [5] *Christiani nominis* (for *Romani imperii*) Pam. Men.   [6] *principum* Pam. Men.; V. as text (see note [10] on lvii *supra*).
[7] *subsidiis pasce corporeis* Leon.; V. Pam. Men. as text. The alteration has been made, very possibly, to fit the Postcommunion for its place in V. Pam. Men. by the mention of peace.

LXI.

ITEM ALIA MISSA.

Deus, in te sperantium salus, et servientium fortitudo, suscipe propitius preces nostras, et Romani imperii adesto rectoribus; ut, tuis consiliis inspirati, tuae opitulatione muniti, adversum omnia resistere sibi[1] arma praevaleant. Per.

Deus, et temporalis vitae auctor et aeternae, miserere supplicum in tua protectione fidentium, ut per virtute[2] brachii tui omnibus qui nobis adversantur revictis, nec in terrenis nec a caelestibus possimus excludi. [Per.]

Omnipotens sempiterne Deus, miserere supplicum in tua protectione fidentium, et propter gloriam nominis tui barbararum³ gentium comprime feritatem; ut dexterae tuae virtute defensi, liberis tibi mentibus serviamus. Per.

Secreta.

B.
Gerb. 277.
Deus, qui subiectas tibi glorificas potestates, suscipe propitius oblationes nostras, et Romanis⁴ vires adde principibus, ut qui se dextera tua expetunt protegi⁵, nulla possint adversitate superari. Per.

Postcommun.

Leon. 375.
Fidelem populum, quaesumus, Domine, potentiae tuae muniat invicta defensio⁶; ut pio semper tibi devotus affectu, et ab infestis liberetur inimicis, et in tua iugiter gratia perseveret. Per.

Item alia.

Gerb. 277.
Populi tui, quaesumus, omnipotens Deus, propitiare peccatis, et totius hostilitatis a nobis errores⁷ averte; ut Romani⁸ nominis secura libertas in tua devotione semper exultet. Per.

Leofr. 186.
Protector noster aspice, Deus, et ab hostium⁹ nos defende periculis; ut omni perturbatione submota, liberis tibi mentibus serviamus. Per.

¹ *resistere sibi* so V., perhaps for *resistentia sibi*.   ² *virtute* so V. (ungrammatically).   ³ *barbarum* V.   ⁴ *Christianis* B. Gerb.   ⁵ *expedint protege* V.; B. Gerb. as text.   ⁶ Leon. inserts a clause, omitted by V.   ⁷ *terrores* Gerb.; V. as text.   ⁸ *Christiani* Gerb.   ⁹ *a paganorum* Leofr.

LXII.

Item Missa pro Regibus.

R.
Gerb. 276.
Pam. 426.
B.
Deus, regnorum omnium et Romani¹ maxime protector imperii, da servis tuis regibus nostris *Illis*² triumphum virtutis tuae scienter excolere; ut cuius³ constitutione sunt principes⁴, eius³ semper munere sint potentes⁴. Per. y

Gerb. 277.
B.
Deus in cuius manu corda sunt regum, inclina ad preces humilitatis nostrae aures misericordiae tuae, et principibus nostris famulis tuis *Illis*⁵ regimen tuae appone sapientiae;

ut haustis de tuo fonte consiliis, et tibi placeant[6], et super omnia regna praecellant[7]. Per. y

Secreta.

Suscipe, Domine, preces et hostias ecclesiae tuae, pro salute famuli tui *Illius* supplicantis, et[8] protectione fidelium populorum antiqua brachii tui operare miracula[9]; ut[10] superatis pacis inimicis, secura tibi serviat Romana[11] libertas. Per. y

R, Gerb. 277. Pam. 427. B.

Infra actionem.

Hanc igitur oblationem, Domine, famuli tui *Illius*, quam tibi ministerio officii sacerdotalis offerimus, pro eo quod in ipsum[12] potestatem imperii conferre dignatus es, propitius et benignus assume; et, exoratus nostra obsecratione, concede ut maiestatis tuae protectione confidens et aevo augeatur et regno. Per. y

R. Gerb. 277. Pam. 427.

Postcommun.

Deus, qui praedicando aeterni regni evangelio[13] Romanum imperium praeparasti[14], praetende famulis tuis *Illis* principibus nostris arma caelestia; ut[15] pax ecclesia·rum nulla[16] turbetur tempestate bellorum. Per Dominum. y

R. Gerb. 277. Pam. 427. B.

[1] *Christiani* B. Pam.; V. R. as text.   [2] *servo tuo imperatori nostro N.* B.   [3] *ut qui tua ... tuo* B. Pam.; V. R. as text.   [4] *est princeps ... sit potens* B.   [5] *imperatori nostro famulo tuo N.* B.   [6] *placeat* B.   [7] *praecellat* B.; Gerb. substitutes for this clause *et tua semper beneficia consequantur*.   [8] R. inserts *in*.   [9] *brachio tuo operante miracula* R.; V. Pam. as text; B. omits *operare*.   [10] *et* V.   [11] *Christiana* (for *Romana*) B. Pam.; *Christianorum Romana* R.   [12] *ipso* Pam.; V. R. as text.   [13] *ad praedicandum aeterni regis evangelium* Pam.; V. R. B. as text.   [14] *Christianum imperium dilatasti* B.   [15] *et* V.   [16] *nullo* V. R.

LXIII.

MISSA CONTRA IUDICES MALE AGENTES[1].

Ecclesiae tuae, Domine, preces[2] placatus admitte; ut destitutis adversitatibus[3] universis secura tibi serviat libertate. Per. y

Pam. 448. Leon. 352.

Secreta.

Protege nos, Domine, quaesumus, tuis mysteriis servientes; ut divinis rebus et corpore famulemur et mente. Per. y

Pam. 448. Leon. 379.

Postcommun.

Pam. 448.
Leon. 363.

Quaesumus, Domine Deus noster, ut quos divina tribuis participatione gaudere, humanis non sinas subiacere periculis. Per Dominum.

¹ *agentibus* V. ² *voces* Leon.; V. Pam. as text. ³ *ut destructis adversantibus* Leon.; *et distitutis adversitatibus* V.; Pam. as text.

LXIV.
Item alia Missa.

Leon. 352.

Praesta, Domine, quaesumus, ut toto tibi corde subiecti timentium voluntatum respuamus affectus¹. Per.

Secreta.

Hostias, Domine, quaesumus, quas immolamus placatus assume et pro nostri² expiatione peccati et pro acceleratione caelestis auxilii. Per.

Postcommun.

I. xxvii
supra.
Pam. 238.

Da plebi tuae, Domine, piae semper devotionis affectum ; ut quae prava sunt respuens, sancta conversatione firmetur, et a peccatis libera nullis adversitatibus atteratur. Per.

Praesta, quaesumus, Domine, ut ecclesia tua prompta tibi voluntate deserviat ; quia propensius audiri poterit et defendi, quum eam tibi digne praestiteris famulari. Per.

¹ *afflatus* Leon. ² *nostris* V.

LXV.
Orationes in contentione ad Missas.

Pam. 447.
Leon. 353.

Omnipotens sempiterne Deus, qui superbis resistis et gratiam praestas • humilibus, tribue, quaesumus, ut non indignationem tuam provocemus elati, sed propitiationis tuae capiamus dona subiecti. Per. γ

Concede nobis, misericors Deus, et studia perversa deponere, et sanctam semper amare iustitiam. Per.

Secreta.

Pam. 447.

Ab omni reatu nos, Domine, sancta quae tractamus absolvant¹, et eadem² muniant a³ totius pravitatis incursu. Per. γ

Postcommun.

Quos refecisti, Domine, caelesti mysterio, propriis alienisque, quaesumus⁴, propitiatus absolve delictis, ut⁵ divino munere purificatis mentibus perfruamur. Per. γ

Pam. 447.
Leon. 357.

¹ *absolvat* V.   ² *ad eadem* V.   ³ *ad* V.   ⁴ *propriis alienis quaesumus* V.; *propriis et alienis quaesumus* Pam.; Leon. as text.   ⁵ *et* V.; Pam. Leon. as text.

LXVI.

ITEM ALIA MISSA.

Praesta, quaesumus, omnipotens Deus, ut semper rationabilia meditantes, quae tibi sunt placita et dictis exequamur et factis. Per. γ

Pam. 447.

Deus, qui unanimes nos in domo tua praecipis habitare, dissensionum causas placatus depelle nostrarum¹, ut competentibus adiuti subsidiis, te largiente, possimus esse concordes. Per.

Concede nobis, omnipotens Deus, ut despectis falsitatibus iniquarum², quae animae nostrae conveniunt rationabilia exequamur. Per Dominum.

Secreta.

Suppliciter te rogamus, Domine Deus noster, ut huius operatione mysterii³ et vitia nostra purgentur, et iusta desideria compleantur. Per Dominum.

Postcommun.

Sanctificationem tuam nobis, Domine, his mysteriis placatus operare, quae nos et a terrenis purgent⁴ vitiis, et ad caelestia dona perducant⁴. Per Dominum. γ

Leon. 358.

¹ *nostrum* V.   ² *iniquarum* so V. (perhaps with an accidental omission of *mentium*; see the first Collect of the following section).   ³ *operationem mysterii* V. (perhaps ungrammatically, but not improbably by error of the scribe).   ⁴ *purget . . . perducat* Leon.; V. as text.

LXVII.

ORATIONES AD MISSAM CONTRA OBLOQUENTES.

Praesta, quaesumus, Domine, ut mentium reprobarum¹ non curemus. obloquium, sed eadem pravitate calcata, exoramus ut nec terreri² nos lacerationibus pateris³ in-

Pam. 448.
Leofr. 184.
cf. Leon.
442.

iustis, nec captiosis adulationibus implicari, sed potius amare quae praecipis. Per. γ

Conspirantes, Domine, contra tuae plenitudinis firmamentum, dexterae tuae virtute prosterne; ut iustitiae non dominetur iniquitas, sed subdatur semper falsitas veritati. Per.

Secreta.

Pam. 448.
Leofr. 184.

Oblatio, Domine, tuis aspectibus immolanda, quaesumus ut et nos ab [4] omnibus vitiis potenter absolvat, et a cunctis defendat inimicis. Per. γ

Postcommun.

Pam. 448.
Leofr. 184.

Praesta, Domine, quaesumus, ut per haec sancta quae sumpsimus, dissimulatis [5] lacerationibus improborum, eadem gubernante [6], quae recta sunt cautius exequamur. Per Dominum nostrum Iesum Christum. γ

[1] *reproborum* Pam. Leofr.; V. Leon. as text.   [2] *terrere* V.; Pam. Leofr. as text. The Collect in Leon. does not agree further than *calcata*.   [3] *patiaris* Pam. Leofr.; V. as text (ungrammatically).   [4] *in* V.; Pam. Leofr. as text.   [5] *desimulatis* V.   [6] *eadem gubernante* so V.; Pam. Leofr. have *eadem te gubernante*, which seems like an ineffectual attempt to correct the corrupt reading of the text.

LXVIII.

Orationes ad Missas pro irreligiosis.

Deus, qui fidelium devotione laetaris, populum tuum, quaesumus, sanctis tuis fac esse devotum; ut qui ab eorum officio [1] impia pravitate mentis abscedunt, per tuam conversi gratiam, diaboli, quibus capti tenentur, laqueis resipiscant. Per.

Deus, qui infideles deseris, et iuste indevotis irasceris, populum tuum, quaesumus, converte propitius: ut qui te per duritiam irreligiosae [2] mentis semper offendunt, ad sanctorum beneficia promerenda, tuae miserationis gratia inspirante, convertas. Per.

Secreta.

Cor populi tui, quaesumus, Domine, converte propitius, ut ab his muneribus non recedant, quibusque [3] maiestatem tuam magnificare [4] deposcimus. Per.

Postcommun.

Da nobis, quaesumus, Domine [5], ambire quae recta sunt, et vitare quae noxia; ut sancta quae capimus, non ad iudicium nobis, sed potius proficiant [6] ad medelam. Per.   Leon. 351.

Ad Populum.

Adesto, Domine, supplicationibus nostris [7], et nihil de sua conscientia praesumentibus ineffabili miseratione succurre; ut quod non habet fiducia meritorum, tua [8] conferat [9] largitas invicta donorum. Per.   S. (alibi.) Gerb. 239. xvii supra.

[1] *offitia* V.   [2] *in relegiosae* V.   [3] *quibusquae* V., probably for the reading of the text, with the sense of *quibus et*.   [4] *magnificare* so V., probably for *magnificari*.   [5] *Domine quaesumus* Leon.   [6] *proficiant potius* Leon.   [7] *supplicibus tuis* V. in xvii *supra*, S.; V. here, Gerb. as text.   [8] *tuorum* S² Gerb.; V. S¹ as text.   [9] *consecret* V. in xvii *supra*, S.; V. here, Gerb. as text.

LXIX.

Oratio super Infirmum in Domo.

Deus, qui facturae tuae pio semper dominaris affectu, inclina aurem tuam supplicationibus nostris, et famulum tuum ex adversa valetudine[1] corporis laborantem[2] placidus[3] respice, et visita in salutari tuo, et [4] caelestis gratiae praesta medicinam. Per. γ   R. Gerb. 300. Pam. 453. Men. 235.

Deus, qui humani generis et salutis remedii[5] vitae aeternae munera contulisti, conserva famulo tuo tuarum dona virtutum, et concede ut medelam tuam non solum in corpore sed etiam in anima sentiat. Per. γ   R. Gerb. 310. Pam. 453. Men. 235.

Virtutum caelestium Deus, qui ab[6] humanis corporibus omnem languorem et omnem infirmitatem praecepti tui potestate depellis, adesto propitius huic servo tuo; ut fugatis infirmitatibus et viribus revocatis, nomen sanctum tuum, instaurata protinus sanitate, benedicat. Per. γ   Pam. 453. Men. 235.

Domine sancte, Pater omnipotens, aeterne Deus, qui fragilitatem conditionis nostrae infusa virtutis tuae dignatione confirmas, ut salutaribus remediis pietatis tuae corpora nostra et membra vegetentur, super hunc famulum tuum propitiatus intende; ut omni necessitate corporea[7] infirmitatis exclusa, gratia in eo pristinae sanitatis perfecta reparetur. Per. γ   Pam. 453. Men. 235.

¹ *adversam valetudinem* V.; R. Pam. Men. as text. ² *laborante* V.; R. Pam. Men. as text. ³ *placatus* Pam. Men.; *placitus* R.; V. as text. ⁴ *ac* Pam. Men. ⁵ *humani generis et salutis remedii* so V. R. (ungrammatically); R. adds *et* before *vitae*; Pam. Men. have *humano generi et salutis remedium et*. ⁶ *in* Pam.; V. Men. as text. ⁷ *corporeae* Pam. Men.; V. as text.

LXX.

ITEM ORATIONES AD MISSAM PRO INFIRMUM [1].

R.
Gerb. 311.
Pam. 453.
Men. 240.

Omnipotens sempiterne Deus, salus aeterna credentium, exaudi nos pro ⋆ famulis tuis *Illis*, pro quibus misericordiae tuae imploramus auxilium [2]; ut reddita sibi sanitate gratiarum tibi in ecclesia tua referant actionem. Per. γ

736

Omnipotens sempiterne Deus, qui aegritudines et animorum depellis et corporum, auxilii tui super infirmos nostros ostende virtutem; ut ope misericordiae tuae ad omnia pietatis tuae reparentur officia. Per.

Secreta.

R.
Gerb. 311.
Pam. 454.
Men. 240.

Deus, sub [3] cuius nutibus vitae nostrae momenta decurrunt, suscipe preces et hostias famulorum [4] famularumque tuarum, pro quibus misericordiam tuam aegrotantibus imploramus; ut de quorum periculo metuimus, de eorum salute laetemur. Per.

Postcommun.

R.
Gerb. 311.
Pam. 454.
Men. 240.

Deus, infirmitatis humanae singulare praesidium, auxilii tui super infirmos nostros ostende virtutem; ut ope misericordiae tuae adiuti [5], ecclesiae tuae sanctae repraesentari mereantur. Per Dominum nostrum. γ

¹ *infirmum* so V. (ungrammatically). ² *auxilio* V. (ungrammatically); R. Pam. Men. as text. ³ R. Pam. omit *sub*; V. Men. as text. ⁴ V. inserts *et*; Men. has *famulorum tuorum*. ⁵ R. omits *adiuti ecclesiae tuae*.

LXXI.

ORATIO PRO REDDITA SANITATE.

R.
Gerb. 312.
Pam. 454.

Domine sancte, Pater omnipotens, aeterne Deus, qui benedictionis tuae gratiam [1] aegris infundendo corporibus facturam tuam multiplici [2] pietate custodis, ad invocationem nominis tui benignus assiste, et hunc famulum tuum liberatum aegritudine et sanitate donatum [3] dextera tua erigas, virtute confirmes, potestate tuearis, ecclesiae tuae sanctisque altaribus tuis cum omni desiderata prosperitate restituas. Per Dominum nostrum. γ

[1] *benedictionis tuae gratiae* R.; V. Pam. as text.   [2] *multiplicas* V.; R. Pam. as text.   [3] *liberatam egritudinem et sanitatem donatam* V.; *liberatum aegritudine et sanitatem donatam* R.; Pam. as text.

LXXII.

ORATIONES INTRANTIBUS IN DOMO[1], SIVE BENEDICTIO.

Adesto, Domine, supplicationibus nostris, et famulos tuos, quos caritatis visitamus • officiis, gratiae tuae largitate locupleta; ut in eorum prosperitate continua gaudeamus. Per Dominum.

Exaudi nos, Domine sancte, Pater omnipotens, aeterne Deus, et humilitatis nostrae officiis gratiae[2] tuae visitationis admisce; ut quorum adimus habitacula, tu in eorum tibi cordibus facias mansionem. Per Dominum nostrum.

Adesto, Domine, supplicationibus nostris, et hanc domum serenis oculis tuae pietatis illustra: descendat super habitantes in ea gratiae tuae larga benedictio; ut his manufactis cum salubritate manentibus[3], ipsi tuum semper sint habitaculum. Per Dominum. γ   Pam. 465. Men. 234.

Exaudi nos, Domine sancte, Pater omnipotens, aeterne Deus, ut si qua sunt adversa, si qua contraria in hac domo famuli tui *Illius*, auctoritate maiestatis tuae pellantur. Per Dominum nostrum.   Pam. 466. Men. 234.

[1] *in domo*, so V. (probably ungrammatically for *in domum*). The third and fourth prayers of this series appear in Pam. Men. with the title *Benedictio domus*.   [2] *gratiae* so V., probably for *gratiam*.   [3] *in his manufactis cum salubritate manentes* Pam.; *in his manufactis cum salubritate manentibus* Men.; V. as text, perhaps for the reading of Pam.; but the text gives a sense as it stands.

LXXIII.

ITEM ORATIONES AD MISSAS.

Protector in te sperantium Deus, et subditarum tibi mentium custos, habitantibus in hac domo famulis tuis propitius adesse dignare: veniat super eos speratae[1] a te benedictionis ubertas[2], et pietatis tuae repleti muneribus, in tua gratia et in tuo nomine laeti semper exultent. Per.   R. Gerb. 307. Sacr. Gall. 916.

Protector fidelium Deus, et subditarum tibi mentium frequentator, habitantibus in hac domo famulis tuis propitius adesse digneris; ut quos nos humana visitamus sollicitudine tu divina munias potestate. Per.

Secreta.

R.
Gerb. 307.
Sacr. Gall.
916.
cf. lxxx
infra.

Suscipe, Domine, quaesumus, preces et hostias famulorum tuorum, et muro custodiae tuae hanc domum circumda; ut omni adversitate depulsa sic hoc semper domicilium incolumitatis et pacis. Per.

Infra actionem.

R.
Gerb. 307.

Hanc igitur oblationem, [Domine[3],] famuli tui *Illius* quam tibi offert pro votis et desideriis suis, atque[4] pro incolumitate domus suae, placatus suscipias deprecamur: pro quo in hac habitatione auxilium tuae maiestatis deposco, ut mittere ei digneris angelum tuum sanctum, ad custodiendos omnes in hac habitatione [consistentes[3]]. Per.

Postcommun.

R.
Gerb. 307.

Omnipotens sempiterne Deus, qui facis • mirabilia magna 738 solus, praetende super hos famulos [tuos[3]] degentes in hac domo spiritum gratiae salutaris; et ut complaceant tibi, Deus, in veritate tua, perpetuum eis rorem tuae benedictionis effunde. Per. γ

R.
Gerb. 307.
cf. Sacr.
Gall. 916.

Omnipotens sempiterne Deus, insere te[5] officiis nostris, et in hac[6] manentibus domo[6] praesentiae tuae concede custodiam; ut familiae tuae defensor, et totius habitaculi huius habitator appareas. Per.

[1] *spirante* V.; *sperantes* Sacr. Gall.; *spirate* R.; Gerb. as text.   [2] *benedictio ne subvertas* Sacr. Gall.; *benedictio ubertas* V.; R. Gerb. as text.
[3] V. omits the words in brackets, which are restored from R.   [4] *atque et* V.
[5] *in certe* R.; *in secretis* Sacr. Gall. (where the words connect with what precedes, in the opening of a *Contestatio*); V. as text.   [6] *hanc ... domum* V. Sacr. Gall. (ungrammatically); R. as text.

LXXIV.

ORATIONES SUPER VENIENTES IN DOMO[1].

Pam. 441.

Deus humilium visitator qui nos fraterna dignatione[2] consolaris, praetende societati nostrae gratiam tuam, ut per eos, in quibus habitas, tuumque nobis[3] sentiamus adventum. Per. γ

Deus qui nobis in famulis tuis praesentiae tuae signa manifestas, mitte super nos spiritum caritatis, ut in adventu fratrum conservorumque nostrorum gratia nobis tuae largitatis augeatur. Per Dominum.

---

[1] So V. (probably ungrammatically). The first of the two prayers has in Pam. the heading *Oratio in adventu fratrum supervenientium.* [2] *dilectione* Pam. [3] *tuum nobis* Pam.; V. as text, probably in the sense of *et tuum nobis.*

LXXV.

BENEDICTIO AQUAE SPARGENDAE IN DOMO.

Deus, qui ad salutem humani generis maxima quaeque sacramenta in aquarum substantia [1] condidisti, adesto [2] invocationibus nostris, et elemento huic, multimodis purificationibus praeparato, virtutem tuae benedictionis [3] infunde, ut creatura mysteriis tuis serviens [4] ad abiciendos [5] daemones morbosque pellendos divinae gratiae sumat effectus [6], ut quidquid in locis [vel] [7] in domibus fidelium haec unda resperserit [8] careat immunditia, liberetur a noxia [9]: non illic resideat spiritus pestilens, non aura corrumpens: abscedant omnes insidiae latentes [10] inimici; et si quid est quod incolumitati habitantium invideat [11] aut quieti [12], aspersione huius aquae [13] effugiat, ut salubritas per invocationem tui nominis expetita [14] ab omni [15] sit impugnatione [15] defensa. Per Dominum nostrum Iesum Christum Filium tuum, qui venturus est iudicare vivos et mortuos et saeculum per ignem. γ

Pam. 464.
Men. 233.
Sacr. Gall. 953.
cf. Stowe
M. 211.

---

[1] *substantiam* Pam. Men.; V. Sacr. Gall. as text. [2] Pam. inserts *propitius.* [3] *virtutis tuae benedictionem* Sacr. Gall. [4] *mysterii tui tibi serviens* Men. [5] *ablegandos* Sacr. Gall. [6] *effectum* Pam. Men. Sacr. Gall.; V. as text. [7] V. omits *vel*; Sacr. Gall. omits *in locis vel*; Pam. Men. have *in domibus vel in locis.* [8] *asparserit* Sacr. Gall. [9] *noxia,* so V. Sacr. Gall. (for *noxa* which is the reading of Pam. Men.). [10] *latentes insidiae* Sacr. Gall.; *insidiae latentis* Pam. Men.; V. as text. [11] *invidet* Pam. Men.; V. Sacr. Gall. as text. [12] *saluti* Sacr. Gall. [13] *aquae huius* Sacr. Gall. [14] *expedita* V.; Pam. Men. as text; Sacr. Gall. has *per invocationem sancti nominis permaneat impugnatione defensa.* [15] *omnibus . . . impugnationibus* Pam. Men.; V. as text.

LXXVI.

ITEM ALIA [1].

Exorcizo te, creatura aquae, in nomine Dei Patris omnipotentis, et in nomine Iesu Christi Filii eius, et Spiritus

cf. I. lxxv *supra.*

sancti. Omnis virtus adversarii, omnis incursio diaboli, omne phantasma, [omnem inimici potestatem²] eradicare et effugare ab hac creatura aquae. Unde exorcizo te, creatura aquae, per Deum verum et per Deum vivum, per Deum sanctum, et per Dominum nostrum Iesum Christum, ut efficiaris aqua sancta, aqua benedicta, ut ubicumque effusa fueris, vel aspersa, sive in domo, sive in agro, effuges omnem phantasiam, omnem inimici potestatem: Spiritus sanctus habitet in domo hac. Per Dominum nostrum Iesum Christum, qui venturus est iudicare vivos et mortuos, et saeculum per ignem.

Item ad consparsum faciendum.

cf. Pam. 465.
cf. Men. 234.

Exaudi nos, Domine sancte, Pater omnipotens, aeterne Deus, et mittere dignare angelum tuum sanctum de caelis, qui custodiat, foveat, protegat, visitet, et defendat omnes habitantes in hanc habitaculum famuli tui *Illius*³: et praesta, quaesumus, ut sanctificatio sit domui huius noster⁴ introitus. Donet cunctis intra eum habitu constitutos divinarum beatitudine largitatem, dominis ac familiae gubernaculum, ad custodiendam obedientiam et irreprehensibilem disciplinam, infantibus bonae indolis gratiam, adultis immaculatam adolescentiam, senibus sanctam seriae conversationis aetatem, omnibusque longam ac sibi placitam senectutem: et ita patrocinantibus sanctis perenni domui huic beatitudinem praestet, ut iugi super eam angelicae protectionis custodia perseveret. Per Dominum. γ

Post haec benedicet sal, et dicit

R.
Gerb. 306.
cf. Sacr.
Gall. 953.
cf. Drum.
Miss. 1.

Exorcizo te, creatura salis, in nomine Patris et Filii et Spiritus sancti, qui te per Heliseum in aqua mitti iussit ut sanaretur sterilitas⁵; qui divini⁶ oris sui voce discipulis⁷ ait, Vos estis sal terrae; et per٠apostolum inquit⁸, Cor vestrum sale sit conditum⁹. Ideoque efficiaris¹⁰ sal exorcizatum, ut omnes qui¹¹ te sumpserint sis eis animae tutamentum, atque huic domui [protectio¹²] in remissione¹³ peccatorum, in sanitate¹³ mentis, in protectione¹³ animae, et confirmatione¹³ salutis, ad expellendas et excludendas omnes daemonum tentationes, in nomine Dei Patris omnipotentis, et Iesu Christi Filii eius¹⁴, qui venturus est iudicare¹⁵ saeculum per ignem. Per.¹⁶

Deinde mittis ipsum sal in aqua, et exsufflas in ea, et dicis

Deus qui ad salutem humani generis maxima quaeque sacramenta in aquarum substantia condidisti, *et caetera sicut superius scriptum est.*

Hic mittis vinum in ipsa aqua, et benedic eam : dic :

Domine sancte, Pater omnipotens, aeterne Deus, exaudi precem meam, sicut exaudire dignatus es famulum tuum Moysen in mari [17] rubro hoc quod Pharao in populo tuo exercebat, ipse marinus exercitus negaretur. Sic et Heliseus sacerdos, quum populus tuus aquam gustare non posset, eo quod esset amara, salem accepit, et proiecit ad exitus aquarum et benedixit eam, et dixit, Sanavit Dominus aquas istas ; non erit ex eis moriens, neque infirmans ; et sanatae sunt aquae illae. Ita tu, Domine, dignare sanare aquas istas, ut ubicumque aspersae fuerint per angulos domus, ubi inimicus celatus fuerit, statim arreptus [18] effugiat ; et sit illi, Domine, hanc aquam aspersionis velut clibanus ardens ignis inextinguibilis. Sit nobis, Domine, haec aqua aspersionis aqua virtutis, aqua refrigerans, diaboli ritu [19] ut liberati hospitales agamus tibi, Domine, Pater omnipotens, laudes et gratias. Per Dominum nostrum.

Post haec mittis oleo sanctificato in aqua, et sic aspergis ea cum hyssopo per domus.

ORATIONES PRO ASPERSIONE AQUAE.

Deum omnipotentem, fratres carissimi, in cuius domum mansiones multae sunt, supplices deprecemur ut habitaculum istum una cum habitatoribus benedicere • atque custodire dignetur, tenebras ab ea repellat, lumen infundat, nullam saevienti adversario tribuat potestatem ; sed propria Deo dicata sit domus, ut nullam in ea inimicus licentiam habeat nocendi, per virtutem et nomen Domini nostri Iesu Christi, qui venturus est iudicare saeculum per ignem. Per Dominum [16].

Benedic huic domui, Domine, benedic dominis domus huius ; respice de caelo, et vide oculos misericordiae tuae ; aperi aures pietatis tuae, et inclina super habitaculo isto atque habitatoribus suis, et mitte custodem angelum in circuitu supplicantium, qui in lateribus domus istius iugiter excubet, et ad custodiam illius perpetuo perseveret, cuius sit obumbratio salus omnium et patrocinium, beatitudo cunctorum. Per Dominum nostrum.

Benedic, Domine, hanc domum et omnes habitantes in ea, sicut benedicere dignatus es domum Abraham, Isaac et Iacob, ut in his parietibus angelus lucis inhabitet: sentiant in ea commanentes rore caeli abundantiam, et per indulgentiam laetentur pacifici atque securi: mittas ad eos angelum pacis qui introitum nostrum exitumque custodiat. Per.

---

[1] Throughout this section the text of V. (both in the prayers and rubrics) contains many grammatical errors, which it seems unnecessary to note in detail. The exorcisms and benedictions are partly parallel in some instances to forms in Pam. Men. and the Sacramentarium Gallicanum; but the forms in Pam. Men., if taken from the same source as those in the text, have evidently been revised. Except as noted below, no alteration, other than obvious corrections of spelling, has been made in the readings of V. [2] *omnem inimici potestatem* so V.; but the appearance of the accusative following after a series of vocatives, and the absence of the words in 1. lxxv *supra*, suggest that the words may have been accidentally inserted. They occur again a few lines further on, following the word *phantasiam*, while they here follow *phantasma*. [3] *Illi* V. [4] *nostre* V.; Tommasi reads *nostrae*, but the correction in the text is perhaps the more probable of the two. [5] *sterilis* R. Sacr. Gall.; *stirilitas aquae* in Drummond Missal. [6] *divina* R. Sacr. Gall.; the Drummond Missal omits the clause. [7] Sacr. Gall. omits *discipulis*. [8] *et per apostolum suum* (omitting *inquit*) Sacr. Gall.; *qui per apostolum Paulum dicere dignatus est* Drum. Miss.; *et idem per apostolum dicit* R. [9] *Sit sermo noster sale conditus* Sacr. Gall.; *Sit cor vestrum sale conditum* Drum. Miss. From this point V. and R. differ considerably from the others, but are more in agreement with Sacr. Gall. than with the Drummond Missal, which at the end, as at the beginning, of the form agrees with the later texts. [10] *efficere* R. [11] R. inserts *ex*. [12] *protectio*, omitted by V., is restored from R. [13] R. gives all these in the accusative. [14] R. omits *et Iesu Christi Filii eius*. [15] *et iudicaturus est in Spiritu sancto* R. [16] This double ending is probably an error of the scribe. [17] *mare* V.; the clause following is probably corrupt, and certainly obscure. [18] *areptus* V. [19] Tommasi's punctuation connects *diaboli ritu* with *refrigerans*, a conjunction which seems unlikely, whatever the sense of *diaboli ritu* may be.

LXXVII.

ITEM ORATIONES PRO FULGURIBUS.

R.
Gerb. 303.
Pam. 466.
Men. 211.

Omnipotens sempiterne Deus, parce metuentibus, et propitiare supplicibus[1]; ut post noxios ignes nubium et vim procellarum, in materiam transeat laudis comminatio[2] potestatis. Per. γ

R.
Men. 211.

Deus, sub[3] cuius imperio nihil non verbo regitur, nihil non oratione mutatur, parce metuentibus, propitiare supplicibus; ut post noxios[4] ignes nubium et turbines procellarum, in materiam transeat laudis comminatio potestatis. Per.

¹ *supplicationibus* R. ² *communicatio* V.; R. Pam. Men. as text, and so V. in the prayer following. ³ Men. omits *sub*. ⁴ *innoxios* V.; R. Men. as text, and so V. in the prayer preceding.

LXXVIII.

BENEDICTIO AQUAE EXORCIZATAE AD FULGURA.

Exorcizo te, creatura salis et aquae[1], in nomine Domini nostri Iesu Christi Nazareni, Filii Dei vivi, ut sis purgatio et purificatio in his locis in quibus as·persa fueris, ad effugandos [immundos][2] et erraticos spiritus, omnemque nefariam vim diaboli pellendam, et omnes figuras et minas phantasmatis Satanae exterminandas; et fulgura et sidera quae missa[3] videntur in hanc arborem non hominibus, aut pecoribus, aut frugibus noceant, sed abscedant et fugiant per invocationem nominis Domini nostri Iesu Christi, et Spiritus sancti, qui venturus est iudicare[4] vivos et mortuos et omne saeculum per ignem. Per.

R. Gerb. 303. cf. Gerb. 306.

¹ *aqua* V. ² V. omits *immundos* which is restored from R. ³ *emissa* R. ⁴ R. does not give the reading beyond *iudicare*; but it agrees with V. in the insertion of *et Sp. s.* before *qui venturus est*, which, like the double ending in V., is probably due to an error of some early scribe.

LXXIX.

ORATIONES IN AREA NOVA.

Omnipotens sempiterne Deus, multiplica super nos misericordiam tuam, et preces nostras benignus exaudi, ut in hac area[1] famuli tui *Illius* Spiritum tuum sanctum Paraclitum mittere digneris: et veniat speratae benedictionis ubertas, ut repleti de frugibus tuis in tuo nomine et in tua gratia laeti semper exultent. Per Dominum.

Multiplica, Domine, super nos misericordiam tuam, et preces nostras propitius exaudire dignare, sicut exaudisti famulum tuum regem David, qui te in area hostias offerendo placavit[2], iram avertit, indulgentiam impetravit. Ita veniat, quaesumus, speratae benedictionis ubertas, ut repleti frugibus tuis de tua semper misericordia gloriemur. Per Dominum. γ

Pam. 470.

¹ *in hac area* so V. (ungrammatically). ² *placuit* V.; Tommasi corrects as text, from Pam.

LXXX.
ITEM ORATIONES IN MONASTERIO.

Pam. 440.

Deus qui renuntiantibus saeculo mansionem paras in caelo, dilata sanctae huius congregationis habitaculum temporale caelestibus bonis, ut fraternitate teneant compagine[1] caritatis unanimiter[2] continentiae tuae[3] praecepta custodiant; sobrii, simplices, et quieti, gratis sibi datam gratiam fuisse cognoscant; concordet illorum vita cum nomine, professio sentiatur in opere. Per. γ

cf. lxxiii supra.

Suscipe, Domine, preces nostras, et muro custodiae tuae hoc sanctum ovile circumda; ut omni adversitate depulsa, sit hoc semper domicilium incolumitatis et pacis. Per Dominum nostrum Iesum Christum. γ

[1] *fraternae teneantur compagine* Pam.; V. as text, either *fraternitate* or *compagine* being abl. for acc. [2] *unanimes* Pam. [3] Pam. omits *tuae*.

LXXXI.
ORATIO IN DOMO ANCILLARUM DEI.

Ingredientes, Domine, in hunc[1] tabernaculum ancillarum tuarum tibi servientium, angelo tuo visitante custodias, et ab huius saeculi adversitatibus defendas. Dona eis propositum mentis, ut tibi exhibeant pudicitiam castitatis; adiuva contra vitia certantes, et victoriae sumant[2] coronam ad te pervenientes. Per.

[1] *hunc* so V., which treats *tabernaculum* as masculine also in lxxvi *supra*.
[2] *summa* V.; Tommasi corrects as text.

LXXXII.
ORATIO PRO RENUNTIANTIBUS SAECULO.

Praesta, Domine, quaesumus, famulis tuis renuntiantibus secularibus pompis gratiae tuae ianuas aperiri[1], qui, despecto diabolo, confugiunt sub titulo Christi. Iube venientes ad te sereno vultu suscipere, ne de eis inimicus valeat triumphare. Tribue eis brachium infatigabile auxilii tui; mentes eorum fidei lorica circumda, ut felici muro vallati, mundum se gaudeant evasisse. Per.

[1] *aperire* V.

LXXXIII.

ORATIO PRO EO QUI PRIUS [1] BARBAM TONDET.

Deus, cuius providentia [2] creatura omnis crementis [3] adulta [4] congaudet, propitius super hunc famulum tuum, iuvenili aetatis decore [5] laetantem, et florem primis auspiciis attondentem, adesto : in omnibus tuae protectionis muniatur auxilium [6], aevo longiore provectus, et praesentis vitae praesidiis gaudeat et aeternis. Per Dominum nostrum. γ

R. Gerb. 257.

[1] *pro his qui prius* R.   [2] *providentiam* V. ungrammatically; R. as text. [3] *crementes* V.; R. as text: the word may be equivalent to *incrementis*, or may be an error for that word.   [4] *adalta* R.   [5] *iuvenilia aetatis decorem* V.; R. as text.   [6] *auxilium*, so V. R. (ungrammatically).

LXXXIV.

ORATIONES AD MATUTINAS.

Gratias tibi agimus, Domine sancte, Pater omnipotens, aeterne Deus, qui nos transacto noctis spatio [1] ad matutinas horas [2] perducere dignatus es; quaesumus, ut dones [3] nobis diem hunc [4] sine peccato transire, quatenus ad vesperum [5] gratias referamus. Per. γ

Gerb. 241. Sacr. Gall. 960. Pam. 472. Men. 203.

Exurgentes de cubilibus nostris [6], auxilium gratiae tuae matutinis, Domine [7], precibus imploramus ; ut discussis tenebris vitiorum, ambulare mereamur in luce virtutum. Per Dominum. γ

Gerb. 241. Sacr. Gall. 960. Pam. 473. Men. 202.

Matutina supplicum vota, Domine, propitius intuere, et occulta [8] cordis nostri remedio tuae clarifica [9] pietatis ; ut [10] desideria tenebrosa non teneant [11], quos lux caelestis gratiae [12] reparavit. Per Dominum nostrum. γ

R. Gerb. 241. Sacr. Gall. 960. Pam. 472. Men. 202.

Te lucem veram, et lucis auctorem, Domine, deprecamur, ut digneris a nobis tenebras depellere vitiorum [13], et clarificare nos luce virtutum. Per. γ

Gerb. 241. Sacr. Gall. 961. Pam. 473. Men. 202.

Auge in nobis, Domine, quaesumus, fidem tuam, et Spiritus sancti lucem in nobis semper [14] accende. Per. γ

Pam. 473. Men. 202.

Deus, qui diem discernis a nocte [15], actus nostros a tenebrarum distingue caligine, ut semper quae sancta sunt meditantes, in tua iugiter laude vivamus. Per. γ

R. Gerb. 241. Men. 203. Leon. 373.

Emitte, quaesumus, Domine, lucem tuam in cordibus nostris, et mandatorum tuorum lucem perpetuam [16] ; et in via tua ambulantes nihil patiamur erroris [17]. Per. γ

R. Gerb. 241. Men. 202.

Pam. 473. Veritas tua, quaesumus, Domine, luceat in cordibus
Men. 202. nostris, et omnis falsitas destruatur inimici [16]. Per. ɣ

Pam. 473. Gratias agimus inenarrabili [19] pietati tuae, omnipotens
Men. 203. Deus, qui nos, depulsa noctis caligine, ad diei huius
principium perduxisti, et abiecta ignorantiae caecitate, ad
cultum tui nominis atque scientiam revocasti: illabere [20]
sensibus nostris, omnipotens Pater, ut, in praeceptorum
tuorum lumine gradientes, te ducem sequamur et principem.
Per. ɣ

Pam. 473. Deus, qui tenebras ignorantiae verbi tui luce depellis,
Men. 202. auge in cordibus nostris virtutem fidei, quam dedisti, ut
ignis, quem gratia tua fecit accendi, nullis tentationibus
possit extingui. Per. ɣ

Pam. 473. Sensibus nostris, quaesumus, Domine, lumen sanctum
Men. 202. tuum benignus infunde, ut tibi semper simus devoti, cuius
sapientia creati sumus, et providentia gubernamur. Per. ɣ

[1] *de transactae noctis spatio* Gerb.; *de transacto noctis spatio* Pam. Men.; V. Sacr. Gall. as text.   [2] *ad matutinis horis* V.; Sacr. Gall. Gerb. Pam. Men. as text.   [3] *donis* V.; Sacr. Gall. Gerb. Pam. Men. as text.   [4] *hanc* Sacr. Gall.; Gerb. omits *hunc*; V. Pam. Men. as text.   [5] Pam. Men. Gerb. insert *et semper tibi*; V. Sacr. Gall. as text.   [6] *tuis* Pam.   [7] Sacr. Gall. omits *Domine*.   [8] *occultis* V. R. Gerb.; Sacr. Gall. Pam. Men. as text.   [9] *glorifica* Gerb.   [10] *et* Pam.   [11] *teneat* R. Gerb.   [12] *gratia* V.; R. Sacr. Gall. Gerb. Pam. Men. as text.   [13] *digneris nobis tenebras repellere peccatorum* Sacr. Gall.   [14] *semper in nobis* Pam.   [15] *et noctem* Leon.; *ac noctem* Gerb.; *ac nocte* R.; V. Men. as text.   [16] *luce perpetua* V. R.; Gerb. as text; Men. has *ut mandatorum tuorum lege percepta, in via*; R. has *ut* for *et*.   [17] *errorem* V.; R. Gerb. Men. as text.   [18] *inimici destruetur* Men.   [19] *inenarrabile* V.; Tommasi reads *inenarrabiles*; *enarrabili* Pam.; Men. as text.   [20] *in labe* V.

LXXXV.
ORATIONES AD VESPERUM.

Sacr. Gall. Omnipotens sempiterne Deus, vespere, et mane [1], et
959.   meridie, maiestatem tuam suppliciter deprecamur, ut ex-
Gerb. 242. pulsis de cordibus nostris peccatorum tenebris, ad veram
Pam. 474.   lucem, quae Christus est, nos facias pervenire. Per Dominum
Men. 200.   nostrum. ɣ

Sacr. Gall. Deus, qui illuminas noctem, et lumen post tenebras facis,
960.   concede nobis ut hanc noctem sine impedimento Satanae
Pam. 474.   transeamus, atque [2] matutinis horis ad altare tuum recur-
Men. 201.   rentes, tibi Deo gratias referamus. Per Dominum. ɣ

Sacr. Gall. Illumina, quaesumus, Domine, tenebras nostras, et totius
960.   noctis insidias [3] repelle propitius. Per. ɣ
Gerb. 242.
Men. 201.

Tuus est [4] dies, Domine, et tua est nox; concede solem iustitiae [5] permanere in cordibus nostris ad repellendas tenebras cogitationum [6] iniquarum. Per Dominum. γ

R.
Sacr. Gall. 960.
Pam. 473.
Gerb. 242.
Men. 201.

Vespertinae laudis officia persolventes, clementiam tuam, Domine, humili prece deposcimus [7], ut nocturni insidiatoris fraudes [8], te protegente, vincamus [9]. Per. γ

Sacr. Gall. 960.
Gerb. 242.
Pam. 474.
Men. 200.

Propitiare, Domine, vespertinis supplicationibus nostris, et fac nos sine ullo reatu matutinis tibi laudibus praesentari [10]. Per Dominum nostrum. γ

Sacr. Gall. 960.
Gerb. 242.
Pam. 474.
Men. 200.

Oriatur [11], Domine, nascentibus tenebris, aurora iustitiae, ut peracto die [12] tibi suppliciter gratias agentes etiam mane [13] respicias vota solventes. Per. γ

R.
Gerb. 241.
Pam. 473.
Men. 201.

Gratias tibi agimus [14], Domine, custoditi [15] per diem: gratias tibi exsolvimus [16], custodiendi per noctem: repraesenta nos, quaesumus, Domine, matutinis horis incolumes, ut nos omni tempore habeas laudatores. Per. γ

Gerb. 242.
Pam. 474.
Men. 201.

[1] Gerb. omits *et mane.*   [2] Sacr. Gall. inserts *ad.*   [3] Men. inserts *tu*; Gerb. inserts *tu a nobis.*   [4] Pam. omits *est.*   [5] Sacr. Gall. inserts *tuae.*   [6] *cogitationum tenebras* Sacr. Gall.   [7] *poscimus* Sacr. Gall.   [8] *nocturnis insidiatoris fraude* V.; Sacr. Gall. Gerb. Pam. Men. as text.   [9] *vitemus* Sacr. Gall.   [10] *matutinis tibi laudes praesentare* V.; *matutinis tibi laudibus repraesentari* Sacr. Gall.; Pam. Men. as text.   [11] Men. inserts *in nobis*; Pam. omits *Domine.*   [12] *diei* V. R.   [13] Gerb. Pam. Men. insert *dignanter*; Pam. has *dignanter recipias.*   [14] *agemus* V.; Gerb. Pam. Men. as text.   [15] *custoditi* V.; Gerb. Pam. Men. as text.   [16] *exsolvimur* V.

LXXXVI.

ORATIONES ANTE CIBUM.

Refice nos, Domine, donis tuis, et opulentiae tuae largitate sustenta. Per. γ

Pam. 467.
Leofr. 7.

Reficiamur [1], Domine, de donis et datis tuis, et tua benedictione satiemur. Per.

Protege nos, Domine Deus noster, et fragilitati nostrae necessariam praebe substantiam. Per.

Leofr. 7.

Benedic, Domine, dona tua, quae de tua largitate sumus sumpturi. Per. γ

Pam. 468.
Leofr. 7.

Deus, qui nos ad delicias spiritales semper invitas, da benedictionem super dona tua, ut ea quae in tuo nomine sunt edenda, sanctificata percipere mereamur. Per.

Leofr. 7.

Tua nos, Domine, dona reficiant, et tua gratia consoletur. Per Dominum nostrum.

Leofr. 7.

[1] *Reficiamus* V.

LXXXVII.

ORATIONES POST CIBOS.

Pam. 468. Satiati, Domine, opulentiae tuae donis, tibi gratias agimus pro his quae, te largiente, suscepimus, obsecrantes misericordiam tuam, ut quod [1] corporibus nostris necessarium fuit, mentibus non sit onerosum. Per. γ

Pam. 468. Satiati sumus [2], Domine, de tuis donis ac datis: reple nos de tua misericordia, qui es [3] benedictus, qui cum [4] Patre et Spiritu sancto vivis et regnas Deus per omnia saecula saeculorum. γ

[1] *quid* V.; Pam. as text.   [2] *Satiasti nos* Pam.   [3] *quia tu es* Pam.
[4] Pam. inserts *Deo*.

LXXXVIII.

ORATIO AD FRUGES NOVAS BENEDICENDAS.

R.
Gerb. 308.
Pam. 467.
Men. 234.

Benedic, Domine, hos fructus novos uvae sive fabae, quos tu, Domine, per rorem caeli et inundantiam pluviarum, et tempora serena atque tranquilla ad maturitatem perducere dignatus es, ad percipiendum nobis cum gratiarum actione, in nomine Domini nostri Iesu Christi. Per quem [1] haec omnia, Domine, semper bona. γ.

Item alia.

R.
Gerb. 307.

Oramus [2] pietatem tuam, omnipotens Deus, ut has primitias creaturae tuae, quas aeris et pluviae temperamento nutrire dignatus es, benedictionis tuae imbre perfundas, et fructus terrae tuae usque ad maturitatem perducas, tribuasque [3] populo tuo de tuis muneribus tibi semper gratias agere, ut a fertilitate terrae esurientium animas bonis affluentibus repleas, et egenus et pauper laudent nomen gloriae tuae. Per.

[1] Instead of the concluding clause of the Canon (indicated by V. R.) Pam. Men. have *Qui tecum*.   [2] *Oremus* V.; R. as text.   [3] *tribuas quoque* R.

LXXXIX.

BENEDICTIO POMORUM.

R.
Gerb. 308.

Te deprecamur, omnipotens Deus, ut benedicas hunc fructum novorum pomorum: ut qui esu interdictae arboris letalis pomi in protoparente iusta funeris sententia [1] multati sumus, per illustrationem[2] unici Filii tui Redemptoris, Dei ac Domini nostri Iesu Christi, et Spiritus sancti benedictione[3], sanctificata omnia atque benedicta, depulsis atque abiectis vetusti hostis atque primi facinoris incentoris[4] insidiis, salubriter ex huius diei anniversaria solemnitate diversis terrae edendis germinibus sumamus. Qui vivis et regnas in unitate.

[1] *iustae funeris sententiae* V.; *iuste funeris sententia* R.   [2] *illustratione* V.; R. as text.   [3] *benedictione*, so V. R., perhaps ungrammatically.   [4] *intentoris* V.

XC.

BENEDICTIO ARBORIS.

Deus qui hanc arboris poma[1] tua iussione et providentia progenitam [esse voluisti[2]], nunc etiam eadem benedicere et sanctificare digneris precamur; ut quicumque ex ea sumpserint, incolumes esse valeant. Per.

R. Gerb. 308.

[1] *pumma* V.; R. as text. The word is apparently treated in the benediction both in R. and V. as a feminine singular (*hanc . . . ex ea*), and also as a neuter plural (*eadem*).   [2] V. omits *esse voluisti*.

XCI.

ORATIONES POST OBITUM HOMINIS.

Pio recordationis affectu, fratres carissimi, commemorationem faciamus[1] cari nostri *Illius*[2], quem Dominus de tentationibus huius[3] saeculi assumpsit, obsecrantes misericordiam[4] Dei nostri, ut ipse ei tribuere dignetur placitam et quietam mansionem[5], remittat omnes lubricae temeritatis offensas, ut concessa venia plenae indulgentiae[6], quidquid in hoc saeculo proprius error attulit[7] totum ineffabili pietate ac benignitate sua compenset[8]. Per[9]. γ

B. Leofr. 199. Sacr. Gall. 951.

Diri vulneris novitate perculsi, et quodammodo cordibus sauciati, misericordiam tuam, mundi redemptor, flebilibus vocibus imploramus, ut cari nostri *Illius* animam ad te datorem proprium[10] revertentem blande leniterque[11] suscipias, et si quas illa ex hac carnali commoratione[12] contraxit maculas[13], tu, Deus, inolita bonitate clementer deleas, pie indulgeas, oblivioni in perpetuum tradas, atque hanc[14] eandem laudes tibi cum ceteris redditurum, et ad corpus quandoque reversuram, sanctorum tuorum coetibus aggregari[15] praecipias. Per Dominum.

Leofr. 201.

R. Gerb. 313.
Leofr. 199.
Sacr. Gall. 951.

Tu nobis, Domine, auxilium praestare digneris, tu opem [16], tu misericordiam largiaris [17]; spiritum etiam [18] famuli tui *Illius* [19] ac [20] cari nostri, vinculis [21] corporalibus liberatum [22], in pace sanctorum tuorum [23] recipias; uti [24] locum poenalem, et gehennae ignem, flammamque tartari in regione viventium evadat. Per eum [25] qui tecum vivit et regnat Deus in unitate Spiritus sancti, per.

Leofr. 199.

Suscipe, Domine, animam servi tui *Illius* [19] ad te revertentem de Aegypti partibus [et] [26] proficiscentem ad te. Emitte angelos tuos sanctos in obviam illius [27], et viam iustitiae demonstra ei. Aperi ei portas iustitiae, et repelle ab ea principes tenebrarum: agnosce depositum fidele quod tuum est. Suscipe [28], Domine, creaturam tuam, non ex diis alienis creatam, sed a te Deo solo [29] vero et vivo, quia non est Deus praeter te solum [30], et non est secundum opera tua. Laetifica, Domine, animam servi tui *Illius* [19]: clarifica, Domine, famulum tuum [31]: ne memineris iniquitatum eius antiquarum et ebrietatum, quas [32] suscitavit furor mali [33] desiderii: licet enim peccavit [34], Patrem et Filium et Spiritum sanctum tamen [34] non negavit, sed credidit, et zelum Dei habuit, et Deum fecisse omnia [35] adoravit. [Per [36].]

R. Gerb. 313.

Suscipe, Domine, animam servi tui *Illius* [19] revertentem ad te: vestem caelestem indue eam, et lava eam sanctum fontem [37] vitae aeternae; ut [38] inter gaudentes gaudeat, et inter sapientes sapiat, et inter martyres coronatos [39] consideat, et inter patriarchas et prophetas proficiat, et inter apostolos Christum sequi studeat, et inter angelos et archangelos claritatem Dei pervideat [40], et inter Paradisi rutilos lapides gaudium possideat, et notitiam mysteriorum [41] agnoscat, et inter cherubin et seraphin claritatem Dei inveniat, et inter viginti quatuor seniores cantica canticorum audiat, et inter lavantes stolas in fonte luminis vestem lavet, et inter pulsantes pulsans [42], portas caelestis Hierusalem apertas [43] reperiat, et inter videntes Deum facie ad faciem videat, et inter audientes auditu caelesti caelestem sonum exaudiat [44]. Suscipe, Domine, servum tuum *Illum* [45] in aeternum [46] habitaculum, et da ei requiem et regnum, id est, Hierusalem caelestem; ut [47] in sinibus patriarcharum nostrorum [48], id est, Abraham, Isaac et Iacob, collocare digneris; et habeat partem in prima resurrectione, et inter surgentes resurgat, et inter suscipientes corpora in die resurrectionis corpus[49] suscipiat, et cum benedictis ad dexteram Dei Patris venientibus veniat, et inter possidentes vitam aeternam possideat. Per Dominum.

Antiqui memores[50] chirographi, fratres carissimi[51], quo primi hominis peccato et corruptioni[52] addicta est humana conditio, sub cuius lege[53] sibi unusquisque formidat, quod aliis accidisse videat[54], omnipotentis Dei misericordiam deprecemur pro spiritu[55] cari nostri *Illius*, cuius hodie depositio celebratur[56], ut eum in aeternam requiem suscipiat, et beata resurrectione[57] repraesentet. Per.

R. Gerb. 314. Sacr. Gall. 952.

Deus, qui iustis supplicationibus [semper][58] praesto es[59], qui pia vota dignaris intueri, da famulo tuo *Illi*[60], cuius[61] depositionis hodie[62] officia pia[63] praestamus, cum sanctis atque electis[64] tuis beati muneris portionem. Per Dominum. γ

R. Gerb. 314. Sacr. Gall. 952. Leofr. 200.

Dic cap[*itulum*] In memoria aeterna.

Item orationes antequam ad sepulcrum deferatur.

Deum iudicem universitatis, Deum caelestium et terrestrium et infernorum Dominum[65], deprecemur[66] pro spiritu cari nostri *Illius*, uti eum Dominus[67] in requiem[68] collocare dignetur, et in parte[69] primae resurrectionis resuscitet. Per Dominum nostrum[70].

R. B. Gerb. 315. Leofr. 200.

Te, Domine sancte, Pater omnipotens, aeterne Deus, supplices deprecamur pro spiritu famuli tui[71] *Illius*, quem ab originibus huius saeculi ad te arcessiri[72] praecepisti, ut digneris, Domine, dare ei locum lucidum, locum refrigerii et quietis. Liceat ei transire portas infernorum et vias[73] tenebrarum, maneatque in mansionibus sanctorum, et in luce sancta, quam olim Abrahae promisisti et semini eius: nullam laesionem sustineat anima[74] eius, sed quum • magnus dies ille[75] resurrectionis ac remunerationis advenerit, resuscitare eum digneris, Domine, una cum sanctis et electis[76] tuis: dones ei[77] delicta atque peccata usque ad novissimum[78] quadrantem, tecumque immortalitatis vitam et regnum consequatur aeternum. Per Dominum nostrum.

Leofr. 201. cf. Sacr. Gall. 951.

Omnipotentis Dei misericordiam, dilectissimi fratres[79], deprecemur[80], cuius iudicio aut nascimur aut finimur, ut

R. B. Gerb. 314. Leofr. 200.

animam [81] fratris nostri *Illius* quem Domini pietas de incolatu mundi huius transire praecepit, requies aeterna suscipiat, et eam beata [82] resurrectione praesentet [83] et in sinibus Abrahae et Isaac et Iacob collocare dignetur. Per [70].

R. B.
Gerb. 315.
Sacr. Gall.
949.
Leofr. 201.

Deus, qui universorum creator et conditor es [84], qui [85] quum sis tuorum beatitudo sanctorum [86], praesta nobis petentibus, ut animam [87] fratris nostri *Illius*, corporis nexibus absolutam [87], in prima [88] resurrectione facias praesentari [89]. Per.

Item orationes ad sepulcrum, priusquam sepeliatur.

Leofr. 201.

Oremus, fratres carissimi [90], pro anima [91] cari nostri *Illius*, quem Dominus de laqueo huius saeculi liberare dignatus est, cuius corpusculum hodie sepulturae traditur, ut eum Domini pietas inter sanctos et electos suos, id est in sinu Abrahae, Isaac, et Iacob, collocare dignetur, et partem habeat in prima resurrectione, quam facturus est, orantibus sanctis [92]. Per Dominum nostrum. γ

Leofr. 201.

Opus misericordiae tuae est, Pater omnipotens, aeterne Deus, rogare [93] pro aliis, qui nobis non sufficimus: suscipe, Domine, animam servi tui *Illius* revertentem ad te. Adsit ei angelus testamenti tui Michael. Libera eam, Domine, de principibus tenebrarum, et de locis poenarum, ne iam ullis [94] primae nativitatis vel ignorantiae confundatur erroribus: agnoscatur a tuis, et misericordia bonitatis tuae ad locum refrigerii et quietis in sinu transferatur Abrahae. Per Dominum nostrum.

Redemptor animarum Deus, aeternitatem concede defunctis, neque vacuari passionis triumphum mundi morte patiaris, qui cum Patre et Spiritu sancto vivis et regnas in saecula saeculorum.

Item orationes post sepulturam. 751

R.
Gerb. 315.
Leofr. 201.

Debitum humani corporis sepeliendi officium fidelium more complentes, Deum, cui omnia vivunt, fideliter deprecemur, ut hoc corpus [95] a nobis in infirmitate sepultum, in virtute et ordine sanctorum resuscitet, et eius animam [96] sanctis et fidelibus iubeat aggregari; cuique in iudicio misericordiam tribuat; quemque morte redemptum, debitis solutum, Patri reconciliatum, boni Pastoris humeris reportatum [97], in comitatu [98] aeterni regis perenni gaudio et sanctorum consortio perfrui concedas [99]. Per Dominum nostrum.

Omnipotens aeterne [100] Deus, qui humano corpori a te ipso animam inspirare dignatus es, dum, te iubente, pulvis pulveri rursus redditur, tu imaginem tuam [101] cum sanctis et electis tuis aeternis sedibus praecipias sociari. Per Dominum nostrum. Leofr. 202.

Obsequiis autem rite celebratis, membris ex feretro depositis [102], tumulo ex more composito, post Israelis exitu [103] ex Aegypto, deprecemur clementiam Dei Patris pro anima [104] cari nostri *Illius*, quem Dominus de laqueo huius mundi liberavit lugubris letali, cuius posse [105] ubique est, et potestas innumerabilis, habens divitias spiritales. Animae huius [106] subveniat sublimis Dominus, ut ardore careat aeterni ignis, adeptura [106] perpetui regni refugium [107]. Coram suo rege gratificet [108] in gaudio genitali, in sublimi solio patrum praeelectorum, in medio [iustorum, in] [109] splendoribus sanctorum, in sede maiestatis, magno in lumine, in regione, in regno vivorum [110]. Per. MS. Magd. 226.

Commendatio animae.

Commendamus tibi, Domine, animam fratris nostri *Illius*: precamur, propter [111] quam ad terras tua pietate descenderas, patriarcharum tuorum sinibus insinuare non renuas, sed miserere [112]: migranti in tuo nomine de hac instabili et tam incerta sempiternam illam vitam ac laetitiam in caelestibus praesta, Salvator mundi, qui cum Patre vivis dominator, et regnas Deus, in unitate Spiritus sancti in saecula. Leofr. 203.

Item alia.

Deus, apud quem omnia morientia vivunt, cui non pereunt moriendo corpora nostra sed mutantur in melius, te supplices deprecamur, ut suscipi iubeas animam famuli tui *Illius* per manus sanctorum angelorum deducendam in sinum amici [113] tui patriarchae Abrahae, resuscitandam in die novissimo [114] magni iudicii; et [si] [115] quid de regione mortali tibi contrarium contraxit, fallente diabolo, tua pietate ablue indulgendo. Per. Gerb. 313. cf. B.

¹ *facimus* B. Leofr.; V. Sacr. Gall. as text. ² *cari nostro Illo* V.
³ Sacr. Gall. omits *huius*. ⁴ B. inserts *tuam vel*. ⁵ *vitam* (for
mansionem) B.; Leofr. inserts *et* after *mansionem*. ⁶ *plenae indulgentiae
venia* Sacr. Gall. ⁷ *saeculo proprio reatu deliquit* B. Leofr.; V. Sacr.
Gall. as text. ⁸ *deleat et abstergat* (for *compenset*) B. Leofr.; Sacr. Gall.
has *indulgeat*. ⁹ Leofr. gives the ending *Quod ipse praestare dignetur* &c.;
B. has *Praest.*; Sacr. Gall. gives no termination. ¹⁰ *proprium ad te
datorem* Leofr. ¹¹ *leviterque* Leofr. ¹² *ut si qua ex carnali contagione*
Leofr. ¹³ *maculam* Leofr. ¹⁴ Leofr. omits *hanc*. ¹⁵ *adgregare* V.
¹⁶ R. inserts *feras*; Sacr. Gall. has *tu per misericordiam* (omitting *opem tu*).
¹⁷ Leofr. inserts *et*. ¹⁸ *animam quoque* (for *spiritum etiam*) Sacr. Gall.
¹⁹ *Ille* V. ²⁰ Leofr. omits *ac*; Sacr. Gall. omits *ac cari nostri*.; R. has
famuli tui et cari nostri Ill. ²¹ *a vinculis* Sacr. Gall. ²² *liberatam*
Sacr. Gall. ²³ R. Leofr. omit *tuorum*. ²⁴ *ut hic* (for *uti*) Leofr.;
Sacr. Gall. has *recipias, et gehennae ignis evadat* (so ending); V. R. as text.
²⁵ *Qui vivis* Leofr. ²⁶ V. omits *et*. ²⁷ *in obviam ei* Leofr. ²⁸ Leofr.
omits the words *depositum ... suscipe*. V. has *fidelem* for *fidele*, probably
by an error of the scribe. ²⁹ Leofr. omits *solo*. ³⁰ Leofr.
omits *solum* and adds *Domine*. ³¹ Leofr. omits *clarifica ... tuum*.
³² *ebrietatem quae* V.; Leofr. as text. ³³ *male* V. ³⁴ Leofr. places
tamen before *Patrem*. ³⁵ *qui omnia fecit* (for *fecisse omnia*) Leofr.; V. as
text. ³⁶ Leofr. adds *Per*. which is omitted in V. ³⁷ *sancto fontem* R.;
V. as text (ungrammatically). ³⁸ *et* R. ³⁹ *coronata* R. ⁴⁰ *semper
videat* R. ⁴¹ *ministeriorum* R. ⁴² *depulsans* R. ⁴³ *apertas
caelestis Hierusalem* Gerb. ⁴⁴ *audientes auditum caelestisonum audiat* R.
⁴⁵ *Illius* V. ⁴⁶ R. inserts *in bonum*. ⁴⁷ R. inserts *eum*. ⁴⁸ R.
omits *nostrorum*. ⁴⁹ R. inserts *suum*. ⁵⁰ *memoreris* (for *memores*) R.
⁵¹ *dilectissimi* Sacr. Gall. ⁵² *corruptione* Sacr. Gall.; V. R. as text.
⁵³ Sacr. Gall. inserts *id*. ⁵⁴ *quod alia investigavit videatque* Sacr. Gall.
⁵⁵ *anima* Sacr. Gall. ⁵⁶ *depositionem celebramus* Sacr. Gall. ⁵⁷ *beatae
resurrectioni* Sacr. Gall. ⁵⁸ V. omits *semper*, which is restored from R.
Sacr. Gall. Leofr. ⁵⁹ *ades* Sacr. Gall. ⁶⁰ *Illius* V.; Sacr. Gall. has
animae famoli tui Ill. ⁶¹ V. inserts *diem*, perhaps for *diei*, but more
probably by confusion with another form; Sacr. Gall. has *transitus* for
depositionis. ⁶² R. omits *hodie*; Leofr. has *die*. ⁶³ R. Sacr. Gall.
Leofr. omit *pia*; Leofr. has *peragimus* for *praestamus*. ⁶⁴ *sanctis et electis*
(om. *tuis*) R. Leofr.; V. Sacr. Gall. as text. ⁶⁵ *Deum* B.; Leofr. omits
Dominum. ⁶⁶ *deprecamur* R. ⁶⁷ R. omits *Dominus*; B. has
pietas Domini. ⁶⁸ *requie* B. ⁶⁹ *partem* R.; V. B. Leofr. as text.
⁷⁰ B. has the ending *Qui venturus est*. ⁷¹ *anima cari nostri* Sacr. Gall.;
V. Leofr. as text. ⁷² *arcessire* V.; *accersiri* Leofr.; Sacr. Gall. has *quem
ab hoc saeculo ad te arcessiri iussisti*, and from this point varies a good deal
from the readings of V. Leofr. ⁷³ *poenas* Leofr.; *vias* V. Sacr. Gall.
⁷⁴ *spiritus* Leofr. ⁷⁵ *ille dies* Leofr. ⁷⁶ *sanctis ac fidelibus* Leofr.
⁷⁷ *deleas ei* Leofr. ⁷⁸ *novissimam* V.; Leofr. has *in novissimum*. ⁷⁹ R.
Leofr. B. omit *dilectissimi fratres*. ⁸⁰ *imploramus* B.; *deprecamur* R.
⁸¹ *spiritum* R. Leofr. ⁸² *et cum beata* B. Leofr.; *et eum in beata* R.
⁸³ *repraesentet* R. B. Leofr. ⁸⁴ *Deus universorum creator et conditor* R.;
Deus qui universorum es creator et conditor B. Leofr.; V. Sacr. Gall. as text.
⁸⁵ Sacr. Gall. omits *qui*; V. R. B. Leofr. as text (ungrammatically). ⁸⁶ *sis
sanctorum beatitudo* B. ⁸⁷ *spiritum ... absolutum* R. Leofr. B., and perhaps the original of Sacr. Gall. which varies the latter part of the Collect, but
retains *absolutum* in agreement with *depositionem*. ⁸⁸ B. omits *prima*.
⁸⁹ *repraesentari* Gerb.; but R. as text. ⁹⁰ Leofr. inserts *Deum omnipotentem*. ⁹¹ *spiritu* Leofr. ⁹² *orantibus nobis* Leofr. ⁹³ *rogariu*
Leofr.; V. as text. ⁹⁴ *ne famulus tuus Ill*. (for *ne iam ullis*) Leofr.
⁹⁵ Leofr. inserts *cari nostri Ill*. ⁹⁶ *spiritum* R. Leofr.; Leofr. inserts
cum. ⁹⁷ R. inserts *Spiritum sanctum protectum*. ⁹⁸ R. inserts *et*.
⁹⁹ *concedatur* R. Leofr. ¹⁰⁰ *sempiterne* Leofr. ¹⁰¹ Leofr. inserts *una*.
¹⁰² This bidding prayer is not in R. Gerb. Leofr. or Sacr. Gall. It appears in
an English Pontifical of about the year 1200, now in the Library of Magd.
Coll. Oxford (MS. Magd. 226), where it begins *Exequiis rite celebratis, membrisque feretro depositis*. ¹⁰³ *post Israel exitum* MS. Magd.; V. as text
(ungrammatically). ¹⁰⁴ *spiritu* MS. Magd. ¹⁰⁵ *cuique possis* V.;
MS. Magd. as text. ¹⁰⁶ *Spiritui huic ... adepturus* MS. Magd. ¹⁰⁷ *re-*

frigerium MS. Magd. [106] *Coram rege suo gratificetur* MS. Magd.; V. as text; perhaps *gratificet* is equivalent to *gratias agat.* [109] V. omits *iustorum, in*, which is restored from MS. Magd. [110] *in sede maiestatis magnae, in lumine regionis vivorum* MS. Magd.; V. as text. [111] *precamurque ut propter* Leofr. [112] *non renuas, miserere qui vivis et regnas* &c. Leofr. [113] *sinu inimici* R. [114] *novissimi* R. [115] V. omits *si*; the kindred Collect in B. has *et quicquid*; R. as text.

XCII.

Item Missa pro defuncto Sacerdote.

Deus, [qui][1] inter apostolicos sacerdotes famulum tuum *Illum* pontificali[2] fecisti dignitate[2] vigere, praesta, quaesumus, ut eorum quoque et[3] perpetuo aggregetur consortio. Per.

R.
Gerb. 315.
Men. 217.
cf. Leon. 454.

Preces nostras, quaesumus, Domine, quas in famuli tui *Illius* depositione deferimus, propitiatus exaudi; ut qui nomini tuo ministerium fidele[4] dependit, perpetua sanctorum societate laetetur. Per.

R.
Gerb. 316.

Secreta.

Suscipe, quaesumus, Domine, pro anima famuli et sacerdotis tui *Illius* quas offerimus hostias[5]; ut cui pontificale donasti meritum, dones et praemium. Per.

R.
Gerb. 316.
Men. 217.
Leon. 454.
xciii *infra*.

Infra actionem.

Hanc igitur oblationem[6], quam tibi pro depositione famuli[7] et sacerdotis tui *Illius* deferimus, quaesumus, Domine, placatus[8] intende: pro quo[9] maiestati tuae supplices fundimus preces, ut eum in numero tibi placentium censeri facias sacerdotum. Per.

R.
Gerb. 317.

Postcommun.

Propitiare, Domine, supplicationibus nostris, et animam famuli tui *Illius* episcopi in vivorum regione aeternis gaudiis iube associari[10]. Per.

R.
Gerb. 317.

---

[1] V. omits *qui* which is restored from R. Men. Leon. [2] *pontificale ... dignitatem* V.; R. Men. as text; Leon. has *fecisti vigere pontificem.* [3] Men. omits *et*; V. R. as text. [4] *fideli* V.; R. has *mysterium fideli.* [5] *Suscipe Domine quaesumus hostias pro anima famuli tui (Ill.) episcopi (famuli et sacerdotis tui* Men.), Leon. Men.; V. R. as text. [6] R. inserts *Domine.* [7] R. inserts *tui.* [8] R. omits *placatus.* [9] *qua* V. [10] *iubeas sociare* V.; *iube associare* R.

XCIII.

ITEM ALIA PRO SACERDOTE.

R.
Gerb. 317.
Men. 217.
Leon. 454.

Praesta, quaesumus, Domine, ut anima famuli tui *Illius* episcopi, quam in hoc saeculo commorantem sacris muneribus decorasti, [1] caelesti sede gloriosa semper exultet. Per Dominum nostrum. γ

R.
Gerb. 317.

Deus, cuius misericordiae non est numerus, suscipe pro anima famuli tui *Illius* episcopi preces nostras, et lucis ei laetitiaeque in regione sanctorum tuorum societatem [2] concede. Per.

Secreta.

R.
Gerb. 317.
Men. 217.
Leon. 454.
xcii *supra*.

Suscipe, Domine, quaesumus, hostias pro anima famuli tui *Illius* episcopi : ut cui pontificale donasti meritum [3] dones et praemium [3]. Per.

Infra actionem.

R.
Gerb. 317.

Hanc igitur oblationem servitutis nostrae, quam tibi offerimus pro anima [4] famuli tui *Illius* episcopi, quaesumus, Domine, placatus accipias, et cum praesulibus apostolicae dignitatis, quorum est secutus officium, habere tribuas sempiternae beatitudinis portionem : diesque nostros.

Postcommun.

R.
Gerb. 317.
Men. 218.

Praesta, quaesumus, omnipotens Deus, ut animam [5] famuli tui *Illius* episcopi in congregatione iustorum aeternae beatitudinis iubeas esse consortem. Per Dominum nostrum.

[1] R. Leon. insert *in*; V. Men. as text. [2] *societate* V.; R. as text. [3] V. and R. agree in transposing *meritum* and *praemium*: but Men. Leon. and the similar *secreta* in the *Missa* immediately preceding seem to justify the reading of the text. [4] R. omits *pro anima*. [5] *anima* V. R. (ungrammatically for *animam* which is the reading of Men.).

XCIV.

ITEM ALIA PRO SACERDOTE SIVE ABBATE.

R.
Gerb. 318.

Deus, qui famulum tuum *Illum* sacerdotem atque abbatem et sanctificasti [1] unctionem misericordiae tuae [2], et assumpsisti consummatione felici, suscipe propitius preces nostras, et praesta ut sicut ille [3] tecum est meritis, ita a nobis non recedat exemplis. Per Dominum.

[Gerb. 318 n.]

Omnipotens sempiterne Deus, maiestatem tuam supplices exoramus, ut famulo tuo *Illi* abbati atque sacerdoti [4], quem

in requiem tuam vocare dignatus es, dones sedem honori-
754 ficatam, et fructum beati-tudinis sempiternae; ut ea, quae
in oculis nostris docuit et gessit, non iudicium nobis pariant[5],
sed profectum attribuant[6], ut pro[7] quo nunc in te gaudemus
in terris, cum eodem apud te exultare mereamur in caelis.
Per.

Secreta.

Concede, quaesumus, omnipotens Deus, ut anima famuli
tui *Illius* abbatis atque sacerdotis per haec sancta mysteria
in tuo conspectu semper clara consistat, quae[8] fideliter
ministravit. Per.

R.
Gerb. 318.

Infra actionem.

Hanc igitur oblationem[9], quam tibi pro anima famuli tui
Illius abbatis atque sacerdotis offerimus, quaesumus, Domine,
placatus intende; pro qua maiestati tuae supplices fundimus
preces, ut eam in numero sanctorum tuorum [tibi][10] placentium facias dignanter ascribi: diesque nostros[11].

R.
Gerb. 318.
cf. xcv
infra.

Postcommun.

Prosit, quaesumus, Domine, animae famuli tui *Illius*
sacerdotis misericordiae tuae implorata clementia[12]; ut
eius, in quo speravit et credidit, aeternum accipiat, te
miserante, consortium. Per Dominum.

R.
Gerb. 319.

[1] *sanctificas* V.; R. as text (ungrammatically). [2] *vocatione misericordiae* R.; V. as text. [3] *illius* V.; R. as text. [4] *et famulo tuo Illo abbate atque sacerdote* V.; *ut famulo et sacerdoti tuo N. atque abbati* Gerb. [5] *pareat* V. [6] *attribuat* V. [7] *per* V. [8] Gerb. inserts *tibi*: but V. R. as text. [9] R. inserts *Domine*. [10] *tibi*, omitted by V. is restored from R. [11] R. makes no mention of the clause *diesque nostros*, but adds *Quam oblationem*. [12] *implorata clementiae tuae* R.

XCV.

ORATIONES AD MISSA[1] IN NATALE[1] SANCTORUM SIVE AGENDA[1] MORTUORUM.

Beati martyris tui *Illius*, Domine, quaesumus, intercessione nos protege, et animam[2] famuli tui *Illius* sacerdotis[3]
sanctorum tuorum iunge consortiis. Per.

R.
Gerb. 319.
cf. Leon.
453.

Adiuva nos, Domine Deus noster, beati *Illius* precibus
exoratus, et animam[4] famuli tui *Illius* sacerdotis[3] in beatitudinis sempiternae luce constitue. Per.

R.
Gerb. 319.
Leon. 453.

Secreta.

R. Gerb. 319.

Suscipe, quaesumus, Domine, hostias placationis et laudis, quas tibi in honore sancti martyris tui *Illius* nomini tuo consecrandas deferimus, et pro requie famuli tui *Illius* sacerdotis tibi suppliciter immolamus. Per.

Infra actionem.   755

R. Gerb. 319. cf. xciv *infra*.

Hanc igitur oblationem, quam tibi in honore sancti martyris tui *Illius*, vel pro requie famuli tui *Illius* sacerdotis offerimus, quaesumus, Domine, placatus intende ; pro qua[5] maiestati tuae supplices fundimus preces, ut eam[5] in numero sanctorum tibi placentium facias dignanter adscribi. Quam oblationem.

Postcommun.

R. Gerb. 319. cf. xcvii *infra*.

Ascendant ad te, Domine, preces nostras[6] et anima[6] famuli tui *Illius* gaudia aeterna suscipiant[6] ; ut quem fecisti adoptionis[7] participem, iubeas hereditatis tuae esse consortem. Per Dominum.

[1] *Missa ... natale ... agenda*, so V. ungrammatically.   [2] *anima* V. ; *animas* R. ; Leon. as text.   [3] Leon. has *episcopi* for *sacerdotis*.   [4] *anima* V. ; R. Leon. as text.   [5] *qua ... eam*, so both V. and R. (as though *anima* had stood in the place of *requie* in the antecedent clause, as in xciv *supra*).   [6] *nostras ... anima ... suscipiant*, so both V. (here and in xcvii *infra*) and R.   [7] *adoptionem* V. here ; but R. and V. in xcvii *infra* as text.

XCVI.

MISSA PRO DEFUNCTI NUPER BAPTIZATI[1].

R. Gerb. 319. Pam. 458.

Deus, qui ad caeleste regnum non nisi renatis per aquam et Spiritum sanctum pandis introitum, multiplica super animam famuli tui *Illius* misericordiam tuam : et cui donasti celerem et incontaminatum transitum post baptismi sacramentum, da ei et[2] aeternorum plenitudinem gaudiorum. Per. γ

Deus, qui omne meritum vocatorum donis tuae bonitatis anticipas, propitiare animae famuli tui *Illius*, quem[3] in finem[4] istius vitae regenerationis unda mundavit ; et quem fecisti non timere de culpa, fac gaudere de gratia. Per.

Secreta.

R. Gerb. 320. Pam. 458.

Propitiare, Domine, supplicationibus nostris pro anima famuli tui *Illius*, pro qua tibi offerimus sacrificium laudis, ut eam sanctorum tuorum [coetibus][5] consociare digneris. Per. γ

Infra actionem.

Hanc igitur oblationem, quam tibi offerimus, Domine, pro anima famuli tui *Illius*, benignus assume, eumque regenerationis fonte[6] purgatum, et periculis vitae huius exutum, beatorum numero digneris inserere spirituum. Quam oblationem. γ

R.
Gerb. 320.
Pam. 458.

Postcommun.

Propitiare, Domine, animae famuli tui *Illius*, ut quem in finem[4] istius vitae regenerationis fonte mundasti, ad caelestis regni beatitudinem facias pervenire. Per. γ

R.
Gerb. 320.
Pam. 358.

[1] *defuncto nuper baptizato* R.; V. as text, perhaps omitting *anima* or *requie*, perhaps simply using the genitive for the ablative case. [2] R. Pam. omit *et*; V. as text. [3] *quae* V., probably for *que*, which elsewhere in the MS. occasionally represents *quem*. [4] *in finem*, probably ungrammatically for *in fine*, which is the reading of Pam. in the Postcommunion. [5] *coetibus*, omitted by V., is restored from R.; Pam. has *consortio sociare*. [6] *fontem* V.; R. Pam. as text.

XCVII.
ITEM ALIA MISSA.

Deus, cuius bonitatis nullus est numerus, quia semper misericordia tibi est causa miserendi, exaudi pro *Illius* famuli tui animam[1] supplicantes, ut illum gratia tua sicut donavit baptismo, ita donet et regno. Per.

Deus, qui caelestis regni nonnisi renatis pandis introitum, auge super anima[2] famuli tui *Illius* gratiae tuae dona; ut quae ab omnibus est purgata peccatis, a nullis sit aliena promissis. Per.

cf. I. lvi
supra.

Secreta.

Oblationes nostras, quaesumus, Domine, propitiatus intende, quas tibi offerimus pro anima famuli tui *Illius*: et cui donasti baptismi sacramentum, da ei aeternorum plenitudinem gaudiorum. Per.

Postcommun.

Ascendant ad te, Domine, preces nostras[3], et anima[3] famuli tui *Illius* gaudia aeterna suscipiant[3]; ut quem fecisti adoptionis participem iubeas hereditatis tuae esse consortem. Per.

R.
Gerb. 319.
xcv *supra*.

[1] *animam*, so V. (ungrammatically). [2] *anima*, so V. (ungrammatically). [3] See note [6] on xcv *supra*.

XCVIII.

ORATIONES AD MISSAS PRO DEFUNCTIS DESIDERANTIBUS POENITENTIAM ET MINIMUM CONSECUTIS [1].

R.
Gerb. 320.
Pam. 459.
Leofr. 196.

Si quis [2] *poenitentiam petens, dum sacerdos venit, fuerit officium linguae privatus, constitutum est, ut si idonea testimonia hoc dixerunt, et ipse per motus aliquos satisfacit, sacerdos impleat omnia circa poenitentem, ut moris est.*

Item ad missas.

R.
Gerb. 320.
Pam. 459.
Leon. 452.

Omnipotens et misericors Deus, in cuius humana conditio potestate consistit, animam [3] famuli tui *Illius*, quaesumus, ab omnibus absolve peccatis, ut poenitentiae fructum, quem voluntas eius optavit, praeventus mortalitate [4] non perdat. Per. γ

757

Secreta.

R.
Gerb. 320.
Pam. 459.
Leon. 452.

Satisfaciat tibi, Domine, quaesumus, pro anima famuli tui *Illius*, sacrificii praesentis oblatio, et peccatorum veniam quam quaesivit inveniat [5]; et quod officio linguae implere non potuit desideratae [6] poenitentiae compensatione percipiat. Per. γ

Infra actionem.

R.
Gerb. 320.
Pam. 459.

Hanc igitur oblationem, quam tibi offert famula tua *Illa* [7] pro anima famuli tui *Illius*, cuius depositionis diem *illum* [8] celebramus, quaesumus, Domine, ut placatus accipias, et ineffabili pietate concedas [9] ut quod exequi praeventus conditione mortali ministerio linguae non potuit mereatur indulgentiam sempiternam [10], quae in eius mente non defuit poenitenti [11]. Quam oblationem [12]. γ

Postcommun.

R.
Gerb. 320.
Pam. 459.
cf. Leon. 452.

Deus, a quo speratur humani corporis [13] omne quod bonum est, tribue per haec sancta [14], quaesumus, ut sicut animae famuli tui *Illius* poenitentiae velle donasti, sic indulgentiam tribue [15] miseratus optatam. Per. γ

---

[1] The title in V. is evidently corrupt: it stands thus *Orat. ad Miss. pro defunct. cuius desiderantibus penitenciam et minimum consecutus.* [2] This direction is drawn from a decree attributed by Ivo of Chartres to Pope Eusebius, which may perhaps have some better claim to be considered genuine than the other decretals which have been assigned to the same author. It is prefixed to the *Missa* in R. Pam. Leofr. as well as in V. The version in Pam. is more, that in R. less correct than that of the text, in which V. and Leofr. almost exactly agree. [3] *anima* V. R.; Pam. Leon. as text. [4] *mortalitatis* V. R.; Pam. Leon. as text. [5] Leon. (perhaps by an error) makes a break

in the Collect at this point, inserting the termination *Per.* and making a fresh beginning with *Et quod*. ⁶ *desiderante* V.; R. Pam. Leon. as text. ⁷ *quam tibi offerimus* Pam.; V. R. as text. ⁸ *cuius diem depositionis* Pam.; both Pam. and Gerb. omit *illum*. ⁹ *concordas* Pam. ¹⁰ *indulgentia sempiterna* Pam. which omits *quae in eius... poenitenti*. ¹¹ *poenitendi* V.; R. as text. ¹² R. Pam. have *diesque nostros*, which V. omits. ¹³ For *speratur humani corporis* Leon. has *inspiratur humanis cordibus*: the reading of the text is probably a corruption, but V. R. Pam. agree in adopting it. ¹⁴ R. omits *per haec sancta*; Leon. omits *tribue per haec sancta quaesumus*; V. Pam. as text. ¹⁵ *tribue*, so V. R. Pam. (ungrammatically): the error is probably caused by the careless insertion of words not contained in the Collect as it occurs in Leon. (see last note).

XCIX.

ORATIONES PRO DEFUNCTIS LAICIS.
ITEM UNIUS DEFUNCTI.

Omnipotens sempiterne Deus, cui nunquam sine spe misericordiae supplicatur, propitiare animae famuli tui *Illius*; ut qui de hac vita in tui nominis confessione decessit, sanctorum tuorum numero¹ facias aggregari. Per. γ

R.
Gerb. 320.
Pam. 457.
Men. 218.

Secreta.

Propitiare quaesumus, Domine, animae famuli tui *Illius*, pro qua tibi hostias placationis offerimus: et quia² in hac luce³ fide mansit catholica, ei⁴ in futura vita eius⁵ retributio condonetur. Per. γ

R.
Gerb. 321.
Pam. 457.
Men. 218.

Infra actionem.

Hanc igitur oblationem, quam tibi pro requie et anima⁶ famuli tui *Illius* offerimus, quaesumus, Domine, placatus accipias, et tua pietate concedas, ut mortalitatis nexibus absolutam⁷ inter fideles tuos habere constituas portionem⁸. Per⁹. γ

R.
Gerb. 321.
Pam. 457.

Postcommun.

Praesta, quaesumus, omnipotens Deus, ut animam¹⁰ famuli tui *Illius* ab angelis lucis susceptam, in praeparatis habitaculis¹¹ deduci facias beatorum. Per. γ

R.
Gerb. 321.
Pam. 458.
Men. 218.

¹ Men. inserts *eum*. ² *ut quid* R. ³ Pam. Men. insert *in*. ⁴ *et* (for *ei*) R.: Pam. Men. omit *ei*; V. as text. ⁵ *ei* R. ⁶ *pro requiem et anima* V.; *pro requie animae* R. Pam. ⁷ *absoluta* R. Pam. ⁸ *mereatur habere portionem* Pam.; V. R. as text. ⁹ R. inserts after *portionem* the clause *diesque nostros*, which V. Pam. omit. ¹⁰ *anima* V. R.; Pam. Men. as text. ¹¹ *praeparata habitacula* Men.; V. R. Pam. as text (ungrammatically).

C.

IN AGENDA PLURIMORUM.

R.
Gerb. 323.
Pam. 460.
Men. 219.
Leon 453.

Praesta [1], quaesumus, Domine, animabus famulorum famularumque tuarum misericordiam sempiternam [1]; ut mortalibus nexibus expeditas lux eas [2] aeterna possideat. Per. γ

Alia.

R.
Gerb. 323.
cf. Leon.
452.

Deus, cui soli competit medicinam [3] praestare post mortem, tribue, quaesumus, ut animae famulorum famularumque tuarum, ab omnibus exutae peccatis, in electorum tuorum societatibus aggregentur. Per.

Secreta.

R.
Gerb. 323.
Leon. 451.
Pam. 460.
Men. 219.

Hostias tibi, Domine, humili placatione [4] deferimus; ut animae famulorum famularumque tuarum [5] per haec placationis officia perpetuam [6] misericordiam consequantur [5]. Per. γ

Infra actionem.

R.
Gerb. 323.
Pam. 461.

Hanc igitur oblationem, quam tibi pro requie et animabus [7] famulorum famularumque tuarum offerimus, quaesumus, Domine, propitius intuere, et concede ut et [8] mortuis prosit ad veniam, quod cunctis viventibus praeparare dignatus es ad medelam. Quam oblationem [9]. γ

Postcommun.

R.
Gerb. 323.
Pam. 461.
Men. 219.

Inveniant, quaesumus, Domine, animae famulorum famularumque tuarum omnium [10] in Christo quiescentium lucis aeternae consortium, qui in hac luce positi tuum [11] consecuti 759 sunt sacramentum. Per. γ

[1] *Propitiare . . . misericordiam sempiternam* R.; *Propitiare . . . misericordia sempiterna* Pam. Men.; *Praesta Domine quaesumus animae famuli tui misericordiam sempiternam* Leon.; V. as text.   [2] *ut eam mortalibus nexibus expeditam lux* Leon.; V. R. Pam. Men. as text (save that Pam. has *expeditae*).   [3] *medicina* V.; R. Leon. as text (the latter part of the Collect. in Leon. differs from V. and R.).   [4] *supplicatione* Leon.; *plicatione* R.; V. Pam. Men. as text.   [5] *anima famuli tui . . . consequatur* Leon.   [6] *tuam* (for *perpetuam*) R. Pam. Men.; V. Leon. as text.   [7] *requiem et animabus* V. R.; *requie animarum* Pam.   [8] *et ut* R.; Pam. omits *et*; V. as text.   [9] R. Pam. have *diesque nostros*, which V. omits.   [10] *omniumque* Pam. Men.; V. R. as text.   [11] *positum* (for *positi tuum*) R.

CI.

ITEM ALIA MISSA.

Pam. 461.
cf. Leon.
453.

Fidelium Deus omnium conditor et redemptor, animabus [1] famulorum famularumque tuarum remissionem

cunctorum tribue peccatorum, ut indulgentiam, quam sem- cf. Gerb. 323.
per optaverunt, piis supplicationibus consequantur. Per. γ

Maiestatem tuam, Domine, supplices exoramus, ut ani- B. cf. Leon. 454.
mae famulorum famularumque tuarum ab omnibus, quae per
humanitatem [2] commiserunt, exutae, in tuorum censeantur
sorte iustorum. Per.

Secreta.

Hostias, quaesumus, Domine, quas tibi pro animabus Pam. 461.
famulorum famularumque tuarum offerimus, propitiatus
intende, et [3] quibus fidei Christianae meritum contulisti,
dones et praemium. Per Dominum. γ

Infra actionem.

Hanc igitur oblationem, quam tibi pro commemoratione
animarum in pace dormientium suppliciter immolamus,
quaesumus, Domine, benignus accipias, et tua pietate concede, ut et nobis proficiat huius pietatis affectus, et illis
impetret beatitudinem sempiternam. Per. γ

Postcommun.

Animabus, quaesumus, Domine, famulorum famularumque Pam. 461. Gerb. 323.
tuarum *Illius* [4] oratio proficiat supplicantium, ut eas et
a peccatis exuas et tuae redemptionis facias esse participes.
Per. γ

[1] V. has *animarum*, perhaps through a confusion with the kindred forms in Leon. and Gerb. which begin *Fidelium Deus animarum*. Pam. as text. The Collects referred to in Leon. Gerb. differ slightly in several points from that in the text, in which V. and Pam. agree. [2] *per humanitate* V.; *quae humanitus commiserunt* B.; the kindred form in Leon. has *quae humanitus attraxit*. [3] *ut* Pam. [4] Pam. Gerb. omit any indication of names; V. as text, perhaps for *Illius atque Illius*, perhaps for *beati Illius*.

CII.

Item alia Missa.

Animabus, quaesumus, Domine, famulorum famularumque Pam. 462. [Gerb. 324 n.]
tuarum misericordiam concede perpetuam; ut eis proficiat
in aeternum, quod in te speraverunt et crediderunt. Per. γ

Secreta.

His, quaesumus, Domine, placatus intende muneribus, Pam. 462. [Gerb. 324 n.]
et quod ad laudem tui nominis supplicantes [1] offerimus, ad
indulgentiam proficiat defunctorum. Per. γ

Infra actionem.

[Gerb. 324 n.]

Hanc igitur oblationem, quam tibi pro animabus famulorum famularumque tuarum venerantes deferimus, quaesumus, Domine, placatus intende; et tua dignatione concede, ut mortis vinculis absoluti[2], transitum mereantur ad vitam. Per[3].

Postcommun.

[Gerb. 324 n.]
Pam. 462.

Supplices, quaesumus[4], Domine, pro animabus famulorum tuorum[5] preces effundimus, sperantes ut quicquid conversatione contraxerunt humana et clementer indulgeas, et in tuorum sede laetantium constituas redemptorum. Per. γ

[1] *supplices* Gerb.; V. Pam. as text.   [2] *absolutae* Gerb.; V. as text.
[3] Gerb. has *Quam oblationem*, agreeing with V. in omitting *diesque nostros*.
[4] *quaesumus*, which is superfluous, is omitted by Gerb., but appears in V. and Pam.   [5] *famulorum famularumque* Gerb. Pam. (the latter adds *tuarum*); V. as text.

CIII.
ITEM ALIA MISSA IN COEMETERIIS.

R.
Gerb. 326.
Pam. 462.

Deus, cuius miseratione animae fidelium requiescunt, famulis tuis *Illis* et *Illis*[1] vel[2] omnibus hic[3] quiescentibus da propitius veniam peccatorum, ut a cunctis reatibus absoluti[4], sine fine laetentur. Per. γ

Alia.

[Gerb. 326 n.]

Omnipotens sempiterne Deus, annue precibus nostris ea quae poscimus, et dona omnibus, quorum hic corpora requiescunt, refrigerii sedem, quietis beatitudinem, luminis claritatem; et[5] qui peccatorum suorum pondere praegravantur, eis[6] supplicatio commendet ecclesiae. Per.

Secreta.

R.
Gerb. 326.
Pam. 462.

Pro animabus famulorum tuorum [*Illorum*] et *Illorum* et hic omnium[7] dormientium, hostiam, Domine, suscipe benignus oblatam: et[8] hoc sacrificio singulari[9] vinculis horrendae mortis exutae, vitam mereantur aeternam. Per. γ

Infra actionem.

R.
Gerb. 326.
Pam. 462.

Hanc igitur oblationem, quam tibi offerimus, Domine, pro tuorum requie famulorum et famularum *Illius* et *Illius*[10], et omnium fidelium catholicorum orthodoxorum in hac basilica in Christo quiescentium, et qui in circuitu huius ecclesiae tuae[11] requiescunt, quaesumus, Domine, placatus accipias, ut per haec salutis humana subsidia in tuorum numero redemptorum sorte perpetua censeantur: diesque nostros[12].

Postcommun.

Deus, fidelium lumen animarum, adesto supplicationibus nostris, et da omnibus[13] quorum corpora hic quiescunt refrigerii sedem, quietis[14] beatitudinem, luminis claritatem. Per Dominum. γ

R. Gerb. 327. Pam. 463.

[1] *Illius* V.   [2] *et* Pam.   [3] R. Pam. insert *in Christo*.   [4] *absolutis* V.   [5] *ut* Gerb.   [6] *eos* Gerb.; V. as text (ungrammatically).   [7] R. Pam. insert *catholicorum*.   [8] *ut* R. Pam.   [9] *sacrificium singulare* R.   [10] *Illi et Illi* V.   [11] Pam. omits *tuae*.   [12] Pam. omits *diesque nostros*.   [13] R. inserts *fidelibus in Christo*; Pam. omits *omnibus* and inserts *famulis vel famulabus tuis N. et N. vel*.   [14] *quietem* V.; R. Pam. as text, and so V. in the second Collect of this *Missa*.

CIV.

ITEM ALIA MISSA.

Adesto, quaesumus, Domine, pro animabus famulorum famularumque tuarum et omnium hic quiescentium, ut si quae carnales maculae in eis de terrenis contagiis inhaeserunt, miserationis tuae venia deleantur. Per.

[Gerb. 326 n.]

Inclina[1], quaesumus, Domine, aures tuas ad preces nostras, pro quibus misericordiam tuam supplices exoramus, ut animas famulorum famularumque tuarum in pacis ac lucis regione constituas, et sanctorum iubeas esse consortes. Per. γ

cf. Gerb. 321.

Secreta.

Munera, quaesumus, Domine, quae tibi pro requie et animabus[2] famulorum famularumque tuarum[3] omnium in Christo quiescentium offerimus, ad earum redemptione[4] proficiant. Per.

[Gerb. 326 n.]

Infra actionem.

Hanc igitur oblationem, quam tibi pro defunctis offerimus, quaesumus, Domine,[5] propitiatus accipias, et miserationis tuae largitate concedas, ut ab omnibus quae per terrenam conversationem traxerunt[6] his sacrificiis emundentur. Per.

[Gerb. 326 n.]

Postcommun.

Multiplica, Domine, super animas famulorum famularumque tuarum misericordiam tuam; et quibus[7] donasti

[Gerb. 326 n.]

baptismi sacramentum da eis aeternorum plenitudine[6] gaudiorum. Per.

[1] This Collect is parallel to that to which reference is made in Gerb., but not identical with it. [2] *pro requie animarum* Gerb. [3] Gerb. inserts *et*. [4] *eorum redemptionem* Gerb.; V. as text (ungrammatically). [5] Gerb. inserts *ut*. [6] *contraxerunt vitiis* Gerb.; V. as text. [7] *cui* V. [8] *plenitudinem* Gerb.; V. as text (ungrammatically).

CV.

Item missa in depositione defuncti, tertii, septimi, tricesimi dierum, sive annualem [1].

R.
Gerb. 327.
Men. 218.

Adesto, quaesumus, Domine[2], pro anima famuli tui *Illius*, cuius in depositione sua[3] officium commemorationis impendimus, ut si quae[4] eum saecularis macula invasit[5], aut vitium mundiale infecit[6], dono tuae pietatis indulgeas et extergas[7]. Per.

R.
Gerb. 327.
Men. 218.

Quaesumus, Domine, ut[8] famulo tuo cuius septimum[9] obitus sui diem commemoramus, sanctorum et[10] electorum largire[8] consortium, et rorem[11] misericordiae tuae perennis[12] infunde. Per.

R.
Gerb. 327.
cf. ciii
supra.

Deus, indulgentiarum Domine, da famulo tui *Illi*, cuius anniversarium depositionis diem commemoramus, refrigerii sedem, quietis beatitudinem, luminis claritatem largiaris[13]. Per.

Secreta.

R.
Gerb. 327.
Men. 218.

Adesto, Domine, supplicationibus nostris, et hanc oblationem, quam tibi offerimus ob diem depositionis septimi vel tricesimi[14], pro anima famuli tui *Illius*, placatus ac benignus assume. Per[15].

Infra actionem.

R.
Gerb. 327.

Hanc igitur oblationem, Domine, quam tibi offerimus pro anima famuli tui *Illius*, cuius depositionis diem[16] septimum vel tricesimum celebramus, quod[17] deposito corpore animam tibi[18] creatori reddidit, quam dedisti[19]: pro quo[20] petimus divinam clementiam tuam, ut mortis vinculis absolutus[20] transitum mereatur ad vitam[21]. Per.

Postcommun.

R.
Gerb. 327.
Men. 219.

Omnipotens sempiterne Deus, collocare dignare corpus et animam et spiritum[22] famuli tui *Illius*, cuius diem septimum, vel tricesimum[23], • sive depositionem[24] cele- 763 bravimus [25] in sinibus [26] Abrahae, Isaac, et Iacob; ut [27] quum dies agnitionis tuae [28] venerit, inter sanctos et electos tuos eum resuscitari [29] praecipias. Per.

[1] *annualem*, so V. (ungrammatically) probably for *annuali, depositio* being used as equivalent to *depositionis commemoratio*. But R. Men. have *in die depositionis defuncti vel (sive* Men.) *iii, vii, et xxx*^{mo} (*iii, vii, trigesimoque* Men.). [2] *Domine quaesumus* R. Men. [3] R. reads *in die depositione sua*, and inserts (misplacing the words, so that they stand before *cuius*) *vel iii, vii, et xxx*^{mi}; V. Men. as text. [4] *qua* V.; *aliqua* Men.; R. as text. [5] *ei saecularis macula inhaesit* R. Men.; V. as text. [6] *fecit* R. [7] *extergeas* V. [8] *ut . . . largire*, so V. R. (ungrammatically); Men. omits *ut*. [9] *tertium vel vii sive xxx* Men. [10] *atque* R.; *tuorum atque* Men. [11] *rore* V.; *rorem ei* Men.; R. as text. [12] *perenne* R.; *perennem* Men.; V. as text. [13] R. adds *oramus*; V. as text. *Largiaris* appears to be superfluous, unless the punctuation is altered so as to divide the series of accusatives, which would seem more naturally to depend upon one and the same verb, as in clii supra. [14] *tertium vel septimum sive trigesimum* Men.; *iii vel vii*^{mi} *xxx*^{mi} R.; V. as text (ungrammatically). [15] R. and Men. place after the *Secreta* a Preface, which is not found here in V., but appears in the next section, where it is no doubt misplaced (see note [12] on cvi). [16] R. inserts *tertium*. [17] *quod*, so V. R. (probably ungrammatically for *quo*). [18] R. omits *tibi*. [19] Some such words as *quaesumus placatus accipias* are required by the sense: but V. and R. agree in omitting them. [20] *qua . . . absoluta* R. [21] R. inserts *diesque nostros*, which V. omits. [22] *corpus et anima et spiritu* V.; *corpus et animam* Men.; R. as text. [23] *iii, vii*^{mum} *et xxx*^{mum} R.; *iii aut vii vel xxx* Men. [24] *depositione* V.; Men. omits *sive depositionem*; R. as text. [25] *celebramus* R. Men.; V. as text. [26] *sinum* Men. [27] *et* R. [28] R. omits *tuae*. [29] *resuscitare* V. R.

CVI.

Item Orationes ad Missam pro Salute vivorum.

Praetende, Domine, misericordiam tuam [1] famulis et famulabus tuis dexteram caelestis auxilii: ut te toto corde [2] perquirant et quae [3] digne postulant assequantur [4]. Per. γ

R. Gerb. 269.
Pam. 438.
Men. 239.

Secreta.

Propitiare [Domine] [5] supplicationibus nostris, et has oblationes famulorum famularumque tuarum quas [6] tibi pro incolumitate eorum offerimus, benignus assume, [7] ut nullius sit irritum votum nullius vacua postulatio: praesta, quaesumus, ut quod [8] fideliter petimus efficaciter consequamur. Per. γ

R. Gerb. 269.
Pam. 438.
Men. 239.

Infra actionem.

Hanc igitur oblationem, Domine, famulorum famularumque tuarum, quam tibi offerimus ob devotionem mentis eorum, pius ac propitius clementi vultu suscipias: tibi supplicantes [9] libens protege, dignanter exaudi, et aeterna

R. Gerb. 270.

eos[10] protectione conserva; ut semper in tua religione laetantes, in sanctae Trinitatis confessione[11] fide catholica perseverent: diesque nostros. γ

Postcommun.

R.
Gerb. 270.
Pam. 438.
Men. 239.

Da famulis et famulabus tuis, quaesumus, Domine, in tua fide et sinceritate constantiam; ut in caritate divina firmati nullis tentationibus ab eius integritate vellantur. Per. γ

Contestatio[12].

R.
Gerb. 327.
Men. 218.

VD. Per Christum Dominum nostrum. Per quem salus mundi, per quem · vita omnium[13], per quem resurrectio 764 mortuorum. Per ipsum te, Domine, suppliciter deprecamur, ut animae famuli tui *Illius*, cuius diem *Illum*[14] celebramus, indulgentiam largiri perpetuam digneris[15], atque contagiis mortalitatis exutam, in aeternam salvationis partem restituas[16] cum angelis et archangelis[17]. γ

INCIPIT AD POENITENTIAM DANDAM[18].

Martène,
lib. I.
cap. vi.

Dicis psalmum vi totum : et iterum dicis[19]: Oremus. *Et incipiens*[20] *psalmum cii usque* Renovabitur sicut[21] aquilae iuventus[22]. *Dicis deinde psalmum quinquagesimum ; post hoc oratio sequitur*[23].

Deum omnipotentem ac misericordem, qui non vult mortem peccatorum sed ut convertantur et vivant, fratres carissimi, supplices deprecemur[24], ut converso ad viam rectam famulo suo *Illo* misericordiae suae veniam propitiatus indulgeat: et si quae sunt culparum suarum omnium vulnera, quae post sacri lavacri unda[25] contraxit[26], ita in hac publica confessione delicta sanentur, ut nulla in eum[27] ultra cicatricum signa remaneant. Per Dominum nostrum.

Martène,
lib. I.
cap. vi.

Deus, iustorum gloria,[28] misericordia peccatorum, da huic famulo tuo *Illi*[29] plenam indulgentiae veniam, et poenitentiae loco[30] exoratus indulge; ut qui praeterita peccata deplorat, futura mala[31] non sentiat, neque iam ulterius lugenda committat. Dimitte ei, Domine, omnia crimina, et in semitas eum iustitiae[32] placatus reinstaura[33], ut securus mereatur deinceps inter tuos bene meritis currere et ad pacis aeternae praemia pervenire. Per Dominum nostrum Iesum Christum.

Domine Deus omnipotens sempiterne, qui peccatorum indulgentiam in confessione celeri posuisti, succurre lapsis, miserere confessis, ut quos delictorum catena constringit, miseratio tuae pietatis absolvat. Per Dominum.

Explicit Liber Sacramentorum. Deo gratias.

SICUT NAVIGANTIBUS DULCIS EST PORTUS
SIC SCRIPTORI NOVISSIMUS VERSUS.

---

[1] Pam. omits *misericordiam tuam*; V. R. Men. as text.   [2] *ut de toto corde* R.   [3] *atque* (for *et quae*) R.   [4] Men. adds a clause which is omitted by V. R. Pam.:—*et medelam tuam non solum in corpore, sed etiam in anima sentiant.*   [5] V. omits *Domine*, which is restored from R. Pam. Men.   [6] *quam* V.   [7] Pam. Men. insert *et*, which Gerb. adds in brackets; V. R. as text.   [8] *quos* Pam.   [9] R. omits *tibi supplicantes*, and inserts *deprecamur* after *suscipias*.   [10] *eius* R.   [11] Gerb. adds *et* in brackets; V. R. as text.   [12] The *Contestatio* here given is clearly misplaced. It belongs to the *Missa* of section cv *supra*, and is found in conjunction with the Collects, Secret, and Postcommunion of that *Missa* in R. and Men. The heading is notable, as separate titles are not as a rule prefixed to the Prefaces which occur in V.   [13] *hominum* (for *omnium*) Men.   [14] Men. inserts *depositionis tertium vel septimum sive trigesimum* (omitting *Illum*); V. R. as text.   [15] *digneris perpetuam* R. Men.   [16] *constituas* R.   [17] Both R. and Men. have the ending *Per quem*, omitting *cum angelis et archangelis.* Perhaps the ending in V. is a mistake for *Et ideo cum*, &c.   [18] This portion was probably placed at the end of the MS. with a view to frequent use. The rubric and form of 'bidding prayer' together make up Martène's *Ordo* xi, which he takes from one of Colbert's MSS., dated by him before 900. The first of the other two prayers occurs in Martène's *Ordo* iii, taken from a MS. belonging to the Cathedral of Tours, to which he gives a similar date (*de Ant. Eccl. Rit.* Lib. I. cap. vi).   [19] *dicit* V.; Mart. as text.   [20] *incipis* Mart.; V. as text, using, as elsewhere, the participle to express an imperative sense.   [21] *ut* Mart.; V. as text, apparently following the Italic version.   [22] Mart. adds *tua*, which V. omits.   [23] Mart. omits *post hoc oratio sequitur* and prefixes *Sequitur Collecta* to the prayer following.   [24] *precamur* (omitting *supplices*) Mart.   [25] *unda*, so both V. and Mart. (ungrammatically).   [26] *contraxerunt* Mart.   [27] *in eum*, so both V. and Mart. (ungrammatically).   [28] Mart. inserts *et*.   [29] *Illo* V.   [30] *locum* Mart.; V. as text (ungrammatically).   [31] Mart. omits *mala*.   [32] *in semitas iustitiae eum* Mart.; V. as text.   [33] *restaura* Mart.

APPENDIX

Showing the Contents and Arrangement of the Gelasian Sacramentaries of Rheinau (R.) and S. Gallen (S.).

This appendix follows, in its first portion, the order of S., the *Missae* and prayers which are not contained in R. being marked by square brackets. Portions marked * show signs of a divergence between the original readings of S. and those of the later recension published by Gerbert. The readings of R., where such portions are common to R. and S., are generally in agreement with the original reading of S. wherever that original reading can be certainly ascertained; and where the matter is common to R. S. and the Vatican MS., the readings of R. and of the first hand of S. are for the most part in agreement with those of the Vatican MS.

In Vigilia Natalis Domini. Ad Nona. Statio ad S. Mariam.   Gerb. pp. 1, 2.
    Deus qui nos redemptionis
    Da nobis o. D. ut sicut
    [Praesta m. D. ut ad suscipiendum]
    Da nobis Dne. ut nativitatis
    Tanto nos Dne. q. promptiore
  *VD. p. X. In confessione
    Da nobis Dne. q. unigeniti Filii tui

De Vigilia Domini in Nocte. Ad S. Mariam.   Gerb. pp. 3, 4.
    Deus qui hanc sacratissimam noctem
    Respice nos m. D. et mentibus
    Accepta tibi sit Dne. q. hodiernae
  *Munera nostra q. Dne. nativitatis
  *VD. p. X. Cuius divinae nativitatis
  *Communicantes et noctem sacratissimam
  *Da nobis q. Dne. D. noster ut qui nativitatem

APPENDIX.

Gerb. p. 5.
Ad S. Anastasiam[1].
Da q. o. D. ut qui b. Anastasiae
Accipe q. Dne. munera dignanter oblata et b. Anast.
VD. Qui ut de hoste
Satiasti Dne. familiam tuam

Gerb. pp. 4, 5.
Item de Natali Domini. Mane prima.
Da (nobis R.) q. o. D. ut qui nova
Cuncta Dne. q. his muneribus
VD. p. X. Quia nostri Salvatoris
*Huius Dne. sacramenti semper natalis (?) (sacramenta semper natalaes R.)
Populum tuum Dne. q. tueantur

Gerb. pp. 5, 6.
In Natali Domini ad S. Petrum (R. adds in die).
*Omnipotens s. D. qui hunc diem per incarnationem
Concede q. o. D. ut nos Unigeniti tui
Oblatio tibi sit Dne. q. hodiernae
VD. Tuae laudis hostiam
Communicantes (ut supra)
Laeti Dne. frequentamus salutis
Praesta q. o. D. ut natus hodie

Gerb. pp. 6, 7.
Alias orationes de Natali Domini.
Adesto Dne. supplicationibus nostris
Largire q. Dne. famulis tuis fidei
[D. qui populo tuo plene praestitisti]
*D. qui humanae substantiae
Omnipotens s. D. creator humanae
Deus qui nativitatis tuae exordium
Deus qui per b. Virginis partum
Concede nobis o. D. ut salutare
O. s. D. qui in Filii tui Dni. nostri nativitate
Da q. Dne. populo tuo inviolabilem

Gerb. p. 8.
vii Kal. Ian. Natale S. Stephani.
Da nobis q. Dne. imitari quod colimus
*O. s. D. qui primitias martyrum
Grata tibi sint Dne. munera q. devotionis
VD. Beati Stephani Levitae
Auxilientur nobis Dne. sumpta mysteria
*Beatus martyr Stephanus Dne. q. pro fidelibus

---

[1] R. has Nall. Stē Anastasiae.

APPENDIX.

Alias Orationes.

Gerb. p. 8.

Gratias agimus Dne. multiplicatis]
Praesta q. o. D. ut beatus Stephanus
Deus qui nos Unigeniti tui clementer

vi Kal. Ian. Natale S. Ioannis Evangelistae.

Gerb. pp. 9, 10.

*Deus qui per os b. Apostoli
Ecclesiam tuam Dne. benignus illustra
Suscipe Dne. munera quae in eius
*VD. Beati Apostoli tui et evangelistae
Refecti cibo potuque celesti
Adsit ecclesiae tuae Dne. q. b. evangelista

Alias Orationes.

Gerb. p. 10.

*Deus qui b. Ioannis evangelistae
Praesta q. o. D. ut excellentiam

v Kal. Ian. Natale Innocentum [1].

Gerb. p. 11.

Deus cuius hodierna die praeconium
Deus qui bonis tuis
Adesto Dne. muneribus Innocentum festivitate
*VD. Pretiosis (enim R.) mortibus
Votiva Dne. dona percepimus
*Discat ecclesia tua D. infantum

Alias Orationes.

[Deus qui licet sis magnus]
Ipsi nobis Dne. q. postulent
[Adiuva nos Dne. q. eorum deprecatione]

Dominica I post Natale Domini.

Gerb. pp. 12, 13.

Deus qui salutis aeternae beatae Mariae virginitate
*Da nobis q. o. D. ut nativitatem (sic)
Muneribus nostris q. Dne. precibusque
VD. Nos sursum cordibus erectis
*Da nobis q. Dne. D. noster ut qui nativitatem
Benedictionem tuam Dne. populus fidelis

Pridie Kal. Ian. Natale S. Silvestri.

Gerb. p. 13.

Da q. o. D. ut b. Silvestri
Sancti tui nos q. Dne. ubique laetificent
Praesta q. o. D. ut de perceptis

---

[1] R. adds *ad scm̄ Paulum*.

Gerb. p. 14.	*Kal. Ian. Octava Domini* [ad S. Mariam].

Deus qui nobis nati Salvatoris
O. s. D. qui in Unigenito
Praesta q. Dne. ut per haec munera
*VD. p. X. Cuius hodie
Praesta q. Dne. ut quod Salvatoris
O. s. D. qui tuae mensae.

Gerb. p. 15.	[*Missa Prohibendo ab Idolis.*

O. s. D. da nobis voluntatem
Ut tibi grata sint Dne. munera
Mysteriis tuis veneranter assumptis]

Gerb. p. 15.	*Item alia Dominica.*

O. s. D. dirige actus nostros in beneplacito
Propitiare m. D. supplic. nostris et populum
Concede q. Dne. ut oculis tuae maiestatis
*VD. Qui [pro] peccato
Per huius Dne. operationem mysterii
*Respice propitius Dne. ad debitam

Gerb. pp. 15, 16.	*Non. Ian. Vigilia Theophaniae.*

*Corda nostra q. Dne. venturae
Tribue q. Dne. ut eum praesentibus
*VD. Te laudare mirabilem Deum
*Illumina q. Dne. populum tuum (et R.) splendore

Gerb. pp. 16, 17.	*viii Id. Ian. Theophania* [ad S. Petrum].

Deus qui hodierna die Unigenitum
*O. s. D. qui Verbi tui incarnationem
Ecclesiae tuae q. Dne. dona propitius intuere
*VD. Nos te laudare omnipotens D.
Communicantes et diem sacratissimum
Praesta q. Dne. D. noster ut quae solemni
*Deus qui per huius celebritatis mysterium

Gerb. pp. 17, 18.	*Alias Orationes.*

Deus illuminator omnium gentium
O. s. D. fidelium splendor animarum
*Da nobis q. Dne. digne celebrare mysterium
Praesta q. o. D. ut Salvatoris mundi

Gerb. p. 18.	*Dominica I post Theophaniam.*

Vota q. Dne. supplicantis populi
Fac nos Dne. D. n. tuis obedire mandatis

APPENDIX.

Oblatum tibi Dne. sacrificium vivificet nos
*VD. Quia quum Unigenitus
Supplices te rogamus o. D. ut quos tuis
Conserva q. Dne. familiam tuam

In Oct. Theophaniae.   Gerb. pp. 18, 19.

Deus cuius Unigenitus in substantia
*Hostias tibi Dne. pro nati Filii tui apparitione
Caelesti lumine q. Dne. semper et ubique
*Illumina q. Dne. populum tuum

xviii Kal. Feb. Nat. S. Felicis Confessoris [1].   Gerb p. 19.

Concede q. o. D. ut ad meliorem
*Da q. o. D. ut qui beatus Felix
Hostias tibi Dne. pro (prae R) commemoratione
*VD. Et confessionem S. Felicis
Sanctorum precibus confidentes

Dominica II post Theophaniam.   Gerb. pp. 19, 20.

O. s. D. qui caelestia simul
Adesto q. Dne. supplicationibus
Oblata Dne. munera sanctifica nosque
*VD. Semperque virtutes
Augeatur in nobis Dne. q. tuae virtutis
Auxiliare Dne. populo tuo ut sacrae

xvii Kal. Feb. Nat. S. Marcelli Papae.   Gerb. p. 20.

Preces populi tui q. Dne. clementer exaudi
[Da q. o. D. ut qui b. Marcelli]
Suscipe q. Dne. munera dign. obl. et b. Marcelli
[*VD. Qui glorificaris in tuorum]
Satiasti Dne. familiam tuam

[*xv Kal. Feb. Nat. S. Priscae Mart.*   Gerb. p. 20.

Da q. o. D. ut qui b. Priscae
*Hostiam (*sic*) Dne. q. quam in sanctorum
Q. Dne. salutaribus repleti mysteriis]

xiv Kal. Feb. Nat. Mariae et Marthae.   Gerb. p. 20.

Exaudi Dne. populum tuum cum Sanctorum
Preces Dne. tuorum respice
Sanctorum tuorum Dne. intercessione placatus

[1] R. has *Nat̃l. Sc̃e. Felicis in pensis.*

Gerb. [xiii Kal. Feb. Nat. S. Fabiani Mart.
pp. 20, 21. Infirmitatem nostram respice o. D.
Adsit nobis Dne. q. sancta precatio
Intercessio q. Dne. sancti pontificis
Refecti participatione muneris sacri]

Gerb. p. 21. [Eodem die] Nat. S. Sebastiani Mart.
Deus qui b. Sebastianum
[*Praesta Dne. q. ut intercedente b. Sebastiano]
Sancto Sebastiano interveniente
[*VD. Quoniam beati martyris Sebastiani]
Sacro munere satiati supplices te Dne.

Gerb. xii Kal. Feb. Nat. S. Agnae [Virg.]
pp. 21, 22. Crescat Dne. semper in nobis
[Praesta q. Dne. mentibus]
*Hodiernum Dne. sacrificium
[*VD. Recensemus enim]
Sumentes Dne. gaudia sempiterna

Gerb. xi Kal. Feb. Nat. S. Vincentii.
pp. 22, 23. Adesto Dne. q. supplicationibus
Hostias tibi Dne. b. Vincentii martyris
Q. o. D. ut qui caelestia

Gerb. Dominica III post Theophaniam.
pp. 23, 24. O. s. D. infirmitatem nostram
Vox clamantis ecclesiae
Haec hostia Dne. q. emundet
*VD. Te benedicere
Quos tantis Dne. largiris
Adsit Dne. q. propitiatio

Gerb. p. 24. [x Kal. Feb. Nat. SS. Emerentianae et Macarii.
Maiestati tuae nos Dne. martyrum
Martyrum tuorum nos Dne. semper
*Accepta tibi sit Dne. sacratae plebis
Iugiter nos Dne. sanctorum tuorum vota]

Gerb. p. 24. [viii Kal. Feb. Nat. S. Praeiecti Mart.
Martyris tui Praeiecti nos
Suscipe Dne. propitius orationem
*VD. Et tuam misericordiam
*Votiva Dne. pro b. martyris tui Praeiecti]

[*Eodem die Conversio S. Pauli Apostoli in Damasco.*]   Gerb. pp. 24, 25.
*Deus qui universum mundum
Apostoli tui Pauli precibus
*VD. Qui ecclesiam tuam
Sanctificati Dne. salutari mysterio]

[*v Kal. Feb. Nat. S. Agnis de Nativitate.*]   Gerb. p. 25.
Deus qui nos annua b. Agnae
Adesto nobis o. D. b. Agnae festa repetentibus
Grata tibi sint q. Dne. munera
*VD. B. Agnis natalitia
Adiuvent nos Dne. q. et haec mysteria]

Dominica IV post Theophaniam.   Gerb. pp. 25, 26.
Deus qui nos in tantis
Familiam tuam Dne. q. dextera
Concede q. o. D. ut huius sacrificii
*VD. Qui genus humanum
*Munera tua nos D. a delectationibus
Porrige dexteram tuam q. Dne. plebi

iv Non. Feb. S. Simeonis. Collecta ad S. Adrianum.   Gerb. p. 26.
Erudi q. Dne. plebem tuam

Ad Missam. Statio ad S. Mariam.
O. s. D. maiestatem tuam supplices
Exaudi Dne. preces nostras et ut digna
VD. Quia per incarnati
Q. Dne. D. noster ut sacrosancta

Non Feb. Nat. S. Agathae (R. adds *Virg.*).   Gerb. p. 26.
*Indulgentiam nobis Dne. b. Agatha
Fiant Dne. tuo grata conspectui
VD. Pro cuius nomine poenarum
Exultamus pariter et de percepto

Dominica V post Theophaniam.   Gerb. pp. 27, 28.
Familiam tuam q. Dne. continua
*D. qui solus es bonus
Hostias tibi Dne. placationis offerimus
*VD. Tibi istam immolationis
Q. o. D. ut illius salutaris
Adesto Dne. populis tuis in tua

APPENDIX.

Gerb. p. 28.   [*iv Id. Feb. Nat. S. Sotheris.*
Praesta q. o. D. ut sanctae Sotheris
Preces nostras q. Dne. propitiatus
Sanctae Sotheris precibus confidentes]

Gerb. p. 28.   [*Eodem die Nat. SS. Zotici, Hirenei et Iacinti.*
Dne. D. noster multiplica super nos
Suscipe q. Dne. munera populi tui
*Sacramenti tui Dne. q. sumpta benedictio]

Gerb. pp. 28, 29.   *Dominica VI post Theophaniam.*
*Conserva populum tuum D. et tuo nomini
*Praesta q. o. D. ut semper rationabilia
Haec oblatio D. mundet nos
*VD. Ad cuius immensam
Caelestibus Dne. pasti deliciis
Adesto Dne. fidelibus tuis

Gerb. p. 29.   [*xvi Kal. Mart. Nat. SS. Valentini, Vitalis, Filiculae et Zenonis.*
Tuorum nos Dne. q. precibus tuere sanctorum
*Ad martyrum tuorum Valentini, Vit. F. et Zen.
*Protege Dne. plebem tuam et in festivitate]

Gerb. p. 29.   [*xiv Kal. Mart. Nat. S. Iulianae.*
O. s. D. qui eligis infirma mundi
In sanctae mart. tuae Iulianae
*Libantes Dne. mensae tuae b. mysteria]

Gerb. p. 30.   *viii Kal. Mart. Cathedra S. Petri.*
Deus qui b. apostolo tuo Petro
Ecclesiae tuae q. Dne. preces et hostias
*VD. Te laudare mirabilem in sanctis
Laetificet nos Dne. munus oblatum

Gerb. p. 30.   [*Non. Mart. Nat. SS. Perpetuae et Felicitatis.*
Da nobis Dne. D. noster sanctorum martyrum palmas
Intende Dne. munera q. altaribus
Praesta nobis Dne. q. intercedentibus]

Gerb. pp. 30, 31.   *iv Id. Mart. Nat. S. Gregorii Papae.*
Concede q. Dne. fidelibus tuis digne S. Gregorii
Has hostias Dne. quas nomini tuo
*VD. Quia sic tribuis ecclesiam tuam
Praestent Dne. q. tua sancta praesidium

APPENDIX.

Incipit in Septuagesima [1]. Gerb. pp. 32, 33.
Deus qui per ineffabilem
Concede q. o. D. fragilitati
Concede nobis m. D. et digne
*VD. Quia per ea quae conspiciuntur
Sacrae nobis q. Dne. mensae
Preces populi tui Dne. clementer

In Sexagesima ad S. Paulum. Gerb. p. 33.
Deus qui conspicis quia ex nulla
Tuere q. Dne. plebem tuam et sacram
*Intende q. Dne. hostiam familiae
*VD. Qui rationabilem creaturam
Sit nobis q. Dne. cibus sacer
Rege q. Dne. populum tuum

In Quinquagesima ad S. Petrum. Gerb. p. 34.
Preces nostras q. Dne. clementer exaudi
Aufer a nobis Dne. q. iniquitates
Sacrificium Dne. observantiae paschalis
*VD. Ut modulum terrenae
*Repleti sumus Dne. donorum participatione
De multitudine misericordiae

[*Ordo Agentibus publicam poenitentiam.* Not in Gerb.
Suscipis eum vi feria, etc.

Orationes et preces super poenitentem. Not in Gerb.
Exaudi Dne. preces nostras et confitentium
Praeveniat hunc famulum
Adesto Dne. supplicationibus nostris nec sit
Domine D. noster qui offensione
Precor Dne. clementiam tuae maiestatis]

Feria iv caput de Ieiuniis. Statio ad S. Sabinam. Gerb. p. 35.
Ad Collectam.
Concede nobis Dne. praesidia

Ad Missam.
Praesta Dne. fidelibus tuis ut ieiuniorum
Fac nos q. Dne. his muneribus offerendis
VD. Qui corporali ieiunio
Percepta nobis Dne. praebeant
Tuere Dne. populum tuum et ab omnibus

[1] R. adds *Stā. ad Scm̄ . . . au . . .* (? *Laurentium*).

Gerb. p. 35.	*Feria v infra Quinquagesimam. Ad S. Georgium Statio.* Da q. Dne. fidelibus tuis ieiuniis Fac nos q. Dne. salutis nostrae Haecque nos reparent (Haec quae nos reparant R.) Inclinantes se Dne. maiestati tuae
Gerb. p. 36.	*Feria vi infra Quinquagesimam. Statio ad SS. Ioannem et Paulum.* *Inchoata ieiunia q. Dne. benigno Adiuva nos D. salutaris noster Praepara nos q. Dne. huius praecipuae Tribue nobis o. D. ut dona caelestia *Praesta famulis tuis Dne. abundantiam
Gerb. pp. 36, 37.	*Sabbato infra Quinquagesimam.* Observationis huius annua celebritate Adesto Dne. suppl. nostris et hoc solemne Suscipe Dne. sacrificium cuius te voluisti Caelestis vitae munere vegetati q. Dne *Fideles tui Dne. per tua dona
Gerb. p. 37.	*In Quadragesima ad S. Ioannem ad Lat(eranis R.).* *Deus qui ecclesiam tuam annua Concede nobis o. D. ut per annua Sacrificium Dne. quadragesimalis initii *VD. Qui continuatis quadraginta diebus Tui nos Dne. sacramenti libatio Super populum tuum Dne. q. benedictio *Ad vesp.* Da nobis q. o. D. et aeternae [*Ad fontes.* Adesto q. Dne. supplicationibus]
Gerb. p. 38.	*Feria ii ad S. Petrum ad Vincula* (R. adds *Eb. i*). Converte nos D. salutaris noster et ut nobis Sanctifica Dne. q. nostra ieiunia Accepta tibi sit Dne. nostrae devotionis [*VD. Qui das escam omni carne] Salutaris tui Dne. munere satiati Esto Dne. propitius plebi tuae
Gerb. p. 39.	*Feria iii ad S. Anastasiam* (R. adds *Eb. i*). Respice Dne. familiam tuam et praesta Pacem nobis tribue Dne. q. mentis et corporis Oblatis q. Dne. placare muneribus [*VD. In quo ieiunantium]

APPENDIX. 327

Sumpsimus Dne. celebritatis annuae
Ascendant ad te Dne. preces nostrae

Feria iv ad S. Mariam ad Praesepe (R. adds *Eb. i*). Gerb. pp. 39, 40.
Preces nostras q. Dne. clementer
Devotionem populi tui q. Dne. benignus
*Sacrificia Dne. propitius (*sic*) ista
*VD. Qui in alimento
Tui Dne. perceptione sacramenti
Da q. Dne. populis Christianis

Feria v ad S. Laurentium ad For.[1] (*ad Formonso* R.). Gerb. pp. 40, 41.
O. s. D. qui nobis in observatione
Precamur o. D. ut de transitoriis
Suscipe creator o. D. quae ieiunantes
*VD. Quia competenter atque salubriter
Percipientes Dne. gloriosa mysteria
Respice Dne. propitius ad plebem tuam

Feria vi ad Apostolos (R. adds *Eb. i Infra* ...). Gerb. p. 41.
Esto Dne. propitius plebi tuae et quam
Da nobis q. o. D. ieiuniorum
Suscipe q. Dne. devotorum munera
*VD. tibi sacrificare ieiunium
Praesta q. Dne. spiritalibus gaudiis
Plebs tua Dne. q. benedictionis

Sabbato ad S. Petrum in xii Lect. (R. adds *Eb. i*). Gerb. p. 42.
[Populum tuum Dne. q. propitius [2]]
Protector noster aspice D. et qui
Adesto q. Dne. supplicationibus nostris ut esse [2]
Actiones nostras q. Dne. et aspirando [2]
Deus qui delinquentes perire non pateris
Post. Bened. Deus quem omnia opera benedicunt
Praesentibus sacrificiis Dne. ieiunia
*VD. Illuminator et redemptor
Perpetuo Dne. favore prosequere
Fideles tuos Dne. benedictio desiderata

Die Dominica vacat. Gerb. p. 43.
Deus qui conspicis omni nos virtute

---

[1] Probably '*ad Formosum*' a name given to the Church of S. Laurence 'in Panisperna.' If so, the name cannot, as has sometimes been supposed, be derived from Pope Formosus, the restorer of the Church, since the later of the two MSS. is earlier than his pontificate by nearly a century.

[2] R. substitutes for the first Collect *Esto Dne. propitius* (Gerb. p. 41) and inverts the order of those beginning *Adesto, Actiones.*

Praesta nobis m. D. ut placationem
Ecclesiae tuae Dne. munera placatus
VD. Maiestatem tuam supplicantes
Refecti Dne. pane caelesti

Gerh. Familiam tuam q. propitiatus
pp. 44, 45.
Feria ii ad S. Clementem.

Praesta q. o. D. ut familia tua
Tuis q. Dne. adesto supplicibus et inter
Haec hostia Dne. placationis et laudis
Percepta Dne. sancta nos adiuvent
Populum tuum Dne. q. ad te toto corde

Gerb. p. 45.
Feria iii ad S. Balbinam.

Perfice q. Dne. benignus in nobis
Deus qui ob animarum medelam
Sanctificationem nobis Dne. his mysteriis
Delicias Dne. [mirabiles] mensae
Da q. Dne. fidelibus tuis et sine cessatione

Gerb. p. 46.
Feria iv ad S. Caeciliam.

Deus qui per Verbum tuum humani
Praesta nobis Dne. auxilium gratiae
Hostias Dne. quas tibi offerimus propitius
Gratia tua nos Dne. q. non relinquat
Populum tuum Dne. propitius respice et quos

Gerb. p. 47.
Feria v ad S. Mariam trans Tiberim.

Ecclesiam tuam Dne. perpetua
Adiuva nos D. salutaris noster
Accepta tibi sint Dne. q. nostri dona ieiunii
*Praeveniant nobis Dne. q. divina tua sancta
*Adesto Dne. famulis tuis et opem

Gerb. *Feria vi ad S. Vitalem* (R. adds *Hic facis scrutinio*).
pp. 47, 48. Da q. o. D. ut sacro nos purificante
Ad hostes nostros Dne. superandos
Haec in nobis sacrificia D. et actione
Fac nos Dne. q. accepto pignore
Da q. Dne. populo tuo salutem

Gerb. p. 48.
Sabbato ad SS. Marcellinum et Petrum.

Da q. Dne. nostris effectum
*Subveni Dne. servis tuis pro sua
His sacrificiis Dne. concede placatus
Sacramenti tui Dne. divina libatio
*Implorantes Dne. misericordiam fideles

APPENDIX. 329

Dominica. [*Statio*] *ad S. Laurentium* [*in xxx*]. Gerb. p. 49.
Q. o. D. vota humilium respice
Propitiare Dne. supplic. nostris et animarum
Suscipe q. Dne. nostris oblata servitiis
*VD. Suppliciter exorare ut cum abstinentia
Cunctis nos Dne. reatibus
Subiectum tibi populum q. Dne. propitiatio

Feria ii ad S. Marcum. Gerb. p. 50.

*Cordibus nostris q. Dne. benignus infunde
*Conserva Dne. familiam tuam bonis
Munus quod tibi Dne. nostrae servitutis
Quos ieiunia votiva castigant
Gratias tibi referat Dne. corde subiecto

Feria iii ad S. Potentianam. Gerb. pp. 50, 51.

Exaudi nos o. et m. D. et continentiae
Prosequere o. D. ieiuniorum
Per haec veniat q. Dne. sacramenta
Sacris Dne. mysteriis expiati
Concede m. D. ut devotus tibi populus

Feria iv ad S. Sixtum. Gerb. p. 51.

Praesta q. nobis Dne. ut salutaribus
*D. qui nos formam humilitatis [1]
[Suscipe q. Dne. preces populi tui cum obl.
Sanctificet nos Dne. qua pasti sumus
Defende Dne. familiam tuam et toto]

[*Feria v ad SS. Cosmam et Damianum.* Gerb. pp. 51, 52.
*Da q. Dne. rex aeterne
Deus qui peccantium animas
Deus de cuius gratiae rore
Sacramenti tui Dne. veneranda
Concede q. o. D. ut qui protectionis]

[*Feria vi ad S. Laurentium ad Tita*(?) [2]. Gerb. pp. 52, 53.
Ieiunia nostra q. Dne. benigno
*Adesto nobis q. o. D. et per ieiunium
Respice Dne. propitius ad munera quae sacramus
Huius nos Dne. perceptio sacramenti mundet
Gaudeat Dne. q. populus tuus semper

[1] Only the first words of this Collect are now in R. which is defective at this point, having apparently lost two leaves.
[2] Perhaps '*ad Titulum.*' The Church of S. Laurence 'in Lucina' was known as 'Titulus Lucinae.'

330 APPENDIX.

Gerb. p. 53. [*Sabbato ad S. Susannam.*
Praesta q. o. D. ut dignitas
*Auge fidem tuam Dne. q. miseratus
*Dne. D. noster qui in his potius
Hos Dne. quos reficis sacramentis attolle
Esto q. Dne. propitius plebi tuae et quae]

Gerb. p. 54. [*Die Dominica. Statio ad Hierusalem.*
Concede q. o. D. ut qui ex merito
Deus qui in deserti regione
Sacrificiis praesentibus Dne. q. intende
*VD. glorificantes et de praeteritis
Da nobis m. D. ut sancta tua
Tu semper q. Dne. tuam attolle]

Gerb. p. 55. [*Feria ii ad SS. Quatuor Coronatos.*
Proficiat q. Dne. plebs tibi dicata
Praesta q. o. D. ut qui in tua
Cunctis nos Dne. reatibus et periculis
Divini satiati muneris largitate
Tueatur q. Dne. dextera tua]

Gerb. pp. 55, 56. [*Feria iii ad S. Laurentium in Damaso*[1]].
Sacrae nobis Dne. q. observationis
*Exercitatio (Exorcicio R.) veneranda Dne. ieiunii
Purifica nos m. D. ut ecclesiae
Caelestia dona capientibus q. Dne.
Miserere Dne. populo tuo et continuis

Gerb. pp. 56, 57. *Feria iv ad S. Paulum* (R. adds *Eb. iiii Hic facis ad aur apertione*).
O. s. D. qui et iustis praemia
Praesta q. o. D. ut quos ieiunia votiva
Supplicis Dne. te rogamus ut his sacrificiis
Sacramenta quae sumpsimus Dne. D. noster
Pateant aures misericordiae tuae

Gerb. p. 57. *Feria v ad S. Silvestrum* (R. adds *Eb. iiii.*).
Praesta q. Dne. ut salutaribus ieiuniis
Tua nos Dne. protectione defende
Efficiatur haec hostia Dne. q. solemnibus
Sancta tua nos Dne. q. et vivificando
Populi tui D. institutor et rector

[1] R. contains the prayers, but has lost the heading, of this *Missa.*

APPENDIX.

Feria vi ad S. Eusebium.
Gerb. pp. 57, 58.

Deus qui ineffabilibus mundum
O. s. D. qui sic hominem condidisti
Haec sacrificia nos o. D. potenti
Haec nos q. Dne. participatio sacramenti
Adesto Dne. populis qui sacra

Sabbato ad S. Laurentium [ad Corpus[1]].
Gerb. p. 58.

Deus omnium misericordiarum
Tua nos Dne. gratia et sanctis exerceat
Oblationibus q. Dne. placare susceptis
Tua nos q. Dne. sancta purificent et operatione
Plebem tuam Dne. q. interius exteriusque

Die Dominica. Statio ad S. Petrum (R. adds Eb. v).
Gerb. p. 59.

Q. o. D. familiam tuam propitius respice
Deus qui sperantibus in te misereri
Munera nos Dne. q. oblata purificent
VD. Maiestatem tuam propensius implorantes
Sacramenti tui q. Dne. participatio[2]
Da nobis q. Dne. perseverantem

Feria ii ad S. Chrisogonum (R. adds Eb. v).
Gerb. p. 60.

Sanctifica q. Dne. nostra ieiunia
Adesto supplicationibus nostris o. D. et quibus
Concede nobis Dne. q. ut haec hostia
Adesto nobis Dne. D. noster et quos tuis[3]
Benedictio Dne. q. in tuos fideles

Feria iii ad S. Cyriacum (R. adds Eb. v.).
Gerb. pp. 60, 61.

Nostra tibi q. Dne. fiant accepta
Afflictionem familiae tuae q. Dne.
*Hostias tibi Dne. deferimus immolandas[4]
Da q. o. D. ut quae divina sunt
Libera Dne. q. a peccatis et hostibus

Feria iv ad S. Marcellum (Marcellinū Eb. v. R.).
Gerb. p. 61.

Sanctificato hoc ieiunio D. tuorum corda
Ieiunia q. Dne. quae sacris
Annue m. D. ut hostias placationis

---

[1] The Church known as 'Foris Muros.' R. omits the words in brackets and adds *Eb. iiii.*
[2] R. has the Postcom. *Adesto nobis* (see Gerb. p. 60).
[3] R. has the Postcom. *Sacramenti tui* (see Gerb. p. 59).
[4] R. does not here agree with S¹ but with Gerbert.

332   APPENDIX.

    Caelestis doni benedictione percepta
    Exaudi q. Dne. gemitum populi

Gerb. p. 62.   *Feria v ad S. Apollinarem* (*Apollonarū Eb. v.* R.).
    Tribue nobis q. Dne. indulgentiam
    Concede m. D. ut sicut nos
    Concede nobis Dne. q. ut celebraturi
    Vegetet nos Dne. semper et innovet
    Succurre q. Dne. populo supplicanti

Gerb. p. 63.   *Feria vi ad S. Stephanum* (*Eb. v.* R.).
    Cordibus nostris Dne. benignus infunde
    O. s. D. clementiam tuam suppliciter
    Sanctifica nos q. Dne. his muneribus
    Sumpti sacrificii Dne. perpetua
    Protege Dne. populum tuum et in sanctorum

Gerb p. 63.   *Sabbatum vacat.* [*Elemosyna datur*[1].]
    Da nobis observantiam Dne. legitimam
    Deus qui iuste irasceris et clementer
    Praesta q. o. D. ut ieiuniorum
    Adesto Dne. fidelibus tuis et quos
    Conserva q. Dne. populum tuum

Gerb.   *Die Dominica ad Palmas ad S. Ioannem*[2].
pp. 65, 66.
    O. s. D. qui humano generi ad imitandum
    ✴Deus quem diligere et amare
    Ipsa maiestati tuae Dne. fideles populos
    VD. per quem nobis indulgentia
    Praesta nobis o. D. ut quia vitiis
    Purifica q. Dne. familiam tuam[3]

Gerb. p. 66.   *Feria ii ad SS. Nereum et Achilleum* (R. adds *Eb. vi*).
    Da q. o. D. ut qui in tot adversis
    Da m. D. ut quod in tui Filii
    Respice Dne. propitius sacra mysteria
    Sacramentorum tuorum benedictione
    Tua nos misericordia D. et ab omni

Gerb. p. 67.   *Feria iii ad S. Priscam* (R. adds *Eb. vi*).
    O. s. D. da nobis ita Dominicae
    ✴Fac o. D. ut quae veraciter

---

[1] R. omits the words in brackets and adds *Eb. v.*
[2] *Diae Dōm ad scm Iohā ad pat. ad Lateranis Eb. vi* R.
[3] R. adds at the end of this *Missa* a *Benedictio Palmae*.

Grata tibi sint Dne. munera quibus
Repleti Dne. sacri muneris gratia
Reminiscere miserationum tuarum

  Feria iv ad S. Mariam (R. adds *Eb. vi*).   Gerb.
Praesta q. o. D. ut qui nostris   pp. 67, 68.
D. qui pro nobis filium tuum
O. s. D. qui Christi tui beata
Praesta q. o. et m. D. ut sicut
Suscipe q. Dne. munus oblatum
Largire sensibus nostris o. D.
Respice Dne. q. super hanc familiam

  [*Feria v Coenae Domini.*   Gerb.
O. s. D. da q. universis   pp. 68-72.
*Concede credentibus m. D. salvum
O. s. D. qui vitam humani generis
Adest o venerabilis pontifex
*Adesto Dne. supplicationibus nostris et me
Praesta q. Dne. huic famulo tuo dignum
*D. humani generis benignissime conditor
*O. s. D. confitenti tibi huic famulo tuo
O. et m. D. qui peccatorum indulgentiam
*Dne. s. P. o. aet. D. respice propitius
*Virtutum caelestium D. de cuius gratiae rore
Communicantes et diem sacratissimum
Hanc igitur oblationem Dne. cunctae
Qui hac die antequam traderetur
Concede q. Dne. ut percepti
D. qui confitentium tibi corda purificas]

  [*Item Missa Chrismalis.*   Gerb.
Dne. D. qui in regenerandis   pp. 72-78.
Da nobis o. D. remedia conditionis humanae
Huius sacrificii potentia Dne. q. ut vetustatem
Communicantes et diem sacratissimum
Hanc igitur oblationem famulorum famularumque
*Emitte q. Dne. Spiritum sanctum
*D. incrementorum et profectuum
*VD. qui in principio
Concede q. Dne. ut percepti
Praesta q. Dne. ut sicut de praeteritis
Exorcizo te creatura olei
VD. Qui mysteriorum]

APPENDIX.

Ad Missam Sero[1].

Not given in this order in Gerb.

D. a quo et Iudas reatus sui poenam
Ipse tibi q. Dne. s. P. o. act. D. sacrificium
Communicantes (*ut supra.*)
Hanc igitur oblationem servitutis nostrae
Refecti vitalibus alimentis

Cf. Gerb. pp. 78-80.

Orationes quae dicendae sunt Sexta Feria Maiore in Hierusalem[2]:

∗D. a quo et Iudas reatus sui proditor

Sequuntur duae Lectiones.

Sequuntur orationes Solemnes.

Oremus dilectissimi in primis pro ecclesia
O. s. D. qui gloriam tuam omnibus
Oremus et pro beatissimo papa
O. s. D. cuius aeterno iudicio
Oremus et pro omnibus episcopis
O. s. D. cuius Spiritu totum corpus
∗Oremus et pro christianissimis imperatoribus
∗O. s. D. qui regnis omnibus
Oremus et pro catechumenis
O. s. D. qui ecclesiam tuam nova
Oremus dilectissimi nobis D. Patrem o. ut cunctis
O. s. D. moestorum consolatio
Oremus pro haereticis et schismaticis
O. s. D. qui salvas omnes
Oremus et pro perfidis Iudaeis
O. s. D. qui etiam Iudaicam perfidiam
Oremus et pro paganis
O. s. D. qui non mortem peccatorum

Not as in Gerb. p. 81.

Sabbato sancto. Benedictio cerei[3].

Exultet iam angelica turba

Cf. Gerb. pp. 83, 84.

Orationes per singulas lectiones in Sabbato (R. adds *sancto*).

D. qui divitias misericordiae

Sequitur Lect. i. In principio fecit

D. qui mirabiliter creasti hominem

Sequitur de Noe ii.

---

[1] R. has only this one *Missa* for the day, with the heading *Fr̄ v ad Cena Dn̄i. ad Miā Sero.*

[2] R. has *Fr̄ vi oratio quae dicende sunt maiore mane in Hierusalem.* It also gives the second Collect, *D. qui peccati veteris* (see p. 75, and note 7 on p. 78).

[3] R. has simply *Ad ceram benedicendam.*

D. incommutabilis virtus
> *De Abraham iii.*

D. fidelium pater summe
> *In Exodo iv cum cant.* Cantemus

D. cuius antiqua miracula
> *In Isaia v.* Haec hereditas

O. s. D. multiplica in honorem
> *In Hieremia vi.* Audi Israel

D. qui ecclesiam tuam semper gentium
> *In Ezechiel vii.* Facta est super me

D. qui nos ad celebrandum
> *In Isaia viii cum cant.* Vinea Dni.

D. qui in omnibus ecclesiae tuae filiis
> *In Exodo ix.* Dixit quoque Dominus,

O. s. D. qui in omnium operum
> *De Iona x.*

D. qui diversitatem
> *In Deut. xi cum cant.* Attendite

D. celsitudo humilium et fortitudo
> *In Daniel xii.* Nabucodonosor

O. s. D. spes unica
(*Post Ps. xli*) O. s. D. respice propitius
> *Inde descendis cum Litania ad fontes.*

Orationes ad Missam in nocte sancta [Statio] ad La (terā R.).   Gerb.
   D. qui hanc sacratissimam noctem gloria   pp. 89-90.
   D. qui per Unigenitum tuum
   Suscipe q. Dne. et plebis tuae
*VD. Adest enim nobis optatissimum
[VD. Te quidem omni tempore sed in hac]
Communicantes et noctem sacratissimam
Hanc igitur oblationem servitutis nostrae
[*Benedictio Agni. D. universae carnis qui Noe]
Praesta q. o. D. ut divino munere
[*Spiritum in nobis Dne. tuae caritatis]
Digne nos tuo nomini
[*Mentes nostras q. Dne. lumine tuae claritatis]

Gerb.
pp. 91, 92.

Dominica sancta ad S. Mariam.

D. qui hodierna die per Unigenitum
D. qui paschale nobis remedium
Suscipe q. Dne. preces populi tui cum oblationibus
*VD. Te quidem omni tempore sed in hoc
Communicantes et diem
Hanc igitur (*ut supra.*)
*Spiritum in nobis Dne. tuae caritatis
O. s. D. qui ad aeternam vitam

Ad vesperum ad S. Ioannem.

*Concede q. o. D. ut qui resurrectionis

Ad fontes.

Praesta q. o. D. ut qui resurrectionis

Ad S. Andream.

Praesta q. o. D. ut qui gratiam
*D. qui nos fecisti hodierna die

Gerb.
pp. 93, 94.

Feria ii [ad S. Petrum] [1]

D. qui solemnitate paschali mundo
*Paschale mysterium recensentes
Paschales hostias recensentes
VD. Nos precari clementiam tuam
[Hanc igitur *ut supra.*]
*Impleatur in nobis Dne. sacramenti
Ad vesp. Concede q. o. D. ut qui peccatorum
Ad fontes. D. qui populum tuum de hostis
Ad S. Andr. Concede q. o. D. ut festa paschalia [2]

Gerb.
pp. 94, 95.

Feria iii ad S. Paulum.

D. qui ecclesiam tuam novo semper fetu
D. ecclesiae tuae redemptor atque protector
Suscipe Dne. q. oblationes familiae
VD. Qui oblatione sui corporis
Hanc igitur (*ut supra.*)
*Concede q. o. D. ut paschalis perceptio
Ad vesp. Concede q. o. D. ut qui paschalis
**Ad fontes.* Praesta q. o. D. ut per haec paschalia
[*Ad S. Andr.* D. qui conspicis familiam tuam]

---

[1] R. omits the words in brackets, perhaps for reasons of space.
[2] R. gives 'Concede q. o. D.' as *Ad Fontes* and 'D. qui populum' as *Ad S. Andream*.

Feria iv ad S. Laurentium. *Gerb. p. 96.*

D. qui nos resurrectionis
*D. qui solemnitate paschali
Sacrificia Dne. paschalibus gaudiis
*VD. Circumdantes altaria tua
Hanc igitur (*ut supra.*)
Ab omni nos q. Dne. vetustate
Ad vesp. Praesta q. o. D. ut huius paschalis
Ad fontes. D. qui nos per paschalia festa
Ad S. Andr. Tribue q. o. D. ut illuc

Feria v ad (scōs R.) Apostolos. *Gerb. p. 97.*

D. qui diversitatem gentium
*D. qui multiplicas sobolem (sobole S.).
Suscipe q. Dne. munera populorum
VD. Quia vetustate destructa
Hanc igitur (*ut supra.*)
Exaudi Dne. preces nostras ut redemptionis
Ad vesp. D. qui nobis ad celebrandum
Ad fontes. Da q. o. D. ut ecclesia tua
Ad S. Andr. Multiplica q. Dne. fidem

Feria vi ad S. Mariam (R. adds ad Marī.). *Gerb. p. 98.*

O. s. D. qui paschale sacramentum
D. qui ad caeleste regnum
Hostias q. Dne. placatus assume
*VD. Qui secundum promissionis suae ... caelestis pontifex
[Hanc igitur *ut supra.*]
Respice q. Dne. populum tuum et quem aeternis
Ad vesp. in Hierusalem. D. per quem nobis et redemptio
Ad fontes. Adesto q. Dne. familiae tuae

Sabbato ad S. Ioannem ad Lat(eranis R.). *Gerb. pp. 99, 100.*

Concede q. o. D. ut qui festa paschalia
*D. qui (*sic*) innocentiae restitutor
Concede q. Dne. semper nos
*VD. Nos te suppliciter obsecrare
Hanc igitur (*ut supra.*)
Redemptionis nostrae munere vegetati
**Ad vesp.* [*ad S. Mariam*]. D. conditor totius creaturae
Ad fontes. D. qui multiplicas ecclesiam tuam in sobole

Die Dominica post Albas. *Gerb. pp. 100, 101.*

Praesta q. o. D. ut qui (festa R.) paschalia
D. qui renatis baptismate mortem

Suscipe munera q. Dne. exultantis
⁎VD. Suppliciter obsecrantes ne nos ad illum
Maiestatem tuam Dne. supplices exoramus
[⁎Exuberet q. Dne. mentibus]
Ad vesp. ad SS. Cosmam et Damianum. D. qui nos exultantibus animis

Cf. Gerb. pp. 101, 102.

Item aliae Orationes Paschales[1].

D. qui omnes in Christo renatos
D. qui credentes in te fonte baptismatis
D. qui pro salute mundi sacrificium
D. qui ad aeternam vitam ... erige
D. qui credentes in te populos
[O. s. D. qui humanam naturam[2]]
[Concede m. D. ut quod paschalibus]
[Praesta nobis o. D. ut percipientes]
[D. qui per Unigenitum]
[Adesto q. Dne. tuae familiae]
Da m. D. ut in resurrectione
[Exaudi nos o. D. et familiae tuae]
[Conserva nobis q. Dne. misericordiam]
[Solita q. Dne. quos salvasti]
[Christianam q. Dne. respice plebem]
[O. s. D. propensius his diebus]
[D. qui sensus nostros terrenis]
[Largire q. ecclesiae tuae Dne. et a suis]

Gerb. pp. 102, 103.

Orationes et Preces de Pascha annotēn (*annotina* R.).

D. [per cuius[3]?] providentiam nec praeteritorum
D. qui renatis fonte baptismatis

---

[1] The series in R. is apparently complete, and differs considerably from that in S.

Order of R.

1–5. As in S., in the same order.
6. Praesta q. nobis o. et m. D. ut in resurrectione
7. Depelle [Dele?] Dne. conscriptum
8. D. qui ad aeternam vitam ... imple
9. D. humani generis conditor
10. Gaudeat Dne. plebs fidelis
11. D. qui renatis ex aqua
12. Fac o. D. ut qui paschalibus
13. Da misericors Deus
14. Familiam tuam q. Dne dextera
15. Paschalibus nos q. Dne.
16. Q. o. D. ut iam non teneamur.

Of these, 13 is in S., where the rest (except 1–5) are wanting at this point: 12 and 14 are not in the series in Gerb.

[2] Imperfect in S.; leaf wanting?

[3] R. has *D. qui per cuius*; S[2] *D. apud cuius.*

APPENDIX.

Clementiam tuam Dne. suppliciter exoramus
VD. Redemptionis nostrae festa recolere
Hanc igitur obl. famulorum famularumque
*Tua nos q. Dne. quae sumpsimus

[*Orationes et Preces in Parochiis.*   Gerb. p. 103.

D. qui humani generis reparator et rector
Renovatos Dne. fontis ac Spiritus tui
*Offerimus tibi Dne. laudes et munera
VD. Nos te suppliciter exorare ut fidelibus
Adiuvet nos q. Dne. sanctum istud
*Populus tuus q. Dne. renovata semper]

[*viii Kal. Apr. Annuntiatio S. Mariae*[1].   Gerb. pp. 31, 32.

O. s. D. qui coaeternum tibi Filium
*Exaudi nos Dne. s. P. o. aet. D. qui per beatae
Altari tuo Dne. superimposita
*Oblationes nostras q. Dne. propitiatus intende
*VD. Qui nos mirabile mysterium
Adesto Dne. populo tuo ut quae sumpsit
Protege Dne. famulos tuos subsidiis pacis]

[*Alias Orationes*
Beatae et gloriosae ... nos Dne. q.
*Beatae et gloriosae ... q. o. D. intercessio
Porrige nobis D. dexteram tuam et per]

Orationes et Preces Dominica post Oct. Paschae.   Gerb. pp. 103, 104.

*D. qui in Filii tui humilitate
D. in cuius praecipuis mirabilibus
Benedictionem Dne. nobis conferat
VD. Quoniam (?) maiestatem tuam precari
*Praesta nobis o. D. ut vivificationis

[*iii Id. Apr. Nat. S. Leonis Papae.*   Gerb. p. 105.

Exaudi Dne. preces nostras quas in s. confessoris
*Praesta q. o. D. ut b. Leo
*S. Leonis confessoris tui atque pontificis
D. fidelium remunerator animarum.}

[*Id. Apr. Nat. S. Eufimiae.*   Gerb. p. 105.

Concede q. o. D. s. martyris Eufimiae
Annue q. Dne. ut s. martyris Eufimiae

---

[1] R. has a different *Missa* (see Gerb. p. 32, note) consisting of one Collect, Secret and Postcommunion.

*Muneribus Dne. te magnificamus oblatis
*VD. In exultatione praecipue solemnitatis
Sanctae nos Martyris Eufimiae]

Gerb. pp. 105, 106.
[(x ?)viii Kal. Mai. Nat. SS. Tyburtii, Valeriani et Maximi.
Praesta q. o. D. ut qui sanctorum tuorum
Suscipe Dne. munera pro tuorum commemoratione
*VD. Te in sanctorum martyrum
*Caelesti munere saginati q. Dne. D. noster]

Gerb. p. 106.
Secunda Dominica post Oct. Paschae.
D. qui errantes(?) ut in viam
Tibi placitam D. noster populo tuo tribue
*His nobis Dne. mysteriis
*VD. Qui humanis miseratus erroribus
Sacramenta quae sumpsimus q. Dne. et spiritalibus

Gerb. p. 107.
[vii Kal. Mai. Nat. S. Georgii Martyris.
Tuus s. Martyr Georgius
*Tanto placabiles q. Dne. nostrae
*VD. Te in omnium martyrum triumphis
B. Georgii martyris tui Dne. suffragiis]

Gerb. pp. 108, 109.
[vii Kal. Mai. Litania Maior ad S. Laurentium in Lucinae.
Mentem familiae tuae q. Dne. intercedente

Ad S. (Valentinum[1])
Deus qui culpas delinquentum districte

Ad pontem Olbi (sic)
Parce Dne. q. parce populo tuo et nullis [2]

Ad Crucem
D. qui culpas nostras piis verberibus [2]

In Atrio
Adesto Dne. supplicationibus nostris et sperantes

Ad Missam
Praesta q. o. D. ut qui in afflictione
Haec munera Dne. q. et vincula
Vota nostra q. Dne. pio favore prosequere

Alia oratio in Atrio
Praesta q. o. D. ut ad te toto corde clamantes]

[1] Name omitted.
[2] These are marked by a later hand for transposition.

[iv Kal. Mai. Nat. S. Vitalis.]

Sancti nos q. Dne. Vitalis natalitia
Accepta sit in conspectu tuo Dne.
Exultet q. Dne. populus tuus.]

Gerb.
p. 109.

Tertia Dominica post Oct. Paschae.

D. qui fidelium mentes unius efficis
*Exaudi Dne. preces nostras ut quod
D. qui nos per huius sacrificii
*VD. De tuo munere postulantes
Adesto Dne. D. noster ut per haec

Gerb.
p. 110.

Kal. Mai. Nat. Apostolorum Philippi et Iacobi.

D. qui nos annua apostolorum
D. qui es omnium sanctorum
Munera Dne. quae pro apostolorum
*VD. Quia tui est operis
Beatorum Apostolorum Philippi et Iacobi

Gerb. pp.
110, 111.

[v Non. Mai. Nat. S. Iuvenalis.

Beati nobis q. Dne. Iuvenalis
Annue q. Dne. ut merita tibi placita
Hostias nostras q. Dne. sanctus pontifex
Laeti Dne. sumpsimus sacramenta]

Gerb.
p. 111.

[Eodem die Nat. SS. Alexandri Eventii Theoduli.

Praesta q. o. D. ut qui sanctorum
Sacrificium laudis tibi Dne. offerimus
Pasce nos Dne. tuorum gaudiis ubique]

Gerb. pp.
111, 112.

Eodem die [1] Inv. S. Crucis.

D. qui in praeclara salutiferae
*D. cui cunctae obediunt creaturae
Sacrificium Dne. quod immolamus
[*VD. Praecipue in die ista.]
*Repleti alimonia caelesti et spiritali

Gerb.
p. 112.

Quarta Dominica post Oct. Paschae [2].

*D. a quo bona cuncta procedunt
[D. qui misericordiae ianuam fidelibus
Suscipe Dne. fidelium preces

Gerb.
p. 113.

---

[1] *V. Non. Mad.* R. (omitting the two *Missae* which precede this in S.).
[2] R. has now only the first Collect of this *Missa*. One leaf appears to be wanting, which probably contained the rest of this *Missa* and the first part of the prayers and *Missae* for the Rogation Days.

∗VD. Tu 'mentes nostras
Tribue nobis Dne. caelestis mensae virtute]

Gerb. p. 113.
[*Pridie Non. Mai. Nat. S. Ioannis ante Portam Latinam*[1].
D. qui conspicis quia nos undique
Sacrificium nostrum tibi Dne. q.
Sumpsimus Dne. divina mysteria]

Gerb. p. 114.
[*vi Id. Mai. Nat. S. Gordiani.*
O. s. D. qui nos s. martyris tui Gordiani
Grata tibi sint Dne. munera nostra
Q. o. D. ut qui caelestia alimenta]

Gerb. p. 115.
[*iv Id. Mai. Nat. SS. Nerei Achillei et Pancratii.*
Semper nos Dne. martyrum tuorum
Sanctorum tuorum Dne. Nerei Achillei
∗VD. Quoniam a te
Q. Dne. ut beatorum martyrum]

Gerb. p. 116.
[*iii Id. Mai. Dedicatio Eccl. B. Mariae ad Martyres.*
Concede q. o. D. ad eorum
Super has q. hostias Dne. benedictio
Supplices te rogamus o. D. ut quos tuis]

Gerb. pp. 120, 121.
In Ascensa Domini[2].
Praesta q. o. Pater ut nostrae mentis
Tribue q. o. D. ut munere festivitatis
Sacrificium Dne. pro Filii tui supplices
VD. In hac praecipue die
Tribue q. Dne. ut per haec
∗Da q. o. D. illuc subsequi.

Gerb. pp. 121, 122.
Item in Ascensa Domini ad S. Petrum.
Concede q. o. D. ut qui hodierna
∗D. qui ad declaranda tua miracula
Suscipe Dne. munera quae pro Filii
VD. Qui post resurrectionem
Communicantes et diem
Praesta nobis q. o. et m. D.

---

[1] R. does not contain this or any of the three following *Missae*. It is now defective at this point, but the missing leaf was probably occupied by prayers and *Missae* for the Rogation Days, the latter part of which are found after the *lacuna* (see Gerb. pp. 118 sqq.). These are not in S., and the *Missa* for the Wednesday is not printed by Gerbert.

[2] *In Vigilia Ascensa Dñi* R.

Alias Orationes.

[D. qui nos resurrectionis Dominicae]
Adesto Dne. supplicationibus nostris
D. cuius Filius in alta

  Dominica post Ascensam Domini.   Gerb. pp.
O. s. D. fac nos tibi semper et devotam   122, 123.
D. vita fidelium, gloria humilium
Sacrificia nos Dne. immaculata
*VD. Ut quia primum tuae pietatis
Repleti Dne. muneribus sacris da q.
*Erectis sensibus et oculis cordis

  [*viii Kal. Iun. Nat. S. Urbani Papae.*   Gerb.
Da q. o. D. ut qui b. Urbani   p. 123.
Munera q. Dne. tibi dicata sanctifica
B. Urbani martyris tui]

Orationes per singulas lectiones in Sabbato Pentecostes.   Gerb.
Da nobis q. Dne. per gratiam   p. 124.
  Sequitur Lect. i in Genesi In principio
O. s. D. indeficiens lumen
  De Gen. ii Temptavit Deus Abraham
D. qui in Abrahae
  In Exodo Factum est in vigilia *cum cantico.*
D. qui primis temporibus
  In Deuteronomio Scripsit Moyses
D. gloriatio fidelium
  In Esaia Apprehendent
*O. s. D. qui per unicum
  In Hieremia Audi Israel
D. qui nobis per prophetarum
(*De Ps. xli*) Concede q. o. D. ut qui solemnitatem
Dne. D. virtutum qui collapsa reparas
  Inde descendis cum Litania ad fontes.

Orationes ad Missam post ascensum Fontis[1]. *Statio ad*   Gerb.
      Lateranis.   p. 125.
Praesta q. o. D. ut claritatis tuae
. D. cuius Spiritu totum corpus ecclesiae multiplicatur
Virtute s. Spiritus Dne. munera nostra

---

[1] R. has *p' Ascensa Dñi Fontes* (sic).

VD. Qui ascendens super omnes caelos
Communicantes et diem sacratissimum . . . praevenientes
Hanc igitur oblationem servitutis nostrae
Praesta q. o. D. ut Spiritus [sanctus]

Gerb. pp.
125-128.

[*Item alia Missa* (S¹ adds *Inf. Ebd.*).
Annue m. D. ut qui divina
Hostias populi tui q. Dne. miseratus
*VD. Qui sacramentum paschale
Sacris caelestibus Dne. vitia nostra purgentur]

Gerb. pp.
126, 127.

Die sancto Pentecostes ad S. Petrum.
D. qui hodierna die corda fidelium
O. s. D. qui paschale sacramentum quinquaginta
Munera Dne. q. oblata sanctifica
*VD. Quia hodie s. Spiritus
Communicantes et diem . . . celebrantes
Hanc igitur (*ut supra.*)
S. Spiritus Dne. corda nostra mundet infusio
Praesta q. Dne. ut a nostris mentibus

Alias orationes.
D. qui sacramento festivitatis
[*D. qui discipulis tuis Spiritum sanctum]
O. s. D. deduc nos ad societatem
Concede nobis m. D. ut sicut in nomine

Gerb.
p. 128.

Feria ii. Ad vincula.
D. qui apostolis tuis s. dedisti Spiritum
Propitius Dne. q. haec dona sanctifica
Adesto Dne. q. populo tuo et quem

Gerb.
p. 128.

[*Feria iii. Ad S. Anastasiam.*
Adsit nobis Dne. q. virtus Spiritus sancti
Purificet nos Dne. muneris
Mentes nostras q. Dne. Spiritus sanctus]

Gerb. pp.
128, 129.

Feria iv. Ad S. Mariam.
Mentes nostras q. Dne. Spiritus Paraclitus
Praesta q. o. et m. D. ut Spiritus sanctus
Accipe q. Dne. munus oblatum et dignanter
[*VD. Post illos enim laetitiae dies]
Sumentes Dne. caelestia sacramenta

Feria vi. Ad Apostolos.   Gerb. p. 129.

Da q. ecclesiae tuae m. D. ut s. Spiritu
Sacrificia Dne. tuis oblata conspectibus
Sumpsimus Dne. sacri dona mysterii

Sabbato in xii Lect. ad S. Petrum.   Gerb. pp. 129, 130.

Mentibus nostris Dne. Spiritum sanctum
Illo nos igne q. Dne. Spiritus sanctus inflammet
D. qui ad animarum medelam
Praesta q. o. D. ut salutaribus ieiuniis
Praesta q. o. D. sic nos ab epulis
[D. qui tribus pueris mitigasti][1]
Ut accepta tibi sint Dne. nostra ieiunia
Praebeant nobis Dne. divina tua sancta

Dominica Oct. Pentecostes.   Gerb. pp. 130, 131.

*Timentium te Dne. salvator
O. et m. D. ad cuius beatitudinem
Remotis obumbrationibus carnalium
VD. Qui cum unigenito Filio
Laetificet nos q. Dne. huius sacramenti
*Ecclesia tua Dne. caelesti gratia

[Kal. Iun. Dedicatio S. Nicomedis.   Gerb. pp. 131, 132.

D. qui nos b. Nicomedis
Munera Dne. oblata sanctifica et intercedente b. Nicomede
Supplices te rogamus o. D. ut quos tuis]

[iv Non. Iun. Nat. SS. Marcellini et Petri.   Gerb. p. 132.

*Laetetur ecclesia tua D. beatorum martyrum
*Votiva Dne. munera deferentes
*VD. Cognoscimus enim
*Q. Dne. ut salutaribus repleti
*Intercedentibus sanctis tuis Dne. plebi tuae]

Hebd. ii post Pentecosten.   Gerb. pp. 132, 133.

D. in te sperantium
D. spei(?) luminis sincerum (*sic*)
Hostias nostras
VD. Qui ecclesiae tuae filios
Tantis Dne. repleti muneribus
Fideles tuos Dne. benedictio desiderata

---

[1] This is perhaps accidentally omitted in R. It is referred to in a marginal note by a later hand.

Gerb. p. 133.	[*v Id. Iun. Nat. SS. Primi et Feliciani.* Fac nos Dne. q. sanctorum Fiat Dne. q. hostia sacranda Q. o. D. ut sanctorum tuorum]
Gerb. p. 133.	[*Prid. Id. Iun. Nat. SS. Basilidis Cirini Naboris et Nazarii.* Sanctorum B. C. N. et N. q. Dne. natalitia Pro sanctorum B. C. N. et N. sanguine Laeti Dne. sanctorum martyrum]
Gerb. pp. 133, 134.	*Hebd. iii post Pentecosten.* Sancti nominis tui Dne. timorem pariter D. qui te rectis ac sinceris Oblatio nos Dne. tuo nomini dicanda ∗VD. Cuius hoc mirificum Sumptis muneribus Dne. q. ut cum
Gerb. p. 134.	*Denuntiatio Ieiuniorum Primi Quarti Septimi et Decimi mensis.* Anniversarii, fratres dilectissimi, ieiunii [Illius mensis ieiunia in hac]
Gerb. p. 134.	[*Mensis iv feria iv. Ad S. Mariam.* ∗O. et m. D. apta nos tuae propitius Da nobis mentem, Dne. quae tibi sit ∗Solemnibus ieiuniis expiatos Quos ieiunia votiva castigant]
Gerb. p. 135.	*Feria vi ad Apostolos.* ∗Ut nobis Dne. terrenorum (*sic*) frugum [∗Fiant tua gratia Dne. fructuosius (*sic*)] O. s. D. qui non sacrificiorum Annue q. o. D. ut sacramentorum Fideli populo Dne. misericordiam tuam.
Gerb. p. 135.	*Sabbato in xii Lect. ad S. Petrum.* ∗Praesta Dne. q. famulis tuis talesque Da nobis Dne. q. regnum tuum iustitiamque D. qui nos de praesentibus adiumentis D. qui misericordia tua praevenis non petentes [D. qui non despicis corde contritos] [D. qui tribus pueris mitigasti] Dne. D. n. qui in his potius creaturis Sumptum q. Dne. venerabile sacramentum Proficiat Dne. q. plebs tibi dicata.

Hebd. iv post Pentecosten.

Deprecationem nostram q. Dne. benignus
Tempora nostra q. Dne. pio favore
Munera Dne. oblata sanctifica ut tui
*VD. Illa quippe festa remaneant
Haec nos communio Dne. purget

Gerb. p. 136.

[xvii Kal. Iul. Nat. S. Viti Mart.
Da ecclesiae tuae Dne. q. s. Vito intercedente
Sicut gloriae (?) divinae potentiae
*VD. Beati Viti martyrio gloriantes
*Refecti Dne. benedictione caelesti]

Gerb. p. 136.

[xiv Kal. Iul. SS. Marci et Marcelliani.
Sanctorum tuorum nos Dne. Marci et Marcelliani
Suscipe Dne. munera tuorum populorum
Salutaris tui Dne. munere satiati]

Gerb. p. 137.

[Eodem die Vigil. Gervasi et Protasi.
*Martyrum tuorum Dne. Gervasi et Protasi
Sacrificium Dne. quod pro sanctis
Sumpti sacrificii Dne. perpetua nos]

Gerb. p. 137.

[xiii Kal. Iul. Nat. SS. Gervasi et Protasi.
*Sanctorum martyrum nos Dne. Gervasii et Protasii
Concede nobis o. D. ut his muneribus
VD. Ecce enim iusti tui
*Da q. o. D. ut mysteriorum virtute]

Gerb. pp. 137, 138.

Hebd. v post Pentecosten.

Protector in te sperantium Deus
Propitiare Dne. humilitati nostrae
Respice Dne. munera supplicantis
VD. Omnipotentiam tuam
Sancta tua nos Dne. sumpta vivificent

Gerb. p. 139.

iv Kal. Iul. in Ieiunio S. Ioh. Bapt.

Praesta q. o. D. ut familia tua
Praesta q. Dne. ut populus tuus
Munera populi tui Dne. propitiatus
*VD. Exhibentes solemne ieiunium
*B. Ioannis Baptistae nos q. Dne. praeclara
B. nos Dne. Baptistae Ioannis oratio

Gerb. pp. 139, 140.

Gerb. p. 140.	[*viii Kal. Iul. Nat. S. Ioannis Bapt. In prima missa de Nocte.* Concede q. o. D. ut qui beati D. cuius misericordia praecurrente Praesta q. o. D. ut qui caelestia]
Gerb. pp. 140, 141.	*Ad Missam in Die* [1]. D. qui praesentem diem honorabilem ∗O. s. D. qui instituta legalia ∗Tua Dne. muneribus altaria cumulamus. ∗VD. In die festivitatis Sumat ecclesia tua D. beati Ioannis
Gerb. pp. 141, 142.	*Alias Orationes.* [Da q. m. D. ut mysticis ecclesia] D. qui nos b. Ioannis Baptistae *Ad fontes.* O. s. D. da cordibus nostris D. qui conspicis quia nos undique [Da q. o. D. intra sanctae ecclesiae uterum] [D. qui nos annua b. Ioannis] [∗O. et m. D. qui b. Ioannem]
Gerb. p. 142.	*vii Kal. Iul. Vig. SS. Ioannis et Pauli.* Beatorum martyrum Ioannis et Pauli Sint tibi q. Dne. nostri munera grata Protege Dne. plebem tuam et quam martyrum
Gerb. pp. 142, 143.	*vi Kal. Iul. Nat. SS. Ioannis et Pauli.* Q. o. D. ut nos geminata Hostias altaribus tuis Dne. placationis ∗VD. Beati etenim martyres Sumpta munera Dne. nostrae
Gerb. pp. 146, 147.	*Hebd. vi post Pentecosten.* Da nobis Dne. q. ut et mundi cursus Exaudi nos D. salutaris noster Oblationibus q. Dne. placare susceptis et ad te VD. Maiestatem tuam suppliciter deprecantes Mysteria nos Dne. sancta purificent
Gerb. pp. 143, 144.	*iv Kal. Iul. Vig. Apost. Petri et Pauli.* D. qui nobis apostolorum beatorum Praesta q. o. D. ut nullis nos permittas ∗Munera Dne. tuae glorificationis offerimus

[1] R. has *viii K?. Iul. Nat̄l. Sc̄i Iohannis Baptiste ad Missa.*

APPENDIX. 349

*VD. Apud quem [quum] beatorum
Quos caelesti Dne. alimento
Ad Vesp. Apostolicis nos q. Dne. beatorum
[*Ad Vigil. Noct.* D. qui ecclesiam tuam apostoli]
[*Ad Matut.* D. qui ligandi solvendique

   iii Kal. Iul. [*Nat. Apost. Petri et Pauli*][1].   Gerb. pp.
D. qui hodiernam diem apostolorum   144, 145.
*Largiente te Dne. beatorum Petri et Pauli
Hostias Dne. quas nomini tuo sacrandas
VD. Te Domine suppliciter exorare
Sumptis Dne. remediis sempiternis
Ad Vesp. O. s. D. qui ecclesiam tuam in apostolica

    Alias Orationes.   Cf. Gerb.
O. s. D. qui nos beatorum apostolorum   pp. 145,
[Familiam tuam D. propitius]   146.
[Concede q. o. D. apostolos tuos]
[*O. s. D. qui nos omnium]

   Pridie Kal. Iul. Nat. S. Pauli.   Gerb.
D. qui multitudinem gentium   p. 146.
*Praeveniant nobis Dne. q. apostoli
Perceptis Dne. sacramentis subdito corde

  [*vi Non. Iul. Nat. SS. Processi et Martiniani.*   Gerb.
D. qui nos sanctorum tuorum confessionibus   p. 147.
*Suscipe Dne. preces et munera
Corporis sacri et pretiosi sanguinis]

   Hebd. vii post Pentecosten.   Gerb.
D. qui diligentibus te bona invisibilia   p. 148.
D. qui in sanctis habitas et pia corda
Propitiare Dne. supplicationibus nostris et has obl.
VD. Verum aeternumque pontificem
Quos caelesti Dne. dono satiasti

 [*Prid. Non. Iul. Octav. Apostolorum. Ad vincula.*]   Gerb. pp.
*D. cuius dextera b. Petrum apostolum   147, 148.
Offerimus tibi Dne. preces et munera quae ut tuo
*Pignus aeternae vitae capientes
Protege Dne. populum tuum et apostolorum
Beatorum apostolorum Dne. Petri et Pauli

   [1] R. has *Nail. Scī Petri.*

Gerb.
p. 149.

[*iv Id. Iul. Nat. vii Fratrum.*

Praesta q. o. D. ut qui gloriosos
Sacrificiis praesentibus Dne. q. intende placatus
VD. Donare nobis suppliciter exorantes
Q. o. D. ut illius salutaris]

Gerb.
p. 149.

Hebd. viii post Pentecosten.

*D. virtutum cuius est totum
Da nobis Dne. q. ut in tua gratia
Propitiare Dne. supplicationibus nostris et has populi
[*VD. Tibi vovere contriti]
*Repleti sumus Dne. muneribus tuis

Gerb. pp.
149, 150.

v Id. Iul. Nat. S. Benedicti Abbatis.

Intercessio nos Dne. q. b. Benedicti
Sacris altaribus Dne. hostias superpositas
VD. Gloriam tuam Dne. profusis
Protegat nos Dne. cum tui perceptione

Gerb.
p. 150.

Hebd. ix post Pentecosten.

*D. cuius providentia in sui dispositione
*Custodi nos Dne. q. in tuo servitio
D. qui legalium differentias hostiarum
*VD. Ut te auctorem
Tua nos Dne. medicinalis operatio

Gerb.
p. 151.

Hebd. x post Pentecosten.

Largire nobis Dne. q. semper spiritum
Concede q. o. D. ut viam tuam
*Suscipe munera q. Dne. quae tibi
*VD. De tua gratia confidentes
Sit nobis Dne. reparatio mentis

Gerb. pp.
152, 153.

viii Kal. Aug. Nat. S. Iacobi (apostoli R.) fratris S. Ioannis.

Esto Dne. plebi tuae sanctificator
Oblationes populi tui Dne. q. beati
*VD. Quia licet nobis salutem
Beati apostoli tui Iacobi
Solemnitatis apostolicae multiplicatione

Gerb.
p. 153.

[*v Kal. Aug. Nat. SS. Simplicii, Faustini, et Beatricis.*

Praesta q. Dne. ut sicut populus Christianus
Hostias tibi Dne. pro sanctorum
Praesta q. o. D. ut sanctorum tuorum]

APPENDIX. 351

[*iv Kal. Aug. Nat. S. Felicis.*   Gerb. pp.
S. Felicis Dne. confessio recensita   154, 155.
Hostias tibi Dne. pro commemoratione
Repleti cibo potuque caelesti]

[*iii Kal. Aug. Nat. SS. Abdo et Sennis.*   Gerb.
D. qui sanctis tuis Abdo et Sennen   p. 155.
Munera tibi Dne. pro sanctorum martyrum
Populum tuum Dne. perpetua munitione]

Hebd. xi post Pentecosten.   Gerb. pp.
Praesta q. o. et m. D. ut inter huius   155, 156.
*Pateant aures misericordiae tuae
Concede nobis haec q. Dne. frequentare
VD. Tibi debitam servitutem
Tui nobis Dne. communio sacramenti.

[*Kal. Aug. ad S. Petrum ad Vincula. Catenae eius osculantur.*   Gerb.
Ipso die Nat. Machabaeorum.   p. 156.
Fraterna nos Dne. martyrum tuorum
Praesta q. Dne. ut sicut nobis
*Intemerata mysteria Dne. pro sanctorum
VD. Quia licet in omnium
Praesta q. o. D. ut quorum memoriam]

iv Non. Aug. Nat. S. Stephani Episcopi.   Gerb.
D. qui nos b. Stephani martyris tui   p. 157.
Munera tibi Dne. dicata sanctifica
Haec nos communio Dne. purget

[*viii Id. Aug. Nat. S. Sixti Episcopi.*   Gerb. pp.
*Beati Sixti Dne. tui sacerdotis et martyris   157, 158.
*S. Sixti Dne. frequentata solemnia
Suscipe Dne. munera propitiatus oblata
*VD. In die festivitatis hodiernae
*Repleti sumus Dne. munere solemnitatis]

[*Eodem die Nat. SS. Felicissimi et Agapiti.*   Gerb. pp.
D. qui nos concedis sanctorum martyrum   158, 159.
Munera tibi Dne. nostrae devotionis
Praesta q. Dne. D. noster ut quorum]

[*vii Id. Aug. Nat. S. Donati Episcopi.*   Gerb.
*D. tuorum gloria sacerdotum   p. 159.
*Praesta q. Dne. ut sancti confessoris
O. et m. D. qui nos sacramentorum]

APPENDIX.

Gerb. pp. 159, 160.

Hebd. xii post Pentecosten.

*D. qui omnipotentiam tuam
D. qui iusta postulantes
Tibi Dne. sacrificia dicata reddantur
*VD. [Ut te] postposita vetustate
Q. Dne. D. noster ut quos divinis

Gerb. p. 160.

[*vi Id. Aug. Nat. S. Cyriaci.*
D. qui nos annua b. Cyriaci
*Suscipe Dne. sacrificium placationis
Q. Dne. D. noster ut intervenientibus]

Gerb. pp. 160, 161.

v Id. Aug. Vig. S. Laurentii.
Adesto Dne. supplicationibus nostris
*B. Laurentii martyris tui Dne.
Hostias Dne. quas tibi offerimus
*VD. [Praevenientes ?][1] natalem
Da q. Dne. D. noster ut sicut b. Laurentii
[Da q. o. D. ut triumphum]

Gerb. p. 161.

[*iv Id. Aug. Nat. S. Laurentii in Prima Missa.*
Excita Dne. in ecclesia
*Respice Dne. munera quae in S. Laurentii
*Q. o. D. ut muneris divini]

Gerb. pp. 161, 162.

Item ad Missam (R. adds *in die*).
Da nobis q. o. D. vitiorum
D. mundi creator et rector qui
*Praesta q. Dne. ut beati sancti
*VD. In die solemnitatis
Prosit nobis Dne. S. Laurentii celebrata

Gerb. pp. 162, 163.

Item alias Orationes.
[*D. cuius caritatis ardore]
[S. Laurentii nos Dne. sancta precatio]
Adsit nobis Dne. q. sancti Laurentii
Praesta q. Dne. ut semper nos

Gerb. p. 163.

[*iii Id. Aug. Nat. S. Tiburtii.*
B. Tiburtii nos Dne. foveant
Adesto Dne. precibus populi tui
VD. Qui dum beati Tiburtii
Sumpsimus Dne. pignus aeternae]

[1] *Venientem natalem* R.

APPENDIX.

[*Id. Aug. Nat. S. Hippolyti.*   Gerb. p. 163.
S. Hippolyti martyris Dne. q. veneranda
Respice Dne. munera populi tui
*VD. Qui non solum malis nostris
Sacramentorum tuorum Dne. communio]

Hebd. xiii post Pentecosten.   Gerb. p. 164.
O. s. D. qui abundantia pietatis
O. s. D. a quo sola (*sic*) sancta desideria
Respice Dne. q. nostram propitius
VD. Qui nos castigando sanas
Sentiamus Dne. q. tui perceptione

. [*xix Kal. Sept. Nat. S. Eusebii Sac.*   Gerb. p. 164.
D. qui nos beati Eusebii
Laudis tuae Dne. hostias immolamus
*S. Eusebii natalitia celebrantes]

[*Item ipso die Vig. S. Mariae.*   Gerb. p. 165.
Sanctae Mariae semper virginis
Suscipe Dne. sacrificium placationis
*Adiuvent nos q. Dne. haec mysteria]

xviii Kal. Sept. Assumptio S. Mariae.   Gerb. pp. 165, 166.
Concede nobis q. o. D. ad b. Mariae
Veneranda nobis Dne. huius est
Intercessio q. Dne. beatae Mariae
VD. Nos te in tuis
*Caelesti munere satiati (?) o. D. tua nos
*O. s. D. qui terrenis corporibus

[*xvi Kal. Sept. Oct. S. Laurentii.*   Gerb. pp. 166, 167.
*B. Laurentii nos faciat Dne. passio
Iterata festivitate b. Laurentii
B. Laurentii martyris honorabilem
*VD. B. Laurentii natalitia repetentes
Solemnis nobis intercessio]

[*xv Kal. Sept. Nat. S. Agapiti.*   Gerb. p. 167.
Sancti martyris Agapiti merita
Suscipe Dne. munera quae in eius
Protegat q. Dne. populum tuum et participatio]

[*xiv Kal. Sept. Nat. S. Magni.*   Gerb. pp. 167, 168.
Adesto Dne. supplicationibus nostris et intercedente
Praesta nobis q. o. D. ut nostrae

VD. Qui humanum genus de profundo
Tua sancta sumentes q. Dne. ut b. Magni]

Gerb.
p. 168.

[xi Kal. Sept. Nat. S. Timothei.
Auxilium tuum nobis Dne. q. placatus
*Offerimus tibi Dne. quaesumus (sic) preces
*VD. Tibi enim festa solemnitas
Divini muneris largitate satiati]

Gerb.
p. 168.

Hebd. xiv post Pentecosten.
O. s. D. per quem coepit esse quod non erat
*O. et m. D. de cuius munere venit
Hostias q. Dne. propitiatus intende
*VD. Quia tu in nostra semper
Vivificet nos q. Dne. huius participatio

Gerb. pp.
168, 169.

ix Kal. Sept. Nat. S. Bartholomaei Apost.
O. s. D. qui huius diei venerandam
*B. apostoli tui Bartholomaei cuius
*VD. Qui ecclesiam tuam sempiterna pietate
Sumpsimus Dne. pignus salutis
Protege Dne. populum tuum et apostolorum

Gerb. pp.
169, 170.

[vi Kal. Sept. Nat. S. Rufi.
Adesto Dne. supplicationibus nostris
Oblatis q. Dne. placare muneribus
VD. Quoniam supplicationibus
Caelestibus refecti sacramentis et gaudiis]

Gerb.
p. 170.

[v Kal. Sept. Nat. S. Hermetis[1].
Intercessio Dne. b. Hermetis
Munera nostra Dne. q. propitiatus
VD. Quoniam fiducialiter
Repleti Dne. benedictione caelesti]

Gerb. pp.
170, 171.

Hebd. xv post Pentecosten.
O. s. D. da nobis fidei spei et caritatis
O. s. D. fac nos tibi semper
*Propitiare Dne. populo tuo
VD. Qui nos de donis
*Sumptis Dne. caelestibus sacramentis

[1] R. has here v Kl Sep. Nat Sti Augustini (Gerb. p. 170). The Collect of the Missa is not at this point in Gerb.

APPENDIX.

[*iv Kal. Sept. Nat. S. Sabinae.*   Gerb. p. 171.
Exaudi nos D. salutaris noster ut sicut
Gratanter Dne. ad munera dicanda
Purificet nos Dne. q. et divini]

[*Eodem die*]. (*iii K. Sep. R.*) *Passio S. Ioannis Baptistae.*   Gerb. pp. 171, 172.
Sancti Ioannis Baptistae et martyris
Perpetuis nos Dne. s. Ioannis Baptistae
Munera tibi Dne. pro. s. martyris
Conferat nobis Dne. s. Ioannis utrumque

[*iii Kal. Sept. Nat. SS. Felicis et Adaucti.*   Gerb. p. 172.
Maiestatem tuam Dne. supplices
Hostias Dne. tuae plebis
Repleti Dne. muneribus sacris]

Kal. Sept. Nat. S. Prisci.   Gerb. p. 172.
O. s. D. fortitudo certantium
*Eius tibi precibus Dne. q. grata reddatur
VD. Qui sic tribuis ecclesiam
Praesta q. Dne. ut sacramenti tui

Hebd. xvi post Pentecosten.   Gerb. p. 173.
Custodi Dne. q. ecclesiam tuam
Praesta nobis m. D. ut placationem
Concede nobis Dne. q. ut haec hostia
*VD. Qui aeternitate sacerdotii
Purificent semper et muniant

vi Id. Sept. Nativitas S. Mariae. Eodem die Nat. S. Adriani.   Gerb. pp. 173, 174.
*Adiuvet nos q. Dne. sanctae Mariae
Adesto nobis o. D. beatae Mariae festa
[Supplicationes servorum tuorum D. miserator]
*Accipe munera Dne. quae in b. Mariae
[Suscipe Dne. q. hostias placationis]
[Unigeniti tui Dne. nobis succurrat]
*VD. Vere dignum ... salutare nos tibi
Sumptis Dne. sacramentis intercedente
[Famulis tuis Dne. caelestis gratiae munus]

[*v Id. Sept. Nat. S. Gurgonii.*   Gerb. p. 174.
Sanctus Dne. Gurgonius sua nos
Grata sit tibi Dne. nostrae servitutis oblatio
*VD. Teque in sanctorum tuorum confessionibus
Familiam tuam D. suavitas illa contingat]

Gerb. pp. 174, 175.	[*iii Id. Sept. Nat. SS. Proti et Iacinti.* Beati Proti nos Dne. et Iacinti Pro sanctorum Proti et Iacinti Percepta nos Dne. tua sancta purificent]
Gerb. p. 175.	*Hebd. xvii post Pentecosten.* Ecclesiam tuam Dne. miseratio continuata *Da q. Dne. hanc mentem populo tuo Tua nos Dne. sacramenta custodiant VD. Ut qui te auctore *Mentes nostras et corpora possideat
Gerb. p. 175.	*xviii Kal. Oct. Exaltatio S. Crucis.* *D. qui nos hodierna die exaltatione Devotas Dne. humilitatis nostrae *Adesto familiae tuae q. clemens *Ad crucem salutandam.* D. qui Unigeniti tui Dni. nostri
Gerb. pp. 175, 176.	[*Eodem die Nat. SS. Cornelii et Cypriani.* Beatorum martyrum pariterque pontificum Adesto Dne. supplicationibus Plebis tuae Dne. munera benignus *VD. Tuamque in sanctorum *Sacro munere vegetatos sanctorum]
Gerb. p. 176.	[*Item Missa Propria Cypriani Episcopi.* *Salutarem nobis dedit hodierna die Sacrificium nostrum Dne. ipsa tibi sit VD. Beati Cypriani natalis Satiati sumus Dne. muneribus]
Gerb. p. 177.	[*xvii Kal. Oct. Nat. S. Nicomedis.* *Adesto Dne. populo tuo ut b. Nicomedis Intercessio S. Nicomedis misericordiae Purificent nos Dne. sacramenta]
Gerb. p. 177.	[*xvi Kal. Oct. Nat. S. Eufimiae.* O. s. D. qui infirma mundi Praesta q. Dne. D. noster ut sicut Sanctificet nos Dne. q. tui perceptio]

APPENDIX. 357

[*Eodem die Nat. SS. Luciae et Geminiani.* Gerb. pp.
Infirmitatem nostram q. Dne. propitius 177, 178.
Vota populi tui Dne. propitius intende
Exaudi Dne. preces nostras et sanctorum]

Orationes Mensis Septimi. Die Dom. ad S. Petrum [1]. Gerb.
Absolve q. Dne. tuorum delicta p. 178.
Q. o. D. preces nostras respice
Pro nostrae servitutis augmento
VD. Quia quum laude
Q. o. D. ut quos divina

xii Kal. Oct. Vig. S. Matthaei Ap. et Evang. Gerb.
Da nobis o. D. ut beati Matthaei p. 181.
Apostolicae reverentiae culmen
B. Matthaei evangelistae q. Dne

xi Kal. Oct. Nat. S. Matthaei Evang. Gerb.
Beati evangelistae Matthaei Dne. precibus p. 181.
Supplicationibus apostolicis b. Matthaei
VD. Qui ecclesiam tuam in tuis
Perceptis Dne. sacramentis beato Matthaeo

Aliae Orationes.
Sit Dne. b. Matthaeus evangelista
Praesta q. o. D. ut qui iugiter

Feria iv ad S. Mariam. Gerb. pp.
Misericordiae tuae remediis q. Dne. fragilitas 178, 179.
Praesta q. Dne. familiae supplicanti
*D. qui de his terrae fructibus
[VD. Qui nos ideo collectis]
Sumentes Dne. dona caelestia

Feria vi ad Apostolos. Gerb.
Praesta q. o. D. ut observationes p. 179.
Accepta tibi sint Dne. q. nostri dona ieiunii
[*VD. Sub tuae maiestatis pio iustoque moderamine]
Q. o. D. ut de perceptis muneribus

Sabbato ad S. Petrum in xii Lect. Gerb. pp.
Tribue q. fidelibus tuis 179, 180.
Da nobis q. o. D. ut ieiunando
D. humanae salutis operator

[1] R. adds *Ebdōm xviii post pentecosten.*

[Omnipotentiam tuam Dne. prompta mente]
Ut nos Dne. tribuis solemne tibi
Post Bened. D. cuius adoranda potentia
Haec hostia Dne. q. et vincula
[*VD. Et tibi sanctificare]
Perficiant in nobis Dne. q. tua sacramenta
Suscipe Dne. preces populi supplicantis

Gerb.
p. 180.

Dominica Vacat.

O. s. D. misericordiam tuam ostende
Tuere q. Dne. familiam tuam
Huius te Dne. muneris oblatione
VD. Qui vicit diabolum
*Caelestis mensae q. Dne. sacrosancta

Gerb.
p. 182.

[*v Kal. Oct. Nat. SS. Cosmae et Damiani.*
Magnificet te Dne. sanctorum Cosmae et Damiani
In tuorum Dne. pretiosa morte
VD. Clementiam tuam suppliciter
Sit nobis Dne. sacramenti tui]

Gerb.
p. 183.

iii Kal. Oct. Dedicatio Basilicae Angeli Michaelis.

D. qui miro ordine angelorum
Da nobis o. D. b. archangeli Michaelis
Hostias tibi Dne. laudis offerimus
[Munus populi tui Dne. q. dignanter]
VD. Sancti Michaelis archangeli merita
Beati archangeli tui Michaelis
Adesto plebi tuae m. D. et ut gratiae
Perpetuum nobis Dne. tuae miserationis

Gerb.
p. 184.

Hebd. xx post Pentecosten.

*Fac nos Dne. q. prompta voluntate
Tua nos Dne. q. gratia semper praeveniat
Munda nos Dne. sacrificii praesentis
VD. Precantes ut Iesus Christus
Purifica Dne. q. mentes nostras benignus

Gerb.
p. 185.

[*Non. Oct. Nat. S. Marci Episcopi*[1].

Exaudi Dne. preces nostras et interveniente
Benedictio tua Dne. larga descendat
Da q. Dne. fidelibus populis]

---

[1] R. has here *vi Nō. Oct. Nat̄l Sc̄i Leudegarii.* See Gerb. p. 184.

APPENDIX. 359

[*Eodem die Nat. SS. Marcelli et Apulei.*]   Gerb. p. 185.
∗Sanctorum nos Dne. Marcelli et Apulei
Maiestatem tuam nobis Dne. q. haec hostia
∗Sacramentis Dne. muniamur acceptis]

Hebd. xxi post Pentecosten.   Gerb. p. 185.
Da q. Dne. populo tuo diabolica vitare contagia
Custodi nos o. D. ut tua dextera
Maiestatem tuam Dne. suppliciter
∗VD. et suppliciter exorare ut sic bonis tuis
Sanctificationibus tuis o. D. et vitia

[*Pridie Id. Oct. Nat. S. Calisti Episcopi.*]   Gerb. pp. 185, 186.
D. qui nos conspicis ex nostra
Mystica nobis Dne. prosit oblatio
Q. o. D. ut et reatum nostrum]

Hebd. xxii post Pentecosten.   Gerb. p. 186.
Dirigat corda nostra Dne. q. tuae
Tuis Dne. q. adesto supplicibus et inter
D. qui nos per huius sacrificii
VD. Qui propterea iure punis
Gratias tibi referimus Dne. sacro munere

xi Kal. (sic: R. has *xvi K̄.*) *Nov. Nat. S. Lucae Evang.*   Gerb. p. 187.
Interveniat pro nobis Dne. q. sanctus tuus
Donis caelestibus da q. Dne. libera
[∗VD. Te in confessorum tuorum]
Praesta q. o. aet. D. ut id quod

Hebd. xxiii post Pentecosten.   Gerb. p. 188.
O. et m. D. universa nobis adversantia
∗Da q. o. D. sic nos tuam veniam
Haec munera q. Dne. quae oculis
VD. Clementiam tuam suppliciter exorare
Tua nos Dne. medicinalis operatio

vi Kal. Nov. Vig. Apost. Simonis et Iudae.   Gerb. pp. 188, 189.
Concede q. o. D. ut sicut apostolorum
Muneribus nostris Dne. apostolorum
[∗VD. Quia tu es mirabilis]
Sumpto Dne. sacramento suppliciter

v Kal. Nov. Nat. Apost. Simonis et Iudae.   Gerb. p. 189.
D. qui nos per beatos apostolos
O. s. D. mundi creator et rector

*Gloriam Dne. sanctorum Apostolorum
*VD. Te in tuorum apostolorum glorificantes
Perceptis Dne. sacramentis suppliciter
Exaudi nos D. salutaris noster et apostolorum

Gerb.
p. 190.

Hebd. xxiv post Pentecosten.

Largire q. Dne. fidelibus tuis indulgentiam
*Delicta nostra Dne. quibus adversa
Caelestem nobis praebeant haec mysteria
*VD. Maiestatem tuam Dne. suppliciter
Ut sacris Dne. reddamur digni

Gerb.
p. 190.

[*Kal. Nov. Nat. S. Caesarii. Ad collectam ad SS. Cosmam et Damianum.*

Adesto Dne. martyrum deprecatione sanctorum

Ad Missam.

D. qui nos b. martyris tui Caesarii
Hostias tibi Dne. b. Caesarii
Huius nos Dne. perceptio sacramenti]

Gerb.
p. 191.

Hebd. xxv post Pentecosten.

D. qui nos regendo conservas
Familiam tuam q. Dne. continua pietate
Suscipe Dne. propitiatus hostias
*VD. Per quem sanctum et benedictum
Immortalitatis alimoniam consecuti

Gerb. pp.
191, 192.

[*vi Id. Nov. Nat. SS. iv Coronatorum.*

Praesta q. o. D. ut qui gloriosos
*Annua martyrum tuorum Dne. vota recurrimus
Hostias tibi Dne. pro martyrum
VD. Celebrantes sanctorum natalitia coronatorum
Sanctorum tuorum coronatorum q. Dne.]

Gerb.
p. 192.

[*v Id. Nov. Nat. S. Theodori.*

*Praetende nobis Dne misericordiam tuam
Suscipe Dne. fidelium preces cum oblationibus
Sancti nos q. Dne. Theodori]

Gerb.
p. 192.

[*iii Id. Nov. Nat. S. Mennae.*

Praesta q. o. D. ut qui b. Mennae
B. Mennae martyris tui Dne. solemnia
Benedictio tua D. impleat corda fidelium]

APPENDIX. 361

Eodem die Nat. S. Martini Episcopi[1].

D. qui conspicis quia ex nulla
O. s. D. solemnitatem diei huius
B. Martini pontificis q. Dne. nobis pia
VD. Te in b. Martini pontificis
Tua Dne. sancta sumentes suppliciter
Exaudi Dne. populum tuum tota tibi
Praesta q. o. D. ut sicut divina laudamus

Gerb. pp. 192, 193.

Hebd. xxvi post Pentecosten.

D. refugium nostrum et virtus
D. quem docente Spiritu sancto
*Da m. D. ut haec nobis salutaris oblatio
VD. Tibi debitas laudes
Sumpsimus Dne. sacri dona mysterii

Gerb. p. 194.

[*xv Kal. Nov.* (sic) *Nat. S. Augustini Episcopi.*
Adesto supplicationibus nostris o. D. et quibus
S. confessoris tui Augustini nobis
*VD. Et in omni loco ac tempore
Ut nobis Dne. tua sacrificia dent]

Gerb. p. 195.

Hebd. xxvii post Pentecosten.

Excita Dne. q. tuorum fidelium voluntates
Excita Dne. tuorum corda fidelium
*Propitius esto Dne. supplicationibus nostris
VD. Tuum est enim omne quod vivimus
Concede nobis Dne. q. ut sacramenta

Gerb. p. 196.

xi Kal. Dec. Vig. S. Caeciliae.

S. martyris tuae Caeciliae Dne.
Muneribus nostris Dne. S. Caeciliae
[*VD. Beatae Caeciliae natalitium Dne.]
*Q. o. D. ut quorum nos tribuis communicare

Gerb. p. 196.

x Kal. Dec. Nat. S. Caeciliae.

*D. cui beata Caecilia ita castitatis
Haec hostia Dne. placationis et laudis
*VD. Qui perficit in infirmitate
*Haec nos Dne. gratia tua q. semper

Gerb. pp. 196, 197.

ix Kal. Dec.[2] *Nat. S. Clementis.*

O. s. D. qui in omnium sanctorum
Sacrificium tibi Dne. laudis offerimus

Gerb. pp. 197, 198.

---

[1] R. has *iii Id. Nov. Nat̄l Sc̄i Martini ad Mis.*   [2] *viii K̄. Decēm.* R.

[✱VD. Quoniam per sancti Spiritus largitatem]
✱Beati Clementis Dne. natalitio

Gerb. pp.
198, 199.

[*Eodem die Nat. S. Felicitatis.*
Praesta q. o. D. ut beatae Felicitatis
Munera tibi Dne. pro s. Felicitatis
Supplices te rogamus o. D. ut intervenientibus]

Gerb.
p. 199.

[*viii Kal. Dec. Nat. S. Crisogoni.*
✱Praesta nobis o. D. ut quem fidei
✱Offerimus Dne. preces et munera
VD. Qui nos assiduis martyrum
✱Annue Dne. q. ut mysteriis]

Gerb. pp.
199, 200.

Incipiunt orationes de Adventu. Dom. v ante Nat. Dni.
Excita Dne. potentiam tuam et veni et quod
Conscientias nostras q. o. D. quotidie
Sacrificium tibi Dne. celebrandum placatus
VD. Qui nos tanquam
✱Animae nostrae q. o. D. hoc potiantur

Gerb.
p. 200.

[*iii Kal. Dec. Nat. SS. Saturnini Crisanti Mauri et Dariae.*
Beatorum martyrum Dne. Saturnini et Crisanti
Populi tui Dne. q. tibi grata sit
Mysteriis Dne. repleti sumus votis et gaudiis]

Gerb. pp.
200, 201.

[*Eodem die*] (*iii Kl. Decēm.* R.) *Vig. S. Andreae Apostoli.*
Q. o. D. ut b. Andreas apostolus tuus
Tuere nos m. D. et b. Andreae
Sacrandum tibi Dne. munus offerimus
VD. Reverentiae tuae dicato ieiunio
Perceptis Dne. sacramentis suppliciter

Gerb. pp.
201, 202.

Prid. Kal. Dec. Nat. S. Andreae Apostoli.
Maiestatem tuam Dne. suppliciter exoramus
D. qui humanum genus tuorum retibus
Sacrificium nostrum tibi Dne. q. b. Andreae
✱VD. Adest enim nobis dies magnificus
Beati Andreae apostoli Dne. q. intercessione
Beati Andreae apostoli supplicatione
Ad vesperum. Da nobis q. Dne. D. noster b. Andreae
Exaudi Dne. populum tuum cum s. apostoli

Gerb.
p. 202.

Dom. iv ante Nat. Domini.
Excita Dne. q. potentiam tuam et veni et ab
Praeveniat nos q. o. D. tua gratia

Haec sacra nos Dne. potenti virtute
VD. Cui proprium est ac singulare
Suscipiamus Dne. misericordiam tuam

Orationes de Adventu (*Domini* R.) *quotidianis diebus ad Missam.*   Gerb. p. 202.
    D. qui conspicis quia in tua pietate
    Subveniat nobis Dne. misericordia
    Grata tibi sint Dne. munera quibus
    Da q. o. D. cunctae familiae tuae

Item alia Missa.   Gerb. p. 203.
Excita Dne. potentiam tuam et veni ut tua
Festina ne tardaveris Dne. D. noster
Intende q. Dne. sacrificium singulare
Hos quos reficis Dne. sacramentis

[*Alia*   Gerb. p. 203.
Exultemus q. Dne. D. noster omnes recti corde
Fac nos Dne. q. mala nostra toto corde
Concede q. o. D. ut huius sacrificii
Spiritum in nobis Dne. tuae caritatis
Preces populi tui q. o. D. clementer]

Alias orationes de Adventu.   Gerb. pp. 209, 210.
✻Concede q. o. D. ut magnae
Mentes nostras q. Dne. lumine tuae visitationis
Preces populi tui q. Dne. clementer
Praesta q. o. D. ut Filii tui
Concede q. o. D. ut quia sub peccati
[Q. o. D. preces nostras]
[✻Concede q. o. D. hanc gratiam]
[Voci nostrae q. Dne. aures tuae pietatis]
[✻Porrige nobis Dne. dexteram tuae venerationis]
[Festinantes o. D. in occursum]
[✻Praesta q. o. D. ut quia pro peccatis]
[✻D. qui nos(tram?) conspicis semper]
[✻Adesto q. o. D. atque in cunctis]

[*vii Id. Dec. Oct. S. Andreae Apostoli.*   Gerb. p. 203.
Protegat nos Dne. saepius b. Andreae
Indulgentiam nobis praebeant haec munera
Adiuvet familiam tuam tibi Dne. supplicando]

APPENDIX.

Gerb. pp. 203, 204.

[*iii Id. Dec. Nat. S. Damasi Papae.*
Misericordiam tuam Dne. nobis q. interveniente
Da nobis q. Dne. semper haec tibi
Sumptum Dne. caelestis remedii sacramentum]

Gerb. p. 204.

Dom. iii ante Nat. Domini.
Excita Dne. corda nostra ad praeparandas
Praecinge q. Dne. D. noster lumbos mentis
Placare Dne. q. humilitatis nostrae
[*VD. cui proprium est veniam]
Repleti cibo spiritalis alimoniae

Gerb. pp. 204, 205.

[*Id. Dec. Nat. S. Luciae.*
Intercessio nos q. Dne. s. Luciae
*Q. virtutum caelestium D. ut sacrificia
*Laeti Dne. sumpsimus sacramenta]

Gerb. p. 205.

Dom. ii ante Nat. Domini.
Aurem tuam q. Dne. precibus nostris
Fac nos q. Dne. D. noster pervigiles
Devotionis nostrae tibi q. Dne. hostia
VD. Referentes gratiarum de praeteritis
Imploramus Dne. clementiam tuam

Gerb. pp. 205, 206.

Mense Decimo Fer. iv ad S. Mariam.
Praesta q. o. D. ut redemptionis
Festina q. Dne. ne tardaveris
Ecclesiae tuae Dne. munera placatus
VD. Ieiunii observatione quaerere
Tuorum nos Dne. largitate donorum
Gratiae tuae q. Dne. supplicibus

Gerb. p. 206.

Feria vi ad Apostolos.
Excita q. Dne. potentiam tuam et veni ut hi
Prope esto Dne. omnibus invocantibus
Praesta Dne. q. ut dicato
VD. Qui non solum peccata dimittis
Prosint nobis Dne. sumpta mysteria

Gerb. pp. 206, 207.

Sabbato ad S. Petrum in xii Lect.
D. qui conspicis quia ex nostra
Adesto Dne. supplicationibus nostris et praesentis
*Indignos q. Dne. famulos tuos
[D. qui pro animarum expiatione]
[Miserationum tuarum Dne. q. praeveniamur]

Post Bened. D. qui tribus pueris
Ecclesiae tuae Dne. munera sanctifica
VD. Quoniam salubre meditantes
Q. Dne. D. noster ut sacrosancta
Veniat Dne. q. populo tuo supplicanti

Die Dominica Vacat.   Gerb. pp. 207, 208.

Excita Dne. potentiam tuam et veni et magna
Adiuva Dne. fragilitatem plebis tuae
Sacrificiis praesentibus Dne. placatus
VD. Sanctificator et conditor
Sumptis muneribus Dne. q. ut cum

xii Kal. Ian. Nat. S. Thomae Apostoli.   Gerb. p. 208.
Da nobis q. Dne. beati apostoli Thomae
Debitum Dne. nostrae reddimus servitutis
VD. Qui ecclesiam tuam in apostolicis
Conserva Dne. populum tuum et quem

Denuntiatio Natalitii unius Martyris.   Gerb. p. 214.
Noverit vestra devotio
Item pluraliter Quo diaboli

In Vigilia[1] *unius sancti.*   Gerb. pp. 214, 215.
Q. o. D. ut nostra devotio
Magnifica Dne. beati *Ill.* solemnia
[VD. Gloriosi *Ill.* martyris *vel* confessoris]
*Sancta tua Dne. de beati *Ill.*

In Nat. Unius Martyris.   Gerb. pp. 215, 216.
Votivus nos Dne. q. b. martyris
[D. qui sanctam nobis huius diei]
Praesentia munera q. Dne. ita serena
*VD. Te semper in laude
Sumpsimus Dne. s. *Ill.* martyris
Plebs tua Dne. sancti martyris tui
Sancti *Ill.* martyris tui Dne.
[*Beati martyris tui *Ill.* nos q. Dne. precibus]
[Beati martyris tui *Ill.* nos q. Dne. patrociniis]

In Nat. Unius Confessoris.   Gerb. p. 221.
Adesto Dne. precibus nostris quas in s. Confessoris
Sancti confessoris tui *Ill.* nos q. Dne.
Propitiare Dne. q. supplicationibus

[1] *In Natl.* R.

[VD. Qui in omnium sanctorum]
Ut nobis Dne. tua sacrificia dent
Misericordiam tuam Dne. nobis
[*O. s. D. cui cuncta famulantur elementa]
[*Sancti Dne. confessoris tui *Ill.*]

Gerb. pp. 223, 224.

In Nat. Virginum.

D. qui inter caetera potentiae tuae (Gerb. 223)
[D. qui nos hodie beatae et sanctae]
Hostias tibi Dne. beatae *Ill.* martyris
[*VD. Maxime hodie in beatae]
Adiuvent nos q. Dne. et haec
D. qui inter caetera potentiae tuae (Gerb. 224)

Gerb. pp. 225, 226.

In Nat. Plurimorum Sanctorum.

Praesta Dne. q. ut sicut sanctorum
Sancti tui q. Dne. iugiter nobis
Munera plebis tuae Dne. q. beatorum
VD. Et te in tuorum honore
Et natalitiis sanctorum Dne. et sacramenti
[Adesto Dne. populo tuo cum sanctorum]
[Magnificantes Dne. clementiam tuam]
[Da nobis o. D. in sanctorum tuorum]
[Sanctorum tuorum *Ill.* suffragiis]
[Exaudi nos o. et m. D. et sanctorum]
Tribue q. Dne. sanctos tuos iugiter

Gerb. pp. 217, 218.

In Nat. Plurimorum martyrum.

O. s. D. qui per gloriosa bella
[O. s. D. qui in sanctorum tuorum cordibus]
Salutari sacrificio Dne. populus tuus
VD. qui sanctorum martyrum
*Celebrantes quae pro martyrum
[Ad defensionem fidelium Dne. q. dexteram]
[*O. et m. D. fidelium lumen animarum]
Concede q. o. D. ut sanctorum
[*Sanctorum martyrum tuorum *Ill.* nos]
[O. s. D. qui nos idoneos non esse]

Gerb. p. 220.

[*In Basilicis Martyrum.*

Indulgentiam nobis Dne. q. s. *Ill.*
*Sacrificium Dne. quod desideranter
VD. Quia dum b. *Ill.* merita
Beati *Ill.* martyris Dne. suffragiis]

APPENDIX.

Missa votiva in Sanctorum [*Commemoratione*¹].   Gerb. p. 281.
∗O. et m. D. cui redditur votum in Hierusalem
∗Exaudi o. D. deprecationem nostram pro famulo
[∗VD. Cuius potentia deprecanda]
Muneris divini percepti q. Dne.

*Incipiunt orationes quotidianis diebus ad Missam*².   Gerb. p. 230.
Perpetua q. Dne. pace custodi quos in te
Adesto nobis m. D. et tuae pietatis
Adesto nobis q. Dne. et preces
Mysteria sancta nos Dne. et spiritalibus
Protector in te sperantium D. et subditarum

Item alia Missa.   Gerb. pp. 230, 231.
Exaudi nos miserator et m. D.
Plebis tuae D. ad te corda converte
Hostias q. Dne. suscipe placatus oblatas
Sancta tua nos Dne. q. et a peccatis
Suscipe q. Dne. preces nostras

[*Item alia Missa.*   Gerb. p. 231.
Q. o. D. ut plebs tua toto tibi corde
Miserere nostri D. et tuae
∗Suscipe Dne. q. hostiam redemptionis
Da q. o. D. ut mysteriorum
Adsit Dne. fidelibus tuis sacrae]

[*Item alia Missa.*   Gerb. p. 231.
Rege nostras Dne. propitius voluntates
Da famulis tuis D. indulgentiam peccatorum
Tua sacramenta nos D. circumtegant
VD. Ut quia tui est operis si quid
Tua sancta nobis o. D. quae sumpsimus
Familiam tuam Dne. pervigili pietate]

[*Item alia Missa.*   Gerb. pp. 231, 232.
Comprime Dne. q. noxios semper incursus
Tu Dne. semper a nobis omnem remove
In tuo conspectu Dne. q. talia
VD. Ut non in nobis nostra malitia
Quotidiani Dne. q. munere sacramenti
Respice Dne. propitius plebem tuam]

¹ The word in S. is over an erasure; R. omits it.
² R. adds *cum canone*.

APPENDIX.

Gerb. pp. 232–238.

Item alia Missa.

Ecclesiae tuae Dne. voces placatus
Ab omnibus nos defende q. Dne. semper
Offerimus tibi Dne.

⟨Here follows the *Canon Actionis*.⟩

[Quod ore sumpsimus Dne. mente capiamus]
*[Conservent nos q. Dne munera tua]

⟨R. inserts here a series of Postcommunions. See pp. 236, 237 *supra*.⟩

Gerb. pp. 238–240.

Item Benedictiones super Populum.

Dne. s. P. o. aet. D. de abundantia
Gregem tuum Pastor bone placatus
[Benedic Dne. hanc familiam tuam]
Benedicat vos D. omni benedictione
Plebis tuae q. Dne. ad te corda
Propitiare populo tuo D. ut a suis
Tuere Dne. familiam tuam et spiritalibus
[Familia tua D. et ad celebranda]
[Fideles tuos Dne. q. corpore]
[Propitiare Dne. populo tuo et ab omnibus]
*[Adesto Dne. supplicibus tuis et nihil]
[Da q. Dne. populo tuo et mentem]
[Plebem nomini tuo subditam Dne.]

Here the S. Gallen MS. now ends, the last gathering of the volume having apparently lost its last leaf. The Rheinau MS., which omits the last six of the *Benedictiones super Populum* contained in the S. Gallen MS., adds one which does not appear at this point in the latter:—

Familiam tuam Dne. pervigili (see Gerb. p. 239).

After the eight *Benedictiones super Populum* follows:—Expliciunt benedictiones anni circuli est numerus lxxii. Incipit Liber secundus de extrema parte. Orationes ad matutinis.

Matutina supplicum vota
Emitte q. Dne. lucem
D. qui diem discernis ac nocte (*sic*)

Gerb. pp. 241, 242.

Al. orationes ad Vespr̄.

Oriatur Dne. nascentibus
Tuus est dies Dne. et tua

Alias orationes.

[The series agrees with that in Gerbert beginning with
    Vox nostra, &c. (p. 242),
and ending with
    Iniquitates nostras, &c. (p. 243).
Then follow the prayers for Prime, Terce, Sext, and None given by Gerbert, p. 243.]

The contents of the latter portion of the Rheinau MS. may be indicated by the headings of the various parts.

Ordo Baptisterii. (Gerb. pp. 248-256.)
In Dedict. Basilice anniversarii. (Gerb. pp. 228, 9.)
Ad Clericum faciendum. (Gerb. pp. 256, 7.)
Pro his qui prius barbam tundit. (Gerb. p. 257.)
Missa consecracio presbiteri. (Gerb. p. 257.)
Missa pro regibus. (Gerb. pp. 276, 7.)
Orat. pro sterilitate terrae. (Gerb. pp. 300, 1.)
Orat. ad pluviam postulandum. (Gerb. p. 301, Roman type.)
Orat. ad poscendum serenitat. (Gerb. pp. 302, 2, Roman type.)
Orat. pro fulgoribus. (Gerb. p. 303.)
Benedict. aq. et salis ad exorciz. ad fulgora. (Gerb. p. 303.)
Orat. pro tempest. et fulgora. (Gerb. pp. 303, 4, Roman type.)
Orat. de Lacram. (?) vel de quacumque tribulat. (Gerb. pp. 275, 6.)
Orat. tempore quod absit mortalitas. (Gerb. pp. 304, 5.)

[There is a leaf wanting in R. at this point, the last mentioned Missa breaking off with the title *Post Com.* while the next leaf begins with the end of a Secret, followed by the Postcommunion, *Sanctificati divino mysterio*, which Gerbert treats as part of the *Missa in tempore mortalitatis*. Probably the missing leaf contained *Orat. ad proficiscendum in itinere* and the first part of the *Missa pro navigantibus* to which the fragment of the Secret and the Postcommunion *Sanctificati divino mysterio* belong].

Bened. aque et salis ad spargen. in domum.	(Gerb. p. 306.)
Bened. aque.	,,
Bened. salis.	,,
Exorcismus salis et aque.	,,
Ad spargendum faciendum exorcis. salis.	,,
Ben. salis.	,,
Ben. domus noue.	(Gerb. p. 307.)
Orat. ad missa in domo nouo.	,,
Ad frug. nouas bened.	,,
Bene uuae sive fabe.	(Gerb. p. 308.)
Bened. pomorum.	,,

APPENDIX.

Bened. arboris.	(Gerb. p. 308.)
Bened. ad omnia que volueris.	"
Bened. panis.	"
Benedictio vini.	"
Bened. salis.	"
Item al. ad salis Ben.	(Gerb. p. 309.)
Orat. in domo infirmorum.	(Gerb. pp. 309, 10.)
Oratio super infirmo in domo.	(Gerb. p. 310.)
Orat. ad Missa pro infirmo.	(Gerb. p. 311, Roman type.)
Orat. pro reddita sanitate.	(Gerb. p. 312.)
Missa pro salute vivorum.	(Gerb. pp. 269, 70, Roman type.)
Mis. votiva pro remedium animae.	(Gerb. pp. 286, 7.)
Mis. pro tribulantibus de quavislibet extra [? et contra] flagella corporis.	(Gerb. pp. 273, 4.)
Missa votiva pro eos qui sibi in corpore vivi mis. cantare rogant.	(Gerb. p. 282.)
Item alia missa votiva.	(Gerb. pp. 282, 3.)
Missa votiva cum lectiones.	(Gerb. pp. 283, 4.)
Item alia missa pro devoto.	(Gerb. pp. 285, 6.)
Mis. votiva.	(Gerb. pp. 279, 80.)
Mis. in Natl. sanctorum vel pro memoria vivorum sive agenda mortuorum fidelium in Christo.	(Gerb. pp. 266, 7.)
Oratio pro infirmo.	(Gerb. p. 312.)
Item alia.	"
Reconciliatio peñt. ad mortem.	"
Alia.	"
Ordo ad commendationem anime.	(Gerb. pp. 312, 3.)
Orat. super defunctis vel commendat. anime.	(Gerb. pp. 313, 5.)
Missa pro defuncto sacerdote.	(Gerb. pp. 315, 7.)
Item al. mis. pro sac. epi.	(Gerb. p. 317.)
Item alia mis. pro sacerdote sive abb.	(Gerb. pp. 318, 9.)
Orat. ad Mis. in Natl. Scorum. siue agenda mortuorum.	(Gerb. p. 319.)
Missa pro defuncto nuper baptizato.	(Gerb. pp. 319, 20.)
Missa quam sacerdos pro semetipso debet canere.	(Gerb. pp. 291, 2.)
Item alia Mis. pro semetipso.	(Gerb. pp. 292, 3.)
Orat. pro defunctis desiderantibus penitentem (*sic*) et minime consecrantem (*sic*).	(Gerb. p. 320.)

APPENDIX.

Mis. unius defunctis (*sic*) laici. . . . (Gerb. pp. 320, 1.)
Item al. Mis. in agenda plurimorum. . . (Gerb. p. 323, Roman type.)
It. alia Mis. in cimiteriis. . . . . (Gerb. pp. 326, 7, Roman type.)
Item alia Mis. in die depositio defuncti vel iii vii^{mi} et xxx^{mi}. . . . . . (Gerb. pp. 327, 8.)
Orat. pro defunctorum ad Mis. . . . (Gerb. pp. 328, 9, Roman type.)
Inpositio manū. inergumin. catecuminum. . (Gerb. p. 253.)
It. alia prouolus (*sic*) energumen.
Item alia in nergumen (*sic*) baptizatum.
    Super hominem qui a demonio vexatur. (Gerb. vol. ii. p. 128.)
    [A leaf is lost, containing part of the exorcism: this appears both from examination of the gatherings of the MS. and from a comparison of the text with that of the same exorcism as it appears in Muratori's Gregorian Sacramentary, *Liturg. Rom. Vet.* ii. 237–40].
In dei nomine incipit Breviariumapostolorum. (Gerb. pp. 453, 4.)
Incipit Martlogium anni circuli. . . . (Gerb. pp. 455 *sqq.*)
    [The Martyrologium is imperfect. What remains of it is printed in M. Delisle's *Mémoire sur d'Anciens Sacramentaires*, pp. 310–13.]

INDEX OF LITURGICAL FORMS

[This Index includes both the forms contained in the Text and those of which the opening words are cited in the Appendix. Numerals below 316 refer to the Text, numerals above 316 to the Appendix. Where words or letters are enclosed in brackets there is a difference in respect of those words or letters between the forms referred to under the heading.]

A domo tua q. Dne., 261.
A plebe tua q. Dne., 164.
Ab omni
  nos q. Dne. vetustate, 337.
  reatu nos, 278.
Ab omnibus nos defende, 244, 368.
Abrenuntias Satanae, 79, 115.
Absolve q. Dne. tuorum, 357.
Accepta
  sit in conspectu, 341.
  tibi sint Dne. q., 36, 328, 357.
Accepta tibi sit Dne.
  nostrae, 18, 40, 326.
  q. hodierna, 165, 317.
  sacratae, 211, 322.
Accepta tibi sit in conspectu, 212.
Accipe et
  commenda, 145.
  esto verbi, 145.
Accipe munera Dne., 193, 355.
Accipe q. Dne.
  munera, 318.
  munus, 344.
Accipe signum crucis, 113.
Actiones nostras q. Dne., 327.
Ad
  defensionem fidelium, 212, 366.
  gloriam Dne. tui, 153.
  hostes nostros, 32, 328.
  martyrum tuorum, 167, 324.
  preces nostras, 149.
  te nos Dne. clamantes, 260.
Adest o venerabilis, 63, 333.
Adesto Dne.
  Deus noster ut per, 104, 341.
  famulis tuis et opem, 32, 328.
Adesto Dne. fidelibus tuis et
  quibus, 249, 324.
  quos, 43, 332.
Adesto Dne.
  invocationibus, 250.
  martyrum deprecatione, 360.
  muneribus, 8, 319.

Adesto Dne. populis
  qui sacra, 40, 274, 331.
  tuis in tua, 323.
Adesto Dne. populo tuo
  cum, 210, 366.
  ut beati, 356.
  ut quae, 339.
Adesto Dne. precibus
  nostris, 189, 365.
  populi tui, 352.
Adesto Dne. propitius plebi, 33.
Adesto Dne. quaesumus
  nostrae redemptionis, 92, 93.
  populo tuo, 123, 344.
  redemptionis, 34.
Adesto Dne. supplicationibus nostris et
  beati Ruffi, 195, 354.
  famulos, 264, 283.
  hanc domum, 283.
  hanc oblationem, 265, 269, 312.
  hoc solemne, 17, 326.
  institutis, 265.
  intercedente, 194, 353.
  intercessione, 352.
  me, 64, 333.
  nihil, 281.
  populum, 5, 318.
  praesentis, 221, 364.
  sperantibus, 340.
  viam, 245.

Adesto Dne. supplicationibus nostris
  nec sit, 14, 325.
  quas in, 356.
  ut qui, 322.
  ut sicut, 108, 343.
Adesto Dne.
  supplicibus tuis et nihil, 241, 368.
  tuis adesto, 116.
Adesto familiae tuae, 198, 356.
Adesto nobis
  Dne. D. noster et quos, 331.
  misericors D., 242, 367.

(Adesto nobis)
  o. D. beatae, 165, 323, 355.
  q. Dne. et preces, 367.
  q. o. D. et per, 329.
Adesto plebi tuae m. D. et ut, 200, 358.
Adesto quaesumus Dne.
  familiae tuae, 337.
  fidelibus, 197.
  pro anima, 312.
  pro animabus, 311.
Adesto q. Dne. supplicationibus nostris et in tua, 321, 326.
  ut esse, 327.
Adesto q. Dne. tuae
  adesto, 100.
  familiae, 338.
Adesto q. o. D.
  ac ieiunio, 21.
  atque in cunctis, 221, 363.
  honorum dator, 26.
Adesto supplicationibus nostris o. D. et quibus, 331, 361.
Adiuva Dne. fragilitatem, 216, 365.
Adiuva nos D. salutaris noster
  et ad, 13.
  et in, 42, 328.
  ut quae, 16, 326.
Adiuva nos Dne.
  D. noster beati, 303.
  q. eorum, 8, 319.
Adiuvent nos q. Dne. (et) haec, 165, 323, 353, 366.
Adiuvet familiam tuam, 208, 363.
Adiuvet nos q. Dne.
  sanctae, 197, 355.
  sanctum, 98, 339.
Adsit Dne.
  fidelibus tuis sacrae, 244, 367.
  q. propitiatio, 322.
Adsit ecclesiae tuae, 7, 319.
Adsit nobis Dne. q.
  sancta, 164, 322.
  sancti, 191, 352.
Adsit nobis q. Dne. virtus, 124, 344.
Aeternam ac iustissimam, 49.
Afflictionem familiae tuae, 331.
Altari tuo Dne. superimposita, 339.
Animabus q. Dne. famulorum, 309.
Animae nostrae q. o. D. hoc, 217, 362.
Anniversarii fratres, 124, 346.
Annua martyrum tuorum, 203, 360.
Annue Dne. q. ut mysteriis, 362.
Annue misericors Deus ut
  hostias, 331.
  qui divina, 344.
Annue q. Dne. ut
  merita, 172, 341.
  sanctae, 170, 339.
Annue q. o. D. ut sacramentorum, 126, 346.
Antiqui memores chirographi, 297.
Aperturi vobis filii, 50.
Apostoli tui Pauli, 323.
Apostolicae reverentiae culmen, 206, 357.
Apostolicis nos Dne. q. 183, 349.

Ascendant ad te Dne. preces, 304, 305, 327.
Audi maledicte Satanas, 48.
Aufer a nobis Dne., 15, 325.
Auge
  fidem tuam, 37, 330.
  in nobis Dne. q. fidem, 291.
Augeatur in nobis Dne., 237, 321.
Aurem tuam q. Dne. precibus, 364.
Auxiliante Dno. D. et salvatore, 22.
Auxiliare Dne. populo tuo, 62, 202, 321.
Auxilientur nobis Dne. sumpta, 233, 318.
Auxilium tuum nobis Dne. 354.
Averte Dne. q. a fidelibus, 258.

Beatae et gloriosae, 169, 339.
Beati Andreae apostoli, 207, 362.
Beati apostoli tui
  Bartholomaei, 354.
  Iacobi, 350.
Beati archangeli (tui) Michaelis, 200, 358.
Beati Clementis
  Dne. natalitio, 205, 362.
  sacerdotis, 205.
Beati evangelistae
  Ioannis, 7.
  Matthaei, 357.
Beati
  Georgii martyris, 340.
  Illius martyris, 366.
  Ioannis Baptistae, 177, 179, 347.
Beati Laurenti martyris
  honorabilem, 193, 353.
  tui, 190, 352.
Beati
  Laurenti nos faciat, 192, 353.
  Martini pontificis, 361.
  martyris tui, 303, 365.
  Matthaei evangelistae, 357.
  Mennae martyris, 360.
Beati nos
  Dne. Baptistae, 178, 347.
  q. Dne. Iuvenalis, 172, 341.
Beati
  Proti nos Dne. 356.
  Sixti Dne. tui sacerdotis, 188, 351.
  Tiburtii nos Dne., 352.
  Urbani martyris, 343.
Beatorum apostolorum, 171, 341, 349.
Beatorum martyrum
  Dne. Saturnini, 206, 362.
  Ioannis et Pauli, 179, 348.
  pariterque pontificum, 199, 356.
  tuorum Ioannis, 179.
Beatorum Petri et Pauli, 180.
Beatus
  Andreas pro nobis, 207.
  martyr Stephanus, 7, 318.
Benedic Dne.
  dona tua, 293.
  et has fruges, 107.
  familiam tuam, 110.
  hanc domum, 288.
  hanc familiam, 240, 368.

INDEX OF LITURGICAL FORMS. 375

⟨Benedic Dne.⟩
  hos fructus, 294.
Benedic huic domui, 287.
Benedicat vos D. omni, 240, 368.
Benedictio Dne. q. in tuos, 43, 331.
Benedictio tua
  D. impleat corda, 360.
  Dne. larga, 171, 358.
Benedictionem
  Dne. nobis conferat, 102, 339.
  tuam Dne. populus, 257, 319.
Bonorum D. operum institutor, 160.

Caelestem nobis praebeant, 233, 360.
Caelesti
  lumine q. Dne. semper, 12, 321.
  munere saginati, 213, 340.
Caelesti munere satiati
  o. D. tua, 194, 353.
  q. Dne. D. noster, 163, 188.
  q. Dne. ut haec, 180.
  q. o. D. tua, 194.
Caelestia dona capientibus, 39, 330.
Caelestibus
  Dne. pasti deliciis, 244, 324.
  refecti sacramentis, 354.
Caelestis
  doni benedictione, 65, 250, 332.
  mensae q. Dne. 201, 358.
Caelestis vitae
  munere vegetati, 17, 326.
  munus accipientes, 271.
Catechumeni recedant, 79.
Celebrantes quae pro martyrum, 366.
Christianam q. Dne. respice plebem, 100, 338.
Clementiam tuam Dne. suppliciter, 97, 339.
Commendamus tibi Dne., 299.
Commune votum communis oratio, 28.
Communicantes et diem Pentecosten, 123.
Communicantes et diem sacrat. celebrantes
  in quo incontaminata, 4, 318.
  quo Dnus. noster unigenitus, 107, 342.
  quo traditus est, 67, 333, 334.
  quo Unigenitus tuus, 11, 320.
Communicantes et
  diem sacratissimum Pentecosten, 120, 344.
  memoriam venerantes, 234.
  noctem, 89, 317, 335.
Comprime Dne. q. noxios, 244, 367.
Concede
  credentibus misericors D., 63, 333.
  Dne. electis nostris, 42.
Concede misericors D. ut
  devotus, 35, 101, 329.
  quod paschalibus, 99, 338.
  sicut nos, 40, 332.
Concede nobis Dne. praesidia, 121, 125, 325.

Concede nobis Dne. q. ut
  celebraturi, 43, 332.
  haec hostia, 230, 257, 331, 355.
  sacramenta, 3, 166, 361.
Concede nobis haec q. Dne. frequentare, 31, 227, 351.
Concede nobis misericors D.
  et digne, 12, 325.
  et studia, 278.
  ut sicut, 124, 344.
Concede nobis o. D. sanctae, 170.
Concede nobis o. D. ut
  despectis, 279.
  his muneribus, 177, 347.
  per annua, 17, 326.
  salutare, 318.
Concede nobis q. o. D. ad beatae, 353.
Concede o. D. ut paschalis, 121.
Concede q. Dne.
  apostolos tuos, 183.
  fidelibus tuis digne, 324.
  fragilitati nostrae, 36.
  semper nos per haec, 94, 337.
Concede q. Dne. ut
  oculis, 320.
  percepti, 68, 73, 333.
  sicut famulus, 140.
Concede q. o. D.
  ad eorum, 342.
  apostolos tuos, 349.
  fragilitati, 12, 325.
  hanc gratiam, 217, 363.
  sanctae martyris, 339.
Concede q. o. D. ut
  ad meliorem, 321.
  anima, 303.
  ecclesia, 101.
  festa paschalia, 336.
  huius sacrificii, 323, 363.
  magnae, 363.
  paschalis, 89, 121, 336.
Concede q. o. D. ut qui
  beati, 348.
  ex merito, 330.
  festa paschalia, 337.
  hodierna, 342.
  paschalis, 336.
  peccatorum, 336.
  protectionis, 329.
  resurrectionis, 336.
  solemnitatem, 343.
  sub, 219, 363.
Concede q. o. D. ut
  qui(a) sub, 219, 363.
  sanctorum, 163, 366.
  sicut apostolorum, 184, 359.
  Unigeniti, 2, 318.
  viam tuam, 226, 350.
Concurrat Dne. q. populus, 42.
Conferat nobis Dne. sancti Ioannis, 196, 355.
Confirma Dne. tuorum corda, 248.
Conscientias nostras q. o. D., 215, 362.
Conserva Dne.
  familiam tuam, 35, 329.

⟨Conserva Dne.⟩
populum tuum, 209, 365.
Conserva
(in) nobis q. Dne., 100, 338.
populum tuum D. et tuo, 244, 324.
Conserva q. Dne.
familiam tuam, 321.
populum tuum, 332.
Conservent nos q. Dne. munera, 368.
Consecramus et sanctificamus, 134.
Consecrare et sanctificare digneris, 134.
Consecrentur manus istae, 148.
Consolare Dne. hanc famulam, 291.
Conspirantes Dne. contra, 280.
Contere q. Dne. hostes, 273.
Converte nos D. salutaris, 221, 326.
Copiosa beneficia q. Dne., 138.
Cor populi tui q. Dne. converte, 280.
Corda nostra q. Dne. venturae, 10, 320.
Cordibus nostris
Dne. benignus infunde, 332.
q. Dne. benignus infunde, 19, 329.
Corporis sacri et pretiosi sanguinis, 349.
Corpus Dni. nostri, 117.
Creator et conservator humani, 133.
Credis in Deum Patrem, 86, 116.
Credo in unum Deum, 53, 55.
Crescat Dne. semper, 164, 204, 322.
Cuncta Dne. q. his muneribus, 3, 318.
Cunctis nos (q.) Dne. reatibus, 39, 329, 330.
Custodi Dne. q. ecclesiam, 229, 355.
Custodi nos
Dne. q. in tuo, 225, 350.
o. D. ut tua, 231, 359.

Da ecclesiae tuae Dne.
q. sancto Vito, 176, 347.
non superbe sapere, 248.
Da famulis et famulabus, 314.
Da famulis tuis
D. indulgentiam, 243, 367.
q. Dne. in tua, 264.
Da misericors D. ut
haec nobis salutaris, 361.
in resurrectione, 100, 338.
quod in tui, 61, 332.
Da nobis Dne. D. noster sanctorum, 168, 324.
Da nobis Dne. q.
ipsius recensita, 5.
observantiam, 36.
pluviam, 260.
regnum, 127, 346.
unigeniti, 317.
ut et mundi, 348.
ut in tua, 225, 350.
Da nobis
Dne. ut nativitatis, 3, 317.
mentem Dnc. quae, 125, 346.
misericors D. ut sancta, 330.
observantiam Dne., 22, 332.
Da nobis o. D.
beati archangeli, 200, 358.
in sanctorum, 212, 366.

⟨Da nobis o. D.⟩
remedia, 69, 333.
ut beati Matthaei, 357.
ut sicut adoranda, 1, 317.
Da nobis q. Dne.
ambire quae recta, 281.
beati apostoli Thomae, 208, 365.
de tribulatione, 249.
Da nobis q. Dne. D. noster
beati Andreae, 362.
ut qui nativitatem, 317, 319.
Da nobis q. Dne.
digne celebrare, 320.
imitari, 318.
per gratiam, 118, 121, 343.
perseverantem, 331.
piae supplicationis, 258.
semper haec tibi, 364.
Da nobis q. o. D.
et aeternae, 326.
ieiuniorum, 327.
ut ieiunando, 357.
ut nativitatem, 319.
ut qui nova, 318.
vitiorum, 352.
Da nostrae summe conditionis, 39.
Da plebi tuae Dne. piae, 40, 278.
Da q. Dne.
D. noster ut sicut b. Laurentii, 352.
electis nostris, 34.
famulae tuae, 159.
fidelibus populis sanctorum, 358.
Da q. Dne. fidelibus tuis
et sine, 31, 62, 328.
ieuniis, 16, 326.
Da q. Dne.
hanc mentem populo, 230, 356.
nostris effectum ieiuniis, 19, 328.
populis Christianis, 19, 30, 327.
Da q. Dne. populo tuo
diabolica vitare, 231, 359.
et mentem, 241, 368.
inviolabilem, 318.
salutem, 328.
Da q. Dne.
rex aeterne cunctorum, 35, 329.
ut tanti mysterii, 44, 155.
Da quaesumus
ecclesiae tuae m. D., 345.
m. D. ut mysticis, 178, 348.
nobis o. D. ieiuniorum, 20.
Da quaesumus o. D.
cunctae familiae, 218, 363.
illuc subsequi, 109, 342.
intra sanctae ecclesiae, 348.
sic nos tuam veniam, 233, 359.
Da q. o. D. ut
abstinentiae, 35.
b. Laurentii, 189.
b Silvestri, 319.
divino munere, 141.
ecclesia tua, 337.
in tua spe, 154.
mysteriorum, 177, 347, 367.
quae divina sunt, 100, 331.

INDEX OF LITURGICAL FORMS. 377

Da q. o. D. ut qui
  b. Anastasiae, 318.
  b. Priscae, 321.
  b. Marcelli, 162, 321.
  b. Urbani, 343.
  b. Felix, 162, 321.
  in tot adversis, 332.
Da q. o. D. ut
  sacro nos, 328.
  triumphum, 352.
De multitudine misericordiae, 15, 325.
Debitum
  Dne. nostrae reddimus, 208, 365.
  humani corporis sepeliendi, 298.
Defende Dne. familiam tuam, 36, 329.
Dei Patris omnipotentis misericordiam, 134.
Dele q. Dne. conscriptum, 100, 338 *note*.
Delicias Dne. mirabiles, 31, 328.
Delicta
  Dne. q. miseratus, 259.
  nostra Dne. quibus, 233, 360.
Deprecationem nostram q. Dne., 347.
Deum indicem universitatis, 297.
Deum omnipotentem
  ac misericordem, 314.
  fratres, 287.
Deum Patrem omnipotentem
  supplices, 147.
  suppliciter, 147.
Deus a quo
  bona cuncta, 104, 341.
  et Iudas, 74, 334.
  sancta desideria, 271.
  speratur humani, 306.
Deus Abraham D. Isaac D. Iacob
  D. qui Moysi, 48.
  D. qui tribus Israel, 49.
Deus
  aeternorum bonorum, 157.
  apud quem omnia morientia, 299.
  auctor pacis et amator, 272.
  caeli D. terrae, 48.
  castitatis amator, 159.
  castorum corporum, 156.
  celsitudo humilium, 83, 335.
  conditor mundi sub cuius, 271.
Deus cui
  b. Caecilia, 361.
  cunctae obediunt, 172, 341.
  in hodierna die, 165.
  soli competit, 308.
Deus cuius
  adoranda(e) potentia, 127, 358.
  antiqua miracula, 82, 335.
  arbitrio omnium, 150, 254.
  bonitatis nullus, 305.
  caritatis ardore, 190, 352.
  dextera (b.) Petrum, 186, 349.
  Filius in alta, 107, 343.
  hodierna die praeconium, 8, 319.
  miseratione animae, 310.
  misericordia praecurrente, 348.

(Deus cuius)
  misericordiam caelestium, 256.
  occulto consilio, 270.
Deus cuius providentia
  creatura, 291.
  in sui, 225, 350.
Deus cuius regnum
  est omnium, 273.
  nulla saecula, 275.
Deus cuius
  Spiritu totum corpus, 120, 343.
  tanta est excellentia, 256.
  Unigenitus in substantia, 11, 321.
Deus
  de cuius gratiae rore, 36, 329.
  ecclesiae tuae redemptor, 91, 336.
  et temporalis vitae, 275.
Deus fidelium
  lumen animarum, 311.
  Pater summe, 82, 335.
  receptor animarum, 141.
  remunerator animarum, 163, 339.
Deus
  gloriatio fidelium, 119, 343.
  honorum omnium, 151.
  humanae salutis operator, 201, 357.
  humani generis, 65, 132, 333, 338 *note*.
Deus humilium
  consolator, 253.
  visitator, 284.
Deus illuminator omnium, 11, 320.
Deus in cuius
  manu corda, 276.
  praecipuis, 102, 339.
Deus in te sperantium
  fortitudo, 106, 272, 345.
  salus, 275.
Deus
  in quo vivimus, 258.
  incommutabilis virtus, 82, 335.
  incrementorum, 70, 333.
  indulgentiarum Dne., 312.
Deus infinitae misericordiae
  et bonitatis, 252.
  et maiestatis, 246.
Deus
  infirmitatis humanae, 282.
  innocentiae restitutor, 95, 337.
  iustorum gloria, 314.
  largitor pacis, 248.
Deus misericors D. clemens qui
  indulgentiam, 66.
  secundum, 66.
Deus mundi
  conditor auctor luminis, 80.
  creator et rector, 153, 352.
Deus omnipotens in cuius honore, 134.
Deus o. Pater Dni. nostri I. C.
  qui regenerasti, 87, 117.
  qui te, 86, 117.
Deus
  omnium misericordiarum, 41, 331.
  patrum nostrorum, 47.

INDEX OF LITURGICAL FORMS.

Deus per
  cuius providentiam, 97, 338.
  quem nobis, 99, 337.
Deus quem
  docente Spiritu, 361.
  diligere et amare, 60, 332.
  omnia opera benedicunt, 327.
Deus qui absque ulla, 141.
Deus qui ad
  aeternam vitam, 99, 338, 338 *note.*
  animarum medelam, 345.
  caeleste regnum, 94, 304, 337.
  declaranda, 107, 342.
  imaginem tuam, 42.
  mutandam aeris, 259.
  salutem, 285, 287.
  vitam ducis, 246.
Deus qui
  anxietate, 270.
  apostolis tuis, 344.
  b. Ioannis, 7, 319.
  b. apostolo tuo Petro, 181, 324.
  b. Sebastianum, 322.
  bonis tuis, 8, 319.
  caelestis regni, 305.
  confitentium tibi corda, 65, 67, 333.
Deus qui conspicis
  familiam, 336.
  nos omni virtute, 327.
Deus qui conspicis quia
  ex nostra, 364.
  ex nulla, 325, 361.
  nos undique, 342, 348.
Deus qui conteris bella, 272.
Deus qui credentes in te
  fonte, 95, 338.
  populos, 96, 272, 338.
Deus qui culpas
  delinquentum, 340.
  nostras piis, 340.
Deus qui
  de his terrae, 200, 357.
  delinquentes perire, 21, 327.
  diem discernis, 291, 368.
  dierum nostrorum, 155.
Deus qui diligentibus te
  bona, 224, 349.
  facis, 247.
  misericordiam, 245.
Deus qui
  discipulis tuis, 124, 344.
  diversitatem, 83, 335, 337.
  divitias, 82, 334.
Deus qui ecclesiam tuam
  annua, 326.
  apostoli, 349.
  novo, 120, 336.
  super gentium, 335.
Deus qui
  emortuam, 269.
  errantes, 102, 340.
  es omnium sanctorum, 171, 341.
  ex omni, 139.
  facturae tuae, 281.
  famulum tuum *Illum*, 302.

(Deus qui)
  famulum tuum Isaac, 269.
Deus qui fidelium
  devotione, 280.
  mentes, 103, 141.
  precibus, 260.
Deus qui
  habitaculum, 160.
  hanc arboris, 295.
Deus qui hanc sacratissimam noctem
  gl.ria, 88, 335.
  veri, 2, 317.
Deus qui hodierna die
  corda, 344.
  per Unigenitum, 366.
  unigenitum, 320.
Deus qui
  hodiernam diem apostolorum, 349.
  hominem ad imaginem, 132.
  homini ad imaginem, 262.
Deus qui humanae
  fragilitati, 257.
  substantiae, 5, 318.
Deus qui humanam naturam, 94.
Deus qui humani generis
  es et reparator, 98.
  et salutis, 281.
  ita es, 46.
  reparator, 339.
  utramque, 258.
Deus qui
  humano generi, 60.
  humanum genus tuorum, 362.
  hunc diem beatorum, 181.
  illuminas noctem, 292.
Deus qui in
  Abrahae, 343.
  deserti regione, 330.
  Filii tui, 102, 339.
  omnibus ecclesiae, 83, 335.
  praeclara salutiferae, 172, 341.
  sanctis habitas, 188, 224, 349.
Deus qui
  ineffabilibus mundum, 331.
  infideles deseris, 280.
  innocentiae restitutor, 95, 337.
Deus qui inter
  apostolicos, 301.
  caetera potentiae, 366.
Deus qui
  invisibili potentia, 85.
  iusta postulantes, 352.
  iuste irasceris, 332.
  iustis supplicationibus, 297.
  iustitiam tuae legis, 247.
  laboribus hominum, 257.
  legalium differentias, 225, 350.
  licet sis magnus, 319.
  ligandi solvendique, 183, 349.
Deus qui loca nomini tuo
  dedicata, 140.
  dicata, 133.
Deus qui
  mirabiliter creasti, 334.
  miro ordine angelorum, 358.

INDEX OF LITURGICAL FORMS. 379

⟨Deus qui⟩
  misericordiae ianuam, 104, 341.
  misericordiae tuae, 272.
  misericordia(m) tua(m), 127, 346.
Deus qui multiplicas
  ecclesiam, 337.
  sobolem, 94, 337.
Deus qui multitudinem gentium, 182, 349.
Deus qui mundi
  creator, 190.
  crescentis, 266.
Deus qui nativitatis tuae, 6, 318.
Deus qui nobis
  ad celebrandum, 337.
  apostolorum, 180, 348.
  in famulis tuis, 285.
  nati salvatoris, 9, 320.
  per prophetarum, 343.
Deus qui non
  despicis, 127, 343.
  mortem, 255.
  propriis, 153.
Deus qui nos ad
  celebrandum, 83, 335.
  delicias, 293.
  imaginem, 247.
Deus qui nos annua
  apostolorum, 341.
  b. Agnae, 323.
  b. Cyriaci, 352.
  b. Ioannis, 348.
Deus qui nos
  b. Eusebii, 353.
  b. Ioannis Baptistae, 348.
  b. martyris tui Caesarii, 360. *
  b. Nicomedis, 345.
  b. Stephani, 351.
  concedis sanctorum, 351.
  conspicis ex nostra, 359.
  de praesentibus, 127, 346.
  et sanctorum, 210.
  exultantibus, 95.
  fecisti die hodierna, 336.
  formam humilitatis, 36, 329.
  gloriosis remediis, 20.
  hodie beatae et sanctae, 366.
  hodierna die exaltatione, 198, 356.
  in tantis, 323.
Deus qui nos per
  beatos, 185, 359.
  huius, 103, 232, 341, 359.
  paschalia festa, 337.
Deos qui nos
  redemptionis nostrae, 219, 317.
  regendo conservas, 360.
  resurrectionis, 90, 337, 343.
  sacramentis tuis, 155.
  sanctorum tuorum, 349.
  Unigeniti tui clementer, 319.
Deus qui
  nostram conspicis, 221, 363.
  ob animarum, 31, 328.
  offensionibus servorum, 251.
  omne meritum, 304.
  omnes in Christo, 93, 338.

⟨Deus qui⟩
  omnipotentiam tuam, 227, 352.
  omnium rerum, 260.
  opprobrium sterilitatis, 270.
  paschal(ia) nobis, 92, 336.
  peccantium animas, 329.
  peccati veteris, 75, 334 *note.*
Deus qui per
  beatae, 3, 318.
  huius celebritatis, 12, 320.
  ineffabilem observantiam, 12, 325.
  os beati apostoli, 7, 319.
Deus qui per Unigenitum tuum
  aeternitatis, 90, 335.
  devicta, 99, 338.
Deus qui per Verbum tuum, 32, 328.
Deus qui
  populo tuo plene, 5, 318. *
  populum tuum de hostis, 336.
  post baptismi, 262.
  praedicando aeterni, 277.
  praesentem diem, 178, 348.
  primis temporibus, 119, 343.
Deus qui pro
  animarum, 222, 364.
  nobis Filium, 333.
  salute, 93, 338.
Deus qui
  profundo consilio, 33.
  prospicis quia, 219.
  providentia tua, 275.
Deus qui quum
  omnes, 248.
  salutem, 42.
Deus qui regnis omnibus, 274.
Deus qui renatis
  baptismate, 96, 337.
  ex aqua, 338 *note.*
  fonte, 97, 338.
  per aquam, 100.
Deus qui
  renuntiantibus, 290.
  sacramento festivitatis, 122, 344.
Deus qui sacrand. tibi auctor es munerum
  ad sanctificationem, 137.
  effunde super hanc, 139.
Deus qui
  saeculorum omnium, 268.
  salutis aeternae, 319.
  sanctam nobis huius, 365.
  sanctis tuis Abdo et Sennen, 351.
  sanctorum tuorum, 247.
  sensus nostros, 101, 338.
  solemnitate paschali, 92, 336, 337.
  solus es bonus, 323.
  spe salutis aeternae, 193.
  sperantibus in te, 331.
  sub tuae maiestatis, 274.
  subiectas tibi, 276.
  te rectis, 109, 346.
  te sinceris, 200.
  tenebras ignorantiae, 292.
  tribus pueris, 201, 222, 345, 346, 365.

(Deus qui)
  tuorum corda fidelium, 262.
  unanimes nos, 279.
  Unigeniti tui, 356.
  universorum creator, 298.
  universum mundum, 323.
Deus refugium
  nostrum et virtus, 361.
  pauperum, 251.
Deus regnorum omnium
  et Romani, 276.
  regumque, 272.
Deus
  sanctificationem o. dominator, 133.
  servientium tibi fortitudo, 275.
  spei luminis sincerum, 106, 345.
Deus sub cuius
  imperio, 288.
  nutibus, 282.
  oculis, 252.
Deus
  totius conditor creaturae, 337.
  tuorum gloria sacerdotum, 189, 351.
  universae carnis qui Noe, 335.
  verae beatitudinis, 247.
  vita credentium, 142.
Deus vita fidelium
  gloria humilium, 105, 343.
  timentium te, 269.
Deus virtutum cuius est totum, 225, 350.
Devotas Dne. humilitatis nostrae, 198, 356.
Devotionem populi tui, 327.
Devotionis nostrae tibi (Dne. q.), 218, 364.
Dignare Dne.
  calicem, 135.
  D. o. rex, 135.
Digne nos tuo nomini, 92, 335.
Dilectissimi
  fratres inter caetera, 161.
  nobis accepturi, 53.
Diri vulneris novitate, 295.
Dirigat corda nostra, 232, 359.
Discat ecclesia tua, 8, 319.
Divini
  muneris largitate, 354.
  satiati muneris, 59, 330.
Domine D. noster
  in cuius, 33.
  multiplica, 213, 324.
  qui in his, 37, 127, 330, 346.
  qui offensione, 14, 325.
  verax promissor, 254.
Domine D. omnipotens
  Pater Dni., 130.
  sempiterne, 315.
  sicut ab initio, 134.
Domine Deus
  preces nostras, 26.
  qui ad hoc, 250.
  qui in regenerandis, 69, 333.
  virtutum qui collapsa, 119, 343.

Domine sancte Pater o. aet. D.
  aquarum, 116.
  benedicere digneris, 147, 148.
  de abundantia, 240, 368.
  exaudi precem, 287.
  honorum, 23.
  iteratis, 267.
  qui benedictionis, 282.
  qui es et eras, 114.
  qui fragilitatem, 281.
  respice, 65, 333.
  virtutem tuam, 112.
Domine sancte spei, 28.
Dominus et salvator noster, 57.
Donis caelestibus da q. Dne., 359.

Ecclesia tua Dne. caelesti, 130, 345.
Ecclesiae tuae Dne. munera
  placatus, 30, 220, 328, 364.
  sanctifica, 222, 365.
Ecclesiae tuae Dne.
  preces placatus, 277.
  voces placatus, 368.
Ecclesiae tuae q. Dne.
  dona, 320.
  preces, 181, 324.
Ecclesiae tuae q. o. D. placatus, 255.
Ecclesiam tuam Dne.
  benignus illustra, 319.
  miseratio, 230, 356.
  perpetua, 31, 328.
Effeta quod est adaperire, 79, 115.
Efficiatur haec hostia, 32, 330.
Eius tibi precibus Dne. q. grata, 197, 355.
Eligunt te fratres tui, 147.
Emitte q. Dne.
  lucem, 291, 368.
  Spiritum, 70, 333.
Erectis sensibus et oculis, 108, 343.
Ergo maledicte diabole, 48.
Erudi q. Dne. plebem, 323.
Esto Dne. plebi tuae sanctificator, 221, 350.
Esto Dne. propitius plebi tuae
  et, 18, 326, 328.
  ut, 37.
Esto q. Dne. propitius plebi tuae, 330.
Et natalitiis sanctorum, 210, 366.
Exaudi Dne. populum
  cum sanctorum, 209, 321.
  tuum cum sancti, 362.
  tuum tota tibi, 361.
Exaudi Dne. preces nostras
  et confitentium, 14, 325.
  et interveniente, 358.
  et ne velis, 255.
  et profectioni, 245.
  et sanctorum, 357.
  et ut digna, 323.
  quas in sancti, 162, 339.
  ut quod tui, 103, 341.
  ut redemptionis, 337.
Exaudi Dne. q. populum tuum de tua, 256.

INDEX OF LITURGICAL FORMS. 381

Exaudi Dne. q. supplicum preces
  et devoto, 29.
  ut quod, 151.
Exaudi nos D. salutaris noster
  et apostolorum, 184, 360.
  et dies, 348.
  et super nos, 23.
  ut sicut, 204, 355.
Exaudi nos Dne. sancte Pater o. aet. D.
  et humilitatis, 283.
  et mittere, 286.
  qui per beatae, 169, 339.
  ut quod, 283.
  ut si quae, 267.
Exaudi nos miserator et misericors, 242, 367.
Exaudi nos o. D. et
  familiae, 100, 338.
  famulos tuos, 42.
  in huius aquae, 115.
Exaudi nos o. et m. D. et
  continentiae, 329.
  sanctorum, 366.
Exaudi o. D. deprecationem, 367.
Exaudi q. Dne. gemitum, 332.
Excita Dne.
  corda nostra, 364.
  in ecclesia, 352.
Excita Dne. potentiam tuam et veni
  et magna, 214, 365.
  et quod ecclesiae, 214, 362.
  ut hi, 218.
  ut tua, 219, 363.
Excita Dne. q.
  corda nostra, 215.
  potentiam tuam et veni et ab, 362.
  tuorum corda fidelium, 61, 361.
  tuorum fidelium voluntates, 361.
Excita q. Dne. potentiam tuam et veni
  ut hi, 364.
Exercitatio veneranda Dne., 39, 330.
Exorcizo te creatura
  aquae in nomine, 116, 285.
  aquae per Deum, 115.
  olei in nomine, 72, 333.
  olei per Deum, 118.
  salis in nomine Dei, 47.
  salis in nomine Patris, 286.
Exorcizo te immunde spiritus
  in nomine, 49.
  per Patrem, 49.
Exuberet q. Dne. mentibus, 99, 338.
Exultamus pariter et de percepto, 166, 323.
Exultemus, q. Dne. D. noster, 218, 363.
Exultet
  iam angelica turba, 334.
  q. Dne. populus, 196, 341.
Exurgentes de cubilibus, 291.

Fac nos Dne. q.
  accepto pignore, 328.
  mala nostra, 218, 363.
  prompta, 231, 358.

⟨Fac nos Dne. q.⟩
  sanctorum, 211, 346.
  tuis obedire, 231.
Fac nos q. Dne.
  D. noster pervigiles, 216, 364.
  his muneribus, 16, 325.
  salutis nostrae, 16, 326.
Fac. o. D. ut
  quae veraciter, 61, 332.
  qui paschalibus, 100, 338 *note*.
Fac. q. Dne. famulos tuos toto, 263.
Familia tua D. et ad celebranda, 241, 368.
Familiam tuam Deus
  propitius, 349.
  suavitas, 198, 355.
Familiam tuam Dne.
  pervigili, 241, 367, 368.
  q. dextera, 323.
Familiam tuam q. Dne.
  continua, 323, 360.
  dextera, 338 *note*.
  propitiatus, 30, 328.
Famulis tuis
  Dne. caelestis gratiae, 355.
  q. Dne. sperata, 264.
Famulos tuos q. Dne.
  benignus, 264.
  placatus, 263.
  tua semper, 264.
Festina
  ne tardaveris Dne., 219, 363.
  q. ne tardaveris Dne., 217, 364.
Festinantes o. D. in occursum, 219, 363.
Fiant
  Dne. tuo grata conspectui, 166, 188, 323.
  tua gratia Dne., 346.
Fiat
  Dne. q. hostia sacranda, 211, 346.
  q. Dne. per gratiam, 43.
  tua gratia Dne., 126.
Fidelem populum q. Dne. potentiae 276.
Fideles tui Dne. per tua, 326.
Fideles tuos Dne.
  benedictio desiderata, 21, 106, 327, 345.
  q. corpore, 241, 368.
Fideli populo Dne. misericordiam, 126, 346.
Fidelibus tuis Dne. perpetua, 17.
Fidelium D. omnium conditor, 308.
Filii carissimi
  ne diutius, 51.
  revertimini, 79.
Foveat nos Dne. sanctae, 170.
Fraterna nos Dne. martyrum, 213, 351.

Gaudeat Dne.
  plebs fidelis, 338 *note*.
  q. populus tuus semper, 329.
Gloriam Dne. sanctorum, 185, 360.
Grata sit tibi Dne. nostrae, 198, 355.

Grata tibi sint Dne. munera
    quaesumus, 6, 318.
    quibus, 217, 333, 363.
Grata tibi sint
    munera nostra, 195, 342.
    q. Dne. munera, 165, 323.
Gratanter Dne. ad munera, 355.
Gratia tua nos q. Dne. non, 32, 328.
Gratiae tuae q. Dne. supplicibus, 364.
Gratias agimus
    Dne. multiplicatis, 6, 319.
    inenarrabili, 292.
Gratias tibi agimus Dne.
    custoditi, 293.
    sancte Pater, 291.
Gratias tibi
    referat Dne. corde, 35, 126, 329.
    referimus Dne., 142, 232, 359.
Gregem tuum Pastor bone, 44, 68, 240, 368.
Guberna q. Dne. temporalibus, 258.

Haec hostia Dne. placationis, 328, 361.
Haec hostia Dne. q.
    emundet, 322.
    et ab occultis, 253.
    et vincula, 202, 340, 358.
    solemniter, 210.
Haec
    in nobis sacrificia, 328.
    munera q. Dne. quae, 233, 359.
Haec nos
    beata mysteria, 35.
    communio Dne. purget, 347, 351.
    Dne. gratia tua q., 204, 361.
    oblatio D. mundet, 244, 324.
    q. Dne. participatio, 331.
Haec
    quae nos reparent, 23, 326.
    sacra nos Dne. potenti, 363.
    sacrificia nos o. D., 40, 331.
    summa est fidei, 55.
Hanc igitur obl. Dne.
    cunctae familiae, 67, 333.
    fam. tui *Ill.* quam tibi ministerio, 277.
Hanc ig. obl. Dne. fam. tui *Ill.* quam tibi offert
    ob desiderium, 245.
    ob diem, 269.
    ob iustis, 262.
    pro salute, 246.
    pro votis, 284.
Hanc ig. obl. Dne. famulorum ... quam tibi
    offerimus ob devotionem, 313.
    offerunt ob devotionem, 263.
    offerunt ob diem, 265.
Hanc igitur obl. Dne.
    quam tibi offerimus pro anima, 312.
    servitutis meae, 254.
    ut propitius, 34.
Hanc ig. obl. famulae tuae *Ill.* quam tibi
    offerimus ob diem, 160.

(Hanc ig. obl. famulae tuae *Ill.* quam tibi)
    offert ob diem, 159.
Hanc igitur obl. famularum tuarum, 265.
Hanc igitur obl. famuli tui
    et antistitis, 155.
    Ill. quam tibi offerimus ob diem, 149.
Hanc ig. obl. famuli vel famulae ... quam tibi
    in huius templi, 139.
    offerunt hanc dedicantes, 138.
Hanc ig. obl. famulorum ... quam tibi offerunt
    annua, 97, 339.
    ob diem in qua, 69, 333.
Hanc ig. obl. quam tibi in honore, 304.
Hanc ig. obl. quam tibi offerimus
    Dne. pro anima, 305.
    in huius consecratione, 143.
    pro anima, 141.
    pro famulis, 29.
Hanc ig. obl. quam tibi
    offero ego, 150.
    offert famula, 306.
Hanc ig. obl. quam tibi pro
    anima, 303.
    animabus, 310.
    commemoratione, 309.
    defunctis, 311.
    depositione, 301.
    requie et anima, 307.
    requie et animabus, 308.
    tuorum requie, 310.
Hanc ig. obl. sancti patris, 154.
Hanc ig. obl. servitutis nostrae sed et ... tuae
    quaesumus, 235.
    quam tibi offerimus ob diem, 334.
    quam tibi offerimus pro famula, 270.
    quam tibi offerimus pro his, 89, 335, 344.
Hanc quoque obl. quam offero, 154.
Has hostias Dne. quas nomini, 324.
His
    Dne. sacrificiis q. concede, 248.
    nobis Dne. mysteriis conferatur, 103, 340.
    q. Dne. placatus intende, 309.
    sacrificiis Dne. concede placatus, 328.
Hodiernum Dne. sacrificium, 164, 322.
Hos Dne.
    fonte baptismatis, 34.
    quos reficis sacramentis, 36, 330.
Hos quos reficis Dne. sacramentis, 30, 363.
Hostiam Dne. q. quam in sanctorum, 321.
Hostias altaribus tuis Dne. 180, 348.
Hostias Dne.
    famulorum tuorum, 263.

INDEX OF LITURGICAL FORMS. 383

(Hostias Dne.)
  q. placatus assume, 92.
  q. quas immolandas, 278.
  quas nomini tuo, 349.
  quas tibi offerimus, 328, 352.
  tuae plebis, 355.
Hostias nostras
  Dne. tibi dicatas, 106, 345.
  q. Dne. sanctus, 172, 341.
Hostias populi tui q. Dne. miseratus,
  121, 344.
Hostias q. Dne.
  placatus assume, 337.
  propitius intende, 229, 354.
  quas tibi pro animabus, 309.
  suscipe placatus, 367.
Hostias tibi Dne.
  beatae *Ill.* martyris, 366.
  b. Caesarii, 360.
  b. Vincentii, 322.
  deferimus immolandas, 331.
  humili placatione, 308.
  laudis offerimus, 358.
  placationis offerimus, 253, 323.
Hostias tibi Dne. pro
  commemoratione, 162, 321, 351.
  martyrum tuorum, 203, 360.
  nati tui Filii, 11, 321.
  sanctorum, 187, 350.
Hostium nostrorum q. Dne. elide, 273.
Huius
  Dne. q. virtute mysterii, 274.
  Dne. sacramenti semper, 318.
  nobis parsimoniae, 20, 221.
Huius nos Dne.
  perceptio sacramenti, 329, 360.
  sacramenti semper, 2.
Huius
  operatio nos Dne. sacramenti,
    256.
  sacrificii potentia, 69, 333.
  te Dne. muneris oblatione, 201, 358.

Ieiunia nostra q. Dne. benigno, 329.
Ieiunia q. Dne.
  nos sacrata, 21.
  quae sacris, 43, 221.
Illius mensis ieiunia, 125, 346.
Illo nos igne q. Dne., 345.
Illumina q. Dne.
  populum, 10, 320, 321.
  tenebras, 292.
Immortalitatis alimoniam, 95, 360.
Impleatur in nobis, 91, 336.
Imploramus Dne. clementiam, 31, 364.
Implorantes Dne. misericordiam, 33, 328.
In
  memoria aeterna, 297.
  sanctae martyrae, 168, 324.
  tuo conspectu Dne., 244, 367.
  tuorum Dne. pretiosa, 199, 358.
Inchoata ieiunia q. Dne., 15, 201, 326.
Inclina q. Dne. aures tuas, 311.
Inclinantes se Dne. maiestati, 326.

Indignos q. Dne. famulos, 219, 364.
Indulgentiam nobis Dne.
  beata, 166, 323.
  praebeant, 208, 363.
  q. sancti *Ill.*, 366.
Ineffabilem misericordiam, 248.
Infirmitatem nostram
  q. Dne. propitius, 357.
  respice o. D., 322.
Ingredientes Dne. in hunc, 290.
Innumeras medelae tuae, 110.
Intemerata mysteria Dne., 351.
Intende Dne. munera q., 168, 324.
Intende q. Dne.
  hostias, 13, 61, 325.
  sacrificium singulare, 363.
Intercedentibus sanctis tuis, 174, 345.
Infercessio
  Dne. b. Hermetis, 354.
  nos q. Dne. sanctae, 205, 364.
Intercessio nos Dne. q. b. Benedicti,
  350.
Intercessio q. Dne.
  beatae Mariae, 353.
  pontificis, 164, 322.
  sancti tui Ruffi, 195.
Intercessio sancti Nicomedis, 356.
Interveniat pro nobis Dne. q., 359.
Inveniant q. Dne. animae, 308.
Ioannes habet similitudinem, 52.
Ipsa maiestati tuae Dne. fideles, 60,
  332.
Ipsi tibi q. Dne. sancte Pater, 334.
Ipsi nobis Dne. q. postulent, 8, 319.
Iram tuam q. Dne. a populo, 257.
Iterata
  festivitate b. Laurenti, 193, 353.
  mysteria Dne. pro sanctorum, 213.
Iugiter nos Dne. sanctorum, 212, 322.

Laetetur ecclesia tua D.
  beatorum martyrum, 345.
  martyrum, 174.
Laéti Dne.
  frequentamus salutis, 2, 318.
  sanctorum martyrum, 346.
  sumpsimus sacramenta, 172, 236,
    341, 364.
Laetificet nos
  Dne. munus oblatum, 181, 324.
  q. Dne. huius, 345.
  q. Dne. sacramenti, 129.
Largiente te Dne. beati Petri et Pauli,
  181, 349.
Largire nobis Dne. q. semper spiritum,
  226, 350.
Largire q. Dne.
  famulis tuis fidei, 5, 318.
  fidelibus tuis indulgentiam, 233,
    360.
Largire
  q. ecclesiae tuae, 101, 338.
  q. o. D. ut anima, 141.
  sensibus nostris, 333.
Laudis tuae Dne. hostias, 353.

384   INDEX OF LITURGICAL FORMS.

Libantes Dne. mensae tuae, 168, 176, 204, 324.
Libera
  Dne. q. a peccatis et hostibus, 43, 331.
  nos Dne. ab omni malo, 247.
  nos q. Dne., 236.
Lucas evangelista speciem, 52.

Magnifica Dne.
  beati *Ill.*, 365.
  beati Laurenti, 190.
Magnificantes Dne. clementiam, 212, 366.
Magnificare Dne. D. noster, 137.
Magnificentiam tuam Dne. praedicamus, 261.
Magnificet te Dne. sanctorum, 199, 358.
Maiestatem tuam Dne. supplices deprecamur ut
  huic, 66.
  sicut nos, 355.
Maiestatem tuam Dne. supplices exoramus ut
  animae, 309.
  quos viam, 97, 308.
  sicut ecclesiae, 183.
Maiestatem tuam Dne. suppliciter deprecamur ut
  haec, 231, 359.
  sicut ecclesiae, 207, 362.
Maiestatem tuam
  nobis Dne. q. haec, 202, 359.
  q. Dne. sancte, 66.
Maiestati tuae nos Dne. martyrum, 211, 322.
Marcus evangelista Leonis, 51.
Martyris tui Praeiecti nos, 322.
Martyrum tuorum
  Dne. Gerbasi et Protasi, 176, 347.
  nos Dne. semper, 211, 322.
Matutina supplicum vota, 291, 368.
Memento Dne. famulorum famularumque tuarum
  et omnium, 234.
  qui electos, 34.
Memor esto Dne. fragilitatis, 249.
Mensa tua nos D. a delectationibus, 237.
Mentem familiae tuae, 340.
Mentes nostras
  Dne. Spiritus Paraclitus, 124.
  et corpora possideat, 230, 356.
Mentes nostras q. Dne.
  lumine, 363.
  Spiritus Paraclitus, 344.
  Spiritus sanctus, 344.
Mentibus nostris Dne. Spiritum, 345.
Miseratio tua D. ad haec, 34.
Miserationum tuarum Dne. q., 222, 364.
Miserere
  Dne. populo tuo et continuis, 330.
  nostri D. et tuae nobis, 243, 367.
Misericordiae tuae remediis, 357.

Misericordiam tuam Dne nobis, 364, 366.
Misericors et miserator Dne. qui, 253.
Multiplica Dne. benedictionem, 143.
Multiplica Dne. super
  animas, 311.
  nos, 289.
Multiplica (fidem q. Dne.) populi, 99, 337.
Munda nos Dne. sacrificii praesentis, 231, 358.
Munera Dne. oblata sanctifica
  et intercedente, 345.
  ut tui, 347.
Munera Dne.
  quae pro apostolorum, 341.
  q. oblata sanctifica, 344.
  tibi dicata q. sanctifica, 242.
  tuae glorificationis, 180, 348.
Munera nos Dne. q. oblata, 331.
Munera nostra (Dne. q.)
  nativitatis, 2, 317.
  propitiatus assume, 195, 354.
Munera plebis tuae Dne. q. beatorum, 366.
Munera populi tui Dne.
  placatus, 177.
  propitiatus, 347.
Munera q. Dne.
  famulae et sacratae, 159.
  quae tibi pro requie, 311.
  tibi dicata sanctifica, 343.
Munera tibi Dne.
  dicata sanctifica, 351.
  nostrae devotionis, 351.
  pro sanctae Felicitatis, 205, 362.
Munera tibi Dne. pro sancti martyris Agapiti, 194.
  Ioannis, 196, 355.
Munera tibi Dne. pro sanctorum, 187, 351.
Munera tua nos D. a delectationibus, 323.
Muneribus Dne. te magnificamus, 170, 340.
Muneribus nostris Dne.
  apostolorum, 184, 359.
  precibusque susceptis, 150, 319.
  sanctae Caeciliae, 361.
Muneribus nostris (q.) Dne. precibusque, 184, 359.
Muneris divini percepti, 367.
Munerum tuorum Dne. 254.
Muniat q. Dne. fideles, 252.
Munus
  populi tui Dne. q. dignanter, 200, 358.
  quod tibi Dne. nostrae, 329.
Mysteria
  nos Dne. sancta purificent, 237, 348.
  sancta nos Dne. et spiritalibus, 242, 367.
Mysteriis
  Dne. repleti sumus, 206, 362.

INDEX OF LITURGICAL FORMS. 385

Mysteriis
  tuis veneranter acceptis, 10, 320.
Mystica nobis Dne. prosit oblatio, 242, 359.

Nec te latet Satanas, 78, 113.
Nobis quoque peccatoribus, 235.
Nostra tibi q. Dne. fiant, 331.
Noverit vestra devotio, 161, 365.

Oblata Dne. munera sanctifica, 321.
Oblatio Dne. tuis aspectibus, 280.
Oblatio nos Dne. tuo nomini
  dicanda, 109, 346.
  dicata, 105, 229.
Oblatio tibi sit Dne. (q.) hodiernae, 4, 318.
Oblationes nostras q. Dne. propitiatus
  intende
  quas in honore, 169, 339.
  quas tibi offerimus, 305.
Oblationes populi tui Dne. q., 182, 350.
Oblationibus (q.) Dne. placare suscceptis, 251, 331, 348.
Oblatis
  Dne. placare muneribus et opportunum, 259.
  hostiis Dne. q. praesenti, 159.
  q. Dne. placare muneribus et a cunctis, 326, 354.
Oblatum tibi Dne. sacrificium, 321.
Obsequiis autem rite celebratis, 299.
Observationis huius annua celebritate, 16, 326.
Offerimus Dne.
  laudes et munera, 98, 261, 339.
  preces et munera, 362.
Offerimus
  sacrificium Dne. quod pro, 186.
  (tibi) Dne. laudes et munera, 98, 261, 339.
Offerimus tibi Dne.
  munera quae dedisti, 41, 368.
  (q.) preces, 349, 354.
Omnipotens aeterne D. qui
  humano, 299.
  primitias martyrum, 6.
Omnipotens Deus
  fac nos tibi semper, 237.
  Romani nominis, 273.
  Trinitas inseparabilis, 136.
  ut sancti nos, 171.
Omnipotens et misericors D.
  ad cuius beatitudinem, 129, 345.
  apta nos, 125, 346.
  cui redditur, 367.
  de cuius munere, 228, 354.
  fidelium lumen, 366.
  in cuius humana, 306.
  maiestatem tuam, 117.
Omnipotens et misericors D. qui
  beatum Ioannem, 348.
  nos sacramentorum, 351.
  peccantium, 250.
  peccatorum, 65, 333.

(Omnipotens et misericors D. qui)
  universa nobis, 232, 359.
Omnipotens Pater misericordiarum, 131.
Omnipotens sempiterne Deus
  a cuius facie, 111.
  a quo sola, 228, 353.
  adesto magnae pietatis, 84.
  annue precibus, 310.
  clementiam tuam suppliciter, 44, 332.
  collocare dignare, 312.
  confitenti tibi, 65, 333.
  creator humanae, 6, 318.
Omnipotens sempiterne Deus cui
  cuncta famulantur, 366.
  nunquam sine spe, 307.
Omnipotens sempiterne Deus cuius
  aeterno iudicio, 75, 334.
  munere elementa, 259.
  Spiritu totum corpus, 76, 334.
Omnipotens sempiterne Deus da
  cordibus nostris, 348.
  nobis fidei, 229, 354.
  nobis ita Dominicae, 332.
  nobis voluntatem, 10, 320.
  q. universis, 63, 333.
Omnipotens sempiterne Deus
  deduc nos, 100, 124, 344.
  dirige actus nostros, 320.
  ecclesiam tuam spiritali, 38.
  effunde super hunc, 139.
  fac nos tibi semper, 105, 229, 343, 354.
  fidelium splendor, 320.
  fons omnium virtutum, 143.
  fortitudo certantium, 196, 355.
  hoc baptisterium, 142.
  indeficiens lumen, 119, 343.
  infirmitatem nostram, 322.
  insere te officiis, 284.
  maiestatem tuam supplices, 302, 323.
  miserere supplicum, 276.
  misericordiam tuam ostende, 358.
  moestorum consolatio, 76, 334.
  multiplica in honore(m), 83, 335.
  multiplica super nos, 289.
  mundi creator et rector, 359.
  parce metuentibus, 288.
  Pater Dni. nostri I. C., 46.
  per quem coepit esse, 228, 354.
  petimus divinam, 259.
  propensius his diebus, 100, 338.
Omnipotens sempiterne Deus qui
  abundantia, 228, 353.
  ad aeternam, 91, 336.
  aegritudines, 282.
  caelestia simul, 321.
  Christi tui beata passione, 62, 333.
  coaeternum tibi, 339.
  continuum, 270.
  ecclesiam tuam in apostolica, 349.
  ecclesiam tuam nova, 76, 334.

(Omnipotens sempiterne Deus qui)
  eligis infirma, 168, 204, 324.
  et iustis praemia, 40, 330.
  etiam Iudaicam, 77, 334.
  facis mirabilia magna, 263, 284.
  gloriam tuam, 75, 334.
  gregalium, 137.
  hanc sacratissimam, 88.
  humanam naturam, 338.
  humano generi, 332.
  huius diei venerandam, 354.
  hunc diem per incarnationem, 4, 318.
  hunc locum Iudaicae, 142.
Omnipotens sempiterne Deus qui in Filii tui Dni. nostri nativitate, 318.
  omnium operum, 82, 335.
  omnium sanctorum, 361.
  sanctorum tuorum cordibus, 366.
  Unigenito, 320.
Omnipotens sempiterne Deus qui
  infirma mundi, 356.
  instituta legalia, 178, 348.
  maternum affectum, 270.
  nobis in observatione, 18, 327.
  non mortem, 77, 334.
  non sacrificiorum, 126, 346.
Omnipotens sempiterne Deus qui nos
  beatorum apostolorum, 183, 349.
  et castigando, 261.
  idoneos non esse, 366.
  omnium apostolorum, 183, 349.
  sancti martyris, 192, 342.
Omnipotens s. D. qui (omnes salvas), 77, 334.
Omnipotens s. D. qui paschale sacramentum
  in reconciliatione, 337.
  quinquaginta, 122.
Omnipotens sempiterne Deus qui per
  abstinentiam, 44.
  continentiam, 18, 22, 32.
  gloriosa, 366.
  unicum, 119, 343.
Omnipotens sempiterne Deus qui
  primitias martyrum, 318.
  regenerasti famulum, 117.
  regnis omnibus, 76, 334.
  (salvas omnes), 77, 334.
  sic hominem, 331.
  superbis resistis, 278.
  terrenis corporibus, 193, 353.
  timore sentiris, 252.
  tuae mensae, 9, 320.
  Unigenito tuo novam, 9.
  Verbi tui incarnationem, 11, 320.
  vitam humani generis, 63, 333.
Omnipotens sempiterne D. respice propitius
  ad devotionem, 84, 335.
  super hunc famulum, 263.
Omnipotens sempiterne Deus
  salus aeterna, 282.
  solemnitatem diei huius, 361.
  spes unica mundi, 83, 335.

(Omnipotens sempiterne Deus)
  totius conditor creaturae, 268.
  vespere et mane, 292.
Omnipotentiam tuam
  Dne. prompta, 201, 358.
  q. Dne. sanctus, 140.
Omnipotentis Dei misericordiam, 297.
Omnium nostrum Dne. q. ad te, 21.
Opus misericordiae tuae est, 298.
Oramus pietatem tuam, 294.
Orate electi flectite genua, 79.
Oremus Deum ac Dnum. nostrum ut super, 148.
Oremus dilectissimi
  Deum Patrem o. ut super hos, 22, 26.
  fratres ut Dnus. D. noster calicem, 135.
  nobis Deum Patrem o. ut cunctis, 76, 334.
  (nobis) in primis, 75, 334.
  nobis omnipotenti Deo, 261.
  nobis ut his viris, 151.
Oremus et pro
  beatissimo papa, 75, 334.
  catechumenis, 76, 334.
  Christianissimo imperatore, 76, 334.
  haereticis, 77, 334.
  omnibus episcopis, 76, 334.
  paganis, 77, 334.
  perfidis Iudaeis, 77, 334.
Oremus fratres carissimi
  pro anima, 298.
  ut D. o. hoc ministerium, 135.
Oriatur Dne. nascentibus tenebris, 293, 368.

Pacem nobis tribue Dne., 19, 326.
Parce Dne. parce
  peccantibus, 248.
  peccatis, 249.
  supplicibus, 251.
Parce Dne. q. parce populo, 340.
Pasce nos Dne. tuorum gaudiis, 341.
Paschale mysterium recensentes, 91, 336.
Paschales hostias recensentes, 95, 336.
Paschalibus (nobis) q. Dne. remediis, 99, 338 note.
Pateant aures misericordiae, 227, 330, 351.
Pater mundi conditor, 266.
Pater noster, 58, 236.
Pax Domini, 72, 236.
Per haec (q. veniat) Dne. sacramenta, 256, 329.
  huius Dne. operationem, 320.
  quem haec omnia, 236.
Percepta
  Dne. sancta nos adiuvent, 31, 328.
  nobis Dne. praebeant, 41, 325.
  nos Dne. tua sancta, 356.
Perceptis Dne. sacramentis
  beato Matthaeo, 357.
  subdito corde, 183, 349.

INDEX OF LITURGICAL FORMS. 387

Perceptis Dne. sacramentis suppliciter exoramus, 362.
rogamus, 185, 360.
Percipientes Dne. gloriosa, 36, 327.
Perfice Dne.
 benignus in nobis, 15, 328.
 q. benignus, 254.
Perficiant in nobis Dne. q., 202, 358.
Perpetua q. Dne. pace custodi, 242, 367.
Perpetuis nos Dne. sancti Ioannis, 196, 355.
Perpetuo Dne. favore prosequere, 20, 327.
Perpetuum nobis Dne. tuae miserationis, 200, 358.
Pignus aeternae vitae, 186, 349.
Pio recordationis affectu, 295.
Pisteuo his ena theon, 53.
Placare Dne.
 muneribus semper, 259.
 q. humilitatis, 214, 364.
Plebem
 nomini tuo subditam, 241, 257, 368.
 tuam Dne. q. interius, 41, 331.
Plebis tuae
 D. ad te corda, 242, 367.
 Dne. munera, 199, 356.
 q. Dne. ad te (semper) corda, 240, 368.
Plebs tua Dne.
 capiat sacrae, 260.
 q. benedictionis, 20, 327.
 sancti martyris, 365.
Plenum q. Dne. in nobis, 152.
Populi tui
 D. institutor et rector, 39, 330.
 Dne. q. tibi gratia sit, 206, 362.
 q. o. D. propitiare, 276.
Populum tuum Dne.
 perpetua munitione, 187, 351.
 propitius respice et quos, 328.
 q. (ad te) toto, 31, 61, 328.
 q. propitius respice atque ab, 327.
 q. tueantur, 3, 318.
Populum tuum q. o. D. ab ira, 255.
Populus tuus q. Dne. renovata, 98, 339.
Porrige nobis
 D. dexteram tuam, 170, 339.
 Dne. dexteram tuae, 219, 363.
Porrige dexteram tuam q. Dne. plebi, 323.
Praebeant nobis Dne. q. divin(um), 32, 345.
Praeceptis salutaribus moniti, 236.
Praecinge q. Dne. D. noster lumbos, 216, 364.
Praepara nos Dne. q. huius, 16, 326.
Praesenti sacrificio nomini tuo, 32.
Praesentia munera q. Dne. ita, 365.
Praesentibus sacrificiis Dne. ieiunia, 31, 327.
Praesta Dne. fidelibus tuis, 325.

Praesta Dne. q. famulis tuis
 renuntiantibus, 290.
 talesque, 127, 346.
Praesta Dne. q. ut
 dicato munere, 221, 364.
 illius salutis, 104.
 intercedente b. Sebastiano, 322.
 per haec sancta, 280.
 sacramenti tui, 206.
 sicut populus, 186.
 sicut sanctorum, 209, 366.
 terrenis affectibus, 252.
 toto tibi corde, 278.
Praesta famulis tuis Dne. abundantiam, 16, 326.
Praesta misericors D. ut
 ad suscipiendum, 1, 317.
 natus hodie Salvator, 4.
Praesta nobis Dne.
 (q.) auxilium, 32, 328.
 q. intercedentibus, 168, 324.
Praesta nobis m. D. ut placationem, 30, 230, 327, 355.
Praesta nobis o. D. ut
 percipientes, 99, 338.
 quem fidei, 362.
 quia vitiis, 30, 332.
 vivificationem, 102.
 vivificationis, 18, 339.
Praesta
 nobis q. o. D. ut nostrae, 192, 353.
 q. D. noster ut familia, 5.
 q. Dne. animabus, 308.
Praesta q. Dne. D. noster ut
 quae solemni, 320.
 quorum, 351.
 sicut, 356.
Praesta q. Dne.
 familiae supplicanti, 357.
 fidelibus tuis ut ieiuniorum, 200.
 huic famulo tuo digno, 64, 333.
 mentibus, 164, 322.
 spiritalibus, 20, 327.
Praesta q. Dne. ut
 a nostris, 123, 344.
 anima famuli, 302.
 beati sancti, 191, 352.
Praesta q. Dne. ut Ecclesia tua
 et martyrum, 187.
 prompta, 278.
Praesta q. Dne. ut
 [et de] nostrae, 149.
 intercedente b. Sebastiano, 163.
 mentium reproborum, 279.
 observationes, 36, 43.
 per haec munera, 9, 320.
 populus tuus, 177, 347.
 quod Salvatoris, 9, 320.
 sacramenti, 197, 355.
 salutaribus ieiuniis, 40, 330.
 sancti confessoris, 189, 351.
 semper nos beati, 191, 352.
Praesta q. Dne. ut sicut
 de praeteritis, 73, 333.
 nobis indiscreta, 213, 351.

⟨Praesta q. Dne. ut sicut⟩
    populus, 350.
Praesta q. nobis
    Dne. ut salutaribus, 329.
    o. et m. D. ut in resurrectione,
    338 *note.*
Praesta q. o. aet. D. ut id, 359.
Praesta q. o. D. sic nos ab epulis, 345.
Praesta q. o. D. ut
    ad te toto, 340.
    animam, 302, 307.
    b. Felicitatis, 362.
    b. Leo, 339.
    b. Marcellus, 162.
    b. Stephanus, 6, 319.
    claritatis, 343.
    de perceptis, 319.
    dignitas, 37, 330.
    divino munere, 89, 232, 335.
    excellentiam, 7, 319.
    familia, 328, 347.
    Filii tui, 219, 363.
    huius paschalis, 337.
    ieiuniorum, 43, 332.
    illa fides, 142.
    natus hodie, 318.
    nullis nos, 348.
    observationes, 357.
    per haec paschalia, 336.
Praesta q. o. D. ut qui
    b. Mennae, 360.
    caelestia, 348.
    gloriosos, 350, 360.
    gratiam, 336.
    in afflictione, 340.
    in tua, 330.
    iugiter apostolica, 184, 357.
    nostris, 333.
    paschalia, 337.
    resurrectionis, 336.
    sanctorum . . . natalitia, 341.
    sanctorum . . . solemnia, 340.
    se affligendo, 201.
Praesta q. o. D. ut
    quia pro peccatis, 219, 363.
    quorum memoriam, 351.
    quos ieiunia, 43, 330.
    redemptionis, 218, 364.
    salutaribus, 345.
    salvatoris mundi, 320.
    sanctae Soteris, 166, 324.
    sanctorum tuorum, 187, 350.
    semper rationabilia, 279, 324.
    sicut divina, 6, 361.
    Spiritus, 122, 344.
Praesta q. o. et m. D. ut
    inter huius, 226, 351.
    sicut, 62, 333.
    Spiritus, 344.
Praesta q. o.
    Pater ut nostrae mentis, 107, 342.
    sempiterne D. ut fidelibus, 154.
Praestent Dne. q. tua sancta, 324.
Praetende Dne. misericordiam tuam, 313, 360.

Praeveniant nobis Dne. q.
    apostoli, 183, 349.
    divina tua, 328.
Praeveniat
    hunc famulum, 14, 325.
    nos q. Dne. gratia tua, 260.
    nos q. o. D. tua gratia, 215, 362.
Precamur o. D. ut de transitoriis, 19, 327.
Preces
    Dne. tuorum respice, 209, 321.
    famulae tuae *Ill.*, 160.
Preces nostras q. Dne. clementer exaudi
    atque a peccatorum, 325.
    et contra, 327.
    et hos electos, 46.
Preces nostras q. Dne.
    propitiatus admitte, 167, 324.
    quas in famuli, 301.
Preces populi tui
    (Dne.) clementer exaudi ut qui, 222, 325, 363.
    (q. D.) clementer exaudi ut qui, 222, 325, 363.
Preces populi tui q. Dne. clem. exaudi
    ut beati, 321.
    ut qui de adventu, 219, 363.
Preces populi tui (q. o. D.) clem. exaudi, 222, 325, 363.
Precibus populi tui Dne. q. placatus, 259.
Precor Dne. clementiam, 14, 325.
Pro
    anima famuli tui *Ill.*, 141.
    animabus famulorum, 310.
    nostrae servitutis augmento, 357.
Pro sanctorum
    (Basilidis) Cyrini, 175, 346.
    Proti et Iacinti, 356.
Proficiat q. Dne. plebs tibi dicata, 39, 128, 330, 346.
Prope esto Dne. omnibus, 364.
Propitiare Dne.
    animae famuli tui, 305.
    familiae tuae, 143.
    humilitati nostrae, 347.
    in te sperantibus, 274.
Propitiare Dne.
    populi tui propitiatus, 249.
    populo tuo et ab, 241, 368.
    populo tuo propitiare, 354.
    preces et hostias, 275.
    q. supplicationibus, 365.
Propitiare Dne. supplicationibus nostris
    et animam, 301.
    et animarum, 329.
    et has oblationes, 224, 245, 313, 349.
    et inclinato, 151.
    pro anima, 304.
Propitiare Dne. vespertinis, 293.
Propitiare
    m. D. supplicationibus nostris, 320.
    populo tuo D. ut a suis, 240, 368.
    q. Dne. animae, 307.

INDEX OF LITURGICAL FORMS. 389

Propitius
  Dne. q. haec dona, 344.
  esto Dne. supplicationibus, 361.
Prosequere
  nos o. D. et quos, 35.
  (q.) o. D. ieiuniorum, 40, 329.
Prosint nobis Dne. sumpta, 222, 364.
Prosit nobis Dne. sancti
  Laurentii, 352.
  Tiburti, 192.
Prosit q. Dne. animae, 303.
Protector fidelium D. et subditarum, 284.
Protector in te sperantium D.
  et subditarum, 283, 367.
  sine quo, 347.
Protector noster aspice D.
  et ab, 276.
  et qui, 327.
Protegat nos Dne.
  cum tui perceptione, 350.
  q. hostia, 256.
  saepius b. Andreae, 208, 363.
Protegat q. Dne. populum tuum, 353.
Protege Dne. famulos tuos subsidiis, 275, 339.
Protege Dne. plebem tuam et
  (in) festivitate, 167, 324.
  quam martyrum, 179, 348.
Protege Dne. populum tuum et
  apostolorum, 349.
  in sanctorum, 44, 332.
Protege nos Dne.
  D. noster et fragilitati, 293.
  q. tuis mysteriis, 277.
Purifica
  Dne. q. mentes nostras, 94, 231, 358.
  nos m. D. ut ecclesiae, 39, 330.
  q. Dne. familiam tuam, 61, 332.
Purificent
  nos Dne. sacramenta, 230, 253, 356.
  semper et muniant, 207, 237, 355.
Purificet nos Dne.
  caelestis executio, 150.
  muneris, 122, 344.
  q. et divini, 355.
Purificet nos (q. Dne.) muneris, 122, 344.

Quaesumus Dne. D. noster ut
  intervenientibus, 352.
  quos divinis, 227, 278, 352.
  sacrosancta, 323, 365.
Quaesumus Dne.
  nostris placere muneribus, 249.
  salutaribus repleti, 321.
Quaesumus Dne. ut
  beatorum martyrum, 174, 342.
  famulo tuo, 312.
  salutaribus repleti, 174, 345.
Quaesumus o. D.
  familiam tuam propitius, 331.
  iam non teneamur, 99, 338 *note*.

(Quaesumus o. D.)
  instituta, 265.
  preces nostras respice, 219, 357, 363.
Quaesumus o. D. ut
  b. Andreas, 362.
  de perceptis, 357.
  et natum, 359.
  iam non teneamur, 338 *note*.
  illius salutaris, 323, 350.
  inter eius numeremur, 18.
  muner(e) divin(o), 233, 237, 352.
  nos geminata, 180, 348.
  nostra devotio, 189, 365.
  plebs tua toto, 243, 369.
  qui caelestia, 322, 342.
  quorum nos tribuis, 361.
  quos divina, 357.
  sancti nos, 171.
  sanctorum tuorum, 211, 346.
Quaesumus
  o. D. vota humilium, 329.
  virtutum caelestium (Dne.), 204, 364.
Quam oblationem, 235.
Qui hac die antequam traderetur, 67, 333.
Qui pridie, 235.
Quod ore sumpsimus, 37, 368.
Quos caelesti
  Dne. alimento, 169, 236, 349.
  Dne. dono, 224, 349.
  recreas munere, 169, 236, 349.
Quos
  ieiunia votiva castigant, 35, 126, 329, 346.
  munere Dne. caelesti, 251.
  refecisti Dne. caelesti, 279.
  tantis Dne. largiris, 237, 322.
Quotidiani Dne. q. munere, 226, 367.

Redemptionis nostrae munere, 337.
Redemptor animarum D., 298.
Refecti cibo potuque caelesti, 319.
Refecti Dne.
  benedictione solemni, 175, 347.
  pane caelesti, 30, 328.
Refecti
  participatione muneris, 322.
  vitalibus alimentis, 221, 334.
Refice nos Dne. donis tuis, 293.
Reficiamur Dne. de donis, 293.
Rege
  nostras Dne. propitius voluntates, 243, 367.
  q. Dne. populum tuum, 13, 325.
Remedii sempiterni munera, 38.
Reminiscere miserationem tuarum, 61, 333.
Remotis obumbrationibus carnalium, 129, 345.
Renovatos Dne. fontis, 98, 339.
Reparet nos q. Dne. semper, 20.
Repleantur consolationibus tuis, 154.

Repleti
  alimonia caelesti, 173, 341.
  cibo potuque caelesti, 351.
  cibo spiritalis alimoniae, 214, 364.
  Dne. benedictione caelesti, 354.
Repleti Dne. muneribus sacris
  da q., 105, 343.
  q. ut, 355.
Repleti Dne. sacri muneris gratia, 62, 333.
Repleti sumus Dne.
  donorum participatione, 15, 325.
  munere solemnitatis, 188, 351.
  muneribus tuis, 225, 350.
Respice Dne.
  familiam tuam et praesta, 326.
  famulae tuae tibi debitam, 159.
Respice Dne. munera
  populi tui, 353.
  quae in sancti, 192, 352.
  quae in sanctorum, 171.
  supplicantis, 347.
Respice Dne. propitius
  ad munera, 329.
  ad plebem, 19, 327.
  plebem tuam, 241, 367.
  sacra mysteria, 61, 332.
Respice Dne. q.
  nostram propitius, 228, 353.
  propitius ad plebem, 221.
  super famulos, 16.
  super hanc familiam, 333.
Respice nos o. et m. D. et mentibus, 3, 317.
Respice propitius Dne.
  ad debitam, 320.
  super hanc famulam, 156.
Respice q. Dne.
  famulos tuos, 264.
  nostram propitius, 155.
  populum tuum et quem, 337.

Sacrae nobis
  (Dne. q.) observationis, 38, 330.
  q. Dne. mensae, 13, 33, 325.
  (q. Dne.) observationis, 38, 330.
Sacramenta quae sumpsimus
  Dne, D. noster, 330.
  q. Dne. et spiritalibus, 103.
Sacramenti tui
  Dne. divina libatio, 328.
  Dne. q. sumpta benedictio, 214, 324.
  Dne. veneranda, 35, 329.
  q. Dne. participatio, 331.
Sacramentis Dne. muniamur, 202, 359.
Sacramentorum benedictione satiati, 40.
Sacramentorum tuorum
  benedictione, 332.
  Dne. communio, 353.
Sacrandum tibi Dne. munus, 362.
Sacrificia Dne.
  paschalibus, 91, 337.
  propensius ista restaurent, 44.
  propitius ista nos salvent, 19, 327.

(Sacrificia Dne.)
  tibi cum ecclesiae, 250.
  tuis oblata, 345.
Sacrificia nos Dne.
  celebranda, 252.
  immaculata, 108, 343.
Sacrificiis
  Dne. placatus oblatis, 257.
  praesentibus Dne. 217, 330, 350, 365.
Sacrificium Dne.
  observantiae paschalis, 15, 325.
  pro Filii tui, 107, 342.
  quadragesimalis, 18, 326.
Sacrificium Dne. quod
  desideranter, 366.
  immolamus intende, 273.
  immolamus placatus, 173, 341.
  pro sanctis martyribus, 176, 347.
Sacrificium laudis tibi Dne. 341.
Sacrificium nostrum
  Dne. ipsa tibi, 356.
  tibi Dne. q. b. Andreae, 207, 362.
  tibi Dne. q. b. Ioannis, 342.
Sacrificium tibi Dne.
  celebrandum, 216, 362.
  laudis offerimus, 205, 361.
Sacris
  altaribus Dne. hostias, 350.
  caelestibus Dne. vitia, 122, 123, 344.
  Dne. mysteriis expiati, 329.
Sacro munere
  satiati supplices te, 61, 322.
  vegetatos, 199, 356.
Sacrosancti corporis et sanguinis, 273.
Salutarem nobis dedit, 356.
Salutari
  munere Dne. satiati, 16.
  sacrificio Dne. populus, 210, 366.
  tuo munere Dne. satiati, 201.
Salutaris tui Dne. munere satiati, 326, 347.
Sancta tua Dne. (de) b. Laurenti, 190, 365.
Sancta tua nos Dne.
  q. et a peccatis, 242, 367.
  q. et vivificando, 40, 61, 330.
  sumpta vivificent, 230, 256, 347.
Sanctae
  Mariae semper virginis, 353.
  martyr(ae) tuae Caeciliae, 203, 361.
  nos martyris Euphemiae, 171, 340.
  Soteris precibus, 167, 324.
Sancte Pater o. D. qui famulum, 131.
Sancti
  confessoris tui Augustini, 361.
  confessoris tui *Ill.*, 365.
  Dne. confessoris tui, 366.
  Eusebii natalitia, 353.
  Felicis Dne. confessoris, 162, 351.
  (Hipp)olyti martyris, 192, 353.
  Ill. martyris tui Dne. 365.

INDEX OF LITURGICAL FORMS. 391

⟨Sancti⟩
Ioannis Baptistae, 196, 355.
Ioannis natalitia, 178.
Laurenti nos Dne., 191, 352.
Leonis confessoris, 339.
Marcelli confessoris, 163.
martyris Agapiti, 194, 353.
nominis tui Dne. timorem, 109, 346.
nos q. Dne. Hermis, 195.
nos q. Dne. Theodori, 360.
nos q. Dne. Vitalis, 341.
Sixti Dne. frequentata, 188, 351.
Spiritus Dne. corda, 124, 344.
tui nos Dne. Abdo, 187.
tui nos q. Dne. ubique, 319.
q. Dne. iugiter nobis, 210, 366.
(Yp)oliti martyris Dne., 192, 353.
Sanctifica
Dne. q. nostra ieiunia, 18, 326.
nos q. Dne. his, 44, 332.
q. Dne. nostra ieiunia, 331.
Sanctificata ieiunio corda, 44.
Sanctificati Dne. salutari, 323.
Sanctificationem (tuam) nobis Dne., 279, 328.
Sanctificationibus tuis o. D., 359.
Sanctificationum omnium auctor, 24.
Sanctificato hoc ieiunio, 331.
Sanctificent nos Dne. sumpta, 42.
Sanctificet nos Dne.
qua pasti, 329.
q. tui perceptio, 356.
Sancto Sebastiano interveniente, 163, 322.
Sanctorum
(Basilidis) Cyrini, 175, 346.
Gerbasi et Protasi, 176.
martyrum nos Dne. 176, 347.
martyrum tuorum *Ill.*, 366.
nos Dne. Marcelli et, 202, 359.
precibus confidentes, 162, 321.
Sanctorum tuorum
Coronatorum, 203, 360.
Dne. intercessione, 209, 321.
Dne. Nerei et Achillei, 173, 342.
Dne. precibus confidentes, 140.
Ill. suffragiis, 366.
nos Dne. Marcelli et, 202, 359.
nos Dne. Marci et, 175, 347.
Sanctum ac venerabilem, 261.
Sanctus Dne. Gurgonius sua nos, 198, 355.
Satiasti Dne. familiam tuam, 318, 321.
Satiati Dne. opulentiae, 294.
Satiati sumus Dne.
de tuis donis, 294.
muneribus sacris, 356.
Satisfaciat tibi Dne. q. pro anima, 306.
Scrutinii diem dilectissimi fratres, 45.
Semper
Dne. sanctorum martyrum, 175.
nos Dne. martyrum, 173, 342.
Sempiternae pietatis tuae, 258.
Sensibus nostris
Dne. spiritum, 129.
q. Dne. lumen, 292.

Sentiamus Dne. q. tui perceptione, 228, 353.
Si iniquitates nostras observaveris, 253.
Sic age quasi redditurus, 145.
Sicut
gloria(m) divinae potentiae, 175, 347.
qui invitatus renuit, 26.
Signum Christi, 117.
Sint tibi q. Dne. nostri munera, 179, 348.
Sit Dne. b. Matthaeus, 357.
Sit nobis Dne.
reparatio, 226, 350.
sacramenti tui certa, 199, 358.
Sit nobis fratres communis, 24.
Sit nobis q. Dne.
cibus sacer potusque, 13, 325.
medicina mentibus, 251.
Solemnibus ieiuniis expiatos, 125, 346.
Solemnis nobis intercessio, 193, 353.
Solemnitatis apostolicae, 184, 350.
Solita q. Dne. quos salvasti, 338.
Sollicita q. Dne. quos lavasti, 100.
Spiritum (in) nobis Dne. tuae, 248, 335, 336, 363.
Subiectum tibi populum q. Dne., 329.
Subveni Dne. servis tuis, 33, 328.
Subveniat nobis Dne.
misericordia, 220, 363.
q. sacrificii, 255.
Succurre q. Dne. populo, 332.
Sumat ecclesia tua D. b. Ioannis, 178, 348.
Sumentes Dne.
caelestia, 344.
dona caelestia, 357.
gaudia sempiterna, 164, 322.
Sumentes gaudia sempiterna, 195.
Sumpsimus Dne.
celebritatis annuae, 19, 327.
divina mysteria, 342.
pignus redemptionis, 352.
pignus salutis, 182, 354.
sacri dona mysterii, 345, 361.
sancti Fabiani, 164.
sancti *Ill.* martyris, 365.
Sumpta munera Dne. nostra(e), 180, 348.
Sumpti sacrificii Dne perpetua, 176, 194, 249, 338, 347.
Sumptis Dne.
caelestibus sacramentis, 229, 354.
remediis sempiternis, 182, 349.
sacramentis intercedente, 197, 355.
sacramentis q. ut intercedente, 192.
Sumptis muneribus Dne. q. ut cum, 110, 216, 346, 365.
Sumpto Dne. sacramento suppliciter, 184, 359.
Sumptum
Dne. caelestis remedii, 364.
q. Dne. venerabile, 128, 346.
Super
has q. hostias Dne. benedictio, 242.

392 INDEX OF LITURGICAL FORMS.

(Super)
   populum tuum Dne., 18, 37, 326.
Supplicationes servorum, 355.
Supplicationibus apostolicis
   b. Ioannis, 7.
   b. Matthaei, 357.
Supplices
   Dne. te rogamus ut his, 330.
   q. Dne pro animabus, 310.
Supplices te rogamus
   D. ut quos, 254
   Dne. D. noster ut sicut, 44.
Supplices te rogamus o. D.
   iube haec perferri, 235.
   ut intervenientibus, 362.
   ut quos, 321, 342, 345.
Suppliciter
   Dne. sacra familia, 34.
   te rogamus Dne. D., 279.
Supra quae propitio, 235.
Sursum corda, 234.
Suscipe creator o. D., 19, 327.
Suscipe Dne.
   animam servi tui, 296.
   fidelium preces, 341, 360.
Suscipe Dne. munera
   pro tuorum, 340.
   propitiatus oblata, 188, 351.
Suscipe Dne. munera quae
   in eius, 319, 353.
   pro Filii, 342.
   tibi offerimus, 152.
Suscipe Dne.
   munera tuorum, 176, 347.
   preces et hostias, 277.
   preces et munera, 349.
Suscipe Dne. preces nostras
   cum muneribus, 270.
   et muro, 290.
Suscipe Dne. preces populi
   supplicantis, 201, 353
   tui cum oblationibus, 88.
Suscipe Dne propitiatus hostias, 251, 360.
Suscipe Dne. propitius
   hostias quibus, 274.
   munera famulorum, 90.
   orationem, 322.
Suscipe Dne. q.
   hostiam redemptionis, 243, 367.
   hostias placationis, 197, 355.
   hostias pro anima, 302.
   munera populi tui, 213.
   oblationes familiae, 336.
   preces et hostias famulorum, 284.
Suscipe Dne. sacrificium
   cuius te voluisti, 17, 326.
   placationis, 203, 352, 353.
Suscipe m. D. supplicum, 253.
Suscipe munera q. Dne.
   exultantis, 95, 338.
   quae tibi, 226, 350.
Suscipe q. Dne.
   devotorum munera, 20, 327.
   et plebis tuae, 88, 335.

Suscipe q. Dne. hostias
   famuli et Levitae, 149.
   placationis, 304.
   redemptionis, 93.
Suscipe q. Dne. munera
   dignanter oblata, 321.
   populi tui, 324.
   populorum, 337.
Suscipe q. Dne.
   munus oblatum, 62, 72, 333.
   nostris oblata servitiis, 329.
   oblationes familiae, 96.
Suscipe q. Dne. preces
   nostras cum oblationibus, 143.
   nostras et ad aures, 367.
   populi tui cum, 249, 329, 336.
Suscipe q. Dne. pro anima, 301.
Suscipiamus Dne. misericordiam, 363.

Tantis Dne repleti muneribus, 106, 345.
Tanto
   nos Dne. q. promptiore, 1, 317.
   placabiles q. Dne. nostrae, 340.
Te
   deprecamur o. D. ut benedicas, 294.
   deprecor Dne. sancte, 114.
   Dne. sancte Pater o. aet. D., 297.
   Dne. supplices exoramus, 113.
   igitur clementissime, 234.
   invocamus Dne. sancte, 158.
   lucem veram et lucis, 291.
   q. Dne. famulantes, 169.
Tempora nostra q. Dne., 347.
Terram tuam Dne., 258.
Tibi
   Dne. sacrificia dicata, 227, 352.
   placitam D. noster, 103, 340.
Timentium te Dne. salvator, 129, 345.
Tribue nobis
   Dne. caelestis mensae, 104, 342.
   o. D. ut dona caelestia, 16, 326.
   q. Dne. indulgentiam, 44, 332.
Tribue q. Dne.
   fidelibus tuis ut ieiunio, 201.
   sanctos tuos iugiter, 366.
   ut eum praesentibus, 10, 320.
   ut illuc, 101, 337.
   ut per haec, 109. 342.
Tribue q. fidelibus tuis, 357.
Tribue q. o. D.
   ut illuc, 101, 337.
   ut munere festivitatis, 108, 342.
Tu
   Dne semper a nobis, 244, 367.
   famulis tuis q. Dne. bonos, 38, 264.
   nobis Dne. auxilium, 296.
   semper q. Dne. tuam, 38, 330.
Tua Dne. muneribus altaria, 178, 348.
Tua nos Dne.
   dona reficiant, 293.
   gratia et sanctis, 41, 331.
   medicinalis, 237, 244, 350, 359.

INDEX OF LITURGICAL FORMS. 393

⟨Tua nos Dne.⟩
  protectione defende, 330.
  (q.) gratia et sanctis, 41, 331.
  q. gratia semper, 358.
  sacramenta custodiant, 230, 356.
Tua nos misericordia D. 332.
Tua nos q. Dne.
  quae sumpsimus, 98, 339.
  sancta, 331.
Tua sacramenta nos D., 243, 367.
Tua sancta Dne. sumentes, 361.
Tua sancta nobis o. D.
  et indulgentiam, 367.
  quae sumpsimus, 243, 367.
Tua sancta sumentes q Dne. ut beati, 195, 354.
Tueatur q. Dne. dextera tua, 39, 330.
Tuere Dne.
  familiam tuam, 368.
  populum tuum, 325.
Tuere nos Dne. q.
  divinis, 252.
  tua sancta, 255, 259.
Tuere nos m. D. et b. Andreae, 206, 362.
Tuere q. Dne.
  familiam tuam, 241, 358.
  plebem tuam, 13, 325.
Tui
  Dne. perceptione sacramenti, 327.
  nobis Dne. communio, 237, 243, 351.
  nos Dne. sacramenti libatio, 326.
Tuis Dne. q.
  adesto supplicibus et inter, 31, 232, 359.
  operare mysteriis, 29.
Tuis q. Dne. adesto supplicibus
  et haec, 328.
  et inter, 31, 232, 359.
Tuorum nos Dne.
  largitate donorum, 19, 221, 364.
  q. precibus, 167, 234.
Tuus
  est dies Dne., 293, 368.
  sanctus martyr Georgius, 340.

Unde et memores, 235.
Unigeniti tui Dne. nobis, 355.
Ut accepta sint Dne., 35, 345.
Ut nobis Dne.
  terrenorum, 126, 346.
  tua sacrificia, 361, 366.
Ut
  nos Dne. tribuis solemne, 358.
  sacris Dne. reddamur, 360.
  tibi grata sint Dne., 10, 320.

Vegetet nos Dne. semper, 43, 332.
Veneranda nobis Dne. huius, 353.
Veniat
  Dne. q. populo, 222, 365.
  ergo o D. super hunc, 81.
VD. Ad cuius immensam, 324.
VD. Adest enim nobis
  dies magnificus, 362.

⟨VD. Adest enim nobis⟩
  optatissimum, 88, 335.
VD. Apud quem quum beatorum, 182, 349.
VD. Beatae
  Agnis, 323.
  Caeciliae, 361.
VD. Beati
  apostoli tui, 319.
  Cypriani, 356.
  etenim martyres, 348.
  Laurentii, 353.
  Stephani, 318.
  Viti, 347.
VD. Celebrantes sanctorum natalitia, 360.
VD. Circumdantes altaria, 93, 337.
VD. Clementiam tuam suppliciter
  exorare ut Filius, 359.
  obsecrantes, 358.
  obsecrare ut spiritalis, 69.
VD. Cognoscimus enim, 345.
VD. Cui proprium est
  ac singulare, 214, 363.
  veniam, 364.
VD. Cuius
  divinae nativitatis, 2, 317.
  hoc mirificum opus, 109, 346.
  hodie octavas nati, 9, 120.
  potentia deprecanda, 367.
VD. De
  tua gratia confidentes, 350.
  tuo munere postulantes, 104, 341.
VD. Donare nobis suppliciter, 350.
VD. Ecce enim iusti, 347.
VD. Et
  confessionem s. Felicis, 321.
  in omni loco, 361.
  suppliciter exorare ut sic, 359.
  te in tuorum honore, 366.
  tibi sanctificare ieiunium, 359.
  tuam misericordiam, 322.
VD. Exhibentes solemne ieiunium, 347.
VD. Gloriam tuam, 350.
VD. Glorificantes et de praeteritis, 330.
VD. Gloriosi (Laurenti) martyris, 190, 365.
VD. Ieiunii observatione, 364.
VD. Illa quippe festa, 347.
VD. Illuminator et redemptor, 327.
VD. In confessione, 317.
VD. In die festivitatis hodiernae
  qua b. Ioannes, 348.
  qua b. Sixtus, 351.
VD. In
  die solemnitatis, 191, 352.
  exultatione, 340.
  hac praecipue die qua I. C., 108, 342.
  quo ieiunantium, 326.
VD. Maiestatem tuam
  Dne. suppliciter, 360.
  propensius, 331.

(VD. Maiestatem tuam)
  supplicantes, 328.
  suppliciter, 348.
VD. Maxime hodie in beatae, 366.
VD. Nos
  clementiam tuam suppliciter, 96.
  precari clementiam, 91, 336.
  sursum cordibus erectis, 3, 319.
VD. Nos te
  in tuis, 353.
  laudare o. D., 320.
VD. Nos te suppliciter
  exorare ut fidelibus, 98, 339.
  obsecrare, 95, 337.
VD. Nos tibi semper et ubique, 102.
VD. Omnipotentiam tuam, 347.
VD. Per quem maiestatem, 234.
VD. Per quem nobis
  indulgentia, 332.
  regenerationis, 143.
VD. Per quem
  salus mundi, 314.
  sanctum et benedictum, 360.
  te supplices deprecamur, 139.
VD. Post illos enim laetitiae, 126, 344.
VD. Praecipue in die ista, 341.
VD. Praevenientes (?) natalem, 352.
VD. Precantes ut Iesus Christus, 358.
VD. Pretiosis [enim] mortibus, 319.
VD. Pro cuius nomine poenarum, 323.
VD. Quem in hac nocte, 72.
VD. Qui
  aeternitate sacerdotii, 355.
  ascendens, 120, 344.
  continuatis, 326.
  corporali ieiunio, 325.
  cum unigenito, 129, 345.
  das escam, 326.
VD. Qui dum
  beati Tiburtii, 352.
  confessores, 263.
VD. Qui ecclesiae tuae filios, 106, 345.
VD. Qui ecclesiam tuam
  in apostolicis, 207, 365.
  in beati apostoli, 323.
  in tuis, 357.
  sempiterna, 185, 354.
VD. Qui
  foedera nuptiarum, 265.
  genus humanum, 323.
  glorificaris, 321.
  humanis miseratus, 103, 340.
  humanum genus, 354.
VD. Qui in
  alimento, 327.
  omnium sanctorum, 366.
  principio, 71, 333.
VD. Qui mysteriorum, 72, 333.
VD. Qui non solum
  malis, 353.
  peccata, 364.
VD. Qui nos
  assiduis martyrum, 362.
  castigando, 353.

(VD. Qui nos)
  de donis, 354.
  ideo collectis, 357.
  mirabile mysterium, 339.
  tanquam, 362.
VD. Qui
  oblatione sui, 92, 336.
  perfecit in infirmitate, 361.
  post resurrectionem, 342.
  pro peccato, 320.
  propterea iure punis, 359.
  quum ubique sis, 137.
  rationabilem creaturam, 29, 325.
  sacramentum paschale, 121, 344.
  saluti humanae, 107.
  sanctorum martyrum, 366.
  secundum promissionis, 95, 337.
  sic tribuis ecclesiam, 355.
  tribuis ut tibi fideles, 140.
  ut de hoste, 318.
  vicit diabolum, 358.
VD. Quia
  competenter, 327.
  dum b. *Ill.* merita, 366.
  hodie sancti Spiritus, 123, 344.
  in saeculorum saecula, 150.
  licet in omnium, 351.
  licet nobis salutem, 350.
  nostri salvatoris, 318.
  per ea quae, 325.
  per incarnati, 323.
  quum laude, 357.
  quum Unigenitus, 10, 321.
  sic tribuis ecclesiam, 324.
  tu es mirabilis, 359.
  tu in nostra, 354.
  tui est operis, 171, 341.
  vetustate destructa, 94, 337.
VD. Quoniam
  a te, 342.
  beati martyris, 322.
  fiducialiter, 354.
  maiestatem tuam, 339.
  per sancti Spiritus, 362.
  salubre, 365.
  supplicationibus, 354.
  tanto iocunda sunt, 193.
VD. Recensemus enim, 322.
VD. Redemptionis nostrae festa, 97, 339.
VD. Referentes gratiarum, 220, 364.
VD. Reverentiae tuae dicato, 207, 362.
VD. Sancti Michaelis, 358.
VD. Sanctificator et conditor, 365.
VD. Semperque virtutes, 321.
VD. Sub tuae pietatis, 357.
VD. Suppliciter
  exorantes ut gregem, 186.
  exorare ut cum, 329.
  obsecrantes ne nos, 338.
VD. Te
  benedicere, 322.
  Dne. suppliciter exorare, 349.
VD. Te in
  beati Martini, 361.

INDEX OF LITURGICAL FORMS. 395

(VD. Te in)
   confessorum, 359.
   omnium martyrum, 340.
   sanctorum martyrum, 340.
   tuorum apostolorum, 360.
VD. Te laudare mirabilem
   Deum in omnibus, 11, 320.
   in sanctis, 324.
VD. Te semper in laude, 365.
VD. Te quidem omni tempore
   sed in hac, 89, 335.
   sed in hoc, 90, 336.
VD. Teque in sanctorum, 355.
VD. Tibi
   debitam servitutem, 351.
   debitas laudes, 361.
   enim festa solemnitas, 354.
   istam immolationis, 323.
   sacrificare ieiunium, 327.
   sanctificare ieiunium, 127.
   vovere contriti, 350.
VD. Tu mentes nostras, 105, 342.
VD. Tuae laudis hostiam, 4, 318.
VD. Tuamque in sanctorum, 356.
VD. Tuum est enim omne, 361.
VD. Ut
   modulum terrenae, 325.
   non in nobis, 367.
   qui te auctore, 356.
VD. Ut quia
   primum, 104, 347.
   tui est operis, 367.
VD. Ut te
   auctorem, 350.

(VD. Ut te)
   postposita vetustate, 352.
VD. Venientem (?) natalem, 352 *note*.
VD. Vere dignum . . . nos tibi, 355.
VD. Verum aeternumque, 349.
Veritas tua q. Dne. luceat, 292.
Vespertinae laudis officia, 293.
Vide ut quod ore cantas, 145.
Virtute s. Spiritus Dne. munera, 120, 343.
Virtutum caelestium D.
   de cuius, 67, 333.
   qui ab, 281.
Visita q. Dne. plebem tuam, 45.
Vitia cordis humani, 250.
Vivificet nos
   Dne. sacra, 249.
   q. Dne. huius, 229, 354.
   q. Dne. participatio, 274.
Voci nostrae q. Dne. aures, 217, 363.
Vota
   nostra q. Dne. pio, 340.
   populi tui Dne. propitius, 357.
   q. Dne. supplicantis, 320.
Votiva Dne.
   dona percepimus, 210.
   munera deferentes, 174, 345.
Votiva Dne. pro beati
   confessoris, 189.
   martyris tui Laurenti, 191.
   martyris tui Praeiecti, 322.
Votivis q. Dne. famulae, 160.
Votivus nos Dne. q. beati, 365.
Vox clamantis ecclesiae, 322.

INDEX OF SUBJECTS

Abbot, *Missa* for one deceased, 302.
Abel-Simson, xliii *note.*
Acolyte, Ordination of, 145.
Adrian I, Pope, xlvi, xlvii, liii, lxxvi.
Advent, *Missae* and Prayers for, lxiv, 214–9, 362–365.
Agape, Prayers and *Missa* for, 261, 262.
Alcuin, liv, lv.
Ambrosian rite, xxi, lii, lxxiv *note.*
Angoulême, Sacramentary of, lvi.
Apples, Benediction of, 294.
Aquileia, Sacramentary of, l.
Ascension Day, 107, 108, 342, 343.
Aurium apertio, 50–9.

Bäumer, Dom S., liv *note*, lv *note*, lvi *note.*
Ballerini, edition of S. Leo, li.
Baptism, Order for, 84; at Pentecost, 110; of the sick, 110.
Baptisterii Ordo, arrangement of, in Rheinau MS. xxxvii.
Baptistry, Consecration of a, 142.
Battifol, Abbé, xlvi.
Beans, Benediction of, 294.
Beard, Prayer on first shaving, 291.
Bede, lx *note.*
Benedictions omitted in Rheinau MS. xxxvi sqq.; of catechumens, 46, 47, 48–9, 110 sqq.; of salt, 47, 286; of Chrism and oils, 70, 72, 118, 333; of Paschal candle, 80, 334; of incense, 81; of the Font, 85; of the Font in clinical Baptism, 115, 116; of water, 116, 285 sqq., 289; of converts from heresy, 130, 131; *super Populum*, 240, 368; of a widow, 271; on entering a house, 283, 284; of a threshing-floor, 289; of persons renouncing the world, 290; on shaving the beard, 291; at meals, 293–4; of fruits, 294; of a tree, 295; of the lamb, xlv, 335.
Birth, *Missa* for anniversary of, 268.
Bishop, Ordination of, 144, 151; *Missa* on day of Ordination, 153; *Missae* for one deceased, 301, 302.
Bodleian Library, MSS. in, see *Manuscripts.*
Bona, Cardinal, xvii, xlv *note.*
Burial of the Dead, 295 sqq.

Candle, Paschal, 80, 334.
Canon Actionis, 234, 368.
Caput Ieiunii, xxvii, 15–17.
Catechumens, Forms relating to, 46–59, 78, 110 sqq.
Cattle-plague, *Missa* in time of, 257.
Cemetery, *Missae* in a, 310, 311.
Charles the Great, xvii, xliii, xliv, lii, liii, lxxvi.
Chrism, *Missa Chrismatis* (or *Chrismalis*), 69, 333; absent from Rheinau MS. xxxvi.
Christina, Queen of Sweden, xvii.
Christmas, *Missae* for, 1–5, 317, 318; *Missa* for Octave, 9, 320.
Chronicon Centulense, liv.
Chur, Bishops of, xliii sqq.
Churches, Consecration of, 133–142.
Clausum Paschae, lxx.
Coena Domini, 63, 69, 72, 333–4.
Collects in Gelasian Sacramentaries, lxxiv *note.*
Commendatio animae, 299.
Confirmation, Form of, 86–7, 117; absent from Rheinau MS. xxxvii.
Constantius, Bishop of Chur, xliii.
Converts from Heathenism, 113; from Arianism, 130; from Heresy, 130, 131.
Creed, Delivery of, 53, 78; form of, 53, 55; peculiar form of, in Bodleian MS., l.

Deacons, Ordination of, 26, 28, 144.
Dead, Burial of the, 295 sqq.
Dearth, *Missa* in time of, 258.
Death, Prayers after a, 295 sqq.
Departed, *Missae* and Prayers for the, 295–312.

INDEX OF SUBJECTS. 397

Delisle, Léopold, xxv, xxxii, xxxv, xlii, l, lvi.
Denis, S., Monastery of, xvii.
Drought, *Missae* in time of, 258, 259.
Duchesne, Abbé L., xvii *note*, xxiv, xxvi, xxxii *note*, xxxvi *note*, xxxix *note*, xlv, xlvii, liii, liv, lxi.

Easter Even, 78 sqq., 334.
Eastertide, 90–99, 335–339; *Pascha Annotina*, 97, 338; *Missa in Parochia*, 98, 339; Vesper prayers, 99; Sundays *post Clausum Paschae*, 102 sqq.
Electi, see *Catechumens*.
Ember seasons, lxv, lxix, lxx, 21, 124, 125, 200, 220, 327, 344, 346, 357, 364.
Epiphany, 10, 11, 320, 321.
Episema, use of, xxv.
Evening, Prayers for, 292.
Exorcisms of salt, 47, 286; of catechumens, 37–49, 78; of oil, 72, 118, 333; of energumens, 111, 112; of water, 116, 285, 286, 289.
Exorcist, Ordination of, 145, 147.

Festivals of S. Gallen MS., xlvi sqq.
Festivals and Vigils:—
SS. Abdo and Sennes, 187, 351.
S. Adrian, 355.
S. Agapitus, 194, 353.
S. Agatha, 166, 323.
S. Agnes (Passion), 164, 322.
S. Agnes (Nativity), 165, 323.
SS. Alexander, Eventius, and Theodulus, 341.
S. Andrew, 206, 207, 362; Octave, 208, 363.
Annunciation, 169, 339.
The Apostles, 184, 185.
Ascension, 107, 108, 342, 343.
Assumption of S. Mary, 193, 353.
SS. Audifax and Abacuc, 163.
S. Augustinus, 361.
S. Bartholomew, 354.
SS. Basilides, Cyrinus, Nabor, and Nazarius, 346, *see* 174.
S. Benedict, 350.
Brothers, Seven, 350.
S. Caecilia, 203, 204, 361.
S. Caesarius, 360.
S. Calixtus, 359.
Christmas, 1–5, 317, 318; Octave, 9, 320.
S. Chrysogonus, 362.
S. Clement, 205, 361.
SS. Cornelius and Cyprian, 199, 356.
SS. Cosmas and Damian, 199, 358.
Crowned Martyrs, Four, 203, 360.
S. Cyprian, 356.
S. Cyriacus, 352.
SS. Cyrinus, Nabor, and Nazarius, 174, *see* 346.

Festivals and Vigils:—
S. Damasus, 364.
S. Donatus, 189, 351.
Easter, 88–95, 336–337.
SS. Emerentiana and Macarius, 322.
Epiphany, 10, 11, 320, 321.
S. Euphemia (Apr. 13), 170, 339; (Sept. 16), 356.
S. Eusebius, 353.
Exaltation of the Cross, 198, 356.
S. Fabian, 164, 322.
SS. Felicissimus and Agapitus, 351.
S. Felicitas, 205, 362.
S. Felix (of Nola), 162, 321.
S. Felix (of Rome), 351.
SS. Felix and Adauctus, 355.
S. George, 340.
SS. Gervasius and Protasius, 176, 347.
S. Gordianus, 342.
S. Gregory, 324.
S. Gurgonius, 198, 355.
S. Hermes, 195, 354.
S. Hippolytus, 192, 353.
The Holy Innocents, 8, 319.
Invention of the Cross, 172, 341.
S. James, 350.
S. John Baptist (Nativity), 177, 178, 347, 348.
S. John Baptist (Passion), 196, 355.
S. John Evang., 7, 319.
S. John Evang. ante Portam Latinam, 342.
SS. John and Paul, 179, 180, 348.
S. Juliana, 168, 324.
S. Juvenalis, 172, 341.
S. Laurence, 189, 190, 352; Octave, 192, 353.
S. Leo, 339.
S. Lucia, 364.
SS. Lucia and Geminianus, 357.
S. Luke, 359.
The Maccabees, 188, 351.
S. Magnus, 194, 353.
SS. Marcellinus and Peter, 345 (*see* 174).
S. Marcellus, 162, 321.
SS. Marcellus and Apuleius, 202, 359.
S. Marcus, 358.
SS. Marcus and Marcellianus, 175, 347.
S. Martin, 361.
SS. Mary and Martha, 163, 321.
S. Mary *ad Martyres*, Dedication, 342.
S. Matthew, 357.
S. Mennas, 360.
S. Michael, 200, 358.
Nativity of S. Mary, 197, 355.
SS. Nereus, Achilleus, and Pancratius, 173, 342.
S. Nicomedes, 356; Dedication of, 345.

Festivals and Vigils:—
S. Paul, 182, 349.
S. Paul, Conversion of, 323.
Pentecost, 118 sqq., 343 sqq.
SS. Perpetua and Felicitas, 168, 324.
S. Peter, 181.
SS. Peter and Paul, 180 sqq., 348, 349; Octave, 186, 349.
S. Peter's Chains, Veneration of, 351.
S. Peter's Chair, 324.
SS. Peter and Marcellinus, 174 (see 345).
SS. Philip and James, 171, 341.
S. Praeiectus, 322.
SS. Primus and Felicianus, 346.
S. Prisca, 321.
S. Priscus, 196, 355.
SS. Processus and Martinianus, 349.
SS. Protus and Iacintus, 356.
Purification of S. Mary, 165, 323.
S. Rufus, 195, 354.
S. Sabina, 355.
SS. Saturninus, Crisantus, Maurus, and Daria, 206, 362.
S. Sebastian, 163, 322.
S. Silvester, 319.
S. Simeon (The Purification), 323.
SS. Simon and Jude, 359.
SS. Simplicius, Faustinus, and Viatrix (or Beatrix), 187, 350.
S. Sixtus, 188, 351.
S. Soteris, 166, 324.
S. Stephen (Bishop), 351.
S. Stephen (Deacon), 6, 318.
S. Theodore, 360.
S. Thomas, 208, 365.
S. Tiburtius, 192, 352.
SS. Tiburtius, Valerianus and Maximus, 340.
S. Timotheus, 354.
S. Urban, 343.
SS. Valentinus, Vitalis, Felicula (and Zeno), 167, 324.
S. Vincent, 322.
S. Vitalis, 341.
S. Vitus, 175, 347.
S. Ypolitus (or Hippolytus), 192, 353.
SS. Zoticus, Irenaeus, and Iacintus, 324.
Fintan, S. (Patron of Rheinau), xxxiv.
Fleury, Abbey of, xvii *note*.
Font, Benediction of, 84; for Clinical Baptism, 115, 116.
Fruits, Benediction of, 294.

Gallican books, xxvii, xxx; texts of, li.
'Gelasian,' Use of the term, xix, liv sqq., lx, lxi; its origin, lviii sqq.
Gelasian Sacramentary, see *Sacramentary*.
Gelasius, S., Liturgical work of, lviii sqq.

Gellone, Sacramentary of, l, lvi.
Gennadius, lviii.
Gerbert, Martin, xix sqq.; manuscripts used by, xx sqq.; referred to, xxxii, xxxiii, xl *note*, li, lv.
Good Friday Prayers, xxv, xxxv, xliv, 74, 334.
Gospels Exposition of, 50.
'Grace' at meals, 293-4.
Grammatical errors, xxxi, xxxiv, xli.
Grapes, Benediction of, 294.
Gregorian Sacramentary, see *Sacramentary*.
Gregory, S., Addition of clause in Canon, xxix, lx *note*; revision of Sacramentary ascribed to him, lviii sqq.; mentioned in Vatican MS., xxix; 'capitulum' of, in Vatican MS., 26.
Gregory II, xxvii, xxxvi, lxxv, lxxvi.
Grimoldus, liii.

Hereford, Pontifical formerly belonging to, li.
Hincmar, of Rheims, lv.
House, Prayers at entering, 283, 284; *Missa* for dwellers in, 283.

Ince, Dr., xxx *note*.

John the Deacon, lix, lx.
John, Patriarch of Aquileia, li *note*.
Journey, *Missa* and prayers for, 245-7.

Kings, Prayers for, 276.

Lamb, Blessing of, at Easter, xlv, 335.
Le Brun, Pierre, xix, lv, lvi.
Lent, *Missae* for, 15-21, 30-45, 60-2, 325 sqq.; Sunday *Missae* of, in Rheinau and S. Gallen MSS., lxvi; Ferial *Missae*, lxvii sqq.
Leodegarius, S. mentioned in Rheinau MS., xxxv.
Leofric Missal, lii.
Leonine Sacramentary, see *Sacramentary*.
Liber Pontificalis, lviii, lx *note*, lxi.
Litany of S. Mark's Day, xlv, 340.
Lord's Prayer, 236; exposition of, 57.

Mabillon, Jean, xvii *note*, li, liii *note*.
Madan, Falconer, l.
Manuscripts:—
  Bodleian Library, Bodl. Add. A. 173, l.
    Douce f. 1, lvii.
    Liturg. Miscell. 319, l.
    B. N. Rawlinson, 99, xxxv. *note*.
  Magdalen College, MS. 226, li.
  Rheinau MS. (now Zürich MS. Rheinau 30), used by Gerbert, xx; description of, xxxii sqq.;

INDEX OF SUBJECTS. 399

Manuscripts:—
  Grammar and spelling of, xxii, xxxiv; tradition concerning, xxxiv; place of writing uncertain, xxxv; peculiar clause in Canon, xxxv; traces of Gallican influence in, xxxv; contents of, xxxv sqq.; second book of, xxxvi sqq.; differences of, from S. Gallen MS., xlix; comparison of, with Vatican MS., xxxvi sqq., lxi sqq. (see the Appendix for outline of the contents of the MS.).
  S. Gallen MS. 348, used by Gerbert, xx-xxiii; relation of, to Gerbert's principal MS., xxi, xlii; known as Gelasian, xxi; description of, xl. sqq.; grammar and spelling of, xli; corrections in, by later hand, xxii, xxiii, xli, xlii; contents of, xli *note*, xlv; date and place of writing, xliii sqq.; possible traces of Gallican influence in, xlv, xlvi; *Proprium sanctorum* of, xlv sqq.; differences of, from Rheinau MS., xlix; comparison of, with Vatican MS., lxi. sqq. (See the Appendix for outline of the contents of the MS.)
  Vatican MS. *Reginae* 316, xvii; description of, xxiv sqq.; arrangement of, xxvi sqq.; grammar and spelling of, xxxi-xxxii; comparison of, with Rheinau and S. Gallen MSS., xxxvi sqq., lxi sqq.
  Zürich MS. used by Gerbert, xx sqq.
  (See also *Angoulême, Gellone, Ottobonianus, Prague*.)
Marriage, Forms relating to, 265.
Martène, Edmond, xxxi, l, li, lv.
Martyrologium of Rheinau MS., xxxv, xl.
Mattins, Prayers at, 291.
Maundy Thursday, see *Coena Domini*.
Meals, Prayers at, 293, 294.
Ménard, Hugues, xviii, xxiv, l, lii, liii.
Migne, Abbé, edition of the Gelasian Sacramentary, xviii *note*.
Minor Orders, Forms relating to, 145.
Missa Chrismalis, xxvi, xxxvi, xxxvii, xlv, xlviii *note*, lvii.
Missae of Rheinau and S. Gallen MSS. compared with those of Vatican MS. and Gregorian Sacramentaries, lxii sqq.
Missae Dominicales, 224-33.
Missae quotidianis diebus, 242-4, 367-8.
Missae for Saints' Days (*Commune*) 209 sqq., 365 sqq.; for special *Missae* see under *Festivals*.

Missae for Thursdays in Lent, xxvii, xxxvi, xlvii, lxxv, lxxvi.
Missae for various special purposes:—
  ad pluviam postulandam, 258-9; ad poscendam serenitatem, 260; ad proficiscendum in itinere, 245; contra iudices male agentes, 277-8; contra obloquentes, 279; de sterilitate, 258; in coemeteriis, 310-11; in contentione, 278-9; in domo, 283: in monasterio, 263; in natali genuino, 268; in nuptiis, 265; in parochiis, 98, 339; in tempore belli, 272-5; in tempore mortalitatis, 255-6; in tribulatione, 248-53; post tempestatem et fulgura, 261; pro caritate, 247-8; pro defunctis, 301-12; pro his qui agapen faciunt, 262; pro infirmis, 282; pro irreligiosis, 280; pro mortalitate animalium, 257; pro pace, 271; pro regibus, 276; pro salute vivorum, 313; pro sterilitate mulierum, 269; prohibendum ab idolis, 10, 320.
Morinus, J. B., xvii.
Morning, Prayers for the, 291.
Monastery, Prayers in a, 263, 264, 290.
Muratori, L. A., xviii, xix, li, lii, lxiv.

Neale and Forbes, li.
Nunnery, Prayers in a, 290.
Nuns, Profession of, 145; Habit of, 145, 157; Benediction of, 156, 158; *Missae* for anniversary of profession, 159, 160.

Orationes solemnes, see *Good Friday*.
Ordination, Forms and regulations for, xxv, xxvi, xxxviii, xxxix, 22 sqq., 144 sqq.; *Missae* for anniversary of, 149, 150, 154, 155.
Ordo Baptisterii, in Rheinau MS., xxxvii.
Ostiarius, Ordination of, 145, 147.
Ottobonianus, Codex, lxvi.

Palm Sunday, 60, 332.
Pamelius, xviii, xxiv, l, lii, lxiv *note*.
Pascha annotina, 97, 338.
Paschal candle, 80, 334.
Passio Domini, see *Good Friday*.
Penitents, Forms relating to, xxvi, 14, 15, 63-7, 314, 325, 333.
Pentecost, 118-29, 343-5.
Pestilence, *Missae* in time of, 255-6.
Petau, Paul, xvii.
Photius, xlv.
Planta, P.C., xliii *note*, xliv *note*.
Pontifical, of Hereford (?), li; of Poitiers, lv.
Postcommunions, 236.
Prague, MS. Sacramentary at, lvi.
Prefaces, Large number of, in later Gelasian Sacramentaries, lxiii *note*.
Priests, Ordination of, 22, 144.

Printed texts used, li, lii.
Probst, F., lxvi *note*.
Prohibendum ab Idolis, 10, 320.

Quinquagesima, 15, 325.

Rappagliosi, Sign., xxx *note*.
Reader, Ordination of, 145, 147.
Reconciliation of Penitents, 63, 65, 314, 333; of Heretics, 130, 131.
Redditio Symboli, 78.
Relics, Translation of, 161.
Remedius, Bishop of Chur, xliii sqq.
Rhaetia Curiensis, xliii, xliv, lxxvi.
Rheinau, Monastery of, xxxii *note*; Sacramentary of, see *Manuscripts*.
Riquier, S., Inventory of, liv.
Rocca, A., xviii.
Rogation Days, xxxv, xlv.

Sabbatum in xii Lectionibus, see *Ember seasons*.
Sabbatum sanctum, 68 sqq., 334-5.
Salt, Benediction of, 47, 286.
Sacramentaries, Roman, in early use in the Frankish kingdom, lii, liii.
Sacramentary:—
  Gelasian, used at S. Riquier, liv; used in parish churches, lv; outside the Frankish kingdom, lxxvi; use long continued, lv; existing specimens of Gelasian, lvi, lvii; two types of Gelasian compared, lxi sqq.; revision of the Gelasian, lxii sqq., lxxv; revision in part as late as Gregory II, lxxv, lxxvi; the later Gelasian more akin to the Gregorian, lxiii; conclusions regarding the Gelasian Sacramentaries, lxxiv sqq. (See *Gelasian, Gelasius*.)
  Gregorian, sent by Adrian I to Charles the Great, liii; early MSS. of, how divided, liii; preface to supplement, liii; authorship of supplement ascribed to Grimoldus, liii; and to Alcuin, liv, lv; supplement borrowed from later Gelasian Sacramentaries, lxxvi; relation of first part to Gelasian Sacramentary still requires elucidation, lxxv *note*, lxxvi. (See *Gregory, S.*)
  Leonine, xxx, l, li.

Saints' Days, *Missae* for (*Commune*), 209-13, 365-7; Notice of, 161, 365 (for particular Saints' Days, see *Festivals*).
Scrutinies, xxxvii, lxvi; Forms relating to, 34, 38, 42, 45, 46-59.
Secreta, Title used in Vatican and Rheinau MSS., xl.
Septuagesima, 12, 325.
Sexagesima, 13, 325.
Sick, Prayers and *Missa* for, 281, 282; on recovery, 282.
Singer, Admission of, 145.
Soul, Commendation of, 295 sqq.
Stations, xxvii, xxxvi, xlv, lxix, lxxv, lxxvi, *note*.
Stowe Missal, lvi.
Strife, *Missae* in time of, 278, 279.
Subdeacon, Ordination of, 145, 148.
Sundays, *Missae* for, 224-33; in Rheinau and S. Gallen MSS., lxx sqq.; after Christmas, 319, 320; after Epiphany, 320, 321, 322, 323, 324, 325; Septuagesima, 12, 325; Sexagesima, 13, 325; Quinquagesima, 15, 325; in Lent, 17, 30, 34, 38, 42, 60, 326, 327, 329, 330, 331, 332; after Easter, 102, 103, 104, 105, 106, 337, 339, 340, 341; after Ascension, 109, 343; after Pentecost, 345-61; in Advent, 214-18, 362-65.
Symbolum, 53, 78.

Tello, Bishop of Chur, xliii.
Tempest, *Missae* in time of, 260, 261.
Threshing-floor, Benediction of, 289.
Thunderstorm, Prayers in 288; Benediction of water in, 289.
Thursdays in Lent, *Missae* for, xxvii, xxxvi, xlviii.
Tommasi, Cardinal, xvii, xviii.
Traditio Symboli, 53.
Tree, Benediction of, 295.
Trouble, *Missae* in time of, 248-53.

Vespers, Prayers at, 292.
Vezzosi, F., xviii, lv.
Victoridae, Bishops of Chur, xliii.

Walafrid Strabo, lviii.
War, *Missae* in time of, 271-5.
Warren, F. E., lii, lvi.
Water, Benediction of, 116, 285 sqq., 289.
Widow, Benediction of, 271.

THE END

www.ingramcontent.com/pod-product-compliance
Lightning Source LLC
Chambersburg PA
CBHW051239300426
44114CB00011B/807